The Northern Counties from AD 1000

A Regional History of England

General Editors: Barry Cunliffe and David Hey
For full details of the series, see pp. xv–xviii.

Buck's 1738 view of Carlisle from the north-west, depicting what was essentially still a medieval walled and fortified town with little industrial development or suburban expansion. (From S. and N. Buck, *The Castles, Abbeys and Priories of the County of Cumberland* (1739, re-published by Hudson, Scott & Sons, Carlisle 1877.)

The Northern Counties from AD 1000

Norman McCord and Richard Thompson

LONGMAN
London and New York

Addison Wesley Longman Limited
Edinburgh Gate,
Harlow, Essex CM20 2JE,
United Kingdom
and Associated Companies throughout the world

Published in the United States of America
by Addison Wesley Longman Inc., New York

First published 1998

ISBN 0 582 49334X PPR
ISBN 0 582 493331 CSD

British Library Cataloguing in Publication Data

A catalogue record for this book is available from the British Library

Library of Congress Cataloging-in-Publication Data

McCord, Norman.
    The northern counties from AD 1000 / Norman McCord and Richard
Thompson.
        p.   cm. — (A regional history of England)
    Includes bibliographical references and index.
    ISBN 0-582-49334-X (ppr). — ISBN 0-582-49333-1 (cds)
    1. England, Northern—History. I. Thompson, Richard, 1947- .
II. Title. III. Series.
DA670.N73M38   1998
942.7—dc21   97-38880
                                                              CIP

Set by 35 in 10/12pt Sabon
Produced by Addison Wesley Longman Singapore (Pte) Ltd.,
Printed in Singapore

Contents

List of plates

List of maps

Acknowledgements

N.Mc. wishes to thank the staff of the Local Studies Department of Newcastle Central Library for their friendly and invaluable help and co-operation during his share of the writing of this book, most of which was carried out in that place.

R. T. wishes to thank the staff of the Cumbria Records Office, Carlisle Library, Tullie House Museum, and the Abbot Hall Museum at Kendal for their help. Particular thanks are due to Stephen White and Susan Dench for their efforts. Nigel Holmes of Radio Carlisle provided kind support. Above all Dr June Barnes and Adrian Barnes provided unfailing support and encouragement as well as much practical help.

The publishers would like to thank the following for their permission to reproduce illustrative material:

Abbot Hall Art Gallery, Kendal, Cumbria for 8.1; British Nuclear Fuels Ltd for 21.1; Carlisle City Council for 17.3; Carlisle Public Library for 4.1, 6.1, 13.2 (M. Fair/Carlisle Public Library), 14.1, 17.4, 19.3 and 20.1 (Mrs M. I. George/Carlisle Public Library); Cumbria Record Office for the frontispiece and 3.1, Earl of Lonsdale/Cumbria Record Office for 1.1 (the property of The Lowther Family Trusts, with whom copyright resides), Mr J. Scott Plummer/Cumbria Record Office for 13.1; Museum of Lakeland Life and Industry for 19.2 and 22.1; Newcastle Central Library Local Studies Department © City of Newcastle upon Tyne for 6.2, 8.2, 10.1, 10.2, 15.4, 16.2, 19.1 and 20.2; North Tyneside Central Library Local Studies Department © Borough of North Tyneside for 16.1 and 20.2; Tullie House Museum, Carlisle, for 18.1 and 18.3; © University of Newcastle upon Tyne for 1.2, 1.3, 2.1, 2.2, 4.2, 5.1, 7.1, 9.1, 12.1, 13.3, 15.3 and 17.2 (all taken by N. McCord).

General preface

England cannot be divided satisfactorily into recognizable regions based on former kingdoms or principalities in the manner of France, Germany or Italy. Few of the Anglo-Saxon tribal divisions had much meaning in later times and from the eleventh century onwards England was a united country. English regional identities are imprecise and no firm boundaries can be drawn. In planning this series we have recognized that any attempt to define a region must be somewhat arbitrary, particularly in the Midlands, and that boundaries must be flexible. Even the South West, which is surrounded on three sides by the sea, has no agreed border on the remaining side and in many ways, historically and culturally, the River Tamar divides the area into two. Likewise, the Pennines present a formidable barrier between the eastern and western counties on the Northern Borders; contrasts as much as similarities need to be emphasized here.

The concept of a region does not imply that the inhabitants had a similar experience of life, nor that they were all inward-looking. A Hull merchant might have more in common with his Dutch trading partner than with his fellow Yorkshireman who farmed a Pennine smallholding: a Roman soldier stationed for years on Hadrian's Wall probably had very different ethnic origins from a native farmer living on the Durham boulder clay. To differing degrees, everyone moved in an international climate of belief and opinion with common working practices and standards of living.

Yet regional differences were nonetheless real; even today a Yorkshireman may be readily distinguished from someone from the South East. Life in Lancashire and Cheshire has always been different from life in the Thames Valley. Even the East Midlands has a character that is subtly different from that of the West Midlands. People still feel that they belong to a particular region within England as a whole.

In writing these histories we have become aware how much regional identities may vary over time; moreover how a farming region, say, may not coincide with a region defined by its building styles or its dialect. We have dwelt upon the diversity that can be found within a region as well as upon common characteristics in order to illustrate the local peculiarites of provincial life. Yet, despite all these problems of definition, we feel that the time is ripe to attempt an ambitious scheme outlining the history of England's regions in 21 volumes. London has not been included – except for demonstrating the many ways in which it has influenced the provinces – for its history has been very different from that of the towns and rural parishes that are our principal concern.

In recent years an enormous amount of local research both historical and archaeological has deepened our understanding of the former concerns of ordinary men and women and has altered our perception of everyday life in the past in many significant ways, yet the results of this work are not widely known even within the regions themselves.

This series offers a synthesis of this new work from authors who have themselves been actively involved in local research and who are present or former residents of the regions they describe.

Each region will be covered in two linked but independent volumes, the first covering the period up to AD 1000 and necessarily relying heavily on archaeological data, and the second bringing the story up to the present day. Only by taking a wide time-span and by studying continuity and change over many centuries do distinctive regional characteristics become clear.

This series portrays life as it was experienced by the great majority of the people of Southern Britain or England as it was to become. The 21 volumes will – it is hoped – substantially enrich our understanding of English history.

Barry Cunliffe
David Hey

A Regional History of England

General Editors: Barry Cunliffe (to AD 1000) and David Hey (from AD 1000)

The regionalization used in this series is illustrated on the map opposite.

*The Northern Counties to AD 1000 *Nick Higham*
*The Northern Counties from AD 1000 *Norman McCord & Richard Thompson*

The Lancashire/Cheshire Region to AD 1000 *G. D. B. Jones with Denise Kenyon & Nick Higham*
*The Lancashire/Cheshire Region from AD 1500 *John Smith*

Yorkshire to AD 1000 *T. G. Manby*
*Yorkshire from AD 1000 *David Hey*

The Severn Valley and West Midlands to AD 1000 *R. T. Rowley*
*The West Midlands from AD 1000 *Marie B. Rowlands*
The Welsh Borders from AD 1000 *R. T. Rowley*

The East Midlands to AD 1000 *Jeffrey May*
*The East Midlands from AD 1000 *J. V. Beckett*

The South Midlands and Upper Thames to AD 1000 *David Miles*
The South Midlands and Upper Thames from AD 1000 *John Broad*

The Eastern Counties to AD 1000 *W. J. Rodwell*
The Eastern Counties from AD 1000 *B. A. Holderness*

*The South West to AD 1000 *Malcolm Todd*
The South West from AD 1000 *Bruce Coleman & R. A. Higham*

*Wessex to AD 1000 *Barry Cunliffe*
*Wessex from AD 1000 *J. H. Bettey*

*The South East to AD 1000 *Peter Drewett*
*The South East from AD 1000 *Peter Brandon & Brian Short*

*already published

1. The Northern Counties
2. The Lancashire/Cheshire Region
3. Yorkshire
4. The Severn Valley and West Midlands
5. The East Midlands
6. The South Midlands and the Upper Thames
7. The Eastern Counties
8. The South West
9. Wessex
10. The South East

This book is dedicated with affection and gratitude to Iris Thompson (who endured a great deal during its composition), and to the memory of Stanley Thompson, Dorothy McCord and Norman Charles McCord.

Introduction

This series of regional histories was planned before the destruction of many old administrative boundaries under the Local Government Act of 1972. The region described here reflects an older pattern and includes the four pre-1972 counties of Cumberland, Durham, Northumberland and Westmorland. Despite their antiquity, these units were never entirely self-contained, and there were many links with adjacent areas. Southern Westmorland had much in common with northern Lancashire, north Northumberland shared many features with south-east Scotland. For our purposes the Furness district, which was part of Lancashire before being included in 1974 in the new administrative county of Cumbria, has been annexed to the study area involved here. Its leading historian has recently told us that 'Furness had . . . closer affinities with Cumberland and Westmorland than it had with central and southern Lancashire.' (Marshall 1996, 42) We have also included references to the northern Cleveland district of the North Riding of Yorkshire, where that has seemed sensible in relation to developments on Teesside.

In his Introduction to the companion volume which dealt with the region's evolution before AD 1000, Nick Higham stressed that for much of its history the region as recognized here had little separate identity. (Higham 1986, 1) In addition to variations in its natural inheritance, during the long slow millennia of the early evolution of human societies the boundaries of our region possessed no recognizable validity. Such concepts as a Forth–Humber cultural province in the Iron Age, or an Anglo-Saxon kingdom of Northumbria which stretched further both to north and south, knew nothing of even medieval county boundaries. Early tribal territories did not match the convenient administrative units of a later society. Human capacity to impose new forms of economic, social and political organization upon the inherited environment developed over time, especially within the centuries covered by this book. Within that period the four northern counties of England possessed sufficient common attributes and experiences to make their joint history a viable project. (Smailes 1968, 3–4)

1

Despite political and administrative changes, the contemporary northern scene owes much to the natural inheritance which shaped the past. Distribution of population and industry, forms of farming, main transport links, still reflect basic physical features such as rock formations, principal river valleys, or mineral deposits which were laid down millions of years before the first human beings set foot within the region. In his first chapter, 'The Formation of the Landscape', Dr. Higham gives a full discussion of the region's physical make-up, and it would be wasteful to repeat more than a brief summary here. Our region inherited a varied environment. On the east, an attenuated continuation of the coastal plain of eastern England provides a belt of generally fertile land along the North Sea coast. The west is less fortunate, with smaller lowland areas, although the Solway plain offers one broad low-lying tract. There are extensive stretches of moorland and mountain territory, proportionally larger than in any other region of England, which have had a marked effect on the region's evolution. (Smailes 1968, 9–71)

The early history of the region has been discussed in detail by Dr. Higham. It may, however, be helpful to preface our present study with a brief outline of these developments. It is important to bear in mind the time scale with which we are dealing in considering the region's past. The Roman occupation of our region is often thought of as something which occurred a very long time ago. It is salutary to remember that before the first Roman soldier reached our area three-quarters of the story of human life in this region had already passed, as far as the dimension of time is concerned. The present volume deals with only a relatively small chronological segment of the region's history, perhaps only one-eighth of it, although it includes developments and changes which moved much faster than in earlier periods.

The first penetration of the region by human visitors began after the end of the last Ice Age, although southern Britain had seen occasional migrants before the last Ice Age developed. In some parts of the region, including much of Northumberland, rounded contours of the landscape still reflect grinding down effected by the last generation of glaciers. Final retreat of the ice sheet from our region occurred about 15,000 years ago, and by about 8000 BC forests of trees such as oak, birch, hazel and alder already clothed much of the countryside. About two thousand years later the first human visitors appeared, making their adventurous way up the coastal plain and penetrating some distance inland along river valleys. These were nomads, supporting themselves by hunting, fishing and food-gathering. About 6,000 years ago primitive farming techniques had been introduced and permanent or semi-permanent habitations became established. During the Bronze Age, beginning about 4,000 years ago, climatic improvement saw occupation reach higher into hilly districts of the region than it had ever done before; the Cheviot Hills may have carried a higher population 4,000 years ago than they have ever done in later periods. A subsequent deterioration in climatic conditions saw settlement fall back to lower levels.

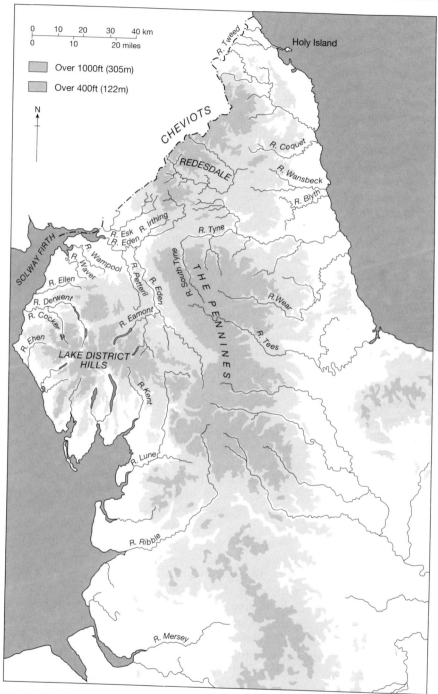

Map 1 Northern England: geographical features

Unlike some areas of southern England, it is not possible to identify in the poorer upland regions of the north a clearly demarcated sequence of cultural phases separating Neolithic from Bronze Age, or Bronze Age from Iron Age. Instead, change seems to have been a slow and gradual evolution stretching over many centuries. However, by the end of the pre-Roman Iron Age, archaeological evidence provides a reasonably clear picture. The population was organized in broad tribal groupings, with some regional centres in the shape of hill forts, but lived for the most part in small homesteads scattered over the countryside, practising a mixed farming which included the growing of crops and the maintenance of livestock. No doubt such older resources as hunting and fishing still played an important part. Society must have been hierarchical in structure, with local chieftains exercising authority within their own districts. Life expectancy cannot have been long, and comforts were very limited.

The Roman invaders reached our region towards the end of the first century AD. In thinly populated areas such as most of north Cumbria, introduction of a Roman garrison may have brought considerable increase in population, perhaps by as much as a third. By the end of the Roman period, settlements around forts had accumulated concentrations of population in comparison with the countryside. Although large areas continued to be forested, the centuries of Roman rule saw extension of native farming into more hilly areas. This development reflected local variations in farming opportunities rather than any political or military factors. There is some evidence to suggest that in both the North East and the North West this expansion was particularly marked in the second century AD. (Higham 1978, 5–16)

During three centuries of Roman rule much of the native life of the countryside continued its traditional pattern, but those in immediate contact with Roman resources received a taste of a more sophisticated society. There is little to suggest that much of this survived withdrawal of Roman power by the early fifth century AD, although Roman roads and perhaps Roman forts and civil settlements remained in use for some time. They could certainly provide a ready supply of worked stones for building purposes, although building in stone did not revive on any substantial scale for many years. The dearth of evidence about the immediately post-Roman period in the region's history is in itself eloquent testimony to the nature of this Dark Age and has led to some pessimistic assessments of prevailing conditions. One modern work suggests that in the early Anglo-Saxon period, 'Between the Tees and the Tyne lay a region almost uninhabited except for wild beasts . . .' (Finberg 1972, 402) This is unduly gloomy. No doubt some kind of sub-Roman authority structure survived and there is no reason to suppose that native homesteads of the countryside ceased to function. There is some evidence of continuity in territorial organization, reflected for instance in the nature of charters recording grants of estates to churches in the early Christian era. Few of these survive, but there are sufficient to indicate persistence of established blocks of land or estates over a long period of time, something which has been demonstrated for other regions too. In some cases local boundaries which may have been established before the Roman occupation were to survive recognizably into the modern world.

It seems likely that the first Anglo-Saxon immigrants from the continent of Europe arrived at the invitation or at least with the acquiescence of local chiefs for whom they might be useful allies. The first Anglian invaders from north Germany must have been few in number and vulnerable, but in the course of the fifth and sixth centuries migrants gradually strengthened their position, pushing their control inland from such early bases as the fortified crag of Bamburgh on the Northumberland coast. (Dark and Dark 1996; Lomas 1992, 1–7) By AD 600, native British authority had been pushed far to the west and the areas which were to be Northumberland and Durham were controlled by the invaders. Distribution of surviving stone crosses from the early Anglo-Saxon period, including one at Kirkhaugh, far up the South Tyne valley near the Cumberland border, and another at Falstone in the North Tyne valley, suggests extensive areas of early settlement. (Miller 1976 for 1975, 4) In Cumbria, in more fertile districts, place-name evidence indicates at least a scatter of Anglo-Saxon immigrants, though such names are absent from the main highland areas.

There is no reason to suppose that these developments involved wholesale displacement of existing native population in any part of the region. Archaeological discoveries from the seventh century and later suggest some kind of cultural fusion between native Celtic traditions and styles imported by newcomers. The Celtic language did not survive the medieval centuries, but elements within it, including some place-names, like Carlisle and Penrith, and natural features, including names of some rivers, remained in current use. Celtic place-names are more common in less fertile areas, suggesting that Anglo-Saxon invaders were content to leave less attractive farming areas to native occupiers. Throughout the North, it is probable that the new masters simply took over pre-existing positions of dominance, represented by old territorial divisions, without expelling the native population needed to work them. No doubt the fertile coastal plain of the North East attracted more intensive new settlement than the rougher territory of the North West. Certainly Anglian place-names occur more commonly in the former area. The medieval North, at least down to the early thirteenth century, still possessed a wide range of Celtic personal names such as Duncan, Malcolm and Cospatric, and there is evidence for survival of the Gaelic language at least as late as that. (Barrow 1969, 6–7)

Early Christianity within the region incorporated Celtic elements in its symbolism and artistic traditions, testifying again to survival of earlier traditions and practices. There is nothing to suggest that the post-Roman population of the North evinced much in the way of common sentiments in resistance to newcomers. On at least one early occasion when the Anglians of Bernicia, the northern part of the future kingdom of Northumbria, were in imminent danger of defeat and expulsion, only dissension among their enemies enabled them to survive. (Lovecy 1976, 31, 44–5)

Our historical evidence begins to pick up again during the seventh century and increases during the eighth. The writings of Bede, for example, provide information about the conversion of pagan Anglo-Saxons to the Christian faith and the establishment of new churches and monasteries. The survival of masterpieces such as the *Lindisfarne Gospels* and the *Codex Amiatinus*, two magnificently illustrated biblical texts, testifies to the high level of civilization attained by monastic centres within the new kingdom of Northumbria. It would be unwise to assume that such exceptionally fine productions reflected a level of civilization which was widespread within the region. Instead they represent peaks of cultural achievement limited in both time and place. The discovery through aerial photography of royal centres such as the eighth-century palace complexes at Yeavering and Milfield illustrated the reality of royal secular power.

Surviving scraps of evidence suggest that the organization of the new Christian faith soon had more than merely religious implications. Villages where important churches were established acted as local centres for a kind of political and social organization which was the ancestor of the later long-lasting system of local government based on parishes. This probably represents establishment of new churches in communities which were already local centres for surrounding districts in a way which is poorly documented for earlier years. It may well be that this form of local organization already had a long history of which we know little or nothing. Political or administrative functions acquired by the new religious organization may be one factor in the scale of land grants made by kings and other magnates to the developing Church. By the eleventh century, churches of the region had accumulated property on a scale which foreshadowed their secular importance during the medieval centuries. (Jones 1995)

In the late Anglo-Saxon period there is some evidence to suggest that monarchs appreciated that royal power had already been weakened by the scale on which religious institutions had been endowed by grants from Crown estates. Not all ecclesiastical dignitaries were prepared to accept royal authority meekly, as the careers of mettlesome saints like Dunstan and Wilfrid demonstrated. (Jones 1995) Royal resources were further depleted by the need to reward followers, which led to creation of hereditary local magnates administering large districts within the kingdoms of the north. Such grants to secular magnates or churches seem to have represented signing away royal rights to revenues and services from the districts concerned, rather than a simple concept of property in estates.

In Northumbria, decline of the kingdom in late Anglo-Saxon times led to the emergence of powerful families who governed extensive territories with a considerable measure of independence. Bamburgh was the principal seat of one such leading house. These established dynasties were not always amenable to royal control. Aristocratic influence was not confined to the secular world, for scions of noble families frequently appeared in control of monasteries and bishoprics. Leading churchmen might use church property to enrich their families, and hereditary succession to ecclesiastical positions was by no means unknown. One of the north's most influential religious centres, St Cuthbert's shrine, was served by a community of married priests which was to survive until 1083. In the late tenth century the acknowledged daughter of a bishop of Durham was married to a leading member of the House of Bamburgh, Uhtred, who came to his father-in-law's rescue in 1004 by relieving Durham from a siege by Malcolm II of Scotland. (Higham 1993, 220, 224)

The eighth century is sometimes known as 'The Golden Age of Northumbria', but by its end that flowering of power and culture was already endangered. Before 800, Viking raids threatened northern centres of learning. The monastery at Lindisfarne, one of the richest landowners within the region, was sacked in 793. About forty years later that community left its exposed coastal situation, carrying with them sacred relics of the principal Northumbrian saint, Cuthbert. Their long search for security saw them settle at Chester-le-Street by 883, after years of wandering which included temporary stopping-places in Cumbria as well as Northumbria. By this time Christianity was spreading among the Vikings themselves, and a Viking king granted the Community of St Cuthbert an endowment which would later form most of the eastern part of County Durham. This was an addition to extensive grants which this holy community had received from Northumbrian kings and other benefactors in earlier years. The seat of the bishopric, and the shrine of St Cuthbert, were to be moved again, to the fine promontory site at Durham, in 995. An early sacrist scoured the region in search of additional sacred relics, bringing to Durham acquisitions of this kind from Tyningham, Hexham, Jarrow and Tynemouth. (Higham 1993, 222) The sanctity of Cuthbert's name, the fame of his miracles, and the wealth of the community, provided a formidable mixture of ecclesiastical and secular power before the close of the Anglo-Saxon period. (Bonner 1989; Rollason 1994) Not all of the monastic communities weathered the storms as well. Monkwearmouth, after many earlier troubles, was finally destroyed by Viking raiders in 870.

The Viking raids were only one among a range of vicissitudes for the region. The kingdom of Northumbria suffered from internal disputes about royal succession and a variety of attacks from external enemies. Although the old sub-Roman native authority had been driven out of north-east England by 600, it still survived to the west in the kingdom of Strathclyde in south-west Scotland and Cumbria. A native British dynasty succeeded in maintaining authority over a population which must have included minority elements drawn from both Anglo-Saxon and Viking immigrants. This kingdom remained capable of taking advantage of any weakness in the Northumbrian regime, and during the early tenth century its hold on south-west Scotland, Cumberland, and probably Lancashire too, made it increasingly formidable. There is no evidence of the presence of English power even in southern Lancashire until early in the eleventh century, and indications that in the late tenth century Chester was not far from Strathclyde's southern border. Strathclyde's Church mirrored its secular power: the bishopric of Glasgow, associated with the saint known both as Kentigern and Mungo, was a major ecclesiastical power, and dedications to its patron saint extend over much of the north-west of the future kingdom of England. British kings in the west continued to be important and independent potentates until at least the early eleventh century.

Viking raids developed quite quickly into substantial invasions which led to the creation of a Danish Viking kingdom based on York which also cherished expansionist ambitions. Scandinavian place-names clustered in the Hartlepool area of south-east Durham indicate one Viking takeover within our region. (Scott 1959, 280) Extending around the Scottish island groups, Viking power became established in the Isle of Man and in Ireland, with a powerful and prosperous kingdom based on Dublin. From these bases, it was easy to move into northern England from the west, and these adventures led to replacement of the ruling Danish dynasty at York by a Norwegian rival from Dublin during the latter stages of that kingdom's existence. (Sawyer 1995) Even after King Athelstan of Wessex established his supremacy in Yorkshire in 927, the people of the shire were suspected of Viking sympathies for many years. After Athelstan's death his successor Edmund had to repeat much of his northern work, and the last Norwegian king of York was not killed until 954. For many years, men of York continued to pay taxes assessed by the carucate, met in wapentake not hundred courts, and counted their money by a duodecimal system of Scandinavian origin. (Higham 1993, 212) Even a century after 954, with some justification, Englishmen doubted which way men of York would go in the event of further Viking invasions.

Penetration of northern England by Viking influences from the west is still reflected in groups of Scandinavian place-names in Cumbria and upper valleys of the Tees and the Wear. Archaeological work has reinforced this with examples of Viking homesteads established in uplands of west Durham by immigrants from the west. Place-name evidence from parts of Cumbria suggests that during the late eighth and early ninth centuries tough Viking settlers succeeded in wresting a scanty living from land which had not been cultivated before or had lain barren for many years, even in such unpromising areas as the heart of the mountainous Lake District. (Whyte 1985) Many areas of the North, even in relatively fertile districts, still offered opportunities for expansion of settlement.

To the north the kingdom of the Scots was emerging as a potentially aggressive rival on the borders of both Northumbria and Strathclyde.

Although relationships between the northern kingdoms fluctuated markedly, the early eleventh century saw an extension of conflict. The kingdom of Northumbria, at the peak of its power, had controlled much of what was to be south-east Scotland, certainly as far north as the Forth, but that position was lost in the troubled centuries which followed. At a time when English kings were distracted by Viking invasions, the Scots sought to make gains at the expense of both Northumbria and Strathclyde. By the tenth century, the border in the east must have lain somewhere near its later line along the Tweed. (Barrow 1966, 31–4) This frontier shift did not involve a major change in the settlement of Lothian, the great region covering south-east Scotland. During Northumbrian control there, Anglo-Saxon elements had come to dominate the region. Even after the Scottish takeover, the border was primarily a political and military line, while social and cultural links remained between folk on both sides of the frontier.

Weakened by internal strife, and with royal authority increasingly unable to control local magnates, Northumbria sometimes seemed close to total collapse, while in the west the kingdom of Strathclyde experienced its own internal and external conflicts. Northumbria, Strathclyde and Scotland suffered from repeated raiding across their nebulous borders, in ways which foreshadowed border conflicts during the medieval period. Beset with all of these cumulative problems and rivalries, in the tenth century our region endured a period of decline and confusion.

The year AD 1000 does not therefore provide a clear-cut starting point, but instead the period covered by this later volume must begin at a time when our region was particularly vulnerable, disturbed and confused. (Kapelle 1979) A further element in the complex interplay of conflicting forces had also entered the picture, in the ambitions of the expanding southern English kingdom of Wessex to extend its control over the weakened powers of the north. The midland kingdom of Mercia, once the leading power in England, had already fallen. After some time as an indirectly ruled dependency, Mercia was effectively incorporated in the kingdom of the English in 918. One of the leading magnate families of Northumbria, based on Bamburgh and descended from the old royal line of Northumbria, acted as an ally of Wessex in the North East, and served as a channel by which the House of Alfred could extend its northern power. By AD 1000 the northern region could be seen as nominally incorporated in the kingdom of the English, but it was by no means clear that this situation would be permanent.

Part One

*c.*1000–*c.*1290

Chapter 1

The Early Medieval North

For these early years the scanty evidence means that there are many gaps in our understanding. In some later periods, the evidence, both primary and secondary, is so extensive that it is impossible to cover it all. For the years immediately after AD 1000, the historian is trying to make sense of a jigsaw puzzle with most pieces missing.

The North in Late Anglo-Saxon Times

We know little of northern political arrangements during the last phase of Anglo-Saxon England. Although by this time the south and midlands of England had been welded into a reasonably coherent state, northern territories presented a different picture. In social organization, concepts of law, and structure of local authority, there remained an uncertain mixture of Celtic, Anglo-Saxon and Scandinavian influences. Elements survived from earlier political entities, the kingdoms of Northumbria and Strathclyde. Scottish claims to suzerainty over Strathclyde involved demands for Cumberland which were not abandoned until the Treaty of York in 1237. Cumbria had been a peripheral dependency of Strathclyde, but the North East contained the heartland of the former kingdom of Northumbria and inherited traditions of independence which inspired resistance to both English and Norman kings. If in Northumbria conditions were far from stable, there was more homogeneity of settlement than in Cumbria. That area held an uneasy mix of settlers of British, Anglian and Norse-Irish origins, with control disputed between various neighbours. Diversity of its peoples' origins was reflected in religious affiliations. All now at least nominally Christian, each group possessed its own saints to whom reverence was due. The northern part of the area looked to the Scottish see of Glasgow as its ecclesiastical authority, and many churches were dedicated to Celtic saints associated with that diocese. The observances associated with these cults exhibited distinctive elements of belief or superstition. The Glasgow connection was a survival of relationships established in the heyday of the kingdom of Strathclyde, and indicated that much of Cumbria was still orientated northwards.

Northern Cumbria may have remained under Scottish control after AD 1000. The southern districts, roughly those south of Shap, naturally inclined more to the English connection. (Stenton 1970) Overall, the future counties of Cumberland and Westmorland were in the eleventh century pioneer territory. They were poor, with a wet climate, much inferior acid soil, and a high proportion of forest, moorland and mountainous country. The meagre evidence indicates that extensive territorial units were needed to maintain the aristocracy. This may also have led Cumbrian leaders to supplement scanty incomes by pillaging and slave-gathering raids into Northumbria. Nowhere in the North West is there as yet evidence for towns. (Summerson 1993, I, 7)

Little revenue reached the English king from his nominal subjects in our region. There were few royal estates in Yorkshire and further north to serve as counterweight to the possessions of northern magnates. Although the king retained the power to appoint earls and bishops, his choice was constrained by the need to choose men capable of dominating a rough and divided society.

The disturbed state of the north was enhanced by the invasion and conquest of England by the Scandinavian king Cnut (Canute) in 1015–16. This involved the fall from power of the Bamburgh dynasty of earls. (Morris 1992) The Scottish threat culminated in a defeat of the Northumbrians at Carham, probably in 1018, which ended any possibility of a recovery of Lothian, the extensive region between Tweed and Forth which had previously been dominated by Northumbria. Our region now comprised a vulnerable border territory. Scotland could threaten the north of England on two fronts, east and west, or a combination of the two. (Kapelle 1979, 34, 38–9, 93)

The Role of Siward

Intervention by English kings in the troubled affairs of the North was sporadic. Cnut moved north some time around 1030, and enjoyed sufficient success to receive the formal submission of the king of the Scots. About ten years later the Scots took the offensive, but King Duncan's siege of Durham ended in failure. For some time a measure of stability returned when Siward, who had been earl of York since 1033, also became earl of Northumbria, probably in 1041. He was a shrewd adventurer from Denmark, who had risen to prominence under Cnut and his sons. His success allowed him to retain his position after 1042, when the House of Wessex in the person of Edward the Confessor was restored to the English throne, if only because he was needed if order was to be maintained in Northumbria. Edward added to the resources of his northern viceroy, granting the earl the shires of Northampton and Huntingdon in addition to his northern satrapy.

In the north, Siward seems to have exercised a pre-eminence similar to that built up by Earl Godwin in the south, even if his relationship with Edward the Confessor was not clearly established. (Higham 1993, 232) His position was stronger in Yorkshire, where Viking influence remained strong, but Viking predominance was not popular further north. It is unlikely that the earl's hold on Cumbria was more than precarious overlordship, with local magnates enjoying practical autonomy. Even this degree of success depended on diminishing the influence of the Scots, whose position in the North West may have been maintained since the later tenth century. One of the earliest documents relating to Cumbria's history, a mid-eleventh-century charter issued by Gospatrick, contains only a 'gesture of deference' towards Siward, rather than recognition of effective suzerainty. (Summerson 1993, I, 8; Rose 1982, 122; Barrow 1973) Despite the extent of his apparent jurisdiction, Siward had problems, although his resistance to Scottish aggression helped to sustain his authority. He strengthened his position by marrying Aelflaed, daughter of one of the last native earls of Northumbria, from the house of Bamburgh, who brought him some of her family's northern estates as well as its prestige. (Morris 1992)

Siward's power depended upon his household retainers, trained and well-equipped professional soldiers. Maintenance of this household and its governing functions was sustained by substantial landed estates and shrewdness in balancing potential sources of trouble against one another. Events in Scotland provided him with unexpected opportunities to consolidate his position.

The death in 1034 of the aggressive Malcolm II of Scotland, who had frequently invaded Northumbria and Strathclyde, was followed by the murder of King Duncan in 1040 by Macbeth, who seized the Scottish throne. Duncan's son, Malcolm, with other leading princes, fled to England and asked for help to overthrow the usurper. Siward took advantage of Scottish difficulties to undermine Scottish control of Cumbria, and took over southern Strathclyde at least as far as the Solway by mid-century. Even if his authority there was limited, this brought English control over routes for possible attacks from the west, the Tyne–Solway gap and the Stainmore pass.

In the mid-1040s, Siward tried unsuccessfully to replace Macbeth with a friendly king from among the Scottish exiles. In 1054 Siward invaded Scotland, accompanied by Prince Malcolm. The importance of the expedition is shown by its wide support. The situation in the North West at this time remains obscure. At some time in the 1050s the Carlisle area was held by a member of the Northumbrian house of Bamburgh, possibly as a Scottish satellite ruler, but Siward's army included a large Cumbrian contingent. King Edward contributed some of his own household troops. Although Siward was victorious, the decisive battle of Dunsinane, on 27 July, brought heavy casualties on both sides. The deaths of Siward's son, Osbeorn, his nephew, and other prominent members of the next generation of leaders of the English North were to have serious consequences. Macbeth fled and survived for three years before being killed. The new Scottish king, Malcolm Canmore, owed the English a debt of gratitude, but Scottish goodwill could not be counted on at times of English weakness.

Siward died the year after his Scottish campaign, having ruled the North for more then twenty years. His dominance had provided relative stability after the confusion and conflicts of earlier years. If Siward's subordination to the English king was limited, these years saw progress towards establishing the region as part of the wider English kingdom. Siward enforced appointment to the see of St Cuthbert of its first bishop from the south, rather than any of the Northumbrian factions. The bishopric was already developing a special status, associated with the sanctity of St Cuthbert, and its control was crucial for the Durham area. (Bonner 1989; Rollason 1994) The overlordship of Edward the Confessor was now at least nominally recognized in virtually the whole of what was to be the kingdom of England during the centuries to come.

The Problem of the North

The succession to Siward as earl of York and Northumbria in 1055 posed problems. His surviving son, Waltheof, was only a boy. (Morris 1992) Edward did not choose the local alternative from the House of Bamburgh, but instead appointed an outsider from the south, Tostig, third son of his most powerful subject, Earl Godwin. This may have been intended to further integrate Northumbria within the English kingdom. (Lomas 1992, 9) The House of Godwin was powerful and ambitious, but the appointment was something of a gamble, as Tostig had no power base in the north and none of Siward's prestige and influence.

Tostig failed in the difficult task of controlling Northumbria, although his catastrophe was postponed until ten years after his installation in 1055. To establish his power, he needed resources to sustain an adequate retinue, and this meant squeezing more revenue from the earldom. Some local feuds were deeply entrenched, including disputes between the bishop and the Durham quasi-monastic community. Siward's bishop retired soon after the old earl's death and Tostig secured the appointment of that bishop's brother to the see. Quarrels broke out again, and the community of St Cuthbert was alienated from the new earl. The Durham *Congregatio* had originated as an orthodox Benedictine community at Lindisfarne, but its subsequent adventures had transformed it into a society of men who performed monastic duties but could marry and have children. Many of them were drawn from influential northern families, and the marriage of a daughter of their bishop to an earl of Northumbria had seemed normal enough in the early eleventh century. (Bonner 1989; Morris 1992) Tostig's alienation of a community possessing both spiritual and secular power was a serious weakness.

Tostig did not possess the resources with which to resist Scottish aggression. Malcolm had established his authority by 1058 and no longer needed English support. The Scots remembered how Siward had taken advantage of their troubles to move into Cumbria. Scottish raids began again, but in 1059 negotiations produced an apparently amicable settlement of current Anglo-Scottish disputes. Trusting in this, Tostig departed on a pilgrimage to Rome in 1061, accompanying Ealdred, the bishop of Durham. (Higham 1993, 235) This was the signal for a Scottish invasion. On the east, a devastating incursion ravaged parts of Northumbria. The Scots reoccupied Cumbria, which they were to hold for another thirty years. Their acquisitions probably went further, with places like Hexham and Corbridge uncomfortably close to the new border. North Tynedale seems to have been under Scottish control at this time. The Scots had acquired territories which enabled them to threaten the region from west as well as north.

Tostig's failure to reverse this situation on his return further impaired his hold on his earldom. His financial exactions continued, and attempts to reduce hostility by murdering three prominent Northumbrian noblemen were counter-productive. In 1065, while the earl was away, his enemies struck. The Durham community played a part in fomenting rebellion, but the first blow was struck at York. A party of disaffected nobles and their followers broke into the city and killed the heads of Tostig's household troops and many of their followers. There followed a general rising and massacre of the earl's followers. The rebels moved south in force and enlisted outside support by installing Morcar, brother of Edwin, earl of Mercia, as their new earl. In this way they recruited the principal rival dynasty to the House of Godwin and avoided damaging disputes about the succession within their own ranks. The continuance of Viking influence was shown by the rebels' demand that Edward the Confessor should accept that the Laws of Cnut were still valid; presumably Tostig had failed to honour edicts of the Viking king. A modern assessment of the 1065 northern rising considers it 'a coup conceived and executed . . . with consummate skill, which reveals . . . full grasp of the intricacies of contemporary English politics'. (Higham 1993, 236–7)

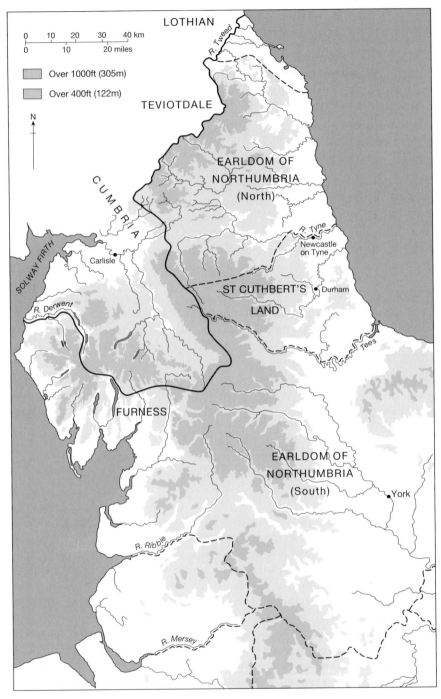

Map 2 The probable northern border of England, 1066–1092
After G.W.S. Barrow, *Feudal Britain* (London 1956)

After negotiations in which Harold, Tostig's elder brother and the most powerful man in the kingdom, took a leading part, a settlement emerged. The ailing king and Harold acquiesced in Tostig's overthrow and the installation of Morcar as earl of York and Northumbria. Other claimants were also bought off. Osulf, head of the House of Bamburgh, was to become Morcar's lieutenant in the north of the earldom; Siward's son Waltheof became earl of Huntingdon and Northampton, part of his father's old possessions. Tostig's financial exactions were to cease.

Tostig fled abroad after his rejection by the dying king and his own brother, Harold. The childless Edward died on 5 January 1066 and Harold was crowned the next day. Despite his lack of hereditary right, Harold's election was generally accepted. The new king possessed great influence within a kingdom which had recently seen little in the way of orderly hereditary succession. Edwin and Morcar made no demur, and presumably Harold's acceptance of Tostig's expulsion had taken account of the need to conciliate this rival family as Edward's death approached. Before the 1065 northern revolt, Harold had married the widowed sister of the Mercian earl, and made a friendly visit to Morcar at York before Easter 1066. (Higham 1993, 238) Tostig had no reason to support his brother and resorted to raiding the south and east of England, before swearing allegiance to the king of Norway and joining him in a major invasion project. Harald Hardrada intended to restore England to Scandinavian rule as it had been in the days of Cnut, and gathered a powerful fleet. In seeking to understand Tostig's behaviour, we should remember that concepts of nationality were embryonic, and that England represented a recent mingling of Anglo-Saxon, Celtic and Scandinavian inheritances.

The Norman Conquest in the North

The survival of Viking influences in Yorkshire made a landing there attractive to the Norse invaders. The Norwegian fleet was joined by Vikings from the Orkneys and Ireland as it approached England. At first the new English king waited with his highly trained household troops in the south, facing another rival, William, duke of Normandy. When he learned that the Norwegians had landed and routed Edwin and Morcar at Fulford Bridge near York, Harold set off north with picked forces. His speed enabled him to catch the invaders by surprise. In the Battle of Stamford Bridge on 25 September Harold won a smashing victory; Tostig and Harald Hardrada were killed. During victory celebrations, news arrived that William had landed in Kent. Harold set out by forced marches to meet this threat, but on 14 October he was defeated and killed. (Le Patourel 1971, 2–5) With few exceptions, surviving leaders of the kingdom accepted the Norman victory, and William was crowned at Westminster on Christmas Day 1066, claiming to inherit as legitimate heir of the Saxon rulers. For the time being, Morcar remained earl of Northumbria and attended William's coronation, although the king did not allow him to return north.

The new regime inherited difficult problems, none more troublesome than the situation in the far north. English control was not yet solidly established, and opposition to southern interference remained potentially strong. Among nobles still holding out against William was Osulf of Bamburgh, while the new king must have had at least a suspicion that northerners had co-operated with Viking invaders a few months earlier.

William tried to deal with his northern province by installing Copsig as his chief representative there. Copsig had influential Northumbrian connections, though he had sided with Tostig in the Norwegian invasion of 1066. The new earl, with his household troops, came north early in 1067 to establish his authority, but failed to dispose of Osulf, whose followers surprised Copsig on Tyneside on 12 March. He fled into the church at Newburn, whereupon his enemies set the wooden building on fire, and Copsig was killed when he emerged. This catastrophe may be connected to Copsig's attempts to gather taxes for William within a region always suspicious of southern tax-gatherers. The rebellion was weakened by the death of Osulf in a minor affray later in 1067, and this gave William a breathing space to try again to establish his authority in the north.

The failure of Copsig, and the king's need for money with which to reward his followers of 1066, led to what was virtually the sale of the earldom of Northumbria to Cospatric, a nobleman with family connections in Northumbria and Scotland. His father was a Scottish prince, and his mother's parents were a former earl of Northumbria and a daughter of Ethelred, king of England.

William I's need for money led him to employ the tax-raising powers of his English predecessors. His first geld may have contributed to Copsig's death, his second led to a rising against him in 1068. Edwin and Morcar rebelled in the spring, and Cospatric also joined the uprising. At the same time, the Saxon prince Edgar the Atheling, closest heir by blood to Edward the Confessor, was at large as a claimant to the English throne. William moved swiftly, forced Edwin and Morcar into submission, and occupied Yorkshire.

The northern surrender was only skin-deep. Cospatric and Edgar the Atheling fled to the Scottish court, where they were seen as useful recruits. The Scottish king married one of Edgar's sisters. William placed a strong garrison in his new castle at York, and appointed Normans to govern the surrounding region. Robert de Comines became the new earl of Northumbria, leading 700 trained troops. By late January 1069, he had reached Durham and his followers began to ransack the houses of the little town which had

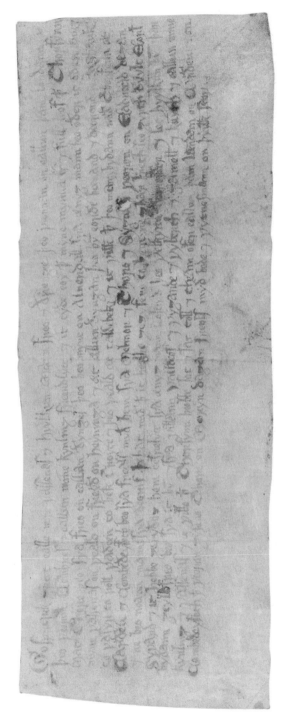

Figure 1.1 Gospatric's writ, amongst the earliest extant Cumbrian documents. Written in Anglo-Saxon and thought to have been issued *c*.1066, the text survives here in a thirteenth-century copy.

grown around the monastic community. During the night, the Norman force was taken by surprise and massacred by local people.

This sparked off another rebellion in Northumbria. The governor of York Castle was caught away from his stronghold and killed with his escorting retainers. The castle at York was besieged by a northern army accompanied by Cospatric and Edgar the Atheling. William gathered an army and moved so rapidly that he surprised the besiegers and scattered them. The rebel leaders escaped and sought help from Swein, king of Denmark, who, as Cnut's nephew, nurtured claims on the English throne. A Danish army landed in Yorkshire in September 1069 and eventually captured York, with the support of northern rebel leaders. The Norman garrison there was routed and many of them killed.

Again William came north with an army and by a series of battles, negotiations and bribes obtained the departure of the Danish invaders, leaving northerners to endure widespread punitive raids. When William reached the northern boundary of Yorkshire some leading rebels, including Cospatric and Siward's son Waltheof, submitted. Devastation of rebel territory continued in parts of Northumbria, with two main forces moving in parallel trains of destruction through eastern and central Durham. Most of the population fled to safety away from the lines of march, but buildings and fields were wasted in what has been described as 'perhaps the most destructive single campaign in England's history'. (Higham 1993, 232) By January 1070 the worst of the retaliation was over and the North was left to lick its wounds. Starvation or migration must have been a choice faced by many.

Insecurity in the North

The harrying of the North had suppressed any immediate threat to William's position there, but sporadic Viking raids and the threat of large-scale Viking invasion continued. A Viking force seized York briefly in 1075 and as late as 1085 the Danes were making preparations for another invasion, though nothing came of this. Northern people had not developed an instinctive loyalty to their Norman rulers, but punitive campaigns had destroyed any capacity for large-scale rebellion. There was an escalation in petty disorder and brigandage, partly due to the presence of many ex-rebels and men deprived of their livelihood during harrying campaigns.

Some kind of settlement now had to be patched up for the North. A new archbishop of York, imported from Bayeux, was installed to bring the northern Church under control. Combined efforts of harrying and confiscation of rebel estates placed the king in a stronger position in Yorkshire than

English rulers had enjoyed earlier. Further north, restoration of order presented intractable problems. Despite his unreliability, William reappointed Cospatric to the earldom of Northumbria. At least Cospatric, with his ties to the old Bamburgh dynasty, could deploy some personal influence north of the Tees. The appointment, which can hardly have been an enthusiastic one, achieved some early results. In 1070, Cospatric reacted vigorously against an incursion by the Scots from their western base in Cumbria. He also accepted installation of William's nominee, Walcher, another Continental priest, as bishop of Durham. It is unlikely that William trusted Cospatric, whose record was dubious and who was a cousin of the Scottish king.

For some time, William was engaged in dealing with remnants of the Danish invading force of 1069 and suppression of resistance in East Anglia, but in 1072 his attention returned to the North. (Lomas 1992, 13) A combined military and naval expedition invaded Scotland. Malcolm withdrew north rather than risk a pitched battle, and the English army reached Fife. Negotiations produced the Treaty of Abernethy, whereby Malcolm recognized the English king as overlord. English rebels, including Edgar the Atheling, were to be expelled from the Scottish court, and a group of eminent hostages, including Duncan, Malcolm's heir, came to England. William also took the opportunity to get rid of the unreliable Cospatric.

Because of other responsibilities in England and Normandy, William could not linger in the north. To cope with the situation north of the Tees, he chose another earl with family links to the region, Waltheof, Siward's younger son. (Scott 1952) Waltheof had been high in the king's favour, receiving Siward's southern earldom of Northampton and Huntingdon. He had joined the 1069 rebellion but subsequently made his peace with the king, a reconciliation marked by marriage with the king's niece Judith. The king believed that his hold on Yorkshire was now secure, but still had doubts about the situation further north, despite the peace with Scotland. That settlement left Malcolm in control of Strathclyde territories in the North West and in a position to cause trouble on two fronts whenever an opportunity occurred. On his return south, William paused to supervise construction of a castle at Durham, providing a refuge for his bishop if things were to turn ugly. By 1074, with the English king at a safe distance, Malcolm, despite earlier promises, welcomed to his court both Edgar the Atheling and Cospatric. Though Edgar, never a successful challenger for the English throne and apparently aware that he was not likely to succeed, made his peace with William some time later, the danger remained acute.

Evidence for ensuing months remains patchy. In 1074 Waltheof was again in arms against the king, perhaps because of another attempt by William to levy taxes on his northern subjects. The rising failed but Waltheof was again pardoned. In 1075 William discovered a more dangerous conspiracy, involving Waltheof, the earls of East Anglia and Hereford, and a Danish invasion which came too late and achieved little except a temporary seizure of York. William was lucky in that his enemies failed to co-ordinate their movements and the plot was detected in time. Waltheof tried to obtain another pardon, but he was imprisoned and executed after trial in the king's court.

Once again, support for royal authority in the north had collapsed. William tried another expedient, entrusting Bishop Walcher of Durham with the secular authority of an earl north of the Tees. The bishop paid a substantial price and the king tried to bolster his position by timely concessions to the influental *Congregatio* at Durham. In other ways too the Church in Northumbria was strengthened. The 1070s saw the founding or restoration of northern monasteries, including Jarrow (1074) and Monkwearmouth (1076–78). (Baker 1970, 5)

For a few years Walcher seems to have moved warily, relying on local advisers in framing his policies. Perhaps some of his imported followers were less careful of native sensibilities, or the bishop himself later adopted less conciliatory policies. There is some evidence that he imposed additional burdens on his estates in the years after the punitive campaigns of 1069 and 1070. (Kapelle 1979, 188–9) His prestige must have been shaken when in 1079 he made no effective resistance to a Scottish incursion mounted when William was fighting in Normandy. An internal quarrel in Walcher's household culminated in 1080 in the murder of an influential nobleman from the House of Bamburgh who had been the bishop's chief counsellor. Walcher, realizing the enmity which this would cause, retired into his castle at Durham. During negotiations with the victim's family, Walcher rode with a hundred knights to a rendezvous at Gateshead. When he entered the church there the Northumbrians massacred his escort and Walcher and his immediate retinue were then killed.

The rebels had no plans for following up this success. A siege of Durham Castle was given up after a few days and the rebellion then fizzled out. Retribution for the Gateshead massacre was not long in coming. Later in 1080 the king's half-brother Odo, bishop of Bayeux, led a punitive expedition north of the Tees, and instituted another harrying sufficiently thorough to ensure that the native nobility of the North East could no longer serve as a serious threat.

The Founding of Newcastle

There had been no effective co-operation between the rebels of 1080 and the Scots, but Malcolm had never been repaid for his incursion in 1079. Later in 1080, the eldest son of the English king, Robert, led an army into Scotland. After marching as far as Falkirk, he secured reaffirmation of the

Figure 1.2 St Paul's Church, Jarrow, successor to the monastery founded in 681. The greater part of the church, to the left, is eighteenth- and nineteenth-century re-building. The tower was probably built by Aldwyn, Prior 1074–83, while the chancel is the most substantial survival of the original seventh-century structure.

Abernethy agreement, an unreliable basis for future relations. English doubts as to how far Scots could be trusted to observe this treaty were illustrated by Robert's action on his march south. He paused to supervise construction of a new base for royal authority in the new castle he erected on the Tyne opposite Gateshead, at a point where there had been a Roman bridge and fort and some kind of Anglo-Saxon religious foundation. (Lomas 1992, 15; Harbottle 1966, 83; Tullett and McCombie 1980, 127) Under the castle's protection, a civil settlement soon sprang up, providing the nucleus for early urban development. By 1091 at latest, the first parish church, St Nicholas, had been established. Newcastle upon Tyne was to play a leading role in the region's history, but it would be an exaggeration to see here a town of any significance by the end of the eleventh century. Durham was larger, and even its claim to urban status was uncertain. (Miller 1976 for 1975, 5)

Odo's punitive campaign had chastened the Northumbrians and ended older forms of native resistance to English rule. Robert's invasion of Scotland temporarily diminished danger from that source. William could once again try to arrange some kind of stable regime north of the Tees. One of his own ministers, the Benedictine monk William of St Calais, was promoted to hold the religious and secular influence of the bishopric of Durham. (Lomas 1992, 15) He set about replacement of the old quasi-monastic *Congregatio* at Durham, which had shown dubious loyalty as well as religious unsoundness, with more orthodox, celibate, and possibly more obedient, Benedictine monks from Jarrow and Monkwearmouth. This change was effected in May 1083. The bishop began negotiations to obtain amicable division of Church property between the bishop and the reformed monastic community, although this was not finalized until the episcopate of his successor, Ranulf Flambard. The division was reflected in neighbouring settlements of Bishopwearmouth and Monkwearmouth at the mouth of the Wear.

Robert de Mowbray in the North

A suitable secular government proved more elusive. The first appointment to the earldom was short-lived, for the nominee gave up the position after a brief experience of its problems. The next earl, Robert de Mowbray, son of one of William's 1066 companions, was of sterner stuff, and set about reducing his province to order. If Mowbray seemed to have the qualities needed to establish authority, his subsequent career provided another illustration of problems of delegated government in a remote region. For effective rule, a powerful magnate was needed, but it was difficult to ensure that such a man would subordinate his interests to those of his sovereign.

William died in 1087, and the next year brought a baronial revolt against his successor. The bishop of Durham and the earl of Northumbria were among the plotters, but eventually William Rufus accepted the submission of both men and retained them in their positions, though the bishop suffered three years in exile, during which the king exploited the Durham estates to his own profit.

New Baronial Appointments

Well aware of problems entailed in trying to make their rule effective in the North, the first two Norman kings embarked upon creation of consolidated baronial fiefs able to provide effective military resources. These were entrusted to strong men, deemed capable of managing their own territories and contributing to the general security of the region. At some date before 1092 William

II conferred on Ivo Taillebois an extensive lordship which included southern Westmorland, southern Cumberland, and probably Furness. This was intended to block incursions into England from the north-west. South of the Scottish border in the east, similar grants were given to Guy de Balliol. He received the upper part of the Tees valley, and his son Bernard was to strengthen his hold by building a castle at Barnard Castle to serve as centre of his estates. He was also given the barony of Bywell in the Tyne valley west of Newcastle. This placed a powerful baron in another well placed position to frustrate threats from north or west. William de Merley, another of William I's 1066 followers, received the barony of Morpeth and built a castle there. (Ryder 1992, 63; Lomas 1966, 16–21) It is unlikely that Northumberland border areas like North Tynedale or Redesdale were yet under effective English control, but Redesdale was to become part of another baronial complex, that of the Umfravilles, in the near future. By 1090 much had been done to buttress the English position in the North.

This was enough to alarm the Scots. In May 1091 Malcolm Canmore invaded Northumberland and pushed further south. The castle at Newcastle must have been either taken or bypassed, and Durham was besieged. William II responded briskly, leading a large army north in the early autumn. The Scots retreated and refused battle. The English pushed further north, straining communications and supply routes. Once again peace was patched up. Malcolm did homage to Rufus, who returned some English properties which the Scots king held.

This was no more than a truce, for William II was not satisfied. In 1092 he took his army north again and made himself master of Cumberland. Evidence relating to the North West in the years before 1092 is thin, but this probably involved takeover of an area which had remained under Scottish control since Tostig's time. (Summerson 1993, I, 47–9) A castle was built at Carlisle and a community established under its protection. Carlisle stood at the lowest crossing over the Eden, and had previously served as the centre of an important territorial holding. It cannot have been more than a village when its future was determined by this decision. (Summerson 1993, I, 13) Like Newcastle, the site's selection for a border stronghold was based on strategic grounds. Carlisle remained under royal control, with the king responsible for maintenance of its castle and garrison. Until 1106, when Henry I bolstered the castle's position by establishing around it the large lordship of Carlisle under Ranulf Meschin, the fortress with the tiny supporting settlement remained an isolated enclave in advance of effective limits of Norman colonization. To establish any kind of viable community there involved enforced transplantation of settlers from the south. (Summerson 1993, I, 16–17)

Establishment of an Anglo-Scottish border running east and then north-east from Carlisle ignored cultural, racial and economic conditions, and was determined on military and topographical grounds. The rise of English power and consolidation of the Scottish kingdom necessitated some kind of frontier across a disputed and ill-organized region. William II's decision to incorporate the Carlisle area within England involved occupation of an area of little wealth or attraction but considerable strategic importance for defence of the more valuable North East. (Barrow 1973, 114; Kapelle 1979, 38–9, 146–7)

The events of the following months, until late 1093, are unclear, though they included another breakdown of Anglo-Scottish relations. Malcolm led a hastily organized invasion of Northumberland in November 1093, but the English were prepared. On 13 November Robert de Mowbray surprised the Scots near Alnwick and routed them with heavy losses. Malcolm and his heir Edward were both killed. This led to disputes over the succession between the king's surviving sons and his younger brother Donald Bane. One of Malcolm's sons was a hostage in England and provided Rufus with an opportunity for fishing in the troubled waters of the Scottish succession. With English support this prince succeeded in displacing his uncle temporarily, but Scotland was torn by civil war which culminated in the death of the English nominee in 1094. Donald Bane returned to a weakened Scottish throne.

The English king's opportunity to profit from these events was reduced by another baronial conspiracy against him in 1095, which involved Mowbray. This may have been because the king had taken advantage of Malcolm's defeat and death to remove the estates of the Durham church from the earl's jurisdiction, an important limitation on his regional power. Rufus was lucky in that the plotters were unable to achieve a co-ordinated attack. He was able to deal with Mowbray in isolation, by besieging the earl's castles. The spirit of the times was demonstrated during the siege of Bamburgh Castle. The formidable fortifications were defended by troops under the command of Mowbray's wife, after the earl himself had been captured. The surrender of the fortress was only obtained after Rufus threatened to have his prisoner blinded before the castle gate if the countess refused to yield. The earl lived for another thirty years, but may well have spent all of them in prison.

For the time being the king had had enough of earls of Northumbria. Mowbray was not replaced, his estates were retained as royal property, and Northumbria north of the Tees was now to be governed either by the Durham church of St Cuthbert in the person of its bishops, or by the king's sheriff of Northumberland. This dispensation could be held as long as Scotland, weak and divided, presented no urgent threat requiring the presence of a military commander of high status. This situation was maintained by William II's success in 1097 in replacing Donald Bane with an English nominee, Edgar, another of Malcolm III's surviving sons. Edgar succeeded in establishing himself, but remained loyal to his English alliance. In the year of his accession, for instance, he gave 'the village of Berwick with all its appurtenances' to the bishop of Durham, the earliest surviving reference to a place which was to play a prominent role in border history. (Hunter 1982, 68) The next thirty years provided one of the relatively rare periods of peace on the border.

Henry I in the North

Henry I consolidated the English position, spending more time in the North than any of his predecessors, which helped the assimilation of the region into a normal pattern of administration. (Barrow 1969, 26) Reconciliation with Scotland was marked by marriages between the two royal houses. Edgar's successors, his younger brothers Alexander and David, followed his policy of friendship with England. David had strong English connections, marrying the heiress of Earl Waltheof and therefore holding the earldom of Northampton and the honour of Huntingdon as vassal of the English king.

In the early years of his reign, Henry I's position was insecure, and the North provided land with which to reward his supporters. This brought new baronial families and extension of their control of the countryside, accelerating a process which had begun under his two predecessors. (Tuck 1986, 3–4; Lomas 1992, 20–30) Some of these families were to play leading roles in the region. The Bertrams received estates in south-east Durham, and the Bruces, initially established by William I in the Cleveland district, saw their holdings increased. In Northumberland the Bolbecs obtained a new barony with its centre at Styford on the Tyne. The Umfravilles received Prudhoe, also in the Tyne valley, and eventually Redesdale also. This vigorous family soon established control there and set about development of cattle and sheep farming. Long before the end of his reign, Henry had done much to fill the northern region with new noble dynasties. Baronial centres like Alnwick, Mitford, Bothal, Morpeth, Wooler and Wark were now occupied by incomers from among the king's followers. To protect their acquisitions, new lords erected castles which served to strengthen border defences. At Mitford, in Northumberland, almost certainly centre of a pre-Conquest estate, Bertram lords cleared civilians from the site of their new castle and removed them to a village on lower ground, where they established a parish church. (Honeyman 1955, 28) The bishop of Durham's fortress at Norham on the Tweed, founded in 1121, formed part of the new defences, and a chain of motte and bailey castles stretched north from Hexham up the valleys of the Rede and the North Tyne.

Parallel changes took place in the North West, with new lords established in places like Carlisle, Kendal, Burgh by Sands, Greystoke and

Copeland. Another chain of castles, including Appleby, Brough and Bowes, guarded the route through Stainmore. The linchpin of these defensive arrangements was the barony of Ranulf Meschin, with his main base at Appleby, but also holding the lordship of Carlisle. Henry I increased the family's holdings by grants to William Meschin, who built a castle at Egremont in about 1125. (Kapelle 1979, 204, 210–14; Turnbull and Walsh 1994, 77) The threat from Scotland had receded, and the new establishment in the North provided a ruling group with incentives and resources to cut down on brigandage in border counties which recent troubled decades had fostered.

Establishment of new noble families did not involve redrawing the territorial map. Tenacity of old-established boundaries was reflected in the original Bruce barony in Cleveland, almost certainly comprising holdings of earlier lords of the area. The additional Bruce estates around Hartlepool and Hart, obtained *c.*1106, had probably been held in earlier years by a dynasty of local Viking lords. (Austin 1976, 73) Sometimes a clutch of old-established estates separated by distance were joined to make up a single barony. The barony of Ellingham or Jesmond contained estates in south Northumberland – Cramlington, Hartley, Heaton, and Jesmond – coupled with a group much further north in the county – Doxford, Ellingham, Newstead. (Offler 1967, 183) Other evidence suggests continuance of ancient groupings with traditional centres. Many Northumbrian townships were grouped around a local capital. In later years, the south Northumberland townships of Blagdon, Northweetslade, Plessey and Shotton paid a standard fee of multure for the services of the same mill, and this may reflect a very old grouping. Similar evidence comes from the North West, especially in southern districts. (Halcrow 1956, 59; Winchester 1987, 17–19)

Henry I's favours were not confined to families of recent immigrants, for there was a minority of English names among those given positions of influence, reflecting a wider surviving English society. (Barrow 1969, 5–9) A series of sheriffs of Northumberland bore English names; they received estates in return for their services. Henry installed Athelwold as the first bishop of Carlisle in 1133. This priest had originally been a native landowner in Yorkshire and after entering religious life became the king's confessor. Eilau, a member of the community of hereditary priests at Hexham, was one of the important native priests still active in the North after the Conquest. His son Ailred or Ethelred was one of the country's most distinguished churchmen in the twelfth century, canonized in 1191. Henry even gave northern lands to descendants of the House of Bamburgh, including the sons of Earl Cospatric.

While Henry was establishing his new mixed aristocracy, David of Scotland, himself the product of Norman upbringing, was introducing a Norman baronage to his own country, including border counties. Even before he succeeded his brother, David occupied a position of importance in southern Scotland, and like Henry he set about placing his own men in key positions.

These new lords had an obvious interest in encouraging orderly development of their acquisitions during the generation of border peace. Some of them already held lands in David's English possessions. Others, like the Bruces and the Umfravilles, were also beneficiaries of the Norman settlement in the English North. Families with names like Boiville, Derman, Morville, Vaux and Mulcaster held lands on both sides of the border. (Summerson 1993, I, 22) This duality survived impaired Anglo-Scottish relations in Stephen's reign.

One interpretation of the settlement of the new aristocracy suggests that Henry was recruiting new men who were inclined to accept estates in poorer border lands more willingly than leading men of 1066. (Kapelle 1979, 27–30) We may doubt whether there was ever a shortage of ambitious men willing to accept land grants. The number of landholders of comparatively lowly origins in Cumbria may reflect the relative unattractiveness of that area before the amity between Henry and David of Scotland made peaceable development easier. Some of those now given northern estates already possessed richer holdings elsewhere, and do not seem to have been forced to accept additional acquisitions of inferior quality.

The changes in the first half of the twelfth century went further than establishment of a more extensive aristocracy. Many of the baronies were of modest size and in addition principal landowners conveyed much of their land to followers in return for service. This made available a range of lesser barons and knights who could carry on the work of county administration, whether under the king or, in the peculiar position attained by Durham, under a palatinate regime headed by the bishop. The system of royal courts was established within the region, and surviving writs show that royal authority was now exercised as elsewhere in the kingdom. There were even stirrings of urban activity. The developing community of Newcastle remained under royal lordship, but Henry granted an early form of municipal charter to its inhabitants. They now possessed their own officials, their own common seal and their own locally enforceable code of laws and customs. (Hunter Blair 1955, 2)

The Situation in the North *c.*1100

The situation by the end of the eleventh century is tolerably clear, even if some of the details remain obscure. After several setbacks, Norman kings established their authority at least as far as the Tyne in the east and Carlisle in the west. After suppression of a series of risings, pre-Conquest ruling families had been largely replaced by followers of Norman rulers. The most important new lords were given consolidated baronies strong enough to enable them to resist incursions from Scots or other enemies. Within the region, the richly endowed church of Durham occupied an exceptional position of combined secular and spiritual influence. As yet, none of the northern barons enjoyed status equivalent to that of the greatest lords in the more prosperous south.

Civil War in England

The civil war which erupted after Henry's death offered irresistible temptation to the Scots. When Henry's nephew Stephen seized the throne, King David declared his support for Matilda, Henry's daughter, and exploited this to Scotland's benefit. The Scots invaded Cumbria and made Carlisle an important base. Leading northern nobles supported rival claimants to the English throne and united resistance to the Scots was impossible. (Summerson 1993, I, 39–41; Lomas 1992, 32–41) Some northern areas had already developed stronger connections with Scotland than others. Where cross-border links were close, this weakened loyalties to the English Crown. During the twelfth century Carlisle's trading connections seem to have been mainly with its northern neighbours, although the little town cannot have looked with favour on potential rivalry growing at Dumfries by the late twelfth century. Coins minted at Carlisle have been found as frequently in Scotland as in England.

In 1138 the Scots invaded northern England. Some recently established baronial families, including men with holdings in both kingdoms, vainly tried to negotiate a peaceful settlement. As David marched south, he met little resistance. Norham and Bamburgh Castles surrendered without a fight. The recently annexed Cumbrian territories contributed a contingent to the Scottish army. The aged archbishop Thurstan of York succeeded in raising an army, headed by Yorkshire barons, and the Scots were badly beaten near Northallerton, on 22 August. This engagement became known as the Battle of the Standard, as the English rallied around a standard bearing the banners of St Peter of York, St John of Beverley and St Wilfrid of Ripon, together with a casket containing the consecrated host.

Despite this defeat, the invasion earned dividends in the Treaty of Durham, concluded in 1139. Stephen, faced with a rival claimant to the throne, bought peace on the border. The Scots kept Cumbria, including Carlisle. In addition, David's heir, Henry, was created earl of Northumberland as Stephen's vassal. Through his mother, he had some hereditary claim to the earldom, and its possession had been a Scottish demand since fighting began after Henry I's death. The new earl was given possession of the county except

Figure 1.3 Bamburgh Castle. One of the principal northern castles for many years, with a long and complex history. There was prehistoric occupation nearby and the site was an early Anglo-Saxon stronghold, while during the medieval centuries it became an important royal castle. In the eighteenth century it was the headquarters of a charitable trust under the will of Bishop Lord Crewe, and in the years around 1900 there was extensive re-building after the castle was bought by Lord Armstrong.

for the royal castles of Bamburgh and Newcastle, and the liberty of Hexham, held by the church of York.

Once again England's troubles had proved Scotland's opportunity, and the takeover of Northumberland and Cumbria was accepted with little resistance. A member of the Umfraville dynasty, of Prudhoe-on-Tyne and Redesdale, was happy to serve as Earl Henry's steward. The insecurity of Stephen's position continued to encourage Scottish ambitions. In the 1140s King David pressed his candidate for the bishopric of Durham against Stephen's nominee. David's man, William Cumin, managed to hold Durham from 1141 to 1144, but this attempted takeover ultimately failed. (Hedley 1959, 293; Young 1994)

Matilda's claim to the English throne passed to her eldest son, Henry of Anjou, the future Henry II, who was also willing to buy Scottish support. In a ceremony at Carlisle in 1149, Henry was knighted by the Scottish king, and promised that if he gained the English throne he would confirm recent Scottish gains and add Newcastle. In the same year, David accompanied

Henry on an invasion of England from Cumbria, which reached Lancaster before Stephen could repel it.

Unexpected developments then intervened. The deaths of Henry of Scotland (12 June 1152), David (25 May 1153) and Stephen (25 October 1153) gave Henry of Anjou, now King Henry II, an opportunity which he readily exploited. David was succeeded by his 11-year-old grandson Malcolm, and this was the signal for internal strife. The new king was in no position to refuse Henry II's demands for return of the Scots' recent acquisitions. The two kings came to an agreement at a meeting at Chester in 1157. England resumed control of Cumbria and Northumberland, though this was not finally accepted by the Scots until the Treaty of York in 1237. Malcolm was given the rich English honour of Huntingdon, to which his family had some hereditary claim. The Scots king was also to hold the lordship of Tynedale as a vassal of the English king, consolation for the loss of the earldom of Northumberland. Again this fief represented a recognition of claims which went back to the days of Siward and Waltheof. Thereafter the monarchs co-operated. Malcolm brought a contingent to an English expedition against Toulouse in 1159 and was knighted by the English king during the campaign. His reign was punctuated by outbreaks of internal strife, but all of these were overcome. Malcolm died as accepted king of Scotland in December 1165 and was succeeded by his brother William the Lion.

Henry II in the North

After the 1157 settlement, Henry II established his authority in the North, enforcing justice, collecting taxes, and maintaining order with a firm hand. In 1166, leading men of the North, like their fellows elsewhere, were required to satisfy the king that their tenure of possessions and privileges was legitimate. Henry was determined to vindicate his authority, and collection of such information was a prerequisite here. For example, Walter, son of William, established his title to the barony of Whalton, and informed the king that three knightly families were settled on parts of the barony to fulfil the military service which he owed; these arrangements had been implemented before the death of Henry I. William, son of a man with the Scandinavian name of Siward, held Gosforth and half of Middleton, a small barony which owed the service of one knight, an obligation which the demesne property fulfilled.

Before the end of the century, the northern counties, outside the privileged liberties of the bishop of Durham, were visited by royal justices on their itinerant assizes. The king had accepted that the bishop should hold his own courts, issue writs and appoint justices. There was never any serious doubt about the superiority of royal power even within this privileged palatinate. Over most of the North, surviving records show that remote areas and relatively trifling affairs could come within the purview of royal justice in the later twelfth century. (Hunter Blair 1952, 2–3; Barrow 1969, 26–7)

William the Lion

The accession of William the Lion in 1165 brought renewed border warfare, as he set about pursuing Scotland's old claims. In 1166 Henry refused to restore Cumbria or Northumberland to Scottish control. Two years later, William began the first negotiations for alliance with France against England. In 1173, after the murder of Becket, Henry II faced a coalition which included not only the kings of France and Scotland but also his own sons. A Scots army invaded Northumberland in 1173 and again in 1174, but a stroke of luck brought Henry an unexpected reprieve.

Riding with a small escort near Alnwick, the Scottish king was surprised by an English force and captured. His freedom was subsequently bought at a high price. The Treaty of Falaise, in December 1174, embodied a solemn promise to subordinate Scotland to England. The English king was given custody of a group of Scottish castles as a guarantee of the treaty and Scottish prelates and nobles were obliged to swear to accept the terms imposed.

This treaty, unlikely to have taken permanent effect in any case, proved short-lived. Henry died on 6 July 1189, and Richard I was eager to depart on crusade. In return for a Scottish subsidy, he agreed to abrogation of the Treaty of Falaise. Three years later the Scottish king contributed a substantial sum to Richard's ransom, presumably on account of his English possessions rather than tribute from Scotland. Despite frequent requests, the English king refused to consider any cessions of territory to the Scots. Instead, in the years after 1174 there was continuing assimilation of northern districts into the normal pattern of county administration. These years saw the formalization of Cumberland and Westmorland, and consolidation of county government in Northumberland. After Richard's death in 1199 his brother John repeated the refusal of territorial concessions. Although war threatened on occasion, no major fighting occurred until after William the Lion's death on 4 December 1214.

When civil war erupted with conflict between John and many of his barons, the new Scottish king, Alexander II, intervened on the side of the rebels, in return for their promise to restore Cumbria and Northumberland. Again opinion among the northern nobility was divided. John had continued the policy of tightening royal control in the border counties and this, together with demands for taxation, provoked unrest. Some prominent men joined the rebels, but John also had his local supporters, like Philip of Ulecotes who became a leading royal agent. (Lomas 1996, 164–7; Harbottle and Salway 1960, 130–2)

The king's urgent needs for support, and for money, enabled influential elements to obtain useful royal grants. In Durham, knights and lesser freeholders took advantage of troubled times to buy from the king a charter which guaranteed that proceedings in the bishop's courts would be conducted according to procedures followed in the king's courts. This suggests that some earlier practices were outdated or at least unsatisfactory to some of the bishop's dependants. (Offler 1988, 195) Similarly, leading men of Newcastle secured in 1213 a charter which allowed them to take over administration of this royal borough in return for an annual rent or farm of £100. Three years later, they bought the right to incorporate themselves into a guild merchant with privileges consolidating their control of the growing town. Hartlepool was another town which bought privileges from John. It was developing into the principal port of the bishopric of Durham, and hoped that by buying a royal charter of privileges the town might escape, at least partially, from the increasingly irksome domination of its episcopal landlord. (O'Brien 1989, 202; Scott 1959, 279)

As in Stephen's reign, English civil conflict provided the Scots with an irresistible opportunity. A Scots army besieged Norham Castle in 1215 and occupied most of Northumberland. Another incursion in 1216–17 seized Carlisle with little opposition. (Summerson 1993, I, 96–8) John marched north, driving the Scots before him and ravaging large areas of southern Scotland. The king's hand fell heavily on barons who had joined the league against him. Their lands were devastated and their castles ruined. Alnwick, Mitford, Morpeth and Wark were among strongholds which suffered for their lords' disloyalty. Their holders had not only joined in the baronial revolt but recognized Alexander II's claim to the earldom of Northumberland. The Scottish king responded to John's invasion by encouraging intervention by Prince Louis of France on the side of baronial rebels, and by another Scottish attack on Carlisle. The tangled situation was resolved by John's death on 19 October 1216, which saw a decline of English support for foreign intervention and growing acceptance of the new infant king Henry III. Reconciliation included return of confiscated estates: the De Merley barony of Morpeth, for example, was restored in 1218. (Hunter Blair 1952, 5–6; Ryder 1992, 63)

Restoration of Anglo-Scottish Amity

In 1219 peace was restored between England and Scotland. England kept the disputed northern counties and Alexander was again given substantial English estates as a vassal of the English king. These included the honour of Huntingdon and the border lordship of Tynedale. For most of the rest of the century, Tynedale was governed by officers of Scottish kings from Wark-on-Tyne. This led to Wark becoming a local capital equipped with castle, prison, bakehouse, brewery, forge, fulling mill for woollen cloth, corn mill and deer park. In addition to the extensive lordship of Tynedale, Scottish kings' holdings in northern England included Penrith, and Castle Sowerby within Inglewood. (Charlton 1987, 30–2; Lomas 1992, 40–1; Fraser 1968, vii)

The thorny question of whether the Scottish king owed homage for his kingdom remained unsettled. Alexander married an English princess and another period of relative calm on the borders began. In the Treaty of York in 1237, Scotland renounced claims to northern counties of England. In 1249 the sheriff of Northumberland held a parley with opposite numbers from the Scottish border counties of Berwick and Roxburgh; a jury of twelve English and twelve Scottish knights advised the sheriffs on prevailing border customs. This produced a statement of conventions which should apply to disputes involving men from both sides of the border. On both sides there was willingness to see such problems resolved without violence. For most of the rest of the century the North enjoyed relative freedom from disorder.

These improved relations were accompanied by increased personal links between leading families in border areas. It was possible for border magnates, like the Muschamp barons of Wooler, or the Roos family of Wark, to take Scottish wives and acquire with them substantial holdings over the border. The Umfravilles of Prudhoe and Redesdale married into the higher Scottish aristocracy and became earls of Angus from 1243. Both co-heiresses of the Muschamp barony of Wooler in Northumberland took Scottish husbands. The Scottish earls of Dunbar, descended from pre-Conquest earls of Northumbria, held the Northumberland barony of Beanley. The king of Scotland was an English territorial magnate. Coldingham Priory in Berwickshire was a daughter house of Durham. Coldstream Priory owned lands in north Northumberland; Melrose Abbey also held English lands. Jedburgh Abbey's grazing rights extended across the border line. The cult of St Cuthbert was not confined to one side of the frontier. As yet such divided loyalties could be acquired without serious problems. (Tuck 1971, 22–4) High-level links of this kind reflected the continuing similarity of society on each side of the border, and even if evidence is largely lacking it is likely that cross-border personal and family links existed at lower levels of society. One modern study has concluded that

The border line itself . . . divided a people who had more in common with each other than with their fellow-countrymen to the north or south. The English and Scottish borderers were similar in their social structure, their speech, their way of life, and their way of gaining a livelihood. (Tuck 1968, 28)

An illuminating incident took place during the judicial eyre of 1292. The court at Carlisle hanged a man for a theft committed in Scotland, as if the border could be conveniently ignored in jurisdictional matters. (Summerson 1982) Such manifestations were encouraged by greater prosperity brought to the North by the coming of peace.

It seemed as if an established tradition of peaceful co-operation might continue indefinitely, although English border defences were not entirely neglected. After the settlement of 1157, Henry II strengthened Cumbrian defences by conferring on Hubert de Vaux the barony of Gilsland, in return for military service. (Summerson 1993, I, 67) Henry III strengthened defences of the royal fortress at Newcastle by adding the Black Gate in 1247–50. The developing town of Newcastle was equipped with perimeter defences, if at a slow pace. Newcastle's first grant of murage, a special tax for building the town walls, was made in 1265. The perimeter ditch was not completed until 1316, and the town wall was still unfinished then. (Nolan 1989, 29–30) Such expenditures were not always popular, especially during periods when there seemed to be no urgent threat of war. At Carlisle, repeated exaction of tolls to maintain the town's defences was part of the Crown's policy of shifting such burdens to local shoulders and increasing revenues from border shires. Such taxes increased prices of goods locally and may have produced disaffection among local people who resented them.

There were limits to what could be done during times of reduced tension. During the Scottish siege of 1216, Carlisle Castle's defences had been damaged by siege engines. An English commission which reported in 1256 noted that nothing had been done to repair the damage (Summerson 1993, I, 121, 123) Generally the northern region experienced relative tranquillity during most of the thirteenth century.

Chapter 2

Early Medieval Society in the North

Within our region, only a few southern districts of Cumbria, already permeated by English influences, were included in Domesday Book. It was not until 1183, with Boldon Book, a survey of the bishop of Durham's estates, that any comparable source survives for the far north. A scatter of chance survivals is all that comes down to us from earlier documents. It is however possible to re-create a general pattern for eleventh-century society.

A highly unequal society was dominated by landowners, religious or secular, who had acquired estates by grants over previous centuries. These grants involved control over inhabitants of estates as well as rights to revenues. More powerful elements, such as leading churches and principal aristocratic interests, controlled wide areas, composed of a number of separate estates, in which a centre, sometimes called a *caput* or head, acted as local capital for smaller communities and scattered homesteads within its attributed territory. Examples include places like Escomb, Gainford, Heighington and Staindrop in Durham, where these villages served as centres for surrounding 'shires'. These units of territorial organization differed in extent, although in parts of the North East there was a recurring pattern of association of twelve villages. In Cumbria, and in upland areas of the North East, such as the Cheviots, Weardale and Teesdale, shires were larger than in more fertile areas, reflecting lower productivity. Dues paid to landowners tended to be lower in poorer areas than in areas of tillage, and often included cornage, paid in cattle rather than crops. Upland landowners controlled access to higher summer pastures as well as the area closer to their main centres. (Winchester 1987, 4–5)

Sometimes a whole shire or group of shires had been granted to a secular magnate or a great church. Some of the clearest examples are found in estates which represented substantial grants to churches, such as Bedlingtonshire, Heighingtonshire and the long-established northern territory of Norham-Islandshire. Their nature has been the subject of prolonged arguments, but it now seems reasonably clear that these north-eastern shires resembled the sokes already recognized as territorial units in much of eastern England further south. (Kapelle 1979, ch. 4)

It is probable that there was a similar pattern within the old king-dom of Strathclyde. Penrith may have already served as headquarters of an important estate within the central area of the Eden valley. As in ecclesiast-ical matters, Cumbrian landowning boundaries retained many old British ar-rangements, which had been more radically altered in the east during Anglian dominance of Northumbria. Carlisle may offer one exception here, with indications that older territorial conventions were undermined there during eleventh-century changes. The scattered evidence which survives suggests that resemblances continued between Cumbrian arrangements and other 'British' areas like Wales. This included survival of large compact territorial hold-ings which may represent very ancient boundaries. Some of these continued into baronial holdings of the years after 1066. (Winchester 1987, 4–5, 18; Barrow 1969, 23; Summerson 1993, I, 11)

Little evidence survives to indicate detailed organization or numbers of the population. Certainly the total must have been small in contrast to that of much later periods. This fundamental difference has implications for the nature of local society in a variety of ways, even if limitations in our evid-ence prevent us from comprehending all aspects of life in a less numerous and more primitive society. (Lomas 1996, 69–71)

The troubled centuries which followed the end of Roman rule may have seen some drop in population, but there is no reason to doubt con-tinuity of an economic pattern which reflected mixed farming carried on in scattered homesteads. Predominance of pastoral farming was more marked in Cumbria, where oats probably represented the only widely grown crop and management of sheep and cattle was the main preoccupation. This in itself imposed limitations on the population which could be supported. Such practices as summer pasturing in outlying uplands were already well estab-lished. When St Cuthbert was a young man, in the seventh century, he once sheltered near Chester-le-Street in some shepherds' huts 'which had been roughly built during the summer and were then lying open and deserted'. (McDonnell 1988, 3) A local lord would have his *caput* in the more fertile part of his holdings, from which he would control the use of surrounding pastoral areas. By the end of the Anglo-Saxon period, population increase had seen summer pasturing spread into many upland areas. Extension of pasturage was often reflected in different tenurial arrangements. Original holdings might carry traditional dues such as cornage or seawake, while later acquisitions might never incur such obligations. The distinction could have wider significance. Over time, administration of longer-settled areas was influenced by developing communal conventions, while land obtained later might be more under the untrammelled authority of its lord. (Winchester 1985, 95–7; Winchester 1987, 20–2)

Within a great estate, the owner, whether secular or ecclesiastical, re-tained some land in his own hands to be farmed by direct dependants. In an economy in which money played a minor role, local magnates rewarded principal servants with grants of land in return for service and contributions in cash or in kind. King Alfred once remarked that a ruler needed men who work, men who pray and men who fight, and no doubt this applied to noble magnates too. (Finberg 1972, 525) Larger estates developed hierarchies of specialists such as soldiers, priests, and craftsmen like smiths, masons and carpenters. Less sophisticated contexts must have seen metal working and similar activities carried on in a part-time and less skilful manner, though there is no reason to suppose that the work of travelling smiths had come to an end. Artistic traditions maintained at least a slender foothold, including production of a variety of sculptured items with religious implications, such as tombstones and decorated crosses. The richest churches aspired to a limited use of such luxuries as small glass windows, perhaps even including early examples of stained glass.

Despite the troubled political history of the region during the tenth and eleventh centuries, there was development on at least a local basis. The few reliable pollen analyses which have been made in recent years suggest continued forest clearance and farming expansion. Long before 1000 there seems to have been little woodland left on anciently settled lowland areas of the north. Even in upland areas, such as the Lake District hills, there were partial clearances to provide summer pastures for nearby lowland settlements. In Cumbria, Inglewood Forest, with its poor soils, resisted colonization until much later, but this was exceptional. (Higham 1986) In some areas political instability in the eleventh century interrupted settlement expansion, with some renewed enlargement of forests instead. Subsequent spread of settlement may have been encouraged by some improvement in climatic conditions in the twelfth and thirteenth centuries.

Identification of the early Northumbrian shire with the soke suggests the existence, under the dominant groups of earl, thegn and dreng, of the peasant hierarchy of sokemen, villeins and bordars already established within sokes further south. Boldon Book shows three such categories in villages of County Durham in the late twelfth century, and there is no reason to suppose this a recent innovation.

There were changes after the Norman conquest and the punitive campaigns which followed subsequent northern rebellions. New lords occupied an unusual position, in that, after earlier destruction within the region, their new possessions were often in a state which allowed them a freer hand than settled conditions might have offered. The Norman takeover in ravaged areas involved, especially in Durham, re-creation of village communities, with lords willing to offer help in resettlement and peasant holdings, in return for payment in produce or labour. (Barrow 1969, 9–11; Kapelle 1979, ch. 6, especially 181–90) There is little contemporary evidence, but reasonable inferences from such later sources as Boldon Book suggest that most of the peasantry held villein status, cultivating a small amount of land for themselves and rendering labour to the lord, either in farming work on his

demesne land or in a variety of individual personal services. On the bishop's estate at Boldon, the landlord could command ninety man-days each week in unpaid labour services from villagers. New lords frequently reserved large areas of demesne land on which villeins performed labour services, evidently unusual in the North in pre-Conquest times. Before the Norman conquest, Northumbria had contained many free men who nevertheless owed some service to a lord. Thegns had been lesser nobility, holding hereditary tenures but liable for some rent in money or goods to their lords. Drengs provided a lower order, but still of free men, who might owe their lords any of a wide variety of services or dues. Sometimes a dreng's holding consisted of a smaller appanage attached to a village. These customs in the North in the later eleventh century represented survivals of forms already extinct in much of the more prosperous south. (Miller 1976 for 1975, 3; McDonnell 1994, 24–5)

In general, labour services in Northumbria increased with the Conquest. Rights of lordship in late Anglo-Saxon Northumbria consisted more in a variety of customary rents and services than in power to compel regular labour. Pre-Conquest northern tenants might be expected to work for their lord at harvest time, but ploughing would probably be done by the lord's own animals and ploughmen, who would be more skilful at such a task. More onerous conditions were imposed over much of Durham in the later eleventh century. Even here there were exceptions. Many of the estates of the monastic community of Durham had been in their hands since pre-Conquest years and for their income they continued to rely on customary rents and dues and on profits from demesne lands.

Newly established communities had working practices which might differ from older settlements. In Durham both Wardley and Westoe were owned by the bishop. At Westoe, most estate work was carried out by the tenants' labour services, whereas at Wardley the bishop relied on a larger paid work force. Wardley was only brought under cultivation in the mid-thirteenth century, which explains the absence of a tradition of labour dues. Similarly, where woodland was cleared for cultivation in thirteenth-century Northumberland, settlers usually paid a simple money rent. (Fraser 1955, 36; Fraser 1968, ix)

The post-1066 changes were not uniform. Much of Northumberland must have escaped early reorganization, since Norman control was not effective until appreciably later and in different circumstances. At the end of the eleventh century, the county's sheriff held the king's castles of Newcastle,

---

Figure 2.1   Carlton, south Durham. It is probable that this village was created in the aftermath of the Norman punitive campaigns of the late eleventh century. Although all of the buildings have been re-built in subsequent periods, the general layout may well reflect the community's original plan, with twin rows of houses alongside a narrow green, their gardens stretching to the boundaries of the surrounding open fields.

Bamburgh and Tynemouth and there were a few recently settled Norman barons, but as yet control of much of the countryside must have been slight. Down to the thirteenth century and even beyond, thegns and drengs continued to appear in such varied Northumberland communities as Beadnell, Halton, Mousen and Whittingham, puzzling lawyers trained in southern conventions.

The situation in Cumberland must have been broadly similar, with the castle colony at Carlisle held for the king but much of the countryside imperfectly subjugated. As in Northumberland, some areas must still have been largely unsettled. Much land between Carlisle and Penrith remained undeveloped natural woodland (Miller 1976 for 1975, 5), and the little civil settlement around the royal castle at Carlisle was no more than a village.

A noticeable feature of the emerging society of the North West was that communities there held a smaller proportion of bondsmen than in the North East. The best calculation suggests that whereas more than half of recorded tenancies were 'bondi, nativi, or villani' in Northumberland and Durham, the figure for the North West was only about 16 per cent. This may be due to the fact that Norman dominance of the countryside came later than in the North East. A distinguished Scottish historian has claimed that 'Cumberland . . . can hardly be thought of as English, in any sense but the political, until the last quarter of the twelfth century'. (Miller 1988, 685; Barrow 1969, 7)

Economic Development

During periods of relative peace after the 1157 and 1219 Anglo-Scottish agreements, there was expansion of economic activity. (Winchester 1987, 6; Miller 1988, chs. 3g, 4g, 6g) The North possessed large reserves of under-exploited land, and colonization of these allowed more rapid growth than in other areas of England. There were variations in the pace of change within the northern counties. Westmorland lagged behind, even in the peaceful decades of the thirteenth century, and it was many years before that county saw significant growth. There was some assarting (taking in new land for cultivation) by the later twelfth century, but it was on a small scale, mainly in the Eden valley and around Kendal. In Cumberland, Durham and Northumberland, growth in rural population and expansion of settlement quickened during the thirteenth century, with farming reaching higher up into the hills than in most earlier periods.

Colonization of waste land created communities such as the small Northumberland village of New Pendmoor, founded in the twelfth century in an area not previously cultivated. Near Bishop Auckland, three settlements sharing the name Thickley were carved out of moorland before 1183. At Bearpark, the monks of Durham created one of their principal granges or estate management centres out of moorland. On the banks of the Solway, marshes at Burgh-by-Sands were developed for grazing and corn-growing before the end of the century. At Gosforth in Cumberland, early seasonal pastures on coastal sand dunes were permanently settled by 1165, with shieling grounds now established in vacant lands to the east, a good example of permanent settlements following earlier seasonal activity. In Cheviot valleys which had been used only as summer pastures, permanent communities were now established, and summer shieling grounds moved further out again. In North Tynedale, where officers of the Scottish king provided effective lordship, several new communities are recognizable by the end of the thirteenth century, even if they were small and poor. (Fraser 1961, 136; Fraser and Emsley 1969, 48–67) They included Charlton, Chirdon, Donkleywood, Tarset, Tarsethope, and Thorneyburn. The subsidiary valleys which fed the North Tyne were called hopes, and Tarsethope must be an example of a summer pasturage or shieling area developing into a permanently occupied hamlet. In the mid-twelfth century, Donkleywood was only a hunting lodge, but well before 1300 there was a small village there, with its shieling grounds further out in lesser valleys. There was an increase in individual home-steads in northern hills, though life in them must have been primitive and hard. (Charlton 1987, 30–2; Harbottle and Newman 1973, 138–41; Lomas 1996, 69–87)

Even in more intensively settled areas, established communities brought into cultivation areas drawn piecemeal from manorial waste or woodland. This happened in old woodland south of the Tyne near the Umfraville seat at Prudhoe in both the twelfth and thirteenth centuries; other examples occurred at Bactansford and Finchale in Durham during the last years of the twelfth century. By the beginning of the thirteenth century, expansion of the villages of Cowpen and Horton in south-east Northumberland made their fields contiguous. The land was increasingly filling up. Increased population in the Lake District is indicated by subdivision of some large parishes, and building of permanent stone parish churches. (Millward and Robinson 1970, 168) Where settlements possessed waste land, expansion often swallowed these. This was a more varied and patchy process than colonization of upland areas.

While much lowland colonization represented peasant farmers responding to population increase, colonization of uplands, much of them subject to forest law, was more directed by secular and ecclesiastical lords. The bishop of Durham's estates included extensive forests. These were not necessarily all wooded, but represented wide areas under the jurisdiction of the bishop's own forest law and forest officers. Royal foresters would not normally interfere in these districts. In this as in some other respects the bishop was coming to exercise quasi-regalian rights in his own territory. (Drury

1978, 87–91) Upland forest law areas were not usually woodland, but areas of waste unencumbered by manorial custom. Population pressures were effective here too, with much assarting, or taking in of patches for farming development, reflected in increasing numbers of payments for assarting in baronial accounts. (Winchester 1987, 42–4; Farrer 1923, I, xiv)

There were exceptions. The royal forest of Inglewood remained substantially intact and mainly wooded throughout medieval centuries, despite local population increases which brought minor encroachments for cultivation on the forest's fringes. Royal policy here resisted encroachments. The forest generated income from timber and wood products, and from rents for grazing and pannage for pigs. This policy retarded the forest's economic exploitation and may have hindered early development of nearby Carlisle. (Parker 1909; Summerson 1993, I, 29)

Where new communities appeared in forest law areas, it was at the discretion of the lord of the forest. Extensive colonization of Lake District valleys in the twelfth and thirteenth centuries was controlled in this manner, including new communities created in the forest of Derwentfells which covered valleys and high ground running east and south from Cockermouth. Colonists in such districts were tenants at will of the lord, usually one of the greater lords of the region. New holdings were held by money rents, in contrast to more complex systems of payments of rents in labour, produce or money common in longer-settled lowland manors. (Winchester 1987, 39–40, 62) In new communities, individual land holdings were often smaller than in the lowlands, but compensation for this came in access to grazing grounds at higher levels. Most newly developed territory was cattle country, or later sheep ranges, and these settlers were pioneers of a frontier society.

The Economy of the Greater Estates

Forest law allowed lords to engage in direct exploitation of upland areas which could be treated as an extension of their demesnes. In the Lake District, upper reaches of valleys were often reserved to the lords' use because of their rich grazing, which could be rented out for money or directly used as vaccaries (cattle ranches). Monastic houses exploited upland grazing areas, and their operations are relatively well documented. The monks of Newminster Abbey, near Morpeth, created sheep ranches in the Cheviot foothills in an area subject to forest law; there were at least 3,000 sheep in their pastures above Bowmont Water and Kilham, with other extensive grazing in the Kidland area of Coquetdale. A new grange, or permanent centre for sheep farming, was established far up the Coquet valley at Caistron; in 1245 it was noted that the land there had never been exploited 'ante tempus monachorum'. The monks were fully involved in the shieling system of 'inbye/ outbye' farming, whereby flocks and herds moved up to outer pastures to feed during summer months. This involved organization on a considerable scale and employment of many shepherds and herdsmen.

Cistercian monasteries became vigorous entrepreneurs in Cumbria, at the cost of eroding their original ethos of retreat from the world and ascetic emphasis on hard labour and prayer. From the mid-twelfth century, Furness Abbey (founded 1127) expanded commercial farming from lowland manors on the Furness peninsula into upland forest areas of southern Lakeland and upper Eskdale. (Millward and Robinson 1970, 158) Further north, the monks of Holm Cultram (founded 1150) were also active. Like Newminster, these Cumbrian houses operated outlying granges administered by lay brethren or *conversi*, while the monks themselves became involved in commercial management. Initially these farming activities had concentrated on more or less subsistence farming in wilder and more remote areas, but the need to finance ambitious building programmes pushed monks into commerce, exploiting for cattle ranching large upland areas within their endowments. This was followed by involvement in sheep farming and the wool trade. By the thirteenth century Holm Cultram was selling wool from 10,000 sheep, while Furness was not far behind at 8,000. (Hallam 1972, 409) The extensive commerce of Holm Cultram was indicated by ownership of properties in such trading centres as Newcastle, Hartlepool and Boston. The abbey shipped wool from its own port at Skinburnness on the Solway Firth; Furness used the Walney Channel. Holm Cultram's status as a daughter house of Melrose facilitated Scottish trading contacts, and this abbey's ships were engaged in wool trade around the Irish Sea, carrying wool from smaller producers as well as their own. Both Furness and Holm Cultram had lost most of their original ascetic zeal by the late thirteenth century. (Summerson 1993, I, 24, 77, 102, 138; Wilson 1901, 167)

Entrepreneurial activities of northern landowners, especially exploitation of upland holdings for commercial farming, constituted a dynamic element in the regional economy in early medieval years. Each estate developed its own economic organization, as opportunity and resources offered. Within Tynemouth Priory's lordship, specific lands at Preston were burdened with the duty of carting millstones the considerable distance from the Slaley quarries near Hexham to all mills on priory estates. (Jobey 1986, 67) In more fertile areas of the North, as in the uplands, agricultural management became more sophisticated. The process of commuting customary rents in kind to money began early and continued to increase. Boldon Book, in the late twelfth century, shows the process well advanced on the bishop of Durham's estates. (In parts of Cumberland, holdings were still being leased at oatmeal rents in the thirteenth century.) By the end of the thirteenth century, monks administering the estates of Durham cathedral priory had eliminated many customary life tenures, replacing them with tenancies at will which made control of farming practices easier. After generations of dispute, the bishop of Durham and his cathedral priory settled long-standing property disputes in an agreement, known as 'Le Convenit', in 1229. On most large estates, lay and ecclesiastical, the need to reward key administrators was well recognized. Secular and clerical landlords conferred lands, gifts and favours on those who served them well. (Lomas 1977, 34; Halcrow 1957, 7–21)

Farming and Rural Society

Apart from the relative sophistication of the large-scale farming already considered, there is little to suggest that expansion of the cultivated area yielded any dividend other than support of a larger population. In terms of soils and climate, the region was poorly endowed and this was reflected in the unsophisticated communal organization of arable farming. (Miller 1976 for 1975, 9–11; Miller 1988, chs. 3g, 4g, 6g)

> Two and three field arrangements were not characteristic of the north as a whole and they were practically unknown in the north-west . . . in the disposition of the ploughland of many villages, therefore, order and system were often conspicuously absent. Far from being neatly disposed in fields, the arable has the appearance of a loose federation of furlongs, interspersed with tracts of meadow or rough grazing. (Miller 1976 for 1975, 9)

This 'unfinished' look may not be a simple reflection of a lack of farming sophistication, but may represent the North's greater concentration on pastoral as against arable farming. (Dilley 1972, 19–20; Winchester 1987, 61) Over most of the North, communal arable resources were organized in open fields, within which individual farmers held dispersed holdings or strips. Any pressure to divide and enclose open fields was resisted because of the value placed on unrestricted grazing by cattle and sheep during winter months after the crops had been harvested. These rights were highly valued, entrenched in manorial custom and enforced by manorial courts throughout the middle ages. There was also pressure to extend them to areas newly taken in from waste.

In the North East, where there was a drier climate and better soils, a few areas escaped this pastoral emphasis sufficiently to develop some kind of three-field system with a stronger arable base: they included Alnwick, Fulwell and Wolviston. References to 'the field' of a village are frequent in

Cumbria. In the more common single open fields, crops were limited by the requirement that they should be spring-sown in late March or early April, after livestock had been driven from its winter 'closing' on the common field, and harvested before they returned from summer pastures in late October or early November. This limited cultivation to spring-sown crops of wheat, oats and sometimes barley. Wheat was grown in the more favourable climate of the east, and on southern fringes of Cumbria. From the thirteenth century, monks of Furness fixed rentals from customary tenants of lowland manors in both money and produce, which sometimes included wheat in favourable areas, but more commonly barley and oats. (Rollinson 1963, 21) In the poorer conditions in most of the region, oats became virtually a monoculture crop. Peas and beans were sometimes grown in the open field, and crops of hay to provide winter animal food were almost universal. Cattle fitted into the early pattern of near-subsistence peasant farming, but sheep increased during the thirteenth century with the development of a more sophisticated wool-trading system. In the twelfth century keeping pigs was common, but later declined with the reduction in woodland areas available for pannage. Near Alnwick, land which had only seen seasonal use before, including summer feeding for pigs, saw conversion to meadows and arable fields accompanying permanent settlements. Where woodland survived, as in some of the Lake District's upper valleys, or in the considerable area of Inglewood Forest, pigs continued to be kept in large numbers into the fourteenth century, but appear to have been generally in decline. This was reflected in baronial accounts by a drop in income from pannage. (Winchester 1987, 101–2) Domesticated goats existed in some hilly areas, but were much less common. The frequent mention of hens and eggs as part of rents in kind indicates that fowls were widely kept. The breeding and keeping of cattle, sheep and horses were the principal mainstays of northern farming.

It was not possible to apply a sophisticated scheme of crop rotation in communities where land allotment was unsystematic. In many open fields the only form of rotation was alternation of oats and hay. The principal fertilizing agent employed was the dung of over-wintered stock. Only on more ambitiously managed estates were there more advanced techniques. Marling, a form of soil enrichment, was used on the estates of Tynemouth Priory, and in coastal areas seaweed might be used as a manure. Some wealthy estates bought in additional supplies of dung for cultivated land. In the early thirteenth century, monks of Furness Abbey, involved in large-scale cultivation as well as extensive stock farming, inaugurated reclamation of coastal marshes for cultivation and erected dykes on Walney Island to prevent high tides inundating farmland. (Rollinson 1963, 18) More generally, peasant farming was increasingly constrained by communal obligations, with few innovations to challenge customary manorial practices.

Social Organization

There were still men who owed nothing to any lord even though they were far from rich. Men who were generally considered to be freemen might be saddled with obligations usually born by unfree tenants. Some men were serfs who could be sold with the land. The limited evidence available shows that variations in conditions relating to land-holding were so extensive that no neat pattern can be established.

The largest element in rural society was the unfree families, living together in village communities, holding some arable land within the community's common field or fields and bound to their lord by the terms of their holding. Labour services were frequently confined to a few 'boon days' on which peasants were obliged to work on the lord's fields. This may reflect the small role of arable farming, with its higher labour requirements. Examples of two or three days' labour per week being exacted can be found, but they were unusual and the tendency was towards their reduction.

Payments in money, produce or labour owed by individuals to their lords were, by the thirteenth century, especially in the long-settled lowlands, increasingly defined by manorial customs. This varied between manors, but in practice increasingly consolidated tenant right. The tendency may also reflect a weaker conception of tenurial obligations in the North. By the thirteenth century customary tenants in Cumbria enjoyed considerable security in their holdings, and the later middle ages saw continued erosion in the dominant position of lords of the manor. (Winchester 1987, 62)

The size of arable holdings varied greatly. A person might hold separate plots by different obligations. Opportunities to extend holdings, by assarting from woodland or waste for example, varied in both time and place. Without this outlet, population pressure might lead to subdivision of holdings, as was the case in more settled areas of Northumberland at East Acomb by 1270, at Halton by 1287 and at Great Whittington by the end of the thirteenth century. Such pressures might explain the large numbers of landless cottagers in lowland manors of Cumberland, who sometimes outnumbered tenants holding land. They presumably found employment as labourers or craftsmen or possibly in early rural industries. Such groups provided much of the direct labour on the manorial demesne, and specialists such as ploughmen, shepherds and herdsmen required by larger estates. (Winchester 1987, 67)

Relatively standardized units of land occupation are often visible. On older estates of Tynemouth Priory, a 36-acre tenure was long established in East and Middle Chirton, but not in West Chirton which was only acquired in the later thirteenth century. Established patterns often showed long continuity. A surviving episcopal lease from 1070 indicates that a unit of 30 acres with two oxen and three cows was then a frequent Durham holding;

Figure 2.2 The deserted village of South Middleton, Northumberland, showing remains of the village itself, surrounded by the ridge and furrow markings indicating medieval ploughing in the open fields. There were twelve tax-payers here in 1296, and the community still existed on a modest scale in the seventeenth century.

a thirteenth-century lease at Billingham involved 30 acres with two oxen and a horse. This resembles estimates of the size of standard holdings in lowland Cumberland manors at between 20 and 40 acres, with a substantial number of double holdings comprising twice the standard plot. (Winchester 1987, 66) Presumably, such standard units had initially reflected the needs of subsistence farming in individual communities. In coastal settlements, the frequency of smaller holdings reflects the contribution of fishing. Any consideration of the size of arable holdings must take into account common grazing rights which supplemented the produce of the common field.

Market Centres

Development of greater estates often included exploitation of the commerce of local markets. Colonization of land brought money rents and growing numbers of peasant farmers engaged in pastoral activities who needed to buy some items, perhaps including oatmeal, and sell produce in order to pay rents. This boost to a money economy encouraged development of markets, often initially in small communities within larger estates. Examples in Northumberland included Bamburgh, Chatton, Elsdon, Rothbury, Warkworth, and Wooler. The right to hold a market derived from a royal grant, which specified conditions in each case and which might well have to be paid for. Implications of market arrangements were illustrated by the De Merley barony of Morpeth. A market at Morpeth was granted in 1199, and a second at Netherwitton in 1257; when the barony descended to co-heiresses in 1266, the division left each half with its market. The Kendal barony was similarly divided in 1246, with the market at Kendal serving its northern division, while a second market at Warton (Lancs.), which did not develop as a borough, catered for the southern section. (Munby 1985) Such divisions represented a sharing of assets, for markets generated tolls, profits for the borough court and rents for burgage tenements. If the centre prospered, additional income might come from such items as rent from mills of various kinds. (Lomas 1996, 87–93)

Warton's fate indicated that commercial success needed more than a baronial initiative. Cumberland provided other examples of unsuccessful market foundations, including Greystoke on the southern fringes of Inglewood Forest, and Newton Arlosh on the north Cumberland plain, the last of three unsuccessful attempts by monks of Holm Cultram to establish a market town under their control. Success required not only seigneurial initiative, but genuine commercial opportunities, as in the case of foundations around the Lake District hills in positions well sited for trade between highlands and lowlands and for the gathering of local upland products. These included Cockermouth, Penrith, Kendal, Ulverston and Egremont. The limited extent of royal intervention in Durham may be partly responsible for the paucity of markets granted there. By 1293 the bishop had two markets on his estates, while the powerful families of Bruce and Balliol held one each.

Creation of market centres in the twelfth and thirteenth centuries reflected a desire to control trade which already existed. There is evidence of informal exchanges, often in local churchyards, preceding establishment of regular markets. Such unpoliced facilities could be the scene of quarrels or bloodshed, or of disorder, desecration or unseemly popular celebrations in holy places. This was at least the nominal basis of a complaint in 1300 from merchants using Cockermouth market against their unchartered brethren at Crosthwaite churchyard. The commerce there was of long standing, with regular gatherings on Sundays and festival days to trade corn, flour, beans, peas, linen, cloth, meat and fish; no profit to the lord and no royal licence to hold a market were involved. Repeated complaints produced a royal order to the sheriff to suppress this market in 1306, in order to divert its trade to markets which were regulated and profitable. (Wilson 1905, 40–2)

Trade, Industry and the Beginnings of Urban Society

In contrast to the south of England, at the time of the Norman Conquest there was little evidence of urban continuity in the North. In the more backward parts of the North West, there is little evidence even for the existence of a money economy. (Miller 1976 for 1975, 5; Summerson 1993, I, 10) Durham, the only community with pretensions to urban status, might instead be regarded simply as the administrative centre of the bishop's extensive estates. The consolidation of royal power brought the foundation of new communities at Newcastle and Carlisle. The original stimulus to their growth was the necessary supply of goods and services to Norman administrative and military centres. Development of Carlisle, for many years directly controlled by the Crown, was more clearly influenced by this original basis. Much depended on the determination of Henry I and Henry II to control Cumberland. This brought royal expenditure on castle and garrison, creation of a walled town, and foundation of the bishopric in 1133. (Summerson 1993, I, 27) Beyond serving these secular and ecclesiastical establishments, the city's commercial development was handicapped by an undeveloped hinterland and poor communications with southern England. During the twelfth century, Carlisle looked naturally to trade with Ireland; there were Carlisle merchants in Dublin by the late twelfth century and a *vicus hibernicorum* at Carlisle by the early thirteenth century. (Summerson 1993, I, 41–4, 76) By 1130, the small mercantile community was sufficiently well organized to lease a royal silver mine at Alston, and five years later Carlisle acquired its own mint. The decision in the mid-twelfth century to detach Alston from Northumberland and attach it to Cumberland may have been intended to secure the safe transport of silver to Carlisle, instead of the risky journey to Newcastle through the liberties of Tynedale and Hexhamshire, where royal authority was less secure. (Fraser and Emsley 1981, 164–5) While under Scottish occupation, the Carlisle mint supplied Scotland with much of its coinage, and the town's importance was indicated by the frequency of visits by David I, who may have conceived of it as a kind of southern capital. He died there in 1153. The city's growth was recognized by the grant of a charter by Henry II in 1158.

Carlisle benefited from cross-border co-operation during periods of Anglo-Scottish amity, which led to population growth, expansion of commerce and existence of almost a cross-border economic zone in those years. During the twelfth century, the use of money grew, and mints were established at Durham and Newcastle, as well as Carlisle. Coins minted by David I at Carlisle, using silver from Alston, were quickly followed by others struck at Corbridge during Scottish occupation of that area. At the time of David's death, he had also opened mints at Berwick, Roxburgh and Edinburgh. (Summerson 1993, I, 42)

Carlisle's development during the twelfth and thirteenth centuries, though considerable, lagged behind the more rapid growth of Newcastle. Newcastle was the biggest English town north of York. Other boroughs developing within the region, often under baronial initiative, and even Scottish towns, adopted the customs of Newcastle as the basis of municipal organization. Newcastle grew rapidly in the thirteenth century. The work of building up the quayside area, previously a marshy and undeveloped tidal desolation, accelerated and was virtually complete by 1300. This provided a more extensive base for the town's trade and ability to handle shipping. (Lomas 1996, 93–101)

Coal was already part of this trade. London had its Sea-coal Lane by 1228. By 1285 complaints were heard in the capital that use of sea-coal for burning lime caused pollution. Leading northern churches profited from coal under their lands, usually by leasing mines to lay entrepreneurs. At Newminster Abbey, the monks were doing this before the end of the thirteenth century, while the bishop of Durham leased mines at Darlington, Ferryhill, Hett, Lumley and Rainton. The prior of Tynemouth owned mines at Benwell, Cowpen, Denton, Elswick, Tynemouth and Wylam. No doubt coal income helped the priory to install a new water supply, employing a skilled workman from Hexham to lead the supply from springs two miles away. By 1269 the priory was embroiled in conflicts with Newcastle merchants who, like urban oligarchies elsewhere, claimed a monopoly of profitable trade, including Tyneside coal shipments. In 1281, an official enquiry concluded that the town of Newcastle had doubled in value 'on account of coal' in recent years. A few years later, a large quantity of coal was shipped from the Tyne, presumably for lime-burning, during building operations at Corfe Castle. At the end of the century, the bishop of London imported Newcastle coal for building work at Gravesend.

Lead from mines in South Tynedale and Weardale was carried by packhorse towards Newcastle, to be shipped to destinations at home and abroad. Monastic roofs and pipes in France or Flanders used 'Newcastle lead', and lead from his Weardale estate contributed to the bishop of Durham's large income. Ship-building and boat-building were established at Newcastle before the end of the twelfth century. The town's increasing prosperity produced other than merely commercial fruits: religious life extended with the endowment of five houses of friars. The Hospital of St Mary the Virgin was in existence by 1190.

Newcastle, because of contacts with the more developed eastern seaboard of England and the Continent, shipped produce of the pastoral interior to wider markets. Wool was the most important item, with Newcastle drawing on supplies from as far away as the northern Lake District. Although wool from northern uplands commanded prices appreciably lower than those earned by some southern regions, it formed a significant part of Newcastle's seaborne trade. In 1275, Newcastle ranked sixth among England's wool-shipping ports. As with coal, the wool trade fostered links between producers, merchants and shipping which reflected growing sophistication in the economy.

Berwick consolidated a position as Scotland's principal port and a major element in that kingdom's economy. The town held a Scottish mint, and its prosperity is shown by the fact that by 1286 its customs contribution to Scottish revenue was, at £2,190, worth approximately a quarter of the total English customs revenue. (Fraser 1969, 44–6; Conway Davies 1953, 175–97; Blake 1967, 1–24; Barrow 1969, 4; O'Brien 1989, 70–83; Barrow 1966, 23)

Stirrings of urban life were felt in other places too, including Alnwick, Darlington, Gateshead, Hartlepool, Kendal, Penrith, Sunderland and Yarm, even if Newcastle outshone them all. Bishop Le Puiset (1153–95) gave a charter to 'weremouth', the terms of which show that there was already an active port there. Few concessions were made and the future borough of Sunderland still effectively belonged to the bishop. (Royal Commission 1992, 6) In Northumberland, Newcastle and Bamburgh were royal boroughs, farming their own borough rents; Corbridge was a royal borough until granted by King John to the lord of Warkworth in 1205. All three places sent two representatives to Edward I's 1295 parliament.

It was difficult in smaller, less successful market towns to maintain a distinctively urban existence. Northern towns, like rural settlements, possessed common fields cultivated by members of the community, but in prosperous towns the relative importance of farming declined as commerce expanded. In the early thirteenth century, burgesses of the new baronial market town of Egremont were granted lands and permission to take in assarts and plant shielings in nearby lands, while at Cockermouth tilling of the townsfield continued into modern times. (Summerson 1993, I, 56) Yarm, 17 miles from the mouth of the Tees, was already a port by the twelfth century. A new bridge there, built in the thirteenth century, provided the lowest river crossing. Agricultural produce of the surrounding area provided most of the trade. (Rennison 1994, 21) Roots of urban life lay, not in physical separation of towns from surrounding countryside, but in the special nature of burgage tenure, allowing a degree of personal freedom and property rights. These privileges were conferred on burgesses in order that the town might prosper and bring enhanced dues to its lord. In the extent of their exemption from immediate lordly supervision, and in their acquisition of self-governing powers, as in so much else, the burgesses of Newcastle were in the van of urban development in the North.

The Role of Fairs

The development of more specialized commerce was reflected in the expansion of fairs, held at much wider intervals than local markets and offering more variety in goods. Furs and finer varieties of cloth might be bought in places like Corbridge and Darlington. Markets and fairs differed in goods traded. Corbridge fair served as a centre for the Tyneside iron trade, selling nails in 2,000 lots, horse-shoes by the 100, and iron itself by the pack-horse load or cartload. At other fairs purchasers could find wine, salmon, herrings, white fish, salt, cheese and butter, onions and garlic, wool, cloth, sheepskins, goatskins, linen, hemp, flax, potash, copperas, woad, lead, lard and millstones. Costly exotic goods like cinnamon, almonds, figs and raisins could be bought in ports like Newcastle, Berwick and Newbiggin, and also in the market at Durham. (Fraser 1968, x)

Scattered references show traders in northern England from Florence, Lucca, Lübeck, Cologne and Brabant, and there must have been many more such visitors. At the end of the thirteenth century a royal enquiry found many ships from the Netherlands and Baltic states in north-east ports, trading in timber, hides, herrings, salted fish, wax, grease and oil, pitch and tar, and butter. A trading concentration on north-west Europe was already established and Newcastle merchants were knowledgeable about maritime and trading interests.

The towns, as well as providing facilities for collection and distribution of goods, also served as industrial centres. This was not universally true, because some processes preferred rural locations. In the woollen industry, the application of water power to one of the finishing stages of cloth manufacture saw fulling mills established where swift running water was available. Cockermouth had a fulling mill by *c*.1200, and during the thirteenth century they proliferated in the Lake District, providing local centres around which a range of domestic outworkers was organized as the textile industry developed. (Winchester 1987, 117)

There was small-scale iron-mining, mostly to meet local needs, with Egremont one local centre. Scotland needed to import iron, and this was a significant part of Carlisle's trade into southern Scotland in the thirteenth century. (Summerson 1993, I, 198) Early in the following century, Scottish raiders plundering the Furness Abbey estates, 'Seized all the manufactured iron they could find and carried it off with the greatest of joy although so heavy of carriage and preferred it to all other plunder'. (Rollinson 1963, 21, quoting Holinshed) Other Cumbrian monasteries, including St Bees and Holm Cultram, were involved in the iron industry, as were some northern secular lords. Another northern industry in which ecclesiastical and secular interests were involved was production of salt from sea water, providing another vital commodity for medieval society.

The Limits of Expansion

These developments must be seen in perspective. The North still contained much that was backward. Despite expansion, population density remained lower than in richer regions to the south. Most buildings were of wood or wattle construction, although the peaceful years of the thirteenth century did see improvement in comfort at least in homes of richer folk. In Northumberland, Aydon Castle and Halton Castle were among substantial new houses built before the end of the thirteenth century. The North could provide few magnates, one the bishop of Durham, who could play a major role on the national stage. Most great men came from further south. (Borne and Dixon 1978, 138; Barrow 1969, 2–3) In economic terms the North was still a relatively poor agricultural area, with less sophisticated management than richer southern regions. (Miller 1976 for 1975, 9–11; Miller 1988, chs. 3g, 4g, 6g)

Relative peace on the border was a prerequisite for peaceful growth and economic expansion. The reduction in violence and disturbance was never complete. Disorder continued to exist in many forms, if at a lower level than in periods of acute border tension or conflict. During a dispute between the archbishop of York and the monks of Durham Priory in the 1280s, messengers on both sides were beaten up and horses mutilated; the prior of Durham tried to obtain favourable court verdicts by bribery. In 1269, the mayor and burgesses of Newcastle were brought before a royal court for violence and intimidation towards traders at North Shields. Incidents such as these, and worse, punctuated the generally more orderly years of the thirteenth century. Courts dealing with crime and violence, as well as other judicial business, continued to sit fortnightly in the North East, even after a statute of 1234 prescribed three-weekly meetings. There was sufficient business to bring royal justices to Northumberland in 1218, 1227, 1235, 1241, 1256, 1269, 1279, and 1293. (Fraser and Emsley 1971, 167)

Not even royal authority provided protection in some cases. On more than one occasion, Newcastle mobs, amounting in one case to a force of 500 armed men, attacked the sheriff of Northumberland while he was arresting prisoners who had aroused local sympathy, or seizing property in the town in cases of debts by townsfolk. There was ample work for other forms of jurisdiction too. At the end of the thirteenth century twenty-three lords in Northumberland, and five in Durham, claimed that they possessed the right to try thieves caught on their estates, and to possess an ordeal pit and gallows. Several maintained prisons. (Fraser and Emsley 1969, 67)

The Church in the North

Kings and nobles took part in the establishment of the northern Church on a sounder footing, including the foundation of monasteries, both in Scotland and in northern England. William of St Calais, bishop of Durham, planned a magnificent setting for the shrine of St Cuthbert. The foundation stone of the Romanesque cathedral was laid with great ceremony in July 1093, after part at least of the Saxon cathedral had been demolished. The Saxon minster had probably stood on the site of the later cloister, and part of the old building must have remained in use until the Norman cathedral could take its place. When the bishop died in 1096, building was well under way. The see remained vacant for three years, but the new community's prior kept the momentum alive. St Cuthbert's shrine was translated to its new home in 1104, and the great nave vault, a design probably borrowed from the abbey church at Jumièges in Normandy, was finished in 1133, forty years after the laying of the foundation stone. (Curry 1986, 31–2; Jarrett and Mason 1995)

Henry I established a bishopric at Carlisle in 1133, which freed the area from ecclesiastical control by the see of Glasgow. At Brinkburn in Northumberland the Augustinian priory of St Peter and St Paul was founded by a Bertram lord of Mitford, probably in the early 1130s. In January 1138, Ranulph de Merley, lord of Morpeth, installed St Robert and twelve other Cistercian monks in Newminster Abbey, the first daughter house of the great Yorkshire abbey at Fountains. Most monastic foundations were established, at least in part, to reflect the status of their founders and that of their families. Hubert de Vaux established the Augustinian priory of Lanercost after Henry II gave him the barony of Gilsland; it was situated in a remote area and not lavishly endowed. (Fairclough 1980, 143; Harbottle and Salway 1964, 87; Todd 1991, 30–44) Thurstan, archbishop of York from 1114 to 1140, worked with King David in developing Scottish ecclesiastical institutions, including the great border abbeys of Kelso (1128), Melrose (1136) and Jedburgh (1138). Co-operation between English and Scottish elements was common. The new Scottish abbeys drew on northern English monasteries, especially Yorkshire houses, for early priors and abbots. Prince Henry of Scotland, who became earl of Northumberland, founded the Cumberland abbey of Holm Cultram as a daughter house of Melrose. Such co-operation survived renewal of Anglo-Scottish hostilities after Henry I's death in 1135 and the succession dispute which followed. When Dryburgh Abbey was founded in 1150, its first monks were drawn from Alnwick in Northumberland.

Most northern monastic houses had modest endowments. The house of Augustinian canons at Carlisle, founded by Henry I, was never wealthy and received no additional resources when it became the seat of the bishopric. This poverty was a principal reason for the prolonged vacancy in 1156–1204, after the death of the first bishop, Athelwold. The building of the

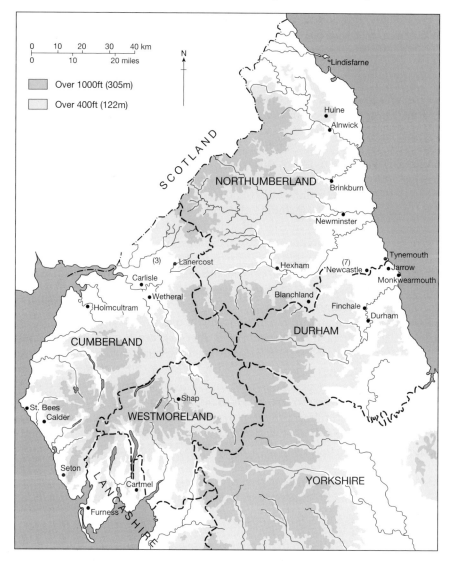

Map 3   Principal religious institutions

cathedral took until almost the end of the thirteenth century for the same reason. Even Cistercian houses established within the region, such as Cumbria's Holm Cultram, Calder and Furness (originally a Benedictine house), enjoyed only modest endowments, although later they contrived higher levels of prosperity and expansion. The initial fervour of the Cistercians favoured settlement in remote sites appropriate to their austere life of labour and prayer.

59

While information on foundation of monasteries and succession to bishoprics is reasonably full, it is difficult to measure the nature and significance of religious belief. Christian belief in these years was often expressed through cults surrounding saints thought of as possessing particular efficacy in mediating between God and man. The most important of these in our region was the cult of St Cuthbert, centred on Durham but powerful throughout the four northern counties and beyond. Some continuing Celtic and Norse Irish influence can also be seen in this sphere. Cumbria possessed churches dedicated to such Celtic saints as Kentigern, Ninian, Bridget, Patrick and Columba. There were pagan survivals, exemplified in the wheelheaded cross at Gosforth in Cumberland with its integration of Norse and Christian motifs. (Rose 1982, 132–3; Rollinson 1967, 65–6) The Norman conquest reinforced Continental influences, including the cult of the Virgin Mary, to whom the Augustinian house at Carlisle (subsequently the cathedral) was dedicated. Norman rulers bore no hostility towards older cults such as that of Cuthbert and in general Christianity was a force for integration rather than conflict in the post-Conquest era. The reformed Benedictine community at Durham was at pains to establish claims to Northumbrian traditions derived from St Cuthbert. Translation of the saint's relics to their new shrine at Durham involved an examination which found his body miraculously incorrupt just as on inspection in 698, eleven years after his death. A Durham manuscript recording this marvel deliberately used the same language as employed on the first occasion. (Aird 1992) Early in the twelfth century, Durham monks refounded a dependent house on Lindisfarne, intended to tie the cult of St Cuthbert more closely to Durham and providing a centre for the saint's veneration in Northumberland. The prior there could also safeguard revenues due to the mother house from estates in the north of the county. The popularity of the cult of St Cuthbert may have reached its peak during the twelfth century. (Tudor 1989, 447)

By 1092 the system of ecclesiastical parishes was operating in the northern counties, and tithes supported churches and priests. Cumbrian parochial boundaries were often coterminous with large secular estates, sharing their extensive nature for similar reasons of small populations and limited incomes. (Winchester 1987, 22–7) Subdivisions of parishes were common in the twelfth century, often associated with individual manors within baronial estates. These developments produced contrasts between extensive upland parishes and smaller units within manorialized fertile districts. From the inception of the parochial system, the communal ability to support the church reflected local variations in prosperity. The North West, with its wide areas of poor pastoral or barren land, struggled from the beginning to maintain an adequate ecclesiastical establishment, a recurring theme in the area's history.

With few exceptions, early monastic foundations remained set apart from the world rather than active pastoral or evangelical agencies. It was not until the arrival of the Dominican and Franciscan friars in the early thirteenth century that preaching orders achieved any prominence. Popular experience of early medieval Christianity was primarily in terms of the ceremonies of the Church, and its power was seen in terms of its supposed magical interventions to ease uncertainties about both this world and the next. (Summerson 1993, I, 153–62)

Part Two

*c.*1290–1603

Chapter 3

The Later Medieval North

The Scottish Succession Crisis

Co-operation between the kingdoms survived a series of unexpected Scottish royal deaths in the early 1290s, and failure of plans to link the dynasties by marriage of Edward I's heir to the 7-year-old Scottish queen, Margaret, the Maid of Norway, who died in 1290. Denied this opportunity for peaceful union of the crowns, Edward sought to exploit the succession crisis to establish English control of Scotland.

There was little initial opposition to Edward's assumption of the role of arbiter of the Scottish succession by virtue of the suzerainty which English kings claimed. The principal claimants were drawn from the Anglo-Scottish nobility, and Edward's choice of John Balliol, rather than Robert Bruce, was equitable. Bruce accepted the verdict. He died in 1294, and his heir spent most of his life on his English estates; when he died in 1304, he was buried at Holm Cultram Abbey in Cumberland. (Prestwich 1988, chs. 14, 18–19; Barrow 1965)

Edward's attempt to dominate Scotland led eventually to prolonged warfare, ending the long thirteenth-century interlude of peaceful development on the borders and destroying many cross-border connections, perhaps most importantly the links within the Anglo-Scottish nobility with interests in both kingdoms. The English Crown's control over its border counties was impaired with consequences lasting until the late fifteenth century.

When the new Scottish king did homage to Edward, there seemed few problems. Edward interfered in Scottish affairs, accepting appeals from Scottish courts and demanding support and subsidies for his own overseas policies. When Anglo-French hostilities broke out in 1294, Balliol repudiated his allegiance and rejected English control. At Easter 1296, a Scottish army led by seven earls ravaged parts of Cumberland, although an attack on Carlisle Castle failed.

Believing that he had settled Scottish affairs satisfactorily, in 1292–93 Edward had taken the opportunity to crack down on his own northern subjects by *quo warranto* proceedings, forcing vassals to prove the legality of any privileges they held. During hearings at Newcastle in January 1293, twenty-three lords from Northumberland and five from Durham successfully defended their right to a gallows on which they could hang thieves caught on their lands. (see p. 00 above; Fraser 1969, 44; Fraser and Emsley 1969, 67)

Another display of power in the border counties saw royal justices in 1292 abrogate Carlisle's embryonic municipal status and self-government, restoring direct Crown control, on the grounds that after a disastrous fire, which had destroyed much of the city, Carlisle could not produce a charter granting these privileges. (Summerson 1993, I, 178–9)

Balliol's rebellion provoked rapid response. Edward gathered an army at Newcastle and invaded Scotland. His first success was the capture of Berwick, the Scots' main trading port, at the end of March 1296, involving a massacre of many townspeople, further undermining Anglo-Scottish amity. The construction of new defences began four days later, and in 1297–98 the large sum of £122 was spent on improving them. (Ryder 1992, 99; Bishop 1992, 117–19). The Scots retaliated with a raid into Northumberland which was said to have burnt 120 settlements. An attack on Carlisle, led by the earl of Buchan, pillaged the neighbourhood, but city and castle held out as the Scots lacked siege equipment. (Barrow 1966, 23; Fraser 1969, 60; McNamee 1990, 40; Summerson 1993, I, 194–5)

The Scots could not field an army capable of facing the English in battle and by the end of the summer of 1296 most of Scotland seemed to be in the hands of the English and their numerous Scottish allies. Balliol submitted, enduring public humiliation, before he and his son were led captive into England. In August 1296, a Scottish parliament assembled at Berwick and its members, including many Scottish nobles, swore fealty to the English king. Edward felt secure enough to leave England in August 1297 on an expedition to Flanders. It seemed possible that with English power established on both sides of the border the links which had bound border folk of both kingdoms might be resumed.

The events of 1296 had implications which made this impossible. Previously the border aristocracy, with interests often straddling the frontier, could serve two masters. Balliol's defiance polarized allegiances. Some chose the Scottish side, and Edward confiscated their estates, using them as a reservoir of patronage with which to reward his followers. The extensive English holdings of the Balliol and Bruce families were eventually confiscated. (Tuck 1971, 25–38; Lomas 1992, 65–6)

These changes produced results which were not immediately obvious. In these crisis years, Edward often made temporary rather than permanent settlements of confiscated estates. The consequent instability is well illustrated in the liberty of Tynedale, which during the forty years after 1296 was held by six different lords, all of them primarily concerned with affairs elsewhere. Exposed to Scottish raiding and internal feuding, this territory lost the stability it had when held by Scottish kings as an English fief. Lacking an energetic and interested lord, local government deteriorated and Tynedale inhabitants, as in similarly affected areas, turned to their own protective devices. Family linkages came to mean more than allegiance to a distant lord. Organization of much of the border areas under the great 'names' like Charlton and Graham owed as much to dislocation of lordship arrangements as to dangers of Scottish incursions.

Even where there was no disloyalty among border landowners, renewed warfare could diminish effective lordship. The Umfraville dynasty remained loyal, but after the loss of their Scottish estates, and the fall in value of their Redesdale lordship after Scottish raiding, their north-eastern estates gradually assumed a lower priority in their interests than their Lincolnshire holdings. In such ways the old Anglo-Scottish aristocracy, with its divided interests, could not survive the renewal of border warfare.

New Aristocratic Dynasties

Fighting brought forward new families, who earned rewards in border warfare. Before the early fourteenth century, the Percies held estates in Yorkshire and Sussex but had no Northumberland connection. Henry Percy, who became first Lord Percy of Alnwick, served Edward in his Scottish wars, including the 1296 campaign, and was rewarded with Northumberland estates, as well as briefly held Scottish estates. (Bean 1957, 91–9; Hislop 1991, 88–90; Lomas 1992, 66–8)

By the middle of the fourteenth century the Percies were entrenched in Northumberland. Among possessions which consolidated their influence, Alnwick was acquired in 1309 and Warkworth in 1332. The first Percy earl of Northumberland (1368–1407) increased family holdings. Some acquisitions were confiscated from Anglo-Scottish nobles choosing the Scottish side, including English lands of the Scottish earls of Dunbar, acquired in 1335. Alnwick was bought some years after the line of its Vesci lords expired in 1297; money earned by military service helped to make this possible. By the late fourteenth century Percies had established a dominant position in Northumberland, while retaining holdings in Yorkshire and Sussex and acquiring considerable influence in Cumberland. Cleverly chosen marriages brought in additional estates, including the barony of Prudhoe when the main line of the Umfravilles died out in 1381. Their extended possessions, and the military power which they represented, raised them to a position of eminence in more than local or regional terms. Lord Percy was a member of the English Regency Council as early as 1340. (Tuck 1992; Ormrod 1990, 13) Towards the end of the fourteenth century, family power reached a peak, with control of almost all English border defences. The leading part which Henry 'Hotspur' Percy played in the campaign which led to the battle of Otterburn in 1388, and the Chevy Chase ballad which it inspired, added to the family's fame. In the next decade, the Percies played a leading role in the deposition of a king and installation of another in his place. Long before then, ties which had linked many of the northern aristocracy with Scotland had been broken and the border was more of a reality than ever before. (Wesencraft 1988; Bean 1959; Tuck and Goodman 1992)

Other changes brought older elements in northern society to new eminence. The Nevilles, acquiring a prominent position from a base within the palatinate of Durham, claimed descent from pre-Conquest lords of Staindropshire. By the thirteenth century they were ensconced as lords of Brancepeth and Raby, and Scottish wars brought further aggrandizement. In Cumberland, Dacres and Greystokes avowed descent from pre-Conquest noble families, vindicating claims to local leadership. A future head of the Dacre family noted that his power rested upon 'my kinsmen and my friends', and in the heart of his territory it could be asserted that 'This countrey has been so overlayd with Dacres, they thought there was no other king'. (Tuck 1986, 1–17; James 1967, 8)

Renewed Scottish Rebellion

The collapse of Scottish resistance in 1296 proved illusory. When Edward tried to raise revenue in Scotland to support Continental ambitions, latent hostility exploded. In May 1297, William Wallace, scion of a minor land-holding family, killed the sheriff of Lanark, a representative of English dominance, and took the lead in organizing Scottish resistance. He shattered the English hold on Scotland and followed this up by devastating English border districts. By one account 715 English communities were burned, and this single campaign put an end to the peaceful development which those areas had known during much of the century. (McNamee 1990, 40–58)

Despite this destruction, and collection of a mass of booty, the Scots failed to take any major border castles, although the town of Berwick was taken by October 1297. English merchants planted there fled, and Wallace informed Hanseatic ports that Scotland was again independent in overseas trading. Even at Berwick the castle held out. Carlisle Castle resisted a Scottish siege. There were hurried attempts to improve Newcastle's defences, still far from completed, but the Scots made no attempt to capture the defended town, although ravaging parties came within a few miles. A few minor castles like Mitford fell to the invaders. Wallace's incursion, though damaging, was a large-scale raid rather than an invasion.

By the winter of 1301–2, efforts to restore the English position had succeeded sufficiently to persuade Robert Bruce, grandson of the original Bruce claimant to the Scottish throne, to enlist under Edward's banner. Wallace was captured in 1305 and brutally executed. By the end of that year, Edward could believe that he had come close to destroying Scottish opposition.

Bruce was dissatisfied with the rewards of his change of side. (Barrow 1965; Duncan 1992) On 10 February 1306, he disrupted the king's peace by murdering John Comyn, nephew of John Balliol and a leading Scottish noble. Bruce decided to renew his grandfather's claim to the Scottish crown. His rebellion took the English by surprise and in March 1306 he was crowned King of Scots at Scone (although Edward had earlier carried off the famous coronation stone to England).

In 1306 the English offensive at first made good progress. Bruce became a hunted fugitive, but Edward's harsh treatment of captured rebels increased Scottish hostility towards English domination. Edward's plans to recover Scotland were interrupted by his death at Burgh-by-Sands on 7 July 1307.

His ambitions in Scotland and on the Continent had been impeded by disputes in England, including quarrels between the king and some of his principal barons. Under his weaker successor, similar disputes were renewed and became more debilitating. This delayed intervention in Scotland, and allowed Bruce to consolidate his position. When Edward II moved north in 1314, the catastrophe of Bannockburn ended his attempt to fulfil his father's ambitions. For some time afterwards, the Scots controlled much of the English border counties, including the lordship of Tynedale, while the remainder lay open to devastating raids. During Edward I's northern wars, most fighting and destruction had taken place in Scotland, but this English disaster, and Edward II's powerlessness, exposed the northern counties of England to Scottish vengeance on an unprecedented scale. Bruce could only pay his armies by plunder.

Without royal protection, borderers adopted other expedients. The men of Cumberland and Westmorland petitioned the king for leave 'to be at war or truce with the Scots according as they see most fit for his own honour or their own profit'. In the aftermath of Bannockburn the bishop of Carlisle made a private arrangement with the Scots for protection of his own estates, a widely imitated precedent. (Summerson 1993, I, 228; Bouch 1948, 67)

The Wardens of the Marches

Renewal of warfare brought an emergency military system on the frontier which gradually crystallized into a long-term arrangement. The 'marches' on either side were entrusted to royal representatives known as wardens, experienced soldiers charged with maintenance of border defences, supplanting sheriffs in military functions and accumulating powers which made them governors of the immediate border areas. (Lomas 1992, 86–90; Lomas 1966, 161–3) Instead of following his father's use of national armies, after Bannockburn Edward II's weakness reduced royal participation in border defences to subsidizing local arrangements. During the fourteenth century there was a reversal of the previous trend for the North to be absorbed into normal royal administration.

Salaries paid to wardens by the Crown enabled them to command 'private armies maintained at public expense'. At first, the wardenship was seen as a device whereby royal nominees directed and co-ordinated border defences. Wardens mustered fighting men of the northern counties, and even the bishop's palatinate of Durham was expected to respond to such a summons. Major castles received permanent garrisons, and appointments as warden or castellan offered ambitious men opportunities for income and advancement. (Beckingsale 1969, 67–8; Tuck 1968, 27–34) With English kings often preoccupied elsewhere, including wars with France, the wardenships began to slip into the control of leading northern families, either new or old. Only men with an independent power base and personal status could in practice fulfil the role. Tough borderers would not follow any other type of leader, and their support was essential for effectiveness in a warden. Before the end of the fourteenth century, wardenships were seen as almost a private possession of certain aristocratic dynasties. The tendency was encouraged by absence of the countervailing influence of large royal estates in border counties before the fifteenth or sixteenth centuries. The rise of the Percy family was aided by frequent possession of the wardenship and its substantial salary. For some years in the late fourteenth century the head of the family, by then earl of Northumberland, was Warden of the East March and his heir Warden of the West March, bringing them control of the entire English border.

Some possessors of royal office and favour failed to establish noble dynasties, as the career of Sir Andrew de Hartcla, an early Warden of the West March, demonstrated. He rose as an effective commander, notably by successfully defending Carlisle against the Scots in 1315. In 1322 he became earl of Carlisle, with a grant of 2,000 marks, rewards for his victory at Boroughbridge, which delivered into the king's hands his hated enemy, Thomas, earl of Lancaster. He overreached himself in 1323 by negotiating an unauthorized truce with Robert Bruce, recognizing Bruce's royal title in

Figure 3.1 Detail of illustration on the Carlisle Royal Charter of Edward II (1316), showing military techniques of attack and defence, and the leading role of Sir Andrew de Hartcla. (Source is the copy of the original charter drawn by Albert Hartshorne for R. S. Ferguson (ed.), *The Royal Charters of Carlisle*, CW1 Extra Series 1894.)

return for peace and protection. Hartcla's calculations reflected Edward's powerlessness to endanger him or protect his northern subjects, the hard-pressed 'pauperes et mediocres et agricultores'. Edward was infuriated at one of his subjects impugning his claim to rule Scotland. Hartcla's rapid rise had made local enemies, and it was by local initiative that he was speedily seized, tried for treason and hanged, drawn and quartered at Harraby on the southern outskirts of Carlisle. His quarters were distributed between Carlisle, Newcastle, Shrewsbury and Bristol, his head sent south for Edward's inspection. This brutality was an empty gesture, for Edward himself was driven to accept a similar truce in the following year. (Summerson 1993, I, 230–56; Wilson 1905, 260)

Border Warfare

For much of the fourteenth century, apart from occasional periods of truce, there was border warfare. Anglo-Scottish clashes were accompanied by lesser conflicts, as border magnates and lesser men on both sides maintained private armies and pursued ambitions or enmities. Military and financial weakness of both crowns induced monarchs to offer plunder in return for military support. For example, in 1315, Edward II offered Anthony de Lucy of Cockermouth all the loot he might gain from the Scots if he took the field. Local leaders took part in raiding, but also sought to improve their own security. After the rout of Bannockburn, 'knights and country people' on the west fled to the royal fortress at Carlisle for protection.

In Northumberland the first half of the fourteenth century saw much castle building, including Ford (1338), Etal (1341), Bothal (1343), Chillingham (1344), and Haggerstone (1344). Alnwick and probably Prudhoe were strengthened. In south Durham, Nevilles of Raby transformed an early fourteenth-century manor house into a formidable castle. Bishop Hatfield improved defences at Durham Castle after appointment to the see in 1346. Similar developments took place in Cumbria, and Carlisle complained to the king that neighbouring lords were concentrating on fortifying their own seats, and neglecting protection of the city. (Hislop 1992, 91–7; Hislop 1995; Curwen 1913; Summerson 1993, I, 318)

Lesser landowners tried to protect themselves by building fortified houses, often known as bastles and peles, sufficient to offer some security against raiders. During the earlier relative tranquillity of the thirteenth century, local landowners could live in undefended hall houses, but between 1350 and 1415 scores of fortified towers appeared, as provision of defensive structures percolated down the social scale, from castle to fortified manor house, pele tower and smaller local strongpoints. At Halton in Northumberland, the fortified tower was probably added to an earlier stone hall some time in the later fourteenth century. Although Craster Tower was first recorded in a list of border holds in 1415, this small castle had probably been built by the second Sir Edmund Craster in the previous century. (Borne and Dixon, 1978, 138; Craster 1952, 127) In towns without adequate defences, individual strong houses were constructed. By the end of the Tudor period, Haltwhistle possessed one strong pele tower, two smaller towers and several other fortified houses. In a crisis atmosphere, the need for a royal licence was often ignored, and refuges for 'the saiffing of men there gudis and gere' multiplied. (Tuck 1985, 46) This was not a response to major Scottish invasions, but to lesser disorder and raiding, with such precautions adopted principally where proximity to the border or easy access intensified danger. Remote areas might find protection in distance or difficulties of terrain.

The Expansion of Border Troubles

Brigandage had several roots. Some gentry families learned that raiding could be profitable, as when in 1357 Sir Robert Tilliol and Sir Thomas de Lucy, breaking a truce, launched a raid into Eskdale and seized 1,000 cattle, 1,000 sheep, and many Scottish captives for ransom. (Wilson 1905, 259–60) Lesser men followed such examples, although most brigands were not poor, if only because for most raiding it was essential to be mounted. It took only a few generations to see brigandage established as a way of life among leading families or clans of borderers on both sides,

> from their Cradells bread and brought up in theft, spoyle, and bloode, as they are by use and custome. Neither have they anie other meane (anie of them) to live but stealinge. (Spence 1980, 87)

There were links between prominent raiders and the more numerous lesser fry. When a border magnate acquired a position in royal administration, he might turn a blind eye to depredations by those whose support he might need in future. In 1384 the sheriff of Cumberland complained that he dare not arrest a notorious criminal for fear of being murdered by the latter's friends. (Summerson 1982, 114)

Uncertainty and damaging raids intensified problems in wresting a living from northern upland areas. Raiding was frequent between October and April, when there was less call for work on the land. October and November, when stock was brought in from summer pasturing, were particularly dangerous months. An observer noted that

> there be more inhabitants . . . than the said countries may sustain . . . the people of the country . . . be loath to depart forth from the same but had rather live poorly there as thieves than more wealthy in another country. (Beckingsale 1969, 81)

The Extent of Disorder

The disorder, reflecting weakened central control of the frontier region, was not confined to the borders. Feuds between rival groups erupted in Newcastle, although the Newcastle oligarchy united in using any available methods, including violence, to inhibit the commerce of Gateshead or Tynemouth. Newcastle merchants, who often saw their ships conscripted into royal service in wartime, indulged in piracy along the east coast. During Edward I's Scottish wars, they were accused of dishonestly seizing goods from foreign ships interned in the Tyne by royal orders. Some were suspected of profitably supplying an invading Scottish army. (Fraser 1969, 48–9; Conway Davies 1953, 190; Fraser 1959, 315, 319)

The border had never been completely peaceful. The War of Scottish Independence brought about 'the intensification, almost institutionalization, of the feuding and raiding which were in any case endemic in the region'. In taxation records there were many references to inability to contribute because of the destruction, as when, in 1313, Northumberland, Cumberland and Westmorland were exempted from taxation for the remainder of Edward II's reign. Durham was not included because of its palatinate status. (Tuck 1968, 28; Harbottle 1969, 78)

Effects of Disorder on the Church

The Church, already handicapped by large and often thinly populated parishes and poor clerical incomes, did not escape ravages. Tithe payments from the bishop of Durham's outlying territories of Norhamshire and Islandshire never regained in the later medieval period their level before Wallace's 1297 incursion. The nave of Hexham Priory was destroyed by Scots in 1296, while a few miles to the east the parson's house at Ovingham was destroyed in 1293, 1312 and 1316. (The last Augustinian canon to live there defended his home wearing armour at the Reformation.) (McNamee 1990, 55; Honeyman 1953, 135)

In 1316 Bishop Halton reported that the Priory of Carlisle had suffered at the hands of Scots who 'robbed their lands and possessions, killed their men and farmworkers, and many times lamentably destroyed their moveable and unmoveable goods up to the walls of the city'. The value of church property in the North West fell disastrously before temporary respite brought by a truce in 1323. Destruction reached outlying religious houses like Furness, St Bees and Cartmel. Income of Furness Abbey fell from £176 in 1291 to £13 6s. 8d. in 1318. Lanercost Priory fared worse: its lands produced £74 12s. 6d. in 1291, but in 1319 they were described as waste and producing nothing. Lanercost never recovered during the following two centuries. In the early fifteenth century its canons were reduced to begging. In 1336 the bishop of Carlisle received permission to fortify his principal residence. Monks of Holm Cultram erected a fortified church at Newton Arlosh to protect local tenants. (Summerson 1993, I, 220; Bouch 1948, 69, 75; Moorman 1948; Dobson 1992; Turnbull and Walsh 1994, 79; Wilson 1905, 257)

Others preferred a more active response. John de Kirkby, bishop of Carlisle, accompanied Lords Clifford and Dacre on a raid into Scotland in 1337, which was sufficiently successful for his fortified manor at Rose to be singled out for retaliation by Scots who held him 'in the utmost hatred through having marched against them in war'. Kirkby remained undeterred, and a sequence of military adventures against the Scots culminated in his spirited performance during the victory at Neville's Cross in 1346.

The extent of disorder was illustrated in an incident of 1317, when Gilbert de Middleton ambushed south of Durham a party which included two cardinals, legates of the pope; Louis Beaumont, bishop-elect of Durham, was carried off and held to ransom. In 1327 a Scots army camped within Stanhope Park killed or removed many of the bishop of Durham's cattle and deer. (Offler 1988, 193; Drury 1978, 94). After Wallace's raid in 1297, a northern chronicler recorded that

> At that time the praise of God ceased in all the monasteries and churches of the whole province from Newcastle to Carlisle. All the monks, canons regular and the rest of the priests and ministers of the Lord, together with almost the whole of the people, fled from the face of the Scot. (McNamee 1990, 40)

Effects of Scots Raiding

It was sometimes possible to buy off the Scots, but only on a temporary basis and at the cost of bleeding white communities affected. One Durham magnate, a kinsman of Robert Bruce through his mother, was involved in at least eight such negotiations during the years 1311–27. On one occasion desperately needed money was raised by ransacking Durham city and seizing every penny found there. In 1297 the Northumberland monasteries of Hexham and Newminster scraped together enough money to buy immunity during Wallace's incursion. (Offler 1988, 197; McNamee 1990, 57) These blackmail payments mostly occurred during post-Bannockburn years when, as the *Lanercost Chronicle* noted, 'the King of England neither knew how to rule his realm nor was he able to defend it against the Scots'. Carlisle paid £200 in protection money during the 1346 invasion. Even in 1385, Holm Cultram paid £200 to Earl Douglas to avert destruction of abbey property. Durham was more effective at scraping together money to buy temporary immunity than other northern counties. (Offler 1988, 197; McNamee 1990, 57; Towill 1991, 33; Bouch, 1948, 95)

Wallace's large-scale raid of 1297 began the destruction, but Bruce's incursions after 1311 and especially after Bannockburn were more damaging. None of his successors inflicted as much harm as Bruce's onslaught of 1314–28. Northern parts of Northumberland and Cumberland suffered most from repeated raids, including damaging irruptions in the 1380s. Over much of the English border country the transhumance system of farming was disrupted. Newminster Priory had extensive upland pastures in the Kidland area of Northumberland during the previous century, but this did not survive Scots raids; even at the Dissolution of the Monasteries, these pastures were worthless. Where local kinship ties, such as those of Armstrongs, Ridleys, Grahams and Routledges, were sufficiently consolidated to preserve some kind of mutual security, the shieling system persisted, but elsewhere disruption was widespread. (McDonnell 1988, 14–15)

Some areas escaped the worst disasters. West Cumberland was only hit once, in 1322. In 1380 Darlington could still provide its episcopal landlord with an annual rent of nearly £100. (Sunderland 1967, 15) In a few exposed areas, improvements were still possible. There were church building schemes in Northumberland at Alnwick, Kirkharle, Morpeth and Widdrington, and additions to churches at Bolam, Bywell St Peter and Embleton. (Briggs 1989, 79) In contrast, a survey of the diocese of Carlisle in 1319 showed that none of the 23 churches in the northern third of Cumberland was able to provide for a priest because of devastation, and nearly half were destroyed.

The blows were so savage that it is unlikely that during the later medieval period Northumberland and Cumberland ever reached again the level of prosperity attained during the thirteenth century. Apart from destruction, persistent danger of attack played a part in destabilizing local society and discouraging attempts at improvement. (Tuck 1985, 33–52)

March Law and Custom

Warfare and raiding did not only produce destruction, insecurity and a form of military government under the wardens of the marches. The needs of defence consolidated border laws and customs differing from those accepted in most of England, including less threatened areas of the northern counties. Despite strains brought by border conflict, the royal system of justice remained, but it was supplemented by another concept of law which developed for settling cross-border disputes in times of peace. Border magnates, including wardens, devised rules for conduct of warfare and settlement of cross-border complaints. During the fourteenth century these crystallized into a body of customary or Marcher law, which was roughly accepted on both sides of the frontier. For instance, 'March treason' was committed when an Englishman joined with a Scotsman to despoil a fellow Englishman. (Tuck 1968, 32; Tough 1928, Part VI; Neville 1994)

The marches were distant from centres of national administration and not welcoming or accessible areas. Royal justice, increasingly effective over most of the two kingdoms, was not always easily applied among clannish borderers on both sides. Occasional meetings between English and Scots wardens to settle local disputes and dispose of cross-border criminal cases led to something approaching a regular system. From 1373, English wardens were expected to meet Scottish counterparts twice a year at trysting places on the border to hear together cases involving subjects of both countries. In practice, these meetings were intermittent, with modest success in repressing disorder. One account of the border areas noted that

> if the poor subjects there complain, or prosecute any offender of any great surname, they are either murdered or their houses burned, so that no man dares complain or give evidence against such offenders. (Spence 1977, 70–1)

There was no fixed line to define where Marcher law operated in addition to the kingdom's common law, nor was Marcher law well codified and consistently applied. Yet its existence showed that there was some vigour in the system, which sometimes worked, even if the justice involved was rough. Over time, conventions of Marcher law showed increasing sophistication, including written bills of complaint and minutes of wardens' meetings. Tables of standard ransom payments were compiled. (Neville 1983, 48; Neville 1994)

In areas like Redesdale and Tynedale, and other districts where danger of war or raiding was greatest, tenant right became established to secure the supply of warlike recruits. Edward I recognized that border services required from Cumberland and Westmorland involved special privileges. This recognition, repeated and extended in later years, became consolidated during the fourteenth century into the concept of border tenant rights in the later medieval period. It is possible that this reflected traditions dating back to pre-Norman times. Knights of Cumberland had argued for similar privileges in their dealings with King John. Some historians have argued that northern tenant right represented the survival of pre-Conquest drengage tenures or even earlier practices. Under these arrangements, in return for security of tenure (including rights of inheritance), tenants paid low rents or other payments to their lord, but provided military service in time of need. Such conventions conferred some security of tenure on tenants, and reduced the lord's need to pay for permanent troops. (Wilson 1905, 251–2; McDonnell 1994)

Border tenant right included the tenant's right to dispose of all or part of his holdings, with at most a nominal role for the landlord. Conventions governing amounts of rent or services due, and inheritance patterns, varied from district to district. In areas close to the borders, supply of fighting men was encouraged by partible inheritance, whereby on a tenant's death holdings were divided among his sons. Even in the late Tudor period, these northern systems of tenant right were recognized in remote and troublesome areas like upper Weardale, and cases invoking these privileges occurred generations later. (Drury 1987, 71–100; McDonnell 1994, 28)

Both the Crown and the nobility had interests, over three centuries of insecurity, in tapping the military potential of the border. Most magnates recognized that this entailed caution in exploitation of estates, for income was often subordinated to 'good lordship' to obtain a loyal following in dangerous times.

Disorder in the North has to be seen within a context of lawlessness in other parts of Britain. If juries could not always be trusted in wardens' courts or other tribunals, this was not a northern monopoly. Local and regional power struggles were common elsewhere, with influential men guilty of intimidation. Among maritime interests, it was not only northerners who showed fondness for piracy and privateering. London saw more violence than Newcastle during medieval and early modern periods. The frequency of border warfare and raiding merely gave a peculiar flavour and intensity of disorder to frontier areas. Of more than 80 petitions to parliaments between 1400 and 1460, complaining of disorder, more than one-third came from Northumberland, Cumberland and Westmorland. (Neville 1983, 47) When the house of Trinitarian friars was established in Newcastle in 1360, one-third of its revenues was routinely devoted to ransoming prisoners. English and Scottish governments were wary of alienating border men of violence who might be invaluable soldiers in time of need.

In early days of the wardenship system, salaries paid by the Crown to wardens were enough to enable them to pay for an effective military force. By the fifteenth and sixteenth centuries this was no longer the case, and wardens relied upon their retainers and the often uncertain support of local levies, for many of whom raiding was a common habit.

Civil Wars

Apart from military campaigns on the borders, and smaller-scale raids and counter-raids, these centuries saw English and Scottish kings embroiled in internal conflicts, rebellions and civil wars. The consequent weakening of royal authority in both kingdoms affected the borders, as northern magnates led their troops in support of causes they favoured.

The troubled reign of Edward II inaugurated these recurring crises. The fall of Thomas, earl of Lancaster, in 1322 was partly due to his failure to enlist support in the North, where he had enemies, and his apparent indifference to Scots raiding during his ascendancy in England. (Maddicott 1970)

The northern frontier was affected by events elsewhere. Anglo-French wars tempted Scotland to take advantage of England's Continental preoccupations, an attitude encouraged by France. The temptation to attack northern counties while much of England's strength was embroiled elsewhere could be irresistible, but also dangerous. In 1346, responding to French appeals, David II invaded northern England while Edward III was in France. Considerable destruction was inflicted before the invaders were caught at Neville's Cross near Durham by an army raised by northern English magnates. Not only were the Scots badly beaten, but their king, together with many leading Scottish noblemen, was captured. David remained a prisoner for eleven years and his eventual ransom strained the Scottish economy.

The Wars of the Roses

During the struggle for the throne in the fifteenth-century Wars of the Roses, northern elements played an important part. (Pollard 1990; Lomas 1996; 167–73) By the mid-fifteenth century, the two dominant families in the North were those of Percy and Neville, and their regional rivalry spilled over into national politics. Although there was no overall loyalty to either York or Lancaster, when the Wars of the Roses began the Lancastrian cause was stronger in the North. In the North East, the Percies were prominent Lancastrians; in Cumbria, the Cliffords, who held the barony of Westmorland, were also Lancastrians. Cliffords' alliance with Percies on the Lancastrian side owed much to recent aggrandizement by the Nevilles, who were incidentally Yorkists but feared by Cliffords as rivals in Cumberland. (Tuck 1986, 14–16) Edward IV, during his struggle for the crown, made no attempt to levy troops in Northumberland, Cumberland or Westmorland. There were exceptions to this situation. In Northumberland, the Crasters of Craster, tenants of a Lancastrian landowner, adhered to the Yorkist side. (James 1966, 46; Craster 1952, 128; Charlesworth 1952, 61) The Percies were weakened by their unsuccessful rising in 1402 against Henry IV, whom they had helped to the throne. Although they were subsequently restored to titles and most of their estates, royal authority was employed from the reign of Richard II to balance Percy pre-eminence in the North with the ambitious Nevilles, who built upon earlier favours to establish a powerful position in both Yorkshire and Cumberland by 1461.

In the fighting of 1459–61, Percies, like most northern magnates, sided with the Lancastrians. The third earl of Northumberland, together with Lord Dacre of Gilsland and other northern leaders, was killed in March 1461 at Towton. This victory was followed up by pursuit of remnants of the

Figure 3.2 Seal of Henry Percy (1272–1315), founder of the family's Northumberland eminence. Frequently employed as military leader, including the Bannockburn campaign, he was created Lord Percy of Alnwick at end of the thirteenth century.

Lancastrian forces in the North, culminating in the battle of Hexham in May 1464, when the Lancastrians were routed. The Yorkist regime finally consolidated its authority in the North. The duke of Somerset, a leading Lancastrian champion, was executed at Hexham immediately after his defeat there. The old fugitive king, Henry VI, had remained at Bywell on Tyne during the battle of Hexham; he then fled, but was soon captured. By the end of June 1464 Edward IV's position seemed securely established. (Charlesworth 1953, 69–81; Charlesworth 1952, 57–67; Hicks 1984, 23)

The Neville family were among the victors, and received a large slice of the spoils. During their years as leading Yorkist supporters, Neville earls of Warwick and Salisbury established a strong northern power base. Warwick became hereditary sheriff of Westmorland, and in the 1460s the Nevilles repeatedly interfered to ensure that Carlisle and Appleby chose MPs of their nomination. (Jalland 1976 for 1975, 40–7)

Warwick's break with Edward in 1470 saw a reversal of fortunes. The king responded by restoring the Percy heir to the earldom of Northumberland and forfeited estates, but without re-establishing their northern hegemony. The king's brother, Richard, duke of Gloucester, the future Richard III, received the lion's share of Neville properties in the North, and emerged as Yorkist viceroy there. This led to friction between Richard and the Percies, with heavy spending by both in maintaining retainers among northern gentry. Both men had important holdings in Yorkshire and Cumberland, which involved competition for regional pre-eminence. Richard, as Warden of the West March, was given royal backing. The struggle for influence precipitated a financial crisis for the earl of Northumberland, who spent too much in trying to keep the allegiance of important gentry, while his income fell. Revenue from his Cumberland properties fell by at least 25 per cent between 1416 and 1470; shortfall from his Northumberland estates was higher. There was a compromise at the end of Edward's reign, which recognized Richard's hegemony in Yorkshire and Cumberland but allowed the earl primacy in Northumberland. A judicious sharing of patronage cemented the deal. (Tuck 1985, 42–3; Hicks 1978, 81–8)

By 1483, the earl was among northern noblemen following Richard's banner, including Lord Greystoke, Lord Dacre of Gilsland, and the reconciled surviving Nevilles. This northern following was crucial for Richard's seizure of the throne in 1483. In return, the earl of Northumberland was given additional grants, though not as generously as he expected. Richard had no intention of abandoning his northern interests, and continued to keep a wary eye on northern matters, which cannot have pleased the earl. At Bosworth Field in 1485, the earl of Northumberland, though present with Richard's army, did not fight for the king; many contemporaries thought that he had betrayed his benefactor. Although Henry VII released the earl after brief imprisonment, and restored him to wardenship of the East and Middle

Marches, he did not trust him. Lord Dacre became Warden of the West March as a balancing factor.

Northumberland continued to consolidate his position by enlisting gentry as paid retainers, spending by 1489 over 40 per cent of his revenues on such payments. He remained loyal to the Tudor regime, although warning Henry of the dangers of imposing more taxation on the North. It was while trying to enforce Henry's financial demands that the earl was murdered by a Yorkshire crowd in April 1489. Although accompanied by a well-armed escort, they seem to have made no serious effort to defend him, which for some seemed a proper reward for his disloyalty at Bosworth Field. This lynching may have owed something to lingering affection for Richard III in the North. The earl's murder was a reminder that, however powerful a magnate might seem to be, it could be dangerous to alienate local opinion. Northumberland's death brought a vacuum of power to the North. His heir was a mere boy and Henry found it difficult in these years to control the border counties. Only someone with a strong local power base could hope to be an effective warden. Changes of fortune and shifts of allegiance during fifteenth-century civil wars disrupted networks of support whereby leading gentry and other influential elements were tied to greater families. The strains of war, forfeitures and shifting allegiances had done much to shatter old loyalties, as the fourth earl of Northumberland's attempts to buy support, and their limited success, demonstrated. (Hicks 1978, 80–102; James 1994, 111)

It is not clear how far the Wars of the Roses were responsible for breakdown of normal government in the North. In 1471 Pope Sixtus IV ordered an investigation into one violent episode illustrating the influence of over-mighty subjects. The earl of Warwick's brother, John Neville, marquis of Montagu, had forced Dr Robert Mason, rector of Richmond and prebendary of Norton, to resign these lucrative livings in order that they could be given to Oliver Bland, Neville's own chaplain. In more secular concerns, great men were frequently guilty of more or less open intimidation or violence. It is unlikely that there was anything new in this. (Donaldson 1960, 170; Brentano 1959, especially ch. VIII) On the whole it seems that dynastic wars of the fifteenth century were less disruptive than cross-border raiding and feuding, and the competing ambitions of the region's leading families. This is borne out by a study of the working of some elements of royal justice in Northumberland, Cumberland and Westmorland in 1439–59. (Neville 1983, 45–60)

Chapter 4

The Tudor North

Border conflicts and disorder remained a challenge to Tudor sovereigns as to their medieval predecessors. Some long-standing border disputes were removed, as when in 1552 the western border was fixed between the English parish of Kirkandrews-on-Esk and the Scottish parish of Canonbie across the old 'Debateable Lands'. (Barrow 1966, 26–7) There was never anything like the extended thirteenth-century period of peace, confidence and expansion.

Border military organization became more sophisticated. Some northern communities specialized in production of military equipment. An account of the village of Bywell, on the Tyne, in 1569, described a long street, closed by gates at each end, inhabited by workers in metal, making arms, armour, bits, spurs and other horse trappings. (Howlett 1975, 123)

Under regulations of 1538, substantial tenants of Holm Cultram Abbey (holding 15–20 acres) had to muster in time of war mounted and fully armed, the next category (10–15 acres) served mounted but less well armed, while those with 2–6 acres provided footmen armed with bows and spears. Similar obligations provided an early warning system to detect incursions. In the *Order of the Watches upon the Middle Marches*, issued by the warden Lord Wharton in 1552: 'FROM *West-Whelpington* to *Raye*, to be watched with four Men nightly of the Inhabitors of *West-Whelpington* and *Raye*: Settlers and Searchers *William Elsden* and *John Rotchester*.' (Bouch and Jones, 1961, 26; Jarrett 1962, 191)

The region's aristocracy was essential for effective mobilization. In one early sixteenth-century campaign, the earl of Northumberland accompanied Henry VIII to France with a force of 500 men drawn from his Yorkshire estates. At the same time 1,500 men from his Cumberland holdings rode at the earl's bidding against the Scots. (Reid 1921, 20) Such military forces, available at need, were made possible by the system of partible inheritance, willingness of border lords to multiply tenancies, and enlistment of local gentry as lieutenants of northern magnates in an intricate system of patronage and kinship links. (Lomas 1996, 145–7)

The system was expensive. During the turbulent years of the Wars of the Roses, such great lords as the Percy earls of Northumberland strained their resources to buy support, while the inflation of the sixteenth century compounded these problems. (Tuck 1992; Bean 1958, 94–104) Financial pressures lay behind Percy attempts to squeeze more income from tenants – even at the expense of 'good lordship' – in the late fifteenth and early sixteenth centuries. The first Clifford earl of Cumberland was forced into efforts of this kind on his Westmorland holdings, and the resultant loss of loyalty undermined his effectiveness as a marcher lord. Monarchs had their own problems with over-mighty subjects, and encouraged their role as courtiers, which consumed their resources and kept them under the royal eye. The Crown was well aware of the need to cultivate the military resources of northern counties. Crown tenants on the borders were given liberal treatment in relation to border tenant right. Borderers were quick to use the need for military service as an argument buttressing whatever privileges they might claim. These often included the convention that in return for border service, tenants could not be compelled to serve elsewhere, a privilege often exploited to obtain further concessions from lords needing such support.

Wartime needs encouraged liberality in dealing with border folk. A section of a 1538 muster roll noted that 391 men 'able with horse and harness' could be expected from the 'Northe Tyndell Theiffs'; neighbouring Redesdale was credited with 185 men 'able with horse and harnes and all speres . . . beside all the foot theves'. (Tuck 1985, 51) The reluctance of royal agents to alienate such groups was shared by northern magnates, whose own ambitions might make them less than reliable agents of royal authority. Even if they could act effectively, they might regard the supply of tough fighting men, amenable to their summons, as a more attractive option than evenhanded enforcement of peace and order.

One well-documented example of endemic border disorders was a large-scale Scots raid on Haydon Bridge in 1587, at a time when Scots attacks had been intensified by the execution of Mary, Queen of Scots. The English government established that some local officers, including John Heron of Chipchase, Constable of Tynedale, had made no attempt to intercept raiders and were instead implicated in this and other similar plundering. (Charlesworth 1957, 73–6) In 1597, Lord Scrope, Warden of the West March, wrote to Richard Lowther, an influential Cumberland landowner, to say, almost despairingly, 'I Pray Cozen Lowther, be a meane to stay your owne men from spoyling ther countrey, for thoug I have forgiven them often, yet there is noe amendment yet.' (Spence 1977, 70–1)

Even wardens' trysts could be dangerous. Sir George Heron, Keeper of Tynedale, was murdered during a wardens' meeting in 1575. Ten years later, a meeting between English and Scottish Wardens of the Middle Marches was in progress near Windy Gyle, high in the border hills, 'when it chanced a sudden accident and tumult to arise among the rascals of Scotland and

England about a little pickery among themselves'. Shots were fired and Lord Francis Russell, son-in-law of the English warden, Sir John Forster, was killed. With difficulty, the wardens succeeded in containing the situation and the meeting ended peacefully.

The Battle of Flodden

Danger from Scotland persisted and in 1513 a renewed Franco-Scottish alliance saw James IV invade Northumberland, when Henry VIII was campaigning in France. The bishop of Durham's fortress at Norham was battered into submission by Scottish guns, and lesser castles at Wark, Etal and Ford taken. These successes were deceptive, for the English government anticipated the danger and reacted vigorously. Reinforcements sent to the border had already brusquely repulsed a Scottish raid led by Lord Home. Royal artillery had been sent north, and the earl of Surrey was soon in the area at the head of an army. Skilful English generalship, and Scottish errors of judgement, brought catastrophe for the invaders. The battle of Flodden, on 9 September 1513, involved the deaths of James IV, his son, the archbishop of St Andrews, two bishops, two abbots, twelve earls and fourteen lords. Although this rout crippled Scotland's ability to field a substantial army for some years, it did not bring peace to the border. The magnitude of the disaster may have induced Scotland to cling to the French alliance, as the only means of preserving independence.

Attempts by Henry VIII and his successors to establish English influence in Scotland proved unsuccessful, and there were repeated Anglo-Scottish collisions, as well as smaller-scale cross-border raiding and feuding. In December 1542, the Scots suffered another reverse, when an invading force was routed by a smaller English army at Solway Moss. Three years later, the English were badly beaten at Ancrum near Jedburgh. Later in 1545, an English force commanded by the earl of Hertford ravaged the Scottish borders, destroying the border abbeys of Kelso, Melrose, Dryburgh, Roxburgh and Coldingham. In September 1547, another English invading army scored a major victory at Pinkie, near Edinburgh. Although Scotland was racked by internal disputes, the spirit of independence, coupled with English miscalculations, undermined English ambitions in the North.

The Pilgrimage of Grace

Apart from the Scottish threat, Tudor monarchs faced other problems. In 1536 the rebellion known as the Pilgrimage of Grace saw much of the North in arms against Henry VIII. (Dodds 1915; Hoyle 1985, 53–63; Summerson 1993, II, 484 *et seq.*; Lomas 1996, 173–6) This outbreak did not have any simple origin. It owed something to northern resentment against the king's religious policies. The rebellion's leader, the Yorkshireman Robert Aske, condemned the dissolution of northern monasteries, with exaggerated accounts of their contribution to northern society. (Keeling 1987, 36; Keeling 1979, 32–3) The principal rebel banner bore a representation of the five wounds of Christ. There was resentment at the loss of charitable facilities provided by monasteries, although religious houses had a declining role within the region. Most priests steered clear of the rising, although a few, including the vicar of Brough and the abbot of Holm Cultram, were active supporters. Resentment at clerical tithes in a time of rising prices seems to have been a more effective spur than doctrinal zeal. A harvest failure in 1535–36, and grievances against grasping landlords and their bailiffs, inspired disaffection. The rebellion was conservative, with resentment expressed against central interference in regional affairs, including religious changes. A modern judgement sees it as 'conservative in character, directed against unwanted change and the evil counsellors seen as responsible for it'. (Summerson 1993, II, 486)

In Lincolnshire and Yorkshire, where the Pilgrimage began, threatened taxation was the principal spur. The four northern counties had been exempted because of their poverty and Scottish ravages, but rising rents and prices provoked discontent here. Antipathy to religious innovations may have provided some kind of loose link with rebels in other regions.

In Cumbria, support, concentrated in the Penrith and Cockermouth areas, was due almost entirely to local factors, including rapacious landlords. Rivalries between local magnates, especially Cliffords and Dacres, prevented a united front by the established order in time to prevent the outbreak. The consequence, with perhaps 15,000 rebels in the field, proved alarming enough to create a belated aristocratic coalition which turned the tide. Henry Clifford, the earl of Cumberland's son, saved Carlisle from rebel attack and at the critical moment was given Dacre support. (Summerson 1993, II, 488) In Cumberland and Westmorland rebels failed to secure backing of significant numbers of gentry or clergy. Dacre tenants followed their lord, and mustered to raise the rebel siege of Carlisle.

In Northumberland, the imminent dissolution of the priory at Hexham affected opinion there. Inhabitants of Redesdale and Tynedale joined the rebels, scenting opportunities for loot, although this reduced the chance that respectable inhabitants in places like Newcastle would join the rising. At the end of the rebellion it was noted that the border mosstroopers had

Figure 4.1 Askerton Castle, manor house close to the border in east Cumberland, illustrating the defensive priorities of northern landowners in the sixteenth century. Home of a branch of the Dacre family, much involved in border conflicts.

exploited the disturbed conditions to ravage more prosperous areas 'so sore that many are weary of their lives'. Redesdale's participation in the rising had been prompted by Sir Reynold Carnaby, a prominent Northumberland figure experienced in various intrigues. It is unclear what his aims were. By February 1537, the Redesdale 'names' had come to terms with royal agents. Tynedale men had risen after being persuaded by John Heron of Chipchase, one of Sir Thomas Percy's henchmen among Northumberland gentry. In March 1537, when the Keeper of Tynedale, Roger Fenwick, went to Bellingham to receive hostages for the dale's future behaviour, he was murdered by three leading members of the great 'names' of the dale, two Charltons and a Dodd. Subsequently heads of the Tynedale families came to terms with the king's general, the duke of Norfolk, agreeing to remain quiet and give up some plunder.

At the outbreak of the rebellion there was widespread belief that if the people's grievances could be brought to the king he would redress them. In Northumberland some gentry who joined the Pilgrimage seem to have thought that they were obeying a royal summons. More recalcitrant rebels would have been happy to invite the Scots in as rescuers. Luckily for the English government, James V was in France during the worst of the 1536–37 crisis. The south of England offered no support to the rebels, although the North provided Aske with a force which at one time was said to amount to 30,000 armed men. Henry VIII at first temporized, and his ministers conceded negotiations on the people's grievances. The rebels then agreed to disperse, though a rash of continuing disorders gave the government justification for repudiating earlier concessions. The king instructed Norfolk that

> before you shall close upp our said baner again, you shal in any wise cause such dreadfull execution to be done upon a good nombre of the inhabitauntes of every towne, village and hamlet that have offended in this rebellion as well as by hanging of them uppe in trees as by quartering of them, and settings of their heddes and quarters in every towne, great and small, and all such other places as they may be a ferefull spectacle to all others hereafter. (Wilson 1905, II, 270–4)

The unfurling of the royal banner symbolized suspension of normal judicial proceedings in affected areas, and imposition of martial law, under which the king's vengeance was carried out. When royal forces gained military superiority there came retribution, with many executions in the North. Among the victims was Robert Hodge, curate of Whitburn, near Sunderland, who had reputedly wished the duke of Norfolk hanged on one side of a tree and Thomas Cromwell on the other, and solicited intervention by James V of Scotland, claiming that the rebels would have carried him triumphantly to London. In Cumbria 74 rebels were executed, including some ringleaders who had tried to make terms with their sovereign. (Dodds 1915, II, 253–4)

A principal reason for the severity of the 1536–37 crisis, and subsequent retribution, was that northern magnates, including the Percy sixth earl of Northumberland and the Clifford first earl of Cumberland (a title conferred in 1525), could not exercise effective authority. This stemmed in part from policies of Tudor sovereigns. Royal payments to wardens of the marches were never high enough to provide military resources capable of threatening the monarchy. In addition, like previous kings, Tudor sovereigns pursued a policy of 'divide and rule'. Encouragement of the Cliffords was one instance of this, strengthening a rival influence against Percy hegemony.

By the later medieval period, Percy earls of Northumberland had acquired dangerous eminence in the North. In Cumberland and Northumberland, Cockermouth and Alnwick formed the twin centres of 'a true regional court'. (Bean 1958, 134; James 1965, 7) The original prominence of the Cliffords was due to their inheritance (in two separate stages) of estates of the old-established Vipont family, but their continued rise owed much to royal favour. The son of the tenth Lord Clifford was an early friend of Henry VIII, who gave him the earldom of Cumberland, grants of estates in Nottinghamshire and Yorkshire, and employed him for seventeen years as Warden of the West March, despite his ineffectiveness. The Cliffords, although they became much richer, were never as successful as the Dacres in enlisting support of the western border 'names'. (James 1966, 44; Reid 1921, 92–3)

The tortuousness of royal policies was further exemplified by encouragement of Dacres, lords of Gilsland, to ensure that Cliffords did not become too strong. The Crown also used its patronage and the opportunity provided by the Dissolution of the Monasteries to buy support by judicious distribution of monastic estates among northern gentry. (Beckingsale 1969, 72; James 1965, 36; James 1994)

Already in 1531, the financial difficulties of the earl of Northumberland had induced him to relinquish the honour and castle of Cockermouth to the king, who felt strong enough to appoint his new steward of the Cockermouth estates, Sir Thomas Wharton, drawn from a relatively unimportant Westmorland family, as a kind of *de facto* Warden of the West March, though he was not given that title. Tenants of this substantial holding were now royal rather than Percy dependants, strengthening the Crown's military resources within the region. Wharton's position was buttressed by enlisting Thomas Dacre among his lieutenants, detaching him from his own family, who regarded Wharton as an upstart. (James 1965, 28, 38) No doubt the grant of the estates of Lanercost Priory to Thomas Dacre was influential here. When the Crown chose to deploy its patronage fully, it had no equal. Wharton rose from knighthood (1529) to the wardenship of the West March (1544) then for a time wardenship of all three English marches (1552), with a peerage (1544) supported by grants and leases of Crown lands. Sir William Eure of Witton, County Durham, achieved similar distinction by service to the crown, primarily as a general. The duties performed by such men in extended royal service showed that such honours had to be worked for under the Tudor regime, but their successful careers also indicated strengthening of royal authority in the border counties. (James 1994)

The Pilgrimage of Grace showed that rival aristocratic agents no longer provided security. Percy and Clifford earls, in face of rising prices, had tried to wring more income from their estates, alienating tenants upon whom aristocratic influence depended. In 1537 Norfolk told Thomas Cromwell that if the earl of Cumberland was to be of use as warden 'he must . . . not be so greedy to get money of his tenants'. Despite Cumberland's loyalty to Henry VIII, he was deserted by most of his followers and tenantry and besieged in Skipton Castle. Cumberland's heir defended Carlisle Castle and his half-brother held out at Berwick. The Cliffords learned from their experiences in 1536–37, for the second earl reversed his predecessor's rapacious policies and restored rents to their level in the reign of Henry VI. (James 1966, 44–58)

The Neville fourth earl of Westmorland, 'one of the few noblemen who cared less for place and power than for a quiet life and a safe head', also found that he could not depend on his own household. He fell into the hands of rebels but refused to give them his support. The king's minister Thomas Cromwell was told that 'the people of his own country had deceived him'. After the rising, he was reported ridding himself of those servants who had failed to stand by him in 1536. (Dodds 1915, II, 253; Hoyle 1985, 62–3)

There were good reasons to question the role of the Percies, as one of their Yorkshire estates was an early centre of discontent. Percy kinsmen and tenants were responsible for encouraging the Pilgrimage in Northumberland, partly by misrepresenting the nature of the outbreak. Two of the earl's brothers exploited the crisis to pursue personal vendettas. One, Sir Thomas Percy, was executed after the rising's failure, the other, Sir Ingram, eventually emerged from imprisonment in the Tower broken in health. The earl, Warden of the Middle and East Marches, was, fortunately for his own safety, ill when the rising began, although suspected of complicity in it. He was dismissed as unreliable in 1537, and died the following year, bequeathing his possessions to the king. His nearest Percy heirs by blood were the disinherited sons of Sir Thomas. Percy influence was eclipsed until the heir was restored in title and estates by Mary I in 1557. By then the family's preferred residence and main income had shifted from Northumberland to Yorkshire, although the earl contemplated a return to Alnwick in the 1560s, perhaps appreciating that absence was eroding Percy influence in Northumberland. (Batho 1957, 49–50)

Growth of Royal Power

There were other reasons for erosion of aristocratic power. Apart from financial problems common on border estates yielding smaller incomes than lands held by southern nobles, border conflicts, civil wars and extinctions affected baronial families and provided monarchs with extended patronage resources with which to reward followers.

After Richard III's defeat and death in 1485, the new king Henry VII had at his disposal not only Richard's northern possessions and offices but also extensive estates forfeited by the defeated party. Such resources were used to establish Tudor supporters in the North. (Hicks 1978, 92, 95) When the Crown acquired the remaining Dacre estates after Thomas Dacre's attainder in 1589, Elizabeth I became the dominant landowner on the Cumberland border, and local gentry were given a role in administration of these estates as well as her officers of the Exchequer and Duchy of Lancaster. (Spence 1977, 66) In addition to these lucrative opportunities, local figures could be bound to the Crown by judicious distribution of such posts as sheriff, or salaried custodian of a royal castle. (Hedley 1957, 5–6)

As Parliament increased in importance, northern boroughs could be induced to elect royal nominees as their MPs, as Newcastle did on several occasions in the fifteenth century. Smaller boroughs seem to have been even more amenable to this kind of pressure. Although kings were willing to sell privileges to developing towns, including various levels of municipal self-government, royal authority swiftly suspended such concessions for disorder or breaches of royal commands. (Jalland 1976 for 1975, 39; Fraser 1961, 142)

The Council in the North

One aftermath of the Pilgrimage of Grace was the establishment in 1537 of a Council in the North. This body of royal nominees, based at York, was entrusted with administrative and judicial functions in northern counties, another brake on northern magnates. One of their functions was to transmit to local agencies orders from the Privy Council. Repeatedly, such orders sought to compel northern magistrates and other royal officials to act energetically in the preservation of law and order, although the frequency with which these orders were issued induces doubts about their effectiveness. The Privy Council was capable of misjudgements of the northern situation. It over-optimistically believed that great border family groupings, especially the Grahams in the North West, could be cajoled, placated or bribed to became supporters of the rule of law instead of freebooters.

Shifting relationships between leading aristocratic interests with influence in the North, such as the Percies, Cliffords, Dacres and Howards, complicated the problems of royal officers for most of the Tudor period. In 1596, one of the leaders on the Scottish borders, Scott of Buccleugh, led eighty followers on a raid on Carlisle Castle, the English West Warden's headquarters, in which the notorious freebooter 'Kinmont Willie' Armstrong was rescued from prison. The ambitious 'name' grouping of the Grahams had connived at this raid. This was too much for the queen, who ordered retaliation. Lord Scrope, Warden of the West March, seized six leading Grahams, with the intention of making examples of them, but he was not backed by the Privy Council. The Grahams were released, sneering at the warden's impotence. Attempts to promote border security in the last years of Elizabeth's reign were frustrated by 'divers insolent broken borderers of the greatest clans' on both sides of the frontier. (Tough 1928; Spence 1977, 70–1, 77, 82–3)

In other ways, royal intervention increased. During the fourteenth and fifteenth centuries there were repeated complaints of neglect of royal

Figure 4.2 Berwick upon Tweed, showing the perimeter defences built in 1558–69, designed to exploit the strength of defensive artillery, with each sector covered by fire from two adjacent bastions.

strongholds. Under the Tudors, Carlisle Castle was modernized to take account of progress in artillery and a new citadel was built to guard southern approaches to the city. The magnificent fortifications of Berwick, begun in the reign of Mary I, became the most expensive building project of Elizabeth I's long reign. The Spanish Battery at Tynemouth, and Holy Island Castle, provide other examples of Tudor military engineering. Significantly, these schemes were carried out not by a prince bishop or a baronial magnate but at the order of, at the expense of, and under the control of, the English Crown. (Summerson 1993, II, 493–4; Towill 1991, 44–5)

Military Changes

Changes in military science and equipment diminished aristocratic power, as artillery and other firearms became increasingly important but so expensive that no magnate could hope to maintain equipment equal to that of the Crown. Border castles and pele towers, many in poor condition, offered little protection against royal artillery. The two effective border fortresses at Berwick and Carlisle were kept in royal hands. After the building of its new defences, Berwick was one of the most important bases of royal power, and its garrison was given policing duties far beyond the town walls.

The eclipse of the feudal levy as first-line troops was a lengthy development. In the initial Norman settlement of the North most Northumberland baronies had been liable to provide men for the garrisons of neighbouring royal castles, but as early as the fourteenth century this had been commuted to a cash payment. (Hunter Blair 1952, 4) Although financial difficulties frequently occurred, royal revenue was greater than that of any subject, and could more easily bear the cost of paying mercenary troops. The Spanish Battery at Tynemouth traditionally was named from Spanish soldiers in the pay of Henry VIII; in 1545 Spanish mercenaries were in garrison at Alnwick and Morpeth, while a force of Italians was in post near Berwick. (Bush 1971, 61)

Such developments provoked disaffection among northern nobles, whose earlier power as almost independent potentates in their own territories was undermined. Even where feudal tenantry remained loyal to lords, their support was no longer militarily decisive. Sixteenth-century inventories show that they rarely possessed firearms. Northern lords did not adapt willingly, finding it difficult to fulfil the role of a court nobility demanding education and culture, rather than a warrior nobility.

The Rising of the Northern Earls

Earlier interpretations of the 1569 Rising of the Northern Earls emphasized its relationship to disputes between court factions. Later research has cited regional and personal causes, explaining why the northern rising took place after principal plotters at the centre had taken fright and abandoned attempts to coerce or replace Elizabeth. (Wood 1975; Marcombe 1987; MacCaffrey 1969; Reid 1906; James 1973; Lomas 1996, 176–80)

The rising was connected with one of the conspiracies against Elizabeth I. Mary, Queen of Scots, and the duke of Norfolk were involved. The seventh earl of Northumberland and the sixth earl of Westmorland were enrolled, but not as prime movers. Both had Catholic sympathies, and had seen their traditional authority in the region undermined by Reformation changes and consequences of the Pilgrimage of Grace. Elizabeth's accession ended the brief interlude of revival of Catholic fortunes under Mary.

At first the new regime moved cautiously. The fifth earl of Westmorland was appointed Lord Lieutenant of Durham in 1559, but the pace of change in the North soon increased. Cuthbert Tunstall, the conservative bishop of Durham, had been restored by Mary after earlier deprivation because of opposition to Protestant innovations. In 1559 he was deprived again for refusing to accept the new Elizabethan religious order. Bishop Oglethorpe of Carlisle, although a Marian appointee, consented under pressure to crown the queen, after senior bishops had refused, but he too was subsequently deprived of office after objecting to Protestant innovations.

At first Tunstall's deprivation was not followed by major changes in Durham's affairs, although Robert Horn, the Protestant dean of Durham, returned to the position he had lost under Mary. The bishop's long-serving officials continued to administer secular and ecclesiastical affairs. They included Christopher Wandisford, steward, Robert Meynell, bishop's chancellor in temporal affairs, and Robert Tempest, the Durham sheriff appointed by Tunstall. All were influential figures with local connections. For the first two years of the new reign, they were allowed to continue in office. The earl of Westmorland remained as Lord Lieutenant of Durham until his death in 1564, when he was replaced by Sir George Bowes, a more reliable agent of royal policy.

The bishopric of Durham was left vacant until 1561, when the Protestant James Pilkington was appointed. He used the new statutory Oath of Supremacy to eject officers with Catholic loyalties, and set about changes in the bishopric's ecclesiastical and secular affairs. Wandisford, Meynell and Tempest were among victims of this purge, being replaced by gentry loyal to the new regime. Vacancies of all kinds, including appointment of William Waddington as dean on Horn's death, saw patronage exercised in favour of militant Protestants, often young men with few local ties, who made little effort to conciliate conservative opinion.

Pilkington openly criticized the established order within his diocese. He was determined that assets belonging to his church should be restored, despite grants or laxity under his predecessors. His attempts to recover episcopal rights, often by court proceedings, and his support of similar actions by other clerics, alienated important interests within the diocese. By 1568, several lawsuits of this kind were awaiting settlement. Some leading families, including the Tempests and Lambtons, were obliged to disgorge properties which friends or relatives within the cathedral community had contrived to lease to them. On both episcopal and chapter estates, scrutiny of leases and similar documents faced tenants with demands for payments which had been conveniently forgotten or allowed to fall into arrears. Energetic action was taken to enforce payment of rent arrears. The new earl of Westmorland was an early victim, complaining to the queen's principal minister of the 'greedy covetousness' of the Durham clergy. The earl's lax morals provided one reason why the queen and puritanical clergy were unsympathetic.

The new order was not free from favouritism to relatives and associates. Despite accumulating resentment, by 1568 Pilkington and his allies believed that they had successfully imposed their authority upon the diocese. Because of the unique combination of ecclesiastical and secular powers possessed by the bishop, and Pilkington's uncompromising Protestantism, the campaign of uprooting Catholicism and establishing the Protestant religion proved more vigorous than in many other dioceses. The work of 'purifying' churches from popish images and decorations was vigorously pursued. The Durham cult of St Cuthbert was not spared. The dean of Durham's French wife burned the holy Banner of St Cuthbert, which had been credited with English victories at Neville's Cross and Flodden. The principal statue of the saint in the cathedral was smashed.

An increasing party of the disaffected included men like Robert Tempest and John Swinburne, prominent gentry whose standing and reputation had been adversely affected by the new regime. Christopher Neville, the militant nephew of the earl of Westmorland, was embittered by his family's treatment by Pilkington and his associates. Together with Swinburne and Tempest, he overcame the earl's preference for peace and encouraged him to join the 1569 rising.

It is obvious to us that the reaction to the new regime in the North was doomed to failure. This was not so at the time. Elizabeth's rule seemed vulnerable. Some of the country's leading men, including the duke of Norfolk, were notoriously pro-Catholic, and in the imprisoned Catholic Mary, Queen of Scots, a possible rival to Elizabeth was at hand after her arrival in the north of England in 1568. Although some Catholic clergy had been deprived, others had shown more flexibility or enjoyed powerful patronage and survived the purges. Even in the Durham cathedral chapter, several old incumbents managed to stay in place. Some possessed secret Catholic sympathies, although only one took an open part in the 1569 rising.

Some leading members of northern society, including peers and gentry, were prepared to protect Catholic priests and worshippers. The Reformation in Scotland brought a stream of Catholic refugees into northern England. Commercial connections of Newcastle provided contacts with the Catholic Church on the Continent and with other parts of England. Catholics and their supporters fostering schemes for Elizabeth's overthrow hoped for support from European Catholic powers.

The participation of the earls of Northumberland and Westmorland in pro-Catholic plotting against the Elizabethan regime reflected hostility to changes introduced into the region, and acute sensitivity on matters of family and status. They resented loss of their traditional authority to the new men at the centre of English politics and their northern agents. Wounded pride helps to explain their persistence after the collapse of the principal conspiracy.

The main plot misfired, partly because Norfolk lost his nerve and submitted to the queen. He urged Westmorland, his brother-in-law, to remain quiet, but both northern earls rebelled. They claimed to be actuated by zeal for Catholicism and in the early stages of the rising, when they briefly controlled most of Durham, they restored Catholic worship there. On 14 November, in Durham Cathedral the English Bible and Book of Common Prayer were destroyed, the communion table broken up, altars restored and the mass heard again. Similar events took place in other churches in the county. Again the five wounds of Christ were emblazoned on the rebels' banners, together with the red cross of crusaders. At first the rebels received a welcome within the bishopric of Durham, and support of Catholic sympathizers among northern gentry, some of whom had personal reasons for hostility to the new dispensation. Other Durham leaders remained quiet; some, including the Lord Lieutenant, Sir George Bowes, who had replaced Westmorland's father in that office in 1564, energetically opposed the rebels. Well-established Northumberland gentry names, including Bates, Carnaby, Carr, Collingwood, Errington, Fenwick, Horsley, Ogle and Swinburne, appear among those attainted for complicity in the rising. Nevertheless, the decline of Percy influence was indicated by the limited support obtained in Northumberland. There were few recruits from the Alnwick area, partly because some gentry were more concerned with battening on Percy wealth there than with supporting its lord. There were conflicts between those who welcomed the restoration of the Percies in the 1550s and those who regretted it. Most of the earl's followers in 1569 came from his Yorkshire estates. (Meikle 1992, 84–5)

At Newcastle, a Catholic citizen and ex-mayor made an abortive attempt to seize that town. A number of northern clergy rallied to the Catholic cause in 1569, including monks from both Furness and Holm Cultram abbeys and Roger Venys, the vicar of Mitford in Northumberland, who said mass for the rebels. William Watson, vicar of Bedlington from 1557 to 1575, had survived the purge of 1561 and was among those who came to Durham to hear mass in the cathedral. At Sedgefield, one of the centres of the rising, the rector was one of Pilkington's principal officers. His attempts to suppress Catholic vestiges in the church there had aroused opposition. During the rising, altars and holy water stoups were re-erected in the parish church and Protestant service books publicly burned. Those who begged for pardon after the rising's failure included 53 men from Sedgefield.

The earls' hopes of enlisting support rapidly evaporated. Aristocratic decline since the demonstration of royal power after the Pilgrimage of Grace was illustrated by the small numbers raised by the earls. Northumberland's following amounted to only 80–100 horsemen and Westmorland's only 60. (Hilton 1977, 46–7) Like Robert Aske and the other leaders in 1536–37, the earls avowed loyalty to the queen and claimed to be in arms to rescue her from evil advisers. Their attempts to raise recruits generally ended unconvincingly with the words 'God Save the Queen'. Sir George Bowes and other loyalist gentry raised their own followings. The release of Mary, Queen of

Scots, had been one of the earls' objectives, but she was moved south out of reach. The earl of Sussex, President of the Council of the North, soon had at his disposal forces much superior to the earls' following and by 18 December the rebels had dispersed and fled. Apart from an abortive attempt to seize York, and the siege of the decayed Barnard Castle, where Sir George Bowes' small and ill-equipped garrison defied the earls for eleven days, the only fighting of any note took place on 19 December, when the Newcastle garrison sallied out to try to catch the rebel leaders on their way to seek refuge in Scotland.

Westmorland made his way abroad, where he survived until his death in 1601. Northumberland unwisely remained in Scotland, only to be sold to the English government for £2,000 in August 1572. He was promptly executed at York, claiming that he died 'a catholyke of the Popes churche'. (Hilton 1977, 47) His brother Henry had remained loyal to the Crown and was therefore allowed, despite the attainder, to succeed as eighth earl to most of the family estates in eight counties. He was not able to rebuild his family's influence. In 1571 he became enmeshed in another conspiracy against Elizabeth, the Ridolfi Plot, and was heavily fined and compelled to remain in the south, while a group of greedy Northumberland gentry, such as Sir John Forster, plundered Percy estates under the guise of administering them on the earl's behalf. The earl, again accused of conspiracy, was committed to the Tower at the end of 1584, and died there mysteriously in the following year.

His son succeeded as ninth earl; he was suspected of complicity in the Gunpowder Plot, in which his kinsman Thomas Percy was killed while resisting arrest. The earl had secured for this unreliable relative an appointment as one of the king's bodyguard. Thomas Percy had previously used his position in the earl's estate administration to feather his own nest at the expense both of his employer and of many Percy tenants, which did not increase the family's popularity in the North. The earl spent the years from 1605 to 1621 as a state prisoner in the Tower, and probably never saw the family estates in the North. It was not until 1630 that another Percy visited Alnwick, two years before succeeding his father as tenth earl. (Batho 1957, 48–62)

After the collapse of the 1569 rising, Elizabeth's government, like that of her father in 1536–37, determined on harsh retribution, including the execution of all public officers who had sided with the rebels and 600–700 from among rank and file. In the event proscription proved less severe; many captured rebels successfully obtained influential pleas in mitigation. In districts where the rising had most support, repression was severe. Within an area of south Durham, stretching from Billingham over to Staindrop and Wolsingham, 99 of the 481 captives were executed. Many relatively minor adherents faced fines of varying severity.

The shifting fortunes of the times were illustrated by the Tempest family. Thomas Tempest had risen to a position of wealth and influence in

Durham during the troubles of the early sixteenth century, profiting, often unscrupulously, from official positions under the Crown and the bishop of Durham. After the Pilgrimage of Grace, he demonstrated exaggerated loyalty by suggesting that wives and children of rebels be 'spoiled and robbed when they come to market and other punishment devised for them'. After his death *c.*1545, his nephew and heir Robert continued profitable service to the bishop. His subsequent alienation, and prominent role in the 1569 rising, led to confiscation of the painfully acquired family estate. Despite such examples, even where reprisals against rebels were severe, mercy was often shown to dependants. (Fraser and Emsley 1971, 145–7; Sunderland 1967, 34)

When, as a postscript to the 1569 northern rising, Leonard Dacre, 'that cankred and suttill traitor', rebelled against Elizabeth in 1570, and garrisoned Naworth Castle with his tenantry, a royal army commanded by Lord Hunsdon easily routed his forces, even though Hunsdon told the queen that 'Hys footmen gave the prowdyst charge upon my shott that I ever saw'. The overthrow and flight of Leonard Dacre was a dramatic demonstration of the new balance of military advantage favouring the Crown, and saw some of the Dacre estates, the Cumberland baronies of Gilsland and Greystoke, pass into the hands of the Howards. This effectively completed the erosion of the power of those northern aristocratic dynasties which had risen in the aftermath of Edward I's intervention in Scotland.

Chapter 5

The Church in the Late Medieval and Tudor Periods

The Bishop of Durham

The bishop of Durham occupied an eminent position within the northern counties, but his role was complex. His ecclesiastical influence was handicapped by the turbulent nature of parts of his diocese, especially border areas. His secular lordship, while substantial, was complicated. Hexhamshire was a liberty held by archbishops of York, outside the bishop's control, as were the liberties of Tynedale and Redesdale, both of which were within the diocese but not the palatinate. Most of modern County Durham was within the palatinate, and so were Howdenshire, an enclave in North Yorkshire, Bedlingtonshire and Islandshire, enclaves in Northumberland long held by the see of St Cuthbert, and Norhamshire, surrounding the bishop's castle on the Tweed. (Lomas 1996, 151–2) The diocese extended beyond the palatinate, covering Northumberland and Durham, including the principal town of the region, Newcastle upon Tyne. The bishop of Durham therefore exercised a variety of functions, rather than any simple overall jurisdiction.

In Cumbria, the diocese of Carlisle had been created in 1133 as a matter of political expediency (see p. 28 above). The cathedral community derived from a recently founded and poorly endowed house of Augustinian canons. For some years after its creation survival of the diocese seemed uncertain, and it was always weaker and poorer than Durham.

Quarrels between bishops and their cathedrals, often about financial affairs or disputed jurisdiction, continued, as in earlier years. In 1385 Bishop Thomas Appleby excommunicated the prior of his cathedral and threatened Carlisle with an interdict. Thereafter things quietened down. At Durham there were quarrels between bishop and monks as late as the episcopate of Thomas Booth (1457–76) but thereafter old disputes subsided. This amity may have owed something to the rarity with which bishops visited their cathedrals. Bishops of Durham when in the North usually resided at Bishop Auckland, bishops of Carlisle at Rose Castle. Many bishops were involved

99

in administration, some held key posts in royal government. The time when bishops might have been the independent choice of cathedral chapters had long since passed. Although a substantial majority of episcopal appointments were of men with family connections in the North, they were effectively royal nominees. Of great names among medieval bishops of Durham, Antony Bek had prudently attached himself to the future Edward I before the latter's accession; Thomas Langley enjoyed the patronage of John of Gaunt. The last Durham monk to become bishop of Durham was Richard de Kellawe (1311–16); the last canon of Carlisle to become bishop there was Thomas Appleby (1363–95), who soon became involved in disputes with former colleagues.

The bishop of Durham was one of the great spiritual peers of England, exercising important secular functions as well as ecclesiastical duties. The peak of the quasi-regalian status of the bishop's palatine powers was probably reached in the early years of the episcopate of Antony Bek. The monks of Durham had selected Bek as their preferred choice, at a time when they were involved in a major dispute with the archbishop of York, being well aware that he stood high in Edward I's favour and affection. While this situation continued, and Bek continued to serve the king well, this spirited bishop was allowed to exercise effective independence in his diocese. His services in the early years of Edward I's Scottish wars, when he commanded the palatinate's substantial contingent of troops, reinforced this position. When the king's favour was withdrawn, his position was weakened. The bishop's independence was threatened when he became involved in disputes with the cathedral community, which allowed the king to come forward as arbiter and demonstrate his own ultimate authority. Edward was willing to seize the opportunity, despite Bek's distinguished services, because he was determined that the full resources of the palatinate should be available in support of his Scottish ambitions. Bek, although he had been a loyal royal administrator and a friend of the king, tried to defend palatinate rights. Quarrels between bishop and cathedral convent gave Edward repeated opportunities to interfere. At the time of the king's death in 1307, Bek was in disgrace and the bishopric's revenues were in royal hands, not for the first time in these years.

Such transactions showed that, however extensive quasi-regalian privileges of Durham might be in theory, even a strong bishop could be brought to heel by a determined king. (Fraser 1957; Prestwich 1988, 541–6) There were royal attempts to make the inhabitants of the palatinate contribute to national taxation in 1338, 1344, 1348 and 1371. In 1371 the men of the palatinate ultimately paid £353 16s. 0d. as a 'free-will offering' to the king instead of paying the national tax of that year. (Lomas 1992, 75–84; Ormrod 1990, 128, 204)

Many bishops were conditioned to obedience by earlier service to kings; some continued as royal administrators while holding Durham. Edward III installed two royal clerks as successive bishops of Durham – Richard

Bury (1333–45) and Thomas Hatfield (1345–81). Bury especially had close personal links with the king. In 1341 an amicable agreement was reached whereby felons fleeing into the palatinate to evade justice would be handed back to royal officers for trial. Thomas Hatfield had become Keeper of the King's Privy Seal two years before he came to Durham and continued to take a leading role in royal government thereafter. Silvester de Everdon, bishop of Carlisle 1247–54, was both a long-serving royal official and a conscientious and effective bishop. (Beckingsale 1969, 71; Ormrod 1990, 128–9, 204; Grasse 1970, 30; Summerson 1992, 70–91)

Despite royal powers over the Church, the palatine privileges of Durham conferred on its bishop a position of secular importance beyond that of episcopal brethren elsewhere. This exceptional status necessarily involved a considerable staff. The diocese required a hierarchy of subordinate priests for exercise of spiritual authority. Administration of the bishop's palatine authority in secular matters required another corps of subordinates. Superintendence of episcopal estates involved another network of agents. (Lomas 1996, 104–8)

Even after Elizabeth I seized some episcopal estates for herself and some of her favourites, the bishop's annual rent roll was almost twice that of the cathedral priory. The bishop of Durham was one of the wealthiest clerics in the kingdom, with episcopal manors scattered throughout his diocese and substantial properties elsewhere. Durham Place in the Strand was one of London's finest residences. (Hodson 1979, 86; Loades 1987, 1–2)

For most of the medieval period, the key official on the secular side was the steward. He managed the bishop's extensive estates and presided over manorial courts either in person or by deputy. In addition, he was effective head of the bishop's civil government throughout the palatinate. The bishopric developed a complex administration which resembled a miniature copy of royal government, with its own chancellor, who headed the chancery or writing office which issued judicial and administrative writs. Some bishops applied recent experience in royal government to improve episcopal administration. Before becoming bishop of Durham in 1406, Thomas Langley had served as the king's Secretary, Keeper of the Great Seal, and Chancellor. (Lapsley 1900; Fraser 1957, chs. V, VI; Storey 1961)

Administration of the See of Durham required many officers and provided opportunities for promotion for the ambitious, the able or the fortunate. Senior secular positions were conferred on members of influential gentry families, consolidating their own influence and binding an important group to the bishop. Many leading officials either came to Durham with experience in the king's government or went into royal service after a Durham administrative apprenticeship. Master William de St Botolph became steward under Bishop Antony Bek in 1286, though until 1291 he continued to act as a royal clerk. Before his death in 1309 he accumulated the archdeaconry of Durham (before 1297), canonries at Chester-le-Street (1288) and St Andrew's,

101

Auckland (1298), rectories at West Horsley (Winchester diocese, 1279), Houghton-le-Spring (1286) and North Collingham (York diocese, 1291). Such accumulations were common among senior officials. (Fraser Officers 1957, 22–4; Fraser 1957, ch. VI; Dobson 1973) The bishop of Carlisle was less prominent than his brother of Durham. His estate and income were smaller and his train of dependants fewer, and he was much less of a secular magnate than his palatine brother in the North East.

Durham Priory

The Benedictine convent of Durham cathedral was one of the foremost monastic houses of the kingdom, with the fame of St Cuthbert buttressed by a considerable estate. Around 1300 the community numbered not far short of 100 monks, with about one-third employed outside the priory at any one time. During its latter stages, the community included about 70 monks, the majority based in the cathedral establishment, while less than 30 staffed nine dependent houses (reduced to eight after the final loss of Coldingham in Berwickshire to the see of St Andrews in the 1470s). At the Dissolution, the community still included 66 monks, more than the largest Cistercian houses, which rarely held more than 40 monks. (Dobson 1992)

Around the cathedral community there clustered a numerous ancillary staff, part clerical and part lay, including the 'household chaplains, notaries, unattached and would-be chantry priests, scribes, school- and choir-masters as well as other clerks and *litterati* who formed the clerical underworld of the late medieval cathedral'. (Dobson 1983, 27)

Durham Cathedral employed at least 100 laymen in various capacities, organized in a hierarchy of duties and status. Again Carlisle's resources were much smaller. Probably the best-paid members of the Durham convent each enjoyed an income equal to that of all the Carlisle canons. The total income of the Durham priory in the fifteenth century was about £2,000 p.a., that of the Carlisle canons only about £400. It is not surprising that Durham attracted and kept a better trained and educated body of clergy, officials and assistants. Even this wealthy and powerful house suffered severe losses during the centuries of border warfare. In 1420 its bursar computed that the priory's income in 1292 had been higher by well over £1,000. This reduction was accounted for by loss of revenue from north of the border, destruction caused by warfare, an associated reduction in area cultivated, and the repeated ravages of plague. (Tuck 1985, 33; Pollard 1989, 88–105; Dobson 1973) Despite this, the cathedral priory of Durham remained one of the richest and most powerful religious houses.

Figure 5.1 Ruins of Finchale, the Augustinian priory near Durham founded *c.*1180, which subsequently became a dependent cell of the Durham cathedral priory.

The Durham monastic community was important in the region's economic life. Its estates continued to grow from gifts, legacies and purchases. If much management remained in the hands of monks, they supervised an extensive work force, including building contractors, tradesmen, bailiffs, rent-collectors and many others. Like other great landlords, the prior of Durham, as head of the cathedral community, developed a standing council to advise him, with both monks and laymen involved.

The complexity of estate business had led to management shifting from the convent collectively to a group of senior monks, individually responsible for particular functions. These 'obedientiaries' included the bursar, the terrar, the steward, the sacrist, and the almoner. Specific items of revenue, or individual estates, were earmarked to provide them with an income. Gilly-corn, a tax paid by the priory's older estates, was appropriated to the almoner; the place-name Sacriston represents an ancient manor the revenue of which went to the cathedral's sacrist. Bursar and terrar in particular became estate managers, carrying out some of the duties entrusted in the bishop's administration to his steward; the role of the priory's steward in estate management, though not negligible, was less central. By the fifteenth century, nevertheless, the prior's steward was often drawn from important families within the region, or perhaps from Newcastle's leading merchant dynasties. The bursar, terrar and steward often presided in person over the prior's principal manorial court, the Halmote. If they were not available, another member of the prior's council might perform this duty. Holders of these posts needed to be well informed not only on the nature of the estates, their incomes and their obligations, but also on matters of practical farming. Bursars and terrars must be carefully chosen, usually from among the best trained and educated monks who had accumulated administrative experience; they had usually enjoyed a university education. The bursar was the principal financial officer of the priory and needed accounting skills. Bursars and terrars kept a watchful eye on the farms of the estate, intervening in detailed management of sheep flocks, sale of wool, and schemes for manuring or marling land to improve fertility.

Until the fifteenth century, part of the priory estate was kept in the monks' own hands as demesne. In the course of that century this practice was abandoned in favour of leasing out manors, reflecting a more general trend of the time (pp. 118–19 below). One exception was an estate at Muggleswick, which was kept on as a centre of stock keeping, and stock breeding, for all the priory's lands. The abandonment of demesne farming did not involve any significant reduction in the importance of the monks who held key posts in the priory's administration. If anything their central role in estate management grew in the later medieval period.

Lay officers of the priory might be involved in discussions of important decisions, but their subordinate role was never forgotten. By the fifteenth century, the prior's council regularly included lay experts in land law. Other experts became paid ambassadors from the priory to the courts of kings or popes or served in negotiations with bishop or metropolitan. The prior of Durham was himself a great figure, a senior baron of the palatinate of Durham and representative of one of the region's richest landed interests. He was frequently involved in such high matters as Anglo-Scottish diplomacy or aristocratic marriages and funerals. Kings and queens were guests at the prior's table.

The wealth of the priory, and its extensive patronage, led to priors being pressured by great men, including kings and aristocratic magnates, for favours or preferment for relatives or dependants. Priors soon became accustomed to the company and practices of the great, and developed skills in playing off one unwelcome suitor against another. Counsel or aid of Durham priors was often sought by lesser men involved in some difficulty or dispute. (Halcrow 1955, 70–7; Donaldson 1960, 169–74)

Although the bishop of Durham was titular abbot of his cathedral community, priors and monks tenaciously defended their privileges and sought to obstruct episcopal or metropolitan interference in their affairs. Priory techniques for fending off unwelcome intervention from outsiders such as the archbishop of York included anguished appeals to the pope, the king, the archbishop of Canterbury, cardinals and bishops, assaults on messengers, maiming their horses, and bribery in lawsuits. On one occasion, the archbishop of York was physically attacked by partisans of the monks, and threatened with murder, while attempting to vindicate metropolitan rights. Disputes of this kind could be spectacularly noisy, but the normal course of ecclesiastical relationships was calmer and more cordial. (Dobson 1973; Brentano 1959, 134; Fraser and Emsley 1969, 53; Fraser 1957, chs. VII–VIII: Halcrow 1957, 7–20)

The community's economic significance extended beyond administration of its estates, for the priory, with its many dependants, also had many needs. It may have been the biggest customer for clothing in the North. In the fifteenth century, its agents were active in buying woollen cloth and furs at Leeds. Paper, wine and spices were bought from Newcastle or York. The Augustinians of Carlisle also sent to York for some of their purchases, though always on a less princely scale than Durham Priory. (Dobson 1983, 30, 35)

Carlisle was much the weaker northern cathedral. Perhaps first aiming at a membership of about 26 canons, the community was hit by outbreaks of plague in the fourteenth century. In 1366 there were only 13 canons, 12 in 1379. There was a partial recovery thereafter, to 17 in 1396, 20 in 1438 and 23 at the Dissolution in 1540. While Durham was the most important monastic community of the diocese, it is unlikely that Carlisle's cathedral community was as large or as well endowed as the Cistercian monastery of Holm Cultram 15 miles west of the city. Apart from its estates, that community developed an early industrial resource in the salt industry. At the Dissolution, Holm Cultram owned 21 salt pans. Other Cumberland houses also developed their revenues in this way; the monks of St Bees possessed their own salt works at Salton. (Walsh 1991, 37–40)

Although there were serious weaknesses in ecclesiastical organization over much of the North, and the Church suffered heavily in the renewal of border warfare, the cathedrals of Durham and Carlisle remained important centres. It was common for prosperous citizens to leave legacies to them. Some successful careers began in schools attached to cathedral communities. Both at Durham and Carlisle a high proportion of monks or canons were drawn from local families. Many maintained links with influential families within the region. The last novice admitted to the Augustinian community of Carlisle bore an obviously local name, Thomas Borodale. However weak the Church may have been in much of the northern countryside, at Carlisle the cult of the Virgin Mary and at Durham the cult of St Cuthbert continued to evoke fervent devotion both within the two dioceses and further afield. There was a marked contrast between cathedral communities and the situation elsewhere in much of the two northern dioceses, especially in those areas most exposed to the repeated tensions and destruction of the border areas. (Dobson 1983, 17–40)

The Church and popular belief

Within more troubled areas, services and the condition of the Church were much more shaky. Abuses continued in ways which had largely disappeared elsewhere. In Northumberland, a charter of 1350 mentioned without surprise or disapprobation a priest's marriage, long after such unions had been prohibited by canon law. (Halcrow 1956, 60) In more sophisticated areas, there were small-scale stirrings of dissatisfaction with orthodox teachings. In the early fifteenth century, there was some Lollard activity. Newcastle possessed a small but intensely interested unorthodox religious community which included members who were both literate and prosperous. (Snape 1961, 355–60)

There is evidence of falling support for monasteries in the later medieval period. Hexham Priory had recovered from the disastrous effects of fourteenth-century border warfare by the 1470s, and the nave of the priory church was rebuilt soon afterwards, but this was followed by decline in later years. (Cambridge 1979, 161–2) In much of the countryside the situation was worse. In the sixteenth century, the average value of livings in Northumberland was only £12 per annum, though in more secure Durham the figure was twice that.

It is difficult to know with any accuracy the extent of the Church's hold on the hearts of the people of the North. (Lomas 1992, 92–105) In a world beset by both perilous natural forces (disease, famine, fire and weather) and uncertainties of war and conflict, late medieval Catholicism offered to the believer a framework of explanation and reassurance. Whatever the secular role of the Church as an institution, its power ultimately derived from its claim that it alone mediated between God and the individual Christian. For most believers, participation in sacraments brought merits which offset the sinfulness which Christian doctrine declared to be the common lot of all. Such merit could counterbalance the sufferings to be expected after death. Similar remission might also be acquired through pious activities of various kinds.

These concepts were effective at many different levels. Richard III, whose northern hegemony included close association with Carlisle, gave two tuns of Gascon wine to the prior and canons of that cathedral community, 'that they might pray for the good estate of the king and his consort Anne, queen of England, for their souls after death and the souls of the king's progenitors'. Matthew de Redmane, a Carlisle burgess who died in the late fourteenth century, left in his will 40 shillings for 'someone going by way of St James', i.e. on a pilgrimage to the Spanish shrine of St James of Compostela. There was presumably no doubt that this commission would procure the deceased investor a share in the pilgrimage's merit. In 1363, the endowment of prayers for past bishops of Carlisle could earn remittance of ten years from the donor's term in purgatory, while a similar grant of 40 days' indulgence was available in 1421 to those who contributed to building the cathedral, a collective expression of meritorious work to the glory of God. (Bouch 1948, 91, 113, 130; Summerson 1993, I, 361) By the late medieval period the pervasiveness of such transactions, and their frequent dissociation from genuine individual piety, were inculcating suspicions that the Church was merely supervising and exploiting a spuriously spiritual commerce, although there is little evidence of widespread dissatisfaction in the North.

There are few indications from northern counties of genuine popular piety in the late medieval period, though superstition of one sort or another was common enough. There is no reason to doubt widespread dislike of the Church in its role of landlord and collector of tithes. Equally, there was still a pervasive belief in the Church as a source of special intercession to offset the dangers both of this world and of the hereafter. In 1365 Bishop Appleby of Carlisle ordered special prayers and processions in response to terrible storms which had lately visited his diocese. The citizens of Carlisle believed that they had been saved from besieging Scots in 1385 by the miraculous intervention of the Virgin Mary herself. (Bouch 1948, 92; Summerson 1992; Summerson 1993, I, 359) Although such 'magical' concepts in one form or another were widespread, there is little to suggest that most teachings of the Church achieved more than a superficial penetration, sometimes combined with earlier pagan elements. The imposition of Protestant teachings during the sixteenth century proceeded with little popular resistance.

Dissolution of Northern Monasteries

In the early sixteenth century, Northumberland held ten monasteries, three nunneries and seven houses of friars. Most of these were small, some very small. Alnwick, Hexham and Newminster were among the largest in the county, but each held only 15–20 full members. Although there is little to suggest that northern houses were generally centres of learning, there was a connection between monasteries and the parochial system. Many livings had been placed by patrons at the disposal of monasteries. Within Carlisle diocese, this applied to nearly half of the parishes, and parochial appointments made were often of poor quality. (Lomas 1996, 116–21; Summerson 1993, II, 619) In some cases monks or friars served in these parishes, and here Dissolution sometimes involved a gap in the provision of clergy. Even the scrappy surviving evidence provides instances of parishes, previously served in this way, without priests in the later sixteenth century. In other parishes, a vicar or curate was installed, perhaps with most of the stipend going to the appointing house, and here too Dissolution might bring interruptions in the supply of priests.

As landlords, religious houses were involved in local society, including frequent participation in disputes and rivalries, where their role might differ little from that of secular landowners. (Summerson 1993, II, 619) Some houses were caught up in other secular affairs. Abbots and priors were employed as ambassadors or entertained kings, queens and great nobles. Percy earls of Northumberland sometimes set up headquarters as wardens of the marches in Alnwick Abbey or nearby Hulne Friary. The involvement of northern houses in secular affairs, and their prominent role as landlords, contributed to their failure to maintain healthy reputations for spirituality, learning or philanthropy. (Bouch 1948, 170; Lomas 1996, 121–35)

Confiscation of monastic property played a part in establishing more effective royal authority within the region, but those who profited most from the Dissolution of the Monasteries in the North included a group of important local laymen. Some of them, like Sir Thomas Hilton, who was granted the priory of Tynemouth, had already been active in the affairs of the house concerned. Sir Reynold Carnaby, principal beneficiary of the suppression of Hexham, was a royal official, a supporter of the earl of Northumberland, and had served as the archbishop of York's steward for the liberty of Hexhamshire. The earl of Northumberland obtained grants of Newminster and Blanchland for his henchman Williame Grene, who had also earned such favours as a royal tax-gatherer and court official. In the North West, the lion's share went to gentry families connected to the king, including men with long records in royal service. They included Sir Thomas Curwen (from estates of Furness Abbey), Sir John Lamplugh (St Bees), Sir Thomas Wharton (Shap), Thomas Dacre (Lanercost), Christopher Crackenthorpe (Byland) and Thomas Sandford (Shap). Dissolution of the monasteries, and confiscations following the 1536 Pilgrimage of Grace and the 1569 Rising of the Northern Earls, provided unequalled opportunities which were eagerly seized by those able to do so.

Apart from some short-lived resistance at Hexham, dissolution was peacefully carried out, with pensions and alternative clerical positions going to inmates. The last prioresses of Neasham and Newcastle became farmers. The last abbot of Alnwick, William Harrison, received a pension of £50, became vicar of Chatton, and founded a family of some importance in county affairs. The sub-prior of Hexham became vicar of Alnham and similar appointments were made at Eglingham, Long Horsley and Felton. At least eleven of the fifty friars in Newcastle houses at dissolution appear later as parish or chantry priests. In other cases parishes which had been served by monastic appointments were left to less qualified incumbents, including numerous Scottish curates (32 are mentioned in the area of the English East March in the 1560s and 1570s) who could be employed for a pittance and seem generally to have provided a standard of service appropriate to their income. Sir John Forster, a leading Northumberland figure who profited at the expense of the earl of Northumberland's estate, was a principal recipient of monastic property, notorious for neglecting to continue the supply of priests. The way in which dissolution was implemented, and the need to reward royal officials and influential local figures from the booty involved, ensured that the occasion did little or nothing to remedy the weaknesses of the Church in the North. One modern study has concluded that

> To take over the fabric of the Church in the Northern province was comparatively easy but the inheritance which they acquired did little to provide the reformers with the machinery of reformation. The large and poor parishes, the scant provision for education and the creaking ecclesiastical administration of the pre-Reformation northern province were only slowly improved. What had hindered reform and efficiency in the medieval church continued to hinder its protestant successor. Despite the reformation many parishioners in the North still remained in Elizabeth's reign 'mere ignorant of religion and altogether untaught'. (Beckingsale 1969, 74–9)

It was not just parishioners. The bishop of Carlisle described his parish clergy in 1561 as 'wicked imps of Antichrist and for the most part very ignorant and stubborn'. In Northumberland in the 1580s 'there are not passing three or four preachers in the whole shire, and so the people for want of teachers have been brought up in ignorance'. There were frequent reports of seriously dilapidated churches because of ravaging or neglect. The consensus of modern scholarship is that although there was a great deal of superstition, both Catholic and Protestant religions were weak in border counties, largely because of lack of an adequate body of able priests. (Keeling 1979, 26, 31, 42; Hilton 1980, 41)

In 1565 Bishop Pilkington of Durham complained that 'the parishes be great, the people many, the wage small, priests bad and very few to be had and fewer to be hoped for'. (Marcombe 1987, 131; Stevens Benham 1987, 6–32) Well-educated priests, or those with other useful talents or connections, were not likely to stay in poorly endowed rural parishes. In 1596, a clergyman offered the Northumberland living of Simonburn refused, 'deeming his body unable to live in so troublesome a place and his nature not well brooking the perverse nature of so crooked a people'. (Freeman 1987, 164) Lowly parish priests, especially in areas of insecurity, were likely to be local men of no great learning, talent or ambition. In addition to parish clergy, there were hundreds of priests without livings, some of them employed for many years as chantry priests or in similar callings. The general level was not high.

The Northern Reformation

The installation of the Protestant regime in the North was no more difficult than elsewhere. Counties such as Norfolk and Suffolk produced more Catholic resistance than the four northern shires. In the North, most priests were closely linked to local secular society, and

> virtually indistinguishable socially and culturally from their neighbouring husbandmen and small yeomen . . . a number of parochial clergy kept alehouses to supplement their incomes . . . The majority of Elizabethan country clergy were farmers six days in the week. (Tyler 1969, 91)

In the years 1559–64 the diocese of Carlisle saw only five deprivations of clergy, with nineteen in the Durham see. At Carlisle Cathedral, the first four prebendaries had previously been Augustinian canons there and involved in 'shady financial dealings'. Their first Protestant bishop thought 'three of them are unlearned and the fourth unzealous'. They were happy to accommodate themselves to the new dispensation, outwardly at least. In Northumberland, there was little overt resistance to the Elizabethan Church settlement. (Hilton 1977, 44; Keeling 1979, 35) There was scant local support for northern monasteries, nor does there seem to have been anything about them to inspire such devotion. Their destruction seems to have had slight effect, except for the dearth of parochial clergy in some places.

The older view that the 1536 Pilgrimage of Grace was primarily sparked off by dissolution of the northern monasteries has not been accepted in recent studies, although the rhetoric of the rebels included religious elements and there was certainly some resentment at interference by outside reformers in religious practices of the northern counties. This was not a simple or straightforward defence of Catholic orthodoxy, for northern religious observances often included strong infusions of superstition and regionally based practices. (Keeling 1979, 25; Harrison 1975, 125–6, 274) Those closest to northern monasteries were not often among their most conspicuous defenders. On estates of the Priory of Tynemouth, monastic tenants used the crisis of 1536 to forward grievances against their monastic landlord. Although in 1573 a group of tenants who had held land from Holm Cultram Abbey expressed a sense of loss at the house's dissolution, they were regretting a number of secular perquisites, rather than spiritual deprivation. (Hallam 1988, 839) At Newminster Abbey, the royal commissioners of 1537 were supported by a vociferous mob from the neighbouring town of Morpeth. (Harbottle and Salway 1964, 88) The involvement of the Percy family in the Pilgrimage of Grace and the 1569 Rising was largely political rather than spiritual in origin; the participation of border reivers from Redesdale and Tynedale in 1539 was a cynical exploitation of the opportunity for looting. The duke of Norfolk who suppressed the Pilgrimage was a notorious Catholic sympathizer.

This helps to explain why the religious revolutions of the sixteenth century could be readily absorbed. John Best, the bishop of Carlisle entrusted with the task of reformation there in 1561, found little open resistance. With the exception of priests protected by Lord Dacre, who remained 'very ignorant and stubborn', and similar problems with the earl of Cumberland, Best found little deep attachment to the old religion. No doubt both peers saw Best as agent of a rival royal power undermining aristocratic pre-eminence, as well as any kind of spiritual threat. The failure of the Rising of the Northern Earls removed the most influential lay supporters of the old religion. In 1571 Richard Barnes, Best's successor, could assure the government that there was no gentleman within the diocese who was openly hostile to the new dispensation. Very few clergy found the Thirty-Nine Articles too much to swallow and lost benefices in consequence. By 1597 it was claimed that only four parishes in Cumberland and eight in Westmorland contained recusants. (Bouch 1948, 208, 213)

The altered style of religion, with Protestant emphasis on a teaching ministry, which required clergymen to instruct congregations in doctrines of the Elizabethan state Church, exposed weaknesses which were long-standing but previously less significant. In both the diocese of Carlisle and the sprawling archdeaconry of Richmond, incorporated into the see of Chester from 1541, which covered southern Cumbria, there was little effective super-vision of often remote and badly endowed parishes during the late middle ages. In 1570 Edmund Grindal complained of his fellow-Cumbrians that

> They keep holy days and feasts abrogated; they offer money, eggs, etc., at the burial of their dead: they pray on beads, etc., so that this seemeth to be, as it were, another Church rather than a member of the rest. (Beckingsale 1969, 74)

Bishop Best struggled against a shortage of adequate clergy. Most new ordinands were local men educated only up to the level of village schools of no great worth. Too many existing priests were like the Carlisle cathedral chapter, 'ignorante preistes or olde unlearned monkes' who, far from being an asset, were an impediment to reform. Clergy of 'knowledge and good conscience' were in short supply. (Bouch 1948, 200–13, 244) At the end of the sixteenth century, Bishop Robinson of Carlisle explained to Cecil that his problems were not with the gentlemen of his diocese, who were gener-ally sound in religion, nor with recusants, who were few, but in reaching the mass of the people. He wrote of

> the poorer sort generally willing to hear, but pitifully ignorant of the foundations of Christianity . . . many of them are without all fear of God, adulterers, thieves and murderers. The chief spring of all this woefulness comes principally of the weakness and carelessness of the ministry. (Bouch 1948, 244)

The sixteenth century saw able Cumbrian priests seeking their fortunes elsewhere. They included Edmund Grindal (bishop of London 1559–70, archbishop of York 1570–5, archbishop of Canterbury 1575–83), Edwin Sandys (bishop of Worcester 1559–76, archbishop of York 1576–88), and Bernard Gilpin, 'The Apostle of the North', who carved out for himself a profitable career within the diocese of Durham. Grindal thought that the part of Cumberland where he was born was 'the ignorantest part in religion, and most oppressed of covetous landlords of any one part of this realm'. (*Dictionary of National Biography*; Marcombe 1980, 20–39)

Chapter 6

Northern Society and Economy

It is not possible to give accurate regional population figures for these years; where sources survive, they rarely offer much basis for reliable calculations of population. One bold estimate concludes that it is unlikely that the total for the four northern counties could have been much above 200,000 by 1600. (Fraser 1968, xvi–xvii; Tough 1928, 26–7; Kirby 1972, 85, 95; Hodgson 1978)

The Northern Aristocracy

One characteristic which the northern counties shared with the remainder of England, and indeed with all contemporary European societies, was the continued importance of its aristocracy, even if these years saw progressive erosion of the independent authority of leading magnates. Even as kings consolidated realms into nation states, they continued to rely upon the nobility for many key positions, not least in maintaining control in different regions. Promotion to aristocratic status, or to higher aristocratic rank, remained the ambition of the thrusting and successful. Those, like Lord Wharton, who attained noble status from lesser origins through royal service, were quick to adopt aristocratic notions of state and splendour. (Curwen 1913, 429) Even when their power had passed its peak, nobles emphasized their rank and dignity. In May 1568, when the royal officer Richard Lowther refused the earl of Northumberland's demand that he should be allowed to entertain the fugitive Queen of Scots, he was left in no doubt as to inferior status, although he complained of injury to his own dignity:

> the earl used some rough wordes towards me, adding too that I was too mean a man to have such a charge . . . and afterwards sent for me

to his lodgging and . . . gave me great threatening with many evil words and a like language, calling me a varlet. (Bouch 1948, 20)

For a variety of reasons, not least policies of the Crown, baronial power was weakened before 1603 (pp. 86–91 above). Aristocratic power depended on service from substantial tenantry in return for landholding. By the sixteenth century, the financial needs of even the greatest magnates brought attempts to squeeze more revenue from estates, which often undermined older loyalties. (McDonnell 1994, 28; see also p. 87 above) In the North East especially, there were attempts to replace restrictive hereditary tenures with leaseholds, allowing landlords greater control and opportunities to raise rents. By the end of the fifteenth century, for example, Durham Priory had greatly extended leasehold on its estates, at the expense of customary tenures. (Lomas 1977, 40–3) Even in Cumbria, price rises of the sixteenth century stiffened attitudes of secular and ecclesiastical landlords in their determination to raise more revenue, even if here there was less pressure for wholesale reform of tenancies.

At first custom ensured that leaseholders enjoyed security of tenure, but price rises in the sixteenth century hardened landlord attitudes, resulting in a growing number of local disputes. A confrontation between the Durham cathedral chapter and its tenants came to a head in 1577. Earls of Northumberland increased leasing on Cumberland and Northumberland estates, impairing their political and military standing within the region, as the murder of the fourth earl in April 1489 suggested. This was again demonstrated in the limited support received during the 1537 and 1569 risings (pp. 81–96 above).

No one living in the border areas could suppose that in these years aristocratic magnates succeeded in maintaining law and order. One modern opinion is that 'During the 1520s, Northumberland was in a state of anarchy. Not only were there Scottish inroads but also virtual insurrection by the turbulent inhabitants of Tynedale, Redesdale, Gilsland and Bewcastle wastes.' (Fraser and Emsley 1971, 143) In these circumstances Camden observed that 'There is not a man amongst them of the better sort that hath not his little tower or pile'. (Tough 1928, 38; Curwen 1913) In the latter part of Elizabeth's reign, as the regime's financial problems intensified, this 'self-help' may have experienced tacit official approval.

Tenurial change was not the only source of reductions in noble power. Income and ability to reward adherents declined with ravaging, famine and plague, as these reduced estate revenue. In 1593, a survey of the earl of Northumberland's estates provided a mass of evidence on the extent to which his revenues suffered from constant cross-border raiding. The exasperation of northern landowners at their losses was eventually to make an important contribution to the pacification of the borders under James I (see pp. 142–4 below). (Pollard 1989, 93–105)

As late as the Wars of the Roses, patronage wielded by great families provided an obvious route to wealth and power for northern gentry. Magnates possessed their own councils, and powerful figures like the earl of Northumberland had many offices in his gift; the position of constable of Alnwick Castle was merely one of a group of well-paid posts usually conferred on client gentry such as the Collingwoods, Fenwicks, Delavals or Muschamps. (Batho 1957, 56, 62) Percy earls also had considerable influence in Cumberland; during the latter stages of the Wars of the Roses, supporters there included such leading gentry figures as Christopher Curwen of Workington and John Pennington of Muncaster. In the previous generation, Richard Neville built up a following of lesser landowners who included Sir Robert Ogle of Bothal, Sir Thomas Lumley of Lumley and Sir John Middleton of Belsay. Such groupings were consolidated by kinship and marriage as well as common dependence upon a patron, and led to lucrative opportunities; during Neville ascendancy, Middleton served as ambassador to Scotland in 1459 and sheriff of Northumberland in 1460–1. (Hicks 1978, 81; Pollard 1976 for 1975, 57–64)

As royal power in the region grew in the sixteenth century, aristocratic patronage declined along with their quasi-independent role. The Crown's power also increased as medieval privileges and independent jurisdictions declined (pp. 88–91 above). The Franchises Act of 1535 provided that criminal justice within the palatinate of Durham be administered in the king's name, although for many years there was little change in procedures apart from that, and the bishop retained the right to appoint magistrates for the palatinate. (Loades 1987, 3) With the creation of the office of Lord Lieutenant in the sixteenth century, its holder, usually an aristocrat, exercised similar rights of nomination of magistrates as in other counties. (Fraser and Emsley 1974, 190) Some of the prince-bishop's powers survived, including his courts, but the overall trend was towards greater uniformity under central control. A document of the reign of Edward VI suggests why the bishop's courts survived sixteenth-century changes. (Kitching 1987, 49–70; Loades 1987, 3; Fraser and Emsley 1974, 190)

> The bishop's courts were very commodious, easy and profitable to the inhabiters and dwellers within the jurisdiction, limits and bounds, of the said County Palatine, forasmuch as their causes, matters and titles were ordered, judged and discussed by such ordinary judges, officers and ministers as were appointed within the said County palatine, being nigh to their habitations and dwelling places for the hearing and determination of the same. (Hitching 1987, 52)

During the sixteenth century, the Crown adopted a variety of expedients as substitutes for baronial authority in the border counties, none of which proved successful. Henry VIII told the duke of Norfolk that 'We will not be bound, of a necessity, to be served there with Lords, but will be served with such men, what degree soever they may be of, as we shall appoint to the same'. (Bush 1971, 40) Brave words, but this confidence was misplaced, for in practice for key positions the status and influence of the incumbent was crucial. Neither using lesser landowners from the region, or great men from elsewhere, proved satisfactory, and such expedients could only be made to work with moderate effectiveness by providing paid soldiers on a scale which strained royal finances. In 1542, the earl of Hertford, warden general on the border, wryly reflected that 'he that shall serve here had need to be both kin and allied among them of these parts and such that hath and doth bear rule in the country'. (Keeling 1987, 33) Long centuries of border instability showed that only when the Crown could reckon on loyal support from the region's leading noblemen was it possible to control the northern counties. (Bush 1971, 45–63; Spence 1977, 66, 73–85, 94)

This situation was not present during much of the sixteenth century, so the Crown sought to enlist the services of the gentry, themselves increasingly aware that royal office might offer surer reward than service to aristocratic patrons. From the late fifteenth century, more northern gentry came to possess the literacy necessary to serve in a ministerial capacity; increasing numbers of them attended local grammar schools when young. (James 1994; Hoeppner Moran 1981, 14, 23; Bush 1971, 49, 58–9)

Development of royal authority provided additional opportunities for energetic gentry. After breakdown of the long thirteenth-century period of relative tranquillity on the border, initially wardenship powers were entrusted to commissions of local gentry. Even when wardenships were held by magnates, they required subordinates of gentry status. Leading gentry played a prominent role in the numerous commissions appointed to cope with cross-border disputes. The development of the office of Justice of the Peace added to their importance. During the religious revolutions of the sixteenth century, the effectiveness of central government was dependent upon gentry attitudes. Even after persecution of Catholic recusants hardened in 1581–86, it was difficult for the authorities to act where local gentry protected the old religion. When George Craster of Craster died in 1546 at the age of 31, after his burial in Embleton Church a priest sang for a year masses for the repose of his soul. (Craster 1952, 131; Hilton 1977, 46, 58; Keeling 1979, 39)

Some gentry served in Parliament as MPs representing either counties or boroughs. An early example is Edmund de Widdrington, MP for Newcastle in 1344. Later examples include several fifteenth-century MPs for Appleby and Carlisle. (Hedley 1957, 3; Jalland 1976 for 1975, 43, 47; Lomas 1996, 136–8) Local affairs were often the principal interest of northern gentry, and there was less enthusiasm for performance of public duties which might be troublesome without offering adequate remuneration. Durham men did not always hanker after parliamentary representation for the palatine county, some of them believing it to be 'a privilege, not to be bound to the attendance of the parliament'. Where individual or family interests were involved, greater enthusiasm could be looked for. The loyalty of the Bowes family during the 1569 rising was rewarded by valuable estates forfeited by the rebel earl of Westmorland. (Foster 1987, 183, 199–200)

The Northern Economy

Economic experiences of the region in the late medieval and Tudor periods were neither uniform nor simple. (Lomas 1992, chs. 9–11) There were striking instances of progress, but cumulatively war, uncertainty, bad harvests and epidemics among men and beasts provided an effective brake.

The problems of the North were not solely due to border warfare, for other sources of suffering beset the relatively primitive socio-economic organization. The years 1315–17 brought disastrous famines through crop failure and the 1320s a series of epidemics among livestock. Cattle plagues may have been more destructive than Scots raids. A contemporary reported in 1319, for instance, that plague had recently killed off the draught animals and dairy cattle on the estates of the monastery at Hexham. (Kershaw 1973; Tuck 1985, 39)

The Black Death reached Durham in 1349 and repeated, even endemic, attacks of plague provided another scourge. In the reign of Edward III, two of three Northumberland knights appointed to collect the feudal aid for the knighting of the Black Prince became plague victims. The Northumberland village of Newton lost almost its whole population in an attack of plague in 1379. (Craster 1952, 126–7) In 1351 the sheriff of Cumberland accounted for a shortfall in revenue from Crown lands near Carlisle by noting 'divers lands which after the plague remain untilled from lack of workers, and from divers tenements, mills, fisheries, pastures and meadows which he could not farm . . . for lack of tenants . . . who died of plague'. Perhaps a third of Carlisle's population died during the first great visitation of the Black Death. The Crown recognized in 1352 that the district was 'now wasted and more than usually depressed, as well by mortal pestilence lately prevalent in those parts, as by frequent attacks'. (Summerson 1993, I, 280)

There were few secure refuges. The inaccessibility of the mountainous core of Cumbria offered some protection against both raiding and plague, but even here there were sheep diseases from about 1270 onwards until at least the middle of the fourteenth century. In 1340 much land in the parish of Brigham on the north-west fringes of the Lake District lay uncultivated because of poverty. The market town of Cockermouth had grown rapidly during the first half of the thirteenth century, but by 1280 its fulling mill was already in financial difficulty with falling income; by 1316–18 the mill was derelict, the market in decay and rents from burgage tenements in a decline lasting for the rest of the century. (Winchester 1986)

In upland areas, farmers found it hard to grow food for their families, and depended on sales of upland products such as hides, wool, and tallow for their livelihood. This trade was always difficult and could be cut off by war or raiding in lowland market areas. Where hill farmers relied on a cash economy, war and epidemics of man or beast could easily overturn a precarious livelihood. (Appleby 1978, 39)

There was probably long-term climatic change which made things difficult in marginal farming areas, often settled in the more favourable period of the thirteenth century. Fourteenth- and early fifteenth-century accounts contain many laments about atrocious weather. In the year after Bannockburn, torrential rain caused extensive destruction to the harvest and may have been a factor in forcing the Scots to abandon a siege of Carlisle. (Summerson 1993, I, 22) Epidemics recurred during the following troubled centuries. Plague and famine arrived together in 1438–40, and the bishop of Durham's income dropped severely by 1439. The impact varied, with some places escaping lightly while others suffered. The North East was hard hit in 1438–40. The rival houses of Percy and Neville both incurred heavy losses, which may explain their ambitions during the Wars of the Roses. As late as 1588–90, there were 1,727 plague deaths in Newcastle; in 1597–98 Penrith suffered 608. Plague killed as many as 1,226 in Kendal within three or four months in 1598, amounting to perhaps half the population. (Arvanigian 1996; Tough 1928, 56–7; Pollard 1989; Phillips 1994)

Areas most exposed to raiding suffered worst, including northern parts of Northumberland and Cumberland, which in earlier periods had mirrored the fortunes of much of upland northern England. As we have seen (pp. 42–6 above), the thirteenth century saw population growth and a spread of farming settlements into more hilly areas. Before the end of the thirteenth century this expansion was reaching its limits, even without the intervention of war. Some manors in Cumberland and Westmorland contained unoccupied holdings as early as the 1270s and 1280s.

Growing prosperity was abruptly ended by renewal of warfare, with marginal farming areas bearing the brunt of the setbacks. The cattle-breeding and moorland pasture manor of Tarset in Northumberland had expanded in the period of peace, with outlying settlements multiplying in valleys of the upland streams, reaching a value of £237 a year before the end of the thirteenth century. In 1315, laid waste by repeated Scottish raiding, it was worth less than £4. On the Northumberland coastal plain, Felton was valued at £22 'in time of peace', but around £2 in 1322. In 1324 the village was virtually uninhabited. Even by 1374 this manor was worth less than half its late thirteenth-century value. Some areas of Cumberland attacked by the Scots in the 1290s remained waste until the second half of the following century. (Miller 1976 for 1975, 15; Hallam 1988, 257, 259)

If there was some special pleading to avoid taxes or dues, there is supporting archaeological evidence of diminishing values from excavations at Belling Law and West Whelpington. At the outlying community of Belling Law, a settlement established in the mid-thirteenth century was abandoned early in the fourteenth. The village of West Whelpington declined in size and prosperity during the border wars of the early fourteenth century and never recovered its earlier level of modest comfort. A coin hoard buried in 1311–20 and the destruction of several buildings at about the same time attest the uncertainties of those years. (Jobey 1977, 15, 37; Evans 1988, 142–3)

Instability close to the border delayed arrival of what seems to have been otherwise widespread economic recovery in the North in the latter half of the fifteenth century. By the mid-sixteenth century, there was a contrast between the relative poverty of northern Cumbria and the more prosperous southern district with its developing woollen industry, town growth and rising population. There was similar contrast in the North East between the border dales and the experience of Newcastle and other prosperous districts further south. Studies of seventeenth-century taxation records have identified three main groups of communities in Durham. In the east there were a number of prosperous communities serving more than a local area, as ports or market centres. Chester-le-Street was credited with a population of 4,472, Sunderland (including Bishopwearmouth and Monkwearmouth) with 3,762. Remote villages on poorer uplands were much poorer; Edmundbyers and Muggleswick had only 219 and 183 inhabitants. Parishes in the fertile Tees valley enjoyed high population densities and could raise more for local taxation. (Kirby 1972, 85, 95; Hodgson 1978)

In the early stages of resumption of border conflict, landlords sometimes left ravaged holdings vacant, hoping for a return to 'normal' conditions. Long continuance of warfare and raiding, and attacks of plague down to the early fifteenth century, falsified these hopes. In the North East, there followed a lengthy process in which landowners sought to restore prosperity by replacing older tenurial patterns with leasehold farms. At West Whelpington, after initial destruction caused by Scots raids in the years of Wallace and Robert Bruce, the village was rebuilt on a planned basis in the later fourteenth or early fifteenth century. (Butcher 1978, 67–77; Evans 1988, 142–6) At this early date, such initiatives were unusual in the North East and unknown in Cumbria. In many parts of the North, landowners were still more concerned with the capacity of their land to support armed tenantry. Even where this consideration was less pressing, the sparsely populated North West, with its relatively undeveloped economy, offered little incentive for drastic changes. (Gregson 1980, 166–78; Appleby 1975, 590–1)

In areas exposed to raiding, social and economic organization was different from that of more settled districts. Isolated farmsteads or small settlements of huts built of earth and wood, usually thatched, represented the simple accommodation. Such buildings were easily destroyed, but as

119

easily resurrected, perhaps only a few hours after a raid had receded. (Spence 1977, 59–63) In these territories of largely marginal moorland and uplands there is little evidence of the communal farming practices continuing over most of the North. Apart from destruction of crops, seizing of livestock and attacks on settlements, such local installations as mills were less easily replaced than simple huts. Raiding in some cases became a vital element in the local economy, as over-population and bad harvests, such as those in the 1590s, impeded more productive developments. During the sixteenth century, a growing population on the border was trying to wrest a living out of unpropitious terrain in conditions of continual insecurity.

Recovery and Agricultural Practices in the Fifteenth and Sixteenth Centuries

During the second half of the fifteenth century, there were signs of farming extension in many communities, with both population and areas of common fields growing. The expansion might be into previously waste land, or areas covered by forest law. In the reign of Edward I, the royal forest of Inglewood stretched over 150 square miles. An intermittent process of nibbling by peasant farmers, mainly in the sixteenth century, saw the forest's area dwindle to less than 2,500 acres by the early seventeenth century. Further east, the bishop of Durham's forest of Weardale was partly settled by 1438, but the process accelerated after 1479, when the forest was leased to Richard, duke of Gloucester; by the early sixteenth century the area ceased to be subject to forest jurisdiction. (Wilson 1905, 498–9; Drury 1976, 140–1; Jarrett and Edwards 1961, 233) There seems to have been little effort by landlords to resist these incursions, but rather the legitimization of trespasses by grant-ing tenancies at will. This at least brought extra income, and could multiply a lord's dependants and his supply of fighting men in dangerous times. The Percies were among those who saw advantage in such 'good lordship', although their financial needs compelled changed attitudes during the six-teenth century. (Appleby 1975, 580)

On many lay and ecclesiastical estates large-scale demesne commercial farming proved a casualty of the long period of instability. A culmination of interruption of trading patterns, livestock epidemics and shortages of labour affected demesne farming disproportionately and fifteenth-century recovery was most marked in the more resilient and smaller-scale peasant farming. Crown demesne land around Carlisle was let to tenants during the fourteenth century, reflecting a more general trend. Holm Cultram and Furness abbeys abandoned direct working of most of their land. By 1537,

Borrowdale, formerly occupied by a vaccary staffed by lay brethren of Furness Abbey, was let out to 41 tenants. (Millwall and Robinson 1970, 177; Whyte 1985, 114)

Continuance of the largely peasant colonization of upland may have seen final clearance of natural woodlands in the Lake District under pressure of pastoral farming. (Winchester 1987, 44) At the same time established settlements were drawing in land from surrounding waste. By 1578, 25 per cent of the cultivated land of the north Cumbrian village of Aspatria had been acquired by this process, while the village of Scotby, near Carlisle, had 35 per cent of its arable taken from neighbouring Inglewood Forest. (Winchester 1987, 44; Dilley 1972, 203) As in the thirteenth century, growing population placed pressure on limited arable land and also on waste which was exploited largely for summer grazing. Presentations before manorial courts for encroachments reached a peak in the early sixteenth century, and there were more manorial regulations controlling grazing rights in surrounding waste areas.

In Cumbria, by the late sixteenth century, multiplication of agricultural holdings, often of cottagers clinging to a precarious livelihood on small plots, brought its own dangers. Population growth was checked by three devastating famines in 1587–88, 1597 and 1623, producing a smaller rural population by the early years of the seventeenth century, the result of a classic Malthusian crisis with population outrunning subsistence. (Appleby 1978, 1–38)

The traditional practice of communal farming in most of Cumbria saw stock driven out to open waste or upland pastures during the summer, and brought back in winter to the protection of enclosed common fields, or the closes of individual farmers. In summer, crops were grown on enclosed areas of the common field, generally oats or barley, but sometimes peas and beans. In many communities, individuals possessed different strips of land scattered throughout common fields, some on better land, some on more marginal areas. Systematic crop rotation was rare, manure from over-wintering stock provided the principal aid to fertility. A survey of the Percy honour of Cockermouth in 1570 is instructive:

> The countrie consists most in wast ground and is very cold, hard and barren yett it is very populous and breedeth tall men and hard of nature whose habitacions are mostly in vallies and Dales where every man has a small porsion of ground wch albeith the soile be hard of nature, yett by cantinuall travell is made fertile to their great relief and comfort for their greatest gaine consists of breeding cattle wch are noe charge to them in Somer by reason they are pastured and fedd upon the mountaines and waste.

If relatively primitive, this was not subsistence farming. Even small farmers traded animal products – wool, skins, tallow and meat – for cash. Probate inventories also show them borrowing and lending money, whether in high-land or lowland. (Appleby 1978, 49, 54)

Manorial custom regulated farming practices and was often an effect-ive brake on individual initiative. Seasonal movement of animals into com-mon fields in winter limited arable practices and crops to those which could be harvested before the return of stock. Manorial courts resisted attempts to close or fence off parts of the common ground, as when in 1518 the vicar of Aspatria was fined 6s. 8d. for keeping 'a close called West Flatt in severality in the open season'. To countenance encroachments would under-mine traditional practice, which required the whole open field for winter grazing. Stock must be free to range across the previous year's stubble, though they would also be fed hay during winter. (Elliot 1960, 98; Elliot 1959, 101)

There is more evidence of individual enterprise in raising stock, where market opportunities might seem more obvious. Even here traditional prac-tices inhibited innovation. The injunction from the Cumwhinton manor court in 1567 that 'no tennan do hold catall symerday but the same be fodders wynter day' indicates determination to prevent individuals from holding greater numbers of cattle than their share in common grazing grounds would justify. Significantly, this prohibition was issued in a community close to the market of Carlisle, with the opportunities it offered. (Dilley 1972, 108)

A contrasting pattern could be found in the developing system of lease-hold or copyhold farms on settled estates in the North East, away from the troubled border zone. Unlike other parts of the region, the wealthy Priory of Durham 'depended absolutely on the prosperity of arable agriculture . . . the plough was very much king'. (Dobson 1973, 252, 279) Fairs held at north-country centres catered for the needs of arable farming. In 1338–39 the bursar of Durham Priory bought 20 plough oxen at Corbridge fair and 50 more at Darlington and Hexham fairs. During the next two years he bought a further 121 at various northern fairs. (Fraser 1969, 49)

During later medieval centuries there were some remarkable examples of agricultural improvement in the North East, influenced by commercial opportunities. In one case where records survive, an exceptional farm seems to have seen a 24 per cent increase in cereal production in the later fifteenth century, possibly connected with increasing use of manure. (Lomas 1982, 31–53) There were also examples of lack of progress. Westmorland remained one of the least developed areas of England, seeing little change in farming practices until the sixteenth and seventeenth centuries. Other northern coun-ties were always more advanced, but on a patchy rather than uniform basis.

Variations of terrain and vicissitudes of border conditions made any-thing like a uniform pace of development impossible. Surviving records of great ecclesiastical estates are especially full, and it is sometimes possible to trace variation in individual and family fortunes among tenants. Alongside tenacious survival of tenures and services which went back to a long pre-

Conquest past, changes occurred over time in patterns of holding. By the early fourteenth century, manors belonging to the prior of Durham exhibited a variety of tenancies in size and conditions. William Mayr held 260 acres in Hebburn, John de Hedworth 100 acres in Southwick, blocks more extensive than the holdings of most neighbours. The ravages of the Black Death, which reached Durham in 1349, accelerated the process of consolidation of holdings. Hard-hit townships saw land concentrated in the hands of survivors, who were often able to accumulate integrated blocks rather than scattered strips in open fields, responding to opportunities for profit from improved farming techniques. (Halcrow 1956, 58) On estates of both the bishop and the prior of Durham, changes in tenurial terms operated to the benefit of tenants. The fourteenth century, especially after the first horrific visitations of the Black Death, saw old systems of personal service die out, and commutation payments were soon assimilated into rents. By 1351, customary services owed to the barony of Embleton by the tenants at Craster had been commuted to an annual payment of 8s. 6d. This may have been due to the barony coming into the hands of the absentee house of Lancaster, for whom cash may have been more welcome. (Craster 1952, 123) Even where only short leases were granted, the landowner's need to retain tenants often provided practical security of tenure for farming families, although such distinctions between letter and spirit could hold the germ of future disputes. Changes on well-documented ecclesiastical possessions were paralleled on estates of the secular landed magnates, including Northumberland and Cumberland property of earls of Northumberland. A survey of 1586 noted that the earl's deer park at Rothbury had been replaced by farming settlements 'now as of long time before occupied by his lordship's tenants'. (Lomas 1977, 27–43; Topping 1993, 24)

Well before the great age of statutory enclosure, reorganization of settlements could be effected by agreement or coercion. (Hodson 1979, 89) In Northumberland, some villages, including Longhoughton, Chatton and Rock, were divided into two separate units in the sixteenth century, with individual holdings concentrated in one division rather than scattered over the whole area. In other places, individuals or families acquired such dominance that they could enforce reorganization to their own advantage. The Delavals did this at Hartley and Seaton Delaval. At Tughall, the lord's bailiff, Roland Bradford, used his office to enforce changes which included consolidation of his holdings into a compact area. In some other places, landowners contrived a concentration of demesne, rather than scattered strips in the open fields. A variety of devices enabled energetic or thrusting tenants or landlords to improve their own income and prospects. (Butlin 1967, 149–60; Marcombe 1980, 34–5; Sunderland 1967, 16–17; Hodson 1979) Such changes were already seen in parts of the North East in the sixteenth century, but their main impact lay in the future. On estates of the earl of Northumberland, a rough equality in size of holding was still normal in the sixteenth century, but multiplying individual changes in circumstances was changing this situation. (Thirsk 1984, V, I, 51) As in earlier periods, fortunate marriages or inheritances could facilitate accumulation of property in both gentry and farming families. Unsuccessful rebellions provided confiscated estates, which were often developed and exploited by local interests able to circumvent the control of the distant Crown. Irruptions of plague or other pestilence could kill off existing landholders and provide opportunities for pushful newcomers. The epidemics of 1586–87 and 1596–97 destroyed the established farming families of Stringers, Hoppers and Taylors at Lanchester. Progress elsewhere in the regional economy encouraged landowners and farmers to press ahead with improvements in productivity. One modern scholar has even concluded that 'ultimately, the first wave of enclosure in County Durham was a function of London's demand for coal'. There was no equivalent stimulus in the North West. (Hodson 1979, 90–1)

Overall, even in poor areas and in districts exposed to raiding, there was some increase in domestic comforts among farming communities. This was from a low level, and might still reflect settlements of no great sophistication. Although the existence of a money economy in the North during the medieval period is well attested, there is no reason to doubt that barter and self-sufficiency were also common. During excavations of the upland Northumberland village of West Whelpington, only thirteen coins and one token were found. On the other hand, in other contexts there was a good deal of money in circulation in the North. A selection of cases of theft or burglary around 1330 already showed sums of 240, 288, 1,600 and 8,800 silver pennies involved. (Jarrett 1962, 224; Evans and Jarrett 1987, 254; Fraser and Emsley 1969, 55–6)

Border districts saw further assimilation towards the norm in the latter stages of the frontier's effective existence. Already in the sixteenth century there were signs of a decline in partible inheritance, a key feature in 'border tenure'. It became increasingly common for the eldest son to inherit the family holding, although that inheritance might be burdened with obligations towards younger children. A successful yeoman often left his main property to his eldest son, but bought land elsewhere for other sons. (Marshall 1981, 224)

Northern Towns

Most towns were very small. In the fifteenth century the cathedral cities of Carlisle and Durham each had a population of under 2,000, much smaller than Newcastle.

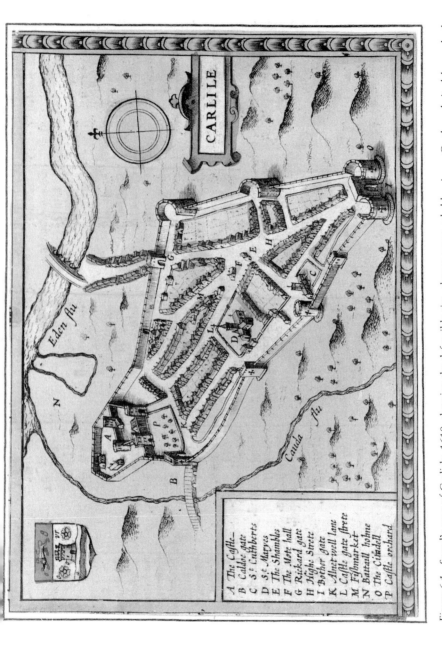

Figure 6.1 Speed's map of Carlisle, 1610, showing the defensible site, almost surrounded by rivers. Castle and citadel were both improved in the 1540s to offer stronger defences against artillery. There were still substantial open areas within the perimeter defences.

125

During the long thirteenth-century peace, Carlisle had profited from growth of trade with Scotland. Border warfare severely affected this trade, although it never entirely ceased. In 1336 orders were given for Scots attempting to buy weapons in England to be arrested, but smuggling continued. In 1343 and 1344, there were further official enquiries into those involved in sending goods from England to Scotland, but in 1366 the bishop of Carlisle, then Warden of the West March, granted a general safe-conduct to Scots coming to Carlisle Fair. (Summerson 1992; Summerson 1993, I, 267)

Suburbs developing beyond the city walls were abandoned in the interests of defence or destroyed by Scots. Carlisle suffered from its undeveloped hinterland. The great royal forest of Inglewood, which stretched almost to the city's southern limits, saw few settlements until the sixteenth century. The city, largely built from the timber of the forest, suffered a series of damaging fires, particularly disastrous in 1292, 1303 and 1391, and recurring outbreaks of plague. (Summerson 1992)

In comparison with Newcastle, Carlisle was small and poor. There was a little professional group, including lawyers, but the city's income largely depended upon local farming, including that of three great open fields surrounding the town, Castlefield, Stanwix and Upperby. In 1346, the people of Carlisle complained that 'the trade from which the citizens and their predecessors used to live is totally excluded from them, the remaining citizens live from the cultivation of fields like the rest of the countryside'. (Summerson 1993, I, 168)

Thirty years later there were reports of depopulation of surrounding countryside, even a warning that the survival of urban society at Carlisle was endangered. (Summerson 1993, I, 316) Local trades, utilizing materials like wool or leather, survived, but scarcely explain retention of a population of perhaps 1,400 in 1377, after years of turmoil on the border. By the later sixteenth century, population may have been as high as 1,700, perhaps reflecting the limit of urban growth in relation to the undeveloped hinterland. (Summerson 1993, II, 511, 513) The city's functions in royal and episcopal government contributed to its resilience, aided by defence expenditure. In 1382, for example, the garrison included 50 men-at-arms, 100 mounted archers and other troops in royal pay. Garrison numbers fluctuated, but their wages must have been important to the local economy. The building of the cathedral, and repeated repairs to defensive walls, also helped. Frequent complaints of neglect of defences may reflect local vested interest in such spending. Expenditure by bishop, cathedral prior and canons, and Dominican and Franciscan communities, helped to boost the economy. There were also windfalls. Edward I was at Carlisle for fifteen weeks in 1307, spending £2,895 18s. 2½d. and holding a parliament.

At Carlisle the king was lord of the manor, and the local sheriff his bailiff. Despite this, the little community made progress towards municipal self-government. In the thirteenth century, a narrow oligarchy of three leading families produced a series of mayors, but by the fifteenth century the ruling group had broadened. In the mid-sixteenth century Carlisle had an administration based on formal organization of trading guilds – merchants, weavers, tailors, cordwainers, glovers, butchers and tanners – reflecting increase in specialization and sophistication within the economy. Much of the limited revenue was deflected from its nominal landlord, the Crown, into the pockets of those who seized opportunities for acquisition or simple appropriation of royal property. (Summerson 1992; Summerson 1993, II, 551–4; Spence 1984, 66, 74–5)

Urban development in the North West depended largely upon exploitation of agricultural produce, both for supplying a local market and for anything further. Poor communications were among factors which impeded development of Carlisle's trading connections, and rival market towns were better positioned. Upland grazing in the mountainous core of Cumbria provided wool, although its quality was poor. During the thirteenth century, Carlisle, Cockermouth, Penrith, Kendal and the monastic foundation of Dalton all profited from the wool trade, and most developed cloth manufacture. By the late fourteenth century, Kendal was emerging as an important centre, controlling most of the wool trade of south Cumbria. By the sixteenth century its cloth enjoyed a national reputation. The trade was concentrated and controlled by a wealthy group of shearman dyers who finished cloth in the town. In earlier years key processes, especially fulling, had often been carried out in the heart of the Lake District, particularly within the large parish of Grasmere, where there was abundant water power for mills. (Chalkin and Havinden 1974, 206–7; Winchester 1987, 118; Armitt 1908; Elliot 1961)

By the fifteenth century, Kendal's dominance in south Cumbria had replaced that of the monastic centre at Dalton in Furness; raw wool was now collected at Hawkshead and carried to Kendal. By the sixteenth century, Kendal was both a collecting centre for raw wool, some of which was transported to Newcastle and thence to the Low Countries, and centre for the manufacture of Kendal 'greens', a coarse woollen fabric which found a ready market among poorer groups. A few local families, including Bensons and Braithwaites, originally with farming backgrounds, profited sufficiently from the wool trade to attain gentry status. (Elliot 1961, 113; Winchester 1987, 63)

Under the Tudors, royal attempts to organize and encourage the English textile trade by means of a virtual monopoly structure, and a ban on export of raw wool, proved disastrous for the North West wool industry. Wool prices collapsed and, even though coarse northern wool was excluded from the ban on export, disruption caused to trade undermined the painfully constructed sheep-farming economy of the Lake District.

Before this disaster, Kendal had reached a population of more than 2,500, perhaps for a while more than 3,000, and had outstripped Carlisle in wealth. (Phillips 1984, 100, 109) It was the most successful of those market towns of the North West which exploited products of local farming. With the single exception of Carlisle, these scarcely exhibited mature characteristics of urban communities. There was little municipal self-government and limited occupational specialization. Even Kendal remained a seigneurial borough until it received a royal charter in 1575. At Cockermouth in the late sixteenth century, inhabitants involved in a variety of economic activities still held and cultivated plots within the common fields. (Winchester 1986, 113)

During the long thirteenth-century peace, Berwick had grown considerably as Scotland's leading port, but resumed warfare brought this to an abrupt end. The town was much fought over, changing hands seven times between 1296 and 1333. Although English and Scots monarchs tried to promote recovery by grants of privileges when in occupation, this was not enough to counterbalance its exposed position. It did provoke loud and repeated protests from Newcastle against encouragement of a potential rival. (Fraser 1961, 136, 141, 146) In 1489, Berwick and Carlisle were the only towns exempted from an English statute forbidding butchers to slaughter cattle within the walls of a town, presumably reflecting their vulnerable position as border fortresses. (Dobson 1983, 31)

The Bishop's Boroughs

A modern assessment puts the total population of County Durham at about 35,000 in the mid-sixteenth century, and all of its towns remained small. (Hodson 1979, 84–5) Bishops issued charters to Bishop Auckland, Darlington, Durham, Gateshead, Hartlepool and Stockton, but none of these came anything like close to challenging Newcastle for regional pre-eminence. On one occasion, James I was to describe Darlington cuttingly as 'Darnton i' the dirt'. In 1585, 273 houses were destroyed there in a great fire, and in 1597 plague killed about 340 townspeople. (Patten 1978, 204; Dodds, *Boroughs*, 1915, 81–185; Sunderland 1967, 35)

Durham city was under the control of its church, which did little to encourage urban growth. The settlement consisted of five separate communities, and it was not until the charter granted by Bishop Pilkington in 1565 that the city's organization began to resemble that of other important northern boroughs. A group of closely connected families, such as the Berehalghs, Tangs and Racketts, much involved in ecclesiastical administration, dominated the small town's affairs. In terms of municipal institutions, Carlisle was well ahead of Durham, with a mayor, bailiffs, chamberlains and a council. The church was less dominant there, and local landowners took a prominent role in managing its affairs.

The city of Durham's population cannot have been more than half that of Newcastle in the fifteenth century, and remained well under 3,000 in the sixteenth. A modern study describes Durham as 'perhaps the most constitutionally retarded' of all northern towns of medieval England. (Hodson 1979, 84–5; Dobson 1983, 30–2) Even after its first full incorporation in 1565, the bishop retained important powers. At Darlington, the bishop appointed the borough's chief officer, the bailiff, until the nineteenth century. The port of Hartlepool enjoyed prosperity in the fourteenth and earlier fifteenth centuries, but then declined. By the sixteenth century, it was primarily a fishing haven. (Dodds, *Boroughs*, 1915, 137)

The bishop of Durham's borough of Gateshead was carefully watched from across the Tyne to ensure that it did not breach any of Newcastle's extensive commercial privileges. (Fraser 1961, 136, 143) Gateshead claimed in the sixteenth century that it contained 'a great number of substantial honest men, faithful and good subjects, some merchants, some drapers and other honest artificers, whom the town of Newcastle doth envy because they do well and thrive so much there'. (Manders 1973, 14)

Despite such spirited assertions of independence, the inhabitants of Gateshead continued to be overshadowed by their larger and more powerful neighbour. (Kitching 1987, 61–4) The bridge between the two towns was important, providing a link in England's principal north–south road, and giving access to the trading centre of Newcastle for merchants and shoppers from County Durham and further afield. It was a vital strategic link for conveying men and military supplies to the frontier zone. The bridge's maintenance was a matter of controversy between Newcastle and the bishop. Newcastle wanted to control the whole bridge, though not necessarily to pay for it all, and on more than one occasion removed boundary stones on the bridge to assert unified control. In 1383, Bishop Langley was forced to defend his rights in the bridge in parliamentary pleadings. Another case dragged on from 1410 to 1417, and there was more litigation in the sixteenth century.

During the brief ascendancy of John Dudley, duke of Northumberland, towards the end of the reign of Edward VI, Newcastle seized the opportunity to bring Gateshead to heel. Strenuous persuasion produced in 1553 'An Act for the Uniting and Annexing of the Town of Gateshead to the Town of Newcastle upon Tyne' (7 Edward VI *c*.10). Before the measure took full effect, Mary I came to the throne and the Act was repealed in 1554 as part of restoration of the old order in the bishopric of Durham. Newcastle tenaciously resisted loss of this long-sought prey, and extracted a high price for relinquishing the victim. A market at Gateshead, suppressed during Newcastle's ascendancy, never reappeared. The price paid for restoration of Gateshead's independence included granting Newcastle a 450-year lease of Gateshead's Saltmeadows, recognized as Gateshead common land by Bishop

Hugh Puiset in the twelfth century. Gateshead's borough tolls were also leased to the town's rival. In 1578 and 1582, Newcastle pressure extorted leases from the bishop of the manors of Gateshead and Whickham with their coal-mining opportunities. (Dodds, *Boroughs*, 1915, 110; Loades 1987, 108–12)

Newcastle upon Tyne

During the later medieval period, Newcastle continued to consolidate its position as leading town in the four northern counties. (Wade 1994; Lomas 1996, 93–101, 158–61) As early as 1334 its taxable wealth was exceeded only by London, York and Bristol. Its customs provided the basis for constitutions of other boroughs of the North East. As one of nine staple towns for the country's wool trade, under a statute of 1353, Newcastle enjoyed a legal monopoly on export of northern wool. This was of inferior quality, but was produced in large quantities. A valuation of 1337 placed a price of 5 marks a sack on wool from Newcastle, as against 9 for Yorkshire and Leicestershire, 10 for Lincolnshire and 12 for Herefordshire. Despite this, wool trading was the keystone of Newcastle's early prosperity. Not all wool was shipped away, for cloth-making was established in the town. There is mention of import of the textile dye woad, and of weavers, fullers and dyers. By 1342, fullers were sufficiently important for their guild to be one of twelve given a voice in election of the mayor. The others included wool merchants, mercers, tailors, skinners, saddlers, tanners, cordwainers, corn merchants, bakers, butchers and smiths. The silversmiths of Newcastle were significant enough to be mentioned in a statute of 1423 stipulating standards of purity. There were also goldsmiths in the town, who received guild incorporation in 1536. (Gill 1980, 2–3) After consolidation of the Tyne foreshore during the thirteenth century, a thriving lime-burning industry developed there during the next few generations, encouraged by availability of water transport and cheap local coal. (Ellison 1993, 151)

The coal trade was already important. During a three-month summer period in 1349, coal was carried in 22 of the 29 ships sailing from Newcastle. Over the winter 1377–78, of 38 foreign ships which called at Newcastle, 25 carried coal when they left. Coal shipped coastwise or abroad was often more valuable than cargoes its carriers had brought into the Tyne. It was common for ships to enter the river in ballast and leave with coal. By 1378, the coal trade had replaced wool as the town's most important source of revenue. Even earlier, Newcastle's placing as third in rank among England's provincial towns owed much to coal. Shipments in the fourteenth century were small in comparison with later periods, but the foundations of both a coasting and an overseas trade were laid. In the mid-sixteenth century, it was claimed that all French industries which depended upon heating metals relied upon Newcastle coal for their fuel. (Blake 1967, 3–26)

In addition to wool and coal, Newcastle acquired a commanding place in north European trade in lead and iron. During Thomas Wolsey's tenure of the bishopric of Durham from April 1523, he inaugurated a shake-up of lead interests on episcopal estates. Within ten years, output and profits increased. There were many small iron-mining sites on the bishop's land. Almost all of this lead and iron was traded through Newcastle. (Blanchard 1973, 64–85) Newcastle grindstones were famous, and production and shipment were highly organized by the early sixteenth century. (Tucker 1987, 185; Jobey 1986, 49–80) More exotic enterprises also contributed to Newcastle's prosperity. At some point before the end of the sixteenth century, a luxury trade in fresh fish was established. Newly caught salmon were taken to London by fast pack-horse, travelling night and day, with frequent changes to ensure speed, and high prices were commanded. Carlisle and Workington developed a similar trade at a slightly later date. (Crofts 1967, 5)

Newcastle established itself as regional metropolis during the medieval centuries. As early as 1377, poll tax returns listed 2,647 liable to pay in the town, suggesting a population of about 4,800. (Butcher 1978, 74) The town had grown during the long thirteenth-century peace on the border. In 1298, the outlying district of Pandon to the east was incorporated, with consequent revision of the perimeter wall.

Development was intermittent rather than continuous, and there were hard times. The relative sophistication of the Newcastle economy meant that it was susceptible not only to regional developments, but to wider European economic cycles. After expansion in 1518–21, 1522–23 were bad years for the European economy. A recovery followed, but then 1527–33 were difficult trading years. A major bankruptcy at the great Leipzig Fair in 1527 sparked off a chain reaction in which confidence sagged along complex trade routes which led from Germany through the Netherlands, where main buyers of Newcastle wool were concentrated. (Blanchard 1973, 64–71)

Variations in the town's fortunes had occurred in earlier years, too. In 1320 a great flood swept back up the Pandon Burn, destroying 140 houses and drowning 120 people. There may have been a drop in population in the late fifteenth century, connected with a serious epidemic in 1478. In 1505, Great Hall (later University College), Oxford, leased property in Clothmarket Street, Newcastle, to a local merchant at reduced rent, because this central site 'is now by desolacion so sore wasted ruynous and fallen in decay so that the recovery and repayring thereof is not likely to be had without the great coast and importable charges of the said John Brandling'. In 1543 and 1559, there were references to properties in the quayside area lying waste. (Heslop and Truman 1993, 3) Overall, though, the three centuries after 1300 saw

131

the regional capital continue to grow. By 1600, most of the area within the walls was built up, and expansion beyond the walls, as in Gallowgate and Percy Street, was under way.

Although already one of England's greatest towns, it would be wrong to over-emphasize the extent to which Newcastle's urban role meant an end to rural habits and connections. The Town Moor remained valuable grazing for animals owned and kept within the town. A town official looked after freemen's beasts, with the aid of four assistants. Every morning they blew horns to warn citizens to have animals ready for collection; every evening they were returned to the town to be reclaimed. (Halcrow 1953, 153)

No other town north of York rivalled Newcastle in size and importance. In 1400, it became one of the few provincial centres to acquire from the king the status of a county. Thereafter Newcastle elected its own sheriff and, apart from the area of the royal castle, was immune from the authority of the royal sheriff of Northumberland. The Lammas and Cow Hill fairs were among the most important commercial events in the north of England. The former dated from the reign of John, the latter, especially important for livestock, was granted by Henry VII in 1490. A building boom in the sixteenth century was indicated by formation of a House Carpenters and Joiners' Company in July 1579, followed by a separate Joiners' Company ten years later. (Louw 1989, 92)

The town's self-confidence was reflected in the way in which most early MPs were drawn from its own leadership, rather than imposed by outside influences. (Jalland 1976 for 1975, 39) None of the other northern towns developed a guild system so early. The system was so well established by the mid-fifteenth century that the book containing the rules of the Bakers and Brewers' Company had been 'casually lost'. (Halcrow 1959, 327) The Newcastle guilds attracted apprentices from all the northern counties, many drawn from lesser landowning families.

Newcastle continued to be dominated by an oligarchy of commercial families, often linked by marriage. As some died out, new dynasties entered the charmed circle, but the general pattern remained unaltered. The Corporation developed procedures for settling disputes between inhabitants, including referring cases to juries selected from aldermen and other leading townsmen. From time to time this hegemony was challenged, not in any democratic spirit, but by other pushful groups anxious to taste dominance themselves. In the later sixteenth century, one such struggle resulted in a victory for the incumbent oligarchy of mercers and coal traders, which included such families as the Carrs, Mitfords, Chapmans, Jenisons and Riddells. (Fraser and Emsley 1971, 147) Royal policy and charters reflected the usefulness to the Crown of keeping control in the hands of a small group. Charters granted by Elizabeth I and James I embodied this approach. The oligarchy could be counted on to maintain the status quo and act as agents of the royal authority which supported them. The profits of the dominant minority and collection of royal revenue could be comfortably secured together. Priors of Tynemouth tried to establish a market and a harbour at the mouth of the Tyne, but Newcastle's opposition to this was long-standing and implacable. It was also generally successful, often by buying royal support. (Howell 1980, 18–19; Fraser 1961, 135–6)

Within Newcastle's ruling group, certain elements came to exercise a particularly important role. Newcastle Hostmen, usually also members of the guild of Merchant Adventurers, acted as 'hosts' or agents for shipping from other ports. Individual hostmen developed connections with ships of particular ports. Although early hostmen generally came from those interested in trade in wool or hides, there was a tendency for such connections to spread, especially into the increasingly important coal trade. Shipments to London saw a dramatic increase during the early years of Elizabeth's reign, with the middle Tyne pits around Ryton, Whickham and Winlaton among the leading suppliers. This trade was largely controlled by hostmen by the end of the Tudor period. (Hodson 1979, 90; Cromar 1970, 193)

Although the incorporation of the Fraternity of Hostmen of Newcastle, with entrenched privileges in the coal trade, did not come until Elizabeth gave them a charter in March 1600, they had been a powerful group long before that. Modern studies have illuminated precocious development of entrepreneurial skills among a group of leading families during the sixteenth century. Seven families, Lawsons, Hodgsons, Selbys, Tempests, Riddells and two dynasties of Andersons, took the initial lead. Conspicuous among their achievements was consolidation of the Tyne's hold on the key London coal market. (Bennett, Clavering and Rounding 1990; Fraser 1984, 169–78) Among active manipulators in the coal trade, a group of women earned a prominent place in the sixteenth and seventeenth centuries, having inherited these interests from a deceased husband or other family connection. Dame Dorothy Lawson, a formidable Catholic matron who lived from 1580 to 1632, was the best known of these redoubtable business women. (Welford 1895, III, 19–25)

The growing importance of Newcastle was reflected in its cosmopolitan connections. Hugh Gerardino, a rich merchant from Lucca, was involved in a lawsuit there in 1293. When war broke out between England and France in 1294, nearly £400 of goods belonging to French merchants were seized at Newcastle. One French trader, from Amiens, regularly employed a Newcastle merchant as his local agent, another rented storage space for his woad from a Newcastle trader, a third owned his own storehouse in the town. Other chance surviving mentions of foreign traders in the fourteenth century include Florence (4), Lübeck (4), Cologne (1), and a partnership from Brabant. Before the end of the thirteenth century, Newcastle had built up extensive trading connections with the Netherlands and north Germany.

Figure 6.2 Newcastle upon Tyne. In the background, the roof of the Black Gate, part of the castle complex, and the intricate fifteenth-century spire of St Nicholas' Church, later the Anglican cathedral. The narrow streets leading from the old riverside town centre were lined with half-timbered houses of the sixteenth and seventeenth centuries, many of which survived in run-down condition into the Victorian period.

A Newcastle jury could display detailed knowledge about commercial shipping in the Baltic. (Conway Davies 1953, 175–99) Ability to exploit foreign commercial contacts was not confined to the merchant oligarchy of Tyneside. As early as 1310, when Henry Percy bought Alnwick from Bishop Antony Bek, part of the purchase price (probably about £5,000) was borrowed from the Lucca banking house of Bellardi. (Bean 1954, 316–17)

The Tyne played an important naval role in addition to its commercial significance. The Privy Council believed that Newcastle was 'the meetest place to mount the sea' against the Scots, although it was difficult for larger ships to make their way up-river to the quay at Newcastle. Warships and larger merchantmen usually anchored lower down the river, although Newcastle retained its legal grip on the whole harbour. By the sixteenth century, there were about fifty sizeable ships owned at Newcastle, and in time of war this resource was drawn on to provide warships for the Crown. In the years on either side of 1500, the appearance of Scottish and French squadrons, threatening English communications with the border and beyond, involved naval campaigning in the North Sea. Armed ships from Newcastle, such as the famous *Elizabeth*, sometimes commanded by their owners, saw hard fighting. The *Elizabeth* mounted as many as 72 guns, no doubt many of them merely small arms; bows, arrows, spears and pikes were also part of the equipment of local ships pressed into the royal navy at time of need. The earl of Hertford's army which invaded Scotland in 1542 owed some of its success to being landed directly in the Forth rather than having to face a long cross-country march. Prizes taken in the course of sea fighting were often disposed of at Newcastle. The town's commercial connections also made the mayor of Newcastle a useful source of intelligence for the English government. (Scammell 1960, 73–96; Scammell 1961, 180–200)

There might be only a nebulous distinction between service by Newcastle ships in the royal navy, authorized privateering and downright piracy. During the winter of 1315–16, the *Falcon* from King's Lynn, carrying supplies for the Berwick garrison, was wrecked on the Durham coast at Whitburn; local people stripped the wreck of cargo and equipment worth about £200. (Fraser 1959, 304–25; Fraser 1969, 49; Spence 1977, 66) Smuggling of dutiable goods, including wool and coal, was a common Newcastle activity. Similar practices were widespread. The prior of Tynemouth required tenants to disgorge for the monastery's benefit one-third of any loot acquired in cross-border raiding. (Blake 1965, 243–56; Tuck 1985, 47)

At Newcastle, unscrupulous citizens continued to impair defences of the castle by encroaching on its territory, contributing to a decline in defensive capacity which had to be made good by repairs in 1336–38. At mid-century the process had to be repeated. By the sixteenth century use of the castle area as a dumping ground for rubbish was well established, and the town council had to pay for its removal from the 'castle moat midden'. (Harbottle 1981, 85–6, 93)

Rural Industry and Mining

The towns of northern England were central to both trade and manufacture, constituting the most economically and socially dynamic parts of the region. Particular rural areas experienced localized industrial activity to meet local demand, or in response to broader trading patterns. Newcastle was the centre of the coal trade on Tyneside, but the stimulus of demand saw mining responding over a wider area, using local water transport where that was practicable. Use of barges of local design, known as keels, to carry coal to the main Tyne harbour area was recorded as early as 1376, but was probably not new then. Landowners were well aware of potential profit in coal-mining. In the fourteenth century, the bishop of Durham owned mines at Winlaton, Whickham, and Gateshead Fell. The prior of Tynemouth had collieries at Elswick and Benwell, while the mayor and burgesses of Newcastle obtained a royal grant to work coal to the north of the town walls. In July 1562, 6s. 4d. was expended on wine, bread and ale for mayor, chamberlains and councillors 'in going to vewe the cooll mynd in the Comon more'. (Mott 1962, 230; Halcrow 1953, 152n.) Even in this relatively well developed and sophisticated mining area, working in collieries was often a part-time activity, a form of by-employment in addition to farm work. This was also the case in other northern areas. Lead-miners in the northern Pennines combined cultivation with mining, as did coal-miners in Cumbria, engaged in what was as yet a part-time activity serving local needs.

With the exception of the Tyneside coal trade, and possibly lead-mining in northern dales, most attempts to exploit mineral resources before the sixteenth century, including copper, gold and silver as well as coal and lead, were small-scale ventures. The sixteenth century brought new awareness of the potential of mineral resources as a source of wealth, shared by a Crown chronically short of money. In 1565, at the behest of the Company of Mines Royal, German capital and expertise were deployed around Keswick to expand copper-mining. This outside initiative was not welcomed by local landowners. Initial friction resulted in the death of one German miner, while the earl of Cumberland pressed his own claims, first by obstructing the transport of ore from the mines and then by attempting, unsuccessfully, to prove his title in the courts. (Donald 1989, 124–44) It would be too simplistic to attribute to this incident disaffection which led to the northern rising against Elizabeth in 1569 (see pp. 91–3 above), but it represented another instance of extended royal intervention in the North which played a part in that breakdown of relationships. The scale of investment in copper-mining in Cumbria was substantial, including smelters and forges in the Keswick area, and provided copper for domestic articles, coinage and sale abroad. These mines achieved technical success, and must have had a considerable impact on local demand for such items as coal and timber, boosting the income of gentry families such as the Curwens and Porters. In the long term, however, they probably represented a financial failure. Selling copper on the international market was not easy, and profitability of the mines was probably never high. (Beckett 1975, 45; Donald 1989, 259)

The northern landscape also supported a variety of rural crafts and industries. Woodland crafts were common in the more afforested southern Lakeland and in Inglewood. (Winchester 1987, 100–16) Besides providing building material, wood was shaped into dishes, cups, wheels, carts and other items for both domestic and industrial use. Oak bark was used for rural and urban leather processing. Wood ash provided potash, usually near textile-manufacturing centres. Charcoal was used in scattered small-scale iron-making.

The most widespread rural industry in the later middle ages was the textile industry. During the thirteenth and early fourteenth centuries, manufacture of woollen cloth, initially largely an urban craft, followed the spread of fulling mills into rural areas, exploiting water power in processes for shrinking, felting and cleaning cloth. (Winchester 1987, 117–18) Woollen cloth was made in many northern pastoral communities, but a concentration developed in southern Lakeland, where fulling mills contributed to a cottage industry which included both spinning and weaving. The extensive, though largely part-time, employment which this brought partially explains disparities in income between southern and northern Cumbria. The pastoral and marginal uplands were more dependent on boosting incomes by non-agricultural earnings, while sheep farming made less demands on labour than lowland arable cultivation. Northern Cumbria saw no equivalent industrial growth, and the northern market towns of Carlisle and Cockermouth were surpassed in development in the fifteenth and sixteenth centuries by Kendal.

Social Mobility

From an early date, successful merchants were able, by legitimate or illegitimate means, to accumulate the necessary resources for social promotion. The Carliol family, immigrants from Carlisle, were leading figures in Newcastle in the later thirteenth century. They acquired the estate of Swarland from the Bertrams of Mitford, taking advantage of a crisis in that baronial family's finances. Other Newcastle merchants who followed this pattern included William of Acton, who acquired West Swinburn, and Richard of Embleton, who purchased Silksworth, near Sunderland. (Fraser 1969, 55–66)

Gentry families were often willing to see their progeny married to the offspring of wealthy commercial families. The Widdringtons of Widdrington in Northumberland made a number of profitable marriages with heiresses. In 1335, Roger Widdrington married Elizabeth, daughter of the wealthy Newcastle merchant Richard de Acton. One of the most famous Newcastle traders of the fifteenth century was Roger Thornton, originally a poor migrant from Bradford. He rose to great wealth, became mayor of Newcastle and a major benefactor of his adopted town and other local causes, including Hexham Priory. His heiress married Sir George Lumley, of Lumley Castle, County Durham. (Fraser and Emsley 1978, 117; Cambridge 1979, 161)

By the sixteenth century, gentry families might provide for younger sons by apprenticing them to wealthy merchants. There was no insuperable gap between country gentry and urban oligarchs. Edmund Craster of Craster, who had married a Newcastle heiress, daughter of the successful trader Christopher Mitford, apprenticed two younger sons, but fortified their prospects with legacies of cash and some detached family property in Yorkshire. (Hedley 1957, 4–5; Craster 1952, 134) In earlier times, ostentatious philanthropy had largely been the perquisite of kings and queens, bishops and lords. Before the end of the fifteenth century, successful merchants were vying with such established groups in gifts to churches and colleges or endowment of schools and hospitals.

Education

An associated development was improvement in educational facilities and the extent of literacy. It was to be some time before the northern counties could equal, and in many instances surpass, achievements of other regions in this respect. (Cressy 1978, 19–23) Nevertheless, before the end of the fourteenth century the number of grammar and elementary schools in the North was increasing, with a consequent spread of literacy among laymen.

Bishop Hatfield of Durham left the huge sum of £3,000 in his will for refounding Durham's college at Oxford. (Harbottle 1958, 82) When Bishop Langley founded a chantry at Durham in 1414, its two priests were charged with teaching as well as religious duties. In 1476, the town of Appleby inaugurated a similar institution. One of the principal traders at Corbridge in the late fourteenth century, Hugo son of Asceline, sent his only son to study at Oxford; the young man returned mentally deranged. (Iley 1974, 204) The Queen's College, Oxford, had important Cumbrian connections from its foundation in 1341, with special provision for scholars from that area because of the 'waste, desolate and illiterate condition of those counties'. At the Dissolution of the Monasteries, the possessions of the Cumbrian abbey of Holm Cultram were granted to Oxford University, reinforcing this local connection. At Cambridge, statutes of St John's College, founded in 1511, provided for special favour to students from eight northern counties, including Northumberland, Cumberland and Westmorland.

By 1400 some Newcastle guilds were trying to impose literacy tests upon apprentices. In 1525, a wealthy Newcastle merchant, Thomas Horsley, left his property for the endowment of a grammar school there. A grammar school founded at Darlington in 1531 under the will of a clergyman who had been born near the town was given a charter by Elizabeth. (Sunderland 1967, 20) The North West saw several new endowed grammar schools during the sixteenth century, including Kendal (1525), Penrith (1564), Kirkby Stephen (1566), Keswick (1571), St Bees (1583) and Kirkby Lonsdale (1591). Evidence of 1545 shows a grammar school in Carlisle continuing at work, while at Appleby the school was refounded in 1574. (Rollinson 1978, 157; Bouch and Jones 1961, 28) By the end of the fifteenth century, it was common for gentry families, often involved in commercial transactions, to send sons to school. An episcopal visitation in 1577 found 21 professional schoolmasters in Northumberland, just over half of them in Newcastle. (Tuck 1968, 242–3) Political tracts in English began to appear, and by the time of the Pilgrimage of Grace circulation of polemical publications was established in northern centres. One estimate suggests that by 1530 perhaps 15 per cent of the northern population was literate to some degree and that the proportion was accelerating. (Hoeppner Moran 1981, 3–23; Jewell 1982, 6–17)

As Elizabeth's long reign drew to a close, the scene was set for changes in the North. Much of the region's history in the previous three centuries had been affected by its role as a frontier district exposed to war, disorder and uncertainty. Accession of a Scottish monarch to the English throne, with effective disappearance of the frontier as a focus of conflict, was to have a crucial influence on the northern region of England, and accelerate trends which were already under way.

Part Three

1603–*c*.1850

Chapter 7

After the Union of the Crowns

Despite conflict and disorder before 1603, there had been some economic and social progress, including advances in farming efficiency in fertile districts. Some towns, notably Newcastle, although still small, developed a more sophisticated economic role. Change accelerated with the ending of the border's military significance, for the threat of warfare had adversely affected the whole region.

Pacification reduced the importance of the fortresses of Berwick and Carlisle, communities heavily dependent on defence spending for income and employment. During the seventeenth and early eighteenth centuries, Carlisle was overshadowed by other towns in the North West, including Kendal, Cockermouth and Whitehaven, until the development of its textile industry in the later eighteenth century brought renewed pre-eminence. Berwick, too, lost in the short term by the coming of peace to the border.

Any hopes of royal power proving effective in Anglo-Scottish unification were doomed by the crisis facing the monarchy during the seventeenth century. In some ways the end of border warfare sharpened differences between the two border regions, as lowland Scotland became increasingly tied to Edinburgh and English border counties developed stronger links with London. The seventeenth century brought into English border counties the parish- or township-based poor-law system established in the rest of the country, with its provisions for relieving the poor and correcting the idle and undeserving. (Spence 1977, 114; Rushton 1989)

The Middle Shires

Change was not immediately apparent. Elizabeth's death was followed by confusion; unruly elements used her death to justify lawlessness. For about ten days, Scots and English brigands were at large in the West March, pillaging as far south as Penrith. Now, however, this was seen as an outrage. An expedition of 200 infantry and 50 cavalry from Berwick suppressed the disorder. Both in England and Scotland, local and central authorities were determined to bring border raiding to an end. James I, after his unopposed accession to the English throne, conceived himself as king of Great Britain. He saw border areas of England and Scotland as 'The Middle Shires' rather than a meaningful frontier, and sought to ensure that 'the verie hart of the country shall not be left in ane uncertaintie'. A proclamation of May 1603 announced his determination to end 'the slaughters, spoyles, robberies, and other enormities' of the border, and replace them by 'a perfect obedience, to the comfort of his Highnesse peaceable subjects'. In subsequent years he kept a wary eye on his northern subjects. (Williams 1963; Macdonald Fraser 1971, 362; Spence 1977; Spence 1989; Spence 1991)

The Graham clan were involved in 'the busy week' which followed Elizabeth's death. Royal forces now destroyed many of their houses and a force of 100 cavalry was based in their territory. By July 1603, 160 notorious robbers in the west had been arrested. A few examples were made, though none of the seven men executed at this time were Grahams or their immediate adherents. By the end of 1603, plans were laid for removing the more infamous brigands. Some were sent to Ireland, others consigned as reinforcements of dubious value to English garrisons serving in the Netherlands.

To establish effective authority in border areas, there was strengthening of aristocratic interests there. Some land was confiscated from marauders and transferred to new landowners who could reorganize these areas to their own profit. (Gregson 1980, 201; Topping 1993, 24) The earl of Cumberland was given additional grants in the west. At Gilsland a branch of the Howards was settled in this troublesome district after Lord William Howard's marriage to a Dacre heiress, and could be expected to keep an eye on such troublemakers as Carletons and Dacres. The earl of Dunbar, influential on both sides of the border, became custodian of much Crown property in Northumberland, including North Tynedale, Upper Coquetdale, Redesdale and parts of Norhamshire. (Williams 1963, 5–6; Fraser and Emsley 1974, 190) Early in 1605 a new Middle Shires Commission, including gentry from both sides of the frontier, was established to carry on the good work in association with aristocratic interests.

Nobles involved in pacification acquired additional power by attachment to the monarch or some great man or party in the state. In their turn, noblemen enlisted gentry by a variety of inducements. Even substantial gentry, influential in their own districts, found it prudent to support a settled aristocratic interest. In a society in which the reign of law was imperfectly established, such protection could be worth loyal service, and such associations could also bring valuable patronage, either directly or from the Crown.

144

Disputes between aristocratic factions, including rivalries at court, could have local consequences. In the early seventeenth century, feuding between Cliffords and Howards hindered pacification of the North West, although this dispute subsided by 1621. (Spence 1977, 127) While Lady Anne Clifford was in dispute with relatives about her inheritance, she encouraged rivals among the nobility to make trouble for her competitors. Such discord slowed but did not prevent greater tranquillity. An early seventeenth-century survey commented upon old habits of thieving, but added optimistically, 'But now these people begin generally to be more civilised.' (Sewell 1978, 159)

Repression was more severe in Scotland than in England, especially before the death of the earl of Dunbar in 1611. The contribution of landowners to pacification was not altruistic, for they had much to gain. The earl of Cumberland's acquisitions included by 1606 Nichol Forest and the old Debateable Lands, which netted about £7,000 when he sold them in 1628. (Edwards 1985, 12; Hodson 1979, 91–2)

Border Tranquillity

The last big border foray, an attack on the Robsons of Teviotdale, led by Elliots and Armstrongs in 1611, illustrated the changed climate, for its leaders were arrested and promptly executed. The severity of repression lessened partly because much work had been done, but also because of rivalries among local leaders. Although an assize judge reported in 1609 that the counties of Cumberland, Northumberland and Westmorland were quiet, there were still outbreaks of trouble. These were centred in the North West, for the active garrison at Berwick curbed the Northumberland border. North Cumberland, with its record of co-operation between brigands and local landowners, was the critical area. Even there, after 1603 most influential interests supported the campaign against lawlessness. By 1621 the situation had improved so much that border areas were no longer subjected to an exceptional military-based system, but had been assimilated into normal patterns of county government.

Members of the Graham clan acquired positions of respectability. The first baronet, Sir Richard Graham, son of a notorious brigand, surmounted family disgrace by service to the royal favourite, the duke of Buckingham. He acquired a considerable estate, including lands bought in 1628 from the financially embarrassed earl of Cumberland, and sired two gentry families, the baronets of Norton Conyers in North Yorkshire and the baronets of Netherby in Cumberland. In Northumberland, the senior branch of the old Charlton 'name' achieved similar respectability. By 1620 their house

Figure 7.1 Chipchase Castle. Fourteenth century tower house, with a Jacobean mansion of 1621, illustrating changes in the border areas following the Union of the Crowns in 1603.

at Hesleyside was being transformed from a border fort into a country mansion. (Spence 1980; Hackett 1960, 162; Bouch 1948, 247) Local chiefs ceased to be war leaders, estimated by the number and quality of fighting men they could muster, and instead were assessed by the votes which their estates could bring to county elections. A warrior élite evolved into gentlemen entrepreneurs, as profitable management of settled estates became more attractive than pillaging.

Border defences deteriorated because, as Defoe noted in the 1720s, while visiting Percy estates in Cumberland, 'there is no enemy to be expected here'. At Newcastle, the second quarter of the seventeenth century saw houses built within the castle's bailey. At Mitford, the gentry family of that name abandoned the castle and built a mansion on lower ground. At Belsay and Chipchase, country houses replaced castles as gentry residences. These are examples of widespread replacement or modification of castles to make them into comfortable homes. Lesser men from border areas sought better opportunities in developing areas like Tyneside, where they would previously have been unwelcome. By the end of the seventeenth century, although not unanimous, most observers thought that old border habits of thieving were 'vary (*sic*) much laid aside'. (Defoe 1928, 274; Harbottle 1966, 84; Honeyman 1955: Fraser and Emsley 1978, 117; Thirsk 1984, 58)

Seventeenth-Century Constitutional Conflicts

Between 1603 and 1688 the region was involved in constitutional struggles. As in other areas, one result of seventeenth-century conflicts was the consolidation of local landed élites, who defeated attempts at centralized power by Stuart monarchs and the Cromwellian regime, and also challenges by political and religious radicals. Even the small towns of the North were under the influence of neighbouring landowning interests. Newcastle was the only town strong enough to maintain independence, and even here there were links between urban oligarchy and local landowners.

Alike in town and country, aristocratic and gentry dominance rested not primarily upon official appointments but on the economic, social and political influence at the disposal of landowners. In Cumberland, for instance, before the Civil War, the magistracy was headed by landowning families such as Dalstons of Dalston, Musgraves of Edenhall, Curwens, Dacres and Lowthers. The influence of the Dalston, Musgrave and Lowther families extended to Westmorland. Even the emergency created by the Civil War only briefly disturbed this pattern, and there is ample evidence of the tenacity with which local oligarchies defended their dominance during this troubled century. (Phillips 1990; Hopkinson 1979; Speck 1992)

In 1640 Charles I's attempts to enforce his preferred religious settlement in Scotland provoked the 'Bishops' War'. The king lacked money and troops to prevent an insurgent Scots army from invading and occupying the North East as far south as Ripon. As early as 1638 the possibility of invasion had seen attempts to improve defences at Newcastle, including the removal of buildings which had encroached on the castle site in recent years. This proved ineffective when put to the test in 1640. After brushing aside an English force at Newburn, Leslie's Scottish army seized Newcastle without serious resistance, and began to exact money and goods for its own maintenance. (Cumberland 1905, 286; Harbottle 1983, 136–8; Middlebrook 1950, 72; Nef 1932, II, 26–7, 204–5, 282–9)

This crisis forced Charles to summon Parliament, in which tension over royal policies fused with puritan sympathies in religion. One source of discontent was arbitrary interference in local affairs to the discomfort of existing local oligarchies. When the Long Parliament met in November 1640 conflict between monarch and legislature escalated. Civil war broke out in August 1642.

The war revealed a confused and complex pattern of allegiance. As in other parts of the country, northern opinion was divided to an extent which makes succinct assessment difficult. Most dominant groups were, with varied degrees of commitment, aligned with the king, although there was a minority of parliamentary and puritan sympathizers. The struggle was reflected in efforts to control local government at county and borough level. This local dimension makes it appropriate to treat the North East and North West separately, though there were similarities between the two areas.

The Civil War in the North East

In the North East, most influential gentry families, including Collingwoods, Tempests, Salvins, Conyerses and Swinburnes, sided with the king, but there were exceptions. The Lilburne family, descendants of minor Northumberland gentry, supported the parliamentary cause and profited in the short run. This family had left Newcastle in about 1600 to settle in Sunderland, a small but growing town untrammelled by guild control. By 1630 George Lilburne was a Durham county magistrate and served as one of the little episcopal borough's first mayors. In 1640 the Arminian rector of Whitburn, Thomas Triplet, complained to Archbishop Laud that a visiting unorthodox minister had been active in the district and that 'To him came the Sunderland puritans like rats over the water'. Lilburne opposed royal financial exactions in 1635 and attempts of the Newcastle oligarchy to obtain a stranglehold on the region's trade. There was local support for this, and resentment at efforts of the bishop of Durham, the Dean and Chapter and other clergy to enforce their authority in both religious and estate matters. There was less sympathy for revolutionary and subversive ideas espoused by that most radical of local parliamentarians, John Lilburne. (Dumble 1987)

At first royalists prevailed in the North, as the earl of Newcastle's forces dominated the military scene. (Spence 1995) Attempts to raise troops for Parliament achieved little, and parliamentary supporters were excluded from local government. Newcastle sided with the king, but not without some opposition. The town, like many other places, had proved restive during the personal government of Charles I. There was hostility to the king's minister Strafford and support for measures of reform in the kingdom's government. (Howell 1964; Howell 1968, 226–7; Howell 1980)

Both MPs elected by the town to the Long Parliament in 1640 opposed the king's personal rule. One of them, Sir Henry Anderson, was a leading figure in Newcastle. If Anderson was a lukewarm and unreliable supporter of Parliament, there were more strenuous adherents. John Blakiston had entered Newcastle's commercial community years earlier and achieved modest prominence. He and Anderson emerged as the town's representatives in the Long Parliament after a disputed election, when Scots occupation buttressed the anti-royalist faction. Blakiston became mayor under the pro-parliamentary regime after the siege of 1644. He was an active judge during the trial of Charles I, attended every one of the court's sittings and signed the death warrant. He died before the Restoration. During his period of influence he exploited his position for personal ends, including the protection of royalist members of his family.

Blakiston was unusually militant. Overall there were good reasons why Newcastle in the early 1640s chose the king's side. Long antipathy to the Scots, and resentment at their recent exactions, influenced the municipal elections of 1640, which rejected puritans and their allies. There were disputes between Newcastle coal traders and merchants of London and East Anglia, mostly supporters of Parliament. Quarrels over division of profits from the east-coast coal trade were connected with southern encouragement of the Scots in the hope of bringing Newcastle hostmen to heel.

Newcastle puritans were a minority. A supporter noted that the town was 'famous for thy mocking and misusing Christ's messengers and all entertainment of his servants'. (Howell 1967) In 1642 Newcastle decided to co-operate with the king by cutting off the rebellious capital's supplies of coal, which had recently become more important. The mayor of Newcastle in 1642–45, Sir John Marley, was prominent in the coal trade and had previously been knighted by the king for loyal service.

After months of indecisive fighting, in September 1643 Parliament called in the Scots again. One motive was the fuel shortage in London caused by interruption of coal supplies. A high price was paid for Scottish aid, in terms of money as well as in political and religious matters. Leslie, now styled earl of Leven, crossed the border early in 1644. Royalists in the North took what hasty precautions they could. Hurried additions and refurbishing did something to place Newcastle defences in better shape. (Bulmer 1958, 73)

On his march south, Leslie besieged Newcastle for three weeks in February, but the town held out and the Scots moved on to take part in the campaign which resulted in the king's defeat at Marston Moor. With the royalist cause in desperate straits, the Scots were free to concentrate on the siege of Newcastle. Their guns breached the medieval curtain wall just north of the Close Gate at the south-west corner of the defences. Undermining and blowing up the White Friar Tower a little further north provided a second breach. The last defenders withdrew to the castle, but that position could not be long defended. Marley had inspired a tough resistance, which was to be commemorated by the addition of the motto *Fortiter Defendit Triumphans* to Newcastle's armorials, but after a three-months' siege the town fell on 20 October 1644. (Harbottle 1969, 82–3; Hunter Blair 1955, 4) The Scots occupied the northern counties for two years, until Parliament could scrape together money to pay them off. During this period they exacted money and goods from occupied areas for their sustenance and profit, which increased local antipathy.

In 1645 Parliament excluded Marley and other royalists from Newcastle's government and its partisans were now in the ascendant. Robert Lilburne raised a regiment of cavalry for the parliamentary army in Durham in 1644. Several friends and relatives served with parliamentary forces. His brother John was a strenuous and radical supporter of the revolutionary cause. A parliamentary garrison remained in Newcastle, and damage to town defences was speedily repaired. Royalist sentiments, though still present, were cowed until shortly before the Restoration of 1660, when royalists began to move openly again.

After the Scottish victory in 1644, there was a shift in power. In Northumberland and Durham, a minority of gentry, such as the Vane family, who had chosen the winning side in recent fighting, were now on the crest of a wave. Their leaders held posts as Lord Lieutenant, High Sheriff, Deputy Lieutenant and leading JPs. Robert Lilburne was a Major-General by 1655 and served as one of Cromwell's regional military governors, taking charge of Yorkshire and Durham. George Lilburne, so recently a merchant, served as High Sheriff of Durham. Such pretensions did not endear these *nouveaux riches* to older interests. A member of an established Durham family complained in 1650 of George Lilburne 'stiling himself Esquire, though it would puzzle a Herald to make it appear'. (Dumble 1987, 227–8) Some leading members of the Newcastle oligarchy came over to the parliamentary side, including Sir Lionel Maddison and James Clavering. Clavering held various posts under the parliamentary regime in the years after 1644, but his loyalty was precarious.

Relations between Parliament and Scots did not always go smoothly, encouraging a royalist reaction early in 1648. Northern gentry, including Sir Richard Tempest, raised a little army of about 1,200 cavalry commanded by Sir Marmaduke Langdale, but it was scattered in an attack on its encampments west of Alnwick by a force from Newcastle under Colonel Robert Lilburne. Prisoners taken then may have been responsible for an unexpected development later the same year. Another Lilburne brother, Colonel Henry, governor of Tynemouth Castle, switched allegiance and declared for the king. It was said that he had been seduced by royalist prisoners in his charge. Sir Arthur Haslerig, commander of the larger garrison at Newcastle, reacted promptly. Tynemouth Castle was taken and Henry Lilburne killed. His brothers denounced his treachery.

During the early 1650s the royalists' enemies seemed firmly in the saddle. It was impossible to conceal their self-interested use of power. This was true of Vanes and Lilburnes and also Sir Arthur Haslerig. In 1648 the Lilburnes' attempts to raise local support for trying the king achieved little success. Even the Vanes and Haslerig showed no enthusiasm.

Ejection of royalist clergy saw puritan ministers intruded into many parishes. During the 1650s, perhaps aware of mutual vulnerability in case of any restoration of the old regime, Independent and Presbyterian elements managed to co-operate or at least to adopt mutual toleration in centres like Newcastle. Both attacked Quakers, who achieved a small but vociferous presence in the North. A few members of the sect acquired powerful protectors. Anthony Pearson was a leading citizen of Appleby and a magistrate there. He experienced spiritual conversion soon after the Quaker James Naylor appeared before the bench. Pearson subsequently sheltered local Quakers and himself became Haselrig's secretary. Elsewhere Quaker activities provoked disturbances, including a riot at Bishop Auckland in 1653. To many in the North, as elsewhere, early Quakers seemed to espouse doctrines subversive of social order. Despite puritan opposition, they established themselves in several places, including Gateshead. (Howell 1979, 192–201)

Replacement ministers were not always satisfactory. Sem Cox, an ex-soldier appointed rector of Middleton in Teesdale by the influence of Sir Henry Vane, was expelled in 1652 because of immoral living and coinage offences. Thomas Weld, the zealous puritan installed in 1650 at St Mary's, Gateshead, stirred up opposition to the revolutionary settlement. Apart from hostility towards Quakers, he proved as oppressive a pastor as any Anglican clergyman could have been. During eight years at Gateshead, Weld excluded from sacraments 'above a thousand soules' whom he considered unsound. He obtained from the Interregnum government an order expelling opponents, including the four churchwardens, from parish administration. Such behaviour, affecting people of local influence, contributed to pro-royalist sentiment. During parliamentary and puritan dominance of Newcastle's affairs, no long-term transformation of authority was achieved. Before 1660, Sir John Marley again occupied a position of influence in the town. As early as 1656, Robert Lilburne reported to the Cromwellian government that in the North East there was great hostility to the regime. (Smith n.d.; Howell 1970; Howell 1981, 310)

Lilburne, who had been a member of the court which tried Charles I as well as a prominent officer in the parliamentary army, had cause for anxiety. Some leaders were in more or less clandestine correspondence with the exiled royal court before the Restoration. James Clavering had deserted the parliamentary cause by 1656 and was suspected of sending money to the exiled Charles II. The weakness of the revolutionary regime became obvious. In 1658 Lilburnes and other adherents forwarded to Cromwell an address of loyalty from Durham magistrates, bearing only seven signatures, including two Lilburnes. The Lilburnes sought to bolster support for Richard Cromwell in the North in 1658–59, but the 1660 Restoration was widely welcomed. Thomas Weld left Gateshead shortly before the Restoration and died soon afterwards; he was replaced by an orthodox Anglican clergyman.

There remained a puritan element in Newcastle which was involved in factional struggles, but events of the 1640s and 1650s had gone far to discredit them. Victorious royalists took some revenge. Henry Vane was executed. Robert Lilburne died a prisoner. George Lilburne lost some of his gains, but remained of local significance in the Sunderland area until his death in 1676. Thomas Lilburne, Cromwellian MP and supporter of the regime, lived unmolested until his death in 1665 on a family estate near Sunderland. At Middleton in Teesdale, the rectory was obtained by Timothy Tully, a northern Vicar of Bray, who had been a 'bright particular star' of Presbyterianism in Cumberland in the 1650s, before timely reversion to orthodox Anglicanism. In this case his predecessor, who had espoused a moderate parliamentary allegiance, continued to live in the parish in modest comfort. (Smith, n.d.) Most men who had risen to local eminence during the Protectorate returned to obscurity after 1660.

The Civil War in the North West

The North West's experiences during Civil War and Interregnum were similar. Loyalties were divided during the crisis of the 1640s. Most influential opinion resented interference in local affairs from any quarter, whether royal personal rule, parliamentary committees or Cromwell's major-generals. (Morrill 1976) Carlisle corporation protested against royal exactions in 1634, and Westmorland magistrates complained against extra-parliamentary taxation in 1640. Nevertheless, most influential sentiment in the North West was royalist, though with varying degrees of commitment. In 1645 a parliamentary supporter complained that 'Here the whole gentry are Malignants, Delinquents, Papists, Popish or base Temporisers; Here not ten of the Gentry . . . nay I dare not say so many, have proved Cordiall to the state . . .'. (Phillips 1978, 169)

When fighting broke out, most leading families supported the king, although few took the field in active campaigning. Only four prominent families declared for Parliament. (Phillips 1970, 38; Morrill 1979, 79) Sir Richard Graham, a royal courtier, helped to hold much of north Cumberland for the king. Graham, one of the most active northern royalists, was wounded at Edgehill early in the war. The Hudleston family of Millom, who had often in the past supplied MPs for the county, were keen royalists with a strong hold on south-west Cumberland. In north Westmorland the parliamentary Lord Wharton was challenged by Sir Philip Musgrave. In the southern area of Westmorland the situation was different. Some royalist champions were preoccupied elsewhere, such as Sir Robert Strickland of Sizergh who based himself on his Yorkshire estates. The influential Bellingham family espoused the parliamentary cause. Among MPs of the North West, Sir Henry

Bellingham alone joined the parliamentary side. Some interests played little part in the conflict. The fifth earl of Cumberland died in 1643 and was succeeded by Lady Anne Clifford, but she did not come north until 1649. (Spence 1979, 47)

At first the contending parties showed little militancy, although individual members of local families proved more bellicose. (Newman 1981, 254) In 1643 royalists mustered tenants to frustrate an attempt to seize Carlisle for Parliament. In the same year Colonel Sir William Hudleston raised a force in Cumberland in an unsuccessful attempt to relieve royalists besieged in Thursland Castle, Lancashire. Carlisle withstood a Scottish siege from October 1644 to June 1645, and only surrendered after defenders were reduced to eating dogs and rats. (Cumberland 1905, 288)

Many local interests kept their heads down during the early stages of the war and avoided being closely linked to either party. When Montrose led a royalist force into Cumberland in 1644, support was disappointing and few showed any inclination to stay with him when he left the area. (Anon. 1644, 2–4) Some gentry families who supported the king in 1643–45 later opted out of the struggle. They were often more concerned for their own affairs than any wider considerations. Sir Christopher Lowther was a royalist, but primarily concerned with defence of Whitehaven. Quarrels occurred among royalist gentry, as when Sir Philip Musgrave was elevated above other colonels of militia by his appointment as county commander-in-chief by the royalist marquis of Newcastle. (Phillips 1978)

Parliament appointed county committees for northern counties at the outbreak of war, but initially these had only a shadowy existence. Their first heads were Sir George Dalston for Cumberland and Sir Henry Bellingham for Westmorland. Both had moved into the royalist camp by the summer of 1644. The situation was transformed by the entry of Scottish troops into Cumberland in early September 1644, which enabled the parliamentary cause to raise its head. Sir Wilfrid Lawson became parliamentary commander-in-chief for Cumberland in October. Several neutral interests agreed to co-operate, but most prominent families held aloof from or opposed the now active parliamentary county committees. Some families were divided. Sir George Bellingham of Levens was now a royalist, but his son James became parliamentary commander-in-chief for Westmorland.

For the most part, the parliamentary regime could not count on old dominant families, but relied on new arrivals among landowning groups. The Westmorland committee included merchants from Carlisle, Cockermouth and Penrith, which cannot have helped to secure the loyalty of established landowning interests. (Phillips 1995) In Cumberland the parliamentary regime presented a more convincing roll of local interests, but this success was more apparent than real. While the region was overawed by Scottish or other parliamentary troops, county committees posed as an accepted and active local government, but deprived of that support the hollowness of their position was soon demonstrated. Local opinion resented having to pay for occupying Scottish troops. Westmorland rose unsuccessfully on this issue in 1645–46. A more serious rising in Cumberland broke out in April 1648. Carlisle was seized and rebels captured Appleby in October 1648. The parliamentary regime in Westmorland disintegrated, and in Cumberland the county committee failed this test. The rising was put down by force, but the restored parliamentary regime was even less prestigious than its predecessors. Only one-third of the Westmorland county committee after 1648 could, even by liberal interpretation, be seen as 'gentlemen'. The Cumberland regime looked more respectable, with a core of gentry, including men like Charles Howard of Naworth, a keen Cromwellian. Even so, there were weaknesses here, and a sizeable garrison remained at Carlisle. By 1653, standards for appointments to the Cumberland magistracy had slipped, and by 1657 the bench contained men who would never have been considered in earlier years. (Phillips 1995) Well before the Restoration, the parliamentary regime in the North West was struggling, and by 1659 it was almost impossible to find men of standing who would implement sequestrations of property of landowners involved in a premature attempt to restore the monarchy headed by Sir George Booth. (Phillips 1970, 66)

After the Restoration, a few old rebels managed to retain influence. (Phillips 1995) Charles Howard, despite his Cromwellian years, emerged as earl of Carlisle and Lord Lieutenant of Cumberland as a result of timely shifts of position and the pragmatism of the Restoration government. Sir Wilfrid Lawson had been well paid as a parliamentary commander and used this income to extend his estates. More typical were cases like Cuthbert Studholme, whose parliamentary attachment had emboldened him to call himself 'esquire' in 1659; by 1664 he had reverted to 'merchant'. Most members of county committees under the Commonwealth were upstarts in the eyes of established county leadership and disappeared from the limelight after 1660.

Even during Commonwealth years, royalist leaders had not been effectively suppressed. The Northern Committee for Compounding sat at Newcastle to assess penalties on royalists. Many victims succeeded in undervaluing estates and so mitigating fines. Survivors embarked upon economic development which could provide enhanced income. Sir Patricius Curwen of Workington was fined more than £3,000 for royalist activities, but this did not curb, and may have encouraged, Workington's expansion. Lowthers wriggled out of the worst consequences of royalist loyalties. The heir to Sir Christopher Lowther retained his inheritance because his lands had been settled on his mother for her lifetime. His brother Sir John Lowther spent more than £20,000 in buying land between 1649 and 1660. Sir Christopher had founded Whitehaven in the 1630s and this family interest was continually encouraged by its landlords. Even Sir Richard Graham managed to recover his estates after brief sequestration. In some cases, friends or relatives bought estates cheaply from the Committee for Compounding with a view to their restoration. Not everyone was as lucky, and some families lost estates. In some cases, losers had been in financial difficulties before the war. Other families emerged from the war with debts which took many years to repay. In general, 'The penalties and taxes of the victors made no marked, lasting impression on the estates of the gentry . . .'. (Welford 1905; Brassley 1985, 24, 55–60; Halliday 1994, 52–63; Phillips 1978, 181–90)

From Restoration to Glorious Revolution

The Restoration was popular in the North as offering escape from political turbulence and oppressive or ineffective government. Yet there was no restoration of monarchy as it had stood before the summons of the Long Parliament in 1640. Effective power remained in the hands of local landowning élites. Institutions which offered rival channels of influence had expired or fallen into desuetude. Prerogative courts such as Star Chamber and High Commission were a thing of the past, as was the Council of the North, and the Privy Council was weakened. The Church had lost much of its control over society with erosion of the powers of Church courts. The discipline of urban trade guilds was increasingly ineffective, while Courts Leet and manorial courts were for the most part either dead or in decline.

James II's attempts to favour Catholicism, and the dubious means adopted for that purpose, undermined Stuart popularity. Newcastle's response provides a good example, welcoming the Restoration, but then rejecting attempts by the later Stuarts to enforce their will. Sir William Blackett headed resistance to a new charter forced on the town at the end of Charles II's reign, which gave the Crown arbitrary powers to dismiss mayor and aldermen. Early in his reign, the openly Catholic James II forced the council to admit a Catholic freeman. Soon afterwards, municipal elections returned a council dominated by the Blackett party. In 1687 James II issued another charter to Newcastle, consolidating royal control, under which he dismissed the mayor, six aldermen, the sheriff, the deputy recorder and fifteen common councillors. The substitute mayor was the recently enrolled Catholic freeman and other appointed officers and councillors were men prepared to follow the king's wishes. Opposition increased, but in January 1688 a Jesuit, Philip Metcalfe, was appointed to preach a sermon before the purged council which he claimed, wrongly, to have 'commanded the hearts of all'. A few months later James II imposed yet another charter, further increasing direct royal control. In the municipal elections which followed, the king's supporters were beaten. Carlisle and Appleby also saw royal interference, with revision of charters and favouritism to an unpopular minority of Catholics. (Cumberland 1905, 297–8)

The efforts of James II to establish regimes dominated by fellow-Catholics saw Catholic gentry appointed to magistracies and other posts of local influence. In December 1686, fifteen Catholics, including two army officers, became Durham magistrates. This ascendancy was brief and resented. The position of Catholic office-holders became impossible when it became clear that the king's policies were leading to disaster.

In October 1688 James cancelled imposed charters in an attempt to conciliate his subjects, but by then it was too late. Northern plotters had concerted plans for taking over garrisons at Berwick, Carlisle, Newcastle and Tynemouth. The king's military commanders appreciated their isolated position and this did much to prevent their resistance. In December 1688, Lord Lumley, who had been one of the seven lords who signed the invitation to William of Orange to intervene against James II, entered Newcastle unopposed, proclaiming support 'for the protestant religion and a free parliament'. Newcastle had welcomed the failure of Monmouth's rebellion a few years earlier, but now there were few in the town willing to stand by the fugitive monarch. (Speck 1989)

During the Glorious Revolution, the old oligarchy regained control of municipal institutions. In previous centuries, dominant elements in Newcastle exploited royal support to prevent other groups from forcing a way into the town's government. By 1688, they had had more than enough of royal attempts to impose unpopular policies in the teeth of resistance. The recently erected statue of James II, paid for by the town, was pulled down by a mob, encouraged by soldiers from the garrison, and thrown into the river. The council did nothing to prevent this, but frugally recovered fragments to dispose of as scrap metal. By the end of the seventeenth century, Newcastle was no longer dependent on royal support in managing its affairs. (Howell 1980, 18–28; Sharp 1980, 35)

In the North West, John Lowther of Lowther spearheaded support for William and Mary's takeover, a role rewarded by appointment as Lord Lieutenant of Cumberland and Westmorland, Privy Councillor and eventually a viscountcy. This enlargement of his influence, together with the patronage which it conferred, aided the Lowther rise to regional hegemony.

Political conflicts of the seventeenth century did not bring about any shift of power from established local élites. Rather, they showed that no stable government could exist without their support. The events of 1688 underlined the dangers of central interference in local affairs. Although northern constituencies elected similar numbers of Whigs and Tories in the general election after the flight of James II, the overwhelming majority were supporters of the Glorious Revolution. (Speck 1989, 203)

Northern Jacobites

There remained a residue of Jacobite sympathies. A few clergymen refused to accept rejection of the anointed king, and this minority retained at least a shadowy existence until the late eighteenth century. Although Lord Crewe, bishop of Durham, found no difficulty in accepting the new dispensation, the dean, Denis Glanville, proved less flexible and chose exile rather than take the new oaths of loyalty. William Andrews, vicar of St Andrews, Newcastle, was appointed in 1688 and survived until his death in 1705. He avoided taking the oaths to the Revolution settlement, and owed his preservation to the support of the Blackett family. Sir William Blackett, despite non-juring religious sympathies, was elected mayor of Newcastle in 1718. Rowland Burdon of Castle Eden in Durham, and Musgrave baronets of Edenhall in Cumberland, were other influential protectors of the non-juring tradition. (Sharp 1980, 37–40)

Cumbrian Jacobites were not strong enough to pose a threat to the new regime. In the Carlisle diocese, Archdeacon Nicholson swallowed initial scruples and supported the new order, with its opportunities for preferment. Rewarded by promotion to the Carlisle bishopric, he strenuously opposed the Jacobite rising of 1715. (Dunn 1972, 15–19; Bouch 1948, 289–312)

The thread of Jacobitism among northern aristocracy and gentry was reflected in treasonable activities. Sir John Fenwick was executed for conspiracy against William III in 1696. Colonel James Grahme of Levens Hall escaped with his life, but spent some time in the Fleet Prison. The earl of Derwentwater and Edward Clavering of Callally paid with their lives for choosing the losing side in 1715. Lord Widdrington survived, but lost his estates, including property at Stella and Winlaton, as well as the Widdrington estate itself. (Gooch 1996; Rounding 1985) Some Jacobites were luckier. William Craster, cousin of John Craster of Craster, was one of the Northumberland gentry who joined the 1715 rising, but survived to die peacefully at Rock in 1725. (Craster 1953, 27) John Thornton was another; his son was able to raise enough money to buy back the family estates, at a high price. Essentially, however, the remnant of old loyalties in Church and state was of little significance after 1715.

After the crushing of the '15, sanctions against disloyalty were tightened. Stringent loyalty oaths were enacted and enforced on Anglican clergy. Some reports suggested that Jacobitism remained strong in the northern counties. In 1718 a letter from Newcastle claimed that the Jacobites there were 'very insolent' and involved in plotting. Alarms proved exaggerated, and sometimes represented no more than a prank to frighten local dignitaries. It was, however, noticeable that in 1745 pro-Hanoverian popular demonstrations only acquired momentum after the failure of the Jacobite invasion. The defeat of Jacobite risings did not reflect triumphs by northern levies. The easy surrender of Carlisle in 1745 was embarrassing, and county militias never matched military exploits of earlier periods. (Sharp 1980; Cumberland 1905, 303)

Forfeited estates provided pickings for those who had chosen the right side and could lay their hands on ready money to buy from the Forfeited Estates Commission. William Cotesworth provides a well-documented example. Second son of a Teesdale yeoman farmer, he ended his life as a rich Tyneside merchant, landowner and coalowner, although it had been a tough struggle to obtain and keep that position. He had no doubt that his successes had been divinely directed by the 'providence of his Goodness'. Rivals would have offered an alternative explanation. It is unlikely that Cotesworth was disturbed by the hostile anonymous letters (including miniature gallows) which followed his zeal in the Hanoverian cause in 1715 and the rewards which this brought. (Ellis 1981)

Those who bought forfeited estates included established families, such as Blacketts of Wallington and Ridleys of Blagdon. The Liddells, already established at Ravensworth a few miles from Newcastle, acquired in 1719 the Eslington estate in north Northumberland, which remains the family seat. These families acquired with their new possessions a commitment to the regime on which these acquisitions depended. Other developments, such as the statute of 1688 which gave landowners mineral rights on their estates, other than gold and silver, also secured support for the Revolution Settlement.

Chapter 8

Religion and Philanthropy

The Church suffered severely during centuries of border warfare and insecurity. After 1603, there were signs of recovery, although reports of ruined churches and poverty-stricken parishes continued. The 1604 Hampton Court Conference on religious affairs considered the northern Church, and a beginning was made in restoration. Much needed to be done. Many years after 1603 an old man at Cartmel Fell told a visiting puritan minister that he regularly attended his local church and that he had

> heard of that man you speak of (Jesus Christ) once at a play at Kendal, called Corpus Christi play, where there was a man on a tree, and blood ran down . . . he could not remember having heard of salvation by Jesus Christ, but in that play.

In the 1630s, churchyards at Barnard Castle and Gateshead were used as urinals by local people. (Lancashire 1914, 254; Tillbrook 1987, 215)

Some northern clergy were more concerned with secular matters than with church restoration. Marmaduke Blakiston accumulated the lucrative pluralities of rector of Sedgefield, canon of Durham, archdeacon of the East Riding and canon of York. He was primarily a country gentleman who happened to be in holy orders. His daughter was married in 1625 to John Cosin, up-and-coming clergyman and future bishop of Durham. When Blakiston died in 1631 his Sedgefield rectory and Durham canonry were inherited by his son Robert. Another son was to take a different course, for John Blakiston became a puritan and regicide.

Although there were only eight clerical JPs in County Durham in 1630, they notched up half as many attendances at quarter sessions as 27 lay colleagues. A clerical magistrate might exercise secular authority in an extensive district. This was true of Cuthbert Ridley, scion of an old Northumberland family, who obtained the living of Simonburn in 1604 and took a prominent part in local and county government. (Fraser and Emsley 1974, 195–6)

159

Religious Controversies

Reform was impeded by national religious disputes. Bishop Neile of Durham was a supporter of Archbishop Laud, but these views were not shared by all northern clergy. By the later 1620s the effectiveness of Durham ecclesiastical administration was affected by quarrels between clergymen. Neile was not a mild man, and built up a party of Arminian supporters which included one of his favourite young clergymen, John Cosin. The bishop's policies involved restoring, altering or re-equipping churches, and this was often disliked by lay folk who had to foot the bill. An insistence upon rights, dignity and privileges of the established Church was a Laudian trait which brought friction with the lay world. Neile was insistent that churchyards must no longer be abused for

> fighting, chiding, brawling or quarrelling, any plays, lords of misrule, summer-lords, morris-dancers, pedlers, bowlers, bearwards, butchers, feasts, schools, temporal courts or leets, lay juries, musters or other prophane usage.

Such crusades were welcomed in some quarters, but caused irritation in others. More significant was hostility aroused when ecclesiastical landlords sought to recover property or dues clandestinely enjoyed by encroaching laymen. The established Church in the North could not count on either internal unity or general lay support in the dangerous years ahead, and could not avoid being associated with the increasingly beleaguered royal government. (Tillbrook 1987, 203–15)

The Church after 1688

One effect of disruptions of Civil War and Commonwealth was a divided Church no longer capable of containing its inherent differences. The Restoration Church was achieved at the price of excluding many who were sympathetic to Presbyterian and Independent congregations which had flourished during the collapse of authority within the state Church. Such groups were now consigned to nonconformity, introducing a division in English life with profound consequences.

War and disruption had other, more visible, consequences. Extensive damage to the west end of Carlisle Cathedral was blamed on parliamentary troops. (Cumberland 1905, 93–4) Corbridge church was burned by the Scots. At Ford the chancel roof had gone, as had much of the nave roof; the parson's house had been demolished and the church had lost most of its fittings. During the Commonwealth, there were few signs of recovery. At Tynemouth, the nave of the old priory church, which had been used as a parish church, was in ruins, but a start was made in 1650 in building a new church at North Shields to replace it. (Jobey 1967, 57) This was unusual, for decay or destruction was the fate of many churches during mid-century decades.

Although its pre-eminence was re-established after 1660, the Church faced problems. The Restoration brought reintroduction of the ecclesiastical regime in the North East. John Cosin was appointed to the restored bishopric of Durham and set about employing religious and secular powers to re-establish the bishop's authority. Episcopal property which had been alienated in recent troubled decades was recovered. Durham Consistory Court was soon sitting again in its old home of the Galilee Chapel of Durham Cathedral, although Church courts never recovered all their earlier powers. Isaac Basire, a prominent northern clergyman exiled under the Commonwealth, returned to show zeal in rooting out error and abuse as archdeacon of Northumberland. A strong hand was needed to deal with men like Humphrey Dacres, incumbent at Haltwhistle, who was so drunk on the first Sunday of 1663 that he could not conduct a service. Cosin and Basire co-operated in attacks on enemies of the Anglican Church, both Catholics and puritans.

A Durham episcopal visitation in 1662 showed many churches needing urgent attention. Near Newcastle, three chapels were still in a ruinous state, and at South Gosforth only the walls of the church were still standing. Cosin spent freely in subsidizing recovery and by the time of his death in 1672 the principal northern diocese had been put upon a sounder footing. (Rogan 1956) His successor, Nathaniel, Lord Crewe of Stene, who came to Durham in 1674, was less conscientious, but continued restoration.

The situation in the North West was less satisfactory, despite efforts after 1660 by diocesan authorities, mainly High Church in inclination. In 1668, Bishop Rainbow lamented that

> The churches of this one diocese of Carlisle are become very ruinous, the Communion plate & linen plundered & stollen away, and many disorders committed to ye great dishonour of Almighty God, the scandall of all good Christian people and the breach of ancient lawes of this land. (Bouch 1948, 364, 368)

Administration had been interrupted during occupation of Carlisle by parliamentary troops from 1644, with ejection of many clergymen. Until the Restoration, the area saw a watered-down form of Presbyterianism in the ascendant, with little ecclesiastical discipline, which may have helped the spread of Quakerism. Southern Cumbria was a neglected part of the diocese of Chester, where a survey of 1714 noted that 56 out of 93 livings were worth less than £10 a year. (Bouch 1948, 333) The rest of Cumbria formed the bishopric of Carlisle, the poorest diocese in England. Low endowments in many parishes almost excused the pluralism and absenteeism among local clergy. Bishop Nicholson noted the example of one of his clergy, who because of poverty 'followed ye plough more than his books'. Others supplemented meagre stipends by working as schoolmasters. Even in the early nineteenth century, a majority of Cumbrian benefices were held in pluralism, and most stipends were well below the national average, despite many subsidies from Queen Anne's Bounty. (Dunn 1931, 52; Bouch 1948, 380–1)

After 1660, bishops of Carlisle did not find diocesan duties attractive; some preferred to apply their energies in seeking better-endowed sees. Between 1660 and 1790, there was only one year in which the bishop spent more than four weeks in his diocese. When Bishop Nicholson embarked upon his first visitation in 1703, there remained much need for reform and restoration. (Burgess 1981, 134)

The Cumbrian Church did not receive full support from major land-owners, some of them non-resident and preoccupied elsewhere. Lady Anne Clifford was an exception, for after she succeeded to her inheritance in 1649 she spent much of her time, and most of her income, in the area. Her disbursements included building new churches and improving existing ones. (Spence 1979, 50, 59) As with other areas of patronage, benefices might carry other than religious responsibility, with bishops and lay patrons requiring political loyalty as well as spiritual exercises.

Increasing prosperity facilitated church building or repairs, either from secular patronage or Church revenues. By the third quarter of the eighteenth century, the bishop of Durham's income was second only to that of Canterbury. (Maynard 1990, 105) Restoration after the troubled seventeenth century did not come immediately or generally. In 1723 the roof of the church at Widdrington was still in a state of collapse, and the rest of the building little better. It was not until 1766 that effective repairs were carried out. (Briggs 1989, 79)

Throughout the eighteenth century, pluralism and absenteeism among northern clergy provoked comment. There were enormous disparities in clerical incomes in both dioceses, but especially in the wealthier Durham see, where rich livings and cathedral prebends provided prizes sought by clerics from prominent families. Some poorer parishes, especially in the North West, could attract only badly educated clergy of lowly origin. (Munden 1990, 196) The surviving evidence makes more of failures and weaknesses than the less exciting tale of modest competence. It is nevertheless clear that the established Church faced problems, often not effectively tackled before the work of nineteenth-century reformers.

Figure 8.1 Portrait of Lady Anne Clifford, at the age of 56, from *The Great Picture* which she commissioned in 1646 when, after prolonged legal wrangling, she had succeeded to the Clifford inheritance. The triptych commemorates the long-standing importance of the Clifford family and emphasises Lady Anne's own status as a great and learned aristocratic lady. Reproduced by kind permission of Abbot Hall Art Gallery, Kendal, Cumbria.

Roman Catholicism

Of rivals to the established Church, Catholicism was reduced by the end of the seventeenth century to a minor role, despite brief encouragement under James II. There were only two priests in Cumbria by 1728–29. Early in the eighteenth century, there were only five Catholic gentry families in Cumberland (Curwen of Workington, Howard of Corby, Howard of Greystoke, Salkeld of Whitehall and Warwick of Warwick), and one (Strickland of Sizergh) in Westmorland. Subsequently the Salkelds died out, while the Curwens were replaced by a Protestant branch. The survival of some Catholic gentry families was imperilled by penalties imposed for recusancy or by entry of heirs into the priesthood. (Halliday 1994) By the late eighteenth century there remained only three Catholic gentry families in Cumbria and probably only a few hundred Catholics within a population of perhaps 100,000. (Hilton 1980; Burgess 1981, 135)

There was similarly patchy survival of Catholicism in the North East. Where gentry patronage continued, pockets survived persecution under penal laws. The first earl of Derwentwater left £400 in 1696 for maintenance of a priest in Newcastle, but the influence of that family did not survive the last earl's fatal participation in the 1715 rising. Whereas Catholic families played a part in early development of the North East coal trade, by 1715 their role there had almost completely ended. (Smith 1976; Nicholson 1975; Nicholson 1978; Forster 1979; Gooch 1982; Gooch 1983; Clavering 1982)

Catholicism in the North received reinforcements from two sources by the end of the eighteenth century. There was an immigration of Irish workers into northern counties; most of these, although not all, came from Catholic areas. (Nicholson 1985) The establishment of a revolutionary regime in France after 1789 saw priests fleeing to Britain. At Heddon on the Wall, the street name 'Frenchmen's Row' represents houses converted to shelter about twenty refugee priests. Despite language problems, such immigrants served a useful purpose where there were Irish communities and a shortage of priests. (Bellenger 1982, 172–4; Nicholson 1980)

Nonconformists

Protestant nonconformity survived the Anglican victory of 1688, but declined thereafter. Gentry families who had espoused the dissenting cause, like the Middletons of Belsay in Northumberland, dropped in number during the late seventeenth and eighteenth centuries. (Halcrow 1958, 105) Where nonconformity enjoyed local support it might continue undisturbed on a modest scale, as with the Presbyterians at Ravenstonedale under Wharton landlords.

Some scattered Baptist congregations in Cumbria, mostly dating from the 1650s, persevered into the twentieth century. Presbyterians and Quakers maintained continuous existence as minority sects, despite persecution during the later seventeenth century. Quakers had already suffered repression, largely because of their rejection of ecclesiastical and secular hierarchies, and other subversive notions. During seventeenth-century troubles, Quakerism attracted thousands, with south and west Cumbria a main centre. Support dwindled during the eighteenth century, to no more than 3 or 4 per cent of the population. (Burgess 1980, 101; Marshall 1983, 188) Presbyterianism, in both the North East and the North West, was understandably stronger near the Scottish border. In Cumbria, it probably enjoyed the support of about 5 per cent of the population during the first half of the eighteenth century. Nonconformity continued in a minority of northern parishes where toleration might be found, but where local church or squirearchy was hostile survival was more difficult. More than half of the Cumbrian parishes were said to contain no more than a single nonconformist. (Burgess 1981, 135–7) Dissent was affected by evangelical movements in the first half of the nineteenth century. Crusades by John Wesley in the later eighteenth century seem to have made little impact, but the Methodist movement gathered strength later and older nonconformist sects shared a significant evangelical revival.

Despite efforts to improve the condition of the Church in the North there remained, especially in poorer and more remote districts, much superstition, including belief in witchcraft, and popular faith in supernatural forces which might be appeased by rhymes, incantations and rituals. (Middleton 1967, 161–6) In the course of the nineteenth century, church and chapel building, on a large scale, tried with only moderate success to keep pace with economic and demographic changes. At Carlisle, for instance, the Ecclesiastical Commission built Holy Trinity Church and Christ Church under legislation of 1818. Both were in districts badly served by existing churches; Holy Trinity served a densely populated textile-manufacturing suburb.

Despite destruction of churches and chapels in recent decades, sufficient physical evidence remains to demonstrate that the building and operation of religious institutions was a compelling preoccupation throughout these years.

Philanthropy

The continuing importance of religion was reflected in expanded philanthropic efforts. Charitable facilities had a long history, including almshouses of various kinds. From the eighteenth century onwards, northern counties, like other regions, saw philanthropic activities proliferate. Prominent figures in local society took the lead, an obligation generally seen as a natural corollary to wealth and privilege. When Lady Anne Clifford established almshouses for women at Appleby, the occupants were subjected to the condition that they must never get into debt. If there was backsliding, miscreants forfeited two weeks' allowances, half of which went to the poor, half to the informant who reported the offence. A second breach involved expulsion from the charity. In a rough world, aristocratic philanthropy was useful, however condescending and grudging it may appear to modern observers. A modern writer notes of Lady Anne that 'To balance her rackrenting against her munificence is not easy.' (Spence 1979, 58–9) Aristocratic bounty inspired gratitude and added to the prestige of donors.

Expansion of Education

Provision of education was seen as a proper exercise of philanthropy, which played a key role in extensions of literacy. By the crude yardstick of ability to sign documents, complete illiteracy among Newcastle shoemakers saw a dramatic and progressive fall, from 52 per cent in 1618–55 to only 3 per cent in 1721–40. Another calculation suggests a literacy rate of something like 50 per cent for craftsmen in the diocese of Durham in the 1630s, with only 20 per cent illiterate a century later. In the late seventeenth century Newcastle was second to London as a centre for publication of chapbooks, used in teaching children to read. Similar evidence comes from Cumbria, which had an unusually large provision of schools by the early nineteenth century. (Houston Durham 1982, 145–6; Marshall and Walton 1981, 15)

Improvement occurred at an uneven rate, with spurts *c.*1666–77, around 1700 and in the early nineteenth century. Progress was most marked among those for whom literacy was an undoubted advantage. Rural areas lagged behind towns, and groups like labourers, keelmen and miners were far behind more sophisticated artisans.

In earlier years, literacy in northern counties had lagged behind other regions, but by 1630 the gap was narrowing. By the end of the seventeenth century the discrepancy between the North East at least and other areas of England outside London had been reduced. Northumberland and Durham were then about equal to Gloucestershire and Oxfordshire. By the end of the eighteenth century, the northern counties probably had a higher level of literacy than any other provincial region, across a wide social range.

The churches took a leading role in school provision. In 1811, Bishop Shute Barrington of Durham founded a Society for the Encouragement of Parochial Schools. When A. F. Foster surveyed elementary schools in mining areas of Durham and Cumberland in 1858 he found that 168 out of the 222 were Anglican foundations. (Heesom, Duffy and Colls 1981, 146, 150) At Kendal, an official survey of 1818 concluded that 'the Poorer Classes have sufficient means of having their children educated'. (Beckett 1976, 142–3) Even if this was optimistic, there is no reason to doubt a significant improvement in literacy.

Although the national government began to make a contribution to schooling in the 1830s, for many years voluntary provision remained more important. Charity schools proliferated in the late eighteenth century and even more in the early nineteenth century. Many parochial schools were either founded or expanded in these years. In the Newcastle parish of St Nicholas in the early 1820s, the church school educated 400 boys and 150 girls. Fees were 1*d.* per week, the school making ends meet by subscriptions and donations. The monitorial system, regarded as an efficient teaching system at that time, was widely adopted. George III's Jubilee in 1810 was marked by his well-publicized wish that every child in his dominions should be enabled to read the Bible, and produced a new flurry of school foundations. By the late 1820s Newcastle Jubilee Schools provided free education for nearly 500 boys and more than 200 girls. Such free provision worried a Newcastle radical, who feared that it

> must tend to blunt the delicate pride of both parents and children, to familiarize the mind to dependence on charitable institutions, and to prepare it for the degradation of pauperism. The demanding of a small weekly sum from the parents is evidently gratifying to their feelings. (Mackenzie 1827, 415–60)

In the early nineteenth century Eneas Mackenzie wrote histories of Durham, Newcastle and Northumberland; in all three there is much evidence for recently founded schools. (Mackenzie 1811; Mackenzie 1827, 415–60; Mackenzie and Ross 1834) The spread of literacy owed something to border pacification. (Houston 1982, 239–51)

The Relief of Poverty

Philanthropy involved much more time, money and energy than the official poor law. (Rushton 1989, 144) It was strongly influenced by religious feeling.

Growing evangelical fervour was a factor in the expansion of provision for the health, comfort and education of the poor. Fear of disaffection was another, and the two often coincided. The Rev. William Carus Wilson, rector of Whittington (model for Mr Brocklehurst in Charlotte Brontë's *Jane Eyre*), inveighed against the 1834 Poor Law Amendment Act because it tended to supplant and subvert proper feelings of Christian duty:

> we have it upon Divine Authority that the poor shall never cease out of the land, and if they, on whose sympathy and succour they are naturally thrown, are found wanting in their duty – if they fail to secure the blessing of those who are ready to perish – the day is fast approaching when they will bitterly repent their unfaithful stewardship. (Carus Wilson 1838)

This concept of stewardship could be strained as local communities became diluted with immigrants. Certain groups were seen as unconnected with local communal responsibility. This was often true of the Irish, but included other groups regarded as outsiders such as the gypsies who grazed their horses on Natland Common and were locally seen by Carus Wilson, perhaps with some justice, as 'a most lawless people' and therefore not deserving. (Searle 1983, 353) For the most part there were extensive reservoirs of sympathy and charity within the northern counties in these years.

The regional capital, Newcastle, was in the forefront of northern charitable activity. The Infirmary resulted from the initiative of a group of prominent local men in 1751 and provided hospital treatment for sick poor of the town. Its first buildings, opened in 1753 on land donated by the town council, cost £3,697. Staffed by eminent local doctors on a voluntary basis, the Infirmary, like many other charities, was governed by its subscribers, who enjoyed the right to nominate patients. Among the Infirmary's first presidents were the earl of Northumberland, Sir George Bowes and Sir Walter Blackett. The Infirmary's architect, Daniel Garrett, had already carried out work at country houses for all three. The Newcastle Dispensary, founded in 1777 on a similar basis, provided poor citizens with free medicines and treatment for minor afflictions. (Miller 1986; Mills 1991; Miller 1990) In 1761 Newcastle acquired a Charity for the Relief of Poor Women Lying-in at Their Own Homes. This employed twelve midwives to attend births where parents would have been unable to pay. If necessary the society paid for attendance of a doctor. Money was given for four weeks to meet incidental expenses. The charity was financed by donations and regular subscriptions, collections in churches, legacies, and an annual charity ball. (Halcrow 1956, 110–12) From 1803, another charitable organization provided a small maternity hospital for difficult births. At Carlisle, the voluntary Infirmary was rebuilt in 1841 at a cost of £6,000. The Dispensary, founded in 1782, received new premises in 1858 which cost £700. As public utilities expanded, it was

To the MEMORY of

M! JOSEPH SAINT.

Late TREASURER of the INFIRMARY

at NEWCASTLE upon TYNE:

This View of that Edifice, which he had ordered to be taken

& engraved at his Expence, is most respectfully inscribed

Figure 8.2 Newcastle Infirmary, 1789. The hospital, founded by voluntary effort in 1751, on the model of a slightly earlier foundation at Northampton, was later extended on several occasions. With a later change of site, the Infirmary developed into the Royal Victoria Infirmary, still one of the north's foremost medical institutions.

normal for gas and water companies to provide free supplies to charitable enterprises.

Smaller places imitated such edifying examples. At Bamburgh, Lord Crewe's trustees, in addition to providing schools for 60 boys and 60 girls whose parents had yearly incomes of less than £60, established a dispensary which gave free medicines to the poor. Local people were given free small-pox inoculations when that technique became available. Midwives were provided for local expectant mothers. A suitable boat and a system of coast-watching were established to try to save wrecked seamen or fishermen. In times of scarcity, cheap food was distributed to poor people within a 40-mile radius. Twice a year a fat ox was killed and meat distributed to the poor. The trustees made grants to individuals with specific needs, sometimes to enable applicants to earn their living by providing such items as milling equipment or a heavy mangle. (Stranks 1978, 142–6)

Individual gifts to meet particular needs were common, the creation of permanent institutions like hospitals and dispensaries was spreading, while

169

influential opinion responded to emergencies, such as bad harvests, ship-wrecks or colliery accidents, by subscriptions to help victims.

The Poor Law

The extent to which northern society comprised small locally orientated communities was reflected in the most pervasive form of local government, the poor law. This was administered on a parish or township basis, domin-ated by men of local influence. Poor-law overseers and churchwardens, often unpaid, levied the poor rate according to local valuations of property. These assessments varied and were often out of date and unrealistic: assessments in Westmorland were only revised once between 1600 and 1800, in 1692. Despite this, an Act of 1730, allowing county magistrates to levy a single rate to meet county expenses, including building and maintaining bridges and prisons, ordered that this should be based on poor-rate assessments.

Poor-relief expedients varied according to local opinions and circum-stances, often with little or no regard for relevant legislation. At Darlington, the old manor house of the bishop had become a workhouse by 1703; much of the old building was destroyed in an 1806 reconstruction. In the late seven-teenth century, Hexham employed paupers in cleaning streets. At Eglingham in the 1650s, poor people were issued with licences to beg throughout the community, supplementing small basic payments of 3*d.* or 4*d.* per week. There is much evidence of kindliness towards respectable poor people by their own communities, although often more relief came from charities than from the poor law. At Elsdon in 1717 there were seven paupers, but local charities made payments to 37 people, including six of the seven paupers. By 1700 it was normal for parishes or townships to give regular payments to paupers, and from about 1720 common for medical attention for the poor to be bought in. As population grew, institutional care expanded. New poor houses were built at Sunderland in 1740, Morpeth 1750, Berwick 1758, Corbridge 1767, Houghton-le-Spring 1775, Stockton 1779. At Berwick the 1758 regu-lations provided for strict administration: the able-bodied would only be relieved inside the poor house, and outdoor relief was to be confined to invalids and sudden adversity. (Rushton 1989; Malden 1991, 113)

Communal attitudes to poor people from elsewhere were frequently hostile. Hexham in the 1630s, Corbridge in 1716 and Morpeth in 1752 issued regulations against admission to the community of poor people who might become chargeable to the poor rates. An anonymous pamphlet of 1755 at Newcastle attacking such 'foreign' paupers followed at least 150 years of similar anger. (Rushton 1989, 140–1)

170

By the early nineteenth century, the poor law in the northern counties did not face the problems presented by rural poverty further south. Although the 1834 Poor Law Amendment Act imposed a pattern on England and Wales, the situation in the North, by contemporary standards, scarcely warranted such intervention. Interference was disliked by communities who believed that they could administer their own poor relief more competently than officials in London. Before 1834, there was no uniformity of poor-law practice in the North, but it was claimed that local conventions reflected particular needs and conditions.

The poor law was controlled by those who paid rates which financed it. This local control and intimacy were pervasive. Ratepayers often knew people to whom poor relief was given. Hard times increased numbers asking for relief while impairing the resources of poorer ratepayers. In such circumstances ratepayer revolts occurred, especially after increases in poor rates in the late eighteenth and early nineteenth centuries. Some of the worst problems were encountered within towns. In the 1790s Sir Frederick Eden observed that citizens of Carlisle, faced with large-scale Irish and Scots immigration, prided themselves 'in their courage and resolution' to preserve their funds for their own native poor. (Thompson 1976, 40)

At Gateshead, spending rose from £568 in 1780 to £4,500 in 1820. In April 1820 a parish vestry meeting resolved that 'on account of the enormous increase of the expenditure of the Parish it is highly expedient that a system of strict economy be appointed ... and particularly in the relief of the poor'. New rules for relief were devised, and expenditure in 1822 dropped to £3,040, 'partly owing to the strict investigation ... which, while it does not prevent those from applying who are really objects of parochial aid, prevents applications from the idle and profligate, whose wants principally arise from their own indolence and improvident habits'. A similar movement at Sunderland brought about publication of lists of applicants for poor relief,

> with the object of awakening a decent and becoming pride, to stimulate industry, to create disposition to economy as regards the future, in opposition to a *lazy and despicable habit* – that of existing on the industry of more provident neighbours ... undistinguishing benevolence offers a premium to indolence, prodigality and vice.

Ratepayers were invited to scrutinize the lists and 'to send them the names of any paupers having means not divulged, but they need not sign their own names'. (McCord 1979, 89–90)

At Kendal and Penrith feelings were similar but the expedient adopted different. There were prolonged attempts to reduce burdens on ratepayers by making profitable use of pauper labour in local workhouses. In north-east Cumbria, parishes invited tenders from private contractors for care of local paupers. (Thompson 1976, 22–33; Thompson 1979, 115–37)

The coming of the 'New Poor Law' after the Poor Law Amendment Act of 1834, at first made little difference to poor-law administration within the region. Financing still depended on local rates and new Poor Law Unions were supervised by the same people who had dominated the parochial system of earlier years. The new Poor Law Commission had little effective power with which to coerce local Boards of Guardians, whose services were crucial to the system's functioning.

This local autonomy was reflected in the ways in which salaried officials were appointed. The ability to manipulate appointments was an outward sign of local power, and often patronage rather than policies provided the politics of Poor Law Unions. Records provide many instances of unsatisfactory officials, some of whom were detected and removed after implementation of the 1834 Act. During the twenty years from 1836, in 11 Poor Law Unions in Cumbria, 22 relieving officers left office in respectable circumstances such as honourable retirement or ill-health; 19 were dismissed or forced to resign for misconduct, mostly in the form of embezzlement of public money drawn from local ratepayers' pockets. Unsatisfactory officials existed not only among lowly officials like relieving officers, but included for instance the first Clerk to the Houghton-le-Spring Poor Law Union, who was so drunk at a Board of Guardians meeting in 1851 that the minutes are a series of doodles and the meeting had to be adjourned. Joseph Brunskill was appointed collector of poor rates in the Whitehaven Union in 1839 despite illiteracy and the consequent need for him to have a deputy. He enjoyed support among local guardians, and this overcame misgivings of the central Poor Law Commission and its regional officer, Sir John Walsham, despite the latter's initial declaration that if the appointment was confirmed 'we would have to eat dirt for the rest of our official careers'. The Poor Law Commission was concerned in 1844 at the behaviour of John Lancaster, Master of the Carlisle Workhouse, 'wandering about in a state of drunkenness in the middle of the night so as to be robbed in a public highway by a prostitute'. (Thompson 1976, 237–40, 476–8)

In the years after 1834, there was a rash of scandals involving peculation among poor-law officials. Since many of these had served under the old poor law, this probably represents belated detection of long-standing abuses. In 1851, a Newcastle poor-law officer, John Scott, left the town ostensibly on a visit to the Great Exhibition; it transpired that he had fled abroad after appropriating £3,000 of public money. (Mawson 1971, 128) There were many similar examples. The overall tendency was towards higher standards of appointment and performance, with professional officers assuming responsibilities which before 1834 had been much more haphazardly distributed and exercised. (McCord 1969; Mawson 1971; Barker 1974; Dunkley 1974; Cadman 1976; Thompson 1976; Wood 1976; Thompson 1979; Manders 1980)

Chapter 9

The Agricultural Economy

The end of border warfare brought acceleration of change in farming, as economic development during the seventeenth and eighteenth centuries saw older patterns of agriculture, with emphasis on subsistence, transformed by more commercial priorities. Transition of clan leaders into respectable gentry was paralleled by transformation of followers into respectable farming folk. Older communal conventions, which had determined and regulated farming practices and the nature of local communities, were increasingly swept aside. Agriculture was reorganized into a new pattern of unitary farms, reflecting more commercialism and individualism in rural life. Change occurred at varying rates in different districts. In general, the North East, with its larger urban population and more developed patterns of trade, was more readily transformed. Even in the eighteenth century, more isolated areas, especially in Cumbria, remained tied to an essentially medieval pattern. In the late eighteenth century, the manorial court at Croglin in east Cumberland could still fine a tenant for the innovation of growing winter wheat in the common field 'contrary to ancient custom'. Such customary restrictions hindered efforts of landowners and tenants to increase farming profitability. (Dilley 1972, 60)

Tenurial Change and Agricultural Reform

Even before 1603 new commercial priorities were evident in efforts of northern landowners to increase rent income. Existing tenurial patterns reflected the desire of local leaders to ensure a supply of fighting men. Obligations involved in border defence were recognized in the system of border tenant right which established tenures characterized by low rents and rights of inheritance in return for military service. In order to buttress border security,

173

the Crown had defended these arrangements in dangerous years, criticizing attempts by landlords to raise income by tightening tenurial conditions. After 1603, conditions had changed and a group of Cumberland gentry told James I in 1604 that they wanted 'to be at lybertye to use our Landes to our most profytt and Comoditie as others in other parties of England being of the like Case do'.

The Crown responded by spearheading from 1609 attacks on tenurial privileges by landowners. It was often difficult for tenants to produce documentary evidence for claims, and in some cases judges held that they were merely tenants at will, while in others customary estates of inheritance were recognized. Prince Charles, the future Charles I, brought a test case against tenants in his barony of Kendal in 1618–19. His lawyers argued that the end of border military obligations invalidated privileged tenure associated with that duty. An eventual compromise, confirmed by the Court of Star Chamber in 1625, allowed the tenants to keep their privileges but imposed heavy payment for this indulgence. Border tenant right generally was declared invalid by a royal proclamation of July 1620, but this still left room for claims that tenants' privileges were common-law rights, enshrined in individual manorial custom. In the North East, landlords succeeded more widely in eliminating tenant right, even in such areas as Wark and Harbottle where it had been strongly established. (Appleby 1975; Watts 1975; Spence 1977, 91–4, 129–52; Spence 1984, 64–87; Watt 1971)

Transformation of tenurial arrangements was less successful in Cumbria. Its achievement depended on the landlord's determination to enforce change rather than be satisfied with increased income within existing landholding patterns. Amongst more determined landowners was Lady Anne Clifford, who inaugurated a review of tenancies when she succeeded to the Clifford inheritance. Within three years, rental from the Skipton and Westmorland estates rose from £600 to £1,050. Law cases between 1650 and 1657 saw this great northern lady eject unsatisfactory tenants and replace them with occupants willing to pay good rents for 21-year leases. (Spence 1979, 47–59) From 1606 the ninth earl of Northumberland enforced leasehold or tenant-at-will tenure whenever a holding fell vacant. Between 1613 and 1630, Lord Howard de Walden replaced tenant right on his border holdings by tenant-at-will status. Such victories were easier where relationships between landowner and tenant had not been fixed by customary conventions.

Most Cumbrian landowners were less successful and some of them more half-hearted than their north-eastern brethren in attempting to undermine customary arrangements. In 1723, the duke of Somerset extracted higher income from his Cockermouth estates, taking advantage of rising prosperity due to commercial and industrial development in west Cumberland, but he did so by increasing entry fines within customary tenurial arrangements. When Lord William Howard attempted radical change on his Cumbrian estate, he allowed himself to be bought off by similar higher payments on changes in occupancy. A campaign in the later seventeenth century by the earl of Northumberland to replace customary tenures of Cumbrian tenants with leasehold arrangements at higher rents, probably copying Northumberland precedents, produced little change. As late as 1797 'formidable combativity' at law in defence of customary arrangements was expressed by the tenants of Soulby and Great Musgrave, 'determined to spend all their estates at Law' rather than acquiesce in destruction of conventional tenures. (Appleby 1975, 575; Searle 1983, 43–7, 101, 108; Gregson 1984, 183)

Such conflicts were no mere legal abstractions, but preserved such features as common fields and manorial regulation in the North West. There was no equivalent to the widespread early introduction of leasehold as in the North East. Leasehold was associated with agricultural progress. It gave landlords more control and greater incentives to invest, while tenants received inducements to work the land efficiently. It implied destruction of common fields and customary practices which often stifled initiative on the part of landlords and tenants. A good example is provided by the Northumberland village of West Whelpington, which was transformed in the late seventeenth century from a communally farmed settlement with inhabitants living in medieval cottage terraces into farming based on unitary leasehold farms. In County Durham, Cowpen Bewley provided another example of such changes. (Evans 1988, 147–9, 177)

Despite variations within the region, there were changes in patterns of land use. Areas previously subjected to forest law, which prohibited dogs and fences high enough to impede deer, were assimilated into normal arrangements during the seventeenth century. Inglewood Forest was freed from forest law and enclosed, with disappearance of many old conventions. In Northumberland, much of the old Rothbury Forest was enclosed by agreement among local landowners and occupiers. (Drury 1976, 140; Drury 1978, 89)

In upland areas, including old forest land, landlords were more readily able to impose their will. A survey of 1604 saw upland pastures at Silloans in Northumberland held in common by members of the Potts and Hedley families, but by the eighteenth century these areas were reorganized as unitary farms with undivided fields. (Charlton and Day 1980, 217) By the end of the eighteenth century, hill farming had changed, with development of upland farms. The duke of Northumberland owned a dozen of these farms in the North Tyne valley, totalling nearly 50,000 acres.

It was, however, on the basis of lowland farming and increased arable cultivation that the North East acquired a reputation for progressive agriculture by the mid-eighteenth century. The Milfield plain and Tweed valley in north Northumberland, and the Tees valley to the south, as well as much of the coastal plain, saw 'better management, better manuring, and better strains of forage crops' which 'significantly increased the productive potential of much land in the North East'. Even here progress remained patchy, and in 1851 *The Times* noted with surprise that in Northumberland a great portion of the county, extending from near Newcastle on both sides of the railway as far as Warkworth, is as little drained and as badly farmed as any district we have yet seen in England, and that the occupiers of the small farms can only eke out a scanty subsistence by careful parsimony, and by employing no labour except that of themselves and their families. (Rowe 1972, xxii)

Despite such reservations, during the eighteenth century the North East came to be regarded as a centre of improved farming, at a time when 'progressive agriculture (was) hard to find' in Cumbria. (Thirsk 1984, 8, 54) What little there was in the North West was limited to land directly farmed by landlords, or to the relatively small leasehold sector, the latter often taken from the lord's demesne or from areas recently brought under landowners' direct control. Even in the late eighteenth century, two-thirds of all farmers in Cumberland held by customary tenures, often with scattered holdings of less than 50 acres. (Beckett 1983, 97; Gregson 1984, 201; Duxbury 1994; Bailey and Culley 1794, 178)

Markets and Agricultural Change

The North exhibited diversity in climate, soils, and contrasts between lowland and upland districts. Climate imposed a pastoral emphasis in the wetter North West and uplands generally, with arable cultivation concentrated in lowlands, especially in the drier North East. Even in Northumberland and Durham, there were wide areas where farming concentrated on stock management, and here for many years indifference to improved techniques was as marked as it was in Cumbria. There were only patches of arable farming in the wetter and colder uplands, usually concentrated in valley bottoms with their alluvial soils. Wide areas of moorland in west Durham possessed only small plots of arable. In extensive but sparsely populated parishes like Edmundbyers and Muggleswick, with only 219 and 183 inhabitants respectively according to a mid-seventeenth century estimate, cultivation, as in many Cumbrian upland areas, was for subsistence and was almost invariably confined to oats. (Brassley 1985; Gard and Shrimpton 1972; Hodgson 1978; Kirby 1972; Thirsk 1984, 30–58)

In other areas, increased population, together with the growing importance of coal-mining and the coastal trade of the North East, had profound significance for farming development. The northern region produced most of its own food. There was a small import trade, which could expand rapidly in times of shortages, as in the dearth year of 1728. Normally, imports provided only a small proportion of food consumption, so that urbanization, and an increase in population not directly involved in agriculture, offered farmers a growing market which provided the biggest stimulus to improved techniques. There were changes in cultivation, and some farmers adjusted stock-keeping to market opportunities, with profitable dairy farming around Newcastle. Maritime connections offered markets for victualling shipping, as did wartime contracts for provisioning the armed forces. In eighteenth-century Durham, some farmers flourished by growing mustard on a considerable scale, responding to a growing demand which was far from merely local. (Bewick 1975, 7; Durham Victoria 2, 365) Berwick, Alnmouth and Stockton benefited in the eighteenth century by supplying food to London, including cheese, butter and eggs, as well as various cereals. In 1816 Berwick sent nearly 5,000 chests of eggs to the capital, valued at around £30,000. (Parson and White, *Northumberland*, 1828, II, 374; Barrow 1995) Throughout the eighteenth century, the North East was able to export food to other British regions. These market opportunities, both local and further afield, encouraged improved productivity, sustained by such means as increased use of lime, manure and improved strains of plants and animals, as well as reorganization of farming communities by enclosures or similar changes.

Cumbria was isolated from wider markets, except for stock which could be driven to market over long distances. In the seventeenth and eighteenth centuries, there was no equivalent urban and industrial development which might have induced Cumbrian farmers to imitate their North East brethren. The most advanced area of Cumbrian farming during the eighteenth century was probably near Whitehaven, which by 1762 had a population of around 9,000 to feed. (Searle 1983, 297) Elsewhere restrictions placed on arable farming by limited markets were stamped on the landscape, with patches of relative sophistication near the small towns. In the late seventeenth century, Celia Fiennes noted on leaving Kendal 'very good land enclosed . . . flourishing with corn and grass, green and fresh'. She soon encountered only 'sad entertainment . . . clap bread, butter and cheese . . . all one can have here . . . they are eight miles from a market town and their miles are tedious to go both from the illness of the way and the length of miles'. A similar pattern of improved agriculture near towns was noted by Arthur Young in 1771. (Dilley 1972, 100–2, 202–3; Morris 1947, 190, 196–7; Pringle 1794, 182; Hutchinson 1794, 76)

By the late eighteenth century, it was fashionable for enthusiasts for agricultural progress to castigate small farmers in Cumbria for lack of 'improvement', and for seeming 'to inherit with the estates of their ancestors their notions of cultivating them'. (Hutchinson 1794, 76; Pringle 1794, 182) Arable practice often involved over-cropping small patches to provide a family supply. This largely subsistence cultivation frequently existed within common fields divided into individual strips. Static local demand created no incentive to increase crops, or adopt new methods which might include recommended rotations, using clover or turnips, or the expensive drainage of wet land, which many small farmers could not afford. One crop change which did make sense was increasing reliance on potatoes, which easily slotted into a pattern of arable subsistence farming. (Hutchinson 1778, 258; Bouch 1948, 226, 340; Marshall 1980, 510, 514; Bailey and Culley 1794, 186)

It was not until the end of the eighteenth century that high wartime food prices, and some increase in demand stimulated by the expanding textile industry of northern Cumbria, saw Cumbrian farming moved on to a more commercial basis. By 1811, Cumberland had about 40 per cent of its population in towns, even if the criterion of 1,000 inhabitants was a modest one. This stimulated farming and was part of a transformation achieved within a generation.

Many village fields were enclosed, as were large areas of common land. The adoption of improved methods encouraged wider arable acreage, with improved performance which during the Napoleonic War moved Cumbria from a grain importer to an exporter. (Searle 1983, 292) Westmorland's farmers, cut off from the sea and without the stimulus of population growth, lagged behind until construction of the canal from Lancaster to Kendal in 1819 established a link with the wider market of Lancashire's textile towns.

Even before the late eighteenth century, there were commercial elements in Cumbrian agriculture, especially in the breeding, rearing and fattening of cattle, 'the surest source of income in the region'. (Thirsk 1984, 12) Even a poor moorland area, such as Bewcastle Fells, had inhabitants who combined indifference to arable farming with awareness that cattle had commercial value. (Hutchinson 1794, 76) From the seventeenth century a growing trade in buying, selling and fattening cattle was embraced by gentry families and percolated down the social scale to small farmers. (Beckett 1982, 47; Marshall 1980, 512–13) Irish cattle were shipped into west Cumberland ports, and Scottish black cattle came over the border and down the Eden valley on the way to southern markets. Price fluctuations gave a speculative dimension to the trade. (Phillips 1973, 145–55) In 1662–63, 18,364 Scots cattle passed through Carlisle along a major drove route; by the mid-eighteenth century an estimated 80,000 passed down the Eden valley annually. The scale of the trade stretched available grazing, which was often under manorial regulation, and such pressures, backed by interested gentry and tenant farmers, hastened moves towards enclosure and unitary farms. As early as 1641, the manorial court of Aglionby, close to Carlisle and major drove routes, was defending its common grazing, stipulating 'that no tenants or inhabitants . . . shall take the beasts of any forreigners to be grazed within the same'. Attempts at regulation proved increasingly ineffective during the eighteenth century as individual farmers evaded restrictions on profits. (Thirsk 1984, 13; Searle 1983, 159; Dilley 1972, 99)

The cattle trade's expansion increased a commercial ethos within Northumberland uplands, where lines etched on the landscape by droving routes can still be seen. Farming and probate inventories often showed cattle as the most important livestock item, especially among upland farmers. They also show that small farmers were involved in the money economy, with mention of savings, mortgages, bonds and debts. Even among upland farmers of Cumbria, there was a slow increase in wealth during the eighteenth century, attributable in part to domestic-based textile industry in the Lake District and Pennine dales, but also reflecting growth in the cattle trade. The 'Great Re-building' on Cumbrian farms in the late seventeenth and early eighteenth centuries indicated rising living standards, although it also represented investment in buildings for over-wintering cattle. Thriving cattle markets developed along the main drove routes, as at Carlisle, Alston, Penrith, Kirkby Lonsdale, Brough and Cockermouth. (Beckett 1982, 47; Thirsk 1984, 12–13; Marshall 1980, 512–13; Marshall 1973)

The Enclosure Movement

Conversion of farming communities from communally worked and regulated settlements into a system based on enclosed individual farms was crucial. A much-quoted estimate was that one acre of enclosed land might produce as much as two acres in dispersed strips within common fields. Enclosure frequently came in stages: after village fields had been enclosed, common grazing might follow, as at Elsdon in Northumberland in 1729, with improving landowners often taking the lead. (Tate 1042, 39–51, 119–40) The general practice was for the Lord of the Manor to compensate commoners for loss of rights by offering shares of the land affected. In 1743 a Cumberland squire was said to be 'dividing his commons which will be a great improvement to his estate' in this way. (Charlton and Day 1979, 215; Beckett 1983, 97) Enclosure was achieved earlier in the North East than in Cumbria. Only about 14 per cent of improvable land, some from village fields and some from common grazing, had been enclosed in Cumberland by 1793. A transformation then followed, with 56 per cent of improvable land enclosed during the war years 1793–1815. In Cumberland, 48 out of the 91 enclosure Acts between 1760 and 1840 came in years of high prices in the first two decades of the nineteenth century. Westmorland saw 29 out of 47 Acts in the same years. (Searle 1983, 291)

Before regular resort to statutory enclosure, changes were procured by agreement between interested parties, with a varying degree of voluntary participation. In Northumberland, there were at least 25 enclosures by agreement in the 1640–99 period, followed by a further 30 before 1750. Examples included Newbrough Ingrounds in 1675, Shilbottle in 1684 and Beadnell in

1701. (Thirsk 1984, 47–9; Tate 1942; Ridley 1974, 213–15; Charlton and Day 1979, 215–17; Austin 1976, 79)

In areas distant from the border, enclosure in the North East began early. Most fields in the Darlington district were enclosed before the mid-seventeenth century, and later enclosure records refer to common pasture. The village of Whessoe disappeared in the course of these changes, and its common fields were replaced by separate farms with fields almost identical with the modern layout. (Sunderland 1967, 16–17) On the land of the Dean and Chapter of Durham, the 1,300-acre Bearpark estate developed during the hundred years up to 1660 into twelve farms worked by rent-paying tenants. In 1726, a writer noted that in lowland Durham 'nine parts in ten are already enclosed, and consequently improved in rents and value to a degree almost incredible'. Enclosure of open fields or common pasture provided opportunity for improved farming techniques, but the scale of the task, and disparities in local conditions, meant that progress was piecemeal and often slow. Even in the eighteenth century, there was work to be done in enclosing common cultivated fields in Northumberland, as at West Whelpington in the late seventeenth and early eighteenth centuries, Kirkwhelpington in 1717–20, Kirkharle in 1724, and Great Bavington soon after 1769. (Tate 1942)

Progress in Cumbria was slower, influenced not only by market conditions but also by persistence of customary tenures. Where there was no demand for greater arable acreages, pressures for enclosure were unlikely to succeed.

Many landowners wanted to rid themselves of customary tenants, who were often troublesome and paid small rents, and appreciated possible increases in income from enclosure. In 1737, the earl of Carlisle offered tenants in Gilsland a chance to convert tenancies into freehold at a price, but the offer was refused. A piecemeal campaign after 1750, proceeding manor by manor, was more successful. Between 1775 and 1790, 100 tenants on this estate accepted these offers, indicating convergence between the interests of the earl and more ambitious tenants. As late as the 1830s Lord Carlisle still had customary tenants in Cumberland, while in remote Westmorland some survived until after 1871. At the other end of Cumberland, earls of Egremont pursued similar tactics, with offers of enfranchisement of holdings going in parallel with enclosure of common grazing land. (Searle 1983, 131–40) Such offers sometimes came when a landowner needed money, but also reflected a lord's willingness to share common land with tenants as a means of facilitating enclosure. The processes of enfranchisement and enclosure precipitated Cumbrian agriculture into a pattern of unitary farms, ending tenurial forms which had endured for centuries. Most of these changes came late, and were compressed into little more than a single generation, a more dramatic change than that experienced in the North East.

While enclosure of common land by agreement was frequent, in cases of dispute or legal complexity local interests resorted to the expensive path of statutory enclosure. During the eighteenth century, agricultural improvement was facilitated by the aristocracy and gentry in Parliament exploiting their power to expedite local changes. Often even statutory enclosures enjoyed a large measure of local consent.

At the middle of the eighteenth century, there were still about 8,000 acres in the unenclosed East and West Commons of Hexham. This was largely open moorland, for common lands closer to the town had over the centuries been encroached on by illegal squatting or formal grants. In 1753, certain freeholders and copyholders of Hexham petitioned Parliament for power to enclose remaining common land. The House of Commons obligingly referred the petition to a committee of local MPs – Allgood, Burrell, Blackett and Ridley, all Northumberland landowners. There was one local opponent of the scheme, but most interested parties agreed to enclosure, and the necessary Act was law less than three months after the original petition. The commissioners for carrying out its provisions were all local men.

Extension of enclosure in the early nineteenth century reflected growing weakness in older institutions or conventions which had controlled land use. At Lyth in Westmorland, the ineffectiveness of manorial regulations against over-grazing was revealed in a late eighteenth-century description:

> When you cast your eyes upon it, it seemed alive with sheep, cows, sterks and calves; horses of all sizes and ages, stags and ponies. Geese were also very numerous being taken down to this marshy pasturage in May and June from all parts of the township . . . not to grow fat, I think . . . for there never was a pasturage so bare, so closely shaved, so incessantly nibbled at as this. (Searle 1983, 164)

Where management systems failed, commoners were more likely to support enclosure.

Whilst not a principal motive for enclosure, fencing and hedging fields allowed improved and healthier animals through selective breeding, and reduced danger from diseases which had affected animals and humans more extensively before 1750. High mortality and economic loss due to animal diseases such as anthrax, tuberculosis and brucellosis declined as a largely unplanned dividend of enclosure. (Butlin 1967, 160; Hodson 1979, 93, 100)

Landlords and Estate Improvement

That the landowners of the North, including aristocracy and gentry, were beneficiaries of improved farming is almost sufficient to explain their leading role. Farming did not stand alone as a source of augmented income for landed estates, but for many landowners it offered the greatest potential. A good example was offered by the Northumberland coastal village of Beadnell, enclosed in 1701 by agreement under the aegis of Ferdinando Foster, Lord of the Manor of Bamburgh. His murder in Newcastle ten days later enabled his brother-in-law Lord Crewe to buy the almost bankrupt Foster estate and inaugurate a campaign of investment and improvement. Local landowners, including the Percy family, promoted estate improvement, involving inter-locking enterprises including commercial fishing, lime kilns, salt-pans and harbour works. Farm leases imposed on tenants the duty of applying pre-scribed quantities of lime. Nearby, the Craster estate received additional income from seaweed burned on the rocks south of Craster village to pro-vide ash sold to the textile industry. (Craster 1952, 24; Craster 1956, 165–70; Edwards 1985, 12; Hodson 1979, 91–2; Charlton and Day 1982, 149–53)

Timber provided additional income, as industrial growth and increased building expanded markets. On the Lawson estate in Cumbria, an estimate of 1718 valued timber at £16,000, and other estates were richer in this respect. By the mid-nineteenth century, shooting and fishing rights were becoming sources of estate revenue.

Various mineral resources – quarrying, coal, lead, copper and iron ore – were exploited by landowners. Those who worked them directly found that profits, though volatile, could be useful. A colliery operated by the earl of Carlisle near Brampton produced over £100 p.a. in the 1730s, over £900 in the 1750s. Such revenues were dwarfed by the £9,000 obtained by the Lowthers from collieries, double their agricultural rent roll. It was scarcely surprising that the Lowthers gave low priority to farming. Their near neigh-bour and rival at Workington, John Christian Curwen, whose fortune also rested heavily on the coal trade, maintained a belief in the primacy of agriculture, 'the English oak', whereas commerce was 'merely the ivy which twined around it'. (Beckett 1983, 102–6; Hughes 1965, 282)

Few landowners would have dissented from Curwen's view, and most estate owners looked to improved farming to increase incomes. In some cases, this option might not be readily available. During the seventeenth century, scope for effective development of farming in Cumbrian uplands was limited, and Sir Daniel Fleming of Rydal recommended to his son direct farming of demesne lands to defray living expenses: 'Live not in the country without Corn and Cattel about thee, for he that must put his hand in his pocket for every expense of household is like him that keeps water in a sieve.' (Phillips 1973, 145) The income which many of Cumbria's lesser gentry drew from their estates was lower than that needed to support gentry status elsewhere, so Fleming's emphasis on subsistence and parsimony was sensible. Even in the North East, where prospects from improvement were more realistic, there remained old-fashioned landed families who were loath to depart from traditional practices, preferring to indulge established farming families. The Herons of Chipchase were among these conservatives, but accumulated debts which brought them to disaster. Much of their property passed to the more innovative Allgood family, who set about efficient estate management. Customary tenancies gave way to leaseholds, with amalgamation of holdings into larger units. This policy involved risks. Improvement implied investment in hedging, fencing and drainage and a variety of other expenses. By the middle of the eighteenth century, the Allgood squires of Nunwick were spending half their rental on servicing mortgages, despite rent increases between 1705 and 1751. (Thirsk 1984, 49–50)

Such uncertainty might explain indifference to agricultural reform on the duke of Northumberland's estates, the most extensive in the region but not prominent in improved farming until the mid-nineteenth century. Other northern aristocrats were more positive improvers. The earls of Carlisle in east Cumberland and Northumberland were conspicuous here, experimenting with turnip and clover as forage crops before 1750 and, perhaps more significantly, trying for improved strains of stock. (Thirsk 1984, 22) Such innovations were not widely imitated at first in Cumbria, except by a few like-minded landowners. Most improvements in stock breeding did not occur until late in the eighteenth century, with improving landlords in the lead. John Christian Curwen was credited with introducing into Cumbria the Shorthorn and Durham breeds of cattle; by the middle of the nineteenth century, these breeds, together with Galloways, had largely replaced the old Longhorn strains. The earl of Egremont sponsored new breeds of sheep, replacing older native types, although the hardy Herdwick survived in upland locations. Eventually, Leicesters proved most popular. Largely because of landlord initiatives, by the mid-nineteenth century Cumbria was recognized as an important stock-breeding region. (Dickinson 1852; Searle 1983, 296–8)

A shift to leasehold tenancies was an effective means of spreading improvement and, as we have seen, the process went further in the North East than in Cumbria (see pp. 172–3 above). From the 1730s the earl of Carlisle used leaseholds on his Naworth estate to impose improved methods. Leasehold spread to other areas of his estates, so that by 1828 half of his Gilsland property was held in this way. The result for the landlord was a rise in rentals from 1s. 4d. per acre in 1770 to 6s. 4d. in 1832. (Gregson 1984, 184; Searle 1983, 300–1)

Influence could also be exercised indirectly. From the late eighteenth century, under patronage of leading landowners, agricultural societies were formed to promote discussion and spread information about profitable innovations among farmers. Agricultural shows, with competitive prizes, also promoted improvement. (Beckett 1983, 101; Durham Victoria 2, 380; Macdonald 1974)

Extension of leasehold in Cumbria, and with it improved farming, was aided by the fact that aristocracy and gentry were buying more land in the latter part of this period, with purchases let as leasehold farms. The largest

Figure 9.1 Wynyard Park, the mansion built in 1820s for the third Marquess of Londonderry on the basis of an abortive design by Benjamin Wyatt for a palace for the Duke of Wellington. It was financed by income from landowning in Britain and Ireland, coal-mining and commerce.

investor was the Lowther family, whose access to mineral wealth encouraged purchases around Whitehaven to secure mineral rights and extend political and social pre-eminence. The earl of Thanet was the second biggest purchaser, building up an estate centred on Appleby, much of it, as with other buyers, from recently created small freehold farms which had replaced earlier customary holdings. (Beckett 1975, 147–50; Searle 1983, 164–223)

Landowners had access to expertise and capital not available to smaller landowners or remaining customary tenants. In the early nineteenth century, despite earlier improvements, Sir James Graham inherited at Netherby an estate 'overburdened with an excessive population; a great portion of it remained unenclosed . . . while one quarter of the estate was completely saturated with water, and a great mass of moss and cold pasture land'. Graham was influenced by John Christian Curwen in embarking on a reform campaign which illustrated the uncertain rewards of such ventures. The estate manufactured drainage tiles, and enforced crop rotations and other desirable practices through leasehold provisions. The number of tenants dropped from 300 in 1823 to only 140 in 1851, with the average size of farms

184

increasing from 40–100 to 100–500 acres. The programme involved heavy investment, and although Graham was able to borrow at favourable interest he was ultimately uncertain as to the overall benefit. An investment of £100,000 between 1815 and 1825 saw rentals increase to £21,638 in 1845, but Graham found the work troublesome and rewards disappointing; more than once he contemplated selling the estate. (Spring 1955; Ward 1967, 61–2; Dickinson 1852, 222) Lower grain prices after 1815, and further agricultural depression in the 1820s (as well as a pessimistic disposition), help to explain Graham's gloom, but the continued programme of change indicated willingness to overcome temporary difficulties and setbacks. Such persistence was easier for major landowners than for poorer men.

Farmers, Farming and Social Change

One reason for slower agricultural change in Cumbria was a distinctive social structure, with survival of a class of yeomanry which had no parallel in the North East. Cumbria's gentry were fewer in number than in Northumberland and Durham and their influence was less. In the early nineteenth century, it was common for Cumbrian farmers to designate themselves as 'farmer' or 'yeoman'. The former were usually farmers holding land by leasehold, representing a growing proportion of farming society. The yeomanry, although declining in numbers and importance, were in many areas the backbone of rural society, predominantly survivors of the former class of customary tenants, whose title to their land gave them a measure of independence. Such holdings could be inherited or sold, and were increasingly transformed into freehold during the eighteenth century. (Jones 1962; Beckett 1982) In 1766 a contributor to the *Gentleman's Magazine* estimated that there were 10,000 customary tenants in Cumberland, and described these 'petty landlords' as 'working like slaves':

> they cannot afford to keep a manservant, but husband, wife, sons and daughters turn out to work in the fields . . . they seldom taste meat and wheat bread . . . Notwithstanding this miserable way of living, they save nothing . . . they cannot feed or dress meaner.

At the lower range, holdings might be less than 10 acres, generating no more than the wage of a farm labourer. (Beckett 1982, 101) By the 1790s, with growing opportunities for urban and industrial employment, it was scarcely surprising that contemporaries were aware that yeomanry numbers were dropping. Economic and social pressures worked to bring rural Cumbria into closer relationship with the commercially oriented society beyond. Once a more homogeneous class, from the sixteenth century onwards there was a developing diversity in yeomanry holdings. (Jones 1962, 208) Successful yeoman farmers bought additional customary estates from unsuccessful farmers, paying usually only a small fine to the landlord. For many years, landowners seem to have taken little interest in these transfers, for it was only with enfranchisement into freehold, often accompanying enclosure schemes, that acquisition of small parcels of land became attractive to them.

Long before the process attracted widespread comment, decline of yeomen was under way. A partial survey of Cumbrian manors between 1650 and 1743 showed a drop in tenant numbers from 456 to 374. Dramatic decline came with accelerated agricultural change in the early nineteenth century, with a drop in yeoman occupiers to around 36 per cent of all farmers. (Searle 1983, 193; Jones 1962, 213) The developing market economy exercised destabilizing effects, even if it brought opportunities to some. During wartime high prices, there was temptation to borrow capital for improvements, or mortgage land, and those who succumbed often faced desperate straits during lean years after 1815. Rent reductions offered protection to leaseholders, but small freeholders were more exposed. Many yeomanry farms, often between 40 and 100 acres, were dependent on family labour, and under-capitalized, without savings or reserves with which to meet adversity. (Searle 1983, 248, 328; Dickinson 1852, 220; Marshall and Walton 1981, 5)

Some, who might 'hardly be termed farmers', relied on supplementary earnings – perhaps carting, textiles, blacksmithing, woodworking, or coal-mining and fishing – to remain viable. This was true of small farmers generally in the North, reflecting a society with fluid occupational boundaries. Small farmers in the North East might work small land-sale coal pits, or act as local carriers of coal or other goods. (Bewick 1975, 28) The first generation of miners at Harrington and St Bees in Cumberland were small yeoman farmers who kept their own cattle. In the late seventeenth century, Sir John Lowther introduced specialist miners to reduce his dependence on local men who might disappear from collieries at peak farming seasons. (Marshall 1973; Wood 1988, 14, 42–5) Hardening occupational boundaries, with greater specialization, contributed to change by diminishing opportunities for supplementary incomes. Better opportunities and less arduous labour existed in other areas of the economy. This may explain abandonment of settlements such as that at Belling Law in North Tynedale. Here a small exposed upland community had eked out a precarious existence from the mid-seventeenth to the early eighteenth century before it was abandoned. (Jobey 1977, 15)

Agricultural reorganization could imply social disruption, and decline in numbers supported on the land. Throughout the North, accumulation of farmland into larger units brought social diversity. More successful occupiers became tenant farmers, or even landowners, while others who lost small customary estates passed into the ranks of landless farm labourers or sought alternative employment. In Cumbria, there was no equivalent to the scale of early agricultural reform in the North East which saw abandonment of some village settlements and their replacement by scattered farms. The century after the Restoration probably saw the peak of this transition, but most villages survived innovations in farming and estate management, although often greatly changed. (Wrathmell 1975)

Villages might disappear or move for various reasons. In the sixteenth century, the Northumberland village of Low Buston had been reckoned able to find 31 able-bodied men for border defence. Decline culminated in abandonment after 1778, when the village stood in the way of Charles Francis Forster's plans for extension of his mansion and the park around it. Other villages which were relocated in order to facilitate emparking around country houses included Little Harle (by 1769), Capheaton (1756–86) and Kirkharle (1758–1828). (Alexander and Roberts, 1978, 110; Wrathmell 1975)

Although landlord power was less pervasive in Cumbria than in the North East, contemporary awareness of 'a remarkable revolution' was heightened by the way in which principal changes were concentrated within a short period. (Gough 1827, 5) The change was captured by the reflections of one prosperous 'Borrowdale farmer' who, although not entirely typical, looked back from the standpoint of 1822 to farming life forty to fifty years earlier:

> upon the family estate we worked hard all day, and at night by rush light, we carded and spun the wool of our sheep, which was made into gowns, petticoats, jackets, breeches and stockings . . . Our sons talk of nothing but Wellington boots, overhauls, dandy waists and neck collar, and a half blood horse to ride a-courting on. Our daughters are sent to a boarding school, to learn music, drawing, French and Italian, which cost £100 a year, and when they come home they can neither make a shirt, nor knit a pile of stockings. (Marshall 1969, 292–3)

These recollections suggest that the shift in farming ethos from subsistence and self-reliance to profit was often seen by contemporaries as moral loss. Such criticisms by 'sentimentalists' were not universally accepted. In the 1790s, one Cumbrian observer concluded that 'Humanity prompts the idea that a man had better labour for certain daily wages, than be in daily hazard of ruin by adversity of season when he and his family are drudging in a little unproductive farm'. (Hutchinson 1794, 998)

Unlike most of England, including the North East, there was little evidence of social polarization between small farmers and labourers in Cumbria. There farmers were often only 'one degree superior' to hired servants, and visitors from the South expressed surprise to find that 'It is usual for the farmer and his labourers to dine at the same table'. (Poor Law Commission 1836, 446–8)

Although Cumberland and Westmorland in the early nineteenth century were amongst the poorest English counties, they shared with Northumberland and Durham low rural unemployment, and farm wages above those in southern counties. Northern counties remained generally tranquil during rural disturbances of the early 1830s. The southern labourer was often seen as demoralized and pauperized, but well-trained northern workers enjoyed a higher reputation. In 1832, the third Earl Spencer, an agricultural reformer, asked a northern friend to find for him 'not only a first-rate ploughman, *but the sort of fellow you have in Northumberland*, who can be trusted to overlook the other labourers'. (Butler 1869, 167)

While many Cumbrian farmers profited from changes in agricultural organization and techniques, the most dramatic instances were evident in successful tenant farmers of the North East. They are illustrated by the example of George and Matthew Culley, scions of a farming family in the Tees valley, who from 1767 rented a farm at Fenton in north Northumberland. After intensive efforts to increase productivity, annual profits exceeded £5,000 by 1799 and almost doubled after 1800, assisted by high wartime prices. This enabled them to buy land, acquire a country mansion, and emerge as an important gentry family. (Rowe 1971; Macdonald 1975) Shortly before his death, George Culley wrote to his son that

> Whenever I am at Fowberry, I am struck with astonishment, when I reflect on our beginning in Northumberland 43 years ago. To think of my son, now inhabiting *a Palace!* altho' his father in less than 50 years since worked harder than any servant we now have, and even drove a *coal cart!*

This example of 'improvement' was not imitated for any intrinsic merit, but because it offered a route to higher profit. (Macdonald 1979, 5) There was no real equivalent in Cumbria, no entrants into the gentry from tenant farmers. Advances in the North East reflected better opportunities in coastal trade and in feeding an expanding urban and mining population, although Cumbria shared to some extent increases in rural prosperity, evident by the early nineteenth century.

Rural Life

In the mid-eighteenth century, it was noted that in Cumbria only 'persons of quality' could afford to eat wheaten bread. (Nicholson and Burn 1777, 11; Jollie 1811, 45–6) During the 1745 rebellion, soldiers visiting Northumberland tried the local breakfast, 'hasty pudding, made of oatmeal and water boiled together, till it comes to the consistency of paste, which some eat with beer, nutmeg and sugar; others with milk; then 'tis tolerable . . . Oatcakes are here also in fashion.' (Thirsk 1984, 38)

Inventories give additional information about life styles. A farmer's widow, in a poor district, who died in 1716, possessed bedding and three bedsteads worth £3, pewter and brass utensils worth £2 10s. 0d., sheets and table linen, two iron pots, a wooden vessel, two spinning wheels and a stock of wool, eight chairs, two tables, a cupboard, a dresser table and a presser. Such inventories demonstrate modest rises in rural wealth and consumption during the eighteenth century. (Coombes 1966, 173; Marshall 1980)

The evidence of rural housing is similar. Most eighteenth-century housing conformed to functional local traditions, employing available building materials for sheltering humans and animals. Standards varied, and houses built at Brandon Hill near Powburn, Northumberland, as late as 1799, possessed only one window and were entered through a cow-byre.

In 1731, travelling from the border to Penrith, Sir John Clerk observed building traditions change with availability of materials. (Prevost 1961) In the North, on both sides of the border, he found 'farmhouses clay without any admixture of stone' but down the Eden valley they were 'built of a kind of red, hard freestone, and their covers are of the same kind in the place of sclaits'. Over much of Cumbria good building stone is lacking, and improvements reflected growing ability and willingness to pay for carriage of stone or bricks. This could be found by the 1790s at Holm Cultram on the north Cumberland plain, where 'The old dwelling houses are poor clay huts, but the more modern ones are genteel stone buildings, or built of bricks.' (Hutchinson 1794, 345) Such improvements did not stand in isolation, but reflected changes in even remote areas, as one witness attested:

> At the beginning of the century, the inhabitants were in a state bordering on extreme poverty. Large families on small estates could but with difficulty earn a subsistence for themselves; they lived barely on the products of their little farms without even *hope or desire* of raising fortunes . . . they were generally very superstitious . . . But things are now assuming a new appearance. The rust of poverty and ignorance is now gradually wearing off. Estates are bought up into fewer hands; and the poorer sort of people move into towns to gain a livelihood by handicrafts and commerce . . . the houses (or rather huts) of clay which were small and ill-built are mostly thrown down, instead of which strong and roomy farmhouses are built. (Williams 1975, 40)

Developments in agriculture not only affected rural society, and enabled northern counties to remain, despite growing population, largely self-sufficient, but also generated greater income which allowed development of other elements within the regional economy.

Chapter 10

Communications and Transport

Economic development, including easier carriage of agricultural produce, was aided by better communications, although for many years this represented only moderate advance. Most early industrial development, including mining, remained dependent on access to the sea because of the cost of overland carriage. As Sir John Lowther observed in the late seventeenth century, 'where there are ships the whole world is the market', but poor communications hindered inland developments. (Beckett 1981, 103) The earl of Carlisle found it difficult to exploit coal on his estate in north-east Cumberland before construction of waggonways. In the 1790s 'peats' were still a common domestic fuel in Carlisle, barely 15 miles from this coal but over routes which incurred heavy carriage costs. (Hughes 1965, 3) In the seventeenth century, it took about five weeks for a book ordered from London to reach Kendal, which had better links with the outside world than most of the North West. Kendal had to await the opening of the Lancaster–Kendal canal in 1819 to obtain cheap coal.

In the seventeenth century, travellers described Cumbrian roads as 'going through such ways as we hope we never shall again, being no other but climbing and stony, nothing but bogs and myres'. Overland carriage was often on railed sleds drawn by oxen, or more commonly by pack-horse; wheeled carts were rare before 1750. (Williams 1975, 19, 23–5) Much of the upland North East was little better, depending on pack-horses in areas remote from coastal shipping. Each pack-horse could carry 2–3 hundredweights, and trains of thirty or forty were common. One witness computed that 354 pack-horses entered and left Kendal each week, carrying woollen goods on which the local economy depended. A trip to London by this method took about eighteen days. It was not until 1772 that Kendal's Nether Bridge was widened to allow vehicles to cross it.

New roads were constructed near Whitehaven under Harbour Improvement Acts inspired by the Lowthers during the first half of the eighteenth century, although at first their impact was only local. Later that century, turnpike trusts extended improved roads, but some districts, including

Figure 10.1 Stage waggon of *c.*1800. Used for carrying goods, and also providing cheap passenger carriage, in the complex net-work of road transport services which had evolved by the end of the eighteenth century.

Cartmel, Furness and south-west Cumberland, remained poorly served until much later.

Stretches of the Great North Road were among early turnpike initiatives, including Darlington to Durham, begun in 1745, and Buckton Burn to Berwick, begun in 1753. In south Durham, turnpike trusts for new roads Barnard Castle–Darlington–Stockton, Durham–West Auckland–Barnard Castle, and Staindrop–Darlington were established in 1749, 1761 and 1795 respectively. (Sunderland 1967, 55) Parliament, dominated by aristocracy and gentry, was unwilling to interfere directly in local affairs but happy to pass permissive legislation allowing road-building, with local gentry taking the lead as investors and trustees. (Williams 1975, 24, 27, 35–6) By the 1830s, the limitations of this piecemeal approach were obvious, and by 1850 Parliament was willing to contemplate mandatory legislation to reintroduce concepts of centralization repudiated in 1688.

Many local farmers supplemented incomes by acting as part-time carriers, and for some this provided most of their income. Much personal correspondence, especially over short distances, was conveyed by carriers rather than the postal system. In the early eighteenth century the historian John Horsley found this a convenient way of eliciting a reply to an enquiry: 'If you can give it to Bates ye Morpeth carrier (at Ralph Emmerson's or next door to him) and desire them to take a particular care of it, it will come very safe to me.' (Birley 1958, 44) By the end of the eighteenth century, partly as a result of road improvements, postal services had improved. A letter posted in Darlington after the Monday market would be delivered in rural north Northumberland via Berwick on Tuesday or at latest Wednesday. (Macdonald 1975, 141) Services were inferior in areas of poor roads and thinly scattered population. The barren moors around Bewcastle retained notoriety for isolation, poverty and backwardness. (Spence 1977, 152) In most towns, it was well into the nineteenth century before letter delivery was facilitated by regular numbering of houses; at South Shields this occurred in 1851.

Long journeys were often unpleasant and expensive, although the Union of the Crowns encouraged an increase in stations where hired horses could be changed on a long journey. (Crofts 1967, 57) To travel on horseback to London from Keswick in the later seventeenth century cost £2 6s. 8d., a substantial outlay. In late June 1747, Sir James Lowther could travel from London to Whitehaven in nine days without undue haste. An urgent trip might only take five days. (Beckett 1983, 90)

Luxury trades moved faster than the postal system, which in the mid-eighteenth century only involved three dispatch days each week for post from London to the North. From 1592 at latest fresh fish was carried to London from Newcastle, using continuous relays of horses. Defoe noted the growth of this specialist traffic, observing that the men of Workington

> carry salmon, fresh as they take them, up to London upon Horses which, changing often, go night and day without intermission, and, as they say, outgo the Post, for that the fish come very sweet and good to London, where the extraordinary price they yield, from 2s. 6d. to 4s. per lb., pays very well for the carriage. They do the same from Carlisle.

A primitive coach service between London and Newcastle existed by the mid-seventeenth century. In 1680, Lord Howard brought heavy goods home from London, first by sea to Newcastle and then by waggon to Naworth along 'that hideous road along the Tyne'. Another description of this route stressed 'the so many and sharp Turnings and perpetual precipices, for a Coach (not sustained by main force) impassable'. Charges for carrying goods from Newcastle to Naworth Castle in the eighteenth century amounted to about 2s. 3d.–2s. 6d. per hundredweight, a significant increase in costs but useful income to those providing the service. (Hughes 1953, 2)

Contemporary vehicles were not calculated to make the roads less 'hideous'. Lady Anne Clifford used a horse litter for progresses around her estates. (Spence 1979, 47) Lord Howard acquired a coach at Naworth in 1633, front wheels weighing 100 lb., rear wheels 200 lb., before the local blacksmith added strips of iron 'strakes', probably adding about 38 lb. to each wheel. This equipage added to its owner's status, but its wheels must have had a devastating effect on ill-made roads.

This aristocratic household relied upon local markets for many supplies. Lord Howard's everyday breeches and jerkins were made for him in Penrith, where Lady Howard found ribbons, silk buttons, silver lace and herringbone lace, and materials for her children's clothes. The increasing sophistication of shipping services along east and west coasts brought a greater range of goods to northern market towns.

Improving landlords knew that the profitability of estates would benefit from better transport. Local landowners sponsored eighteenth-century road-building schemes, such as the 'Military Road' between Newcastle and Carlisle, the 'Corn Road' from Hexham through Rothbury to Alnwick and the port of Alnmouth, and the road from Newcastle to the Scottish border at Carter Bar (on the lines of the modern A696 and A68).

During the 1745 rebellion, it took General Wade's vanguard two days in November to move 20 miles from Newcastle to Hexham. The road west from Hexham to Haydon Bridge was marked on maps as 'Summer Road'. Landowners in Northumberland and Cumberland advocated a new east–west link, and used strategic arguments to persuade Parliament to grant a modest subsidy, although their true motivation was commercial rather than military. (Lawson 1971, 187–201)

After the Union of the Crowns, cross-border trade was slow to increase, but by the mid-eighteenth century it had developed to the point where pressure for better roads became effective. (Spence 1977, 151) The Carter Bar turnpike Act was supported by MPs bearing local gentry names such as Blackett, Middleton and Ogle, while trustees nominated in the Act provide a list of interested Northumberland landowners – Allgood, Airey, Anderson, Bigge, Blackett, Collingwood, Fenwick, Ogle, Shaftoe, Swinburne. Meetings of trustees at the Seven Stars Inn at Ponteland were convivial county occasions. (Lawson 1971, 187–8) The changed situation on the border was shown by conversion of an old fortified house at Horsley, near Otterburn, into an inn, The Redesdale Arms, when the new road opened in 1779.

The so-called 'Corn Road' was the brainchild of Sir Lancelot Allgood, but most of Northumberland's larger landowners backed him in securing the necessary Act in 1752 and contributing to the cost. (Thirsk 1984, 47) Many landowners built shorter roads, serving more local needs. In the mid-eighteenth century, Sir William Middleton built a road from Longhorsley to the Breamish valley and another from Morpeth to Elsdon, both useful for his own estate produce. In Cumberland Dr Robert Graham followed a similar policy. (Lawson 1966, 194; Spence 1977, 153) The influence of landowners facilitated construction during the eighteenth century of bridges, financed by county rates, including crossings of the Tyne. In 1834, local landowners financed a bridge over the North Tyne at Bellingham, replacing earlier fords. The building of a new bridge at Stockton, completed in 1769, provided the Tees with a lower crossing point than the old bridge 17 miles up-river at Yarm. (Rennison 1993–94, 21)

In lead-mining dales, reliance on pack-horses continued into the nineteenth century, but from the 1820s new roads were built. There were no roads worth mentioning in West Allen Dale until 1826. In about 1828, a coach service linked Newcastle to Alston by way of Whitfield. (Coombes 1958, 248, 258) Improved access and cheaper carriage contributed to increased lead production in the early nineteenth century.

Similar improvements saw roads penetrating the Lake District and brought increased tourist traffic, before railways produced a greater effect on this remote region. Development of Carlisle's cotton industry also owed much to road improvements. (Williams 1975, 31–2, 118–23) Progress involved improved road-building methods and parallel advances in bridge-building, exemplified in the iron bridge at Sunderland, built in 1793–96 and designed by a local landowner, banker and MP, Rowland Burdon of Castle Eden. (Miller 1976, 70; Lawson 1971, 194–5)

Coaches and Carriers

Before the end of the eighteenth century, the region was served by an intricate network of regular carriers. A stage-coach from Newcastle reached York in three days by 1764, including overnight stops. A few years later, a Newcastle–London coach would deliver passengers who joined at Darlington in three days 'provided no material accident happens'. (Sunderland 1967, 59) In 1795, Newcastle had seven daily coach services, which included Carlisle, Edinburgh and London, as well as nearer places like Morpeth and Durham. Coaches heading north reached Berwick in $6\frac{1}{2}$ hours, with stops in Morpeth and Alnwick. By 1831 services had quadrupled, and the fastest coaches aimed to reach London in 37 hours, though fares were £6–£7.

Poorer travellers used slower stage waggons, with broad wheels to minimize road wear, primarily designed to carry goods. In the mid-eighteenth century, four waggons left Newcastle for London each Saturday, passing through Darlington on Tuesdays. Some time later, Arthur Young was impressed with the waggon link between Kendal and London, the longest regular service in the country. By the mid-1820s, waggons of Pickersgill and Company left Newcastle for Birmingham on six days each week (omitting Sunday), while a competitor offered services on Tuesdays, Wednesdays and Fridays. A small Northumberland village such as Barrasford received one weekly carrier's visit from Newcastle, as did a small distant town such as Brough in Stainmore. In the mid-nineteenth century several carriers operated waggons along recently built roads up the North Tyne valley and into Scotland.

194

Improved roads and carriage arrangements did not stand alone, but were linked into enhanced shipping services. At varying dates, northern ports saw repeated improvements. Early development of Stockton saw customs transferred there in 1680 from Hartlepool, then in serious decline, but the lower Tees left much to be desired. Lead from mining dales was shipped from Yarm, up-river, but only small vessels could navigate the sinuous course, taking four tides to cover less than 20 miles to the sea. Only minor advances were effected before the establishment of the Tees Navigation Company of 1808, which implemented its first improvements in 1809–10. (Rennison 1993–94, 21–2)

In 1842, advertisements for the six ships of the Stockton and London Shipping Company noted regular weekly services to London and back. Lists of collection and distribution points for goods carried included nearly 100 places in Durham, Northumberland and North Yorkshire. Despite improvements in inland transport, including railways, coastal shipping remained a major artery of commerce, carrying huge quantities of coal and other commodities, and providing a cheap passenger service.

Waggonways and Railways

Some transport improvements existed in embryonic forms in the seventeenth century. For haulage of heavy goods like coal, early waggonways, on which waggons were pulled along wooden rails by horses, were already known, though short and few in number. The first recorded example in County Durham, probably taking a route from Whickham by Lobley Hill to the Tyne at Dunston, was in use before the Civil War. In the Whitehaven district, waggonways began to supplement roads for coal haulage in the 1730s, allowing collieries further inland to be worked profitably. Waggonways continued to expand during the eighteenth century. Short lines brought coal from local collieries to the Northumberland coast at Cullercoats, where in 1708, 36 salt pans used more than 15,000 tons of coal to produce 2,200 tons of salt. Working out of shallow local collieries led to the end of that industry; the last shipment of salt from Cullercoats was in July 1726, and the last six salt pans moved to Blyth where coal was readily available. A map of 1737 showed 17 waggonways in the neighbourhood of Cox Green and Fatfield in County Durham. Waggonways of 1790–1800 linked limestone quarries at Pallion, Southwick, Carley Hill and Fulwell with coal-burning lime-kilns on the river Wear. (Mann 1984, 223; Beckett 1981, 65; Anon. 1985, 4–15)

Development of railways from waggonways impressed contemporaries and has fascinated later generations. Like many nineteenth-century changes, the railway's evolution owed much to piecemeal innovations and experiments. Pioneers of railway expansion in the North had experience with waggonways and stationary steam engines for winding and pumping. The Stanhope and Tyne Railway of 1834 was essentially an extended waggonway. When first completed there were 10.5 miles worked by fixed steam engines, 3 miles of self-acting inclined planes and only 9.5 miles of locomotive haulage.

Colliery engine-wrights were prominent in devising means for bringing earlier elements together and developing locomotive haulage. Such enterprises were often adventurous. When in 1826–27 George Stephenson recommended locomotives for the Liverpool and Manchester Railway, he knew that existing engines were not capable of the necessary performance. From 1827 the young Robert Stephenson concentrated on meeting this requirement. Forming a design team which brought in William Hutchinson, manager of Stephenson's Newcastle works, and George Phipps as design draughtsman, it took only 33 months to develop locomotives which marked advance on earlier models. The *Rocket* of 1829 was an interim design. A combination of necessity, experience and inventive talents brought success. In September 1830 the *Planet* combined improvements affecting several elements in locomotives, with new standards in reliability and pulling power. (Bailey 1988, 10–11)

Technical innovation was not the principal consideration in early railway history. The Stockton and Darlington line of 1825 is celebrated for demonstrating that railways could be profitable. In the early nineteenth century a ton of coal worth 4*s*. at a colliery near Bishop Auckland cost 8*s*. when carted to Darlington and 12*s*. at Stockton. It cost less to carry a ton of coal by sea to London than to move it overland 19 miles between Bishop Auckland and Stockton. Early railways in County Durham reduced the cost of coal carriage from about 4–5*d*. per ton/mile to only 1.3*d*. The Darlington Quaker businessman Edward Pease, a promoter of the Stockton and Darlington line, received in 1839 a dividend of at least £1,000 on his £1,600 capital investment; in 1848 he received £7,000. Coal shipments from Stockton along the railway were 43,600 tons in 1834, 57,000 tons in 1835, 117,000 tons in 1836, 180,000 tons in 1837. The Stockton and Darlington line also demonstrated that a private Act of Parliament could cut through difficulties involved in way-leaves and other access problems. (Kirby 1993; Rennison 1993–94, 25–30)

Railway development established engineering dynasties. When George Stephenson designed the Hetton Colliery Railway, his brother Robert (1788–1837) became resident engineer, supervising building at a handsome salary. George's son Robert, named after this uncle, became one of the most eminent Victorian engineers. Thomas Elliott Harrison (1804–88), son of a lime merchant, founded another dynasty. For seventy years this family was involved in the design of railway bridges in the region. His nephew Charles Augustus Harrison designed the King Edward VII bridge over the Tyne and

Figure 10.2 Newcastle upon Tyne. The Swing Bridge was built in 1868–76 to a design by W. G. Armstrong on the site of earlier bridges serving the old riverside town centres of Newcastle and Gateshead. Behind stands the High Level Bridge of 1845–9, designed by Robert Stephenson, providing both a key link in the developing railway system and a road link between the new centres of Newcastle and Gateshead developing on the higher land above the riverside.

the Queen Alexandra bridge over the Wear. (Pease 1907, 147, 168, 213, 264, 303, 323; Anon. 1985, 27)

Railways began with short lines financed by local investors and meeting local needs. Of the initial 537 £100 shares of the Stockton and Darlington Railway, 267 were owned in north-east England, 75 in Norwich where north-east interests had family and financial connections, and only 100 in London. The second phase, typical of the years after 1840, saw trunk lines linking the region into a national system. Outside investment now played a greater role, because of greater costs and wider implications, but also because arrangements for investment in railway shares had become more sophisticated. The building of early railways encouraged, not only coalfields, but also a variety of other enterprises.

The North East's success in railway development acted as a stimulus to companies which supplied goods to railways. The Tyneside firm of David Haggie & Son won a contract for George Stephenson's Liverpool and Manchester Railway, involving a continuous rope eight inches in circumference and three miles long. A team of 18 horses needed reinforcements

197

before this 13-ton giant could be moved to a point where it could be taken on board a barge for transport to its destination.

Railways served not only industry and commerce, for in Cumbria they brought rapid growth in an existing tourist trade. In 1843–44 there were no more than 8,000 tourist movements into the Lake District along the Kendal–Windermere road link, and there may have been only half as many. In 1847–48, its first full year, the Kendal and Windermere Railway carried 120,000 passengers, mostly between early May and late October. This not only increased the numbers but also extended the social range of those able to afford such trips. (Walton and McGloin 1981, 157–8)

The four northern counties were not among regions in which canals played a large role, and the few schemes which appeared were not successful enough to inspire imitation. (Thornthwaite 1992) Carlisle's quest for links with seaborne commerce bore fruit in 1823 with a canal from the city to Port Carlisle on the Solway Firth. By the 1840s it was hard hit by railway competition, paying no dividends after 1848. In the 1850s, the canal was replaced by a railway. (Sunderland 1967, 62; Walton 1979, 196–7)

Chapter 11

Coal-Mining and Related Developments

Although agriculture remained the largest source of income and employment until well into the nineteenth century, other elements in the regional economy continued to expand. An account in 1605 noted that 'in the countyes of Durham and Northumberland there be no great trades as clothing and suchlike used, by which the poorer sort are sett on worke and relieved from begery saving only the trades of colyery and salting'. (Thirsk 1984, 57)

The northern coalfields helped to meet rising demand for fuel, with Northumberland and Durham the most important district here. (Flinn 1984, 26)

Annual Coal Production (000s of tons)

	1700	1750	1775	1800	1815	1830
North East	1,290	1,955	2,990	4,450	5,395	6,915
Cumberland	25	350	450	500	520	560
Great Britain total	2,985	5,230	8,850	15,045	22,265	30,375

There were early examples of transformation of rural communities under pressures of economic change, especially in areas close to coal-shipping ports. At Whickham, near Gateshead, before the Union of the Crowns, the copyholders 'were all well defended by their customs from seigneurial exploitation, and they were free to pass their lands, their goods, and their rights to their children'. (Levine and Wrightson 1991, 89, 139–41, 150–1) Modern studies have examined how the expanding coal industry brought about decline of such small occupiers, with coalowners accumulating holdings to develop collieries and access routes. (Levine and Wrightson 1991; Clavering and Rounding 1995) Some copyholders profited from mining opportunities; others lost their independence. By the end of the seventeenth century, 'The institutions of the manor were now all but defunct ... The Elizabethan agrarian community had been submerged within a largely industrial and commercial order.' (Levine and Wrightson 1991, 150)

199

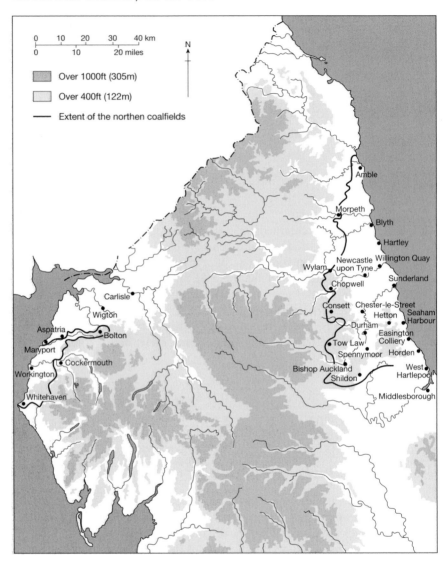

Map 4 The extent of the major Northern coalfields

Between 1640 and 1680 coal output doubled in Northumberland and Durham, and by 1680 this contributed about 40 per cent of the national total. By 1750 there had been another doubling in output. The Tyne continued to dominate the coal trade. In 1609, its nearest rival, the Wear, shipped only 5 per cent of the Tyne total. Although Wear shipments continued to grow, even in the early eighteenth century they amounted to less than a third of the Tyne trade. The Tees did not enter the trade on any substantial scale until 1826.

Invention of the Newcomen engine in 1712 brought steam power to mining, with early installations at Byker, Chester-le-Street, Tanfield Lea and Washington. In the late eighteenth century there were more than 100 engines at work in the North East. Apart from encouraging coalowners who could afford capital investment, this put key workers into a strong position. *Circa* 1719 there were only two men in Cumberland who were specialists in building and working steam engines. One of them, Peter Walker, was paid £1 weekly to work an engine at Whitehaven colliery. Within a few months he had used his leverage here to become colliery manager, exploiting attempts by coalowners elsewhere to lure him away. (Whatley 1976, 71)

Increased production involved greater sophistication in management, organization, financing, distribution and sale. These processes were demonstrated in the organization and financing of the east-coast coal route to London; by 1826, London was annually importing about two million tons of coal by sea, of which only about 125,000 tons came from other coalfields. (Flinn 1984, 212–311)

Expansion of mining encouraged related sectors, including harbours, shipbuilding and shipping, and development of coal-using industry within the region, including salt-making, glass-making, ironworks, and chemical manufacture. By the mid-nineteenth century, the Tyneside chemical industry consumed a quarter of a million tons of coal annually.

This kind of 'knock-on' effect had wide implications. Availability of local coal promoted lime-kilns scattered throughout the region, playing a part in agricultural improvement and helping the region to feed mining settlements. Such uses encouraged mining in remote areas where the quality of the fuel was poor. Coal-burning lime-kilns and tile-works in Upper Redesdale served their local market but also exploited demand in adjacent areas of Scotland. The earliest surviving mention of Redesdale mining dates from 1691. The number of collieries there increased during the eighteenth century, but they remained small and shallow. From about 1800, miners appeared as a distinct element in the population of this remote valley. The duration of mining was limited by demand, and soon dropped away from its early nineteenth-century peak. Demand for lime diminished, partly because farmers learned to avoid excessive use. Demand for drainage tiles failed when most land suitable for draining had been dealt with. (Day and Charlton 1981, 270–3, 290–1)

The Great Northern Coalfield attracted Scots south to work in the mines and they were joined now by 'surplus' manpower from border areas like Redesdale and North Tynedale, who might have been less welcome on Tyneside in earlier and more troubled periods. Other immigrants included ambitious Yorkshiremen such as Leonard Carr. When Carr died in 1658 he was a wealthy member of the Newcastle oligarchy, with coal-mining a principal source of his prosperity. (Fraser and Emsley 1978, 117–19)

Increased coal production saw changes in occupational structure. Miners appeared with increasing frequency in records such as parish registers. As collieries became larger, with higher levels of employment, workers became increasingly differentiated, with separate functions such as hewer, putter, engineman or banksman emerging. By the mid-nineteenth century, South Hetton colliery employed an office and managerial staff of 12, 200 surface workers in 22 categories, and 316 underground workers, including 140 hewers, 140 putters (described as 'many assistants of different styles and ages') and 36 men acting as supervisors or carrying out specialized ancillary tasks underground. (Leifchild 1853, 182–3) Mining communities became more complex and hierarchical, with supervisory grades and their families occupying prominent positions in the community.

In the late eighteenth and early nineteenth centuries, increasing demand saw shafts driven deeper. Although mining ventures were something of a gamble, there were great prizes to be won. In 1819 a Gateshead colliery made a profit of £7,000 on an initial capital of £15,320, and elsewhere profits of 27 per cent and 18 per cent were recorded. Although disastrous losses also occurred, such figures encouraged new sinkings. (Ashton and Sykes 1929, Appendix C) A series of new or extended sea-sale collieries along the lower Tyne included Walker (1765), Willington (1775), Felling (1779), Wallsend Main (1781), Hebburn (1794), Percy Main (1802), Jarrow (1803) and South Shields (1810). All were more than 600 feet deep.

These deeper ventures brought additional hazards. No doubt accidents had been common in earlier mining, but by chance our earliest surviving mention of a fatal mining accident on the Great Northern Coalfield concerns the deaths of James and Thomas Thompson, victims of an accident in a mine at Gateshead in 1621. Mining remained dangerous, as demand for higher production pushed against the limits of contemporary technology. As late as 1787, the deepest Tyneside shaft reached only *c.*630 feet, about as far as contemporary skills could go, but the tendency was to go deeper. (Galloway 1898, I, 294–5)

Although large collieries existed where water transport was within reach, especially access to the east-coast shipping route to London, most mines remained small. There were many small pits serving a local market, often worked on a part-time basis. In 1687, John Hasty leased a small farm near Durham, but worked on his landlord's property for part of the time and also worked part-time in a small local colliery. In his *Memoir*, the engraver Thomas Bewick recalled small-scale mining on his father's farm at Cherryburn in the later eighteenth century. (Thirsk 1984, 57; Bewick 1975, 28)

Coal-mining in the North West was controlled by families who combined landowning with mining, transport and sale of coal and sometimes other minerals too. Growth of the ports of Maryport, Whitehaven and Workington represented the industrial and commercial ambitions of rival landowning entrepreneurs. (Phillips 1978, 190)

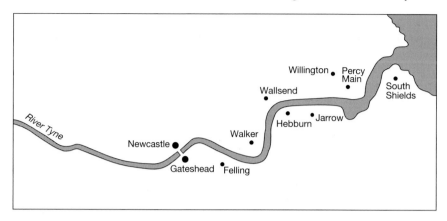

Map 5 Some Tyneside collieries of *c*.1800

It was the coal trade, and especially the Irish coal market, which fostered the growth of west Cumberland ports. For some time Whitehaven profited from the Navigation Acts' protection of British shipping in the colonial trade, and the Lowther port could briefly claim to be the kingdom's second most important harbour. Colonial tobacco must pass through a British port before setting out for destinations like Holland or France, and this enabled Whitehaven to attract a substantial share of the Atlantic tobacco trade in the 1740s. (Beckett 1981, 106) This was a transient success and dependence on the Irish coal trade was soon re-established. The failure in 1763 of Peter How, Whitehaven's largest tobacco merchant, heralded a quick decline in a trade which depended on the fragile protectionist basis of compulsory trans-shipping of colonial cargoes. Whitehaven's pretensions as a rival to Bristol, Liverpool and Glasgow in Atlantic trades were soon eroded. The port's diverse activities had not mixed well, as ports and shipping became increasingly specialized. Whitehaven's Irish trade required large flat-bottomed vessels, unsuitable for Atlantic voyages. (Eaglesham 1977, 53)

For the Great Northern Coalfield of Northumberland and Durham, there were three main markets. Local demand for household and industrial purposes was one, with local industries, such as the salt pans of the seventeenth and early eighteenth century, burning small coal which could not be sold elsewhere. There was growing export to western Europe, an established trade which was to provide future growth but was not yet of primary importance. In 1776, the Tyne exported 77,000 tons, mostly to Germany, France and Scandinavia. (Elliott 1968, 85) A more influential market in promoting technical change and extended production was the coal trade down the east coast, culminating in the London market.

The Irish market meant more to the Cumberland coalfield than any local demand. Early development was initiated by the Whitehaven branch of the Lowther family, whose organization of collieries, and manorial control of Whitehaven, reflected the extended management of a landed estate. (Williams 1951; O'Neill 1982)

Sir Christopher Lowther founded the port of Whitehaven and inaugurated expansion, which was extended by his more effective successors Sir John (1642–1706) and Sir James Lowther (1706–54). They may have spent over £500,000 in acquiring land in a widening circle around Whitehaven to secure mining rights, provide access to the coast and prevent any rival from enjoying these advantages. This huge investment was something of a gamble in its initial stages. Even in 1705, Sir John Lowther considered withdrawing from such a risky trade, but discovery of the rich Howgill mine settled this question. That colliery supplied most Lowther coal during the eighteenth century. By the late seventeenth century, the Lowther interest possessed almost a monopoly in the Dublin coal trade, and could effectively dictate its terms. This encouraged the family to plough resources into colliery development, technical improvements and building waggonways. Pits became larger, and deeper, with use of Newcomen engines from 1716, blasting powder from 1717 and better ventilation from the 1720s onwards. In the mid-eighteenth century, Lowther collieries in Cumbria were at over 600 feet the deepest in the country, and contemporaries marvelled at the way in which coal was mined under the sea. (Wood 1988, 5) Whitehaven grew as a coal port, and the Lowthers exerted every scrap of influence they possessed to prevent development of rival harbours. For almost a century, these machinations succeeded in impeding expansion of Maryport and Workington.

This obstruction of rival interests became less effective by the end of the eighteenth century. At Workington, with harbour developments in 1763–69, John Christian Curwen emerged as the principal competitor in the coal trade, a rivalry which spilled over into regional politics. Humphrey Senhouse laid out Maryport in 1748–49 as his coal-shipping port and this enterprise attracted a smaller proportion of west Cumberland trade. Although Senhouse ambitions received a check in expensive but unsuccessful attempts to win coal at Ellenborough in the early eighteenth century, subsequent investments provided them with happier results in mining and associated ventures. (Wood 1988, 34) By the early nineteenth century shipping registered in these two harbours exceeded the Whitehaven total.

Ships of the Cumberland Ports

	1682	1709	1772	1810	1822
Whitehaven	40	72	197	188	181
Workington			97	134	117
Maryport			76	101	128
Harrington			12	42	38

From time to time, Cumbrian coalowners managed to reconcile their interests in market-sharing agreements, but for the most part they operated competitively.

Despite possession of useful resources, including coal and iron, and a favourable position in relation to several trade routes – western coasting trade, Atlantic trade and a foothold in the Baltic trade – west Cumberland's expansion remained limited. There was no shortage of capital and there were improvements in the technology of coal-mining and shipping, and some awareness of the need to diversify away from over-dependence on the coal trade. Whitehaven merchants embarked on enterprises in iron, glass, pottery, and the production of ropes and sailcloth for the growing merchant fleet. In the 1790s, there were still 3,340 seamen registered in Cumbrian harbours, more than either Bristol or Sunderland, and almost as many as Glasgow. Some Cumbrian landowners became involved in shipyards building small but sturdy vessels of shallow draft for the coal trade, and in shipping operations, another sector with potential for both profit and loss. In the 1790s it was common for 10–12 vessels to be in the process of being built at Whitehaven. Some of these ventures enjoyed modest success, but none of them achieved the breakthrough which could decisively alter the narrow base of the local economy. The coal trade remained the staple of Cumbrian shipping. (Hughes 1965, 64, 72, 150; Eaglesham 1977, 20; Beckett 1981, 119–43; Hutchinson 1794, II, 83)

The availability of cheap coal and expanding markets led to establishment of salt pans and trading in salt by Lowthers and Curwens. In 1629 Sir Patricius Curwen employed an agent in Ireland to push sale of his salt. (Phillips 1973, 196) The coastal location of Curwen estates resulted in the family developing a profitable fishing interest, but coal became their most important enterprise.

Although increase in Whitehaven's population from an estimated 1,089 in 1688 to 11,000 in 1801 was striking, it was left behind by developments in areas like Tyneside and Clydeside. The Lowthers considered schemes for alternative investments, and even ventured into them, but remained preoccupied with the coal industry as an aspect of estate development, and suspicious of more abstract ventures in trade or manufacture.

Whitehaven continued to be hampered by isolation from centres of population. Ready access to the sea provided entry into the coal trade, but this was not balanced by an import trade, given the port's geographical remoteness. In 1739, Sir John Clerk noted that roads in the vicinity of Whitehaven were 'monstrously bad, rough and narrow'. Turnpike roads improved this situation, with better links to Carlisle, but Whitehaven remained stubbornly facing the sea, comparatively isolated even from its near hinterland.

The development of the more substantial coal trade of the North East reflected not so much the activities of eighteenth-century gentlemen entrepreneurs as a longer history which included early control of the coal trade by the Newcastle Hostmen, coupled with their hegemony in Newcastle's municipal affairs. (Cromar 1978, 193) The growth and complexity of the coal trade, and extension of mining districts, made it difficult for them to maintain their grip on production and sale. Increasingly, gentry and even aristocrats appreciated the possibilities of exploiting the mineral resources of estates. The Newcastle oligarchy could not control men of this calibre, nor was it easy to maintain co-operation between rival coal magnates.

Coal Cartels

Waggonways and collieries required the participation or agreement of land-owners, and their construction consolidated control of the industry by those who possessed land needed for collieries or access routes. These groups were tempted to combine and so reinforce their power over production and prices. But here, as in the North West, cartels often foundered because common interest was less powerful than rivalry between individual coalowners.

By the early eighteenth century, landowners whose income and capital were increased by the coal trade, such as the Liddell, Bowes and Cotesworth interests in the North East, were buying up coal-bearing land and properties needed for way-leaves for coal transport. Estates confiscated from Jacobites like Lord Widdrington were snapped up after the 1715 rebellion. (Rounding 1985) The development of groups of leading coalowners impaired dominance of the coal trade by the Newcastle Company of Hostmen, which was dying by 1700. By 1726, the manoeuvres and intrigues of leading coalowners developed into the first 'Grand Alliance' by which Liddell, Wortley, Bowes, Ord and Cotesworth interests came together to regulate the coal trade, to the detriment of other producers and consumers alike. 'Alone, none of them had the power or resources necessary to dominate or subjugate other large coalowners; together they *were* able to do this.' This regulation did not always run smoothly, but for some years it was possible to force other coal-owners to co-operate and restrain rivalries between the allies. For about a quarter of a century, until 1750, the Grand Allies held a dominant and profitable position on the coalfield, manipulating production and prices through agreed quotas. There remained some independent producers, such as the Catholic Silvertop gentry family of Minsteracres, but the cartel of the first half of the eighteenth century enjoyed considerable success. Later attempts at regulation of the coal trade were less effective. (Cromar 1978, 193–207; Taylor 1953; Large 1958–59; Heesom 1974; Sturgess 1975)

By the early nineteenth century, the greater scale of mining enterprises, technical refinements, and risks to capital invested, all worked to widen ownership of collieries. It was not practicable to take collieries deeper than about 600 feet, so resort had to be made to developing wider areas and making greater use of waggonways, which increased capital expenditure before profits began to flow. Before the end of the eighteenth century, some north-east collieries, with access to the sea-sale market, were large, costly and complex enterprises.

Although the cost of sinking collieries continued to rise, when Queen Victoria came to the throne most pits were small and inexpensive. A calculation of 1843, based on a study of 37 collieries, showed only six in Northumberland and Durham which had cost more than £110,000 to bring into production, while 16 more had cost less than £30,000 each. Altogether this large group involved capital expenditure of £2,475,000. If anything, these calculations, which gave an average cost of £67,000, were on the high side. A parallel group of another 33 collieries gave a total investment of £1,782,000, averaging about £54,000.

Towards the end of the first quarter of the nineteenth century, North East coal production was radically altered. In 1820–22 the magnesian limestone which covered the east Durham plateau was penetrated and presence of coal seams below it confirmed. The Hetton Coal Company reached coal at a depth of nearly 900 feet. After the first sinking at Hetton-le-Hole, mining expanded, affecting not only levels of production and organization, but also the coal trade. Within thirty years, 16 large collieries were sunk to exploit concealed coal measures. The lead in technical innovation, once held by Lowther interests in Cumbria, was now in the North East. To obtain greater winding capacity, almost all of these collieries possessed two shafts from their origin, thirty to forty years before safety considerations made this compulsory. In 1843 east Durham collieries produced 910,200 tons, not far short of one-fifth of the coalfield's total. They were so costly, at a time when coal-mines were still risky ventures, that landowners were discouraged from being sole investors. The first shaft at Haswell Colliery had to be abandoned after £60,000 had been spent on it. Sinking began at Shotton Grange in 1841, but it was not until eight years later and after spending £120,000 that the colliery began to show profit. (Sill 1984; Moyes 1969, ch. 7) Increasingly, large collieries were owned by companies or partnerships, with landowners relying on royalty payments instead of active management. Sometimes landowners appeared as part-owners or shareholders alongside colleagues who spread the costs and the risks. In 1829, the Hetton Coal Company consisted of 19 partners who between them held 36 shares. The marquess of Londonderry, the earl of Durham and the earl of Lonsdale remained examples of magnates of sufficient wealth to own and operate collieries independently.

Larger collieries affected surrounding areas in a variety of ways. The increasing use of horses and ponies, both underground and on the surface, expanded demand for fodder, while new mining villages increased demand for food and other household supplies. The mines' needs in leather goods, woodworking, iron articles, all affected the local economy. Some colliery companies farmed leased land to meet some of these requirements. By the time of Queen Victoria's accession, four large mining enterprises in east Durham leased a total of 27,949 acres.

During the first half of the nineteenth century, output of the Great Northern Coalfield rose from some 4.5 million tons to around 10.5 million. The number of miners there increased from 12,000 to 40,000. A witness to the Royal Commission on the Employment of Children in 1842 described how

> Within the last ten or twelve years an entirely new population has been produced. Where formerly there was not a single hut of a shepherd, the lofty steam engine chimneys of a colliery now send their columns of smoke into the sky, and in the vicinity a town is called, as if by enchantment, into immediate existence. (Royal Commission 1842, Appendix, 143)

Well-paid employment brought migration into mining districts. (Thirsk 1984, 41) Hetton Coal Company built a new village at Hetton Downs, close to its first successful sinking; by 1827 there were 110 houses, and by mid-century pitmen headed 198 of its 243 households. Nearby, Hetton-le-Hole, described as a hamlet in a directory of 1821, saw population grow from 264 in 1811 to 5,900 in 1831.

Mining Accidents

Between 1767 and 1815, there were at least seven explosions which caused more than 30 deaths in north-east collieries. The early nineteenth-century expansion of mining probably saw the peak of danger with an annual death rate of around eight per thousand miners employed. Ignorance and human error could have disastrous consequences, as in the Harraton Row explosion of 1817. An overman warned hewers not to use naked lights in part of the mine. As soon as he moved away, one of them lit a candle, complaining that safety lamps gave inadequate light; 38 men died in the following explosion. Between 1821 and 1847, 117 miners lost their lives at Whitehaven through the use of candles or open lamps in many incidents in pits notorious for explosive gases. Attempts by management there to enforce safety precautions at first achieved only limited success. (Duckham 1973; Wood 1988, 139–40)

Figure 11.1   A dramatic indication of rising standards in colliery housing: South Row, Bedlington 'A' Pit, Northumberland, showing a miner's cottage of 1839 embedded in a later colliery row of 1894. This photograph was taken by the late S. B. Martin in 1968, shortly before the terrace was demolished.

From the middle of the eighteenth century, inventors sought safer illumination in mines. One early device was Carlisle Spedding of Whitehaven's idea of producing a stream of sparks from a small steel-and-flint mill, which had a lower temperature than a candle flame. Early safety lamps were cumbrous, of little practical benefit. In the early nineteenth century, after a disastrous explosion in the Brandling Main colliery which killed 92 men and boys, an intensive study was inaugurated by local interests, including mine-owners, clergy and disinterested philanthropists. They commissioned Sir Humphry Davy to carry out research. At the same time the colliery mechanic George Stephenson was working on a similar project, in ways which involved personal danger if a less scientific approach. This dual approach resulted in two similar safety lamps, for both of which Davy's work provided vital information. Stephenson's lamp remained popular in north-eastern collieries, although the Davy lamp obtained wider acceptance. (Duckham 1973, 42–3, 53; Griffin 1978; Griffin 1980)

In earlier years, there were cases of children starting work in northern pits as early as 5 or 6 years old; 7-year-olds were more common in the early nineteenth century. By then, women were not employed underground in North East collieries, though there were still a few female miners in Cumberland. In introducing proposals for statutory reform of coal-mining conditions in 1842, Lord Ashley emphasized that the mining magnates of the Great Northern Coalfield were not his main targets, noting that 'they have exhibited, in many respects, care and kindness towards their people'. (Hansard, 3rd Ser., LXIII, 1323)

Chapter 12

Other Aspects of the Regional Economy

Unlike the failure to develop coal-using industry in Cumbria, the Great Northern Coalfield of Northumberland and Durham fostered new industry on a considerable scale.

Glass and Soap Making

Glass-making was an example, becoming established on Tyneside in the seventeenth century. Admiral Sir Robert Mansell obtained a monopoly in glass-making in 1615, and set about experiments using coal. (Ridley 1962; Ross 1982) After earlier setbacks in Wales and Nottinghamshire, partly due to transport costs, 'for his last refuge he was enforced to make triall at Newcastel upon Tyne, where, after the expense of many thousand pounds, that work for window-glass was affected with Newcastle cole'. Mansell's enterprise made bottles, mirrors, tumblers and spectacle glass as well as window panes. The factory probably produced 6,000–8,000 cwt of glass by the 1620s. Although the monopoly, renewed in 1623, collapsed with the Civil War, the family firm survived for the rest of the century. (Ridley 1962, 146–7)

Other glass-makers, including the Henzell and Tyzack families, came to Tyneside after Louis XIV's Revocation of the Edict of Nantes sent Huguenot refugees fleeing abroad with their expertise. A branch of the Dagnia family, already making glass at Bristol, migrated to Tyneside in 1684 and settled in Newcastle's Closegate, making many different kinds of glass, including finer ranges. In 1697 Onesiphorus Dagnia was fined £200 for evading duty on more than 2,697 dozen glass bottles. By the end of the seventeenth century there were 15–20 glass-works operating in or near Newcastle. Manufacture was paralleled by skilled glass engravers, culminating in the Beilby workshop in the later eighteenth century. Profits were sufficiently attractive to induce leading local interests to invest. In 1759 Matthew Ridley bought the old Henzell glass-works at Howdon Pans, and a few years later his son, the second Ridley baronet, was one of England's largest bottle manufacturers. In 1769 a glass-works was set up by John Hopton at Sunderland, pioneering another centre of the industry. About £50,000 was spent in 1838 on modernizing Hartley's Sunderland glass-works, which became one of Britain's major producers of sheet glass. By the 1830s Cookson's glass-works at South Shields was the largest in the country. When the company was sold in 1845 the purchase price was £140,000.

These successes were achieved despite increasing tax burdens: by the early nineteenth century, duty on glass reached 40 per cent. Eneas Mackenzie claimed in the 1820s that 'more glass is manufactured on the river Tyne than in all the kingdom of France'. Excise duty on glass was repealed by Peel in 1845, part of his policy of freeing trade from harmful restrictions. In 1841 British manufacturers formed a cartel which shared the market to their joint profit, until later in the century when foreign competition became a serious threat. Import duty on glass was removed in 1857 and thereafter Belgian glass in particular flooded the British market.

Glass-workers were a distinctive element in local society. In September 1823, the *Newcastle Courant* gave a description of one of their celebrations:

> The flint glass-makers employed in the houses on the Tyne and Wear, walked in procession in this town. The men all wore sashes and glass stars suspended from their necks by chains or drops of variegated colour, the great majority having glass feathers in their hats. And every individual carried a glass ornament in his hand. (Ridley 1962)

Soap-making also profited from cheap coal. In earlier periods British soap was inferior to that from the Continent; by 1770 it had attained equality. In the early nineteenth century, Newcastle, London and Merseyside were centres of production. Tyneside firms like Doubleday & Company were among leaders of an industry which received a boost when duty on soap was abolished in 1833. (Gittins 1976, 265–73) Many other industries, including paper-making and potteries, prospered from proximity to the coalfield.

Lead-Mining

As in coal-mining, much lead-mining in northern dales was on a small-scale and often part-time basis. Combination of a small farm with part-time lead-mining was a feature of these districts, although some already found mining their main source of income. Many farms were too small to provide a living for a family even by the limited standards of these years. Lead-mining communities were often scattered and isolated, with miners in Weardale and Teesdale having more in common with Cumberland lead-miners of Alston and Nenthead than with coal-miners on the Great Northern Coalfield. (Rowe 1990, 416) As in coal-mining, lead-mining involved hard physical labour. A manuscript owned by the Newcastle Literary and Philosophical Society includes drawings of tools used in the lead industry; they could be mistaken for a set of gardening implements. (Mulcaster *c*.1805)

In lead as in coal there were some large-scale enterprises. By the mid-seventeenth century, the London Lead Company was established in the Alston district and, in addition to westwards extension from that base, sank new mines near Cockermouth. At Nenthead, a mining community established by the company *c*.1760 was rebuilt as a model village in 1825. The company opened the Allen smelt mill at Allendale in 1692 and bought an old smelt mill at Whitfield in 1706. The Allenheads mill was also opened in the early eighteenth century. Another major lead producer, Sir Walter Calverley Blackett, who died in 1777, had been receiving as much as £5,000 p.a. from mines in the Allenheads area. (Phillips 1978, 190; Coombes 1958, 248) By 1840 the London Lead Company had a work force of about 1,500, while Blackett lead interests employed about 2,000. In 1823 Britain produced two-thirds of the world's lead, and about half in 1838. (Raistrick 1977, 17; Hunt 1970, 1–8; Bennett 1993, 14; Banks, Nichol and Bridge, 1994, 215)

As in coal-mining, landlords could profit from lead-mining without direct participation. Much lead-bearing land in County Durham was owned by the Church. Annual lead output from the bishop's Weardale estates rose to an average of about 20,000 tons between 1815 and 1850, the peak period of production. (Dunham and Hobbs 1976, 7) When leases fell due for renewal, ecclesiastical landowners could drive hard bargains. In 1802, when Bishop Barrington renewed the lease of the London Lead Company's Weardale holdings, annual rent rose from £850 to £4,000, with an extra lump sum of £70,000 as a fine for underpayment of royalties. When coal royalties and rent roll from the farmed estate are added, it is easy to understand how the bishop of Durham was one of the richest men in England. From the 1830s the Ecclesiastical Commission began to even out gross anomalies in clerical incomes, and the Durham revenue provided important resources for this. The rector of Stanhope was another beneficiary of the lead industry. In 1832 the living was worth not far short of £5,000 p.a., more than the income of many gentry families. (Maynard 1990, 104–5)

Landowners were not the only beneficiaries. Because of the patchy nature of lead lodes, the level of success was something of a gamble. In 1835 the Newcastle Agent of the Bank of England mentioned one fortunate strike by a group who 'by the unprecedented success of that mine have been

Figure 12.1 Lead mine and ore crushing plant, built 1873–7, at Killhope, county Durham. The ore crushing plant was powered by a water-wheel 34' in diameter.

raised from the condition of labouring miners to very great opulence'. Such strokes of luck were exceptional.

The Iron Industry

Iron-mining and iron-working provided another industry with pockets of activity at the time of the Union of the Crowns. The iron-rich haematite ore of Cumbria had long been known and in the seventeenth century there was iron-making in west Cumberland and in Furness, using expensive charcoal. (Phillips 1977) Experiments using coal for smelting produced inferior iron which blacksmiths 'would not work if they could have it for nothing'. In the North East, small-scale iron-working had existed in south-east Northumberland since at least the early seventeenth century. Scrap iron shipped in by returning colliers provided raw material. Experiments in improved technology occurred but with little success before the nineteenth century. (Wood 1952, 10; Fletcher 1881, 5–21; Evans 1992)

Pressure for change increased as demand for iron rose, including iron rails for waggonways and then railways; coal waggons usually had iron wheels

214

from about 1753. To meet such needs, new iron works were established, especially in the North East where need for additional iron was greater. Problems of smelting with coal were overcome. In Northumberland, new sites included Lemington-on-Tyne (1799), Wylam (1836), Ridsdale (1836) and Hareshaw (1836). Remoter sites suffered from poor communications; iron from Hareshaw had to be carried by cart 17 miles to the nearest railway at Hexham. The pattern of small, scattered works, exploiting local deposits of coal, iron ore and limestone, or reworking scrap metal, began to be replaced by larger centres of production in the mid-nineteenth century.

Some iron-users involved themselves in iron ore mining and processing to secure supplies. During the early nineteenth century the North Shields firm of Pow and Fawcus was one of Britain's biggest manufacturers of anchors, chains and other maritime ironwork. Its founders had backgrounds as rural blacksmiths. As the firm's need for iron grew, it helped to establish the Ridsdale Iron Works despite the remote setting and transport costs involved.

The most spectacular of the region's early iron-working enterprises was the Crowley works west of Gateshead. In the late eighteenth century Arthur Young was impressed, as well he might be, by the firm's annual wage bill of £20,000 and the fact that supervisory workers could earn an annual wage of £200. His fertile imagination was stirred by the metal-working machinery employed. (Young 1771, 10–11; Evans 1992, 184–5; Levine and Wrightson 1991)

> As to the machines for accelerating several operations in the manufacture, the copper rollers for squeezing bars into hoops, and the scissors cutting bars of iron – the turning cranes for moving anchors in and out of the fire – the beating hammers, lifted by the cogs of a wheel; these are machines of manifest utility, simple in their construction, and all moved by water.

During the first half of the nineteenth century, the scattered iron industry of the North was still growing. At Bedlington, an iron works founded in 1736, mainly as a nail-making enterprise, branched out in later years; by 1850 it was employing 2,000 workers. (Evans 1992)

Engineering

Growth of the engineering industry was associated with expansion of related sectors such as coal-mining, iron-working, railways and shipbuilding. The Stockton and Darlington Railway was established to serve coal-mines and led to the Stephenson locomotive building firm in Newcastle, which developed into a major engineering concern. Its progress illustrated the innovator's need for competent assistants. Robert Stephenson's success owed much to George Crow, chief foreman and subsequently works manager, Ralph Whyte and William Wheallans in the drawing office, and William Hutchinson who took over management during Stephenson's absences abroad. These men attained financial and social eminence in Tyneside society and the firm provided an increasing number of shop-floor jobs, well-paid in contemporary terms, numbering almost 1,500 by mid-century.

The Hawthorn brothers provided a parallel success story. Beginning in 1817 with four workers, numbers rose to 10 by 1818, 34 by 1820, 185 by 1830, 550 by 1840 and just under 1,000 by mid-century. Much of the firm's success was due to sound design and good workmanship. By 1850 engineering in various forms, including mining equipment, railway engines and marine engineering, had established an important place in the region's economy.

Shipbuilding

The growing sea-borne trade of the northern counties, both coastal and deep sea, stimulated shipbuilding. Most shipyards were small, and one striking exception in early years did not encourage imitation. Hurry's shipyard at Howdon on the Tyne, founded in 1758, grew to impressive size, with building slips capable of holding four ships at a time, a quay 800 feet long, a ropery, sail-making lofts, etc., only to collapse in bankruptcy in 1806. Most yards were smaller and simpler, and in the early nineteenth century it was common for a group of shipwrights to rent shore land, build a ship, sell her and dissolve the temporary partnership. (Royal Commission 1992, 41)

Tyne and Wear developed into major centres. By 1848 there were 36 shipbuilding enterprises on Tyneside, none of them very large. Sunderland developed into a rival of some pretensions. Growth there, to which shipbuilding made a significant contribution, saw the town made a separate parish in 1719, containing 'six thousand souls and upwards'. (Royal Commission 1992) During the first half of the nineteenth century, Wearside forged ahead, and by the 1830s *Lloyd's Register* claimed (with some exaggeration) that Sunderland was 'the most important shipbuilding centre in the country, nearly equalling as regards number and tonnage of ships built, all the other ports together'. Most ships built on northern rivers were small and designed to serve regional needs. A few larger ships were built on the Tyne, including East Indiamen. The Tyne also saw more experimenting with iron ships than the Wear, in ways which were to bear fruit in the later nineteenth century (see pp. 269–74 below).

The Textile Industry

Although coal, iron and engineering played a more important role in the long run, the textile industry was important in particular localities, especially west of the Pennines at Carlisle and Kendal. The northern counties had a long-established and widely distributed woollen industry in the seventeenth and eighteenth centuries.

In the Lake District, Cockermouth was well placed to gather wool from upland flocks, and processed wool of indifferent quality into coarse woollen articles – fustians. Even relatively backward Carlisle had a small textile industry of this kind during the seventeenth and eighteenth centuries. Kendal was a more important centre. It inherited a long tradition of wool trading and making 'Kendal cottons' – a coarse but hard-wearing woollen cloth with a national reputation. During the eighteenth century, Kendal also became a centre for weaving linsey, a combination of linen and wool, and for hosiery. Textile production was organized in a classic pattern, with out-workers in the surrounding countryside, and small communities working for master manufacturers in the town. In 1772, Pennant noted that the inhabitants of Ambleside, 13 miles distant, were 'much employed in the knitting of stockings for the Kendal market, and spinning woollen yarn, and in making of thread to weave their linseys'. (Pennant 1772, 41) At the height of the 1790s boom in hosiery, as many as 5,000 men, women and children in hamlets, villages and small towns within a radius of about 20 miles were organized by hosiers based in Kendal. Smaller numbers, perhaps another 1,500, were employed as spinners and weavers in other branches of Kendal's textile trade. The rise in Kendal's population during the eighteenth century, almost tripling to reach 8,000 by 1801, is striking, but, because of the scattered work force, underestimates this industrial activity. (Marshall and Dyehouse, 1976, 129; Young 1771, III, 132–5)

By 1801, Kendal had settled into relative decline within the national textile industry. The market for hard-wearing cloth was overtaken by a fashion for 'more elegant fabrics', while export of Kendal cloth for 'negroes and poorer planters' was affected by the American War of Independence. (Nicholson 1861, 241) By this time the once booming hosiery trade was in difficulties. It had rested on a precarious basis, requiring better-quality wool from Leicestershire, Warwickshire and parts of the North East, and now faced unbeatable competition from cotton fabrics which were woven rather than knitted.

The developing cotton industry pioneered technological and managerial changes which affected all textile manufacture. Boom conditions in that branch, which supplanted woollen manufactures as the principal source of Britain's industrial wealth in the first decades of the nineteenth century, encouraged speculation across the North. In its early stages, location of mills was influenced by water power to drive spinning machinery. This saw mills built in dispersed places, including Carlisle, Dalston, Wigton, Warwick Bridge, and Brampton in northern Cumbria, in Furness to the south, but also in remote situations like Kirkby Stephen.

Competition limited survival of cotton manufacture to those areas in proximity to the Atlantic trade, with its supply of raw cotton. The most important of these was that surrounding Carlisle. The city experienced relative decline following the Union of the Crowns, and for many years depended on its farming hinterland. Economic primacy in Cumbria was diverted to Whitehaven, Cockermouth and Kendal. In the 1720s, Defoe attributed the little city's poverty to its having 'little trade'. Modern opinion concurs with this verdict: 'Carlisle was a small and poor city with a population of about one thousand, essentially a market town and a minor port which had developed little in the way of commerce.' (Defoe 1928, 278; Spence 1984, 66)

Subsequently, Carlisle provided an example of an old community transformed by textile enterprises. In the mid-eighteenth century, improved road links with Newcastle and Whitehaven may have inspired the judgement of a Newcastle-based company, Scott, Lamb & Co., that Carlisle was potentially an important centre of calico weaving. Their venture succeeded 'beyond the most sanguine expectation'. (Hutchinson 1794, 662) Within a short period, this encouraged development of water-powered spinning mills, and a Carlisle-centred network of weaving outworkers.

The boom, on the basis of this industry, is indicated by the growth of Carlisle's population from 4,158 in 1763 to 21,965 in 1841, but this is a partial reflection of employment generated by an industry largely carried on by outworkers, many of whom lived in smaller communities nearby. (Barnes 1981, 16) At the height of the 1790s boom, handloom weavers could earn over £1 per week, twice the wage of an agricultural labourer, but this was not sustained. By the first decades of the nineteenth century, handloom weavers were associated with endemic poverty. (Thompson 1976, 126–7, 132) By then, a working day of 12–14 hours might produce a weekly wage of only 5–8 shillings, well below a male factory worker's wage of 18–24 shillings. Factories offered comparatively few jobs for men – most work was carried out by women and children, whose wages were lower although good in comparison with other occupations. Despite low wages, handloom weavers showed little inclination to seek better jobs elsewhere; in 1838 there were still 6,000 of them in the Carlisle area. (Handloom Weavers 1840–41, Reports from Commissioners, 9)

The fall in wages seems initially to have had little to do with competition from power looms, but more with competition from additional workers attracted into the trade by prosperity in the 1790s. Carlisle manufacturers were slow to invest in powered weaving. Until the completion of the Carlisle canal in 1823, coal was expensive. Manufacturers continued to rely on handloom weavers, although these often worked in group 'manufactories' rather than in the individual households of the older domestic system. (Parson and

White 1829, 152–3) There seemed good reasons for reliance on handloom weavers. They required no high capital investment, and were paid by piece-work, so that they provided a flexible resource to tide the local industry over booms and slumps. In 1829, the Carlisle area employed only 89 power looms out of a national total of 58,000, and cotton thread was exported to be woven elsewhere. Powered machinery was used more on the spinning side, still largely reliant on water power. In 1829, the Carlisle area had 80,000 spindles producing cotton thread, but only six steam engines had been acquired. (Parson and White, *Cumberland*, 1829, 152–3)

The development of the textile industry transformed the economy of northern Cumbria. Its effects in Carlisle included rising property values, increase in the number of well-paid jobs, and substantial immigration, includ-ing many Scots and Irish. The rural hinterland was influenced by the need for a larger food supply, and higher food prices affected incomes of local farmers and their employees. Even in 1851, 15.56 per cent of employment in Cumberland was linked to cloth manufacture, concentrated around Carlisle, the largest source of employment after agriculture. By that time the industry was in relative decline, with the growth of Carlisle's population trailing behind cotton towns elsewhere, especially in Lancashire. (Barnes 1981, 17)

Almost the last indication of confidence in the trade was completion of the steam-powered Shaddon Mill in 1836 by Peter Dixon and Son in the Denton Holme suburb of Carlisle. The Dixon dynasty had risen through textile manufacture to influence in the city, and even in the county, briefly providing one of Carlisle's MPs in 1847, but their business was bankrupted after the American Civil War. By that time, the arrival of the railways and population growth had encouraged the settling there of other enterprises. Jonathan Carr from Kendal established an important biscuit factory in 1834. Engineering enterprises included the Cowan Sheldon company whose founda-tion in 1847 coincided with opening of the city's new Citadel railway station. This meant that decline in textile production did not bring catastrophe, for other employment sustained progress and prosperity. (Marshall and Davies-Sheil 1977, 97–8; Bennett 1993, 4)

The application of powered machinery, pioneered in cotton manufac-ture, produced changes in organization which affected other textiles. Some smaller mills in the north faded from the scene. Kendal managed to hang on, catering for a continuing demand for coarser and hard-wearing items like horse blankets, floor cloths, dusters, mops, carpets and trouserings. Wilson's Castle Mill, rebuilt in 1806 as the first local mill to employ steam as well as water power, carried out carding, spinning, dyeing, power-loom weaving, fulling and finishing within one enterprise, abandoning traditional domestic organization in favour of factory processes. By 1850, the district had relinquished the domestic system, and most mills used combinations of water and steam power. As many as 500 hands worked for Braithwaite and Co. at Meal Bank, where they were housed in 'neat healthy cottages', representing changes in organization and working practices. (Nicholson 1861, 240–3) While water power predominated, Kendal was not badly situated, despite its relative isolation, but the shift to steam power imposed disadvantages in spite of the link provided by the Kendal–Lancaster canal. Compared with textile development in Lancashire and Yorkshire, Kendal was a minor centre.

In Cumbria water power retained some of its earlier importance. Of 736 water-powered mills of all kinds known in Cumbria, many were concentrated in southern Lakeland; 206 of this total were involved in textile manufacture. Cumbrian factories included a number of mills making wooden bobbins, feeding demand from the greater textile manufacturing enterprises in Lancashire. (Marshall and Davies-Sheil 1977, 20)

Northumberland and Durham were less dependent on textiles for economic growth. The failure of the textile industry to remain important within north-eastern economic expansion probably reflected the concentration of the industry elsewhere and the existence of more attractive outlets for investment in such sectors as coal and shipping. In its heyday, though, the scattered but cumulatively significant textile industry played a prominent part in the regional economy.

Eighteenth-century Berwick exported woollen stockings produced by an industry based on domestic outworkers in the town and surrounding countryside. Stockings were also knitted around Barnard Castle. Darlington was for some time a centre for linen and woollens; in the 1820s there were nine linen and seven wool or worsted mills there, and the 1831 census showed 25 per cent of the town's adult males dependent on textiles. (Sunderland 1967, 68–9) Durham's long-lived carpet industry existed on a small scale before the end of the seventeenth century. There were textile mills in many Northumberland communities, including Alnwick, Mitford, Corbridge, Haltwhistle, Hexham, Morpeth and Otterburn. Most of these were small and short-lived. Near Castle Eden, in south-east Durham, a large cotton mill was built in 1793, but a directory of 1828 mentioned 'Factory ... formerly an extensive cotton manufactory, but it has long since gone to decay, though the cottages built for the workmen are still remaining'. (Parson and White, *Northumberland*, 1828, II, 265)

During the first half of the nineteenth century, textile interests in the region were eclipsed by the phenomenal growth of the principal British centres of the industry. The North's industrial future was to rest much more on the interlocking interests of coal, iron and steel, engineering and shipbuilding.

Chapter 13

Northern Towns

Although the landed interest retained much of its traditional predominance, there were growing indications of possible rivals. The developing towns were a source of other kinds of influence. By the end of the seventeenth century, but not before, leading townsmen were accorded the status of 'gentleman'. (Morrill 1979, 73) Building or rebuilding of aristocratic and gentry mansions was paralleled by urban building operations. The early Victorian construction of a magnificent new town centre at Newcastle was a striking example, but in the eighteenth and nineteenth centuries there was a broad spectrum of urban improvements, springing from either individual initiative, as in the Lowthers' work at Whitehaven, or communal schemes in provision of new town halls or market buildings.

All northern towns were small by later standards, but there was a quickening of urban growth, on a patchy and unequal scale. The most dramatic evidence of growth occurred in communities exposed to broader patterns of trade. This affected Newcastle and Sunderland, but led also to creation of west-coast ports where before the early seventeenth century there was nothing larger than a village. By the mid-eighteenth century, Whitehaven, Workington and Maryport illustrated the enterprise of their respective Lords of the Manor.

Market Towns

Cumulatively, greater expansion took place in market towns closely integrated with the developing rural economy. By 1811, twelve towns in Cumberland had populations over 1,000, with 40 per cent of the county's people now in towns by this modest criterion. Contemporaries noted that in contrast 'the population of villages . . . is rather decreasing, except where some

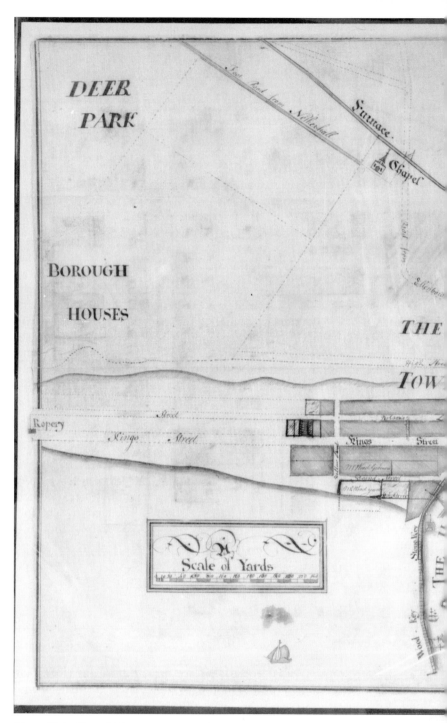

DEER PARK

BOROUGH

HOUSES

THE

TOW

Ropery

Street

Kings Street

Kings Street

Scale of Yards

Figure 13.1 Plan of Maryport, *c*.1760. The town represents a planned development by the Senhouse family, primarily as a coal-shipping port, although the plan shows a variety of

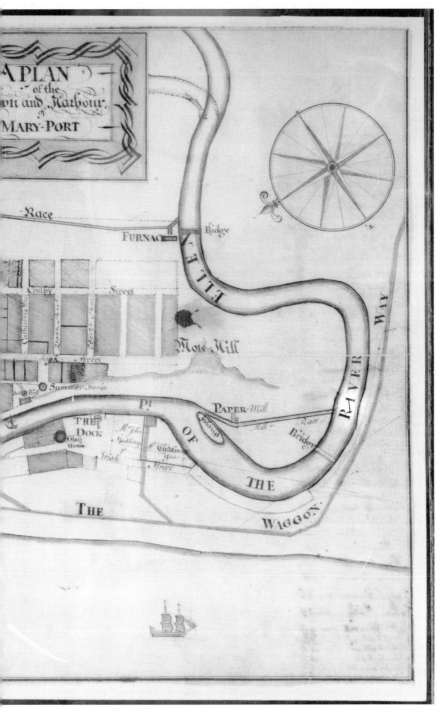

industrial and commercial enterprises created within the manorial framework, including roperies, mill-race, furnace, paper mill, glass-house and harbour installations.

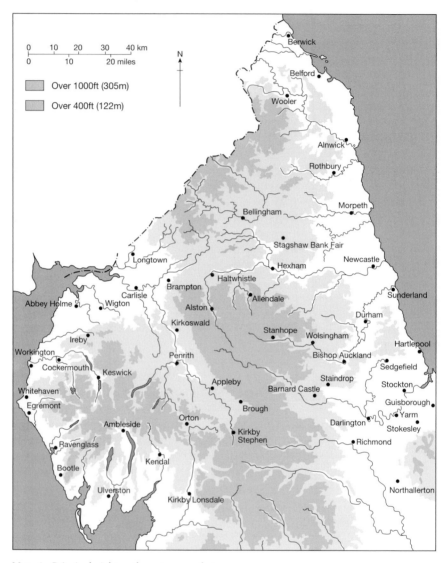

Map 6 Principal eighteenth-century market towns

branch of commerce or manufacture exists'. (Chalkin and Havinden 1974, 209; Housman 1800, 58)

The period 1760–1830 has been described as 'the high noon of the more substantial market town', which provided goods and services for the surrounding rural community. They held blacksmiths, innkeepers, tailors, attorneys, bankers, doctors, etc., and their brewers, butchers, saddlers, fellmongers, flour dealers, etc., marketed and exploited local farm produce. Retailing, largely the province of general dealers in the past, assumed growing specialization as the eighteenth century progressed, reflecting more sophisticated demand and a more complex money economy. By 1787, Kendal had five clock- and watchmakers, and a brandy and wine merchant, in addition to the usual array of market-town trades. In 1829, Carlisle had six clock- and watchmakers and eight nailmakers. (Marshall 1983, 131, 143–8, 155–60; Marshall 1975, 208–9) The principal country towns retained or developed social and administrative functions, as centres for entertainment and education, as well as judicial and local government activities. Implicit in all this was mutual dependence between town and country. As early as the mid-eighteenth century, a decline in the number of farming families who made their own clothes was noted. Although there was an initial reluctance in the Carlisle area to use products of a new commercial brewery amongst inhabitants 'long accustomed to home brewed ales', by the 1790s this prejudice had been 'entirely removed'. (Hutchinson 1794, 662)

Markets held on traditional days had been established for centuries, following a rota as neighbouring towns held markets on different days. (Marshall 1983, 141–2, 145–6, 148–9) Better communications fostered urban growth, without imposing the complex national market which railways were to encourage. The process was not uniform in time or place. Improved communications, especially turnpike roads, reinforced the market town's role in exchange between a national and local economy. On the other hand, better roads enabled Penrith in Cumberland to capture trade which would otherwise have rested with the Westmorland towns of Brough and Appleby, limiting their growth. Kendal was enabled to compete successfully with other towns, including Ambleside, Milnthorpe, Kirkby Stephen and even Kirkby Lonsdale, while Ulverston gathered in much Furness trade despite rivalry from the market at Broughton. Carlisle was increasingly the market centre of north Cumberland. (Marshall 1983, 158–66) Less advantaged towns, like Shap, Ambleside and Kirkby Lonsdale, suffered as centres like Carlisle and Kendal expanded. In Northumberland, the cattle market at Morpeth was by-passed and withered after railways brought easy access to Newcastle and a new cattle market was established there.

Urban Government

In their origins, market towns often reflected ambitions of Lords of the Manor in one aspect of profitable estate development. Ambleside received

Figure 13.2 Industrial housing at Ginns, near Whitehaven, built by Sir James Lowther in 1736. Three rows constructed along a hillside site contained a total of 270 houses.

its first charter thanks to the influence of the countess of Pembroke in 1650. Hawkshead was indebted to the Sandys family, while the regular plan of Broughton in Furness reflected the desire of the Sawreys to establish a planned market community. (Chalkin and Havinden 1974, 211–12; Spence 1977, 153)

Longer-established and larger communities sought to escape the control of landowners. At Darlington, during early Stuart years the bishop still appointed the Bailiff, chief officer of the little borough, who presided over a court which dealt with minor problems and introduced by-laws. This essentially medieval pattern remained intact until, in the mid-nineteenth century, sanitary enquiries produced horrendous accounts of the state of the town. A Local Board of Health was formed in 1848, but it was not until after 1880 that developed local government effected major improvements in public health there. (Sunderland 1967, 89–91)

At Gateshead, from 1287 at latest, the bishop of Durham appointed the little episcopal borough's chief officer, the Bailiff, but this practice died out in the later seventeenth century, by which time there were enough craftsmen for local government to be reorganized on a guild basis. Bishop Cosin's charter of 1671 mentioned freemasons, carvers, stonecutters, sculptors, brickmakers, tilers, bricklayers, glaziers, painters, stainers, founders, nailors, pewterers, plumbers, millwrights, saddlers, bridlers, trunkmakers and distillers of all kinds of strong waters. Increasingly the town's administration was in local hands, mainly the parochial organization of the rector and the oligarchical Four and Twenty. (Rogers 1967) The scale of municipal government remained small, and it was the Ellison family, principal local landowners, who provided the first organized water supply from 1615 to *c*.1700. (Rennison 1977, 179) The first gas supply, in 1818, was provided by a company dominated by leading local figures. As the old local government under the Bailiff appointed by the bishop atrophied, its modest functions fell either to the parish or to the freemen. The Borough Holders, whose holdings gave them traditional status in the bishop's manorial courts, emerged as another organization acting collectively in its own sectional interests.

Compared with its more powerful neighbour across the Tyne, Gateshead remained of modest importance. By the beginning of the nineteenth century, with population approaching 10,000, development reached the point where inadequacies of existing local government were apparent. Local leaders secured an Improvement Act in 1814 which established, under their own control, an Improvement Commission with limited powers for lighting, paving, cleansing and policing the town. A further Act in 1824 brought modest expansion in these powers, but the Commission's achievements never had more than a limited impact upon some central streets. The Commission's functions were taken over by the new Corporation established under the 1835 Municipal Reform Act, which initially did little to expand the effectiveness of local government.

Kendal provides an analogous story. From 1767, a statutory body, the Trustees of Kendal Fell Lands, derived income from enclosure of common lands and was flexible enough to take on tasks neglected by the existing Corporation. (Marshall 1975, 242; Palmer 1972, 29) They organized street lighting and cleaning, as well as aspects of poor relief, and provided an alternative channel of influence for nonconformists excluded from Kendal Corporation.

There were other cases in which chartered boroughs resorted to similar expedients. At Penrith, inhabitants provided for remodelling the congested centre of the town by raising a public subscription. At Carlisle, the Corporation interpreted its chartered functions narrowly, provoking conflicts with other leading citizens. In 1804 a modest initiative in lighting and paving central streets involved creating by local Act of Parliament an independent authority for that purpose. Policing provided a similar issue, with the Corporation striving to avoid expenditure. This produced another local Act, establishing a Carlisle police authority with power to levy its own rate. (Alfrey 1980–81, 3; Brader 1966)

Newcastle upon Tyne

Among the region's towns, Newcastle remained in the forefront, with its influence felt throughout the four northern counties. In Camden's *Britannia* of 1637, this eulogy appeared:

> Now where the wall and Tine almost meet together Newcastle sheweth itself gloriously, the very eye of all the townes in these parts, ennobled by a notable haven which Tine maketh. (Hunter Blair 1955, 1)

Despite vicissitudes during the Civil War, before the end of the seventeenth century revival was under way. In 1698, when Celia Fiennes visited Newcastle, she concluded that 'it most resembles London of any place in England, its buildings lofty and large of brick mostly or stone; the streets are very broad and handsome'. (Louw 1989, 95)

Improvements in thoroughfares were impeded by the town walls. The wall along the quayside was removed under a 1763 order from the town council. In 1797 the Close Gate – by then seen as 'narrow, awkward and dangerous' – was pulled down. Destruction accelerated in the early nineteenth century. The medieval bastion which guarded the town's Newgate, built by Edward III, was demolished in 1823. Another stretch of medieval wall was destroyed in the 1840s to facilitate Amos Spoor's development of Hanover Street. Arrival of railways involved further breaches. (Harbottle 1969, 82–4; Nolan 1989, 33; Summerson 1995)

There were other signs of growth. The lower course of the Lort Burn was culverted in 1636, and new streets included Dean Street and Mosley Street in 1785. The site of the old Carmelite Friary, which had stood with little change since dissolution in the sixteenth century, saw the building of respectable houses in the early eighteenth century. (Harbottle 1968, 178) A new Mansion House was built in the Close in 1691. Newcastle's growing size and prosperity attracted migrants from neighbouring regions. (Fraser and Emsley 1978)

Although by now well established as a northern metropolis, Newcastle remained small in comparison with London. In 1635, Wardens of the London Goldsmiths' Company came to Newcastle on a rare investigation in accordance with chartered privileges, which included supervisory authority over provincial goldsmiths. Many products of Newcastle goldsmiths were rejected as substandard. Condemned plate was broken up and returned to its makers, who were heavily fined. (Gill 1980, 3, 6)

Nevertheless, a modern study notes that 'the area around Newcastle upon Tyne must . . . be considered among the most advanced economic regions of the country'. (Ellis 1981, 117, 119) By the mid-nineteenth century, the town's population had jumped from 28,295 in 1801 to 87,784, emphasizing its status as a regional capital. Building the Newcastle–Carlisle railway in early Victorian years continued and extended Newcastle's long-standing influence in Cumbria.

In the late eighteenth and the early nineteenth century there was an expansion in communal activity as in other regional capitals. The Literary and Philosophical Society of Newcastle upon Tyne, which still plays an important part in the city's cultural life, was founded in 1793, the Newcastle Society of Antiquaries in 1813. The Northumberland Institution for the Promotion of the Fine Arts came in 1822 and the Newcastle Mechanics' Institute in 1824. The Natural History Society was founded in 1829 and five years later local doctors came together to promote the Newcastle College of Medicine.

The guilds still existed, though generally in decline. Some of them acquired better halls, as when in 1716 the Shipwrights or ship carpenters rebuilt with 'four fair turrets' the old Sallyport Tower on the town walls. In 1836 the Skinners and Glovers sold their hall in the ancient Blackfriars; eleven members each pocketed £70 as a result of this deal. (Harbottle and Fraser 1987, 38–40; Hunter Blair 1958, 63)

Newcastle was a centre of printing, at a time when Kendal and Penrith did not possess a bookshop. (Marshall 1983, 137) The Newcastle book trade was sufficiently established and extensive for booksellers and stationers to come together in 1801 to form a cartel to maintain prices. This association broke up in the 1820s as individual members preferred to follow their own interests in such matters as granting discounts to favoured customers. (Hunt and Isaac 1977, 168–9, 174)

Newcastle was the centre for sale and distribution of coal and lead. Newcastle grindstones were already famous throughout the country, with a trade so well established that prices saw little change over two centuries. It was already noticed that an increasing number of Newcastle shops were specialists rather than general dealers. (Tucker 1987, 185)

In the early Victorian period, the co-operative movement tried to challenge urban retail provision by establishment of co-operative stores. Newcastle Chartists were prominent here, but effective retail co-operatives lay well in the future. The early north-eastern societies, including examples on Tyneside, Wearside, and Teesside, all failed within a few years. (Purvis 1986, 201–3) The region's economic success did not depend on such innovations, and in agriculture, industry and commerce, private enterprise and its champions remained dominant.

Newcastle provided the hub of regional economic development. There was industry in the town itself, including engineering works, printing establishments and commercial brewing. In addition, Newcastle became the region's centre for financial and commercial services.

From the late eighteenth century, the town possessed its own banks, which served a variety of regional needs. The record of these early banks was not unmixed. In 1806, the banking partnership of Surtees, Burdon, Brandling and Embleton, which included members of several important local dynasties, failed. Before the acquisition of limited liability by Victorian legislation, bank failure might entail catastrophe for those involved in ownership and management. One partner in this bank was more fortunate than other victims of banking failures. Although Rowland Burdon of Castle Eden, who came from a prominent Durham family and had served as a County Durham MP, was declared bankrupt in July 1806, his popularity ensured that friends worked to secure for the family the core of their estates. In 1828 a branch of the Bank of England was established in Newcastle, and ensuing decades saw a development of banking consistent with the town's role as a regional capital.

Newcastle was a regional centre for insurance, including marine insurance for northern shipping. As the number of local companies grew, dealing in stocks and shares became a regular activity. In early Victorian years there were only nine professional dealers in shares in Newcastle, but this had grown to 20 by 1845, when they felt sufficiently established to found the Newcastle Stock Exchange. (Killick and Thomas 1970, 121)

Newcastle was a centre for entertainment, with an established theatrical tradition and a wide range of visiting shows, including circuses and exhibitions of various kinds. By 1850, Tyneside was a centre of sporting activities too, with competitive rowing, boxing, wrestling and pedestrian events well established in the annual calendar.

The town contained a growing number of merchants and artisans, and there was a running battle between freemen and council about control of the extensive Town Moor. A compromise effected in 1774 and embodied in an Act of Parliament laid down that freemen collectively owned the soil of the moor and rights to pasturage there. The council was allowed to lease no more than 100 acres at a time in seven-year leases, but only to effect improvements on the moor. The race course and other specified areas for public access were to be preserved as open ground. (Halcrow 1953, 155)

The regional capital continued to be dominated by an oligarchy concerned with the town's economic interests. Newcastle's charters prescribed an astonishingly cumbrous system of election for the council, involving seven distinct stages of selection. In practice these complexities mattered little, as the system was manipulated to ensure control by leading families. The early nineteenth century saw growing opposition to this oligarchy. There was little genuinely liberal or democratic about the opposition in Newcastle, which represented a rival would-be oligarchy. The party which controlled the unreformed council was built round a close group of linked leading families.

> Thus, in 1817 Nathaniel Clayton was Town Clerk; he had held that office since 1785, and was to be succeeded in 1822 by his son, John; his brother Robert was mayor and Robert's son, William, was sheriff; in the following year, although Robert and William were out of office, Henry, another son of Robert's, was sheriff. (Burn 1958, 3)

Figure 13.3 Early retail development, Newcastle upon Tyne. The large central block here comprises the new meat, fruit and vegetable markets built 1834–5 as a major element in Richard Grainger's central area development scheme. The triangular block to the right was built in *c.*1867 to house the Central Corn Exchange and News Room. The porticoed building at far centre right is the Theatre Royal of 1836–7, with another substantial building to its left which was originally the headquarters of the Northumberland and Durham District Bank.

A modern study concluded that early nineteenth-century charges of municipal corruption were ill-founded: 'It was highly oligarchical, but, although its accounting system was not such as would satisfy a District Auditor to-day, its members do not appear to have been personally corrupt by the standards of their age or very seriously at fault by ours.' (Cook 1961; Burn 1956) The conclusion was that Newcastle was 'narrowly but not ill governed' and that the old regime 'did not disappear by reason of its own corruption, passivity or incompetence'. There is no reason to suppose that the 'reformed' municipality which followed the Municipal Corporations Act of 1835 was more public-spirited or enlightened than its predecessor. Between 1780 and 1832 the council spent *c.*£90,000 on improvements, despite lack of popular support for higher spending. In 1812 the Corporation acquired the castle and the area around it by buying out the Crown lessees. It was with the co-operation of the Corporation that the property developer Richard Grainger was able to implement his plan for the new town centre which remains the city's finest architectural inheritance.

After 1835, the reformed council tried to wriggle out of commitments to expenditure on improvements, including building new central streets.

231

The municipality from 1835 followed a policy of rigid economy and lack of innovation, often carried to extremes, and evinced no high standards of competence in administration. (Callcott 1988) In January 1837, the Mansion House in the Close, built in 1691, was sold off, with all of its furnishings, pictures, silver plate, books, china and other contents, 'in spite of the strenuous opposition of the majority of the inhabitants of the Town'. A modern scholar noted of this 'insensate and wasteful piece of vandalism' that 'there has probably never been a sale in Newcastle at which collectors' items fetched as little as they did on that occasion'. (Hunter Blair 1955, 3, 10; Burn 1956, 8)

Reformed and unreformed councils shared a common determination to safeguard the interests of Newcastle, even if these were narrowly and selfishly conceived. Under old charters, the town controlled the whole Tyne harbour, from river mouth to a point well above Newcastle. Both before and after municipal changes in the 1830s, the town council fought tenaciously and unscrupulously to maintain this monopoly. An Admiralty enquiry in 1849 calculated that in the past forty years the council had received £957,973 in revenue from shipping, but had spent only £397,719 on port maintenance and improvement. When in 1849 a Bill, backed by other Tyneside communities and port users, was introduced to abolish Newcastle's river monopoly, 'The predominantly Liberal corporation of Newcastle fought it with an obstinacy, an intransigence and a lavishness of expenditure which would have done credit to the most thoroughly dyed-in-the-wool Tory and the Bill failed to pass.' (Burn 1956, 12) This proved a Pyrrhic victory, for evidence of past neglect was too strong. A new Bill passed in the following year, but the council still struggled to save as much as it could of its revenues from the river.

In 1763 and again in 1812, Newcastle Corporation included in local Acts of Parliament powers to install street-lighting. The 1763 Act only referred to the walled area of the town, while the 1812 Act extended to some developing extra-mural suburbs. Little resulted from these initiatives, but when the Grand Duke Nicholas of Russia visited Newcastle in 1816, he was proudly shown the town's new gas-works, on the site now occupied by Pilgrim Street roundabout. At the same time, no doubt he noticed that Newcastle still possessed many windmills; at 37, they probably outnumbered those of any other town.

Problems of Urban Government

By 1850, northern towns had seen changes in local government, both in municipal administration and in the poor law. Such changes did not reflect general public support for wider official activity, and there was much scepticism as to the necessity of improvements and their cost. One of the few specific duties laid on reformed town councils by the Municipal Corporations Act of 1835 was establishment of a police force. This represented a substantial proportion of boroughs' spending and was therefore a focus of ratepayer hostility. Borough police forces remained small and of limited competence for many years after 1835, in the North as elsewhere.

Public Health

If increases in local taxation could disturb ratepayers, they were not enough to provide healthy urban conditions. Overcrowding was a principal cause of higher mortality in towns than in the countryside. Most towns continued to reflect medieval plans of lanes and streets, with growing population crammed into additional building. In his 1850 survey of Carlisle, the inspecting engineer Rawlinson noted competition between private dwellings and businesses for restricted territory 'until every open space is built upon'. The narrow quayside lanes and stairs of Newcastle, and the increasingly unhealthy Blackfriars site, saw severe overcrowding, worsened by absence of effective planning or supervision. Industrial development added pollution to already dire conditions. Parts of Newcastle and Gateshead contained some of the worst slums of Victorian Britain. (Harbottle and Fraser 1987, 38–40; Chronicle 1851)

   The increase of manufacturing and population in Kendal affected living conditions. Much of the town was composed of 'yards' of various sizes and shapes, containing a high density of unplanned houses and workshops. Behind old main streets, noise, smells and disease provided an unpleasant environment. A local census of 1787 showed that the town centre contained an extraordinary mixture of people of different callings and status, with prosperous families living close to slum conditions. Some impression of such areas can still be obtained in Dr Manning's Yard, formerly Braithwaite's Yard, even though the workshops and small factories have gone. (Marshall 1975, 226)

   Places like South Shields (1850) and Tynemouth (1849) received municipal institutions under the Municipal Reform Act of 1835, but there was vigorous local opposition to this because of fear of increased local taxation. Powers of the new councils were limited, and they showed little sign in the early years of initiative in public health, though they were willing to fight for their towns' interests in such matters as opposition to Newcastle's control of the Tyne.

Slums were not confined to centres of economic expansion, for country towns had patches of industry and of slums, though the two were not always connected. In the White Hart yard in the market town of Alnwick in the mid-nineteenth century,

> Great filth of every description may always here be found, and it has long been noticed as much subjected to fever. An open sewer, containing all kinds of putridity, which is seldom or never cleansed, runs ... so far down the yard, and, where it becomes covered, its place is supplied by a large midden, into which all the blood and offals from the slaughterhouses are thrown, and frequently for a considerable time to remain. (Rawlinson 1850, 76)

At about the same time, a government inspector had this to say of Hexham:

> I enquired for the return of the mortality, and found that, for the last 7 years, it was actually some $27\frac{1}{2}$ in the thousand, but with 'cooked' returns it was 24 in the thousand ... I then traced disease to crowded room tenements, undrained streets, lanes, courts, and crowded yards, foul middens, privies and cesspools. The water I found was deficient in quantity and most objectionable in quality, dead dogs being lifted out of the reservoir ... I am staying at the best hotel in town, but there is no water closet, only a filthy privy at some distance. (Cadman 1976, 390)

Mining villages presented similar evidence, as in this County Durham example:

> Where a line of houses opens to the fields, there is generally a foul ditch or channel full of liquid and solid refuse sufficient to poison the atmosphere as it enters the dwelling rooms ... Privies and cesspools are crowded close to many of the cottages, wells and pumps are in some cases close to middens and cesspools. Many cottages have no privies or water supplies. Refuse is thrown out in heaps, or over the surface. Children ease themselves in the road in front of the houses, and not infrequently adults also. (Barker 1974, 124)

Rural villages might not be much better, as in this description of north Northumberland housing in 1842:

> In many, human beings and cows are littered together under the same roof. Of the whole number 174, which I am discussing, there are but 27 which have two rooms each, and which are supplied with that convenience which is indispensably necessary to cleanliness and decency. (Gilly 1842, 14–15)

It is difficult to know how old many black spots were. Some may have existed for many years, but it was only now that from motives of reform they were investigated and publicized.

Chapter 14

Continuity and Change

The eighteenth century possessed an orderly and settled system of government and administration. Local magistrates dominated local government, and the bench reflected the influence pattern within society. A man did not become influential because he was appointed a county magistrate; rather his appointment as magistrate depended upon his possessing the informal status which conferred a prescriptive right to that official position.

A demonstration of the power of deferential ties in society was provided by Sir James Lowther's description of his arrival at Whitehaven in 1734. He was met

> on the high road by the sheriff, chief gentlemen, clergymen and principal freeholders living for above 30 miles in length in that part of the country, who accompanied me to Whitehaven where I was received by thousands in the high streets, the bells ringing, the great guns firing, and the ships putting out their colours. (Owen 1990, 251)

Such a welcome reflects respect for informal authority emanating from possessions, birth and patronage, all linked to ownership of land. Lowther held only the rank of baronet, but his estates were extensive and he enjoyed proportional power and respect. The rise of this family was helped by the withdrawal from Cumbria by some aristocratic leaders. Between 1680 and 1750, peers sold more Cumbrian land than they bought; the duke of Norfolk, the duke of Wharton and the earl of Sussex ceased to be Cumbrian landowners. The appointment of Sir John Lowther, a mere baronet, as Lord Lieutenant of Cumberland and Westmorland in the late seventeenth century reflected a dearth of more appropriate candidates as much as the increasing Lowther influence. Sir John became Viscount Lonsdale in 1696 and his successors, earls of Lonsdale, inherited the prestige of earlier noble interests and ended a relative vacuum in aristocratic influence. (Beckett 1975, 64)

The rise of the Lowther dynasty had its own features, but reflects general truths about the ways in which the landed aristocracy exercised power.

When in the later eighteenth century branches of the family dwindled to one main line, the consolidated family possessions provided an income of at least £45,000 p.a. for the first earl of Lonsdale. His influence included control of nine MPs, a group satirized at the time as the Lowther 'ninepins'. This leverage was based on a large landed estate, and a variety of other associated activities including mining and urban expansion. A hostile account complained:

> E'en by the elements his power's confess'd,
> Of mines and boroughs Lonsdale stands possess'd;
> And one sad servitude alike denotes
> The slave that labours, and the slave that votes. (Ferguson 1871, 408)

Aristocrats appreciated links between their economic, social and political interests. In 1826, Lord Lowther noted that

> Families are continually blamed in the strongest terms for allowing, merely for the sake of saving their money and trouble . . . Parliamentary interest to be undermined. A person should act according to the rank and station he holds in society . . . If they neglect the influence their station gives them, their property will soon be found on a less safe tenure. (Jupp 1973, 21)

Lowther influence helped to consolidate the family's dominance of the west Cumbrian coal trade with Ireland, a mainstay of the dynasty's fortune. Maintenance of that influence necessitated care and expenditure of money and energy; from the early eighteenth century, Lowthers employed professional agents to manage local electorates. (Hopkinson 1979, 109)

Profits of associated economic and political activity were not merely local, but brought access to royal recognition for the family and royal patronage for deserving supporters. In the late seventeenth century, Sir John Lowther boasted to his son of some of the consequences of his influence:

> I gott (a younger son) chose as a Member of Parliament for Carlisle . . . I gott besides my uncle to be made Surveyor of the Port of Newcastle, I gott my brother in lawe to be made commissioner of the Revenue in ireland, which he managed with great integritie and reputation to his death, and my cousin James Lowther to be a Parliament man and of the Board of ordinance. But these things cost me nothing, being pure effects of the King's Goodness to me. (Beard 1990, 285)

These successes extended the family's patronage, already large in terms of its own possessions. Royal bounty reflected Lowther's ability to support the government effectively through personal and family influence. Amongst

236

many examples during the eighteenth century, Lowther influence procured the lucrative appointment of Surveyor General of the Customs at Barbados for William, third son of Humphrey Senhouse of Netherhall, and a second well-paid colonial post for another Senhouse scion. No doubt this important gentry family was willing to buttress the Lowther position in return. (Hughes 1965, II, 104) In its heyday, Lowther approval could secure almost any office in Cumberland or Westmorland. As an impecunious barrister, James Boswell trailed Sir James Lowther about Cumbria in considerable discomfort to secure endorsement as candidate for the post of Recorder of Carlisle. In 1700 a Lowther agent, considering probable electoral behaviour, reminded his employer that in the Whitehaven district 'There is scarce a freeholder but is more or less benefitted by your coal trade.' (Hughes 1965, II, 104) Ecclesiastical patronage could also earn gratitude and support. Clergy appointed by the Lowther family were expected to display the family's yellow colour at election times. (Burgess 1984, 48)

Early in the reign of George III, the regional and parliamentary influence of Sir James Lowther received impressive recognition. In return for supporting the ministry headed by his father-in-law, the earl of Bute, he was allowed control of all Treasury appointments in Cumberland and Westmorland. (Owen 1990, 285) This, added to patronage as Lord Lieutenant of the two counties, brought a mass of official patronage to supplement his formidable unofficial power within the region. In January 1839 the hostile *Kendal Mercury*, complained of the commanding position enjoyed by the Lowther dynasty:

> In every part of the County, the Lowthers have Clergy and Magistrates, and Commissioners and Excisemen, and Surveyors, and Corporators, and Tax-Gatherers, and constables; all eager to gain future favours by promoting the wishes of their patrons. (Marshall and Dyehouse 1976, 131)

If the Lowthers were remarkable in their accumulation of patronage, there were many parallels. In 1706 Mary Clavering of Chopwell, near Gateshead, married William Cowper, Queen Anne's Lord Keeper, soon to become Lord Chancellor and Lord Cowper, whose posts in government carried considerable patronage. Under George I, Cowper remained in favour and became a wealthy earl. His wife became Lady in Waiting to the Princess of Wales. Her family profited by this exalted connection, and in 1714 James Clavering wrote to Lady Cowper to say that 'as it's now in yr. ladyship's power to help and assist yr. poor friends & relations, I doubt not of your kind remembrance'. Despite the fact that one member of the Clavering family was executed as a traitor after the 1715 rebellion, this link enabled the family to prosper and solicit favours for their own supporters. Lady Cowper's brother 'Jacky' Clavering was a Lord of the Bedchamber to George II. In

1714, after Mr Gowland of Durham played a prominent part in celebrating George I's safe accession, James Clavering wrote to his sister Lady Cowper to say, 'I wish my Lord for ye encouragement of friends in these parts wld. remember him with some suitable posts.' (Hughes 1956, 14–21)

In a private capacity the second Duke of Northumberland employed Robert Mylne on improvements at Syon House in Middlesex; his father had also commissioned work by Mylne at Northumberland House in London. Ducal satisfaction helped Mylne to official contracts to design a number of bridges in Northumberland. (Gotch 1955, 87–94)

The combination of political, economic and social influences available to the landowner was illustrated by Lowther control of Whitehaven. The family was the principal agent in the town's development, its coal shipments to Ireland and elsewhere transforming 'a few huts into a wealthy and flourishing town'. Lowther coal also encouraged coal-using industry such as salt, glass and iron. Expanding commerce encouraged shipbuilding and rope-making. (O'Neill 1982, 134–5; Beckett 1981; Williams 1951; Parson and White, *Cumberland*, 1829, 243)

Lowther dominance was reflected in the first form of local government, established in 1708. Town and harbour were governed by 21 trustees chosen every three years. Two-thirds were elected by groups who shared the Lowthers' concern for the town's prosperity, including merchants, shipowners and master mariners. Remaining trustees were appointed by the Lowther Lord of the Manor, who possessed a veto over decisions. Apart from this, as owners of land on which the port grew, and collieries which supplied the principal item of commerce, they controlled patronage among the town's population which ensured that elected trustees behaved. Until well into the nineteenth century, family control of the town was secure, even if some townsfolk resented dependence.

Limitations on Landlord Influence

Despite their advantages, aristocracy and gentry did not enjoy untrammelled control of northern society. In political matters, their freedom of action was limited in two respects. There were lesser men who were not amenable to authority, even if cajolery, flattery, or persuasion might enlist their support. Electoral studies have demonstrated the lengths to which patrons felt obliged to go in expenditure of time, money and effort in cultivating electorates. Each constituency possessed its pattern of influence. Some of them provided patrons with absolute control, but it was more common for county and borough constituencies to exhibit complex political, economic and social attachments which meant that control required assiduous attention. Even where one interest was paramount, such as the Howards in Morpeth, or the Lowther interest in Westmorland, it was sound tactics to conciliate independent support.

The second limitation was more subtle. Leading figures not only wished their influence to be effective, but for it to be accepted as part of the normal working of the communities concerned. When the duke of Northumberland returned to Alnwick Castle, he would be welcomed by a large troop of mounted tenantry. Such attentions were expected, but they were more impressive and more pleasing when they were accorded voluntarily. Even a ducal magnate must show consideration for the interests of lesser men.

Contemporary writers stressed the need for landowners to take a personal interest in their estates. (Beckett 1983, 87–107) Northern landlords might be tempted to spend more time in the attractive social life of London and the south of England, administering estates through agents. High living brought pressures to increase rent income, and several writers pointed out that such a course of action could be disastrous in economic, social and political terms. The Cumberland landowner J. C. Curwen told the House of Commons that he was 'sensible that the residence of gentlemen in the country is a most desirable object, and tends much to the happiness of the bulk of the people'. It was in a landowner's interests not only to employ good stewards but also to ensure that he himself was visible to dependants as directly concerned and a dispenser of patronage in the neighbourhood.

It was not always possible for magnates to be regular residents; estates and responsibilities might extend to other regions. The sixth duke of Somerset visited his Cumbrian estates once between 1682 and 1748. This was exceptional. Some aristocratic landowners rationalized estates by disposing of outlying properties which they rarely visited. It was appreciated that personal attention redounded not only to the landowner's profit but also to his prestige. Most leading members of the Lowther family spent considerable periods in Cumbria. Sir James Lowther of Whitehaven (1673–1755) was assiduous in combining profitable sojourns in London during parliamentary sessions with stays at home in Cumbria. Even while in London he carried on a detailed correspondence with his steward, usually writing by every post.

Accepted conventions moderated even the most powerful local influence and society was not always prepared to acquiesce if a magnate chose to press his authority too far. When the young Sir James Lowther (1736–1802) nominated county magistrates in ways which ignored established custom, selecting men of inferior status while ignoring others better qualified, and attempted to monopolize parliamentary representation of Cumbria, he overstepped the mark and provoked hostility among local gentry which inflicted a rebuff in the general election of 1768. The Westmorland electorate rejected a Lowther nominee, reducing his parliamentary strength to what was virtually the pocket borough of Cockermouth, and a long-standing arrangement with Lord Thanet to share Appleby's representation. In 1789, by now earl of Lonsdale, Lowther used his patronage as Lord Lieutenant in ways which angered other interests. Resentment resulted in a formal county meeting and a memorial of complaint signed by the earl of Carlisle, Sir Henry Fletcher, Sir Frederick Vane and seventy other landowners. (Bonsall 1960, 66; Ferguson 1871, 175, 298) Normally, a less arrogant attitude ensured that social, political and economic influences were effective. The district around Levens Hall provides an example of a resident landlord followed in Westmorland county elections by almost all voters for many years, and similar instances existed in many places. (McCord and Carrick 1966, 100–1; Hopkinson 1979; Beckett 1983, 94–5)

Patronage and deference enjoyed by aristocracy and gentry were paralleled at other social levels. In their own sphere, lesser folk enjoyed political, economic and social influences. At a time when formal agencies of national and local government performed only a narrow range of functions, society was ordered and held together by this intricate network of unofficial influences. Commonly, this influence was buttressed by performance of various duties. It was regarded as a proper activity for those who could afford it to provide charity for those in need. To care for one's own dependants was to acquire a natural claim on their gratitude, but communal responsibilities could go much further.

Whilst aristocracy and gentry retained pre-eminence, individual families saw variations in fortunes. Even the greatest families could find their position altered by marriage with an heiress. The third marquess of Londonderry acquired with his bride a substantial landed estate, eleven collieries, a collier ship, two railways, a quarry, a harbour, the nucleus of a new town and a prominent role in Durham society. (Sturgess 1982, 179) Marriage of the sixth duke of Somerset to the heiress of the Percy earls of Northumberland in 1682 made him one of the most powerful northern magnates. In addition to estates in Northumberland, some of them producing incomes from coal-mining, the duke acquired land in and around Cockermouth in Cumberland. (Hopkinson 1979, 101; Marshall 1983, 188) The Percy inheritance subsequently descended to Somerset's granddaughter Elizabeth Seymour, countess of Northumberland, who married the wealthy Yorkshire baronet Sir Hugh Smithson in 1740. He took the name Percy and was subsequently created duke of Northumberland. This marriage affected not only a major territorial holding but also the pattern of influence within the region. Successive dukes of Northumberland exercised economic, social and political power in the North. For many years this included almost a prescriptive claim to be Lord Lieutenant of Northumberland and to nominate one of the county's two MPs.

Many gentry families after the Restoration, like the Bowes, Lambton and Lumley dynasties, had occupied positions of local influence long before 1640; Delavals had held estates in south-east Northumberland since the twelfth century. Shifts within local dominant groups continued, but they were slow and piecemeal rather than revolutionary. New entrants represented success in legal, ecclesiastical or commercial careers, rarely promotion of farming families. Of new claimants to the style of 'gentleman' in Cumbria during the first half of the eighteenth century, none emerged from the ranks of the farmers, and success in trade, the law or other professional occupations provided a more usual springboard. (Beckett 1975, 97)

During the early eighteenth century, the Ridley family, successful Newcastle merchants, acquired a landed estate in south-east Northumberland, much of it forfeited Jacobite land. Alderman Ridley of Newcastle was hard-pressed financially during a struggle with the coal cartel in the 1740s, but timely marriage to the heiress of Matthew White's considerable fortune relieved the strain. His father-in-law's death in 1750 brought a valuable collection of land, collieries, glass-houses and other interests into the Ridley estate and hastened transition from urban 'gentleman' to important county figure, baronetcy and seat in Parliament. (Cromar 1978, 206) The family were not content merely to achieve the status of landed gentry, but exploited an estate of varied interests. Banking, coal-mining and development of the little port of Blyth were all part of estate management. On 17 January 1744, an advertisement in the *Newcastle Journal* announced:

> At Blyth a good seaport in Northumberland, good convenience for carrying on any trade, with liberty to build warehouses, granaries, and other things necessary: also a new windmill built with stone and well accustomed, a fire-stone quarry for glasshouse furnaces, a draw-kiln for limestones, two large sheds for making pantiles and stock bricks, with a good seam of clay for that purpose.

In the mid-1780s, Sir Matthew White Ridley, Bart., MP, built a brewery at Blyth which earned him an annual profit of some £400. (Sullivan 1971)

Even where newer landowning families absorbed many of the cultural interests of aristocratic contemporaries, the appetite for commercial opportunities remained. In the late eighteenth century, the intellectual and artistic interests of two children of the merchant and landowner Ralph Carr took them on overseas tours, but they were expected to use their eyes and their wits to recognize commercial opportunities. (Purdue 1994, 124)

In the Kendal area the Fisher family made money in trade and bought a landed estate in 1626. (Phillips 1970, 40–2; Phillips 1995) Other families acquired independence after years of service to landed magnates. The Lawson family owed much to paid service of its members as stewards of the earl of Northumberland's manor of Cockermouth, allowing them to attain independent status as landowners. The seventeenth-century Civil War and the Restoration, without altering social norms, provided opportunities for the pushful to elbow their way into the landed interest at the expense of those who chose the wrong side and paid for their loyalties.

A study of landed families in County Durham concludes that, after expansion in the early seventeenth century, numbers dropped, from 91 in 1610 to 72 in 1819. Surviving families acquired additional estates by marriage, inheritance or purchase. Decline among landowners was kept on a small scale, despite failure of families from default of heirs or other causes, by new dynasties replenishing the landowning élite, 175 in Durham over this long period. Of the newcomers, many (45) were already landowners on a more modest scale, some (41) came from the professions; there were 36 merchants and an ironmaster. The most common method of joining the landowners was purchase, 116 of the 175 newcomers acquiring their status by that route. In a region in which many landowners were involved in mining, transport and commerce, and knew some of the potential recruits well, older families seem not to have discriminated against newcomers. (Halliday 1994; Phillips 1973, 36; Purdue 1994, 124–38)

The early nineteenth century saw an increased flow of entrepreneurs from industry and commerce joining the landed interest, acquiring estates or at least a country house with appropriate surroundings. In shipping, ownership had often spread widely in small shares, usually in sixty-fourths of a ship's value, but from the late eighteenth century specialist shipowners, sometimes on a large scale, became prominent and enjoyed a higher social status. By the mid-nineteenth century these shipowners dominated local shipping. (Ville 1989, 205–9) Such men do not seem to have experienced difficulty in gaining acceptance in local society. When the successful industrialist J. W. Williamson attended the mayoress of Newcastle's fancy dress ball on 22 March 1832, he wore a genuine Persian costume 'richly ornamented with jewels of great value'. A fortnight later the 'gentlemen of Durham' sponsored a similar function in the Assembly Rooms, Durham, which brought together landowners, coalowners, bankers, merchants and industrialists. (Yarrow 1992, 142)

Despite a few wealthy families, Cumbrian landowners were generally poorer than in Durham and Northumberland. In terms of income, many Cumbrian gentry families would not have qualified for such status in more prosperous regions. Even here, there was improvement in landowning incomes, as some Cumbrian gentry prospered by involvement in cattle trading; others invested in mining, shipping or commerce. (Beckett 1975, 82; Phillips 1973, 191–213; Jarvis 1954, 230)

It was possible for ruin to come to long-established landed families. Some accumulated debts which threatened their status. The Whitfield squires in south Northumberland embarked upon expensive building without adequate income. Overwhelmed by debt, they were forced to sell their patrimony in 1750. Most families were more fortunate or more prudent.

The survival of some families involved anxious manipulation. An agricultural depression in the 1680s caught some landowners in a vulnerable situation. Edmund Craster of Craster spent the last few years of his life sheltering at Durham, having been forced to allow his principal creditor to occupy Craster for 21 years in return for cash to pay off most pressing debts. His son restored the situation, although forced to sell land in the 1690s, reducing holdings to only 425 acres. By the time he died in 1722, John Craster had improved the position, buying land again and finding portions for younger children as well as a comfortable estate to bequeath to his heir, another John. This John continued the recovery; he was a successful lawyer, and married into the influential Villiers family. By 1737 the Crasters again owned 2,090 acres; many farms had been completely rebuilt. John saw his eldest son George educated at Eton and Gray's Inn, and gave him £100 for a visit to France. George was provided with a profitable marriage in 1757, which brought a dowry of £10,000, a reversion worth another £10,000, and income from £8,000 lent on mortgage.

George Craster died in 1772, having divided his time agreeably between London, overseas travel, and his ancestral estate, where he added a Georgian block to the old tower house. On his death, the house contents were valued at £640. Craster's bedroom had curtains of crimson damask. His library contained 340 books and manuscripts, two terrestrial and two celestial globes, three Italian silk umbrellas, guns and bedding. China included a Sèvres tea service decorated with paintings of partridges and kingfishers by the well-known artist Alonde. The dining room possessed four mahogany tables and twelve leather-bottomed chairs. Chippendale supplied at least some of the room's fittings. No doubt Mr Craster cut a considerable figure among tenant farmers and less adventurous local squires. (Craster 1955, 17–21)

The Craster experience showed how the eighteenth century saw improvements in the standard of living of the well-to-do. The work of Vanbrugh at Seaton Delaval Hall for the Delaval family in the early eighteenth century was on the same scale as ducal rebuilding at Alnwick Castle, where the first duke of Northumberland spent £70,000–80,000 in the years after 1755. In both cases income from non-agricultural sources helped to finance ostentatious building schemes. (Ryle Elliot 1952, 113) The magnificence of leading aristocratic families, with palaces like Alnwick Castle, was followed, at a lower level, by gentry families. In 1691 Sir John Lowther embarked upon rebuilding Lowther Hall, a project which cost £16,500, including £430 paid to the court painter Antonio Verrio for embellishment of walls and ceilings. In the following century Henry Howard of Great Corby covered his tower house at Corby Castle with a classical front. (Owen 1990, 207–8; Beckett 1975, 118)

The Coming of Parliamentary Reform

For a century after the Glorious Revolution of 1688, landed aristocracy and gentry held sway, in both regional and national affairs, with little competition. Even in later years this hegemony showed resilience in face of accelerating social and economic change, although it came under pressure from the late eighteenth century onwards. Although there was deference towards established rank, in the North as elsewhere, society was increasingly altered by economic development and urban growth. A contemporary writer complained in 1794 that opening the earl of Carlisle's colliery near Castle Carrock had resulted in the loss of 'that ancient simplicity of manners which mark the husbandman', with the adoption instead 'of a familiar roughness and austerity, together with a low subtlety, which too often borders on fraud and deceit'. (Hutchinson 1794, I, 180) In 1800 a bread riot by slate quarrymen at Ulverston saw a local magistrate suspended from a window by his heels. Such defiance had happened before, but now seemed more frequent and alarming. In the hard year of 1740, the Guildhall at Newcastle was pillaged by a tumultuous crowd, including men from neighbouring industrial villages. The town's stock of ready cash was looted. During anti-militia riots in the war years of the 1790s, it proved difficult to obtain evidence against ringleaders, even if trouble did not match the Hexham anti-militia riot of 1761, in which the death toll may have been as high as 45, with 300, including women and children, seriously injured. (Marshall 1983, 191; Grierson 1972, 105–6; Dickinson 1979) Although nothing in the North equalled the scale and ferocity of the anti-Catholic Gordon Riots of 1780 in London, there were sufficient incidents of strikes, demonstrations and riots in the late eighteenth and the early nineteenth century to cause alarm. (Stevenson 1979, 76–80) The skilful organization which marked some of these popular eruptions, including the early miners' strike of 1765 and the seamen's strikes of 1815, was an additional worrying factor. (Stevenson 1979, 76–80; Levine and Wrightson 1991, 398–427; McCord and Brewster 1968; McCord 1968; Dickinson 1979)

That manifestations of discontent did not produce serious results owed much to moderation evinced by those in power. Most magistrates, well informed about local conditions, appreciated that draconian repression was unlikely to produce tranquillity. It was more prudent to earn, by restraint and conciliation, the continued respect of local people. Many magistrates, and military and naval officers, appreciated legitimate grievances and responded accordingly. During a noisy protest against the export of food at a time of local scarcity, a magistrate at Whitehaven commented that 'We cannot wonder that people should take umbrage at their (food supplies) being sent off to any other place.' (McCord 1970, 17–18; Price 1980, 36)

There was reluctance to employ armed force against popular demonstrations, a reluctance shared by local dignitaries and officers of army and

Figure 14.1 The Northern Colossus, or the Earl of Toadstool Arm'd with a poll axe. This 1786 print reflects local hostility to Lowther attempts to control parliamentary elections in Carlisle.

navy. The unpaid parish constables, described in the 1834 Poor Law Royal Commission report as 'the most inefficient body imaginable', who provided normal resources for policing communities, would have been almost ludicrously incapable of coping with a northern population which was genuinely disaffected, but that was not the situation faced. (Royal Commission 1834, Appendix A, 310A)

However, increases in size and distribution of population produced situations which guardians of law and order found it increasingly difficult to police effectively. Older communal conventions weakened in the face of large-scale immigration. Carlisle provided a notable if extreme example. By the 1820s only half of Carlisle's population was native born, with Irish and Scots migrants providing most of the remainder. (Barnes 1981, 94, 124–30) This did not make for social cohesion and from an early date there were local protests against 'the numerous hordes of the idle and unsettled (who) ... emigrate to this place from Scotland and Ireland with one fixed idea – that we are compelled to maintain and support them'. Not so much danger of revolution, but such problems as intimidation by beggars, vagrancy and petty crime, exposed inadequacies of the old order. By the early 1850s, 25 per cent of the inmates of Carlisle prison were strangers, born outside the county of Cumberland, many of them Irish immigrants. (Marshall 1970, 228) The *Carlisle Journal* lamented on 29 December 1826 that

> Never in the memory of man were crimes so abundant in the North of England as they now are in the neighbourhood of Carlisle. The current talk is of robbery, robbery ... We are now, indeed, becoming like the inhabitants of ANOTHER IRELAND!

The new, unpopular arrivals congregated in slum suburbs, with hopes of employment in the textile industry often disappointed. In these quarters traditional deference to local magistrates was largely absent. When a local association for the prosecution of felons was formed to fight crime, leading members were assaulted or had their windows broken by a mob from the Caldewgate suburb. During a turbulent election in 1826, the mayor of Carlisle was captured by the mob and ducked, and when troops intervened a woman and a child were shot accidentally. (*Carlisle Journal*, 9 and 29 December 1826; Barnes 1981, 102–3, 289) This resulted in 1828 in the establishment of a small police force for the city, but for many years it remained difficult or impossible to serve warrants in Caldewgate. It was not until 1857, when it was made compulsory, that Cumbria acquired anything like adequate police. In the North East, growth in mining communities was one reason why Durham chose to pay for a county police force as early as 1840. Northumberland ratepayers, like their Cumbrian neighbours, held out until 1857.

In a thinly populated and largely rural society, a limited system of local government might suffice, bolstered by the unofficial power of aristocracy and gentry. As population increased, mining, commerce and industry expanded and towns grew, it became increasingly difficult to administer local affairs on the old basis. Problems such as public health, policing and education became pressing and more appreciated. This attracted intervention by the state, gradually eroding the local independence of earlier years. By 1850 this process was under way, even if changes were limited in extent and effectiveness and much of the older patterns of influence remained intact.

Parliamentary Reform

Traditional patterns of northern parliamentary representation facilitated control by the landed interest. Before 1832, Cumberland and Westmorland returned a total of 10 MPs – two for each county and two from each of the boroughs of Appleby, Carlisle and Cockermouth. In Carlisle freemen provided the electorate, perhaps amounting to no more than 300 in the seventeenth century, but increasing from the early eighteenth century. At Appleby and Cockermouth the vote was attached to particular pieces of property, the burgages. At Cockermouth electors were fewer than at Carlisle, although numbers voting were often higher than the total entitled to do so. In the fiercely contested election of 1710, 237 voted; not more than about 150 qualified electors existed at the time. Appleby's electorate in the seventeenth century was under a hundred.

Northumberland saw only three contested county elections between 1760 and 1830. Even in the early nineteenth century, the duke of Northumberland could normally nominate one of Northumberland's two county MPs, though his candidate had to be suitable for that position. There is no recorded instance of a Northumberland county elector being evicted for defying the voting instructions of his landlord, though no doubt less extreme forms of pressure as well as 'legitimate influence' were employed often enough. The earl of Carlisle dominated Morpeth elections. At Berwick the garrison commander enjoyed considerable electoral clout with merchants; at Durham the Church of England was a political force. Newcastle might be independent enough to choose its own MPs, but often preferred landed gentry with Newcastle connections.

The electoral pattern was already out of symmetry with distribution of population. Towns like North and South Shields, Gateshead and Sunderland were centres of population and economic development without their own parliamentary voice. Kendal was the biggest town in Westmorland, but Appleby the only parliamentary borough, as well as the seat of county government and assizes. Kendal men consoled themselves by establishing the right of burgage holders there to vote in Westmorland county elections, a dubious claim sustained by the 'bold swearing of the Kendallers'. Other forms of electoral distortion were common. As it became clear that electoral influence was a valuable asset, leading local figures such as the Lowthers began to buy up vote-carrying burgages in boroughs. Lesser men might hope to earn a bribe or favour by acquiring a small portion of an old burgage and claiming a vote for this fraction. At Carlisle, as it was increasingly appreciated that votes were worth having, the number of freemen electors grew, doubling in the first two decades of the eighteenth century.

From the late eighteenth century onwards, opposition to the state of parliamentary representation was increasingly vocal. Popular radicalism in this period, and more particularly the Chartist Movement, has been a topic of compelling interest to modern historians. In 1839–40 there were large and sometimes turbulent public meetings in support of the People's Charter, including demonstrations in Newcastle. Despite the weakness of police resources, established authority remained in control. The extent of Chartist support varied widely. In 1839–40 there was considerable support among industrial villages in and around Tyneside; Irish immigrants to Teesside took little interest. In later years Chartism never recaptured the scale of support and enthusiasm displayed in the movement's first phase. (Thompson and Harrison 1978; Ashton 1991; Devyr 1882; Harrison and Hollis 1979; Maehl 1963; Rowe 1971; Rowe 1977; Rowland 1983; Wilson 1983; Chase 1994, 31)

Even in areas displaying a radical tradition from the 1790s to the 1840s, as was the case in Carlisle, it is difficult to demonstrate that Chartism exerted effective influence. In Carlisle, popular radicalism closely corresponded with the fortunes of handloom weaving, and was given political expression by the wide freeman vote in parliamentary elections. These were notorious for their turbulent and often lawless popular element, frequently manipulated by influential groups for electoral advantage. (Barnes 1981, 81, 128, 262) On the other hand, this kind of leverage was utilized by leaders of the weavers, using political means to try to 'recover our lost rank and situation in society'. Despite occasional flirtation with more radical tactics, handloom weavers' spokesmen were more concerned to seek redress through legitimate channels such as repeated petitioning of local magistrates and Parliament. In the North East the situation was similar. Radical groupings emerged from time to time but were often short-lived and ineffective. There was little co-operation between groups of workers pursuing trade grievances of one sort and another, and political radicals concerned with political rights. The most able radical journal of the North East in the early nineteenth century, the *Tyne Mercury*, was an enemy of trade unionism, much given to pontificating about the errors of local workers when they ignored political economy by strikes and other restrictive practices.

The contemporary debate on political reform was less concerned with those excluded from the political nation than with those propertied elements, including commerce and industry, increasingly acknowledged as under-represented in comparison with the landowning élite. These grievances were expressed in such centres as Newcastle, Carlisle and Kendal, reflecting a sense of independent status, sometimes associated with religious nonconformity, and representing interests capable of challenging prescriptive patterns of influence within society.

In religion, first Protestant dissenters and then Roman Catholics were given a political role denied in 1688. Immediately after Catholic Emancipation in 1829, P. H. Howard of Corby was one of the first Roman Catholic MPs, elected for Carlisle in 1830. In that city, as in Newcastle and other northern towns, there were signs of coalition between liberal urban groups, including influential dissenters, with the Whig section of the landed interest.

Another instance of a Liberal–Whig alliance against aristocratic interests was the sustained but at first only moderately successful campaign of the radical lawyer Henry Brougham, allied with Kendal's nonconformist leaders, to wrest at least one of Westmorland's parliamentary seats from Lowther control. Dynasties of leading townsfolk existed in Kendal, with their own corps of dependants and supporters. John Wakefield (died 1829), who founded one of these dissenting interests, set up the first gunpowder mill in the district at Sedgwick, south of Kendal, in 1764, and a local bank in 1788, and was said to have spent £30,000 in supporting the anti-Lowther campaign. Unitarian and Quaker groups in Kendal forged their own networks of marriage connections. (Marshall and Dyehouse 1976, 155) In County Durham politics, the radical earl of Durham could count on organized liberal groups in towns like Gateshead who would marshal county voters in their own districts. (McCord Gateshead 1969) Even if such activities were often unsuccessful in early years, a growing consensus supporting parliamentary reform challenged established political networks such as that of the earl of Lonsdale in the west and the duke of Northumberland in the east. Reformers could mobilize sufficient support to force the existing order into costly defensive measures. It was said that the four well-heeled candidates in the fiercely contested Northumberland county election of 1826 spent £250,000 between them, much of it lavished on fortunate electors, including free drink. In Westmorland, the Lowther interest was obliged to spend freely, combating Brougham's appeals to independence of the county electorate. While no doubt many, perhaps most, electors were subject to influences of one kind or another, some were capable of changing allegiance or defying influential men when they felt strongly on an issue. (McQuiston 1976, 153)

In 1831, enthusiasm for the kind of parliamentary reform offered by Grey's government brought an electoral upset. Lowther candidates were beaten for both Cumberland county seats and one Westmorland county seat. In Northumberland, the influential Tory Matthew Bell abandoned his candidacy after a preliminary canvass showed its hopelessness. Although the Tory cause in Northumberland was usually strong, on the issue of the

Whigs' parliamentary reform scheme, which included doubling the county's representation, both seats went to supporters of change.

The 1832 Reform Act reduced the Lowther electoral empire by removing MPs from Appleby and Cockermouth, although there was compensation in a single seat for Whitehaven. Another new constituency, Kendal, reflected economic importance which enabled the town to nurture opposition to the dominant Lowther interest in Westmorland society and politics.

In Northumberland, the earl of Carlisle saw his borough of Morpeth lose one of its two seats, although the family continued to dominate the constituency until well into the second half of the century. Of borough constituencies created in 1832, Tynemouth and Sunderland tended to elect members closely connected with the towns' interests, but insisted that candidates should pay electors heavily. The 1832 changes left the landowning élites in possession of much electoral influence for a considerable time to come, even if this power had to be exercised in ways less blatant than some past practice. (McCord and Carrick 1966; McCord and Wood 1959–60, 11–21)

The Great Reform Act was very much the work of the landed élite itself, as in Northumberland's Earl Grey, Durham's 'Radical Jack' Lambton, earl of Durham, or Cumbria's Sir James Graham, Bart. This timely concession succeeded in splitting opposition, with moderate liberals rallying to the reformed constitution against radical demands for further political change. This was a principal reason for the failure of Chartism. Whig reforms of the 1830s undermined opposition to the existing order by conferring on its more influential elements much of what they wanted. This included more than admission to the parliamentary electorate and redistribution of parliamentary seats. Related measures such as the Poor Law Amendment Act of 1834 and the Municipal Reform Act of 1835 consolidated the grip of local propertied groups on their own communities, and tied them more closely in support of the reformed order.

The North in 1850

By the middle of the nineteenth century, economic and social change was accelerating transformation of a remote and relatively poor frontier zone into an urbanized and industrialized society.

One of the most striking features of this transformation was increase in population. During the first years in which national censuses were held, in Cumbria numbers grew by 13 per cent in 1801–11 and 16 per cent in 1811–21. County Durham's population was 149,384 in 1801, 390,997 in 1851, an explosive rise of 261 per cent in a couple of generations, the

highest rate for any county in the first half of the century. Northumberland's increase, if less spectacular, was still striking – from 168,000 in 1801
to 304,000 in 1851. In 1836, the bishop of Durham told his clergy that

> Where a barren moor lately presented the appearance of a desert,
> never inhabited, and but rarely visited by man, a railroad may perhaps
> be formed, or a coal-pit opened out; cottages are built, and men,
> women, and children appear diligently employed in gaining their daily
> bread. (Heesom 1979, 139)

Despite this unprecedented demographic change, for many people life
remained bounded by local considerations. Within the swollen population
of Sunderland by 1851, a majority, 60 per cent, lived in the town in which
they had been born, and 10 per cent came from elsewhere in County Durham, 5 per cent from Northumberland. Scotland and Ireland contributed
12 per cent, and 8 per cent had some kind of rural origin. (Fox 1980, 19)

Despite changes since 1603, there remained much that was rough and
uncivilized in northern society, although in 'polite' society violence and
drunkenness were no longer acceptable. The general tendency was towards
higher standards, but the record was mixed. When the prison reformer John
Howard visited Newcastle in 1771, he noted that

> During the Assizes at Newcastle the county prisoners are, men and
> women, confined together seven or eight nights in a dirty, damp dun-
> geon, six steps down in the old Castle, which, having no roof, in wet
> seasons the water is sometimes inches deep. The felons are chained to
> rings in the wall. (Charleton 1889, 133)

At a bull-baiting on Newcastle's Sandhill in 1768 a soldier ventured too
near in his excitement and was fatally gored. Elimination of cock-fighting
was not effected until many years after it became illegal. (Jobey 1992) In
1837 the Chief Constable of Newcastle presented the town council with a
tabulation of less salubrious activities.

> 17 houses for the reception of thieves
> 8 houses the resort of thieves
> 31 the average number of thieves
> 71 brothels where prostitutes are kept
> 4 average kept in each house
> 46 houses of ill-fame, where they resort
> 31 houses where they lodge

> (Rewcastle 1854, 13)

251

In 1850 the head of Tynemouth police reported that

> In one house, the notorious 'Sally Joyce' on the Steam-Mill Bank, I found one night eleven persons who had been living for a considerable period of time on no other visible means of support than that of pilfering. The most of them had been convicted thieves and were the associates of thieves. They were regaling themselves with a piece of beef, eggs, tea and some hot whisky toddy. (Anon. 1949, 56)

Accounts from the late eighteenth and early nineteenth centuries mention many young girl prostitutes.

The northern counties consumed more than their proportionate share of alcohol. Beer duty at Newcastle netted for national revenue a handy £43,000 in 1825–26. In May 1822, a large illicit still was discovered in abandoned workings of an old colliery on the outskirts of Newcastle. Smoke had been emitted into old mining galleries to disperse unnoticed, while fuel was frugally abstracted from the pit's unworked resources. Even in this respect, however, changes were for the better. There were 1,366 prosecutions for drunkenness in Newcastle in 1838, less than 1,000 in 1852.

When Queen Victoria ascended the throne, the four northern counties of England were experiencing rapid transformation. The separateness of early periods had diminished and the region was more firmly established as part of a wider national community. Standard weights and measures were now generally used. Even in rural Cumberland, by the 1790s 'butchers began to sell their meat by weight, and the country frugal housewife to throw away her old pound stone, substituting in its place the standard 16 ounces for weighing her butter'. (Hutchinson 1794, 662) There was decline in locally distinctive patterns of dress, dialects and recreational habits.

Communications and contacts with the remainder of the United Kingdom had been improved, most notably in sophisticated organization of east-coast shipping and extension of the railway system. This does not mean that there was a uniform national process of change and development. The North had its own regional economy. From a thinly populated and poorly endowed section of a predominantly agricultural society, the region, or at least a substantial part of it, was turning into a centre of industrial growth. By 1851, farming had lost its place as the biggest single source of employment and income; in the North East there were then 35,522 workers directly employed in agriculture, but 41,089 in coal-mining. Changes between 1603 and 1850 would have astonished earlier generations. The next couple of generations were to see the pace of change accelerate further and bring about a northern region in many ways different from all that had gone before.

Part Four

1850–1920

Chapter 15

Industrial Revolution

For most of its history, the northern region was relatively poor and backward, its resources exceeded by those of the fertile South and East. The situation was transformed in the nineteenth and early twentieth centuries, when industrial and commercial expansion conferred unprecedented levels of importance. Perhaps the only parallel to this prominence existed during Northumbrian supremacy within Anglo-Saxon England. (Barrow 1969, 1)

These changes were not only important within regional and national history, but possessed wider significance. They reflected opportunities offered by a changing world in the Age of Coal, Iron and Steam, opportunities which the North was well placed to exploit. Total international trade amounted to about £800 million in 1850, nearly £3,000 million in 1880 and passed £8,000 million by 1914. (Ashworth 1975, 14–15) Within this growth, one of the most portentous developments in history, the British share was large, and a substantial portion was taken by the four northern counties. Even if this prominence did not prove permanent, the North's role in making the modern world may have been the region's greatest contribution to the evolution of human society. Before 1850 the transition to an urbanized and industrialized society was under way, but the pace then accelerated. (McCord 1995)

The price of importance was vulnerability to wider events. Rails exported from the region equipped railways which opened fertile interiors of remote continents to world trade with eventual consequences for British agriculture. Distant instability could exercise baleful influence, as in the ill effects of the American Civil War on Carlisle's cotton industry.

Economic transformation had profound demographic results. After 1850, rural districts had static or declining populations, but this was more than matched by population growth in industrial areas. The most dramatic of these was the creation of large new towns at Middlesbrough and Barrow in Furness, startling contemporaries by the pace of their development.

The Northern Élite

In the nineteenth and early twentieth centuries, many industrial and mining companies, commercial and shipping houses, and financial institutions, were controlled by a relatively small coherent group. These leaders were linked together in various ways. There were family connections and personal friendships. (Briggs 1996, 13) There were links in intellectual and cultural societies in main centres, where prominent figures from town and country acted together, and in sport and recreation. There were connections in church and chapel, shared schooling or apprenticeship; Armstrong's Elswick and Palmer's Jarrow works were nurseries of men later to hold key positions in companies within the northern region and elsewhere. (McCord 1994; Briggs 1996, 13; Binfield 1982, 166)

One example of such links was created after 1882 by John Wigham Richardson, who, with his partner J. D. Christie, owned the Neptune shipyard on Tyneside. (Wigham Richardson 1911, 253–4) During the winter he held regular Virgil evenings at his home. A party of friends dined together and discussed passages of Virgil. When the main works of that poet had been covered, Horace came next, though a proposal to move on to Lucretius 'frightened some of our members'. Those involved included Thomas Hodgkin, Newcastle banker as well as distinguished historian, W. S. Daglish, Tynemouth solicitor prominent in Tyneside local government, Benjamin Browne, senior partner of Hawthorns' engineering works, Benjamin Noble, banker, and Theodore Merz, scientist and expert in the industrial application of improved technology, including electric power. We need not suppose that Latin literature was the only topic considered. Gentlemen's clubs provided other meeting places. At Newcastle, the Union Club, founded in 1862, moved into new premises in Westgate Road, which had cost £40,000, in 1878. (Kelly 1925, 223)

By mid-century Newcastle had a community of scientists, with connections to industry, capable of holding their own with other regional centres. Newcastle Chemical Society was founded in 1868 and a College of Science in 1871. In 1885 Dr J. H. Rutherford founded a school providing technical education. The meeting of the British Association for the Advancement of Science at Newcastle in 1863 provided an opportunity for local scientific and technological talent. The town chose as mayor in that year the ironmaster Isaac Lowthian Bell, FRS, who was perfectly capable of taking the lead in the chemical section. An industrial seminar of the highest order was held, calling on the expertise of Maling on pottery, Swinburne on glass, Spencer on steel, Lowthian Bell on iron, Sopwith on lead, Nicholas Wood on mining, Richardson on chemicals, Palmer on shipbuilding, Armstrong on armaments. By the time the British Association visited Newcastle again in 1889, higher scientific education there had developed sufficiently to make local

256

professors among the stars of the meeting, and industrialists were less prominent. (Campbell 1980, 60–2)

The Importance of Coal

At the heart of the transformation was the coal industry, a leading beneficiary of improved technology. As demand for coal for domestic and industrial purposes increased at home and abroad, coalfields affected surrounding areas in two principal fashions. Coal mining, transport and sales became crucial in income and employment, while availability of this cheap energy encouraged development of coal-using industry on the coalfields.

Much of the enhanced output was exported. Northern coal went all over the world, but exports from the principal source, the Great Northern Coalfield of Durham and Northumberland, continued an established pattern. Most went to continental Europe in a wide arc stretching from the Baltic to the Mediterranean. Northern collieries provided a vital energy source for urbanization and industrialization throughout Western Europe, at a time when Europe counted for so much in world affairs. (Elliott 1968; Mitchell 1984, 18–19)

The smaller Cumberland coalfield played a lesser role and lost the dominance of the Irish market which it had enjoyed for two centuries. Competition from larger Lancashire and Scottish coalfields saw the Cumbrian share drop to only 16 per cent by the end of the nineteenth century. (Wood 1952, 126–7; Wood 1988, 203) Despite this setback, coal production increased with expansion of iron and steel industries. Although Whitehaven remained the centre of production, collieries spread inland and to the north. In 1851, coal-mining provided only 3.88 per cent of employment in Cumberland, with farming at 24.07 per cent and textiles at 15.56 per cent, but by 1911 the figure was 9.69 per cent. If iron and lead were added, mining then provided the biggest single form of employment. The relative importance of mining in west Cumberland was greater than county-wide figures suggested.

Cumberland coal was unsuitable for producing coke for iron works, but local coke could be mixed with coke from the North East. The Maryport and Carlisle Railway of 1845, and the Keswick and Penrith Railway of 1864–65, enabled ore to be carried to North East iron works; trains returned with coke for Cumbrian furnaces. Towards the end of the century, improved technology allowed greater consumption of Cumbrian coke, using one-third of the coal produced there, but in the early twentieth century five-sixths of coke used in the Cumbrian iron and steel industry still came from the North East. The Cumberland coalfield reached its highest level of annual production, just over 2 million tons (a little under 1 per cent of the national total), in the early twentieth century. (Marshall and Walton 1981, 52–3; Wood 1952, 331–2; Wood 1988, 173–4)

By mid-century, about one-third of coal shipments from the Tyne were exported. In 1888, when over 6 million tons were shipped, 63 per cent went abroad. Annual east-coast shipments doubled to about 5 million tons during the second half of the century. In the early years of the twentieth century, the Tyne shipped some 17 million tons annually, of which over two-thirds were exported. About half went to France, Germany and Italy. Scandinavia was the next biggest customer, and Spain and Russia took as much as 10 per cent each in peak years. Within coastal shipments, London took about 60 per cent in the 1870s, and about 80 per cent in the years after 1900. (Elliott 1968, 75–87; Smith 1961, 283)

In 1851, Northumberland agriculture employed twice as many as mining, but by 1900 mining outstripped farming. There were nearly 11,000 miners in 1851, 37,000 in 1901, more than 15 per cent of total employment. In Durham, numbers directly employed rose from 30,000 in 1851 to 100,000 in 1901, from 18.5 per cent of total employment to a remarkably high 23 per cent, with many others indirectly dependent on the coalfield. By 1911, there were well over 54,000 miners in Northumberland, nearly 20 per cent of all employment; by then Durham had more than 152,000, not far short of 30 per cent of all employment. (Rowe 1973; Brown 1995)

Demand for different kinds of coal brought shifts in demographic patterns. Rapid growth of Teesside iron and then steel industry increased demands for coking coal from west Durham, while other districts responded to rising demand for steam coal. Household and steam coal of south-east Northumberland was exploited intensively in the years on either side of 1900. Ashington's population rose from 345 in 1851 to 13,956 in 1901, while the older village of Bedlington grew from 5,101 to 18,766. Coal shipments from nearby Blyth rose from 235,000 tons in 1880 to 1.8 million tons in 1890 and more than 4 million by 1914. The Tyneside chemical industry used 250,000 tons in 1853, and the annual figure rose to 300,000 in the 1860s. Accelerating population growth increased domestic consumption. (Rowe 1971, 130)

Greater shipments were facilitated by a technical breakthrough, replacement of wooden sailing colliers by screw-propelled iron steamships. A lengthy process of trial and error culminated in 1852 with demonstration of the profitability of the new type in Palmer's *John Bowes*. She was the first successful modern cargo ship, ancestress of thousands of vessels carrying the spectacular increases in world trade already noted. (Martin and McCord 1971; Davidson 1946, 40; Smith 1961, 285–7) The year after *John Bowes* made her first trips to London, the Gas, Light and Coke Company, a principal coal-shipping firm, decided to change over to the new colliers. By 1855 there were about 60 steam colliers based in the Tyne and the number continued to grow. A good sailing collier might carry about 280 tons, the *John Bowes* and her early sisters between 400 and 750, depending on size. Carrying capacity of steam colliers soon increased. The sailing fleet declined, with remaining ships driven to take risks to survive. In 1862, 100 colliers were listed as missing at Lloyds after a fleet put to sea in doubtful weather. Three years later similar circumstances brought further heavy losses. The improved colliers did not need the keelmen who manned coal-carrying barges on north-east rivers, for they loaded from shore installations served by railways. Keelmen were already in decline, but this final blow brought about the disappearance of a distinctive group of workers.

Most northern collieries were now owned by companies, but a few aristocratic magnates remained. (Ward 1971) Lord Durham's colliery income was over £84,000 in 1856 and reached £380,000 in 1873. By the 1890s he owned fourteen collieries and a small fleet of coal-carrying ships. In 1896 there was an abrupt change, direct exploitation was abandoned and the collieries sold. Londonderry influence lasted longer. Collieries owned by Lord Londonderry dropped from eleven in 1853 to only three by 1919, but these were important concerns, employing about 7,000 miners. He also owned a railway (until 1900), colliers and the little port at Seaham Harbour which was extensively improved in the early twentieth century. In Cumberland the earl of Lonsdale's income from Whitehaven Colliery reached £90,000 in 1873, but was often less than half this. In 1888 the colliery was leased to owners of the Harrington Ironworks, ending 200 years of direct management. A fixed rent, and payments based on tonnage mined, were preferred to unpredictable fluctuations in income. Over the next thirty years mergers and takeovers saw Cumberland coal-mining increasingly controlled by iron and steel companies. (Wood 1988, 160, 315)

Even where aristocratic interests withdrew from management, mineral revenues could be an important part of income. In 1913 the earl of Durham received nearly £60,000 from way-leaves, coal royalties and rents from railways. The duke of Northumberland leased almost all his coal-bearing land, but mineral income amounted to £82,450 in 1918. (Mountford 1966; Mountford 1976) Earls of Lonsdale owned nearly 40,000 acres in Westmorland alone *c*.1874, but their agricultural rent-roll was buttressed by income from railways, iron, coal and urban property. Coal income alone amounted to more than £40,000 p.a. in the early twentieth century. (Marshall and Dyhouse 1976, 155–6)

Increased employment had effects beyond greater numbers. Where collieries opened, there was a rush of male migrants to the scene. In 1871, County Durham had 941 females per 1,000 males, the lowest of any county; the national average was 1,052 per 1,000. By 1900, newcomers to Ashington far outnumbered those born there. Rapid change facilitated shifts in beliefs and attitudes, and may have made support for Labour politics easier to develop. (Rowe 1990, 427; Hodnett 1994, 14)

Figure 15.1 Coal-hewer, wearing standard pit clothing, working in a narrow seam in an early twentieth-century Northumberland colliery.

Simpler occupational structures of earlier periods became more complex and varied. Small land-sale collieries survived, but sea-sale mines were increasingly characterized by diversity of function. Now there were not only hewers and putters, but pony-drivers, shifters, stonemen, sinkers, boiler-minders, enginemen, overmen, deputy overmen, engineers, managers and assistant managers, and labourers. Large collieries possessed surface installations, including offices and workshops, employing trades not specific to mining such as clerks, accountants, secretaries, cleaners, electricians, storemen, loco-motive drivers and firemen, mechanics, joiners and smiths, as well as those responsible for horses and ponies. Ancillary operations produced additional complexities; coke-ovens became more sophisticated:

> These patent ovens and by-product recovery plants employed a wide range of workers – loaders, levellers, cranemen, doormen, door washers, stampers, ram enginemen, and those employed in valve cleaning, regulating gas burners, dealing with the centrifuge, hydraulic mains, exhausters and scrubbers, and in the processing of sulphate of ammonia, benzole and tar distilling. (Emery 1992, 80–1)

Mining communities reflected this complexity, and the expression 'the miners' could bear different meanings. This illustrates a more general transition from a relatively simple pre-industrial society into something much more numerous but also more diverse and complex. (McCord 1995)

In other ways too, organization became complicated. Permanent mining unions were created in mid-Victorian years, and became involved in convoluted arrangements for settling wages and conditions. From the 1870s, printed books, listing wage rates and variations derived from local customs and conditions, were regularly produced by coalowners' associations. Printed minutes of proceedings of mining unions exhibited similar complexity and sophistication.

It is difficult to arrive at general conclusions about mining wages, which varied between different working places, individuals and groups within the hierarchy of mining jobs. Hewers, the cream of the underground work force, were among the region's best-paid workers, but there could be significant fluctuations even here. Their dominance among miners diminished, especially when coal-cutting machinery began to make progress. In 1891, hewers provided 40 per cent of underground workers in Northumberland, only 33 per cent by 1911. Skilled hand-workers, hewers had most to gain by defending traditional working practices, although this played a part in limiting productivity, ultimately to the coalfield's disadvantage. (Hodnett 1994, 14) In Cumberland, coalowners maintained co-ordinated policies which kept miners' wages below the national average, despite growing union membership and competition for workers from iron-mines. This was helped by the continuing supply of immigrant workers from Scotland and Ireland, although the latter were often seen as 'an inferior class of workmen'. (Wood 1988, 181–91)

Coal-mining continued to be dangerous, although for most of the century seafaring was more hazardous. Some jobs in the chemical industry were also very unhealthy. Larger collieries, with more employees, made explosions increasingly dangerous. In the 1860s, the average loss of life in colliery explosions was three per year, but this figure more than doubled over the next twenty years. Catastrophes continued, including New Hartley in 1862 (204 men and boys killed), Pelton 1866 (24), Seaham 1880 (164), Trimdon Grange 1882 (74), Elemore 1886 (28), West Stanley 1909 (168), Wellington Pit, Whitehaven 1910 (136). Minor accidents were cumulatively more dangerous. Increasing efforts were made to improve safety, and Mines Acts of 1887 and 1911 marked substantial extensions of intervention and regulation. This was not always welcomed by owners or miners. In Cumberland there were accusations that local magistrates hearing cases could be influenced by links with defendant companies. (Wood 1988, 193) The industry intensified research into mining dangers. One result was proof, by the early twentieth century, that coal dust increased the destructive power of explosions. It was significant of changing conditions that these tests were organized and financed by coalowners on a national basis. (Redmayne 1942, 159)

At the coal face much continued as before. There were attempts to replace expensive labour by machines, but substantial progress in mechanical coal-cutting did not come until the inter-war years. In some areas, including

Figure 15.2 Richard Logan, electrician at Broomhill Colliery, Northumberland, with his wife and mother-in-law in the parlour of his home at Six Cottages, in the early twentieth century. Logan and his wife both died in 1953 at the age of 77.

west Cumberland, thin seams and many faults made mechanical coal-cutting impracticable. (Wood 1988, 339–40) There was better progress in mechanical conveyors underground and machinery for coal-sorting on the surface. A few companies pioneered electrical equipment, but by 1910 only 2,055 electric lamps were used underground in British collieries. (Wood 1988, 339–40; Redmayne 1942, 154) Increased output was gained by employing more miners; labour productivity in coal-mining declined in the half-century before 1914.

Although important aspects of mining remained old-fashioned, coalfields were at the heart of northern development. Access to cheap coal attracted a variety of coal-using industry. Of these, iron and then steel making provided another growth point in the later nineteenth century.

Iron and Steel

In earlier years, iron-making plants were scattered, as local resources of iron ore, coal and limestone indicated. Some, like rural Northumberland sites at

Hareshaw and Redesdale, were in locations where transport costs were a serious disadvantage. It was only where works were near good water carriage that northern iron-makers could compete with other regions. At Bedlington, a major iron works, said to employ some 2,000 workers by mid-century, found competition too stiff and closed in 1867. The quality of iron ore varied, influencing the location and fortunes of iron works. The expansion of production on lower Teesside was in part due to the low metal content of Cleveland ore, which reinforced incentives to reduce transport costs.

The construction of coal-carrying railways in south Durham, following the success of the Stockton and Darlington Railway, provided early stimulus to the lower Tees area. At mid-century, however, most of its inhabitants were living in rural settings, with farming providing most employment. Stockton and Hartlepool had populations of less than 10,000, Darlington over 11,000, and expanding Middlesbrough not much more than 7,000. Three decades later, the situation had been transformed. The lower Tees district saw population triple from less than 100,000 in 1851 to over 300,000 in 1881. Most increase was urban, with Stockton at 41,000, Darlington 35,000, the new port of West Hartlepool at 28,000 and booming Middlesbrough at 56,000. (Bullock 1974; Briggs 1996, 2–9; Taylor 1996, 53–7; Polley 1996, 154–9)

Early Victorian years saw small-scale development of iron-making, exploiting local iron ore and coal, as at Tow Law and Witton Park. There had been iron-ore mining in the Cleveland Hills since the 1830s, but the situation was transformed when in 1850 the ironmaster John Vaughan recognized the potential of the main deposits at Eston. (Briggs 1996, 10; Nicholson 1996, 42–5) Mining at once increased, with Cleveland producing 188,000 tons by the end of 1851. At first Vaughan and his partner Henry Bolckow sent ore by train to existing blast furnaces at Witton Park, but they soon established new furnaces closer to mines, at Middlesbrough. By 1854 Teesside had nine major iron works, with 29 furnaces in blast. Darlington developed one important works, but the centre of interest shifted to Middlesbrough. Cleveland ore, with cheap Durham coal and easy access to shipping, provided boom conditions despite low iron prices in the 1850s. By 1861 Teesside produced 11 per cent of British iron, and this rose to 19 per cent over the next decade. For twenty years after 1851, the main component of population increase on Teesside was inward migration of workers attracted to the boom in iron production. (Nicholson 1996, 42–5; Taylor 1996, 53–7; Briggs 1996, 2–9; Bullock 1974)

The Teesside industry depended on mass production of low-cost products like iron rails and shipbuilding plates. Much went abroad and even in high-tariff Germany cheap Teesside iron could sell profitably. Dependence on exports involved dangers, illustrated by a sharp recession in the 1870s which saw the failure of some Teesside iron-makers. (Nicholson 1996, 39) Stronger companies weathered the depression and experienced renewed

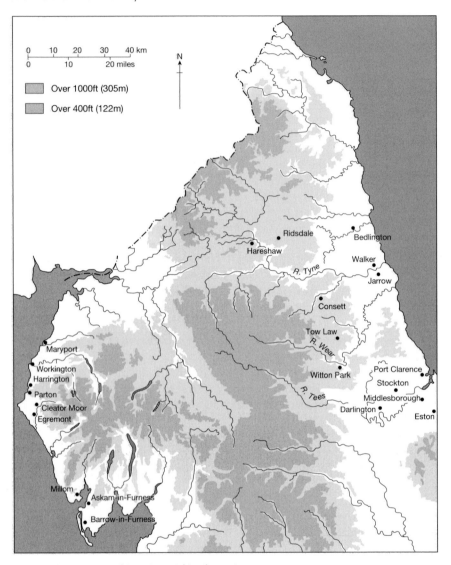

Map 7   Some iron-working sites within the region

growth from the later 1870s. By 1881, Middlesbrough was exporting not far short of half a million tons of iron annually, while coastal shipments took even more. In 1881 Teesside had 27 iron works, operating nearly 100 blast furnaces. Annual output of pig iron was well over two million tons.

Cleveland ore, which fed early expansion, could not be used in the Bessemer steel-making process. As steel began to replace iron for many purposes, Teesside producers had to find alternative supplies. At first they

264

turned to rail-borne ore from Cumberland and Furness, but these sources were limited and expensive. By the 1870s Teesside was making about half a million tons of steel a year, using mostly Spanish ore. The Gilchrist Thomas process of steel-making, available from 1879, could use Cleveland ore. During the later nineteenth century Teesside made acid steel with Spanish ore and basic steel with ore from Cleveland.

As iron and then steel became available on Teesside, manufacturing companies using these products were attracted, including bridge-building, shipbuilding, marine engineering, locomotive and railway rolling stock making, and pipe and tube manufacture. Some steel-makers diversified. Bolckow Vaughan developed collieries, rolling mills, galvanizing and eventually constructional engineering and ownership of ore-carrying ships. Their total work force had reached 10,000 by 1881. Dorman Long grew from a series of takeovers, springing from a small firm making wrought iron and carrying out engineering contracts. Expansion saw Dorman Long a giant among Teesside enterprises by 1914; during the inter-war period Bolckow Vaughan became part of its empire. Its main rival followed a different course. The shipbuilding firm of Furness Withy at Hartlepool moved into coal and iron and steel making to promote economies and efficiency. By 1898 these amalgamations produced another large conglomerate, the South Durham Steel and Iron Company.

There was a tradition of shipbuilding on Teesside, but in the first half of the nineteenth century it was insignificant compared to Wearside and Tyneside. In 1851 there were only eleven small yards, building and repairing wooden ships of moderate size. The eruption in iron-making and shift to iron shipping produced dramatic change. In 1882, shipyards on the lower Tees, with nearby Hartlepools, built 136,000 tons of iron ships, the great majority steamships. By the 1880s, the Teesside iron and steel industry had transformed south-east Durham, and the southern bank of the Tees, into a major industrial region.

Consett Iron Works

Despite locational disadvantages, the iron works at Consett, in the interior of County Durham, provided an important outlier. (Warren 1990) In the 1840s, the Derwent Iron Company was the region's biggest iron works, but its finances were precarious. Involvement with the ill-fated Northumberland and Durham District Bank brought crisis in 1857 and uncertainty until the emergence in 1864 of a stronger Consett Iron Company. This allowed renewed growth, despite remoteness from crucial supplies. Consett is several

Industrial Revolution

miles from the Tyne by the most direct route, 15 miles from South Shields installations from which it drew imported ore in later years. Even in the new company's earlier years, ore had to be transported from Cleveland. These disadvantages were overcome, partly by competent management, including skilful negotiation of favourable railway carriage rates, and exploitation of a variety of ancillary activities. The company acquired collieries, producing coal for sale as well as feeding the company's furnaces. Siting disadvantages were mitigated by drawing iron ore and other supplies by rail from Cumbria as well as north-eastern ports.

Circumstances provided Consett and other iron works with healthy markets. The building of railway systems at home and abroad brought demand for iron rails and associated metal items. The development of iron and then steel steamships provided another fillip when railway markets were falling away with completion of networks. By 1875 Consett employed between 5,000 and 6,000 men and was Britain's biggest supplier of ships' plates. Progress in metal technology involved recourse to different kinds of ore, and the company proved adept at protecting supplies. When Spanish ore was needed, the company negotiated an agreement with Krupps and the Spanish Ybarra firm in 1872, facilitating joint exploitation of the Orconera mines. By 1890, Consett was producing 175,000 tons of steel annually, much of it plates for the North's shipbuilding industry.

By 1900, managers at Consett faced crucial decisions. Competition from other British producers, and increasing rivalry from Germany and the United States, were eroding markets. Modernizing the works involved heavy cost. After long debate, the company decided not to undertake major capital expenditure, but instead joined a cartel of British steel producers. By collusive price-fixing and division of markets, the firm survived profitably, at the cost of operating obsolescent equipment. The reluctance to modernize, at a time of over-capacity, was understandable, and was not followed in all company interests. The profitable collieries saw considerable investment before 1914, including the use of electrical power.

Iron and Steel in Cumbria

There were differences between iron and steel industries in the North East and the North West. Cumbrian haematite ore was richer, with a metal content of as much as 50 per cent, often more than four times that of Cleveland

Figure 15.3 Consett Iron Works. This photograph of *c.*1965 shows the works in its last prosperous phase.

deposits. In 1849 the second richest mine in Britain was discovered at Askam in Furness and this was surpassed by the Hodbarrow mine in Cumberland seven years later, which produced 343,194 tons of ore in 1880. Increasing sophistication was reflected in the involvement of international mining experts in purposeful prospecting. (Harris 1965; Harris 1966)

Cumbrian ore was expensive to extract, but its quality overcame this disadvantage. By mid-century it was profitable to transport ore from Ulverston or Whitehaven, or from the new port of Barrow, to iron works in Staffordshire or South Wales. Railways facilitated shipments, including the Furness Railway (1858) and the Whitehaven and Furness Railway (1850). By 1858 this traffic had already reached 700,000 tons p.a. (Bainbridge 1964, 315; Atkinson 1981, 106–12)

Two years earlier, visiting Workington Haematite Iron Company, Sir Henry Bessemer assured the company that their high-quality iron would make an admirable basis for large-scale production of steel, for which there was expanding demand. This opportunity was seized by Cumbrian producers, but additional rail links, especially the South Durham and Lancashire Union Railway projected in 1862, also enabled high-quality ore to be conveyed economically to steel works in Durham, including Consett. North East coal or coke for Cumbrian steel-making offered return traffic. Furness had no coal of its own, while Cumberland coal was often unsuitable for this purpose. (Lancashire and Wattleworth 1977, 2–3, 40–1, 104; Pollard and Marshall 1854–5, 115–21)

The development of Barrow under the patronage of the duke of Devonshire (the principal landowner), railway companies, and proprietors of the Park iron-mine, was consolidated in the Barrow Haematite Steel Company of 1865, six years after furnaces for iron smelting had been established. Booming demand for steel rails at home and abroad provided early success. By 1870 the enterprise was the largest employer in the area, and the second largest steel firm in Britain. During its first eleven years, the company's Hindpool steel works never paid less than 20 per cent dividend to its 25 shareholders, who included six members of the duke's family as well as H. W. Schneider, the original entrepreneur and largest shareholder. In 1867, dividends reached 30 per cent.

There was more variety in iron and steel enterprises in west Cumberland. None of the landowners there emulated the duke of Devonshire's role in Barrow. Modestly sized companies, including those at Cleator Moor, Harrington, Parton, Whitehaven, Maryport, Distington and Millom, made high-quality iron which was used to make steel elsewhere. The nature of local ore deposits, occurring, with the exception of the great Hodbarrow mine at Millom, in veins rather than concentrated masses, encouraged this modest scale. It was not until 1871 that the West Cumberland Iron and Steel Company began to produce steel rails at Workington. The arrival of Charles Cammell and Company, moving their Bessemer plant from Dronfield in South Yorkshire to Moss Bay near Workington in 1883, signalled higher activity. Assets included not only plant and workers, but a full order book and international trading connections.

Cumbrian iron and steel made an important contribution to the developing national and international economy during the 1860s and 1870s, when steel-making technology relied on haematite ore. The Solway Junction Railway of 1869 carried Cumbrian iron ore and iron to Lanarkshire. In the mid-1880s the steel industry of the North West was still making a significant contribution to British production, with *c*.40 blast furnaces at work, even if the North East's share was larger. (Bennett 1993, 3, 6) Furness iron-mines reached peak production in 1882, and ore production in Cumbria declined during the next twenty years. Despite technical improvements, exhaustion of deposits closed most mines by the earlier twentieth century. The number of miners dropped from *c*.7,600 in the 1890s to only *c*.2,500 in 1931. Growing ore imports eroded the position of Cumbrian mines, while the discovery of the Gilchrist Thomas steel-making process enabled poorer ores, including Cleveland deposits, to be used in steel-making. In this less favourable climate, some Cumbrian enterprises failed, while others were involved in reorganization in which Cammells played a central role. (Bennett 1993, 21) By 1909 this resulted in one principal firm, the Workington Iron and Steel Company, with 22 blast furnaces, five rail-making mills, a colliery with coke ovens, six iron mines, two limestone quarries, a brickworks and its own dock at Workington. Industrial west Cumberland was then heavily dependent on the survival of this company. In 1920 competition pushed concentration further, as that firm joined the wider United Steel Company, with its main base in Lincolnshire. (Wood 1952, 291; Jewkes and Winterbottom 1933, 78 *et seq.*)

Whereas in the North East, growth of iron and steel making was involved in a complex pattern of industrial development, west Cumberland never saw a comparable take-off, although the picture in nearby Furness was somewhat different, as the growth of Barrow demonstrated. The Furness Railway, with profits bloated by iron-ore traffic, and an able manager, James Ramsden, was happy to second the duke of Devonshire's plans for growth. Both supplied capital for new ventures. By 1898 the railway company had invested £2.5 million in Barrow Docks, making Barrow one of the most modern and best equipped of all British ports. In the early 1870s, Ramsden envisaged a future town with 100,000 inhabitants. Local enterprises founded in the early 1870s included Barrow Steam Corn Mill, Barrow and Northern Counties Pure Linseed Company, Barrow Printing and Publishing Company, Barrow Shipbuilding Company, and Barrow Steamship Company. Barrow's population, a mere 900 in 1859, reached 47,259 by 1881. (Pollard 1955; Marshall 1958, 233, 249–53, 393; Stark 1972, 38–42; Leach 1872)

Optimism diminished in the less propitious climate of the 1880s and 1890s. Barrow Haematite Steel Company faced growing problems. The cost of the docks dragged down the fortunes of the railway company and, by the end of the century, enterprises of the 1870s were in trouble. The surviving shipbuilding, milling and textile companies relied on subsidies from the duke of Devonshire to stave off disaster. Towards the end of his life, the duke contemplated the dismal prospect – so much in contrast to the heady aspirations of the early 1870s – that 'Barrow and all its works will become an utter and complete failure'. (Pollard 1955, 221) Barrow never succeeded in matching the success of Liverpool and Glasgow as an Atlantic port. Only the faltering shipbuilding enterprise indicated modest success in diversifying the local economy, and sustained later increases in population.

West Cumberland remained dependent upon iron and steel. Rapid growth in the 1870s and 1880s, broadly centred on Workington (which doubled its population in the 1860s and again in the 1870s, to around 25,000), never bore fruit in development of metal-using industries such as shipbuilding and engineering. Consequently after 1881 the population of west Cumberland remained virtually static and arguably declined in real terms, in contrast to the more diversified North East.

Engineering

Part of the transformation encouraged by the interdependent expansion of coal-mining, iron and steel making and steam power lay in the development of engineering. The three north-east rivers of Tees, Tyne and Wear were principal centres.

On Tyneside, Robert and William Hawthorn built up an important firm from small beginnings during the first half of the century, helped by growing demand for marine engines. Robert Hawthorn died in 1867 and three years later the elderly William Hawthorn sold out to new owners. The principal partner from 1870 was Benjamin Browne, a 30-year-old engineer who had served an apprenticeship in Armstrong's Elswick works, and subsequently worked for the Tyne port authority. To buy Hawthorns, Browne scraped together every penny he could and borrowed more. He brought with him as partner F. C. Marshall, who had expertise in marine engineering and a reputation for enforcing efficient working practices. He had recently reorganized Palmer's Jarrow works, where he rooted out workers and practices not matching his high standards. Marshall's usefulness in improving performance was recognized by the terms on which he came to Hawthorns – a salary of £1,000 p.a., plus a quarter of all profits after a dividend of 5 per cent on capital was met. Marshall set to work to repeat methods already applied at Palmers, purging unsatisfactory workers tolerated under the paternalistic regime of the Hawthorn brothers. A new marine engineering works was acquired in 1871, and the Hawthorn works embarked upon renewed expansion.

Experiences of firms which did not move with the times could be disastrous. While Hawthorns increasingly concentrated on co-operation with ship-builders, amalgamating with Andrew Leslie's shipyard in 1886, some other large Tyneside companies lost their way. At Gateshead, Hawks Crawshay had a history of innovation, including the acquisition in 1844 of the region's first Nasmyth steam hammer. By mid-century the firm had accumulated an untidy range of activities, including bridge-building, lighthouse equipment, and nail-making. This diversity, and weaker management, meant that it was unable to meet competition from better-organized enterprises and collapsed in 1889. A similar fate, for similar reasons, overtook Gateshead's second big engineering firm, John Abbot and Company, which by the end of the century made, among other items, railway engines, water pipes, hydraulic presses, safety lamps and metal tacks. The company was in trouble by 1900, and eventually went under in 1909.

North East Shipbuilding

These were by no means the only failures in an environment of competition and fluctuating conditions, which faced entrepreneurs with multiple problems. In the boom years 1905–7, Sunderland shipyards built one million tons of new shipping, but 1908 was a difficult year with production slumping to only 92,022 tons. (Royal Commission 1992, 8) Maintaining financial viability and productive capacity was not easy in such conditions. These difficulties, however, occurred within a general pattern of growth and success, in which North East shipbuilding was conspicuous. Although the Clyde and the Thames took to iron shipbuilding before northern England, the North was well placed to benefit from the mid-Victorian revolution in shipbuilding. By 1900 more than half of the world's new tonnage was built in Britain and more than half of Britain's share was built in the North East.

Northern yards varied in the ships they built. Some lived by multiple orders for cheap and relatively standardized vessels. It was a local joke that Palmer's built screw colliers by the mile and chopped them into convenient lengths. South-east Durham yards built hundreds of economical cargo steamers for customers at home and abroad. On Wearside, Doxford's built 178 of their more or less standardized turret-deck cargo steamers during the eighteen years after 1893. In 1905, Doxford's had the highest shipbuilding record in the world, producing 20 ships averaging 4,332 tons, and in the following year the yard launched an average of one ship per fortnight. In 1911–14, the firm consistently outbuilt all British rivals. (Corfe 1983, 45) The Tyneside shipbuilder Wigham Richardson noted that 'Over and over again during 40 years, I have demonstrated that our principal profits have been made from simple cargo steamers and from repetitions of them.' (Wigham Richardson 1911, 71, 125, 143–4) At South Shields, Redhead's yard concentrated on small- and medium-sized cargo ships and cultivation of shipowners. In 1878 the yard built its first ship for the Hain Steamship Company of St Ives. By 1899, this connection had resulted in 35 orders, 87 by 1965. Runciman and Strick were other shipping lines successfully cultivated. At Hebburn, Andrew Leslie's yard developed similar links with shipping lines, including Lamport and Holt, Alfred Holt and Company, and Booth and Milburn. Leslie built 41 ships for Lamport and Holt between 1861 and 1892. Dreadnoughts and ocean liners received most publicity, but a high proportion of tonnage from northern yards represented work-horses rather than greyhounds of the seas.

Costs were crucial, as in the development of the oil tanker. Carriage of oil in barrels was inefficient in loading and unloading, and wasteful in cost of barrels. Innovation came from a Newcastle shipowner and shipbroker, James McNabb, who suggested use of large tanks which could be carried in ships' holds. The first vessel incorporating this was converted by Hawthorn's in 1886, but she was already obsolete. Henry Swan, managing Armstrong Mitchell's shipyard at Low Walker, devised the solution of using the ship's hull as the oil container. The first oil tanker appeared in 1886 to Swan's design. Over the next twenty years northern yards built 200 tankers, Armstrong's taking the lion's share with 96.

Naval shipbuilding was a specialized area in which most northern yards could not compete effectively. Two Tyneside giants, Armstrong and Palmer, dominated North East contributions, although other yards obtained minor orders from British and foreign navies. Naval shipbuilding was competitive but profitable.

As the last quarter of the century passed, there was an increasing tendency for shipyards to consolidate into larger groupings, as ships grew larger, more complex and more costly. The success of northern shipbuilders contributed to parallel success in ship repairing and manufacture of maritime machinery and equipment.

Among major firms, Armstrong and Palmer acquired reputations for self-sufficiency in shipbuilding operations, but their independence can be exaggerated. Newton and Nicholson of South Shields, specialists in packing steam joints, were employed by Palmer during construction of the battleships *Resolution* and *Revenge* in the late 1880s. A few years later, Armstrong's employed Donkin & Nichol of Newcastle to provide steering gear, forced draught installation and hauling and winding engines for the ill-fated battleship HMS *Victoria*. Many of her forgings were produced by the Tyne

Forge Works, Ouseburn, Newcastle, a firm employing about 500 workers, which became a subsidiary of Newburn Steel Works. These are examples of an intricate network whereby specialized suppliers of many kinds were now needed for technologically advanced production.

There was marked increase in the work force involved in shipbuilding and kindred activities. In 1851 most northern yards employed less than 50 workers, and only one more than 200. By 1887 one ship-repairing yard, Wallsend Slipway, not the biggest, employed well over 1,000 men. In 1911, shipbuilding provided directly 5 per cent of all work in Northumberland; the Durham figure was 6 per cent. Individual centres saw higher proportions – South Shields 9.4 per cent, Sunderland 15.6 per cent, Stockton 9.6 per cent, West Hartlepool 13.3 per cent. (Rowe 1973, 127 and tables) By 1911 the North East employed nearly half of Britain's shipyard workers.

Overseas orders played an important role. The Tyneside shipbuilder Charles Mitchell nurtured a profitable Russian connection, operating a ship-yard at St Petersburg from 1862 as well as obtaining orders for building Russian ships on Tyneside. Andrew Leslie also cultivated a Russian connec-tion, with 11 of his first 17 ships Russian orders. The most intensive foster-ing of overseas contacts can be seen in the work of Palmer and Armstrong.

Charles Mark Palmer was born into one of Newcastle's merchant families, a breeding ground for commercial skills, though not for over-scrupulous personalities. In 1854 a local banker commented on the Palmer family firm that they were successful, 'but I do not think that they are much liked, being tricky in fulfilling their coal contracts'. (Bank of England, 22/3/1854) During the third quarter of the century Palmer worked hard at building up an industrial empire which included Cleveland iron mines and an integrated Tyneside enterprise which built ships from arrival of iron ore to departure of completed vessels. (McCord 1979, 131–3) His success brought appropriate rewards – country house and London mansion, magistracies, deputy lieutenancies, baronetcy. He dominated the town of Jarrow, which had been called into existence by his enterprise. He was its first mayor, and when Jarrow received a parliamentary seat it was for many years almost a Palmer pocket borough. (McCord 1979, 131–3; Purdue 1982)

William George Armstrong sprang from a similar background, the close-knit Newcastle oligarchy of commercial and professional families. Like Palmer, these connections gave him access to capital needed to prime his career as industrialist. In 1847, solicitor turned engineer, he set up a small factory at Elswick, west of Newcastle, manufacturing hydraulic machinery of his own design. He had three partners – Armorer Donkin, George Cruddas and Addison Potter – established businessmen on Tyneside. Each put up £5,000, to which Armstrong added £2,000 and an estimated £3,000 in the value of his patents. (Cochrane 1909; Dougan 1971; Scott 1962, 24–35) Until his death in 1879, Cruddas acted as financial mentor, putting the firm on a sound footing. The partners restricted dividends and ploughed back

profits; within fifteen years initial capital of £20,000 had grown to £100,000. In an uncertain world, the enterprise obtained a reputation for financial integrity, paying bills promptly and keeping borrowing to a minimum.

There were problems. Armstrong's hydraulic designs did not always work well, and there were disappointed customers to placate. The Crimean War saw Armstrong's involved in gun design, which brought orders from the British services totalling more than £1 million between 1859 and 1863. There was then an abrupt cessation, with only £60,000 of British armaments orders during the next fourteen years. The company was strong enough to weather the storm, and astute enough to find alternative income. In 1867, Armstrong's provided armament for a group of gunboats built by Charles Mitchell at Walker, and this intervention into shipbuilding rapidly expanded. Increasing co-operation brought a merger with Mitchell in 1882, and the Armstrong Mitchell union was involved in shipbuilding both above and below Newcastle, as well as engineering and armaments. In 1897, the company was strong enough to take over a major competitor and become Armstrong Whitworth.

The move into shipbuilding, including warship building, was timely in the late nineteenth and early twentieth centuries. In 1913, building Walker Naval Yard increased Armstrong's stake in warship building. Winning a long series of naval orders, at home and abroad, was not a simple result of high quality of design in a competitive atmosphere, but involved high-powered salesmanship and ruthless exploitation of every channel of influence. (Warren 1989; Dougan 1971; Noble 1925, 82; Hough 1966; Manning 1923, 140)

In 1914–18, the need to mobilize resources in support of the national war effort confirmed the region's dependence on a limited range of interdependent heavy industries, especially coal, iron and steel, engineering and shipbuilding. There had been deliberate attempts at diversification by enterprises like Armstrong's before 1914, but then concentration again on staple activities to supply military and naval materials. During the war Armstrong enterprises built 47 warships, armed another 62 and repaired or refitted 521. They built more than 1,000 aircraft, 13,000 guns, 12,000 gun carriages and 14.5 million shells. At the end of the war the company had large cash balances but also increased dependence on military and naval aspects of its business.

In the early twentieth century, 23,000 jobs on Tyneside were directly dependent upon Armstrong enterprises, with many more relying indirectly upon the company. There were other major Tyneside shipbuilding enterprises, such as Swan Hunter & Wigham Richardson, who built the famous *Mauretania*, launched in 1906. By contemporary standards shipbuilding

---

Figure 15.4 The *Mauretania* leaving the Tyne on her maiden voyage, 1907.

wages were good, especially in skilled trades. Apprenticeships in the Armstrong works were eagerly sought and formed part of a great web of patronage among workers which determined which boys should be admitted to skilled trades in such industries as shipbuilding and engineering. Elswick foremen enjoyed considerable status and influence in the local community; when the British Association made a much-publicized visit in 1886, they showed the distinguished visitors around the works.

Naval shipbuilding contributed to revival at Barrow, at the cost of linking the town with the fortunes of a single company. In 1888 the troubled Barrow Shipbuilding Company was taken over and transformed into a Naval Construction and Armaments Company, which exploited the 'vast and empty docks' there. This was timely as international naval rivalry increased. In 1897 the company became part of the Vickers group, and a major naval shipbuilding enterprise. Thereafter Vickers dominated the social and economic life of the town. Under the favourable circumstances of the years around 1900, shipbuilding employment grew from 2,355 in 1891 to 9,000 by 1909 and 17,000 by 1914. (Stark 1972, 38) This boost was part of a population increase which brought Barrow to over 60,000 by the early years of the new century. Steel production was now of minor importance.

Turbines and Electricity

There were other success stories. Charles Algernon Parsons, son of an Irish earl with scientific interests, worked as premium apprentice at Elswick for four years and then in 1884 moved to another engineering works at Gateshead, where his turbine experiments began. Disagreements within the company brought a break in 1889, with Parsons setting up a small works at Heaton in Newcastle's eastern suburbs. From this base his turbine work succeeded in two fields, electricity generation and marine propulsion. Marine turbines rapidly developed from the tiny installation in the *Turbinia* of 1897 to the 70,000 hp of the *Mauretania* of 1907.

At the turn of the century Parsons was well known in local technical circles. When he demonstrated the potential of his turbines for electricity generation, he found little difficulty in obtaining capital. His first generator produced only 7.5 kW; by 1900 1,000 kW machines were introduced, and by 1910 358,000 kW. In 1889 there were two generating companies on Tyneside, employing steam engines and operating working agreements on pricing and divisions of territory. Parsons turbines brought further progress. The generating station opened at Carrville near Wallsend in 1904 was the first large modern generating station. Enterprising firms nearby, including the North East Marine Company, a maker of ships' engines, became buyers of electrical power. A Tyneside railway was electrified five years before any London suburban line. (Bell 1951, 28–9; Hennessey 1972, 57–61) By 1914, progressive colliery companies in the North were introducing electrical equipment. In 1912 Ashington Coal Company's generators produced more than 5,000 hp. For many years Tyneside was in the forefront of electrical engineering, providing go-ahead local enterprises with cheap electric power, and a growing asset particularly valuable in the lean inter-war years. (Rowe 1990, 431)

Industries in Decline

Interlocking empires of coal, iron and steel, engineering and shipbuilding provided a spiral of interdependent prosperity. Overall the northern region saw increased prosperity, sufficient to support phenomenal increases in population and higher standards of living and opportunity. This success occurred despite some contrary elements such as the failure of some individual enterprises and shrinkage or collapse of some elements within the regional economy.

Textile manufacture in Cumbria had been a success story during the first half of the nineteenth century (pp. 215–18 above), but this was not to last. In 1851, 15.56 per cent of employment in Cumberland was in this sector, but by 1871 only 5.72 per cent. Westmorland saw a smaller but still significant drop, from 8.38 per cent to 4.77 per cent. The leading Carlisle-based firm of Peter Dixon and Sons still employed c.8,000 workers in 1847, and continued to rely on handloom weavers to take up their cotton yarn. This had the advantage of leaving the ill effects of trade depressions to fall on weavers rather than the manufacturer, but technical obsolescence was a weakness in competition with rivals elsewhere.

Allegedly Dixons never recovered from the loss of specialized markets as a consequence of the American Civil War. The firm had supplied cotton ginghams which 'had always adhered to the same pattern' for southern slaves, but following emancipation the demand from the free negro was for 'a gaudier article . . . (he) . . . is capricious, and must be tickled and attracted by new patterns'. (Buller 1882, 52) This, together with isolation from main centres of the industry, brought about the bankruptcy of Dixons in 1872. An unsuccessful attempt to refloat the enterprise as a joint stock company preceded final collapse.

What was left of the Cumbrian textile industry was concentrated in specialist firms in Carlisle and Kendal. Towards the end of the century, there was partial revival of varied textile manufacture at Carlisle – printing of fabrics, woollen spinning, dyeing and finishing. In 1911 Carlisle had over 2,000 textile workers, but they amounted to two-thirds of Cumberland's total. Ferguson Brothers, using fine Egyptian cotton, employed 1,200 workers in the early 1920s, but there was no doubt of the overall decline of the industry. The downturn was more marked at Kendal, although some carpet-making survived. Factors which had brought Cumbria success in textiles were no longer as useful. Water power was of decreasing importance, while isolation from centres of the industry and its main suppliers hindered expansion. (Marshall and Walton 1981, 9–11, 24–7)

By the end of the nineteenth century, the textile industry of the North East had also shrunk. A few centres, such as the city of Durham's carpet-making, continued to flourish, but elsewhere a scatter of small-scale textile enterprises made only a tiny contribution to the region's increasing industrial prosperity.

Lead-Mining

Some other northern industries faced problems in these years. In 1850 lead-mining districts in the Northern Pennines were prosperous, and increasing output matched buoyant prices. In 1851–61, population of Middleton in Teesdale rose from 1,849 to 2,266 because of increased lead working. Thomas Sopwith, a leading expert, could receive as much as £6,000 p.a. for exploration of lead deposits and management of Beaumont lead interests. Expansion continued until the 1870s, followed by disastrous decline. A minor cause was the working out of more accessible lodes of ore, but the principal reason was the collapse of international lead prices at a time when Britain was wedded to free trade policies. British lead was fetching £21.49 per ton in 1877, only £12.25 eight years later. There were attempts to keep going by cutting costs and accepting lower standards; in 1884, it was still common for lead-miners to reach working places either by ladders or footholds cut into high brick walls. The drop in prices, continuing until they bottomed out in 1892, was too steep for such expedients to have significant impact. In the 1920s Britain produced less than 1 per cent of the world's lead output. (Banks, Nichol and Bridge 1994, 215)

Loss of lead-mining in the Alston district precipitated a population fall of 18 per cent there in 1871–81. Many migrants found their way into the industrial North East or to a lesser extent into west Cumberland. In the Allendale area of south-west Northumberland, principal mines closed one by one – Swinhope in 1872, Mohopehead in 1878, Coalcleugh in 1880, Allenheads in 1896. A few managed to hold out. Weardale Lead Company continued to produce lead and by-products until 1931, but they were better survivors than most. By the end of the century, lead-mining was the shrunken remnant of a once great industry. With this contraction came the end of a distinctive local culture in which lead-mining had been combined with small hill farms. (Hunt 1970; Turnbull 1975; Coombes 1958; Dunham and Hobbs 1976)

The Chemical Industry

Another sector in which growth gave way to contraction was Tyneside chemical manufacture. In 1852, Tyneside employed almost half the chemical workers in Britain. By the 1860s more than half the national production of alkali and bleaching powder came from 24 chemical works along the lower Tyne. Leading figures in the industry, including Christian Allhusen and James Cochrane Stevenson, were prominent in social and political life. As with the lead industry, the climate turned sour in the later nineteenth century. (Campbell 1964; Campbell 1968, 1463; Campbell 1969)

Tyneside chemical plants had been based on the Leblanc alkali process, developed in the later eighteenth century. This revolutionized the supply of alkali, needed in increasing quantities for textiles and other industries. The Leblanc process, while superior to older methods, was wasteful and inefficient, although modifications introduced additional by-products. By mid-Victorian times, Tyneside chemical companies had invested heavily in the Leblanc process. In the 1870s a more efficient technique, the Solvay process, was developed, and the competitive position of the Tyneside chemical industry was eroded. Much Tyneside chemical production had been exported, and customers were now able to set up more efficient production methods and undercut old suppliers.

There were other reasons why the Tyneside chemical industry faltered. Brine deposits in south-east Durham offered raw material for advanced processes which could outstrip any locational advantages which Tyneside still possessed. In 1885 J. C. Stevenson reorganized his chemical interests and with another manufacturer acquired extensive brine royalties at Haverton Hill near Teesside. This district was to become an important centre of the chemical industry in future years.

In 1891 the difficulties of older chemical plants led to rationalization in the United Alkali Company, forerunner of Imperial Chemical Industries. This defensive arrangement involved closure of obsolescent or inefficient producers. A number of Tyneside works disappeared under this proviso. Although some plants, including Allhusen's Newcastle Chemical Works, managed to hold on, by 1914 the Tyneside chemical industry had shrunk to relative insignificance.

Other Industries

In Cumbria, quarrying continued on a substantial scale. The Albert Memorial in London includes 'pink' granite from the Shap quarry opened by Curtis of Dalbeattie in 1868. Cumbrian slate found markets outside the region, as railway development facilitated carriage of bulky materials. When the Honister Slate Quarry finally closed in 1985 it had seen two hundred years of working. (Bennett 1993, 9, 11)

Manufacture of gunpowder in the North West continued, with new works opened at Black Beck in 1862 and High Gatebeck in 1898. (Bennett 1993, 28, 31) Soap-making showed modest growth, and at the end of the nineteenth century Tyneside firms produced household and industrial products. Thomas Hedley's firm was established in 1837, and had a considerable future ahead. A local survey of industry in the late nineteenth century claimed that this enterprise relied 'on *quality* rather than *advertising*', but by the end of the century more sophisticated tendencies were manifest. The company expanded, its growth based in part on the import of increasing quantities of African palm oil. From 1898, Hedley's was spending increasing sums on advertising, with Fairy Soap the first of its well-promoted products. (Anon. *c*.1894)

Paper-making was another established industry. By 1862, twelve North East firms were producing about 8,000 tons p.a. Import of esparto grass from the 1860s onwards facilitated expansion. The Ford Mill at Hylton near Sunderland, built in 1864 at a cost of about £40,000, was one of the first to use this material, and deserved success for other reasons too. Early operations showed a profit of around 21.5 per cent, but the owners only withdrew 7.5 per cent in dividends, ploughing the remainder back into the business. Care was taken in profitable recycling of chemicals. A near neighbour, Hendon Paper Works, employed over 400 workers in the early twentieth century. While achieving modest prosperity, paper-making remained one of the lesser northern industries. (Maidwell 1959; Bank of England, 25/5/1868; Mitchell 1919, 157–8)

Pottery and glass making were established before 1850. In the late 1860s there were 13 potteries on Tyneside, employing 1,200. Twenty years later, the Maling company employed 1,200 in mechanized production of huge quantities of earthenware containers and similar cheap items. There was another centre on Wearside, with a similar expansion in production and employment in the third quarter of the century. The industry was then hit by foreign competition, and the late nineteenth and early twentieth centuries saw severe shrinkage. In 1881 Sunderland exported 684 crates of earthenware, but only 222 in 1891 and 26 in 1900. The two principal potteries in Gateshead closed in 1892 and 1909 respectively. At Sunderland two Southwick potteries closed in 1874 and 1897 and the important Deptford pottery in 1918. In the 1860s these three had employed about 3,000 workers. With free trade a national dogma, and relatively high labour costs, northern potters could not withstand competition from cheap foreign imports together with rivalry from other British producers. (Bell 1971; Manders 1973, 65; Mitchell 1919, 149)

In 1851, northern glass-works made major contributions to the Crystal Palace. The old-established Sowerby firm was one of the first British producers to make pressed glass when the technique was imported from America after *c*.1860. New ideas came after Swan exhibited his evacuated carbon filament electric lamp at a memorable meeting at the Newcastle Literary and Philosophical Society on 3 February 1879. The Swan Electric Lamp Company was formed to exploit this discovery, utilizing local glass-making skills. (Ridley 1962; Ross 1982)

Like pottery, the glass industry suffered severely from cheap foreign imports, but it had other problems. In the third quarter of the century this industry provided an early example of trade union influence. By the 1860s a closed shop existed in blown flint glass works, with employers bound to take the next name on the union's list when a vacancy occurred, while in other ways tight union organization ensured good wages by contemporary standards. This dominance was short-lived. It is unlikely that without it the works concerned could have stood up to competition from the new cheaper mechanized production of pressed glass articles, but high labour costs encouraged the rapid collapse of older plants. The removal of import duties on glass in 1857, as part of national free trade policy, brought additional problems.

In sheet glass of various kinds there was early collusion among manufacturers. By 1841, a conference of British companies, including northern firms as well as others elsewhere like Pilkington and Chance, agreed on production quotas. The position of the Sunderland firm of Hartley was enhanced by their introduction of rolled plate glass in 1847. By the 1860s the British sheet glass sector was dominated by a triumvirate of Chance, Pilkington and Hartley, operating in collusion. This tranquillity was disturbed from 1875 by imports of cheap Belgian glass. Attempts by British firms to extend their cartel arrangements failed because 'there is unfortunately no association of window-glass-manufacturers in Belgium and no understanding of any kind amongst them'. (Ridley 1962, 157)

Increasing costs in Belgium helped British market recovery, but the British cartel faltered. Pilkington began to move forward independently; the

St Helens firm owned their own collieries and took the lead in improved glass technology. Gradually more northerly works were squeezed out, with eight closures in Sunderland alone. James Hartley died in 1886 and the enterprise he had founded was already in trouble. His Wear glass-works, which had been one of the industry's giants, finally closed ten years later.

On the Tyne the story was similar. At South Shields the Swinburne company became the Tyne Plate Glass Company in 1868, when the works covered 7 acres and employed about 600 workers. In 1891 it collapsed with heavy debts and by 1900 South Shields possessed only one small pressed glass maker as a survival of what had been one of the district's main industries. (Hodgson 1907, 364) Bottle-making had been another standby of the region's glass industry, with about 4 million bottles produced annually in the 1860s. Here too competition gradually obtained the upper hand.

Glass-making did not disappear from the four northern counties. The first electric light bulb was blown at Lemington on Tyneside, and the region remained an early centre of bulb manufacture. Overall, glass-making never recovered the prominence it had occupied in the third quarter of the century. A contributory cause may have been the superior attraction to available capital provided by the dominant local interests of coal, iron and steel, engineering and shipbuilding.

Chapter 16

Transport, Agriculture and Services

Despite some mixed experiences, the predominant trend in the regional economy after 1850 was one of increases in production, trade and employment. Industrial and commercial growth brought complex developments which were not confined to industry. Transport links, including railways, shipping services and docks, diversified and required more workers. Late Victorian industry needed thousands of work-horses, requiring increased fodder production, breeding, trading and veterinary facilities and manufacture of harness and trappings of various kinds.

On the Tees, Middlesbrough Dock, first opened in 1842, was enlarged three times in the later nineteenth century, and other port facilities were created to cater for Teesside industries. Parallel expansion of the port of Barrow in Furness was more of a speculative endeavour. The Furness Railway Company, very much the creature of the Cavendish family, poured capital generated by mineral traffic – iron ore, copper and slate – into a phased but extensive programme of harbour improvements completed by 1879, but for some time this optimism proved misplaced. The expensive docks were not used to full capacity. Barrow was handicapped by its relative isolation. (Leach 1872, 26; Marshall 1858, 198, 25, 273, 344) On the Wear, successive dock-building schemes produced a total of 210 acres of enclosed docks by the early twentieth century, while at the harbour mouth new pier and lighthouse building was substantially completed by 1903.

The most dramatic changes came on the Tyne. During the second half of the nineteenth century, the Tyne Improvement Commission transformed a dangerous shoal-ridden estuary into a major modern port. In 1847 clearance over the bar at the river mouth could be little more than 6 feet – much the same as in 1818. By 1865 improvements had increased this to 15 feet; by 1875 a 20-foot channel existed to Newcastle. Sizeable ships could now make their way up-river to serve extended industrial and urban communities. Large docks were built on both sides of the river; quays with modern cranes, improved coal-shipping machinery and similar installations multiplied. In 1876, the route up-river beyond Newcastle was opened by building

Figure 16.1 Fish Quay, North Shields, crowded with fishing craft in late nineteenth century.

a swing bridge; without this Armstrong's Elswick works would have been impossible. The bridge worked by hydraulic machinery of Armstrong's design and construction. In carrying out this campaign, the Tyne Improvement Commission drew on advanced technology, but much depended on the way in which the Tyne commissioners were themselves involved in the area's industries, with personal interests in efficient shipping facilities. Capital required came from river dues or was borrowed on the strength of that growing revenue.

Lesser ports saw beneficial changes. At Seaham Harbour the early years of the new century saw considerable investment, including new breakwaters. Blyth harbour had been difficult, dangerous and of limited capacity in earlier years. From 1885 there was heavy spending on improvements, timely in view of the increase in coal shipments which lay ahead.

There was expansion and rationalization of railway networks. (Tomlinson 1915; Hoole 1986; Holt 1986) The North Eastern Railway achieved a dominant position, absorbing the Newcastle and Carlisle Railway in 1862, the Stockton and Darlington Railway in 1863, the Blyth and Tyne Railway in 1874, and the Londonderry Railway in 1900. The NER owned docks and coal staiths as well as railways. It was efficiently managed and found no problems in raising capital. By 1903 there were 40,000 shareholders. In Cumbria, there was similar expansion by the London and North Western

284

Railway, which by 1859 controlled the north–south trunk route between Lancaster and Carlisle, and had established strategic dominance in the North West, consolidated by the takeover of the Cockermouth and Workington Railway, and the Whitehaven Junction Railway, in 1866. This hegemony was partially challenged by the Midland Railway's Carlisle–Settle line, completed in 1877. (Marshall and Walton 1981, 29–43)

Railway companies, like port authorities, were closely linked with the regional economy generally. In 1898, the chairman of the North Eastern Railway was Sir Joseph Pease, of the Darlington Quaker family, who had many local interests. Deputy chairman was Teesside ironmaster Sir Isaac Lowthian Bell; directors included members of the Northumberland aristocratic families of Grey and Ridley, Sir David Dale of Consett Iron Company, the coalowner Sir James Joicey, and Sir William Gray, a leading shipbuilder. This mingling of aristocratic landed families and newer commercial and industrial interests may have served to deflect conflicts of interest and contribute to a common élite. (Lewis 1996, 110) On a smaller canvas, the Furness Railway Company provided a similar coalition, exemplified in the entrepreneurial paternalism of the duke of Devonshire and the ways in which the railway assumed many functions of local government during the early development of Barrow. These included financing schools, a reading room, a market house and a public meeting room. When the town received a charter in 1867, the company secretary, James Ramsden, moved effortlessly into the mayoral seat. (Marshall 1958, 282–3, 298)

Because railway companies were headed by men of influence within the region, there was every incentive to provide efficient service for interests with which they were concerned. Careful planning and systematic use of statistical analysis became features of NER policy-making. There was deliberate recruiting of able young men, who were encouraged to exploit educational opportunities. The NER introduced superannuation in 1882, extended recognition to railway unions by 1908 and established sophisticated conciliation procedures. When the London and North Eastern Railway came into existence after the First World War, the North Eastern Railway was the largest, most efficient, wealthiest and most influential of its constituents.

There was additional construction after 1850. A relatively isolated area was opened up by the Border Counties Railway in the early 1860s. One reason for this predominantly rural line was hope that small local collieries might expand sales in Scottish border counties; among the active promoters was William Henry Charlton of Hesleyside, a leading landowner in the area to be served. (Thornthwaite 1991; Slade 1975, 195–6; Day and Charlton 1981, 270–1) Building a new line down the Durham coast, authorized by an Act of 1894, was essential for development of Horden Coal Company, and served new or rebuilt mining communities, including Blackhall, Easington and Horden. Most coal produced was taken by rail to West Hartlepool, where modern loading equipment expedited turn-round of waggons and colliers.

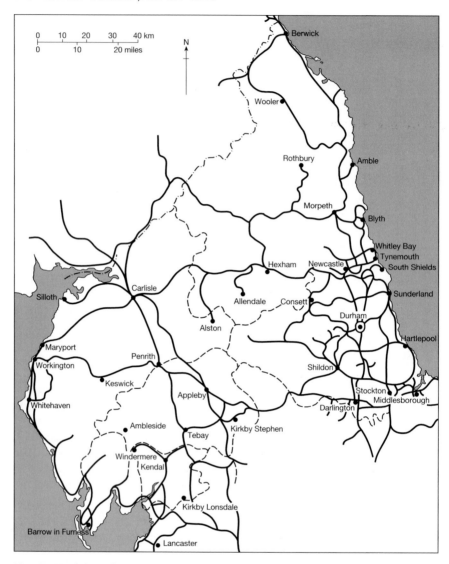

Map 8 Northern railways

The economic effects of railways were profound, and not always an unmixed blessing. Local crafts and industries faced competition in local markets, which brought a decline of rurally based industries and manufacturing functions in smaller towns. (Marshall 1983, 198–209) Commercial functions might be lost to more attractive markets and retail centres. Longtown's market was one casualty here, and in 1885 there were complaints from Aspatria, 20 miles from Carlisle, that cheap excursion trains were draining away local trade. In many small towns, such ill effects were obscured by growth in service and retail functions. Penrith lost industry, but retained importance from its nodal position on the regional railway system. New housing was developed close to the station after construction of the Keswick–Penrith railway in 1864–65. By 1865 about twenty of Cumbria's market towns had rail links, with larger centres the principal beneficiaries. Railways did not wholly replace older forms of horse-drawn transport, and often stimulated carriers' trade, by strengthening trading links between town and country, and feeding a growing appetite for manufactured goods and other products from beyond the region.

Carlisle offers the best example of a local economy benefited by railway development. By 1877 seven railway companies operated from the city, providing direct employment and also opportunities for engineering enterprises. While industrial interests of west Cumberland and Furness rested on a narrow range of activities, development of Carlisle as a railway centre encouraged diverse enterprises relying on cheap transport. This helped to compensate for decline in textile manufacture. The expansion of Carr's Biscuit Company into a nation-wide supplier reflected improved communications. The firm of Hudson and Scott, later the Metal Box Company, developed from general printers into producers of an immense variety of tin boxes with stencilled printing. This depended on convenient and cheap transport of products as well as a rapidly growing market. Its work force rose from 200 in 1882 to 1,200 in 1906; a branch opened in Newcastle in 1910. When the Cowan, Sheldon engineering works was set up in Carlisle in 1847, it was in response to the needs of the expanding railway network; the first important line in Cumbria, the Lancaster and Carlisle Railway, had been created in the previous year. Once established, the company branched out into other activities, becoming a leading crane manufacturer. (Bennett 1993, 3–4) By the early twentieth century its excellent rail links had enabled Carlisle to acquire a population of *c*.50,000 and a broadly based economy which contrasted with most other inland towns in the North West.

Railway development not only affected local industries, but influenced patterns of residence and population. Successive extensions in the 1860s and 1880s improved rail links between Newcastle and the coast. This led to the growth of Tynemouth and Whitley Bay as seaside recreational centres, and enabled these and other places on coast lines to develop as dormitory areas for Newcastle and the rest of industrial north Tyneside. In Cumbria Silloth followed a broadly similar course. Most promoters of the Carlisle and Silloth Bay Railway had Carlisle connections and included a substantial proportion of the city's council. The original development of Silloth, in a windswept and desolate location, was inspired by Carlisle's desire for a new outlet to the sea under the city's control. New docks were built in 1857–59. Disappointing revenues were responsible for its promotion as a seaside resort. After the North British Railway took control in 1862, Silloth was advertised as a sea-bathing and health resort, for those in Carlisle, the Scottish Borders and the Scottish Lowlands, but with only indifferent success. (Walton 1979; Bennett 1993, 7)

Railway extension, together with rising living standards and increased leisure, brought mass tourism. For many years in the late nineteenth and early twentieth centuries, there was annual mass migration of Glasgow holiday-makers to Whitley Bay by train. Development of Tynemouth and Whitley Bay as recreational centres for Tyneside's industrial belt was paralleled by Roker and Seaburn for Wearsiders. Redcar and Saltburn catered for different social groups from industrial Teesside.

Members of Kendal's dominant élite sponsored the Kendal–Windermere railway, completed in 1847, which helped to open up the eastern Lake District to tourism. Earlier, Keswick had been the centre of smaller-scale sightseeing in the lakes, but that was a 'carriage trade' of the wealthy and educated. (Marshall and Walton 1981, 177–203) Arrival of the railhead on Windermere precipitated an era of rail-borne tourism, shifting the centre of the tourist industry to the south, to Bowness and the new community of Windermere, and the growing resort of Ambleside accessible by steamer up the lake. Within its first year, the rail link increased arrivals at Windermere four- or five-fold compared with earlier arrivals by road. (Walton and McGloin 1981, 157) Railways shaped tourism in the Lake District until the arrival of motor transport in the twentieth century, but exposed the paradox already noted by Wordsworth and other opponents of local railway build-ing. It was feared that intrusion of railways into the landscape, and effects of mass tourism on tranquillity, could threaten qualities which made the region attractive. (Walton 1991, 20) Newer railway resorts overtook Keswick, but in 1864 that town received its railway link, as a by-product of the building of the Cockermouth, Keswick and Penrith Railway, designed mainly for mineral traffic. Keswick's expansion may have been slowed initially by the company's preoccupation with mineral traffic and lack of energy in promoting tourism. After 1870 all Lake District railways were increasingly dependent on tourism, and Keswick grew rapidly during the remainder of the century, with something like one-twelfth of the population employed as servants of one kind or another, and perhaps as many as a quarter of the houses taking in lodgers. (McGloin 1977, 40–7, 76)

The nature of tourism in the Lake District – such respectable pursuits as walking, rowing and admiring the scenery – attracted prosperous groups, including those whose education included appreciation of its literary associa-tions. Windermere and Keswick dealt uneasily with more plebeian elements, such as day excursionists, and neither consistently developed commercial entertainments designed to cater for them. The reverse was often the case. Day trippers were generally poor spenders, and there were fears that they might frighten away the more 'respectable' visitors on whom hotels and lodg-ing houses depended. These fears were exaggerated, for popular behaviour remained more restrained than that of some visitors to Blackpool, Redcar, or Whitley Bay. At Windermere, development was restricted for fear of attracting lower-class excursionists; until the 1890s, although there were Sunday train services, there were no Sunday excursions or Sunday steamer services on the lake. (Walton 1991, 27–9) Resistance to commercialism also came from conservationists like Canon H. D. Rawnsley, prominent in the Lake District Defence Society, who fulminated against 'the vulgar intrusions and destructive idiosyncrasies of the nineteenth century excursionist'. Nevertheless, after 1877, as real wages for many workers rose, there was a significant rise in visitors arriving with third-class tickets. In 1865, such tickets amounted to 46 per cent of arrivals at Keswick; by 1911 this had jumped to 93 per cent, 427,000 out of a total of 455,000. (McGloin 1977, 66)

As on coast lines from Newcastle, rail links from Lancashire to south-eastern Lakeland produced exclusive dormitory developments, as well as retirement and summer homes within reach of the railways. This opportunity was recognized with the first rail link in 1847, but the most dramatic expansion at Windermere occurred during the 1890s when express trains enabled commuters to reach Liverpool and Manchester in just over two hours. By the end of the century, Windermere represented a phenomenon among northern communities,

> a playground in which the leaders of Lancashire's industrial and mercantile life could meet and draw from one another self assurance from this association that they were in a group quite separate from the majority of the middle class. (Westall 1991)

An elaborate and exclusive social round centred around the Royal Windermere Yacht Club.

The development of dormitory facilities, and growth of tourism, compensated for decline of rural industries. Southern Lakeland avoided the loss of population which occurred in other rural areas. It is difficult to over-estimate the importance of the railways to such communities, and the various ways in which they contributed to maintaining population there. (McGloin 1977, 40–7)

Suburban Transport

Other transport developments had social as well as economic effects. At Gateshead, the first tramways were authorized by an Act of 1880; the first track was in use three years later. By 1898 there were 6.5 miles of tram routes, served by steam locomotives, which gave way to electric traction early in the new century. Newcastle Corporation obtained powers to run electric trams in 1899, and its first trams appeared in Pilgrim Street at the end of 1901; within twenty-five years tram lines extended to 50 miles. In 1894, Sunderland's horse trams travelled about 265,000 miles and carried 2,300,000 passengers on 6 miles of track. The first electric trams appeared in 1900, carrying during the first nine months 6.25 million passengers and covering nearly 400,000 miles. By 1905 there were 11 miles of track, and by 1914, 14 million passenger journeys a year. (Barke 1992; Staddon 1973)

Motor buses arrived before the First World War, although they were not common until after 1918. In 1904 a half-hourly bus service began between Bishop Auckland and West Auckland. Two years later, a local newspaper carried information about services between Spennymoor and Ferryhill. By 1914 the Northern General Transport Company had absorbed a number of small local ventures and operated 54 buses. (Kennedy and Marshall 1962, 18–25)

By 1914, local tram and bus services covered relatively small areas in or close to urban centres. Elsewhere, communities depended on trains. In places without railways, and for those who could not afford rail tickets, movement was limited to the speed of a man or a horse. Early twentieth century photographs of mining and rural communities often show them with un-made-up main streets, reflecting the limited transport and relative isolation facing many communities before the expansion of buses and motor cars after 1918. In the late nineteenth and early twentieth centuries it was common for poorer people to walk long distances to work or for recreation. Workers' children might walk from Jarrow to Tynemouth and back for a seaside trip, or a miner's children might walk from Boldon Colliery to the Town Moor Fair at Newcastle, saving for more enjoyable use money which might have been spent on railway or tram fares.

Expansion of suburban transport by 1914 had important results. Previously a worker had to live near his work or face long walks in all kinds of weather. With growing suburban train services and the coming of the tram, it was possible for workers to live some distance from work. This helped to reduce urban overcrowding. The spread of housing into peripheral areas, where land was cheaper, provided better houses for the same price. Suburban growth was reflected in urban local government. (Pollard 1996, xi) Newcastle swallowed up the townships of Westgate, Elswick, Jesmond, Heaton and Byker as part of national municipal reform in 1835. As suburban housing spread further, in 1904 the city absorbed another outer ring, Fenham, Benwell, Walker and part of Kenton. Inter-war legislation brought the city's authority, and its higher rates, to parts of Newburn, Castle Ward and Longbenton.

Banking

Northern banks, after catastrophes in 1847 and 1857, developed into stable institutions capable of providing financial support and banking services for northern industries. The Newcastle branch of the Bank of England continued to operate as a linchpin of local banking activity. In 1859, local banks were reinforced by a new banking partnership in Newcastle – Hodgkin, Barnett, Pease, Spence and Company – with ample capital, useful contacts within the region and elsewhere, and competent management. The role of banks in the local economy may be illustrated by two examples of this firm at work. During a short but sharp shipbuilding recession in 1866, the bank shored up more than one local shipyard. Wigham Richardson's enterprise was one of these, and he later recalled:

> There was so little work at Walker that grass grew in the shipyard, and the cartmen requested permission to reap the hay . . . If it had not been for the kind support of our bankers, and especially of John William Pease, I think that we would have lost heart and thrown up the sponge. (Wigham Richardson 1911, 205)

A few years later it was the bank's backing which made possible reconstruction of the engineering firm of R. and W. Hawthorn under new owners and set it on a renewed expansion.

Local control of the economy was coming under pressure by 1900. The process was exemplified in leading local banks. In Cumbria, banks bearing local names such as Wakefield, Crewdson, Mounsey and Heysham were absorbed by more powerful institutions, in the first place provincial banks based in centres like Liverpool. The scale of capitalization of the coastal iron and steel industry attracted Scottish banks as well as Scottish iron and steel companies. (Marshall and Walton 1981, 122–4) Ultimately regional banks succumbed to the evolution of national joint stock banks. In the North East, the long-established bank of Woods and Company was taken over by Barclays Bank in 1897, while Lloyds Bank absorbed Hodgkin, Barnett, Pease and Spence in 1893 and the venerable Lambton Bank in 1908.

Agriculture

The unforeseeable and phenomenal expansion of industry and commerce did not entail disappearance of the old economic order. Even if agriculture did not play the crucial role of earlier years, it remained important. In 1911, farming still provided 1 in 20 of all jobs in Northumberland, although the figure for County Durham was less than half that. Farming still provided 17.42 per cent of all work in Westmorland, but only 12.15 per cent in Cumberland, where mining and industry were more developed. In Cumbria, the proportion of work provided by agriculture had halved during the previous sixty years. By mid-century, the population of some of Westmorland's agricultural parishes was declining; the county's total population was only 58,287 in 1851, but the census listed 23,068 born there but living elsewhere. The countryside was emptying surplus population into urban areas and industries of adjoining counties. (Webster 1968, 1–4) In 1901 the proportion of all work provided by farming in Durham was not much more than a third of the national average. (Rowe 1973, 125)

These developments owed much to changes in transport. Improved steamships allowed products of the Americas and Australasia to compete with home production. The earlier stages of railway development were seen as beneficial to northern farmers. As soon as the Newcastle to Carlisle Railway was in business from 1838, Newcastle wholesale egg merchants travelled to Kendal to buy up local stocks of eggs, carry them by train to Newcastle and thence ship them to London by steamer. Railways could carry fat stock to growing urban populations. If this damaged existing cattle markets, it created larger successors in the growing towns. The new cattle market at Newcastle entailed decline for by-passed older venues like Morpeth. Fortnightly cattle fairs at Kendal and Penrith profited as central selling points. When the Lancaster to Carlisle rail link was opened in 1846, it was soon found that there were not enough cattle trucks to cope with this expanding traffic. (Garnett 1912, 46–7; Maud 1862, 4)

These changes brought more concentration on pastoral farming, so that extended arable and high corn prices of the French Wars became only a memory. Figures of sales at Newcastle's cattle market illustrate this. In 1852 a total of 38,109 cattle, 250,369 sheep and 34,544 pigs were sold, but thirty years later the totals were 111,705; 302,504; 41,747. In 1880 the annual Cow Hill Fair (established in 1490) on Newcastle's Town Moor was still one of the biggest livestock fairs in the north of England, with large-scale dealings in horses, cattle and pigs. (Halcrow 1953, 155)

For much of the North, there was no point in trying to compete with warmer climates and better soils in cereal growing, when mutton, lamb, beef, wool and hides were in demand from urban and industrial communities. Local producers of perishable meat and dairy products seemed to possess a guaranteed market: 'So long as the tall chimneys of Yorkshire and Lancashire smoke, so long will the farmer of Westmorland have a never failing demand for all his produce.' (Webster 1868, 1–4) Northern farmers, who had adopted an increased pastoral emphasis after 1850, initially escaped the consequences of the collapse in cereal prices during the 1870s. By the 1880s, with developments in refrigeration, meat imports were beginning to bite. By

1882 Furness farmers complained of preferential rail rates for imported American meat. Agricultural depression in the North was less harsh than in arable districts further south, but brought falling rents for farmland. Northern farmers faced the problem of higher wages, and found that proximity to urban and industrial communities brought competition for workers. An official enquiry of 1895 noted that 'most capable men seek situations in towns'. (BPP 1895, 10)

Local farms could sell meat and dairy produce, but competition lowered prices. By the 1880s there was import of cattle and sheep from Denmark and Sweden, while pigs were moved from Aberdeenshire and northern Ireland. In September 1884, a Durham co-operative store recorded its first sales of frozen New Zealand mutton. Butter was imported in increasing quantities; about 1890 one Newcastle firm claimed that it regularly held Danish butter worth £20,000. Rising shipments into the Tyne between 1863 and 1883 illustrate rising imports – butter from 32,242 cwt to 332,120 cwt, flour from 12,214 sacks to 334,384 sacks, wheat from 87,995 quarters to 224,070 quarters and cheese from 18,911 cwt to 30,160 cwt. (Dixon 1895, 139; Anon. *c*.1886, 8; Anon. *c*.1894, 135; Lloyd 1916, 188)

Northern agriculture could hold its own in some respects. Butter production increased; in 1891 Westmorland railway stations sent off 185 tons. Local farmers founded an important dairy enterprise, the Vale of Eden Company, as part of the same development. By the early twentieth century, this firm was sending cooled milk by train to Newcastle and South Shields, while farmers at Kirkby Stephen sent milk to London and Liverpool. By 1900 northern farming, especially in the North West, concentrated heavily on cattle and sheep; where crops were grown, they tended, as with oats and turnips, to be ancillary to this pastoral bias. (Garnett 1912, 138–41)

During the years when mid-Victorian farming continued prosperous, there was persistent erosion of small farms, and further acquisitions by greater landlords. This was especially so in Cumbria, where survival of small and often under-capitalized farms had encouraged farming conservatism. Informed contemporaries often saw replacement of small farmers by substantial tenants as change for the better. An official enquiry in 1882 indulged in a side-swipe at the idealized small farmer of sentimental literary convention: 'whole estates in Westmorland have been created by the amalgam of small freeholds . . . however poetry may suffer, the result is a great gain to the public'. (BPP 1882, 43) Among admired examples was William Thompson, successful London alderman and railway director, who acquired 25,000 acres in southeast Westmorland by such methods. After 1880, as agricultural prosperity faltered, this process ended. Falling rents discouraged investment, and depression favoured the small proprietor who could depend upon his family, and harmed larger tenant farmers saddled with expensive labour.

There was a fall in the number of farm labourers, from 21,674 to 8,526 in Cumbria between 1851 and 1911. (Marshall and Walton 1981,

61, 251) This included virtual extinction of full-time female farm servants. The extended pastoral emphasis needed less labour, and many farmers cut costs in face of falling prices. Wages on northern farms were perhaps as much as one-third higher than in southern counties which did not have heavy competition for labour. A Cumberland farmer noted:

> I do not know of any case where a father pays his sons and daughters wages. They give their sons a shilling or two to buy tobacco. A girl is far better off in service than staying at home. (BPP 1895, 40)

This was more typical of Cumbria than of the North East. Where Cumbrian farmers employed paid labour, they commonly relied on indoor farm servants, rather than day labourers. Most of these were young, in the 14–30 age range, perhaps graduating into the ranks of day labourers upon marriage, though many nurtured ambitions to become farmers themselves. (Marshall and Walton 1981, 251) There was often little social distance between labourers and the farmers they served. In 1895 Lord Muncaster's agent claimed to know 'not a few instances' in which labourers had risen to become 'farmers of considerable importance', while in 1940 a survey showed that 60 per cent of Westmorland farmers had begun their careers as farm servants. (BPP 1895, 9–10; Searle 1983, 368) A late Victorian admirer noted how the avoidance of 'more expensive tastes (for) . . . pianos and lawn tennis' enabled Cumbrian farmers to survive agricultural depression. (Little 1880)

Against the background of depression, technical progress slowed. In 1873 Westmorland still had 4,376 landowners, of whom well over a quarter owned less than a single acre. There was further consolidation of farming units, and continued improvement in livestock and farm buildings, but less application of powered machinery than in southern arable areas. (Webster 1868, 12, 25–6; Harbottle 1995) Some of this reflected extended pastoralism, but it was also due to the mixed fortunes of large estates whose farmers had previously been in the van of improvement. In the early twentieth century, the earl of Carlisle was driven by indebtedness to sell off parts of his estates in Northumberland and Yorkshire, and some outlying property in Cumberland. The Grahams of Netherby were also forced to sell land, but the earl of Lonsdale and Lord Leconfield, sustained by mineral revenues, avoided this. (Searle 1983, 332–5, 377–84)

There were examples of a different kind. When the fourth duke of Northumberland succeeded his brother in 1847, he began improvement and modernization which, for the first time, brought the region's largest estate into the ranks of conspicuous agricultural reformers. When Major Brown acquired the Callaly estate in Northumberland in 1877, he set about increasing efficiency. In the second half of the nineteenth century, one of Britain's most distinguished farmers was Jacob Wilson, who farmed at Woodhorn, near Ashington, and served as principal agent for the earl of Tankerville's estates. He pioneered techniques such as ploughing by steam power and was a successful animal-breeder. He was knighted for services to agriculture in 1889, no mean achievement for a man of his position.

The patchiness of improvement disguises the extent to which northern farming adapted to changing market demands and opportunities. In districts close to developing industrial communities on Teesside, farmers increased fodder production, to serve thousands of horses employed in transport, and kept more cows to provide more milk. (Bullock 1974, 92)

Cumberland and Westmorland County Councils created a residential farm school at Newton Rigg. Northumberland County Council, which included many landowning and farming members, founded its own experimental farm and farming school at Cockle Park, after negotiations to join the Cumbrian scheme failed. (Taylor 1989, 39, 87–8) The venture was viewed with suspicion by urban ratepayers and even by some farmers. In 1905 the duke of Northumberland, in his annual address to tenants, was at pains to quieten opposition to this use of county rates. The College of Science at Newcastle received its first professor of agriculture in 1891, although at first the subject attracted few students.

Fishing

As late as 1870, the Tyne produced quantities of salmon, but pollution affected many northern rivers. The North Sea provided most of the increased supply of fish. Recent research has explored the complex relationships between growing demand for food, shifting patterns of fish stocks, and changes in technology, especially railways which facilitated distribution of fresh fish to wider markets. (Muirhead 1992) In 1877 William Purdy of North Shields, owner of steam tugs, conceived the idea of using them as trawlers. By 1909, North Shields was a busy fishing port, with 76 steam trawlers based there, and many more visiting on a seasonal basis.

The herring fishery was a centre of development. John Woodger, agricultural labourer turned fish merchant, helped by inventing the kipper in 1843, applying to herrings a curing process already used for salmon. From small beginnings, the Woodger curing firm had grown into a much bigger business when he died in 1876. By 1910, nearly 20,000 tons of herring were landed at North Shields annually, some by Norwegian boats. In the years before the First World War, 600 herring boats might appear at North Shields at the height of the season. The port's fishing industry normally employed about 2,600 people, but this swelled to almost 6,000 at the peak of the summer seasonal harvest of herring.

The Retail Trade

Distribution of food and other supplies to the swollen population of late Victorian Britain was a remarkable feat of organization, in which northern counties took a prominent place. In Newcastle, the old provision market in the Bigg Market continued every Thursday and Saturday morning. By the later 1880s egg supplies came from Ireland, Scotland, Denmark, Germany, France, Italy and Hungary – an illuminating example of growth in international exchange. (Collingwood Bruce 1889, 43) Markets built in the 1830s remained retailing centres, especially for meat, fruit and vegetables. The increasing supply of meat and dairy produce brought dietary gains, but could worsen public health problems. By the early 1880s, Newcastle possessed 145 slaughter-houses and triperies; in 1895 there were 73 dairies holding a total of 628 cows. (Armstrong 1883, 10; Armstrong 1895, 6)

There was proliferation in shops of many kinds, ranging from large department stores through many intermediate forms to thousands of street-corner general dealers and off-licence holders. (Taylor 1996, 58, 65–70, 77) This played a part in developing a more complex and diverse society. The wealthier society of late Victorian and Edwardian years enjoyed retail facilities on a more extensive and sophisticated scale than at any earlier period. In 1898, for example, Newcastle had 44 ice-cream makers. (Armstrong 1898, 3)

The late nineteenth century brought, especially in Newcastle, department stores such as Bainbridge's and Fenwick's. The Bainbridge store was founded in 1867 and rapidly expanded. The founder of Fenwick's had been a drapery assistant in a Mosley Street shop before branching out on his own. Success came to these ventures not only because of growing market opportunities, but also by hard work, patience and business dexterity. Even when his store had proved a success, J. J. Fenwick was only drawing £700 to £800 p.a. in the later 1890s; his manager-buyer received £500. Both stores operated paternalistic if authoritarian regimes. In 1907 the Bainbridge establishment employed 107 people who had worked there for more than twenty-five years. (Darlington 1893; France 1913; Airey 1979; Anon. 1917, Pound 1972)

Co-operative stores, after a shaky beginning (see p. 227 above), shared in retailing expansion. A parliamentary return for 1875, not a full account, noted 48 co-operative societies in County Durham with membership of nearly 40,000. In the previous year these had a turnover of £1.75 million and distributed nearly £120,000 as dividend. Northumberland was credited with 37 societies, with turnover of £600,000 and dividend payments of nearly £60,000. (*Newcastle Weekly Chronicle*, 30/6/1877)

Figure 16.2 Newcastle upon Tyne. Energetic shopping during the 1898 sale at Fenwick's department store.

Mining areas were centres of co-operative growth. Capital of the Crook society grew from £67 in 1865 to £16,000 in 1876, membership from 40 to about 2,000. By 1915 sales over fifty years totalled well over £7.25 million, and 5,025 members held savings averaging £30 in the society's funds. The Bishop Auckland society began in 1860 with £100 contributed by 118 founder members. By 1910, it was trading at more than £113,000 p.a., with 15 shops and 17,774 members. These societies served mining families, and provided more than retail trading. Annual celebrations and regular social gatherings were part of the pattern. In 1874, in place of their annual tea party, the Crook society determined on a trip to Sunderland 'if possible when the Channel Fleet are in'.

Co-operative societies increasingly provided members with facilities for house purchase and built houses themselves. An influential member of the Windy Nook Society rejected the extreme views that 'private property is robbery', preferring 'the generally accepted view that the more of the people of a nation you can get to own the homes they live in, the more securely you are establishing the foundations of the commonweal on a sound and stable basis'. (Lloyd 1910; Anon. 1912; Potts 1992)

In Cumbria, iron ore mining communities provided centres of retail co-operation, such as the Cleator Moor society with a membership of 1,840 and sales of £80,912 in 1875, rising to 3,592 and £109,734 by 1886. (Marshall and Walton 1981, 254) This mirrored the prosperity of industrial districts which the iron mines served, and societies' success peaked in the 1880s before entering decline. North-eastern societies held their own until much later.

Co-operative stores encountered rivals, even in mining districts. A variety of chain stores challenged established shops. Another competitor was created by J. W. Brough, who came from a family established in wholesale provision dealing. Brough made a planned incursion into mining districts, designed to undercut co-operative stores and other shops by supplying a limited range of essential items which housewives needed to buy regularly. Salesmen toured mining villages and similar communities, canvassing orders which were delivered by horse-drawn vans. By 1906 there were branch depots at Ashington, Bedlington, Crook, Gateshead and Stanley, apart from a group in Newcastle, and the firm continued to grow. Its creator became a wealthy and distinguished member of local society, well known for philanthropic activities and support for his own nonconformist sect in the area around his home. 'The traveller from Brough's' became an established friend in many local families. (Mathias 1967, 73–95; Ellis 1952)

A modern study of Cumbrian towns sums up retailing there:

> if we take towns that were small or even declining in size, like Longtown, Burton, Brough or Brampton, then each had one or several confectioners in the closing years of the century, and greengrocers, fruiterers

and fishmongers were becoming commonplace in the slightly larger towns, as were chemists and druggists, china, glass and earthenware dealers, wool and fancy depositories, mineral water manufacturers, musical instrument dealers, photographers, coal merchants, cycle makers and dealers, cowkeepers (farm-derived persons from the dales who provided fresh milk), dentists, laundry operators, fish, game and poultry dealers, furriers, manure merchants, nurserymen, and timber dealers. (Marshall 1983, 207)

There was increase in 'convenience foods' in various forms, and in advertising. In 1903 the Tynesider Angus Watson, after a successful spell with Lever Brothers, returned home to found a tinned food business. His first successful line was Norwegian sardines – with the 'Skipper' trade name. In 1907 he invested £1,000 in his first advertising campaign. 'Sailor' salmon and 'My Lady' fruit joined the popular products; by 1911, Watson was spending £40,000–50,000 p.a. on advertising in Britain and America. Products were offered to retailer and purchaser with a 'money back if not satisfied' guarantee. Watson was a pioneer in industrial relations, with a sophisticated profit-sharing scheme. Records of employees were kept under joint supervision of management and workers. Products of this enterprising company were not the first tinned goods to be seen in the region, but large-scale production and distribution, and extensive advertising, introduced tinned food to many families. (Watson 1937)

Chapter 17

Society and Government

It is not easy to correlate social problems in any simplistic way with industrial or urban growth. Horrendous descriptions come from rural market towns, mining villages and fishing hamlets as well as major growth points. Some of the worst conditions emerged from old towns, including Newcastle, Gateshead, Sunderland, Morpeth, Alnwick, Carlisle, Whitehaven, Cockermouth and Kendal, with more people crammed into existing central areas and sometimes a shortage of building land. Despite population growth, some newer industrial centres, including Barrow, Cleator Moor and Workington in Cumbria, avoided the direst consequences. Barrow, despite rapid initial growth in the 1850s, consistently returned a death rate below the national average and never approached the mortality figures of older towns like Newcastle, Gateshead, Carlisle or Kendal. (Marshall 1958, 242)

Housing

In many cases slum conditions were already old, but now publicized. Compilation of reliable death rates not only highlighted communities with terrible problems but could distinguish between different areas of the same town. Carlisle had an annual death rate of 25 per 1,000 in 1841–42, but investigation revealed higher mortality within poor areas like the Lanes and Rickergate in the overcrowded old centre, whereas workers of Peter Dixon & Co. in Shaddongate fared much better. Similar detailed surveys followed cholera epidemics. (Reid 1845; Waterson 1987)

To existing problems were now added the consequences of rapid economic change and population growth, especially in some areas of the North East. In the second half of the century, Northumberland's population almost doubled, from 304,000 in 1851 to 603,000 in 1901; the figures for County

300

Durham are more startling, from 391,000 to 1,187,000. Such growth rates would impose strains in any context; in a little-governed society which already possessed social problems pressures were acute.

Even where planning was attempted, the scale of change could have ill effects. The original proprietors of Middlesbrough envisaged a 'garden city' plan for the small town anticipated in the first period of growth, after the building of early railways. A grid layout was planned, with housing plots of 60 feet by 200 feet. These calculations were overthrown by the flood of development which accompanied the boom in the Teesside iron industry in the years after 1850. (Moorsom 1967, 8; Briggs 1996, 2–9; Taylor 1996, 53–7) The wife of a leading ironmaster vividly described the forces determining development:

> There springs, and too rapidly, into existence a community . . . the members of which must live near their work. They must therefore have houses built as quickly as possible; the houses must be cheap, must be as big as the workman wants, and no bigger; and as they are built, there arise, hastily erected, instantly occupied, the rows and rows of little brown streets . . . A town arising in this way cannot wait to consider anything else than time and space: and none of either must be wasted on what is merely agreeable to the eye, or even on what is merely sanitary. (Bell 1907; Briggs 1996, 24–5)

Barrow experienced similar pressures, with such housing expedients as wooden huts on Barrow island. Growing prosperity eventually brought improvements, here as elsewhere; Vickerstown of 1904 echoed Lever's showpiece industrial housing at Port Sunlight. (Trescatheric 1985, 25–6; Marshall 1958, 287; Bennett 1993, 34)

Within some developing centres, the pressure of population growth on inadequate housing stock was worsened by limited building land. At Newcastle the extensive, inalienable Town Moor limited building to the north. Gateshead was ringed by landed estates, and it was only after 1860 that land was released for building. At South Shields the principal landowner was the Dean and Chapter of Durham, whose legal capacity to sell or lease land was restricted. At Carlisle, the rivers Eden and Caldew, and later railways, helped to confine the city to its medieval area and the single sprawling and unhealthy suburb of Caldewgate which held many poorer inhabitants. The new Nelson Bridge of 1853 facilitated development of the healthier mixed industrial and housing suburb of Denton Holme. (Harris 1967) Even where such handicaps did not exist, land in or close to towns was often too expensive for workers' housing to be feasible.

In central Newcastle, growth of large establishments like the Hawthorn and Stephenson engineering works, before effective suburban transport, put pressure on existing housing and helped to create appalling conditions in the

Figure 17.1 Gateshead. Northern towns possessed some of the worst slums in the country. A good example is this area of Gateshead, just to the east of the High Level Bridge, photographed in late Victorian times.

poorest areas, which contained the pool of casually employed quayside labour, and unskilled Irish immigrants. In 1865 the town's population had increased by about half in only twenty years and amounted to some 122,000. A council report listed 9,639 families living in single-room homes, 6,191 with only two rooms. Nearly 14,000 people were without 'water closet or privy accommodation of any sort'. Newcastle's death rate was then 36.7 per 1,000 annually; Liverpool, at 33.1 per 1,000, was the only other major town with a death rate above 30. By 1901, Newcastle's population had grown to 215,000. (McCord and Rowe 1977; Chronicle 1851; Spence 1954, 22; Barke and Callcott 1994, 13–19)

The Public Health Act of 1848 set a yardstick of an annual death rate of 23 per 1,000 as so bad that central government could compel creation of a Local Board of Health with sanitary responsibilities. Newcastle had a crude death rate of 24.8 per 1,000 on average for the years 1874–79,

Figure 17.2 Newcastle upon Tyne. High density terrace housing of *c*.1900 between Barrack Road and Stanhope St., part of an extensive development stretching up from the riverside industrial belt to the west of the city centre.

Middlesbrough 23.96 per 1,000 in 1871–73, and Gateshead 22.9 per 1,000 in 1881–83. It was only after 1901 that Newcastle's death rate fell permanently below 20 per 1,000. Northern towns occupied places at the top of assessments of high death rates, infant mortality and overcrowding. In a table of urban areas, arranged to show density of overcrowding in 1907, the top five towns were Gateshead, South Shields, Tynemouth (essentially North Shields in this context), Newcastle and Sunderland. West Hartlepool, Middlesbrough and Stockton, while not as bad, were still high. (Dewsnup 1907) In 1891, 34 per cent of the population of County Durham lived at a density of more than two per room, while in Northumberland, with a larger rural element, the situation was worse, at over 38 per cent. The figure for Gateshead was 40.8 per cent, for Newcastle 32.9 per cent and for Sunderland 32.9 per cent. Carlisle, 33.9 per cent, and Whitehaven, 33.4 per cent, were black spots in Cumbria. London, at just under 20 per cent, provided the worst overcrowding statistics outside the northern counties. Such problems were not distinctively urban, for mining communities like Ashington in Northumberland at 32.2 per cent, and Houghton-le-Spring in Durham at

303

27 per cent, were black spots. In all four northern counties, rural areas enjoyed lower infant mortality rates than towns.

Such figures do not simply present terrifying testimony to the social effects of rapid industrial growth and urbanization. Evidence collected in 1891 showed the more rural county of Northumberland significantly worse in terms of overcrowding than more industrialized Durham. The intensity of the problem was distinctively regional, shared by all four counties, rather than specifically urban or industrial. (Marshall and Walton 1981, 93, 96–8) Other British regions saw comparable economic development in these years without producing conditions which were as bad; the rural North experienced severe overcrowding without economic development or population increase. There seems to have been a low level of expectation and provision in housing when compared with other regions, and this situation may have roots deep in the past.

Although social problems were not simply urban, their concentration there made them more serious and more obvious. By 1900, the problems were being tackled with more knowledge and ability than in any earlier period. In the 1890s, although population was rising, overcrowding fell slowly. The proportion of those living at a density of more than two per room declined from 34 per cent to 28 per cent in County Durham, and from 38 per cent to 32 per cent in Northumberland.

The provision of additional housing was not smooth or continuous. Gateshead saw two bursts of house building, reflecting availability of land. In the 1860s and 1870s, land was released from Park estate on the east and Shipcote estate on the west. Many small terrace houses were built, with houses increasing faster than population. By 1881 this supply of land had dried up, and the trend was reversed. From the late 1880s more land became available and another building boom occurred. These houses were bigger than those of the earlier expansion. The town's population was now growing so fast that new houses did no more than keep pace until overcrowding was reduced again in the early twentieth century. (Manders 1973, 162–75)

Fluctuations occurred elsewhere. At Middlesbrough, an average of 347 houses p.a. was planned in 1865–70, 1,027 in 1871–76 and then fell from a peak of 1,416 in 1875 to only 31 in 1880. House-building there was at a low level throughout the 1880s, in contrast to Tyneside and even West Hartlepool, only a few miles away. (Polley 1996; 163–8) Despite variations in extent and timing, overall there was a considerable increase of new housing in northern towns in the last quarter of the century.

The late 1860s and early 1870s were good years for many collieries, and increased profits were often reflected in improved living conditions for mining families. Some new mining villages built in these years, such as Cambois in Northumberland and Esh Winning in Durham, embodied significant improvements in housing and sanitation. Much of the worst conditions within mining communities occurred in places like Bedlington, Houghton-le-Spring and Spennymoor, where the core of old villages became tenemented with the poorer strata of mining society, including Irish families. The 1872 Public Health Act was important in clearing up the worst conditions in mining villages and facilitating provision of water supply, drainage and similar improvements. As in the towns, progress although real was patchy, with examples of bad conditions persisting well into the twentieth century. (Seeley 1973; Brown 1995)

Improvements in Health

Improvements in living conditions were reflected in better health. Epidemics of various kinds continued. Some killer diseases were in retreat during the second half of the century, but the process was uneven. In the 1849 cholera outbreak Newcastle suffered 412 deaths; Workington lost 160 out of a population of *c*.6000, and nearby Maryport and Cockermouth suffered heavily. The country town of Alnwick, with dreadful slums, saw 140 deaths in a month – twelve times the town's usual death rate. In the cholera epidemic of 1853, Newcastle paid a horrendous price for neglect of public health, with 1,533 deaths. (Callcott 1984) The same epidemic pointed the way forward, for in North Shields there were only twelve deaths, largely through the exertions of a local sanitary reformer, Dr Greenhow.

At Middlesbrough a smallpox outbreak in 1897–98 saw 1,411 cases and 198 deaths. Newcastle's smallpox epidemic of 1903–5 was the last serious visitation within the region. Smallpox was one disease where official intervention played a role in reducing deaths. Early Victorian statutes, culminating in the 1853 Act for the Compulsory Vaccination of Children (16 & 17 Vict. *c*.100) provided vaccination at ratepayers' expense, without incurring the stigma of pauperism, punishing parents who failed to protect children. This drastic intervention, repudiating any concepts of *laissez faire*, represented acceptance that public interest could override private rights and met with little opposition in northern counties. (Thompson 1976, 316) Typhus saw a marked reduction from the 1870s. A combination of improvements in medical science, public health, housing and diet meant that death rates in the North, though still high by national standards, dropped considerably by the early twentieth century.

Improved water supply was part of the story, though again progress was patchy and intermittent. At North Shields, a report in 1851 noted a correlation between inadequate water supply in North Shields and 'more filth of habitations and uncleanliness of person and much more disease and mortality'. (Anon. 1949, 84) It was not until after an Act of 1897 that the town acquired a decent water supply, when the council took powers to oust the unsatisfactory water company. As recently as 1892, the company had refused to abandon a polluted source until compelled by court injunction. Progress came earlier in east Durham, through the Sunderland and South Shields Water Company, founded in 1852. That company's chain of steam-powered water-pumping stations – Fulwell 1852, Cleadon 1863, Ryhope 1869, Dalton 1877 and Seaton 1896 – provided reliable water supplies to Sunderland, South Shields and smaller communities. Hartlepool benefited from a new water company founded in 1846. (Anon. 1946, 9)

At that time part of east Newcastle received water which had passed through a cemetery and absorbed graveyard drainage. Between 1870 and 1890 there was a programme of new works. The Newcastle water company built new reservoirs in rural areas and continued to increase supplies in the early twentieth century. By 1914 this company, which could not supply 1.5 million gallons of safe water daily at mid-century, provided more than 20 million gallons. (Rennison 1979) As early as the 1880s, some Newcastle workers' houses had bathrooms, although in other districts of the city water closets had not yet been installed.

In Cumbria, the 1870s and 1880s saw much discussion of the need for better water supplies and some achievements, including replacement of polluted wells and streams at Cockermouth, Keswick and Workington with Lakeland water. Clean water was perhaps the biggest factor in reducing urban mortality in the later nineteenth century. (Marshall and Walton 1981, 95) This improvement owed much to technical developments and the emergence of competent specialists. The engineer Thomas Hauxley was responsible for more than 150 waterworks, including Darlington, Durham, Middlesbrough, Newcastle, Stockton, Sunderland and Weardale.

In Northumberland, many small settlements continued to rely on wells or springs until the twentieth century, as water supply companies concentrated on larger communities. Some local sanitary authorities created after the 1872 Public Health Act were active in this field. By 1876 the Bedlington authority had brought a decent water supply to its whole area, at a cost of £15,000 to local ratepayers; nearby Cowpen spent £11,200. In County Durham the contribution of water companies was more widespread. A number of mining communities received a supply from the Weardale and Shildon Water Company. Drawn from moorland sources, this was described by an unkind critic as having 'the colour of India Pale Ale, and a slight taste of pond'. By 1880 almost half of County Durham's mining villages received water supplies from companies, including many of the largest communities. By 1914 polluted water supplies, for so long a killer, were rarely a problem.

Local Government: The Institutional Framework

These years saw expansion in local government activities, and in supervision by central government. This was intermittent rather than continuous, often occurring in response to public concern, following some particular cause for alarm.

The 1834 Poor Law Amendment Act replaced an inchoate structure with a relatively uniform pattern covering England and Wales. Initially narrowly concerned with the poor law, the machinery once established was repeatedly used for other purposes. It provided registration of births, deaths and marriages, vaccination against smallpox, and collection of statistics and other information at the request of Government or Parliament. Outside boroughs, poor-law authorities acquired public health functions, implementing legislation of the 1870s and 1880s.

Mid-Victorian experiments in local government included *ad hoc* institutions dealing with public health, education and burials. By the end of the century, the proliferation of local authorities, usually reflecting piecemeal reactions to some particular scandal, had created an administrative nightmare of overlapping functions, jurisdictions and rates. The Public Health Acts of 1848 and 1872, while marking progress in sanitary matters, were part of this process. The arrival of elected county councils after 1888, taking over most of the administrative functions of the county magistrates in Quarter Sessions, added another dimension, and changes in the early 1890s brought new local authorities within counties. Increasingly local authorities, in such spheres as poor law, public health, care of the mentally ill and education, were subject to modestly effective supervision by inspectors and auditors appointed by central government.

Important as these changes were, it would be easy to exaggerate the role of official agencies in shaping Victorian Britain. The foundation and early growth of new centres such as Middlesbrough and Barrow, the most important new towns of the North, owed little to any local authority, but reflected an uneasy mix of paternalism and private speculation, planned development and responses to expediency and profit. Barrow's expansion was guided by the Furness Railway Company until 1864, when official intervention came in a local committee appointed by Ulverston Poor Law Union to undertake limited public health functions. (Marshall 1958, 288–98) Middlesbrough was dominated in early years by owners of the land on which it was founded. Millom was projected as a model town in Cumbria by its iron-mining company, but development outran this idealism. By 1866, there were outbreaks of typhoid, dysentery and diarrhoea, associated with overcrowding, which compelled Bootle Poor Law Union to invoke public health legislation and intervene. A report of 1874 attributed inadequate and damp housing to 'money speculators', but the generally poor environment, with pigs, goats

Figure 17.3 A heap of privy midden refuse awaiting removal by 'night soil' carts, deposited in front of Charlotte Terrace, Botcherby, Carlisle *c*.1900.

and horses roaming uncontrolled, and large puddles 'in which may be seen floating the decomposing carcasses of drowned cats and puppies' indicates a disastrous breakdown in control. (Harris 1966, 459–61)

Nor could it be assumed that existence of formal structures of local government would produce improvement. There was no sustained public support for more official activity at the expense of taxpayers and ratepayers. (Briggs 1996, 16, 18, 26; Lewis 1996, 107) An investigation into the cholera epidemic of 1853 had this to say of the ways in which Gateshead had used the 1848 Public Health Act:

> in the actual exercise of those powers, the Local Board does not appear ever to have lagged behind, but on the contrary to have been generally in advance of public opinion in the borough, and of the views and

wishes of the ratepayers at large . . . the main objection thereto seems to have consisted in the impatience of sanitary rates on the part of the ratepayers at large, who have hitherto been more alive to the direct pressure of those rates than to the indirect effect of unremedied sanitary evils upon life and death, and ultimately upon the poor rates. (Anon. 1854, xxxix)

During previous decades, Gateshead ratepayers had suffered considerable rate increases; by 1850 a total of 4*s*. 7*d*. in the £ was levied by six separate rating authorities.

It took many years for concepts of legitimate public interest to overcome qualms about increased local government and its cost. Local politics often reflected these issues. For almost a generation municipal politics in Kendal revolved around proposals for spending ratepayers' money on such projects as sewers, schemes, according to the 'Anti-Drainers' there, 'for draining the pocket and suchlike foolish underground work'. (Curwen 1900, 58; Waterson 1987, 192; Marshall and Walton 1981, 126) Even at Keswick, increasingly dependent on tourism for its livelihood, during the 1850s visitors suffered days or even weeks of stomach upsets from the contaminated water table. There was lengthy conflict between 'the clean party' and 'the dirty party' before remedial action could begin. (McGloin 1977, 9–10)

Expenditure and the Politics of Local Government

The key to understanding local government lies in its financing by local rates raised from ratepayers who elected relevant authorities. It was locally intimate, crucially different from modern arrangements whereby most local official spending is financed in a relatively anonymous fashion by grants from national taxation. Much vigour in local politics reflected antagonisms between those willing or eager to see further official activity, and adherents of rigid economy. Repeatedly reformers resorted to prodigies of arithmetic to persuade ratepayers that modest expenditure in prevention might save larger future costs incurred because of defective sanitation. Proposals for sewage works were accompanied by optimistic estimates of profits from the manure trade, or by growing crops on land enriched by proximity to sewage works. In 1892 ratepayers at Alnwick, a country town with serious health problems, were told that

no profit is normally found to arise from Sewage Works, it being considered satisfactory of working expenses and labour, seeds and plants, be about repaid by sale of Crops – the object being to carry on the Works efficiently at the least cost practicable. (Balfour 1892, 7)

Opposition to expenditure was not only widespread among ratepayers, but an entrenched official attitude. In 1893 the District Auditor rebuked Whitehaven Board of Guardians for extravagance in entertainment provided for paupers to celebrate a royal wedding. (Thompson 1976, 247–58; Pugh 1978, 281) At Darlington, a local poll of ratepayers was held in 1866 on the question of creating a council. Votes for a charter were 562, against 472, blank voting papers 388, papers not returned 174. After further controversy a charter was secured in 1867. At the first election, the leader of the incorporation campaign scraped in by two votes, and seven out of ten members of the old Local Board were elected. (Sunderland 1967, 93)

Economy was encouraged because many ratepayers were far from rich. Increased rates imperilled poorer ratepayers, especially in difficult times for the local economy. During depression on Tyneside in 1886, the Newcastle Board of Guardians was reluctant to accept pleas for increases in spending because

a considerable proportion of the rates are drawn from a class very little removed from pauperism, who had a hard struggle to pay the demands made upon them . . . any considerable increase to their burdens would have the effect of causing them to become paupers. (Relief Fund 1885–86)

Attempts to cut back on routine expenditure, such as poor-relief payments to the non-able-bodied, were relatively rare. Likely areas of attack included official salaries or controversial capital projects. Parsimony could be based on principle, including fears that increasing official activity could erode individual responsibility. Opponents of the drainage scheme at Kendal in the 1870s advocated an alternative strategy of improvement in terms of individual self-help coupled with philanthropic support, opposing use of ratepayers' money. (Waterson 1987, 192) Similar attitudes were reflected in a sustained campaign by the *Whitehaven Gazette* during the 1890s, not only against 'excessive' School Board expenditure but also against the principle that ratepayers 'must in addition to educating their own children, educate those of the scum of society and thus place them in a position to rob their own children of their rightful bread'. (Pugh 1978, 191–2)

Nor should such attitudes be seen simply as selfish reaction. There were good reasons why taxpayers and ratepayers were sceptical of the quality and efficiency of official administration. Both central and local government were often incompetent and inefficient. Examples from Hexham Rural Sanitary Authority could be paralleled repeatedly. In 1876 the Local Government Board was so incensed at this authority's persistent failure to reply to letters that it threatened to have it dissolved. A few years later, the Hexham chairman complained to the central Board about its failure to confirm by-laws sent months earlier, and it transpired that the draft had been lost in the central department's office. (Cadman 1976, 70, 405) It is easy to suppose that because a task is entrusted to an official agency it will be carried out with reasonable skill; this was not a view commonly held by Victorian ratepayers or taxpayers.

Scepticism about standards of official performance was not confined to the rich, to dogmatic economizers, or to the so-called 'shopocracy' of small tradesmen and retailers who formed a significant part of local electorates and made their views felt in many local authorities. Popular culture often reflected ambivalence or hostility towards official interventions. In 1876 members of the Crook co-operative society, overwhelmingly drawn from mining families, met to celebrate the opening of a new shop. They applauded views expressed by a visiting radical speaker from Newcastle:

> When, in a country like this, they raise for the government yearly the sum of £70,000,000, and they had the confounded impudence to tell them it is not enough, was it not time the people stood upon their independence, and told the government that, if they could not conduct the business of the nation in a better manner than to be compelled to spend £75,000,000 a year, it was time they went away, and that somebody else took their places? (Lloyd 1916, 141)

There was widespread suspicion of local authorities too, graphically illustrated by a northern newspaper:

> There may be some truth also in the somewhat tart definition that Boards of Health are bodies more prone to poke their noses into the privies of other people than to sit in judgement upon their own. (*Darlington Telegraph and Gisbro' Mercury*, 22/6/1861)

As local government took on an increasingly representative basis, and local electorates widened, such attitudes remained. Sir Wilfrid Lawson described a Cumberland County Council election: '(of) any two candidates . . . one was firmly in favour of efficiency and economy, and the other was strongly approving of economy and efficiency'. (Tufft 1976, 63) Lawson was a member of an élite landed, industrial and professional group which remained influential in local government and parliamentary representation. In Cumberland, party politics had little effect on county council elections. Liberals and Conservatives conspired to avoid contested elections wherever possible; voting behaviour by electors continued to reflect accepted patterns of leadership and deference rather than party or ideological divisions. Between

1889 and 1914, 32 out of 39 chairmen of Cumberland County Council committees had experience as magistrates. The first chairmen of Northumberland County Council were Sir Matthew White Ridley, Bart. (1889–95), Earl Percy, seventh duke of Northumberland from 1899 (1895–1918), and Sir Francis Blake, Bart. (1918–40). (Marshall and Walton 1981, 120; Taylor 1989, Appendix I, i–iii) Such tenures reflected widespread attitudes, seen also in the influence of Sir Charles Mark Palmer in Jarrow or the duke of Devonshire in Barrow.

Local Officials

Parsimony in local government was reflected in reluctance to pay adequate salaries to officials – salaries which must often have been higher than the incomes of many ratepayers. Not surprisingly, it was difficult to recruit and retain adequate staff. Central government agencies tried, often provoking local resentment, to induce local authorities to foster public service by paying decent salaries in proportion to responsibilities involved and qualifications required.

At first, poor-law guardians were happy to appoint trusted paupers to less important posts within workhouses, with only a nominal wage, disregarding protests from central government that such practices weakened the answerability of officials in the event of inefficiency, incompetence or dishonesty. (Thompson 1976, 457) With economy in official expenditure accepted belief, official salaries were a natural and convenient target, partly because official duties were often new and unprecedented, or had previously been performed by unpaid functionaries such as poor-law overseers. The central Poor Law Board and its successor the Local Government Board admired the Hartlepool Poor Law Union for its general economy, but were less happy about attitudes towards salaries, and the guardians' insistence that any application for higher wages must be accompanied by a letter of resignation, allowing them to replace the official if they could find someone to carry out the duties more cheaply. (Gregson 1976, 125) During a depression in 1885–86, ratepayers in the South Shields Union enforced salary cuts, including reducing the stipend of the Union's part-time clerk, G. W. Mitchell, from £220 to £125. When Mitchell retired a few years later, an audit revealed that he had informally evened things up by dipping his hands into public funds. Examples of dishonesty among officials holding cash balances were commonplace, as in the case of Alan Cameron, collector of the water rate for Newbottle and Penshaw in 1899, who was sentenced to 12 months' imprisonment for embezzlement. During the twenty years from 1836, in eleven

Poor Law Unions in Cumbria, 22 relieving officers left office in respectable circumstances such as honourable retirement or ill-health; 19 were either dismissed or forced to resign for misconduct, mostly in the form of embezzlement of public money drawn from local ratepayers' pockets. (Bank of England 16/8/1851; Barker 1974, 91, 152, 206; Mawson 1971, 128; Seeley 1973, 14)

Such anecdotal evidence obscures growing acceptance of improved notions of official responsibility and performance among both local authorities and officials. Evidence from Cumbrian Poor Law Unions indicates a slow but measured improvement both in the standard of officers and salaries paid. (Thompson 1976, 280–462) This reflects a general trend, and one which continued throughout this period. A wider pool of recruitment developed with improving education and increases in employments which were broadly equivalent to many official posts. Initially, finding suitable candidates often posed problems. In 1861, Edward Hurst, poor-law inspector for the northern region, could only suggest 'an old soldier or an ex-policeman' as a suitable workhouse master. (Thompson 1976, 432)

It could not be assumed that local authorities would appoint the most suitable candidate to an official position. Ability to confer salaried jobs reflected local power and prestige. Appointments to official posts were influenced by patronage or nepotism, and although such practices were increasingly controversial, they could for many years be seen as partially legitimized by tradition. There remained an extensive network of patronage which continued to influence nominations to posts in central and local government.

One consequence was that local authorities were tenacious in defending officers against criticism from central government. This was the case with Henry Castley, relieving officer in the West Ward (Westmorland) Poor Law Union, charged in 1869 with being 'drunk in charge of a lunatic at Citadel Station (Carlisle)', while conveying him to the county lunatic asylum. Castley was subsequently also accused of inducing his charge to make indecent advances to a girl in a railway compartment. This was enough to make the central authority enforce his sacking, over protest from the guardians, who later, unavailingly, petitioned for his reinstatement. Castley's father had served the same union as a long-serving and respected official; his own appointment probably spared the guardians from giving the retiring parent a pension. It is unlikely that such expedients would be abhorrent to ratepayers, most of whom had no prospect of pensions themselves. Before proper superannuation, there were cases when officials were kept on for years after they had ceased to be able to give competent service, because otherwise they would have become paupers. An official enquiry demonstrated examples of this in the case of masters of both the Berwick and the Houghton-le-Spring workhouses. (Thompson 1976, 232–3; Hurst 1864) Failures in duty by poor-law officials were more common as causes of scandal than relief policies pursued by boards of guardians.

313

Increased Official Activity

Necessity was the principal cause of greater official activity. Extended intervention affected northern industries, amongst the first areas of the economy
experiencing inspection and regulation. An Act of 1863 stipulated that 90
per cent of hydrochloric acid gas produced in alkali manufacture must
be dissolved in the works rather than emitted into the atmosphere. Coal-
mining was subjected to developing regulation, with Acts of 1887 and 1911
milestones in this process. Merchant shipping was subjected to official controls in loading levels and safety inspections. Resort to statutory force and
official inspection was usually instituted to compel recalcitrant enterprises to
measure up to beneficial changes already adopted by progressive elements
within the industry concerned.

Expanded Concepts of Public Interest

Pressure groups developed notions of public interest to justify legislative intervention and a wider role for government agencies. Railway building in the
Lake District, and plans to develop Thirlmere as a reservoir for Manchester,
aroused controversy in and out of Parliament, and were fought on competing
interpretations of public interest. As early as 1810, Wordsworth advocated
conservation on the grounds that the Lake District represented 'a sort of
national property, in which every man has right or interest who has an eye
to perceive and a heart to enjoy'. (Marshall and Walton 1981, 204) Resistance to the Thirlmere project was led by Robert Somerville, shoe manufacturer
in Kendal. In this instance, opposing views of public interest embodied in
Manchester's need prevailed. Although it failed to stop the project, opposition
was consolidated by Canon Rawnsley into the Lake District Defence Association, with a £5,000 fighting fund. Membership, mostly outside Cumbria,
including Tennyson, Browning, Matthew Arnold, Ruskin, Morris, Octavia
Hill, Lord Coleridge, the duke of Westminster, W. E. Forster, Sir John Simon,
Frederic, Lord Leighton, Alfred Waterhouse, and Edward Burne-Jones, resembled a list of the great and good in Victorian society, and provided the
germ of the later National Trust and the idea of the Lake District as a
National Park. Such notions would have been scarcely conceivable in 1850,
and their maturation during the 1890s indicate how far concepts of legitimate public interest had developed. (Dowthwaite 1991; Marshall and Walton
1981, 204–19)

The Lake District had . . . become a forcing house for new ideas about the proper relationship between man, property, morality and the environment. The issue posed by the pressure to open out and develop central Lakeland played a significant part in the retreat from laissez-faire economic doctrines in the later nineteenth century . . . (Marshall and Walton 1981, 219)

Another symptom was concern for ancient monuments, in earlier years unthinkingly demolished in the name of progress. HM Office of Works made a cautious beginning with early listing for preservation of a number of major sites, including Lindisfarne Priory in 1913. (Craster Peers 1953, 255)

Growing northern towns saw impressive growth of local government during the later part of the nineteenth century. In 1873, Newcastle Borough Council still attached limited significance to its public health role. Although by-laws of 1865 and 1870 prescribed regulations for new houses, including size, size of rooms, compulsory provision of windows, and widths of new streets and lanes, there was little effort to enforce them. The 'Sanitary Committee' was merely a subcommittee of the council's Town Improvement and Streets Committee. By the early twentieth century, the Sanitary Committee was a main standing committee including some of the council's most influential members. It spawned eight standing subcommittees to supervise different aspects of its work. Despite this, Newcastle never produced an equivalent to Birmingham's Joseph Chamberlain, and its administrative record was poor. In the 1880s a major scandal demonstrated slackness and waste in management of the city's finances, which was well publicized in the local press. (Callcott 1984, 172; Callcott 1988)

Despite such weaknesses, there was something like a revolution in local government here, as in other northern towns. This was reflected not only in formal powers and structure, but also in civic consciousness and pride. (Briggs 1996, 18–19) During the 1880s and 1890s pressure for economy and a minimal official role in Kendal relaxed sufficiently to allow a burst of civic enterprise and expenditure: new public baths and washhouses (1884), a Market Hall (1887), a free library (1892), and a Town Hall (1893). There was a similar pattern in Carlisle, with Market Hall (1889), Tullie House Library and Museum (1893). The Public Baths (1884) received an ornate and exotic interior, including Turkish baths, which could not have been contemplated by municipal government in an earlier generation. (Marshall and Walton 1981, 126–9)

At least as important as changes in political culture was increase in resources made available by economic growth. If development of industry, mining and commerce contributed to the worsening of social problems, they provided the increased wealth necessary to finance ameliorative measures. In the mining area covered by Houghton-le-Spring Poor Law Union, population grew from 21,000 in 1836 to 34,000 in 1882, but rateable value of property from £46,000 to £151,000. Similar jumps affected northern urban areas. (Barker, 1974, 150; Coote Hibbert and Wells 1907; Free Trade Union 1909, 14–15) Improved valuations played a minor part in these increases, but the main cause was economic development. Many local authorities acquired additional income without pushing up rating levels beyond ratepayers' limited toleration. Even the most economically minded body could nerve itself to spending in these circumstances. In the 1860s, local reformers in Wallsend succeeded in establishing an administrative local board, only to see its activities undermined by economizers, but the 1880s saw a changed climate. In 1891, the Board determined to spend £6,500 on a new hospital. Rateable value had been under £30,000 when the Board was created; by 1891 it was nearly £80,000 and, with expansion of shipbuilding and other local industries, was to grow to about £250,000 by the early 1920s. In these circumstances the Local Board and its successor, the Borough Council, could face increasing expenditure with an equanimity which would have astonished their predecessors of the 1860s. (Richardson 1923, 413–15)

Rateable Value of Property (£s)

	1870	1907
Newcastle	449,000	1,641,000
Sunderland	258,000	706,000
Gateshead	134,000	427,000
South Shields	125,000	421,000
West Hartlepool	67,000	262,000
Tynemouth	112,000	243,000

County councils and rural district authorities might not enjoy such windfalls, but even here there were increased official responsibilities in public health, education and maintenance of roads and bridges. The era of turnpike trusts was ending, and from the middle of the nineteenth century responsibility for road maintenance shifted to local authorities. County councils assumed control of main roads, including those released by redundant turnpike trusts, while lesser authorities took over minor roads. The main road to Ponteland through Northumberland's Castle Ward became a public road in November 1881, instead of being administered by a turnpike trust. (Lawson 1971, 208) The amount which Cumberland County Council spent on road and bridge repair doubled during the 1890s, an increase which represented *inter alia* a considerable increase in road traffic. It also led to protracted squabbles between county and borough authorities as to respective financial obligations. As the cost of road building and maintenance grew, with increasing traffic and the dawning of motor transport, the burden of financing major trunk routes became too much for the limited revenues of county councils, especially in Cumberland and Westmorland. Eventually, central government was drawn in, exemplified by the creation of the Road Board in 1909 and the Ministry of Transport in 1919. (Williams 1975, 178–201)

As early as 1877, Newcastle Corporation was purchasing land for new stables to house the increasing number of horses required for its activities. (Harbottle and Fraser 1987, 38, 40) In 1882 the city's Medical Officer of Health had a staff of a chief and four assistant inspectors of nuisances, a chief and assistant inspector of provisions, and two clerks. By 1907 this had grown to a chief inspector, assistant chief inspector and nineteen assistant inspectors of nuisances, a chief inspector and two assistant inspectors of provisions, a superintendent of municipal midwives, six health visitors and six clerks, not counting staff employed in the city's own hospitals. By 1911, the cleansing department employed well over 500 men. The tiny band of scavengers who had intermittently cleaned a few principal streets in early Victorian years provided a contrast with such complex and sophisticated operations. Their councillor masters could scarcely have anticipated that in March 1907 the professional who headed Newcastle's cleansing department would be discussing his work with fellow experts at the Annual Conference of Cleansing Superintendents of Great Britain and Ireland. (Harbottle and Fraser 1987, 38, 40; Coote Hibbert and Wells 1907, 161–75; Anon. 1911, 51 *et seq.*)

Police professionalism improved. For many years county forces of Northumberland and Durham were headed by chief constables who combined experience in the armed forces with an assured position in local society. In 1902, after Colonel Eden's retirement, Durham county force was for the first time led by a career policeman, who had headed smaller forces at Reigate and South Shields. (Newcastle Union 1880, 1889; Anon. 1957, 16–17; Anon. 1940, 21–3)

Expansion of central government's role is illustrated by the census figures shown in the table. (Rowe 1973, 128)

Numbers Employed by Central Government

	1851	1911
County Durham	385	2,587
Northumberland	500	2,486
Cumberland	213	772
Westmorland	56	323
Newcastle	141	1,191
Gateshead	34	291
Tynemouth	98	216

Multiplication of official positions and gradual emergence of career structures and professional organizations reflected a more general change in British society, as specialized occupations crystallized out of an earlier simpler structure. In the years before 1914, the Newcastle Municipal Officers' Association reflected the hierarchical pattern of the city's staff and published its own printed journal. National publications such as *The Local Government Chronicle* provided exchange of information and opinions between local government officers and facilitated their emergence as a pressure group in local government matters.

The Relief of Poverty

For many years, poor-law expenditure provided the largest element in local government spending. The North saw no universal acceptance of the 'principles of 1834' which sought to cut outdoor relief to able-bodied poor. Offers of relief to the able-bodied were supposedly limited to support within the workhouse, an expedient seen as sufficiently deterrent to induce applicants to find any available work. Central authority policy throughout the period 1834 to 1909 remained attached to the idea of the deterrent workhouse, but local administration was shaped by such policies only to a minor extent.

The winter of 1862–63 saw 'cotton famine' in Cumbrian textile industries as a result of the American Civil War, and an unusually high peak of male able-bodied pauperism, but this was not reflected in greater use of the deterrent workhouse. (Thompson 1976, 171, 697–711; Thompson 1979, 132–2) Guardians continued to see applicants in terms of 'deserving' or 'undeserving', rather than the often arbitrary division between 'able-bodied' and 'non-able-bodied' advocated by central authority. Even a society inclined to seek causes for crime, poverty, and disease in individual responsibility found it difficult to blame individuals for unavoidable unemployment caused by such events as the cotton famine. The widespread inclination to treat such applicants as 'deserving', and avoid the workhouse test for them, subverted central policies, and brought frequent bickering between central and local authorities. The Poor Law Board and its successor the Local Government Board were unable to persuade guardians that they understood local needs and conditions better than the guardians themselves.

Guardians, and ratepayers whom they represented, often had intimate knowledge of cases which came before them. The overwhelming majority of poor-law cases were uncontroversial – the old, the sick, widows and children – and it is probable that, because communities were more locally orientated than they have since become, fraudulent and 'undeserving' claims were more readily identified. In 1886 the Newcastle Board of Guardians explained reluctance to increase spending during severe unemployment not only in terms of the effect of higher rates on poorer ratepayers but also because 'Relieving officers have found imposture so rife among the applicants that they have wisely done all in their power to put an end to a system so fruitful of evil.' (Relief Fund 1885–86) A widespread malpractice was illustrated by a Durham case of 1910. Houghton-le-Spring guardians discovered that Robert Richardson, who had been receiving relief payments, had concealed £249 in the Post Office Savings Bank. He was ordered to repay £65 9s. 6d. of ratepayers' money obtained fraudulently.

Practice determined by local knowledge was not always generous. Those whose money financed poor relief usually understood that the aged did not always grow old gracefully and that the sick and the weak were not always pleasantly pathetic. Local prejudices could affect poor-law practice. Border counties had annual illegitimacy rates well above the national average (in Cumberland 12 per 1,000 of the population, Westmorland 9.2, in 1863, against a national average of 6.5). Moral outrage from time to time inspired harsher treatment of mothers of bastards and their offspring, although such deterrents seem to have had little effect. (Thompson 1976, 199–200) Cases in the Houghton-le-Spring Poor Law Union around 1900 show continued willingness to punish those considered undeserving. In 1890 Elizabeth Bell, a workhouse inmate, received 14 days' imprisonment for disorderly conduct; later the same year two women from the workhouse were before the magistrates, 'the one for tearing and destroying the bed-clothes, and the other for disorderly and refractory conduct in the workhouse'. In 1902 William Gribbin was given 7 days in prison for drunkenness; after his release, he, 'on presenting himself for admission to the workhouse in a drunken condition had, owing to his violent conduct, been taken before a Justice and committed to prison for a further period of 14 days'. Such examples may have kindled sympathy in a few, but were unlikely to appeal to most ratepayers. (Barker 1974, 170–1, 227)

The casual poor, mainly tramps and vagrants, featured most in complaints of harsh treatment. While most communities accepted an obligation to maintain their own 'settled' poor, this was not willingly extended to include those on the move, sometimes workers genuinely in search of work but including also a considerable proportion who were either criminal or on the fringes of the Victorian underworld. Policemen were routinely appointed as assistant relieving officers dealing with this group. In sharp contrast to the treatment given to most applicants for relief, local practice embraced a variety of deterrent policies – searching, confiscation of property, compulsory task work (commonly stone-breaking), compulsory baths (often cold), and a generally robust treatment by the police. A debate in the 1890s about the greater burden of casual poor at Kendal compared with neighbouring Ulverston evoked claims that at Kendal workhouse beds were more comfortable, the stone for stone-breaking softer, and separation of the sexes not enforced as at Ulverston. (Thompson 1976, 560–3; Pugh 1978, 296)

The concept of the undeserving poor died hard (if it has died). It only required a small number of well-publicized cases of abuse to explain the opinions expressed by Alderman Richardson of Newcastle, in opposing a scheme for council house building in 1891:

> There was a residuum of the population incapable of helping themselves. The residuum was the result, to a large extent, of hereditary causes, but mainly the result of a life of debauchery, sin and often crime . . . If it was right and incumbent upon them to provide shelter for these people, it was equally incumbent upon them to provide food and raiment for them. Therefore the Corporation might begin and erect bakehouses and clothing establishments tomorrow. By that means, they would get themselves upon an inclined plane, which would land them in the vortex of pure municipal socialism. (Newcastle Council 1891)

Such sentiments were shared by many ratepayers, most of whom were far from rich. Poorer ratepayers were no keener than their richer brethren on higher local government spending to tackle social problems.

Workhouses built in this period exhibited growing suitability for the complex demands placed upon them. None of these designs was strongly influenced by the deterrent role of 'the principles of 1834'. Smaller and simpler structures built during the 1840s, such as the surviving early workhouse at Hexham, were replaced by complex and elaborate structures from the 1860s. Not only were these designed by members of the developed architectural profession, but often by architects specializing in institutional buildings. These later workhouses, in contrast to many of their more utilitarian predecessors, increasingly embodied in design and decoration elements of communal prestige and status. The new South Shields workhouse was 'reviewed' in a lyrical account in the *Newcastle Chronicle* of 28 November 1878, demonstrating that contemporaries were impressed. A few years later, its architect, J. H. Morton, wrote to the South Shields guardians to tell them that he had just won the contract for the new Gateshead workhouse, 'the fourth workhouse I have erected on the same principle as that of South Shields'. (Mawson 1971, 111)

Changes were less striking in rural workhouses, including many Cumbrian examples, but by no means wholly absent:

> the union workhouse in Cumbria was consistently adapting its role to meet the needs of the overwhelming proportion of its inmates. The old, the mentally and physically sick, children and single pregnant women, all demanded an institution of care. By 1871, at least in embryonic form, the most developed and larger union workhouses in Cumbria had been adapted to meet this need, being at once hospitals, geriatric

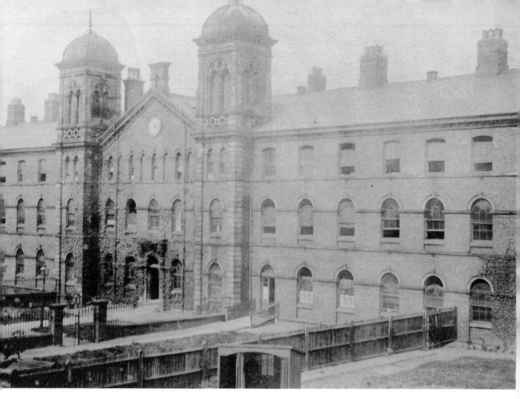

Figure 17.4 Carlisle Workhouse, Fusehill. Opened in 1864, this shows the development of early simple, highly functional workhouses into something more elaborate and ostentatious. This 1890s photograph illustrates the continued policy of classification, with separate yards for different categories of inmates.

homes, places for the care of less chronic mental patients, orphanages, schools, lying-in hospitals, and vagrant wards. (Thompson 1979, 135)

Greater sophistication was paralleled by increased staff, more specialization, and the spread of professional qualifications. In 1880, the Newcastle Poor Law Union employed a headquarters staff of 57, with five added within the next few years. Duties assigned to these officials displayed sophistication in marked contrast to the handful of officers employed by the Union at its inception in 1836. (Newcastle Union, 1885, 1889)

Education

Education also saw expanded official activity. The years before 1870 had seen growth in elementary education, overwhelmingly provided by voluntary organizations, with agencies involved linked to the churches.

Voluntary provision had been backed by increasing subsidies from central government, accompanied by official inspection of aided schools. The 1870 Elementary Education Act brought a leap forward in education provided by official bodies. The Act aimed to supplement voluntary provision, but schools built by new School Boards, elected and financed by ratepayers, played an increasingly important role in providing basic literacy, and sometimes more, for an increasing population.

Levels of achievement varied, depending on local opinion and the capacity of the new education authorities. Sometimes ratepayers were unconvinced of the need to spend more of their money on building and maintaining schools. (Marshall and Walton 1981, 138–49; Everett 1963; Taylor 1964) The Western Board School at North Shields, opened in 1872, was designed to house 582 boys and girls in the main building, with an infants' school for 284 adjoining. The estimated expense was £5,734, and there was grumbling when the final cost, including fittings, reached £7,500. A member of the Tynemouth School Board was at pains to assure ratepayers that 'there is no ornamentation in the building . . . the cost about which so much has been said and written, is simply owing to the present high cost of building operations'.

Robert Spence Watson's role at Gateshead illustrates the importance of individual contributions. He gave devoted service on the School Board for many years and reinforced it with his influence in Tyneside politics and society. The Gateshead School Board was the fourth to come into existence and went on to build 21 schools between 1871 and 1903. The 1902 Education Act ended the separate existence of School Boards; it was not until 1928 that Gateshead received another new school. By 1877 Board schools in Gateshead were teaching more children than voluntary schools, and by 1883 more than twice as many. In 1879 income from school rates there was still higher than central government education grants, but by 1888 this balance had shifted, here as elsewhere.

Cumberland had 934 teachers in 1851, 1,815 in 1891, Westmorland, with much smaller population growth, 318 and 465. Northumberland had 1,354 teachers in 1861, 2,315 in 1881; the Durham figures were 2,086 and 4,349. In towns the story was similar; a rise of 348 to 799 in 1861–81 for Newcastle, from 86 to 368 for Gateshead and from 245 to 559 for Sunderland. The leap forward after 1870 was not maintained, but there was a slower rise, roughly in accordance with increase in population.

Chapter 18

Social Changes

Deep-rooted distrust of official agencies was compatible with increase in private benevolence. Despite extension of government, central and local, unofficial agencies remained important in ameliorating social problems and pioneering charitable activities. As in earlier years, there were numerous examples of individual philanthropy, communal response to emergencies, and the creation of long-term charitable foundations. At Jarrow and Walker on Tyneside, the first hospitals were built by industrialists responsible for the towns' rapid growth – Charles Mark Palmer at Jarrow and Charles Mitchell at Walker. Successive extensions of Durham County Infirmary, founded originally at mid-century, were made possible by gifts of £10,000 by Dean Waddington of Durham in the 1860s and £12,000 by John Eden of Beamish Park in the 1880s. At Newcastle, the Diamond Jubilee of 1897 was commemorated by rebuilding the Infirmary, rechristened the Royal Victoria Infirmary, at a cost of well over £200,000. The Armstrong family and the shipowner John Hall each gave £100,000 for this purpose. The first specialist children's hospital in the region opened in 1863 at Hanover Square, Newcastle. In 1888 the solicitor John Fleming paid for new premises erected in memory of his wife. Lord Armstrong provided a further extension in 1896. (Hume 1951, 52; Anon. 1930, 115) In Carlisle, the Liberal Anglican MP and textile manufacturer, Joseph Ferguson, devoted 20 per cent of his income to philanthropy, and there were other examples of conspicuous benevolence among the city's industrial and commercial élite. (Anon. 1924, 25–37; Burgess 1984, 640, 681–2)

Charitable responses to local depressions or disasters remained common. The cotton famine affected textile workers in Carlisle and prompted an unofficial relief committee which subsidized wages reduced by short-time working. At its peak this committee dealt with 6,000 cases and spent more than £7,000 in the six winter months of 1862–63. During the whole financial year 1862–63 the Carlisle board of guardians spent about £11,000 and never had more than 3,255 cases. A principal, explicitly stated, function of the unofficial committee was to deal with cases which guardians found difficult because of their limited discretionary powers. Given that local poor-law administration and philanthropy were dominated by the same groups, it is not surprising that they provided complementary facilities. (Thompson 1979, 122–6)

The Hartley Colliery disaster of 1862, which killed more than 200 men and boys, was one of the worst mining catastrophes. It was followed by a public subscription for dependants of the victims. Most donations, though by no means all, came from the northern region. They eventually totalled £81,838 19s. 5d. Similar funds had been established earlier, in response to the cholera epidemic of 1853 and the great fire and explosion which devastated much of quayside Newcastle and Gateshead in 1854. Lists of donations show old and new forms of wealth co-operating, with peers, bishops and gentry joined by banks, collieries and factories.

Charitable institutions founded in earlier years often extended their activities. There was a flow of new creations as different needs were recognized. The problems of getting to grips with the condition of the very poor were considerable. Most towns acquired funds providing clothing and footwear. In Newcastle, 2,676 pairs of boots were provided by one charity in 1909. At North Shields, 'The Poor Children's Boot Fund' was set up in 1884 by Alderman Isaac Black, owner of a prosperous clothing and tailoring business. Police forces were involved, identifying cases of need, distributing gifts and trying to ensure that they were used as intended. Boot funds normally marked gifts to try to prevent their being pawned or sold. (Anon. 1908) At Sunderland a shipowner, James Knott, began a similar scheme as a personal activity; his work was eventually taken over by the Poor Children's Holiday Association, with Knott providing an endowment.

This Newcastle-based Poor Children's Holiday Association provides a good example of ways in which charities proliferated and extended their coverage. Its first seaside trip for poor children took 120 boys and girls to Monkseaton for the day in 1891. By 1912 the holiday scheme catered for 12,000 children. The PCHA pioneered special facilities for tuberculosis patients, long before there was official provision. Rescue work among waifs and strays was developed, as the Association became involved in a multiplicity of charitable activities as well as its initial work in providing for convalescence and holidays. (Anon. 1913)

From about 1870, it became common for workers in collieries, shipyards or factories to make regular small donations to hospitals or similar institutions, and for employers to implement these arrangements. Rules of philanthropic institutions changed accordingly, with places on governing bodies reserved for representatives of multiple small donors. In 1861, Sunderland Infirmary established its first collecting arrangement of this kind, and in 1877 the patronage system of presenting patients by subscribers was scrapped. It was also abolished at Newcastle Infirmary in 1887, and provision made for nine workers' representatives to sit on the House Committee. (Miller, 1986, 161–2)

Friendly societies and insurance facilities already had a long history, but expansion quickened during the Victorian period, until a high proportion of working families were covered with some kind of insurance provision. (Turner 1996, 85–97)

Some trade unions developed charitable functions. From 1899 Northumberland coal-miners contributed regularly to provide retirement homes. Many cottages provided in this way can still be seen. In its first six years the Durham Aged Mine-Workers' Homes Association built 200 homes for aged couples and by 1924 the figure had reached over 1,000. (Oxberry 1924, 10–12, 32)

Co-operation between official and unofficial humanitarian agencies grew. Conditions in Middlesbrough during the growth in the third quarter of the century have been neatly caught in Lord Briggs' description of 'The British Ballarat'. (Briggs 1968, 250) The ironmaster Henry Bolckow played an important part in bringing about economic expansion, but his role was a varied one. He lived in the town until 1856, and served as improvement commissioner for both port and town. He was Middlesbrough's first mayor and first MP, one of its first magistrates, a governor of the voluntary infirmary and a benefactor of hospitals, schools, churches and recreational facilities. Bolckow was succeeded as mayor and MP by Isaac Wilson, manufacturer of iron and pottery, and director of the Stockton and Darlington Railway. Wilson became chairman of the Tees port authority, principal agent of the Middlesbrough landlords, chairman of the local School Board from 1870 to 1888, director of the water company and first president of the Mechanics' Institute. With men like these active in public life and charities, Middlesbrough received its first park, a gift from Bolckow, in 1868, before Newcastle possessed such an amenity. (Briggs 1996, 12–13) On Tyneside, the role of Charles Mark Palmer in Jarrow's development provides a good parallel to Teesside ironmasters in this respect. (Purdue 1982, 182–4)

As charitable initiatives proliferated, Poor Law Unions extended the practice of sending paupers in need of special treatment, such as the blind or the deaf and dumb, to appropriate establishments, paying fees from the rates. When a public body placed dependants in private institutions this involved checks to ensure that public money was well spent. Poor-law guardians were punctilious in such matters. In 1913, deputations from the South Shields guardians visited a varied range of institutions in which one or more of their charges were maintained at public expense, mostly within the region but in some cases as far afield as Birmingham, Bristol and Middlesex. (Mawson 1971, 96–7, 121–2) Poor Law Unions were connected with a variety of official and unofficial institutions, paving the way for the eventual takeover by official agencies of much social work originally undertaken by charitable societies.

This was not the only area of co-operation. Especially in later years, unofficial groups often provided extra comforts or treats for workhouse inmates. These might include books, toys, musical instruments, pictures or a barrel of beer at Christmas. Workhouse children were taken to shows, including pantomimes, or for outings to the seaside or the country. In 1887 South Shields poor-law guardians held an unofficial collection among themselves to send workhouse children to the Newcastle Jubilee Exhibition, and received a letter of thanks ending 'We are your children'.

Increased philanthropic activity in the late nineteenth and early twentieth centuries was not the result of benevolence in society at large, but of groups of individuals who developed this interest. In an unequal society, most efficient intervention came from those who possessed resources and influence.

The Influence of Religion

Motivation for charitable activity varied, but religious zeal was important. Wide reaches of society seemed little affected by formal religion, or any Christian observance. The report of the 1861 Royal Commission on Education disclosed a continuing pattern of 'open profligacy' in the Cumbrian countryside, including the claim that eldest children in most families were illegitimately born. (Marshall and Walton 1981, 152–3)

For all its limitations, the 1851 religious census indicated a low level of church or chapel attendances. The rapidly growing towns and mining communities were weak points in religious observance. A survey conducted by the *West Cumberland Times* in 1902 indicated further decline, with only 20 per cent in its circulation area attending church or chapel. (Burgess 1984, 684) At the popular level, concern for religious doctrine or liturgical matters, however absorbing they might be to some élite groups, were infrequent preoccupations. This is not to deny the existence for many of real religious devotion.

There was sectarian division and prejudice. One example saw the central Poor Law Board investigate angry claims that Roman Catholic children were being forcibly converted to Protestantism in the Cockermouth workhouse. The investigation elicited this testimony from 14-year-old John Walker:

> I was a Catholic but have turned now and am a Protestant. I don't know the difference between the two religions. The Catholics worship the Virgin Mary made of stone . . . I never heard of the Trinity. Don't know what it is. The only reason I can give why I wished to be a Protestant is because the Catholics worship a stone . . . (Thompson 1976, 524)

No doubt some other 'conversions' were similarly superficial.

Religious rivalries brought violent and bigoted conflicts, especially where Irish Roman Catholicism confronted evangelical Protestantism allied with Orange lodges. (Steele 1976, 232, 239) Orange sentiment was strong in Whitehaven, while Irish Catholics were a majority in nearby Cleator Moor. Both the North East and the North West saw rioting during tours by the anti-Catholic agitator William Murphy in mid-Victorian years. Murphy never recovered from injuries sustained when he was beaten and kicked by Catholic Irish workers at Whitehaven in 1871, and died the following year. In 1884, a provocative Orange march through Cleator inspired a violent Catholic response which led to a riot. Sectarian and ethnic prejudice were more prominent in such incidents than religious commitment. (Marshall and Walton 1981, 99)

Evangelical Christianity inspired the work of the temperance movement (pp. 329–32 below), but there were notable setbacks, as in the Cumberland county council election of 1889. Teetotal candidates were beaten, including their leader, the devout Sir Wilfrid Lawson, defeated by Thomas Iredale, a self-made brewery magnate with a following among Workington workers. In Kirkby Stephen, the building of a fine Temperance Hall was matched by Richard Winter's impressive brewery opposite. (Tufft 1976, 13–14; Bennett 1993, 13)

Despite reservations about popular knowledge of religion, or levels of attendance at church or chapel, it is difficult to deny the influence of diffuse Christian teaching over wide areas, and the piety of influential religious groups. It requires only modest powers of observation to appreciate that the building and operation of churches and chapels was one of the main communal activities of these years, in towns and smaller communities. During the second half of the nineteenth century Stockton received 17 new churches and chapels, Darlington 20, Sunderland 40, Jarrow 13 and South Shields 30. As Newcastle's Elswick suburb grew with the expansion of Armstrong's works, 15 churches and chapels were built there.

Although pit villages held many ungodly folk, a high proportion of miners who exercised influence among their fellows – as, for example, office-holders in trade unions or co-operative societies – were adherents of church or more commonly chapel. The doomed miners trapped in the wrecked New Hartley colliery in 1862 left notes behind telling of the prayer meetings they held before being overcome by the failing air supply. (Anon. 1862, 2–3)

In lead-mining dales, Primitive Methodists were credited with improving manners in rough communities: 'They have reclaimed and reformed individuals who were enemies to their families and themselves, as well as a perfect pest and a disgrace to the neighbourhood.' (Hunt 1970, 221)

Throughout the later nineteenth and early twentieth centuries, religious festivals, especially Good Friday, were great occasions in communities. Sunday schools recruited many children whose parents were not regular attenders at church or chapel. No doubt children's attendance might be inspired by parents who wanted them out of the way for other than religious motives. (Stigant 1971, 99) Reminders with religious overtones abounded. Workers entering Wigham Richardson's Neptune shipyard passed an inscription exhorting them: 'Watching these fleeting hours soon past, remember that which comes at last.'

Religious faith was not confined to any social level. (Green 1994, 193–4) The elder Sir Wilfrid Lawson (1795–1867) experienced a dramatic conversion in middle age, faced with a dangerous illness 'when the unseen realities of the eternal world seemed breaking upon him'. (Russell 1910, 3; Burgess 1984, 424) T. H. Bainbridge aimed at extending Christian stewardship among staff of his Newcastle department store. In 1912, facing a serious operation, he wrote:

> I am now face to face with the possibility of death. It is therefore a solemn moment. I have been a very unprofitable servant. I have no hope except in a penitent trust in Jesus Christ as my Saviour. The first verse of the hymn *Just as I am* represents, I trust, my attitude to Jesus Christ, on whose promise 'Him that cometh unto me I will in no wise cast out', I now rely for salvation. (France 1913, 21–2, 39)

There were links between the devout of differing status. Inscribed stones on a chapel in Bedlington Station, a mining community in south-east Northumberland, illustrate this. The principal foundation stone was laid by a member of the Bates coalowning family, but walls contain many 'half-crown bricks', inscribed with a name in return for small donations to building funds. They include names of two brick-makers at the colliery brickworks. Two bricks record members of the Garrow family, who for many years combined evangelical religion, local government, trade unionism and the Labour Party as compatible characteristics. A few hundred yards away, the early twentieth-century Anglican church of St John also has a foundation stone laid by a member of a coalowning family, but its congregation included mining families, some of whom made 'clippy mats' in aid of church-building funds. On Tyneside and Wearside, fine Victorian churches were built by leading shipbuilders.

Older aristocratic elements, often with revenues swollen by economic development, continued to play their part. In 1857 the bishop of Durham, congratulating Lady Londonderry on her new church at Seaham Harbour, reflected that

> It shows that if property has its duties and its responsibilities, so it has its Privileges and its pure Pleasures . . . and it is the purest of all earthly pleasures to have the will and power combined to exercise the sacred Trust for the lasting benefit of those whom God has made dependent upon us. (Heesom 1979, 155)

328

The continued importance of religion was also illustrated in the creation of the diocese of Newcastle out of the see of Durham in 1882. The
Anglican Church attracted families making their way into upper reaches of
society. Some leading Kendal dynasties moved from nonconformist activity
in mid-Victorian years. They included the Wakefield family, who graduated
from political liberalism and religious nonconformity as part of Kendal's
urban élite, through a fortune made in banking, to landed gentry status,
with an estate of 7,000 acres; before the end of the century, the family were
pillars of the Conservative Party and the Church of England. (Marshall and
Dyehouse 1976, 154–5; Briggs 1996, 16–17)

Although Carlisle remained the poorest diocese in England, over
£350,000 was spent on building or restoring 158 churches during the long
episcopate of Bishop Harvey Goodwin (1869–91). Goodwin and his predecessor Samuel Waldegrave (1860–69) tried to improve the quality and
public image of clergy, which had in some cases left a good deal to be desired in matters such as drinking and 'lack of general culture and refinement
and in too many cases descent to the level of their flocks in the moral scale'.
(Bouch 1948, 429–30, 435–6; Burgess 1984, 185–7) Reformers, including the
evangelical Bishop Villiers, appointed in 1856, were handicapped by low
stipends in Cumbrian parishes. By 1864 two-thirds of Villiers' ordinations
had already left the diocese, attracted by better livings elsewhere. Villiers only
stayed at Carlisle for four years before translation to Durham. Attempts
to extend the educational role of the diocese were limited by shortages of
funds. In 1856 Westmorland (excluding Kendal) possessed only two fully
certificated schoolteachers; there were none in Cumberland north of Carlisle
or south of Whitehaven. In the 1880s, Goodwin still found slackness or
neglect, and criticized his 'part-time clergy'. Even in the richer see of Durham,
it was not always easy to find money to cope with unprecedented and unforeseeable population growth. (Munden 1990; Rawnsley 1896; Heesom 1979)

Irish immigration into developing industrial districts reversed the decline
of Catholicism, establishing concentrated pockets of adherents. In 1885 about
20 per cent of the population of Jarrow were Irish. Middlesbrough in 1871
had a higher concentration of Irish-born residents than any other English
centre except Liverpool. (Pelling 1967, 334; Chase 1994, 27, 37) There
were ten Catholic churches in West Cumberland by 1902, and well-attended
centres at Carlisle and Whitehaven. Methodism made gains in the same
areas, though not without setbacks when internal disputes or shortages of
money impeded progress. The development of industrial communities like
Barrow and Millom after 1860 facilitated Methodist growth, partly because
of the contribution of Welsh and Cornish incomers. (Burgess 1981, 137,
142–51) Visitation records of the bishopric of Durham often express concern about the success of nonconformist sects. In many northern towns and
mining communities, dissenters pushed the established church into a relatively minor role in religious activity.

Crime and Drunkenness

There is no difficulty in finding religious zeal in these years, but there is equally full documentation of different characteristics. Devout books, tracts and journals poured from presses, but so did publications of other kinds. In the third quarter of the nineteenth century, the *News of the World* and its rival *Lloyd's Weekly News* enjoyed an increasing readership with a taste for the sensational and scandalous. Contemporary society included much that was rough, vicious and criminal to fill popular if unedifying publications.

The rural scene was less turbulent, characterized by lower crime rates and stronger communal discipline. Westmorland had one of the lowest crime rates in Britain, with one murder recorded in fifty years. There were, however, complaints of heavy drinking, and high rates of illegitimate births. (Buss 1974, 63–4; Marshall 1995)

There was improvement in levels of civilization, but it was far from complete. In 1878, Tynemouth police recorded 914 offences of drunkenness and disorderly behaviour, 158 thieves, 157 vagrants, 301 prostitutes and 682 habitual drunkards. (Anon. 1969, 25) Local newspapers often published accounts of violent fights, some on a large scale. One occurred in a rough quayside area of Newcastle, Sandgate, on the evening of Sunday, 11 May 1851, inspiring a local song 'The Horrid War i' Sangeyt'. Police collided with an Irish crowd which refused to disperse and began to gain the upper hand. As news spread, native inhabitants of nearby tenements sallied out to help the police, and this unusual coalition carried the day against the Irish. Leaders of all three groups were referred to by nicknames in the song, in the knowledge that they would be recognized in what was still very much a locally orientated community.

Policemen were not always as lucky, as examples from Northumberland demonstrate. At 3 a.m. one night in 1873, a village policeman surprised a poaching gang; he tried to arrest them but was shot and died of his wounds the next day. In 1880 PC Scott was beaten to death by a poaching gang. In 1913 two policemen were shot dead while trying to make an arrest at Bedlington. (Anon. 1957, 57–65)

Prostitution remained common, with young girls often involved. (Rewcastle 1854, 14) Reports in local newspapers show that some public houses were centres of the trade; a case of January 1877 indicated that George Henry's Plough Inn, Spicer Lane, Newcastle, was one of these. A House of Lords Select Committee on Intemperance was told by Newcastle's Chief Constable in 1877 that, although the poorer brothels of the town were often prosecuted, the better class were conducted so discreetly that it was impossible to obtain evidence against them. The impossibility of stamping out prostitution was recognized by the well-informed, and reflected in police regulations of the 1860s stipulating that policemen should ignore prostitutes who offered no overt offence to public order or decency. These orders were essentially unchanged in the early twentieth century. (Rewcastle 1854, 14; Newcastle Watch 1869, 21; Newcastle Watch 1905, 244)

Drink remained a serious problem. As early as 1854 a Newcastle suburb had one public house to every 22 families. In the early 1890s there were nearly 500 public houses in Sunderland, about 250 at South Shields. National figures of convictions for drunkenness in 1911 saw Northumberland top of the county league with 127.31 per 10,000 population, Newcastle at 97.91 and Middlesbrough 117.51. In 1920 Northumberland still topped the county drunkenness league, with Durham runner-up. (Rewcastle 1854, 25; Robinson 1934, 62; Bennison 1995, 31)

There was drunkenness at many levels. In Northumberland the vicar of Stannington in the 1870s was often found in the fields after being on the spree all night. In the 1850s it was said of clergy in upland Cumbria that many of them were 'more or less intoxicated at one time or another, at parties, fairs or markets'; several of them were 'notorious drunkards'. (Munden 1990, 195) A North Shields firm of solicitors, Fenwick and Crawford, suffered when two generations of Crawfords took to excessive drinking. Dismissals for drunkenness occurred frequently in local police forces. (Dodd 1897, 90–5; Ridley 1958, 192; Bank of England, 8/4/1851, 27/5/1859) At a time when many wages offered little leeway for indulgences, for a man or woman to become addicted to drink might spell ruin not only for an individual but for families.

The Temperance Movement

With this background, the strength of the temperance movement is not surprising. Attempts were made to provide alternatives to public houses, but such innovations as cocoa houses enjoyed little success. The Durham club movement, partly conceived as a respectable alternative to the public house, began to expand early in the twentieth century, with 58 clubs founded in 1898–1905. Northumberland was slower off the mark, with only 15 clubs in the principal union by 1906. In their early years, northern clubs, as in other regions, were interested in education, operated libraries and lecture programmes, and in other ways could be seen as improving as well as social institutions.

The North of England Temperance League was founded at Newcastle in 1858; thirty years later it had 105 affiliated societies, with 15,000 active members. By 1893 there were 202 societies and 50,000 active members. (Anon. 1894–97) This umbrella organization was one of a number active in

these years. In the years around 1900, the temperance movement possessed a wider support than any political movement, without ever exerting more than a limited influence. Bands of Hope, Good Templars, Rechabites, and many others, offered thousands of families not merely a crutch against drink but a range of alternative social activities. In a mining suburb of Sunderland, The Hope of Silksworth Lodge of Good Templars was founded in 1871 and flourished for many years. Its social activities came to include an annual pantomime and election of Rose Queen, choirs, football and cricket teams, and billiards. A new headquarters was built in 1912. In addition to social activities, temperance organizations provided insurance and savings schemes.

There was influential support. Successive Presidents of the North of England Temperance League were Sir Walter Trevelyan, Bart., Edward Backhouse (Sunderland banker), Arthur Pease (Darlington banker and businessman), T. W. Backhouse, and the countess of Carlisle. The Trevelyan baronets of Wallington, the Middleton baronets of Belsay, the Atkinson landowners at Angerton, and the earl of Carlisle, all turned estates 'dry' by closing public houses or transforming them into temperance establishments. This example was imitated by some colliery companies, including those at Throckley and North Seaton. It was claimed that this increased the happiness and comfort of the communities concerned. (Hayler 1897, 23 *et seq.*) Sir Wilfrid Lawson and the countess of Carlisle assembled 16,000 Good Templars and Rechabites at Sir Wilfrid's country seat at Brayton in 1875. Carlisle had six lodges of Good Templars, Penrith three and Egremont two; most Cumbrian towns possessed at least a single lodge. (Marshall 1983, 204)

Campaigns against licences and for reduction in drinking hours were frequent. In mining communities, temperance organizations were strong, but drunkenness was also common. In the 1892 general election at Newcastle, the popular Conservative candidate, Hamond, could campaign effectively by appealing for the support of 'all who loved a glass of beer'. Not surprisingly, elections were still marked by unruly behaviour. (Waitt 1972, 352; Sunderland 1967, 83) Nevertheless there was a change. In November 1902 a Cumbrian newspaper noted a decline in street violence and drunkenness, and this would seem to be broadly true of the region. Improvement might not be secure, and some developments during the First World War seemed to threaten a relapse.

Carlisle and Gretna became centres of military training and munitions manufacture, acquiring army bases and 20,000 well-paid munitions workers. Drunkenness soared, reinforcing Lloyd George's view that 'drink is doing us more damage than all the German submarines put together'. A formidable array of local opinion reinforced government anxieties and pushed through emergency arrangements whereby drink outlets were subjected to official

Figure 18.1 Band of Hope temperance parade in the market place, Carlisle, before the First World War, illustrating the mass support which the temperance movement could command.

control. Of 120 public houses in the Carlisle and Gretna area, 53 were closed and 85 of the 100 off-licences cancelled. A supervisory board, the State Management, prohibited links between wages of those selling drink and levels of sales. Attempts were made to replace alcoholic drinks in public houses with cheap and nourishing food. By the end of the war, the 'nationalized' brewery and drink outlets represented a vested interest which, backed by temperance influences, succeeded in continuing the scheme. In 1919 its General Manager claimed that reversal to the earlier situation would be 'received with dismay by the great majority of the inhabitants'. Local employers, the Chief Constable, the bishop of Carlisle and other religious interests, all added supporting voices. There was trade union support too, although there were dissenting opinions, including the claim that the 'nationalized' public houses were 'about as cold and uncomfortable as a third class waiting room in a country railway station'. This complaint had some justification, as might be expected in public houses administered to discourage the sale of drink. (Burgess 1984, 424–6; Radcliffe 1977, 243–8; Murfin 1990, 76) The North East avoided this draconian reaction to wartime drinking, but there were similar anxieties and some restrictions, including cuts in opening hours and production of alcoholic drinks.

Leisure, Sport and Recreation

The later nineteenth century saw an expansion in leisure time, with reductions in hours, spread of Saturday half-holidays, statutory bank holidays and extension of secular pleasures on Sundays. Leisure patterns changed, with some old-established pastimes, such as cock-fighting and other brutal practices, increasingly condemned by respectable opinion and law. Older celebrations associated with rural life might evolve into fun-fairs attracting both urban and rural customers. Even in rural areas, by the early twentieth century, traditional country dancing had either died out or was in decline under the impact of outside influences, increasingly replaced in village dances by such international imports as the tango, foxtrot, or American two-step. This was part of wider change which saw assimilation of popular culture into more uniform patterns. Although much 'home-made' and family-based recreation continued, popular culture was increasingly urban in origin and commercial in character. (Jobey 1992; Murfin 1990, 39–41, 47, 110, 191–5, 231; Marshall and Walton 1981, 164–78; Godwin 1986, 31; Huggins 1996)

Some older celebrations disappeared. In Westmorland, Christmas had been traditionally celebrated at Brough with pagan overtones centred on the holly tree. 'Intemperance and disorder' were associated with rivalry between supporters of two public houses. Vicar and schoolteacher were responsible for replacing such scenes with more decorous celebrations from about 1860. Where traditional festivities enjoyed influential support, their chances of survival were better. The Curwen family helped to preserve a form of mass football at Workington, even though it could involve damage to property, injuries and even on occasion death among the participants. The 'uppies' (miners) and 'downies' (seamen) who fought these battles believed that they were somehow immune from the intervention of the law.

For many years after cock-fighting had been outlawed, it continued surreptitiously. In 1850, mining communities still saw cock-fighting and dog-fighting; playing cards for money was common, as was pitch-and-toss, a pastime which attracted many miners well into the twentieth century. Certainly there was no cultural uniformity among northern miners. Despite condemnations from church and chapel, gambling attracted many miners, and many other workers too. From the early twentieth century increased interest in football was accompanied by the spread of football pools (which provide illuminating evidence on popular attitudes towards large personal fortunes).

Paternalism which sought to remove the temptation to drink was also exerted against gambling. Proprietors of Throckley Colliery not only banned alcoholic drinks from the village but prohibited pigeons or whippets in colliery houses, to discourage gambling. (Hayley 1897, 25) A YMCA conference at Carlisle in 1894 distinguished between 'noble' recreations such as cricket, golf and football and less savoury activities such as boxing and horse-racing. The former might be allowed on Sundays, not the latter. (Pugh 1978, 147) Despite such concern, the time, energy and money invested in sport and recreation made this one of the most pervasive interests of society. It was northern pressure which ensured that rules of the Amateur Athletic Association did not exclude 'mechanics' from competitions under its auspices.

Some activities maintained wide support; others came and went. There were many running clubs on Victorian Tyneside. Elswick Harriers was founded in 1889 and has prospered ever since. (Watson 1994, 50) Boxing remained popular. Even in the late nineteenth century, open-air bouts drew crowds to watch local contenders – like the 500 present at one fight on Blyth Links in 1881. The memoirs of Eugene Corri, a well-known referee of the 1890s, described the audience at a match between Ben Taylor, 'The Woolwich Infant', and George Crisp, 'The Pitmen's Champion'. (Anon. 1957, 24; Manders 1973, 249, 252; Potts 1991)

> Greater than the fight was the setting of it. The Standard Theatre, Gateshead, was packed with pitmen (Shipcote Colliery was just across the road), who sat in their shirt sleeves, and I early observed that the majority of them had brought refreshments to contend with the great heat. Bottles were being handed about. Glasses were not necessary. (Manders 1973, 252)

Fox-hunting drew support from mining districts. At a meeting of North Durham Hunt in 1873 there was 'a tremendous crowd of lookers on, many of whom were drunk'; about '60 or 70 pitmen' cheered the digging-out of a fox. In hunting accounts there were frequent references to crowds of supporting pitmen. (Apperley 1924, 31–2, 62, 142, 165, 176) Horse-racing, and gambling which accompanied it, were of interest at all levels of society. Newcastle race course moved to Gosforth Park in 1881 from the Town Moor, where it was replaced by an annual temperance festival which developed into a fun-fair which attracted 160,000 visitors in its first year. Race meetings, especially the summer meeting when the Northumberland Plate was run, drew large crowds of diverse social origins. Before tram services reached Gosforth Park, many people walked long distances to attend. Greyhound racing was another recreation with a varied following. Edward John Dent, who acquired the country house of Shortflatt Tower in 1880, earned a national reputation as breeder and trainer of greyhounds, producing six winners of the Waterloo Cup in a single eight-year period. (Raimes 1955, 140)

Competitive rowing preceded soccer as the focus of popular enthusiasm. In the 1840s, local newspapers gave it considerable space, catering for a following which peaked during the third quarter of the century. From the 1850s, North East oarsmen enjoyed national and even international status. At matches between champions of Tyne, Thames and Mersey, river banks were lined with huge crowds and much money changed hands in bets. Harry Clasper and his seven keelmen brothers were among the first oarsmen to achieve celebrity; they also helped to devise and popularize changes in the design of racing boats. Clasper claimed to be champion oarsman of the world. His disciple Robert Chambers, previously a puddler at Walker Iron Works, surpassed his mentor before dying in 1868 at the early age of 37. When Clasper died in July 1870, aged 58, his funeral saw one of the greatest scenes of popular mourning in the century. The *Newcastle Chronicle* put the numbers attending the funeral at between 100,000 and 130,000.

The declining popularity of this sport could be connected with its increasingly unsavoury reputation, illustrated by the death of the local champion, James Renforth, during an international challenge match at New York in 1871. This was apparently due to an overdose of what the *Newcastle Chronicle* called 'Yankee dope' while devoting seven columns of a black-edged edition to an account of Renforth's death, no doubt responding to the priorities of its readership.

In mid-Victorian years, handball and fives were popular among Durham miners, with most pit villages acquiring one or more alleys, often attached to pubs. Over 7,000 came to Coxhoe on 21 May 1870 for a championship match at the Railway Hotel. The popularity of these sports peaked in 1878–88, and again a great deal of gambling accompanied them.

Rowing as the central focus of popular enthusiasm was eclipsed by association football. An account of 1913 described how in pit villages and

Figure 18.2 Newcastle United A.F.C. team poses with their trophies after their successful season of 1907–8.

elsewhere boys became devoted to the game from childhood. Football was played in alleys, yards or any scrap of vacant ground. The ball might be only newspapers tied with string. The daydream of becoming a successful player of national acclaim was shared by thousands of boys. Games could be rough, and it was normal for friendly societies to exclude football injuries from claims on funds.

In 1889 attendance of 10,000 was recorded at a local match at Sunderland; nine years later 20,000 watched Newcastle United's first game in the First Division. In the first years of the new century, Newcastle United's St James' Park was extended to raise capacity to 55,000. The spread of the Saturday half-holiday boosted football gates.

During the early twentieth century, Newcastle United and Sunderland consolidated positions among leading clubs and recruited huge followings. In addition to teams playing in national competitions, there were hundreds of others – including villages, coal-mines, factories, churches, chapels, schools, colleges – organized in many local leagues and competitions. If most football enthusiasts were workers, it was not an exclusive activity. John Fenwick, proprietor of one of Newcastle's biggest department stores, was a regular Newcastle United fan, while in 1887 the officials of Sunderland AFC included the shipbuilders Thompson and Marr, and Tyzack from the local coalowners.

Soccer, and other forms of sport and recreation which attracted a wide social range, provided an indication of social cohesion and often focused a broad-based local patriotism which might offer an explanation of the relative tranquillity of the region during this period of unprecedented change. The thousands who joined the lord mayor and other dignitaries of New-castle in cheering a recent victory over Barnsley were more representative than the radical miner who complained of such distractions at the 1910 Northumberland miners' picnic: 'a crust to a starving being was of more value than all the cups and leagues. Let them combine and not depend on the employer class, but on themselves, and themselves alone.' (Northumberland Miners 1910, 33–4)

By the early twentieth century, the Hartlepools had four theatres (Empress, Grand, Palace and Royal), Jarrow had three (Royal, Palace and King's). In addition to the long-established Theatre Royal (rebuilt 1837), Newcastle had the Tyne Theatre (1867), Grand Theatre (1896), Olympia (1899), Palace (1878, rebuilt 1895), Empire (1890, rebuilt 1903), and Pavilion (1903). Competitive flower and vegetable shows became common, each pro-viding a focus for its own followers. On Saturday 23 August 1879, there were flower shows at Whitfield, Choppington, Shildon, Kenton, Gosforth, Shotley Bridge and Seghill; on the following Monday the Lumley and Harraton Agricultural Society staged its annual show, Ryton Flower Show was held and Warkworth Horticultural Society opened its twentieth annual exhibition.

Music halls became established, not only in towns like Newcastle and Carlisle, but in places like Bishop Auckland, serving as centres for a planet-ary system of nearby mining settlements. (Mellor 1970) On a more intellectual plane, the Tyneside Sunday Lecture Society provided from 1884 onwards attentive audiences for such stars as Charles Bradlaugh, Dr Nansen, Oscar Wilde and Prince Kropotkin. At the turn of the century the first moving pic-tures appeared. In 1899 Newcastle theatre-goers might see a 'Bio-Tableaux' of the Cup Final between Derby County and Sheffield United. Early films included 'The Grenadier Guards at Drill' and 'The Queen's Ships at Sea'. (Manders 1991, 8)

There was a diminution in unsavoury elements of popular entertain-ment, usually as a result of influential pressure groups rather than popular support for higher standards. Public executions provided a good example. Earlier reforms reduced the spectacle involved, but their popularity had not abated, as this account of one of the last public executions at Newcastle, in March 1863, illustrated:

the whole thoroughfare had the appearance of a street paved with human heads. These people had assembled as early as 5.30 a.m. By 8 o'clock the crowd was so dense that dozens of people had fainted; and these were passed over the heads of the multitude to the outside.

The story of the execution is soon told; the condemned man was under a minute in view before he disappeared from the gaze of the bloodthirsty crowd. (Reed 1903, 182–3)

The greatest popular celebrations in these years came with the Queen's Diamond Jubilee. The biggest junketings took place in urban centres, but the atmosphere was the same in this example from rural Northumberland:

> for us, the Jubilee consisted in the local efforts. These took the form of sports, competitions, tea and dancing on Barrasford Green, about a mile from us. The proceedings began with a procession of the school-children from three villages, all waving small Union Jacks and wearing Jubilee medals presented to each child by the Parish Council. (I think.) They marched behind the Gunnerton Brass Band. I was given a flag and marched proudly in the ranks. Arrived at the Green, the races and sports began . . . Music throughout the afternoon was provided by the . . . Brass Band . . . whose members were drawn from all over the estate; our gamekeeper, coachman, and both gardeners, the Station-master, the blacksmith, a road mender, and a few farmers. As the evening came on there was dancing on the Green till 10 p.m. The band then played Auld Lang Syne and God Save the Queen, and the great day was over. (Murray MS)

Throughout the region, similar celebrations indicated the prevalence of patriotic sentiments, essentially expressing cohesive elements in society.

Political Activists

There were minorities who possessed an absorbing interest in politics. When in 1884 Tyneside was preparing for a royal visit, protest meetings were held to oppose spending on such activities; speakers contrasted 'feasting and revelry in high places' with 'semi-starvation and want' alleged to prevail among Tyneside workers. (Anon. 1884) The first socialist candidate to fight a parliamentary election in Newcastle was Fred Hammill in 1895; he obtained 2,333 votes. Only five Labour councillors sat on Newcastle City Council by 1914, with two more after elections that year.

Although the national Labour Party did not become strong within the region until after the First World War, earlier groups associated with the Independent Labour Party or similar movements laid a foundation before 1914. (Purdue 1974) Numbers were small, but the quality of some early socialists commands admiration. Often self-educated but well-educated, their capacity for reading, thinking and organizing might have taken them far in a more propitious environment. Others were less impressive intellectually, but attractive personalities.

In *Two Lamps in Our Street*, Arthur Barton gave a portrait of his 'Uncle Jim', shipyard craftsman and fervent radical. His favourite authors included Chesterton, Bradlaugh, Belloc, Darwin, Dickens and Hume. Professing militant atheism, when he took children to a cathedral he removed his hat, though muttering 'By, it's hot the day'. Books and music were among his principal loves. He thought that '*Messiah* held all the world's glory and grief', and he had a rage for learning. There were not many such men, but they exercised a disproportionate influence, although no doubt they endured leg-pulling from less intellectual or high-principled fellows.

Their interests overlapped with another group of activists, equally interested in self-improvement as a means of reforming society without extreme changes. They included men like Thomas Burt, ex-miner and leader of the Northumberland miners' union, Liberal MP, Privy Councillor, junior minister, honorary Doctor of Letters. Burt was a self-educated man, whose studies did not take him to socialism but to the radical wing of the Liberal Party. He was Morpeth's MP from 1874 until 1918 and his seat was rarely threatened. He worked for the cohesion of society and for its improvement. By the end of the nineteenth century there was a small group of 'Lib-Lab' MPs from northern constituencies, mostly with views similar to Burt.

Others might be found in local government. It was not until after 1918 that labour groups won control of important local authorities, but before then small groups of respectable workers could be found as town councillors, poor-law guardians, school board members and in a few cases magistrates. Trade unionists were elected at Workington, Cleator and Aspatria in the 1890s; they included James Flynn, iron-ore miner, Patrick Walls, iron-worker, and Andrew Sharpe, from a coal-mining background. The Irish vote at Cleator sent a Roman Catholic priest to Cumberland County Council in 1889. By 1920, there were 14 Labour men among the 32 members of Barrow Town Council. (Marshall and Walton 1981, 132–7; Todd 1976, 185)

Joseph Hopper, founder of Durham Aged Mine-Workers' Homes Association, was born at Windy Nook, near Gateshead, in 1856. He was brought up a Primitive Methodist, preached his first sermon at 15 and was a regular preacher by 18. He read avidly in political economy, history and biography, with Macaulay and J. S. Mill among his favourite authors. He became an elected member of Felling Local Board, Heworth School Board and Gateshead Poor Law Guardians. (Oxberry 1924, 10–13) His views differed from those of Uncle Jim, but he was more influential. Jarrow Town Council received its first working-man member in 1886, and there were three by 1895. When Hebburn Urban District Council came into existence in the 1890s, it was dominated by trade union sponsored workers; in 1907, eight out of its twelve members were working men. Militant socialists were rarely seen in elected public office, though there were a few. By 1900 a local Liberal newspaper might differentiate between respectable working men and socialists in its reporting of local government news. (Purdue 1982, 186–7, 192) Worker-politicians on the radical wing of the Liberal Party made the first effective penetrations into public office.

Industrial Relations

Other activists were involved in trade union work, although this often over-lapped with politics. The late nineteenth and early twentieth centuries saw changes in the size and standing of trade unions. Both Northumberland and Durham acquired stable mining unions; by the end of the century the over-whelming majority of miners were union members. The extension of the franchise meant that mining votes dominated some northern constituencies, making them effectively pocket boroughs of mining unions.

There was growth in engineering and shipbuilding unions, although for many years the Amalgamated Society of Engineers included only a small proportion of northern workers eligible to join. During the Tyneside engin-eering strike of 1871 only a tenth of striking workers were members, although the leaders were keen unionists. Levels of recruitment improved in later years, as moderate union leaders did much to establish the respectability of unions. Thomas Burt, William Crawford and John Wilson among miners, John Burnett among engineering workers, John Kane in iron and steel, and Robert Knight of the boilermakers, were broadly willing and able enough to work effectively within limits imposed on them by contemporary society. (Clarke 1966; Porter 1970, 159–68)

It was not always easy to present a united front among workers. Shipbuilding was transformed by technological changes in mid-Victorian years and later. Especially after a sharp depression in the mid-1880s created uncertainty of employment, there was bitter competition for certain categor-ies of work between rival trades. In the years 1900–3 groups of shipyard workers went on strike for thirty-five weeks to enforce claims against those of other workers. Hostility could be bitter and long-lasting. At Barrow in the early twentieth century, scarcely a year went by without serious disputes of this nature. There were conflicts between skilled men and labourers, and disputes arising from work demarcation, control over entry to trades, and resistance to new technology – all of this within the context of the most prosperous years in the town's history. (Stark 1972, 41–52)

Strained relations between skilled tradesmen and labourers were common. The skilled trades, with higher and more regular wages, were first to become unionized and trade privileges were jealously guarded. Apprenticeships were given within a closed circle of contacts. These often reflected family links but could arise from shared chapel membership or friendship with foremen or others in a position to nominate. A good example of this exclusive attitude comes from Durham Colliery Enginemen's Association in January 1886:

> John Charlton, fireman, Stargate colliery, has applied through Blaydon branch to be taught the art of braking. This committee after carefully considering this case cannot see their way clear to depart from the resolution passed at a Delegates' Meeting held in 1875 which stresses that none but enginemen's sons be taught until the Executive deem it prudent to do so. (Hiskey 1974, 20–1)

With increasing technical sophistication, patterns of employment became more complicated and diverse. In some industries, working society was dominated by particular groups of skilled men. In collieries, hewers generally took the lead in the employees' side of industrial relations. Shipyards contained a high proportion of skilled workers; in Palmer's shipyard in 1892 there were 8,886 workers, of whom 4,421 were time-served skilled men, 900 apprentices and 3,464 labourers or other unskilled categories. Some 'helpers' were not directly employed by the firm but paid by skilled workers whom they assisted. On occasion unskilled came out on strike against skilled, with the company not a party to the dispute. During early unionization among shipyard labourers, skilled tradesmen were often less than supportive. (Clarke 1966, chs. 7 and 8)

There were attempts by workers and employers to develop industrial relations to minimize conflicts harmful to both parties. Charles Mark Palmer, while no great friend to trade unions, was careful to maintain good personal relations with his work force. This helped to keep his enterprise at work during the prolonged 1871 strike on Tyneside which paralysed most engineering works. Both in coal-mining and in iron and steel, negotiated agreements prevented many disputes from escalating into strikes. David Dale, Chairman of Consett Iron Works, showed the results which patient employers could obtain in this way. After disputes and strikes between 1860 and 1866, culminating in a lockout lasting months, a Board of Arbitration and Conciliation for the Manufactured Iron Trade of the North of England was set up in 1869. This represented employers and workers and exercised for many years a pacifying influence. (Porter 1970) Mining, shipbuilding and the North Eastern Railway saw similar arrangements.

Arbitration in industrial disputes continued. Robert Spence Watson, a leading Tyneside Liberal, acted in more than 100 disputes, many involving complex issues and potentially serious conflicts. His awards were accepted, though not without grumbling in some cases, which might come from either party involved. David Dale was another local figure often called on for this purpose, both within the region and elsewhere. Industrial conciliators received an interesting recruit in John Burnett, successively a largely self-educated worker, successful strike leader, and general secretary of the largest engineering union, who became the first senior civil servant concerned with industrial relations.

Although there were vociferous groups deriding any concept of common interests between employers and workers, this was scarcely the dominating attitude in industrial relations. By 1914, while conflicts continued to arise, most of the region's industrial interests had seen trade unions recognized as influential, responsible and respectable bodies to an extent which would have seemed incredible half a century earlier.

There had been general advance in the position of workers. Their trade organizations had come of age, and there was the beginning of a penetration into positions of influence in regional and national administration. During these years of economic development it was easier for some workers to rise faster and further. Any list of northern leaders of the early twentieth century included self-made men who in some cases had become important employers. Sir William Allan (1837–1903) began working life in an engineering works, then went to sea as a merchant seaman, before hard work and good fortune brought him ownership of an important engineering company. James Craig (1834–1902), son of a Newcastle brush-maker, made his way in the tough Tyneside business world by hard work and a certain absence of scruple; he became an important shipowner and Newcastle MP from 1886 to 1892. Other workers attained eminence without acquiring wealth. The many books celebrating regional dignitaries around 1900 included, with aristocracy and industrialists, men such as Thomas Burt and Charles Fenwick, miners' leaders and Liberal MPs. When John Burnett died in 1914, there were laudatory obituaries in such places as *The Times* and *The Annual Register*. Society was still far from equal, but the barriers had been lowered somewhat.

Attitudes to Women and Children

Children were increasingly recognized as a group requiring special attention and care. Earlier development of Sunday schools was followed by greater thought as to integration of children into worship. At St James' Congregational Church, Newcastle, Sunday morning service once a quarter was especially designed to serve younger members, something unknown earlier.

(Binfield 1982, 165) Many churches and chapels harboured organizations specially directed towards the young, including temperance, sporting, educational and merely social activities.

Pauper children also received more consideration. Around 1900, Poor Law Unions removed children from workhouses and placed them in homes organized to provide something resembling family life. The provision of toys and treats of various kinds became common. It was not unusual for poor-law guardians to congratulate themselves on providing for children in their care better conditions than those of many poor children outside. This seems to have been all too true. An enquiry into the condition of children in South Shields in 1909 discovered that:

> Many children were very poorly clad and their clothes showed no signs of being repaired and lacked any method of fastening except pins. It was even found at times that a child's underclothing was sewn on ... he often found that the main diet of a child was tea and bread which was not the proper food for the growing child, especially when served as a mid-day meal by parents who were quite able to provide something of a more sustaining nature. It was also found a common practice for children to be sent to school without having a breakfast because the mother was unable to get up early enough in the morning ... (Mawson 1971, 122–3)

Legislation for protection of children was not so much innovation as setting a formal framework for concern which had already made itself felt within society. The idea that children were a special kind of creature needing special facilities tailored to their needs had long before been taken up by other agencies. From 1876 one of the most enterprising provincial newspapers, the *Newcastle Chronicle*, publicized features for children, beginning with articles by 'Uncle Toby'. By 1886 this had grown into a children's organization with about 100,000 registered members. The Dicky Bird Society, as this pioneer enterprise was called, numbered Ruskin and Tennyson among honorary officers and emphasized care and kindness towards animals, including wild creatures, working beasts and household pets. While it remained true that many northern children, and those not always amongst the poor, grew up in conditions of hardship and neglect, there were signs of greater sympathy and helpfulness abroad in society.

Women saw some improvement in their situation. There was suffragette agitation among those who had the leisure and the means to adopt this attitude. (Lewis 1996, 121) The North provided the movement with one of its martyrs, Emily Davidson, killed during the 1913 Derby. There were signs of increasing freedom and opportunity for women, beginning for the most part among the richer and more leisured sections of society. Legislation opened some areas of local government to female voting and membership,

Figure 18.3 Expansion of female employment: women packing biscuits for Carr and Company, Carlisle, in the late nineteenth century.

and a handful of women appeared on elected local authorities. In 1894 Miss Peel became the first woman guardian in Houghton-le-Spring Poor Law Union; Sunderland Union had five women guardians in 1898, though only two a few years later. In 1913 the South Shields board of guardians had a woman chairman. Ladies such as these were drawn from groups with the means, the education and the leisure to forward their interests in social reform. (Lewis 1996, 121–3)

Employment prospects for women improved, though the region remained one of low female employment. The development of professions like teaching and nursing provided openings for a few, though they tended to be relatively poorly paid. In 1932, *Blackwoods Magazine* published recollections of a nurse at Sunderland Royal Infirmary in 1902; she displayed considerable resilience, but remembered stern discipline, long hours, arduous work and poor pay. The shipbuilding firm of Wigham Richardson employed a few women office workers from 1886, despite initial doubts and some disappointment at the initial results. (Wigham Richardson, 283–4) Near this shipyard, Thermal Syndicate was progressive technically, but all office work

345

was carried out by twenty men and boys. In 1905 J. J. Fenwick's secretary was the only female member of the shorthand speed class provided by Armstrong College. (Anon. 1956, 12; Pound 1972, 61) Even in the expanding retail sector, men remained dominant. Shop work did provide increasing numbers of paid jobs for women, and a few reached positions of authority over men; in 1907, four women held supervisory posts with Crook co-operative society. In 1910, the Stanley branch of the grocery firm of Broughs Ltd employed 42, including only eight women; in 1920 there were 23 women in a staff of 65. (Ellis 1952, 44; Lloyd 1916, 208) A few industries, including rope-making and potteries, provided high levels of female employment. Girls frequently migrated to Lancashire or Yorkshire industrial centres, perhaps hoping to escape domestic service by employment in the textile industry. Old forms of female farm work, including Northumberland 'bondagers', were in steep decline by the early twentieth century, and an official enquiry observed that 'they prefer to obtain situations in towns, in shops, or in domestic service in private houses or hotels'. (BPP 1895, 42) Domestic service remained the most common form of paid female work, and 'going into service' was the fate of many unmarried girls from northern colliery villages and similar communities. Such employment could be informal, as was often the case when mining families recruited a maid-of-all-work to assist in the home.

Like other social changes, the tendency was for enlightened concepts of woman's role to filter down from richer sectors of society. Even though women might exercise considerable influence in working homes, the role of the sexes was sharply defined within patriarchal assumptions, as this early twentieth-century account indicates:

> At half past five in the evening my father came back. He smelt of iron and oil and machinery, and he washed his hands with paraffin and dried them on cotton waste before sitting down to his tea. During the 3 or 4 hours left him before bed he did nothing – I mean nothing to help my mother. He might go out, or read *Titbits* or listen to Peter Dawson singing 'Boots' on the old gramophone, but everything he did was for himself. The eight and a half hours in the little cramped cabin of his crane high above the clash and roar of the shipyard were for us. What was left of the day belonged to him. (Barton 1969, 168, 171)

The 1914–18 war increased employment for women, but was far from bringing equality of opportunity. During the war, munitions enterprises, including Armstrong's, recruited thousands of women to work in new or expanded factories, carrying out such work as filling artillery shells. Munitions factories, largely staffed by women, were established in such unlikely centres as Gretna. By 1917, Vickers were employing 6,000 women at Barrow, a town where there had been a low level of female employment. Women replaced men in many jobs, releasing them for military service. Often they took over jobs held by husbands, brothers, or other relatives, but as war continued women were employed in a wider variety of occupations, including many posts in transport, as ticket collectors, porters, or conductresses. Some women had more adventurous experiences, such as tram driving or employment as commercial travellers. Much wartime female employment was essentially temporary. An emergency shell factory set up in the North Eastern Railway's Darlington workshops employed 150 men and 1,000 women, but did not outlast the war years. When war ended, there was intense pressure, most of it successful, for women to relinquish temporary employment in favour of returning menfolk. This did not always happen, and even in the four northern counties, with traditionally low levels of female employment, there were changes. Some women employed by Broughs Ltd as travellers continued to work for the firm after the war, and in retail, transport and secretarial work there remained a higher level of female participation. (Todd 1976, 175; Ellis 1952, 44–5; Bell 1952, 58)

Other Effects of the First World War

When war broke out in August 1914, patriotic enthusiasm erupted. Official recruiting for army and navy took time to improvise, and much initial enlistment was conducted by voluntary agencies. In Cumbria, the fifth earl of Lonsdale raised his own battalion of The Border Regiment. His recruiting poster was couched in terms sufficiently bombastic to arouse protests even in the patriotic atmosphere of those days. (Sutherland 1972, 129–30; Bargett 1993)

Are you a Man

or

Are you a Mouse

Are you a man who will for ever be

handed down to posterity as a Gallant Patriot

or

Are you to be handed down to posterity

as a rotter and a coward?

By mid-November 1914, Scots on Tyneside provided a brigade of 4,000 infantry; by the beginning of 1915 Tyneside Irish raised 5,500 men. Sporting programmes collapsed as the attention of players and public went elsewhere. (Tyneside Scottish 1915; Lavery 1917, 81 *et seq.*; Buchan 1955, 52) Nearly 200,000 coal-miners, or about 19 per cent of the national total, enlisted during the first seven months of the war, and northern coalfields were as much involved as others. (Redmayne 1942, 179) Around 5,000 employees of the North Eastern Railway, 10 per cent of the work force, volunteered during the first two months.

About 3,300 Middlesbrough men were killed in the war. Of 1,543 men employed by Palmer's who joined the forces, 145 were killed. Of 714 men from the main Tyneside gas company who enlisted, 90 were killed. Of principal Newcastle schools, Dame Allan's School had 625 old boys serving, 84 killed; the figures for Rutherford Grammar School were over 830 enlisted and over 150 killed. County Durham police force contributed 420 recruits; 52 were killed and 98 wounded. The Lonsdale battalion of The Border Regiment suffered heavy casualties and was decimated on the Somme in 1916. The battalion lost nearly 800 within the regiment's death roll of over 13,000. Casualties disproportionately affected communities which responded gallantly to Kitchener's appeals for men, accompanied by the pledge that friends who joined together would serve together. War memorials, with their endless columns of names, testify to the slaughter, while the toll of lost merchant seamen was equally tragic. (Jackson 1947, 29; Davidson 1946, 40; Anon. 1929; Anon. 1940, 25; Maw 1964, 113)

There were those who opposed the war and endured unpopularity and risks for their principles. A few Independent Labour Party members in County Durham provided a link in a chain of sympathizers seeking to conceal and protect conscientious objectors. Sympathy for conscientious objectors was not common in a region in which thousands of families had men in the armed forces or facing submarine warfare in the merchant navy. Anti-German feeling sometimes received ugly expression. In Jarrow,

> The few Germans in our town were pork butchers, and they had a bad time. Their windows were constantly being broken, especially if a ship had gone down or an attack failed. Only the fighting men who sometimes came to tea . . . astonished us by speaking of the enemy in almost friendly terms. (Barton 1969, 88)

In the mining area around Crook, the sinking of the *Lusitania* provoked an anti-German riot in which 7,000 people were involved. Two butchers' shops with old German connections were destroyed, and there were many arrests and heavy fines. (Lloyd 1916, 59)

For the devout, bereavement could be mitigated by religious consolation, as in this extract from a letter sent to a Methodist padre from parents in County Durham:

> We were glad to receive your communication with reference to our son's faith and trust in God. It is a great consolation to know that there was no doubts and fears but a faith that would lay hold on the

promises made to us; we know that if we are faithful we shall meet again in the better land. (Wearmouth 1958, 78, 130)

For those who served in the war and survived, memories of shared experiences were strong during inter-war years. The ex-servicemen's and 'Comrades' clubs within the developing working men's club movement demonstrate this. It is odd how often histories of inter-war Britain have failed to appreciate how ex-service organizations such as the British Legion involved more people, at all levels of society, than ephemeral and ineffective political groups which have sometimes received exaggerated attention. In inter-war years, 11 November meant more in British society than, for example, 1 May. Someone who was a child at school at the time recalled early celebrations of Armistice Day:

> The silence really was a silence then. The Armageddon of shipyard and steelworks was cut off at five to eleven like the gunfire on the Western Front that first November Monday. Horses were held; busses stopped; suburban trains sought the nearest station . . . The heroes were all gone and we were young and guilty and alive. When I read Edmund Blunden's line, 'Why slept not I in Flanders' clay with all the murdered men', that seemed to strike our note. (Barton 1969, 77)

The war exercised profound influence upon the generations which lived through it. In immediate post-war years, much energy went into commemorative enterprises, ranging from community war memorials to individual donations in memory of those who died. The language of war memorials offers insights into how the war was regarded in post-war years. A plaque in St Bartholomew's Church, Whittingham, Northumberland, is a good example.

> To the Historic Memory of the Men of the Ancient Parish of Whittingham who died in the Great War with Germany, 1914–1919.
> They enlisted to Vindicate the Cause of an Outraged Humanity.
> They laid down their Lives in a Sacred and Righteous Cause.
> They died for England.

In 1919 Viscount Stamfordham bought from his nephew the old Ovingham vicarage, which had been in secular hands for centuries, and gave it back to the church in memory of his son who had been killed in France in 1915. (Honeyman 1953, 138) The wealthy Tyneside shipowner, Sir James Knott, built the church of St Basil and St James at Newcastle in memory of two sons bearing these names who had been killed. At North Shields the small voluntary hospital was given a large extension as a community memorial, and similar philanthropic reactions occurred in many places.

The North *c.*1920

The end of the First World War closed a significant chapter in the history of northern England. The differences between the northern region in 1850 and in 1920 were enormous. The population had more than doubled, and its distribution had been drastically altered; north Tyneside held 36 per cent of Northumberland's population in 1801, 61 per cent in 1901. Ways in which the region's income was earned had changed: in 1911 almost 50 per cent of employment in County Durham came from only four sectors – coal, shipbuilding, iron and steel, and engineering. (Rowe 1990, 426, 430) The North had acquired much greater relative importance within Britain. There remained areas of poverty, cruelty, vice and crime, but there had been improvements in the standard of living of the overwhelming majority, and a diminution in rougher and barbaric elements.

Other generalizations are less easy to substantiate, especially the imposition of twentieth-century notions of nineteenth-century society as highly polarized in terms of class. Society was much more intricate and complex than this implies. Examples abound, but let several instances of diverse behaviour and experiences indicate these complexities. During engineering strikes in 1871, workers were supported and employers criticized by a wide range of opinion, including *The Times*, *The Spectator* and *The Pall Mall Gazette*. Before the strikes ended, donations to strike funds were coming from many different sources, and strikers enjoyed the support of some leading local employers, including Joseph Cowen, prominent manufacturer and proprietor of the influential *Newcastle Chronicle*. During the strike the men's leaders urged peaceable behaviour, but there was sporadic violence. In one case which came before a local court, evidence seemed clear enough that two local strikers had severely beaten a foreign blackleg; the defendants were acquitted with the following judgement: 'The Bench are not satisfied that there is sufficient evidence to convict the accused, and they are dismissed. And now, my men, take care and don't do it again.' (Allen 1971)

In view of the reputation which the poor law acquired by the early twentieth century, it might be supposed that non-contributory old age pensions after 1908 would have been greeted with universal gratitude from potential recipients. The historical record has too often ignored the point that the poor-law system by 1900 employed a salaried and professionally qualified staff responsible for looking after paupers. Old age pensions provided a small weekly payment without any provision for care. This was a principal reason for the mixed reaction which greeted the innovation. In assessing results in one northern union, the Local Government Board's regional inspector remarked ruefully in 1911 that

> Many even of the outdoor poor showed themselves reluctant to apply
> for the pension, some because the amount was less than they had been

receiving from the guardians, two because 'the guardians have always treated them well', thirteen 'because they are as well off with their out-relief', three more because 'they do not wish to be deprived of the visits of the medical and relieving officers' and so forth . . . The general attitude of the aged paupers on this question, although unconsciously complimentary, proved embarrassing to the various boards of guardians, whose financial advantage obviously lay in the wholesale transfer of cases to the pension list, but whose efforts at 'peaceful persuasion' were often at times unavailing. (Mawson 1971, 134)

Shift in Interdependence

There was another profound and far-reaching development in these years which was not fully appreciated at the time or subsequently. This was a shift towards greater interdependence, particularly marked in areas which experienced rapid economic and demographic changes. In the early nineteenth century, as in all former years, for most people life was bounded by local considerations and, where individuals depended upon each other, they depended on those amongst whom they lived and worked in locally coherent communities. Although there had been some shift away from this situation by 1850, the pace markedly accelerated, so that by 1920 the extent of interdependence had been greatly widened. Alike in social, economic and political spheres, the degree of localization had diminished, and interdependence no longer resided simply within internal coherence of communities. The point can be illustrated by the growth of public utilities. Before 1850 a beginning had been made, which included gas and water companies. By 1920 the network of gas, water and electricity supplies was much more widespread and pervasive. We have seen (p. 304 above) how the Sunderland and South Shields Water Company in the later nineteenth century brought for the first time a reliable water supply to areas of east Durham. This was an undoubted boon. It also meant that the population involved was brought into a new dependence on the operation of pumping stations' steam engines by a few dozen specialized workers, with whom most could have not even the most remote acquaintance. Similarly enginemen of pumping stations were dependent upon others whom they did not know for an increasingly complex range of services and supplies. Miners of the region could, and sometimes did, cut off by strike action the coal supply vital to home and industry. They could no longer live of their own, but depended for food, and for an extending range of other needs, on continuance at work of many

351

specialized groups with whom they were unlikely to have any personal contact. (McCord 1995)

In many ways the economy of the northern counties was an interlocking one, so that, for instance, slackening demand for shipbuilding could have repercussions on employment in iron and steel and coal-mining. Interdependence within the northern economy was more complicated than this. In the early nineteenth century, shipbuilding enterprises were generally small and simple. Where they depended upon outside suppliers, as for timber, sails and ropes, their requirements were few and simple. By 1920, this was far from being the case, and shipyards depended on a complex network of outside suppliers. Similar developments took place in mining, whereby the relatively simple needs of early nineteenth-century collieries developed into inescapable dependence on a wide range of specialist suppliers. If the North Eastern Railway supplied many of its own increasingly complex needs, at the cost of introducing additional complications into its organization and structure of employment, it too increasingly depended on a widening range of outside suppliers. We have already seen (pp. 294–7 above) how the phenomenal growth of retail services depended upon an astonishingly sophisticated and complex system of supply straddling the world.

Elaboration of supply networks of many kinds, themselves often consequences of the twin forces of industrialization and urbanization, facilitated increases in communities dependent on a single economic function. Barrow's concentration on naval armaments, or the evolution of places like Whitley Bay, Redcar, Keswick, Ambleside and Windermere into tourist resorts, were part of this pattern. A similar development saw increasing specialization and concentration of various forms of production. In 1850, brewing was a varied and scattered industry. The quarter-century before 1914 saw the disappearance of much home brewing and then the takeover or closure of many local breweries. More than 40 northern breweries, about 60 per cent of the total in 1890, disappeared in the 1890–1914 period, bringing dependence upon a small number of major producers, mostly situated in the region's principal towns. (Bennison 1994; Bennison Brewers 1995)

There were other shifts in interdependence. Whereas in earlier periods society was effectively managed by unofficial patterns of influence and control existing within local communities, by 1920 both central and local government had expanded. Officers of local and central government depended on a wide range of services provided by many thousands of people whom they did not know; those thousands increasingly lived in a context in which officials played a key role in managing society.

This shift from an intimate and local pattern of interdependence to a complex pattern involving more impersonal interdependence, which was every bit as real, represented a major change. Although the shift occupied only a few generations, it proceeded in a piecemeal manner which meant that its significance was not generally appreciated. The development was to continue and become even more pervasive after 1920, but by then the process was well advanced. Nor was interdependence confined to the northern counties themselves. Northern industry and trade depended heavily on overseas export markets, beyond their control. A region heavily dependent on export markets possessed an external interdependence which paralleled internal changes.

Within northern society there had been changes in patterns of influence, with dominance by older powerful groups diminished. Even in 1920, the territorial aristocracy exercised influence and received respect, although the relative decline in importance of agriculture, expansion of trade unionism and growth of formal agencies of government eroded their previous dominance. Their decline in power, a slow and piecemeal process, was far from complete by 1920, especially in social and cultural terms.

Their dominance of elections in north Northumberland is one instance of continuity. After the Second Reform Act and the introduction of the secret ballot, the 1874 election returned two Conservative MPs without a contest, Matthew White Ridley, heir to a landed baronet and leading Conservative, and Earl Percy, heir to the duke of Northumberland. In 1880 they were opposed by a good local farming candidate whom they defeated. Similarly, in Westmorland there were no contested county elections between 1832 and 1880. (Purdue 1982; McCord and Carrick 1966, 97; Marshall and Walton 1981, 109–10)

For some time after 1850, many borough electorates were sufficiently small to remain manageable by older forms of manipulation. Even in expanding towns such as Gateshead, at mid-century the electorate was small enough to be susceptible to 'influence'. The three candidates in 1852 received 270, 190 and 136 votes. After the Second Reform Act of 1867, swollen electorates required other methods of organization; the 1868 election at Gateshead was won by 2,404 votes to 1,487, and electorates continued to increase. (McCord 1969, 179) Leadership in Cumbrian towns was usually exercised by prominent employers, who assumed some kind of active political responsibility, generally of a vaguely paternalistic character, almost as a matter of course. Barrow, with a small commercial and professional population, was dominated by its industrial leadership; in the early twentieth century, it was almost a Vickers company town. Militant socialists were initially unpopular there; in the 1895 general election, Pete Curran received only 414 votes, as against 3,192 for the Unionist candidate and 2,355 Liberal votes. (Todd 1976, 70) Nevertheless, with a more acceptable candidate and a more propitious year, Barrow returned the North West's first Labour MP, Charles Duncan, in 1906. In Whitehaven, Lowther influence remained even after the earl of Lonsdale withdrew from active management of local collieries. There were no contested elections there between 1832 and 1868. Only after full incorporation in 1894 was town government effectively separated from management of the port. (Marshall and Walton 1981, 125–32)

Never a completely closed caste, the northern élite continued to absorb recruits. There were many points of contact between northern aristocrats and influential newcomers rising in the social scale from industry, commerce or professional success, who might aspire to knighthood, baronetcy and occasionally peerage, and often acquired prestigious country residences and estates. (Briggs 1996, 16–17; Lewis 1996, 110) Socially prominent individuals remained in demand to ornament and support philanthropic, recreational and cultural activities throughout the region. If there was by 1920 a crop of Labour MPs from northern constituencies and Labour members of local authorities of various kinds, the established Conservative and Liberal parties were still the main forces in northern political life, although Labour was poised to make greater gains.

By 1920 the relative autonomy of the region had declined. We have seen how northern banks were increasingly incorporated into larger concerns operating on a national basis (see p. 289 above). Trade unions and employers' organizations were commonly managed upon a national rather than regional basis. The independence of mining unions in Northumberland and Durham diminished in the years before the First World War, which saw increasing cordiality and co-operation with miners elsewhere in Britain. There was diminution in the regional basis of important elements in the economy, indicated for instance in the merger of the great armaments and engineering enterprises of Tyneside's Armstrong and Lancashire's Whitworth in 1897 or the takeover of Tyneside breweries by Scottish interests after 1895. (Bennison 1994, 165; Bennison Brewers 1995) The relative importance of local and national elements in politics shifted in favour of the latter, and there were many examples of sport, recreation and entertainment organized on a national basis.

It was still possible, especially in rural and upland areas, for life to continue on a local basis. In more remote areas, transport and retail facilities remained relatively primitive until after 1918. Regional and local organizations and characteristics had not become defunct, but there had been a shift in their relative weight compared with those deriving from a wider context. It was with this radically changed situation that the North faced problems which the years after 1920 were to bring.

Part Five

After *c*.1920

Chapter 19

Post-War Economic and Social Problems

The economic, social and political transformation after *c*.1850 had been unprecedented and unforeseeable, as were the economic and social problems which afflicted the region in post-war years. At the end of the war, there was a general anticipation of a return to the pre-1914 situation. Demobilization of the forces proceeded with little difficulty, and most of the women who had reinforced the labour force made way for ex-servicemen. By the early 1920s a low ratio of female employment was re-established, with women providing only 20 per cent of the work force, mainly as domestic servants, dressmakers, barmaids, laundry workers, clerks, typists or shop workers. (Robinson 1988, 12)

During the war, industries on which the region primarily depended, such as coal-mining, iron and steel, engineering and shipbuilding, were fully employed, with little indication of future problems. Yet the vulnerability of the regional economy remained, with its concentration on a few interdependent industrial sectors dependent on export markets, increasingly exposed to competition and reliant upon a continuing high volume of international trade.

The Coal Trade

The coal trade had been at the heart of the region's industrial growth, and early post-war experiences suggested an imminent return to pre-war patterns. In 1919, while other exports from Tyneside rose by 19 per cent over the previous year, coal and coke exports were up by 25 per cent. The next year's figure was poorer, but was plausibly explained as a temporary setback. Many wartime controls continued, and the national Coal Controller allocated the North East ports an export quota of only 7 million tons, reached by the middle of the year. There was slackening in home demand, and these two factors resulted in a drop in coal sales and unemployment of colliers and other coal-transporting facilities. (Shaw 1920, 53) After 1920, the coal trade remained at a fairly high level for the remainder of the decade, except when interrupted by major strikes, as in 1921 and 1926. During the French occupation of the Ruhr coalfield in 1923, coal exports boomed; the Tyne alone shipped 21.5 million tons, of which more than 18 million were exported. This exceptional achievement could not be sustained in more normal circumstances.

The traditional pattern of coal trade persisted. During the 1923 boom, Germany, France, Holland and Belgium took more than three-quarters of exports. Within the coastal trade, London remained the biggest market, with other British destinations taking only about 12–15 per cent of shipments. Cumberland coal faced increasing competition in the Irish market from other British producers and its share shrank. (Elliott 1968, 85; Wood 1988, 253–4)

High levels of coal production sustained mining employment. In Durham this peaked at 170,000 in 1923. In 1923 and 1924, unemployment among North East miners only amounted to 2.6 per cent and 3.9 per cent, though the 1926 strike brought 22.6 per cent for 1927. It was still 13.3 per cent in 1929. (Board of Trade 1932, 98) In that year, the Great Northern Coalfield produced 53.5 million tons and employed 208,000, already fewer than in 1924. As depression intensified, the numbers employed continued to fall. Between 1924 and 1934 the coalfield lost almost 50,000 jobs, particularly damaging in that this represented loss of work for adult men, and openings for younger male workers.

Output in Cumberland peaked in 1924, with just over 12,000 miners employed. By 1929 this had shrunk to 9,823, although output remained relatively steady at just over 2 million tons. Productivity still lagged behind other coalfields. Collieries faced financial losses and technical problems resulting from exhaustion of accessible seams. The important Duke Pit at Whitehaven closed in 1933 after a disaster which killed 136. The survival of the Cumberland coalfield depended on the iron and steel industry. The design of coke ovens had improved since the 1890s, and a rising share of Cumbrian coal was earmarked for this use. By the 1930s, the United Steel Companies were consuming nearly half of local production. The integration of coal-mining, iron ore mining, limestone quarrying, coke ovens, iron and steel making and the port of Workington under that firm maintained the west Cumberland industrial base at a higher level than would otherwise have been possible. A corollary was rationalization, with a concentration around Workington, while outliers like Cleator Moor, Distington, and Harrington lost employment. Investment by the United Steel Companies saw Workington expand, while Maryport contracted severely. Collieries shrank from 43 in 1900 to 25 in 1938, making a significant contribution to Cumbria's unemployment problem. A minor Cumbrian industry to go under was gunpowder manufacture, ending in 1937, when ICI concentrated production in Scotland. (Wood 1988, 340, 217, 221; Jewkes and Winterbottom 1933, 96–7; Bennett 1993, 3, 28)

The drop in demand which brought mining unemployment had more than one root. (Economics Dept 1935, 21) Well over a quarter of northern coal had been consumed by domestic and industrial users on or near the coalfields. In 1924 this consumption was already about a million tons lower than in 1913. The figure slumped further, as northern industries were hard hit by depression. The international economic crisis was particularly serious for the Great Northern Coalfield, heavily dependent on exports. In 1929, North East ports sent nearly 21 million tons overseas, but this figure was more than halved by 1932. The slight improvement in coal exports in 1933–34 still left them at 7 million tons below 1929 levels. Germany, France, Belgium and Italy took less than half their earlier share. Coastal shipments held up better, but could not compensate for severe drops in exports and local consumption.

These blows fell heavily on older and less efficient collieries. Loss of employment was most severe in districts where production costs were high owing to the exhaustion of more accessible and profitable seams. This was true of many older Durham pits. In efficient collieries, mechanization also contributed to lower employment. A high proportion of the larger Northumberland collieries were either modern or modernized: 55 per cent of coal there was cut mechanically by 1929, 81 per cent by 1933. Durham and Cumberland were less advanced. Durham's figure rose from 22 per cent in 1929 to only 35 per cent in 1933, reflecting more older collieries. Cumberland too had only reached 35 per cent by 1933, but progress was rapid during the 1930s, rising from a low 11 per cent in 1929 to 71 per cent in 1939. There was an equally dramatic rise in mechanical conveyance of coal, and use of electric motors in mining. These technical advances, which affected both coal and iron ore mining, contributed to overall loss in mining employment despite a recovery of production in both branches of mining during the 1930s. (Wood 1988, 444–7) The effect was marked in west Cumberland, where employment in mining and quarrying plummeted from 48.1 per cent to only 18.6 per cent by 1946, the biggest factor in the unemployment which affected that area for almost a generation. (Whitfield 1975, 106, Appendix G) Market uncertainties and depleted coal seams were other reasons for this lost employment. Overall, Durham collieries lost money in 1931–34, Northumberland in 1932–34.

Such figures conceal diversity, with modern efficient collieries recording better results. The loss of production and employment would have been

Figure 19.1 The survival of older mining practices is shown by this photograph of haulage at Greenside Colliery, county Durham, *c.*1930.

greater without the Coal Mines Act of 1930, which enforced pooling of colliery incomes. This preserved some collieries not otherwise viable, at the cost of limiting profitability of successful pits. There were notable success stories. In Northumberland, the Ashington Coal Company remodelled, and in some cases rebuilt, surface installations of its five major collieries. Although by 1931 there was only one colliery working in the Wallsend area, this Rising Sun Colliery was taken over in 1934 by the Bedlington Coal Company, with new shafts sunk to the deeper Brockwell seam and expensive new surface installations for coal preparation. In Durham, Horden Collieries Ltd paid dividends of 7.5 per cent in 1930 and 5 per cent in 1935, though only 2.5 per cent in 1933. (Ashington Coal Company 1935, 4; Horden Collieries Ltd 1946, 26) In contrast, older pits in the Bishop Auckland district were forced to close, bringing heavy local unemployment. The overall decline in mining income and employment was a principal ingredient in the post-war economic and social problems of the northern region.

Iron and Steel

Some of the collieries' principal customers faced difficulties. The biggest customer of Throckley Coal Company was Newburn Steel Works, closed in 1924. The iron and steel industry was an important buyer of coal and a key producer of materials for engineering and shipbuilding. In 1929, the North East produced 2.3 million tons of pig iron and 2.2 million tons of steel. There followed a catastrophic decline in demand which saw the 1932 figures down to 0.88 and 1 million tons. Slow recovery ensued, with pig iron at 1 million in 1933 and 1.7 million in 1934, steel 1.3 million in 1933 and 1.8 million in 1934. Between 1924 and 1934 the North East's steel industry lost 16,000 jobs. Some of this was due to increases in efficiency, but much more reflected the economic depression of those years. Unemployment in the industry was 14 per cent in 1929, and rose to 46 per cent at the worst of the depression, before falling to 23 per cent in 1934. Thereafter rearmament brought recovery.

Cumberland had similar experiences. Its acid steel lost out to cheaper basic steel from elsewhere. In the Furness district, ore reserves were depleted, foreshadowing the end of iron and steel making at Barrow. West Cumberland fared better, with demand for haematite iron for a variety of special purposes holding up. By the early 1930s, only about two-thirds of this iron was made into steel locally, but Cumberland still produced about one-third of Britain's haematite iron. The Cumbrian iron and steel industry had another weakness. A high proportion of its assets was held by the United Steel Companies, with its main interests, and most profitable plant, elsewhere. Some of the industry's old markets had now been lost. The Bowness-on-Solway railway viaduct had been built in 1869 to carry Cumbrian iron to Lanarkshire; it was declared unsafe in 1921 and demolished in the early 1930s. (Bennett 1993, 6) However, the 1930s saw some recovery in iron ore mining and iron and steel making in west Cumberland. Government protectionist policies played a part, as did interruption of Spanish haematite supplies because of civil war. Rearmament increased demand for acid steel, and the potential profit encouraged such developments as the opening in 1934 of a new Bessemer converter by United Steel at Workington and the construction in 1935–36 of two blast-furnaces by the Millom and Askham Iron Company. (Clarke 1981, 212, 256)

Engineering and Shipbuilding

Despite international depression, in coal and in iron and steel the northern region managed to hold its share of reduced national output and employment.

In engineering, the picture was worse, with the North East losing 41.3 per cent of employment as against a national average of 23.9 per cent. This reflected dependence on heavy engineering, a sector hit hard in these years. Recovery lagged behind too; in 1934 nationally, engineering employment was 10 per cent less than in 1929, but the North East figure was 27.3 per cent. (Economics Dept 1935, 27; Hodgson 1975, 181)

During economic expansion, shipbuilding and marine engineering had been among the major successes of the North, despite some fluctuations. (Dougan 1968, 140) Prosperity continued into the immediate post-war years, as war losses were replaced. The boom was short-lived, and by late 1923 14,000 shipyard workers were unemployed at Sunderland and 6,000 at Jarrow. The early 1930s saw desperate years. In 1929, North East yards launched 679,000 tons of merchant ships, but in 1933 only a catastrophic 37,000 tons, and only 67,000 tons in 1934. In shipbuilding, as in engineering, the northern counties could not hold their share of the reduced British total. The 67,000 tons of 1934 were only 14.5 per cent of the national output, very different from the halcyon years around 1900. In March 1930, northern yards held one-third of British shipbuilding contracts, falling to not much more than 10 per cent in the next few years. Clydeside did better, even in tanker-building, previously an acknowledged North East speciality.

Shipbuilding had known earlier fluctuations in employment, but mass unemployment during the early 1930s had disastrous social consequences. In 1931, with most shipyard berths empty, nearly three-quarters of ship-building workers were unemployed and in 1933 the proportion touched nearly four-fifths before recovery began. Companies which survived took cuts in profitability and dividends. At Swan Hunters, one of the biggest Tyneside builders, profits of a meagre £150,000 in 1931 dropped to only £19,000 in 1933, before recovering to £190,000 in 1935 and nearly £500,000 in 1939. Firms tried to keep a core work force together by taking ship-breaking contracts or by manufacturing caravans, boilers or other more or less desperate expedients. Such palliatives could do little to help an industry with masses of idle but expensive plant. (Smith and Holden 1947, 65)

Rationalization schemes included the National Shipbuilders Security Ltd, devised by the Clydeside shipbuilder Sir James Lithgow and backed by companies which between them launched 93 per cent of British-built tonnage in 1930. A levy of 1 per cent on the value of new ships, and borrowing powers of up to £2.5 million, financed buying up unprofitable shipyards. Initially this was to end shipbuilding on these sites for at least forty years. Many northern yards were victims of this campaign.

The most notorious instance was the purchase and closure of the Palmer shipbuilding enterprise at Jarrow. That town had grown up with the development of mining, engineering and shipbuilding, and depended upon them to a degree unusual even in the northern counties. Before 1934, colliery closures and other losses had hit hard and this made the closure of

Palmer's even more damaging. By the criteria adopted by Lithgow's brain-child, the firm was an obvious target, already in financial trouble, without orders or reasonable prospect of obtaining any. The decision to buy it out and close the yards was taken on commercial grounds which appeared to be sound, but the decision could not remain merely a commercial one. The shipyards were the town's last major employer, and their closure entailed serious social consequences. It was a key element in the concept of 'The Town that was Murdered', to use Ellen Wilkinson's phrase. There was more to come. Early efforts to restore steel-making to Jarrow foundered on the opposition of steel-makers elsewhere, themselves faced with surplus capacity and unemployment. There was some industrial recovery at Jarrow in the later 1930s but it was far from complete by 1939.

Barrow's shipbuilding interests were also affected. In 1910–13, barely 4 per cent of tonnage had been merchant shipping, but Vickers managed to survive lean years for warship orders after 1918. In 1921–26, an average of 32,000 tons of merchant shipping was launched, meagre pickings but enough to enable the yards to survive until rescued by naval rearmament. In the early 1930s Vickers still employed 11,000 in Barrow, about half the insured work force of the Furness district. Despite modest success in adapting to post-war conditions, Barrow was dramatically affected by the coming of peace. Between 1914 and 1918, its population had swollen to around 90,000, but in the immediate post-war years about 17,000 were lost. During the 1920s, slower decline brought loss of a further 10 per cent, only exceeded among centres of inter-war depression by Rhondda in South Wales. (Daysh 1938; Jewkes and Winterbottom 1933, 1, 4, 83)

West Cumberland and Furness lacked the diversification needed to compensate for the vulnerability of staple industries. If anything, they suffered more than the North East. Even in 1930, before the full impact of the depression, the Cumberland coastal belt had unemployment rates of 24.6 per cent and Furness 31.4 per cent, well above the national 16.2 per cent. By 1934 the rate had soared to 57.3 per cent in Maryport and 51.4 per cent for the remainder of the hard-hit areas of west Cumberland, as against a national 29.7 per cent. Henry Daysh of Durham University, an investigator well acquainted with depression in the North East, confessed during his survey of west Cumberland in the mid-1930s that of all the sizeable communities he knew 'Maryport was the one that hit me hardest'. Cumberland lost 5 per cent of its population in the 1930s, despite, as in the North East, frequent reluctance of unemployed workers to move elsewhere. (Daysh 1938; Jewkes and Winterbottom 1933, 119–22, 3; Clarke 1981, 73, 17; Holmes 1983; Wood 1988, 228)

Loss of Major Firms

The region's industrial problems during the depression were illustrated by the fate of its biggest company. Armstrong Whitworth, with complex ship-building, engineering and armaments activities, emerged from the war with considerable profits but with problems ahead in a world with little appetite for expensive warships and similar products. If the company, with its huge work force, was to survive, it must find alternative profitable lines of business. Before 1914, there had been efforts to diversify into motor vehicles and aircraft, and war contracts encouraged these trends. The engineer John Siddeley had designed engines for Armstrong warplanes. In 1919, the Armstrong directors bought Siddeley's company and embarked upon new car and aircraft designs under the Armstrong Siddeley name. Personal relations between Siddeley and the parent company were poor and as Armstrong's finances deteriorated the directors decided in 1926 to sell Armstrong Siddeley to Siddeley and new partners for £1 million. (Tapper 1973, 14)

Armstrong directors pinned their hopes on an ambitious but risky scheme centred on paper-making, extensive timber concessions in Newfoundland and building a fleet of specialized ships for this purpose, but expenditure spiralled without adequate returns. The company had a trading deficit of nearly £900,000 in 1924, and by mid-1925 owed £2.5 million to the Bank of England. Share prices, which had stood at £3 in 1914, plunged to a few shillings by late 1926. The Bank of England finally enforced replacement of unsuccessful management and a merger with Vickers in which Armstrong's was the junior partner. (Scott 1962, 153)

The ill-fated paper-making venture appears startling, but it had not been a wildcat idea and the germ of the scheme attained profitablility in other hands. Failure to diversify successfully saw Vickers Armstrong close Walker Naval Yard in April 1928. It had opened just before the war, in time to build the battleship HMS *Malaya*. In spite of a brief revival in 1930–31, following a contract to build a large liner, the yard had to await rearmament orders from 1936 to become viable again. Earlier in the century, Armstrong's had employed 23,000 workers on Tyneside. The shrinkage of employment in what had been a major company in national terms was part of the story of the depression years, but also illustrates decline in local control of the regional economy.

At Carlisle, the local division of the Metal Box Company also struggled to preserve autonomy within a national company. Its attachment to older lines such as tin plate lithography and decorated boxes fell foul of the dynamic strategy preferred by the London-based managing director, Robert Barlow. He was aware of rivalry from international competitors and this led him to undermine the older company tradition of considerable independence for regionally based subsidiaries. Increasingly, local industrial enterprises were swallowed up in national or even international conglomerates, such as ICI or United Steel, although during inter-war years takeovers only affected a minority of northern enterprises. Parallel developments took place within banking, insurance and other financial services, part of a nation-wide reduction in local autonomy and regional individuality.

Losses of jobs in mining and manufacturing spread ripples throughout the regional economy, as reduced income affected services which developed in the boom period before 1914. Unemployment in the distributive trades mirrored the experiences of many of their customers. Retail companies which had shown marked growth now found sales and profits sharply reduced. Co-operative societies saw reduced sales per member. Local building societies reported lower demand for mortgage lending. (Board of Trade 1932, 417; Southern 1993, 75; Anon. 1961, 4)

Agriculture

Northern agriculture, long surpassed in income and employment, suffered its own problems during the depression years, including a collapse in beef prices in 1933. Change already under way in the previous century continued, as farming patterns were affected by external factors. Competition from producers elsewhere in Britain and abroad, together with transport improvements within the region, saw arable farming decline further and dairy farming increase. In 1936 a survey noted that in the Solway area of Cumberland 'practically every farm now sells liquid milk', with markets as far away as Lancashire and the Midlands. Older balanced farming gave way to specialized types based on dairy produce, the fattening of beef cattle, sheep farming, and to a lesser extent horses, pigs and poultry. The needs of dairy farming helped to protect employment levels until after 1945. Northern industrial recovery in the later 1930s was accompanied by improvement in farming fortunes.

Effects of Depression

Statistics on the inter-war economy conceal a mass of individual tragedy. The word 'deprived', often misused in present-day polemic, may properly apply to the inter-war unemployed. In mines, engineering works, shipyards,

365

Figure 19.2 Photograph of Isaac Cookson, shepherd in Mardale, Cumbria, soon after the First World War, illustrating some of the popular images of Lake District life and farming which exercised a growing appeal among visitors. Reproduced by the kind permission of the Museum of Lakeland Life and Industry, Kendal, Cumbria.

many who found themselves unemployed and poor during the 1920s and 1930s came from groups previously among the most highly paid and prestigious of the region's work force. In the collieries, the lengthy strike of 1921 eroded savings accumulated by mining families; a few years of relative calm and prosperity were followed by the prolonged and bitter struggle of 1926. The harmful effects persisted into the crisis years of the 1930s, marked by a severe fall in demand for coal at home and abroad. Comparable adversity was experienced in other key industries.

The extent of the depression, and its social effects, were severe, but ought not to be exaggerated. In the region as a whole, the majority of workers remained in employment. With international depression lowering prices, the 1930s were years of rising standards of living for many, probably a sizeable majority, even within this hard-hit region. The main impact of depression fell with especial force upon a few sectors, and it was the ill fortune of the northern counties that they depended on these to an unusual extent. Coal, iron and steel, engineering and shipbuilding had been so obviously the basis of the region's expansion in the recent past that the difficulties experienced

366

had psychological as well as material impacts. For other sections of the economy – building, furniture, electrical goods and household appliances, motor cars and motor cycles, clothing and food preparation – the 1930s saw considerable growth. These were under-represented in the northern economy.

Amidst industrial depression, there were still examples of growth. In the years after the creation of Imperial Chemical Industries in 1926, the Teesside chemical industry continued to expand. The ICI base at Billingham replaced Middlesbrough as the local boom town. Employment in the chemical industry rose from a few thousand in 1921 to not far short of 50,000 by 1945. Some other Teesside industries also flourished. Constructional engineering firms won bridge-building contracts at home and abroad. On Tyneside too there were success stories. The old soap-manufacturing firm of Thomas Hedley faced financial crisis in the late 1920s but emerged in 1930, having found sanctuary within the Cincinnati-based Procter and Gamble Group. The rejuvenated firm enjoyed growing markets at home and abroad, with new products backed by skilful and expensive advertising campaigns – Oxydol in 1930, Sylvan Flakes in 1933 and Mirro in 1934. At Wallsend, Victor Products Ltd was founded in 1929 by two engineers, H. Crofton and R. W. Mann. Possessing at first only meagre capital and makeshift premises, this firm flourished by designing and producing mining machinery, contributing to increasing mechanization in mines at home and abroad. The heavy electricity generating enterprises on Tyneside prospered as electrification continued in inter-war years. In 1922, Parsons supplied a 50,000 kW generator to Chicago, and by 1939 was regularly supplying generators of twice that capacity to customers at home and abroad. (House 1969, 135–6; Anon. 1935, 5; Hale 1953, 5, 15)

Some Cumbrian towns, including Carlisle and Kendal, weathered the inter-war storm, largely unaffected by the industrial decline of the west. Carlisle's population grew from from 52,225 in 1921 to 67,798 by 1951. In 1801, Carlisle had held only 5 per cent of Cumberland's population: in 1948 the figure had risen to 23.6 per cent. A varied industrial base helped, including the railways and associated engineering enterprises which provided the largest source of employment. The city's textiles and food processing were expanding sectors during the 1930s. In 1936 the Hudson Scott division of the Metal Box Company began to produce tins for such food products as Nestlé's Carnation Milk; markets for such tinned items increased tenfold between 1924 and 1932. Carlisle also profited from its status as county capital and the general increase in service occupations and white-collar employment. (Reader 1976, 68; Turnbull 1991, 112)

Another bright spot was tourism in the Lake District, encouraged by expanding ownership of motor cars and development of bus services. There were attempts by conservationists to preserve the natural inheritance, which provoked ill feeling, especially if viewed from the perspective of west

Cumberland, which resented opposition to new roads to help local industries. 'Why should the convenience of a population be sacrificed to the penchant of a coterie for wildness and solitude?' (*West Cumberland Times*, 24/2/1923) If tourism was of increasing importance to the Cumbrian economy during the twentieth century, for many years this went unappreciated as attention focused on the problems of older staple industries. (Clarke 1981, 100; Marshall and Walton 1981, 234–5)

Within the four northern counties, additional revenue and employment produced by successful enterprises were not enough to offset the battering experienced by the core northern industries.

Declining Resources

Economic problems imposed strains on local resources available to provide help as most funds deployed for local public purposes were traditionally derived from local taxation in the form of rates and were expended by locally elected authorities. In the nineteenth century, there had been times when economic setbacks reduced the resources of many ratepayers while increased demands were made for greater expenditure in relief payments. Greater stresses in inter-war years intensified such problems, despite extensions of centrally funded national insurance. Increased spending imposed by the scale and endurance of inter-war unemployment involved costs which exceeded available local revenues.

Gateshead provided a good example. Even before 1914 some of the town's main sources of employment and income had failed (see p. 269 above), so that many inhabitants worked for firms in neighbouring local government areas, including Newcastle. Gateshead possessed wide areas of low rateable value housing, without rate income from these outside firms. In the early 1930s, Gateshead's Public Assistance Committee carried a burden of debt accumulated in coping with the mining crisis of 1926 and its aftermath. In 1935, rates amounted to 15s. 6d. in the £, of which almost half went directly in public assistance to the needy. The situation in County Durham was broadly similar. Only about 3 per cent of the county's houses had rateable value of more than £20, while 76.5 per cent were rated at £10 or lower. In 1934, when the worst depression had passed, 73 out of every 1,000 inhabitants were in some degree dependent on public relief, as against a national average of only 25.4. In that year, public assistance required, after taking into account special central grants made to depressed regions, a rate of 6s. 5d. in the £, more than all other county functions put together. The national average rate for this purpose was 2s. 8½d.

Even in the later 1930s, a penny rate in County Durham produced just over £14 per 1,000 inhabitants; the Northumberland equivalent was £20, Middlesex nearly £40. At Jarrow a penny rate raised about £400; the Bedford figure was £1,500 and the London borough of Holborn £6,000. (Wallace 1934, 89–90; Goodfellow 1940, 36–7)

Cumberland, burdened with its distressed western coastal belt, was in 1939 afflicted with rates of 11s. 3d. in the £, the fifth highest of all English counties, despite receipt of grants from the national exchequer which were nearly twice the national average. Since its formation in 1889, the administrative county had lost important revenues. In 1914, Carlisle became a county borough, keeping its considerable rateable value. By 1929 successive statutes had relieved agricultural land from rates, and reduced the liability of productive industry and freight transport. In 1939, the county's rateable value, at £830,000, was not much more than half that of 1889. At the same time there had been drastic extensions of the services in education, health and welfare expected of such authorities, only partly compensated for by central government grants. (Anon. 1939, 78–80) There was no correlation between population, extent of social problems, and the income of local authorities, as the table indicates. (Goodfellow 1940, 70–1) Local authorities with severe problems did not possess the largest income; commonly the reverse was the case.

Population and the Income of Local Authorities in 1939

	Population	Product of Penny Rate (£s)
Newcastle	290,000	10,216
Cumberland	198,940	3,200
Gateshead	118,000	2,125
South Shields	111,000	2,083
Tynemouth	67,000	1,499
Carlisle	62,500	1,640
Jarrow	31,000	436
Gosforth	20,000	731
Newburn	19,000	377

Under the impact of depression, the region increasingly looked for outside help, and especially from Parliament and national government. During the previous period of growth there had been little disposition to invite government intervention, but times had changed. Wartime experience of government control of the economy suggested that intervention might be practicable and beneficial. The economic and social problems which now beset depressed areas faced national government with a regional problem of a new and unforeseen kind. In so far as official attention had been paid to regional problems in earlier years, this concerned rural areas experiencing problems from food imports and declining populations. After the First World War, regional problems changed abruptly, affecting areas which had previously experienced massive industrial development. The northern counties of England, Clydeside and South Wales were dependent upon heavy industries which had been growth points before 1914, but possessed a relatively small share of newer industries. The problem was not so much a national predicament of industrial decline, but disparities in distribution of declining older industries and developing newer industries. A Board of Trade survey listed 646 factories established in 1932: of these, only eleven were in the North East and none on the Durham coalfield. (*The Times*, 22/3/1934)

Increasingly, hard-hit districts were forced to rely on central subsidies to support necessary spending. These developments, unwelcome to both parties, could exacerbate relations between local and central authorities. Depressed districts might see regulations imposed by an apparently remote and uncaring Whitehall as unworthy of punctilious observance. In a row over the granting of supplementary relief payments, at the worst of the depression, a Labour leader on Cumberland County Council told ministers that 'Nobody on this (Public Assistance) Committee is going to do their dirty work.' (Clarke 1981, 77)

Two local authorities exasperated the Ministry of Health sufficiently to use emergency powers to supersede them with appointed commissioners. In 1926 the Chester-le-Street Board of Poor Law Guardians had an overwhelming Labour majority; two-thirds of its members were miners. The Board had a long record of conflict with Whitehall for flouting regulations and paying unduly generous relief. Matters deteriorated with the approach of the 1926 coal dispute. The Board effectively excluded non-Labour guardians from supervision of relief policy, channelling payments exclusively through co-operative stores and preventing relieving officers from full investigation of claimants' resources. In the Birtley sub-district, impropriety went further; recipients of relief were invited to contribute to a fund collected for local guardians. (If these, mostly miners on strike, had been forced to apply for relief they would have been disqualified as guardians.) By July 1926 the Chester-le-Street Union had 14,000 cases of outdoor relief on its hands, and little or no attempt was made to check claims, especially from mining families. After repeated warnings, emergency powers were invoked and the elected Board of Guardians was superseded by commissioners appointed by the minister. By the end of 1926, after a thorough check, the number of outdoor relief cases was down to 3,000. (Rose 1971, 311)

In 1930, the functions of poor-law guardians were vested in public assistance committees of major local authorities. The new authority in County Durham was soon embroiled in similar disputes. After two years of bickering, the county's Public Assistance Committee was replaced by appointed commissioners at the end of 1932. The latter, headed by a Liberal ex-Home Secretary with local connections, Edward Shortt, found that their elected predecessors had been refusing only 1 per cent of relief applications and paying maximum levels of relief to 92 per cent of claimants. The commissioners carried out a review which reduced the payment of maximum scales to 70 per cent and rejected 6.5 per cent of claims altogether. In their published reports, they listed examples of applicants who had been given relief from public funds while possessing concealed assets. No doubt this was true, although these amounted to a tiny proportion of the thousands of cases with which this authority had to cope. We have the frank recollection, published in 1938, of an intelligent and likeable man who during the early 1930s lived in a lodging house in County Durham catering for unemployed men. (Commissioners 1933)

> The lodging was rough, the bedding sparse, and the food consisted mainly of thick slices of bread and margarine, with milkless tea, fried blackpudding and onions and a little cheese. The talk at meal-times was mostly about football or sport and hardly ever about politics or women – the main subject of interest to all was 'fiddling', i.e., the various means by which they could supplement their relief without reporting to the authorities. (Common 1938, 125–6)

Understandable, no doubt, but not calculated to appeal to ratepayers, many of whom were far from rich, in a county paying about three times the national average in relief expenditure. The strict family-based means test for relief in the early 1930s aroused bitter and lasting resentment. A father who lost his job in a skilled and well-paid trade could find his relief payments reduced because of the earnings of adolescent or adult children, and normal patterns of family relationships were strained in consequence.

The task facing elected councillors and poor-law guardians was not simple or easy. The unemployed and their champions pushed for generous relief policies, while ratepayers and their spokesmen pointed to difficulties brought about by rising rate demands, especially for poorer ratepayers, often themselves badly hit by the depression.

There were other sources of friction in the administration of relief. Many skilled workers, previously enjoying good incomes and high status, found that for small sums of relief they must attend upon local official agencies and justify claims to junior functionaries. No doubt some of these officials were both competent and sympathetic, but this was not always the case. John Mill, Secretary of the Boilermakers' Society, made the point in restrained terms in 1934:

> To entrust wide discretionary powers over craftsmen workers to young clerks without industrial experience seems likely to create a dangerous form of official despotism, and to be resented by the workers. (*Newcastle Journal*, 7/12/1934)

371

The Development of Regional Policy

Government intervention in support of the depressed regions during the inter-war period gradually became more overt and extensive. It failed to make substantial inroads into the problems of the affected regions. It is easy now to underestimate the difficulties involved in earlier phases of this development. The scale and persistence of the depression were unexpected and unprecedented. It was by no means clear what government could or should do in response. The prevailing concepts of economics scarcely encouraged large-scale official intervention in the country's economy. Moreover, both government and Parliament faced political constraints. It is difficult to detect any popular enthusiasm for tax increases which were an obvious concomitant to greater government intervention.

Political parties which campaigned for higher levels of government spending and intervention did not fare well in inter-war electoral history, despite the wide electorate. The general elections of 1931 and 1935 sustained the self-proclaimed National Government, and even in the hard-hit northern counties there was a substantial Conservative vote. Although the region came to provide the Labour Party with an invaluable base, its dominance was never unchallenged. With the exception of the electoral disaster of 1931, mining constituencies were generally Labour strongholds, although the minority vote was enough to deny a simple equation of social status with political allegiance. The towns were more mixed and volatile in their results. The Hartlepools sent Conservative MPs to Westminster in 1929, 1931 and 1935, while Darlington, Stockton and Sunderland also contributed MPs to the National Government's majority in 1931 and 1935. In the general election of 1931, Labour fared badly in the North as in the country as a whole. The mining constituency of Seaham Harbour returned Ramsay MacDonald, although with a much smaller majority than in 1929. Even in the 1935 general election, after the worst depression years, Labour's recovery was less marked than sanguine supporters had expected. There were gains in Durham county divisions, but seats like Houghton-le-Spring, Barnard Castle and even Jarrow were won by narrow margins. At Jarrow 46.9 per cent of those voting supported the Conservative candidate.

Labour strength in County Durham, outside separately administered county boroughs, enabled the party to control the county council for many years, enjoying eventually a majority secure enough to exploit county patronage in a partisan fashion and ignore widespread criticism. Other northern counties did not share this monolithic control to anything like the same extent. (Callcott 1973; Callcott 1980)

The turn-out of workers in support of the miners during the General Strike of 1926 might at first sight point to a telling unity of purpose, but even here the evidence is mixed. The solidarity did not last for long. Most union leaders responsible for ending the national strike remained in elected positions after 1926. The only action which might have saved the day for the miners would have been a ban by other workers on the movement of imported coal, but nothing substantial was done to that end. The position is even clearer for the 1930s. Despite the many schemes introduced to help victims of the depression, this was not a general preoccupation at any level of society. Even as the northern coalfields were hit hard by falling demand and ageing collieries, some others were relatively prosperous. There was little enthusiasm in more fortunate areas for the reintroduction of national wage levels to the advantage of miners in troubled coalfields. Even in the northern pits, there was less than general rank-and-file support for the 'county average' arrangements of the 1930s, which imposed limits on earnings in more successful collieries to subsidize less profitable mines.

In the Britain of the 1930s many were prepared to make loud noises of sympathy and protest for the depression's victims, but at any social level those willing to do anything about it were a much smaller number, and those willing to make any significant personal sacrifice fewer still. Even within the northern counties, events like the abdication crisis of 1936 and the coronation of 1937 could attract attention away from social problems of the day. Those who are contemptuous of the failure of the state to solve inter-war economic problems must take account of a lack of will amongst Britain's democratic electorate.

In these circumstances, official intervention was neither urgent nor prodigal. Increased mining unemployment after the 1926 dispute, and the colliery closures which followed, induced the Baldwin government to finance a modest scheme of small removal grants to encourage redundant miners to move to other areas. Inaugurated in 1928, this was later extended to other groups of workers in a similar predicament and then linked with retraining centres. This was a new departure, but modest investment of public funds produced an appropriately modest result in relation to worsening unemployment. Users of the scheme tended to be younger, more ambitious and adventurous workers, and it did little or nothing for older men who lost their jobs. During the worst of the depression, even prosperous regions had little additional employment to offer.

As yet government and Parliament had not ventured beyond small-scale measures, gingerly allocating small sums of public money to encourage some redistribution of labour between depressed regions and more prosperous areas. The idea of using tax revenue in subsidies to firms willing to provide employment in hard-hit districts was a much larger step and one against which telling arguments could be mustered. How competent would government be in deciding which enterprises merited such bounties? Why should taxes drawn from certain regions be used to subsidize competitors elsewhere? Was not the principle of selective government subsidies an inherently inefficient economic policy?

It was not until 1934, with the worst of the depression already over, that there were further significant innovations in regional policy. The Special Areas Act of that year had two main causes. The lesser was a series of special enquiries into the depressed regions, which publicized unemployment and its adverse social effects, involving heavy increases in public spending on unemployment benefits and public assistance payments. Central government had tried to maintain the semblance of local autonomy in official welfare concerns, but by the early 1930s this veil was becoming thin. Repeatedly, central government was forced to bail out hard-hit authorities by such expedients as guaranteed loans or overdrafts. Gateshead Poor Law Guardians advanced £42,019 in loans to miners during the 1921 strike. By mid-1925, only £7,372 of this had been repaid. A total of £214,678 in loans for emergency relief in the 1921–25 period was written off in May 1925. At the same time the Labour-controlled Board of Guardians resolved not to try to obtain repayments of such advances in future. A leading Labour guardian, Kelly, admitted that it was an unfortunate decision for those who had made efforts to pay back their loans. (*North Mail*, 27/5/1925) It was increasingly clear that much of this kind of debt was unlikely to be repaid.

The commissioner who reported upon the North East stressed that depression was beyond local control:

> There is no likelihood that the same forces which have created the present situation will automatically readjust it, except after a lapse of time and at a cost of human suffering which no modern Government would care to contemplate. Durham and Tyneside can only escape from the vicious circle, in which depression has created unemployment, and unemployment intensified depression, by means of some positive external assistance. (Wallace 1934, 106)

He pointed out that in June 1934 the national unemployment figure stood at 16.1 per cent, while that for County Durham and Tyneside was 27.2 per cent. In the Bishop Auckland district, with older collieries closed, the figure was 50.4 per cent and at Jarrow 56.8 per cent. The report calculated that, of the 165,000 unemployed in the areas covered, 63,000 had been unemployed for more than two years, and 9,000 for more than five years. Similar figures came from depressed west Cumberland, with an unemployment level of 51.4 per cent, with almost 25 per cent of these without work for more than two years. Maryport produced an unemployment level of 57.5 per cent. In the North East, unemployment peaked in 1935, but west Cumberland proved more intractable, and high rates remained there until relieved by the coming of war in 1939. Such figures, reflecting official statistics of registered unemployment, are almost certainly underestimates. (Dennison 1939; Odber 1965; Loebl 1988; Clarke 1981, 16, 65, 404)

The principal push behind the 1934 legislation was the cabinet's appreciation that with a general election imminent they must be seen to be doing something to help depressed regions. Articles in *The Times* in the spring of 1934 pressed for drastic action, and may have been decisive in inducing the government to set up the regional enquiries which preceded the 1934 legislation. (*The Times*, 20–23/3/1934) It is unlikely that any minister had much confidence in the effectiveness of the 1934 Special Areas Act. Under the Act, two Commissioners for Special Areas were appointed – one for England and Wales and one for Scotland. The Treasury was to provide them with £2 million annually. There was obvious disparity between the scale of the problems and allotted resources, and grants were additionally limited by specific restrictions. The results of regional legislation, even after the purse strings were somewhat loosened in 1937, were trivial in comparison with the recovery effected by revival in trade and the government's rearmament programmes. (Loebl 1988)

Apart from specifically regional initiatives, there was legislation which helped in other ways. North East shipyards derived some benefit from the British Shipping (Assistance) Act, 1935, which provided low-interest loans for shipping firms to finance new building in British yards, provided they scrapped two tons of older shipping for every new ton built. The Wear won 24 of the 50 orders placed under this scheme, but the boost was only temporary and building there had slumped again by 1938. (Royal Commission 1992, 45)

The state's Forestry Commission was active in the North from 1926 onwards. Large moorland areas became clothed with trees, probably for the first time since before the Roman period. In 1932 the process was intensified by acquisition of most of the duke of Northumberland's upland property in the border area, but forestry's contribution to the northern economy was always a minor one. (Hanley 1936, 67; Pawson 1961, 72)

One innovation of the later 1930s was the creation of subsidized trading estates. The Team Valley Trading Estate, near Gateshead, was one of the earliest of these. By 1939, it had attracted firms employing 2,520 workers. This was a small number in comparison with local unemployment, and few jobs were for skilled adult male workers where the principal need existed.

The tale of regional policy in Cumbria was similar, and here the problems seemed even more deep-seated and intractable. The author of the 1934 report on Cumberland, J. C. C. Davidson, was even more pessimistic than his opposite number in the North East. Cumberland acquired the unenviable distinction of being 'the Cinderella of the Special Areas'. There was tension between central government's commissioner, Malcolm Stewart, and the locally sponsored Development Company representing local authorities, trade unionists and Cumberland industrialists. Stewart was impressed by the problem of surplus labour, and advocated migration schemes and settlement of unemployed workers in small market-garden ventures, while the Development Company pursued more active policies of public works and incentives to attract industry. Only after 1937, with more financial support from central government, was significant new industry attracted to this area, which possessed few obvious advantages and was remote from main centres of growth. The availability of good-quality water prompted some expansion of industry, including textiles, tanning and wood pulp. The secretary of the Development Company, Jack Adams, courted energetic and able refugees from Nazi persecution; by the summer of 1939 such initiatives had created a small number of jobs, but these often represented opportunities for women rather than alternative male employment. As in the North East, rearmament did more than regional policy to improve matters. By the late 1930s there were complaints of shortage of labour at Vickers' warship yards at Barrow. An airfield at Silloth provided work for the Maryport unemployed, while in east Cumberland 1,200 new jobs came with a RAF supply depot north of Carlisle. In 1938, the selection board for a Land Settlement Scheme was faced with a dearth of unemployed applicants in face of industrial revival. By 1939 northern wages had again reached the level attained in the early 1920s. (Dennison 1939, 139; Clarke 1981, 145–6, 233, 396; Hudson 1989, 12)

Economic Recovery

By the mid-1930s there were signs that the northern region was past the worst of the depression, although recovery was far from general. In 1935 a perceptive retail manager observed that 'the time is coming, when people are tired of going to cheap shops to which they were driven in the years of repression, and these people are now coming back to the better shops'. (Mathias 1967, 89–92) In 1935, the Newcastle postal area handled 11.8 million more letters and 2.5 million more telephone calls than in 1931; wireless licences were also up, by 10,500. If the chain of shops which J. W. Brough had built up before 1914 saw profits of only £25,000 in 1932, they were up to £52,000 in 1937 and a record £82,000 in 1939. (Tyneside 1935; Mathias 1967, 89)

By 1937, the recorded national level of unemployment was 11 per cent. The Hartlepools still returned 23 per cent and Middlesbrough 15 per cent, but a few miles away Darlington was below the national average at 9 per cent. There were always disparities within the northern region, including the contrast between hard-hit Jarrow and its relatively prosperous neighbour Hebburn, a centre of the expanding heavy electrical engineering industry.

Figure 19.3 Vasey Crescent, Carlisle. Council housing of 1937 in mock-Tudor style.

Population

The twentieth century saw a marked slowing down in population growth. During the twenty-year period 1931–51 (there was no census in wartime 1941), Northumberland still saw a 5.5 per cent increase, but County Durham, a centre of mining problems, lost 1.5 per cent of its population. In Cumbria, long-term drift from the rural interior combined with industrial decline on the coastal belt meant that the region contained fewer people in 1939 than in 1891, although these broad trends obscure areas of stability or even increase as in Carlisle and Kendal. (Marshall and Walton 1981, 222)

In post-war years, outwards migration from northern counties kept population growth low, effectively cancelling out about half of the natural increase from births. As in earlier periods, there was a complex pattern of individual movements in and out, but now the balance had tilted and the net result was a drop in population. Although overall northern loss was low, a high proportion of those lost were active younger people, an unwelcome trend. (House, 1969, 55)

Chapter 20

Inter-War Social Improvement

The drastic fall in regional resources during the depression slowed down social improvement, especially in communities which saw high levels of long-term unemployment. In statistics of overcrowding, infant mortality, tuberculosis and similar indicators, the region continued in an unenviably high position.

The regional figures conceal marked local discrepancies, as illustrated by 1921 figures for overcrowding – i.e. those living at a density of more than two per room – in communities on or near Tyneside. Similar diversity existed within an overall Cumbrian figure of 8.4 per cent, with Carlisle at 19 per cent, Whitehaven 18.8 per cent, Barrow 11 per cent, Kendal 4.25 per cent.

Overcrowding in the Tyneside Region, 1921

	Numbers living at a density of more than 2 per room	% of total population
National average		9.1
Newcastle	88,000	33.6
Hebburn	11,000	46.9
Jarrow	15,000	42.5
South Shields	42,000	36.5
Tynemouth	21,000	43.4
Gosforth	2,000	13.8
Whitley Bay	2,100	10.4

During 1931–35, the tuberculosis death rate among young women in Gateshead and South Shields was more than twice the average for England and Wales. Cumberland had the unenviable distinction of the worst place among English counties for tuberculosis deaths. This was despite considerable efforts by the county's medical services: there were 398 TB deaths in 1909, only 158 in 1937. West Cumberland was the principal black spot. (Hadfield 1977; Anon. 1939, 75; Fraser 1939)

378

Despite such evidence, the inter-war period, with all its difficulties, saw an increasing attack on social problems. There were local variations and temporary setbacks, but by 1939 there had been a remarkable improvement in the condition of the people in the four northern counties. Although Parliament and governments moved warily in accepting wider welfare responsibilities, there was some increase in resources made available from national revenue for tackling some of the region's old problems.

Many communities faced serious housing shortages and curtailed income in these years. Subsidies from central funds were necessary before such local authorities could tackle housing problems. This applied both to building new houses and improving old ones. In the mid-1920s, local authorities could call upon central grants to pay for the replacement of old dry lavatories by water closets. Gateshead Council had little income to spare, but with such backing nearly 19,000 WCs were installed in 1925–27. Gateshead acquired a new central library in 1926; most of the £27,000 needed came from elsewhere, including a grant of £16,500 from the Carnegie United Kingdom Trust. A new isolation hospital was built in 1936, because 75 per cent of the cost was met from national taxation under Special Areas legislation. Without subsidies, the town would not have been able to afford expensive improvements, at a time when the public assistance committee spent half the rate income, and more than 800 in every 10,000 of the town's people were dependent on relief payments. There were other doles from central sources: for example, Durham County Council received from the Department of Transport 60 per cent of the cost of a new bridge at Brancepeth in 1935. (Cole n.d.)

Subsidies enabled local authorities to undertake new housing schemes and tackle slums inherited from earlier years. At Sunderland, 445 families were re-housed in 1934–36. In their new accommodation, they occupied 1,671 rooms as against 881 in their old homes. Each family now possessed a bath, scullery, garden and WC. (Leonard 1996, 185–7; Dennis, 1070, 150–1)

In North Shields, about a quarter of all babies were born in one-roomed homes in 1920. By the mid-1920s the situation had deteriorated, to about one-third, but thereafter, despite economic problems, there was a change for the better. The council responded to the Housing Act of 1930 and its subsidies with a five-year programme of slum clearance and rehousing, erecting nearly 2,000 new houses. In 1936, only 10 per cent of babies were born in one-room dwellings, and by 1938 the figure was 5.8 per cent, much lower than had ever been the case before. (Goodfellow 1940, 32; Barke and Turnbull 1994)

At Blyth, the council built more than 1,200 houses between 1918 and 1935, with national subventions keeping cost to ratepayers at a tolerable level. Darlington eliminated most of its worst central slums by 1939, while Middlesbrough rehoused more than 4,000 families on new housing estates. In Newcastle, national subsidies helped to provide 5,549 new houses in the

1920s, with the figure leaping to 22,160 for the 1930s. The city council had built only 454 houses between 1890 and 1920, but it provided 8,130 of the new houses of the 1930s; by 1939, 22,000 people were living in council houses there. (Leonard 1996, 185–7; Reynolds 1935, 25; House and Fullerton 1960, 65; Glass 1948, 49; Municipal 1935, 21; Newcastle 1930, 45; Spence 1954, 23)

Carlisle was in the forefront of municipal housing, tackling problems which had been serious since the 1880s at latest. In 1919–38, the city council built 5,065 houses, more than any other local authority in relation to population. This relieved the overcrowded city centre and saw much rehousing from older Caldewgate and Denton Holme suburbs into new estates to the south and west of the centre. The principle of municipal housing was implemented by a council dominated by a Liberal–Conservative alliance but conscious of the challenge offered by Labour. There was little opposition, though by the mid-1930s grumbling on grounds of cost had become vocal. The privately rented housing sector suffered by this extension of subsidized competition. By 1939 it was largely confined to poorer and older houses, inferior in such matters as sanitation and bathrooms. Like County Durham, Carlisle adopted a policy of allocating council housing by a points system according to need, reflecting an awareness of links between housing and general issues of welfare and public health. It remained true that tenants of council housing in these years rarely came from the poorest strata of society. (Perriam 1992, 89; Turnbull 1991, 125, 287, 27–8, 425)

The disappearance of the old poor-law authorities in 1930 brought additional rationalization to local government which, despite the depression, continually improved welfare provisions. The new relief agencies worked under the Relief Regulation Order of 1930 and its successors, which abandoned any policy of deterrence towards the poor and sought rehabilitation and whenever possible re-employment. Cumberland County Council's interpretation of its new public assistance role was to reject 'the former poor law atmosphere' and accept that its clients here were 'very largely the victims of a persistent industrial depression which leaves them little or no chance of finding work'. (Anon. 1939, 76–8) At Newcastle, the Public Assistance Committee of the city council improved medical services provided by the old workhouse infirmary, now Newcastle General Hospital. The number of patients admitted rose from 3,048 in 1930 to 6,695 in 1936, operations from 596 to 2,722. (Newcastle Hospital 1937) The PAC also dropped the traditional practice of different relief scales for summer and winter, and now the more generous winter scales applied throughout. When in 1931 the Ministry of Health, alarmed at the growing cost of relief in depressed regions, asked the Newcastle authority to make economies, the PAC replied that they had given careful consideration to the Ministry's circular but saw no possibility of reduced expenditure. In 1931–32, that committee spent £340,000. (Newcastle Hospital 1937; Newcastle Council 1930, 1932)

Inter-war years brought advances in educational provision. Transport improvements made it easier for bright rural children to attend grammar schools in the nearest towns. New secondary schools, such as Linskill and Ralph Gardner schools at North Shields, provided higher standards of accommodation than their predecessors, although an enquiry of the late 1930s found teachers' salaries within the region below national averages. (Robinson 1988, 91)

The contribution of local authorities to social improvement was important, but did not reflect unanimous public opinion, as a letter of 1921 to a leading local newspaper indicated:

Too much is made by certain members of the council of the council's responsibility for the health of the people. If some of them would use more soap and water and less intoxicating drink there would be no need for this outcry about the health of the poor, whose poverty is often the result of their own folly. (*Newcastle Journal*, 21/7/1921)

Such hostility existed against a background of expanding local government services in matters of health, education, housing and general welfare in the first forty years of the century. Ratepayers' resistance to greater spending may have been mitigated by greater subsidies from national taxation and the piecemeal pace of expanded official activity. When Cumberland County Council established a new Health Committee in 1908, it was given an additional staff of a clerk and two assistant medical officers of health. By 1939, the committee supervised 62 full-time staff, and a variety of activities which included midwifery, antenatal care, gynaecology, child welfare, tuberculosis, cancer, prevention of blindness, venereal disease, orthopaedics, ear, nose and throat treatment, and dental services. While these expanded functions reflected preoccupation with the health of children, and certain major diseases, the outline – and to some extent the conscious striving – for a comprehensive approach was implicit in medical services offered by local government by 1939. (Anon. 1939, 73–5)

Economic adversity still handicapped improvements in welfare services. In 1932, a Durham clergyman told his bishop that

I wish to give you one example of how sickness affects the unemployed. This case is living in a Council's house. His wife was taken to the R(oyal) V(ictoria) I(nfirmary), N'castle, a week ago and has gone through a severe operation. There are five children, aged 15, 5, 4, 2 years and 6 weeks. When this man went for his relief, 10/- was taken off for his wife, leaving him with 25/- for the week, with a house rent of 10/4 per week. He went to see his wife the day after the operation, and in order to get into N'castle he had to go in with a friendly carrier. Next day he was unable to afford 4*d.* to telephone the Infirmary. This, of course, is how sickness has always affected the poor . . . (McCord 1987, 11)

In a variety of ways, although northern counties continued to lag behind national averages, the inter-war years saw a remarkable improvement in social conditions and a narrowing of gaps between different regions. Infant mortality offers a good example. (Goodfellow 1940, 28) In Cumberland the level of infant mortality had been as high as 126 per 1,000 in 1908. Continuing improvement in such places as Jarrow, Gateshead, Cockermouth and Maryport is particularly striking against the background of profound economic distress during the 1930s. By 1939 Gateshead's figure was down to 60 per 1,000, still uncomfortably above the national average, but representing significant improvement.

Infant Mortality (per 1,000 live births)

	1923–25	1935–37
National average	73	58
Gateshead	100	86
Newcastle	96	89
South Shields	104	82
Jarrow	101	97
Whitley Bay	57	67
Gosforth	70	65
Cumberland	72	61
Carlisle	78.4	67.6
Cockermouth	131	40
Maryport	82	54
Whitehaven	78	63
Workington	80	63

Social Reformers

This progress did not reflect widespread popular demand, but efforts of identifiable minorities of social reformers. As in earlier years, these included local doctors, including the more energetic medical officers of health appointed by local authorities. Dr McGonigle, MOH for Stockton, was a good example. In his regular reports he pulled no punches, as far as reporting poor conditions was concerned. He backed descriptions with statistics demonstrating the need for improvements, including comparisons between the health of the unemployed and those at work, and between richer and poorer sections of townspeople. He pointed out that the removal of a poor family from slum conditions to a modern council house did not necessarily produce a great improvement in standard of living; if higher rents impaired a family's ability to feed itself there might even be deterioration.

At Newcastle Dr James Spence, a pioneer in child health care, carried out on behalf of the city council an extensive survey of the health of local children. This brought uncomfortable demonstrations; while anaemia affected 16 per cent of the children of professional groups, the figure could be as high as 81 per cent for children of the very poor. Among the latter there was eight times as much pneumonia and ten times as much bronchitis as in the city's richer families.

Philanthropy and the Depression

The activity of social reformers was part of continuing growth in philanthropic activities, already expanding in earlier years. Official agencies provided more help than in any earlier period, but they were not the only source of alleviation. Families, friends and neighbours, as so often in the past, provided a principal source of support. Many small neighbourhood shops were generous in credit to customers in difficulty; when better times returned, many, though not all, of these loans were repaid. (Taylor 1992)

Help came from further afield. In the 1930s, Jarrow was 'adopted' by organizations in Surrey, while Hertfordshire 'adopted' a group of Durham mining villages. The Lord Mayor of London's Relief Fund channelled substantial sums of money to depressed communities in the North. The industrialist Lord Nuffield endowed his own relief fund with £2 million. Such initiatives were less trammelled by restrictions than the official Special Areas Commissioners. For example, the Nuffield Trust gave a five-year loan of £25,000 to Victor Products Ltd of Wallsend in the mid-1930s to enable the company to extend production and take on more workers. (Anon. 1979) In Cumbria, Lady Mabel Howard organized a branch of the Personal Service League which provided clothing and other gifts; the Carnegie Trust was active in west Cumberland and supported schemes for resettling unemployed workers on the land. A group of students from King's College, London, organized rehabilitation camps near Morpeth, where unemployed workmen were given good food, light work and entertainment in the hope of enabling them to take advantage of opportunities for return to work. These are only examples of a diverse range of ameliorative activity. (Clarke 1981, 82–5; Branson and Heinemann 1971, 61; Honeyman 1955, 27)

Such efforts could not do more than mitigate the social consequences of economic adversity. Groups which suffered most often felt that they were largely forgotten by the rest of the national community, much as many

383

miners felt after the failure of the 1926 General Strike that they had been left to struggle on in isolated weakness. (Hitchin 1962, 81)

The creation of charitable organizations continued. At Newcastle, the Citizens' Service Society worked from 1920 onwards on its own ameliorative programmes and tried to co-ordinate activities of sister societies. It was supported by contributions in cash and kind from wealthier sections of local society, who provided most of the volunteers who staffed it. There were many educated women of means for whom a working career was not possible, and such an organization could call upon this reservoir of talent and interest. In this Society's work there was an emphasis on tailoring help to individual needs; in some cases applicants for help were directed to other specialist societies for appropriate assistance. For others, the Citizens' Service Society itself provided a variety of responses. For those suffering from tuberculosis or other illnesses, it provided money for extra food, spare beds or warm clothing. Home helps were provided for a family while the mother was ill, long before any official agency provided such support. As new council estates developed in the 1930s, the Society fostered community associations on them. Much work was done in rehabilitation of discharged prisoners and Borstal boys. The Society bought up large houses and converted them into flats let at moderate rents. All of this represented only one element in the continued activity of voluntary agencies engaged in social services.

Although much of this work remained essentially local, there was more intervention from national philanthropic institutions, as in the campaigns against cruelty to children and animals. There was also continuing interaction between voluntary and official relief agencies. As in earlier years, public bodies used facilities provided by unofficial initiatives which complemented their own role. Semi-official bodies such as the National Council for Social Service received modest grants from public funds in aid of work in depressed areas. The process by which official agencies took over social services originally provided by voluntary initiative continued. In 1920, for instance, Newcastle Council adopted nine 'mothers' and babies' welfare centres' originally set up by voluntary efforts. On his Wallington estate, Sir Charles Trevelyan, Bart., introduced family allowances for estate workers long before the introduction of similar state benefits in 1945. (Lambert 1995, 39)

During the inter-war years, the Newcastle-based Poor Childrens' Holiday Association (p. 322 above) extended work in tuberculosis treatment, especially among children; in 1930 it opened a large holiday home at Whitley Bay for mothers and children from poor families. The Sutton Dwellings Trust built sizeable housing estates in Newcastle in 1918, 1928 and 1935, with another at South Shields in 1929, together amounting to nearly 1,000 modern homes at low rentals. On a smaller scale, the Bible Class of a North Shields chapel raised the money to build about 100 new homes. Trustees of the estate of the shipowner Sir James Knott spent large sums in improvements on Tyneside, including £100,000 on a large youth centre in North Shields, and the erection of a huge housing block overlooking the mouth of the Tyne. (Anon. 1949)

Old-established medical charities remained important at a time when state provision was limited. An appeal in 1927 raised £143,000 (including £75,000 from Lord Runciman) for extensions to Newcastle's Royal Victoria Infirmary, one of the North's principal hospitals. It was increasingly common for hospitals to be supported by organized groups of voluntary workers, such as the Guild of Help at Sunderland Royal Infirmary, founded in 1931. (Hume 1941; Robinson 1934, 86) Much support for voluntary charities came from richer sections of society, but it was also common for bodies like working men's clubs to make contributions to such institutions as hospitals and convalescent homes.

Popular Culture

A feature of inter-war years was extension of facilities for recreation and entertainment. There was also an erosion of regional distinctiveness, so that by the 1930s even in remoter parts of the region the inhabitants spent leisure time in ways broadly similar to their counterparts elsewhere in Britain. The cinema, gramophone and wireless all exerted pressure towards uniformity, reflected also in the relative decline of local publications and growing readership for national newspapers. (Murfin 1990, 24, 231)

Sport, especially association football, continued to inspire enthusiasm greater than any kind of political activity. Other sports possessed their own, less pervasive, attraction: for example, a modern standard work notes that 'It would be wrong, terribly wrong, to by-pass the North-East in any cricketing review.' (Swanton 1966, 263, 288, 700, 703, 816; Bowen 1970, 271, 284, 290)

These were also the growth years of the cinema, and northern communities displayed above-average addiction to this entertainment. Three cinemas were built in close proximity at West Hartlepool in the 1930s, Sunderland acquired five between 1932 and 1937, Gateshead four in 1936–39 and Newcastle fifteen between 1931 and 1939. As early as 1910, Barrow had its 'Electric' cinema, and two years later Workington had two – the Carnegie Hall and the Hippodrome. In 1927 the Albion Cinema's programme at North Shields included a fervently patriotic film on 'The Battles of the Coronel and Falklands Islands'; in 1929 the RCA Photophone Corporation installed their 'talkie apparatus' there. Early cinemas tended to be makeshift conversions, but by the 1930s a new generation of purpose-built cinemas were more

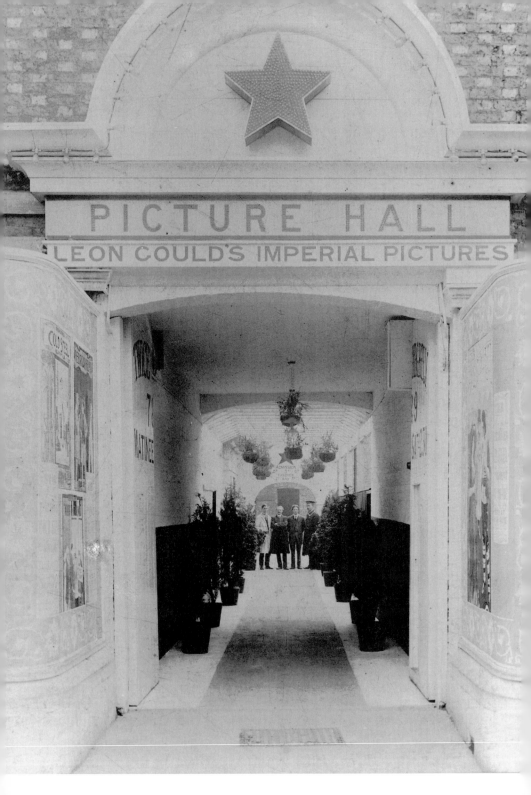

lavish, still offering cheap entertainment for a mass audience. (Elliston Allen 1968, 178; Murfin 1980, 212–13; Manders 1991; Manders 1995; Bennison 1995, 32–3)

Growth in working men's clubs continued. In 1925, Prudhoe Working Men's Club spent £3,000 in buying the Palace Theatre; in 1935, Westerhope Excelsior Social Club spent £5,000 on a new building. From 1921, the Northern Clubs' Federation Brewery provided not only good-quality beer but also a continuing source of income for the clubs which owned it. (Elkins 1970; Bennison 1995)

While there was an unmistakable trend towards uniformity in leisure practices, there were still distinctively northern survivals. Some popular local comedians, such as Bobby Thompson, were barely known outside North East England. Cumbria preserved its own forms of wrestling, hound trailing and hunting.

Development of bus services, including eventually long-distance journeys, brought increased mobility. Services between Morpeth and Ashington existed by 1923 and between Morpeth and Newcastle soon afterwards. Early ventures were helped by availability of cheap ex-service vehicles which could be converted into rough-and-ready passenger carriers. Railways also responded to changing conditions: a new station at Seaburn, near Sunderland, catered for seaside visitors as well as suburban expansion. Nearby, the LNER in 1937 replaced a simple platform at Roker by a more sophisticated station to cope with Sunderland AFC supporters. Older readers may remember long queues for electric trains from Newcastle to nearby coastal resorts on summer weekends in the 1930s. Holidays became more widespread; before 1939 adventurous people even of modest means were embarking on such ventures as cycling holidays in France or the Low Countries. At Ashington, the local colliery magazine encouraged miners to try such ventures.

Inter-War Summary

The inter-war experiences of the region were more complex and varied than is normally remembered. It was a period of shattering blows from large-scale unemployment; the means test of the 1930s still occupies a definite if diminishing place in the region's folk memory. It was also a period of improved housing, health, education and recreation. Areas of poverty remained;

Figure 20.1 The Star Picture Hall, Denton Street, Carlisle, showing some of the self-conscious dignity and formality of the early twentieth-century cinema as a purveyor of mass entertainment.

there were great inequalities of wealth, comfort and opportunity, as in earlier periods. There was a continuing expansion of efforts, by both official and voluntary agencies, to tackle social problems. By 1939, these problems had not disappeared, but many had been significantly reduced, notwithstanding economic difficulties. When the Second World War began, the great majority of the region's inhabitants enjoyed a higher standard of living than in 1920, or in any earlier period. For the first time, there had been a significant attack on slums which had disfigured the region for generations, even if much remained to be done. By 1939, unemployment had shrunk markedly. The improvement in the inter-war years was not equally shared and may have meant little to the long-term unemployed, but for the great majority it was real.

One aspect of economic recovery in the later 1930s which was dangerous was absence of reconstruction of the region's industrial base. The rearmament programme was a godsend to the ailing heavy industries of the North, but reinforced reliance on them, a dependence which had already proved unsafe. Demands of rearmament and then exigencies of war production involved concentration on coal, steel, engineering and shipbuilding. Much effort was expended in making existing plant work more intensively rather than in modernization. Coal-mining and the steel industry were controlled by the Ministry of Supply, which sought, irrespective of long-term consequences, to squeeze out maximum immediate output. By 1944, 30 per cent of all employment in Cumbria was directly connected with war production. Even in the midst of the war emergency, there was some appreciation that 'a grave crisis will arise when armament production stops'. (Clarke 1981, 360–1, 365)

The Second World War

The scale of wartime effort can be illustrated by shipping figures. Wear shipyards produced 240 new merchant ships during the 1939–45 war, with 125 more coming from Teesside. The relatively small Tyneside figure of 74 was due to concentration of warship work there. The old Armstrong base at Elswick worked flat out during war years, including a major contribution in tank manufacture.

The war affected the regional economy in other ways. Coal export markets were lost as many of them came under enemy control. The east-coast coal-shipping route was threatened by enemy action. The collier fleet suffered heavy losses and even late in the war coastal coal shipments were well under half their pre-war figures.

Northern agriculture had contrived to recover by 1939 through con-centration on profitable pastoral farming and specialized production for urban markets in dairy produce and similar lines. In 1939, this was put into abrupt reverse, with a crash programme of extended arable farming to compensate for loss of vulnerable imports. Government initiative and sub-sidies facilitated a transformation in farming over a short period, one of the more remarkable responses to wartime conditions.

Another feature of the war economy was increase in female employ-ment. There were many woman farm workers, and echoes of 1914–18 in female porters, guards and ticket collectors on the railways. The 1939–45 war brought wider changes, with women carrying and laying railway sleepers and repairing multi-core signal and telephone cables. Shipbuilding also called on this reserve work force; at Hebburn, Palmer's old shipyard employed many women, including a force of 350 allocated to ship conversion and repair work. (Crump 1947, 107; Palmers 1946; Price 1993)

By 1940, demands of the war effort had mopped up remaining unem-ployment. Overriding wartime priorities interrupted improvement in such areas as housing, but brought also increased acceptance of communal respons-ibility for the feeding and welfare of the population. Medical resources, whether provided by local authorities or voluntary agencies, were increas-ingly integrated into an emergency system of public services which foreshad-owed the post-war National Health Service. By 1939, central and local government possessed extended resources in trained professional staff which made it relatively easy to implement emergency administrative arrangements. At Darlington, for instance, the staff of the Public Assistance Committee coped with the provision of emergency centres capable of looking after 7,000 people, and homes for about 10,000 war workers and evacuees, as well as conversion of the old workhouse into an emergency hospital. The established tradition of co-operation between official and voluntary welfare agencies proved useful in the improvisation of new administrative and welfare facilities required by war.

The Armed Forces

As in 1914–18, there was large-scale recruiting for the armed forces, though now conscription was available from the beginning. In some cases mobiliza-tion revealed survival of older social patterns. When the Northumberland Hussars mustered for war service in 1939, its squadron commanders were Major Lord Ridley, Major Lord Ravensworth and Major T. Eustace Smith (of the Smiths dock family, now comfortably ensconced among the county's landed gentry). Junior officers showed a considerable sprinkling of North-umberland's landed families. More generally, recruiting depended less on local ties than in the previous war. In 1914–18, casualties in individual actions could come as a catastrophe to local communities, but this was less the case in 1939–45. Overall British casualties were fewer; war memorials provide illustrations of the difference. At Shildon, for instance, the village memorial lists 271 from 1914–18, 138 from 1939–45. The casualties of the later war were serious enough. During a month of hard fighting in 1944, the 50th Division, which included Durham Light Infantry formations, saw 113 officers and 1,045 other ranks killed, 338 and 4,967 wounded. (Bright 1949, 13; Ward 1963, 466; Clay 1950, 313) The northern region, with established maritime traditions, suffered heavy naval casualties and tragic loss among merchant seamen, shared by deep-sea sailors, coastal crews and fishermen. The region provided its contribution to the expanded Royal Air Force and bore its share of losses here too.

Air Raids

Unlike the 1914–18 conflict, when air raids in the North were few and small in scale, danger of death and injury from enemy action was not confined to armed services and merchant navy. Police records from Tynemouth list 329 bombing incidents within the borough between June 1940 and March 1943. Both North and South Shields, like other towns, suffered civilian casualties, including major tragedies when crowded air-raid shelters received direct hits. Ports were among principal targets. Railway stations at South Shields, Sunderland and Middlesbrough were hit, while destruction in 1941 of New-castle's principal goods station was the biggest single instance of material damage in the North. In North Shields, bombing destroyed 166 properties, severely damaged 1,307 and slightly damaged 9,928; equivalent figures for South Shields were 482, 1,324 and 9,706. Proximity to enemy bases and possession of war installations ensured that the North East suffered more from bombing than Cumbria.

Despite the danger to which civilians were exposed, and natural hos-tility towards the enemy, hatred of Germans was less frenetic and more controlled than in 1914–18. Especially in the crisis years of 1940–43, there was a marked spirit of national purpose and unity. It was not universal. One remarkable instance was the existence during the war of 'fiddling' in the administration of Newcastle's emergency services, which emerged as a scandal in 1944 and involved a Home Office enquiry. (Fitzwalter and Taylor 1981, 32; Home Office 1944) There were strikes during the war, some of

Figure 20.2 Ruins of Wilkinson's mineral water factory, North Shields. Bombing on the night of 3–4 May 1941 caused the building and its machinery to collapse into a crowded underground air raid shelter, killing 106 men, women and children.

them damaging, as in coal-mining, but they were generally insignificant in relation to the war effort achieved. There were some who, especially before the German attack on Russia, saw the conflict as a capitalist war in which the people had no true interest, but this was not a prevailing opinion.

Chapter 21

After the Second World War

Victory in 1945 was followed by serious economic problems, though social consequences were less severe than during the inter-war depression. Wartime defence expenditure masked the vulnerability of the regional economy, but problems re-emerged with the coming of peace. The seriousness of the situation was for some time veiled by temporary demands for post-war reconstruction at home and abroad, and then the Korean War's requirements in defence-associated production. These fortuitous circumstances could not erase relatively low productivity and reliance on a narrow range of declining industries. Fundamental problems remained and in some important respects the situation had worsened. (Robinson 1988, 17)

The rebuilding and modernization of the regional economy was not easy. In some ways though, wartime experience helped in post-war years. Tentative moves towards an official policy of regional aid during the 1930s set a precedent followed by later governments. In 1937, the government appointed a Royal Commission on the Distribution of the Industrial Population – the Barlow Commission as it became known. Its terms of reference illustrated the changed climate of opinion in which it was established:

> To inquire into the causes which have influenced the present geographical distribution of the population of Great Britain and the probable direction of any change in that distribution in the future; to consider what social, economic or strategical disadvantages arise from the concentration of industries or of the industrial population in large towns or in particular areas of the country; and to report what remedial measures if any should be taken in the national interest.

The Commission reported in 1940, and, while its main objective had not been study of weaknesses of depressed regions in the 1930s, the report included a reasonably thorough assessment of them. It was less easy to postulate remedies. Nothing much could be done during the war, but in 1944 a White Paper on Employment Policy accepted the case for planned regional policy for employment, and the special needs of the regions which had been hit hard during the inter-war depression. The northern counties made a large contribution to Labour electoral victory in 1945, which reflected *inter alia* confidence in the effectiveness of state intervention to secure social amelioration.

In the post-war era, governments sought to implement such plans, including the state's assumption of an unprecedented role in centralized control of the national economy. In part these measures depended on retaining wartime controls, but there was also new legislation, including the Distribution of Industry Act of 1945. Industrial development in the Midlands and the South was restricted to facilitate expansion and diversification in 'development areas', as the pre-war 'special areas' were now termed. In 1945–47, these areas, containing about one-sixth of industrial workers, received about half the new industrial developments approved under the government's extensive powers.

From government restriction of development elsewhere, and various forms of subsidy, the region did well in these years. This was useful, but two-thirds of its post-war industrial development was financed by private capital. The steel and chemical industries were two sectors with heavy private capital investment. More than £27 million was spent in modernization at the Consett steel works, with annual capacity tripled to a million tons between 1945 and 1960. Thereafter rationalization of the steel industry reduced the work force from 5,000 to 3,500 during the later 1970s and parts of the works closed. Final closure in September 1980 was a disaster for what had been effectively a company town. That the modernized works had remained profitable counted little in face of the nationalized British Steel's pursuit of its master plan of concentrating production on a limited number of coastal sites. The story of the last years of the Consett works is not creditable to the competence or on occasion even the honesty of the nationalized steel corporation. The National Coal Board's policies after nationalization have also earned criticisms, mitigated by the shared responsibility of governments. In steel and coal, the early history of nationalized industries was marked by absence of policy continuity, and ill-thought-out decision-making. When shipbuilding was nationalized in 1977, British Shipbuilders adopted an unrealistic appreciation of its chances in the years ahead, based on an overly optimistic assessment of 1966. In all of these cases, enterprises in the northern counties were prominent victims of this limited competence. In the 1950s and 1960s, the National Coal Board refused to provide Durham County Council with any information about future mining employment within the county. (Robinson and Sadler 1984; Warren 1990; Hudson 1989, 146–210, 371)

In many cases, older interests could not be saved. The coal trade, for so long a principal support, was a spent force. In 1947 coal shipments from the Tyne to foreign buyers totalled only 216,000 tons, the lowest figure since 1832. Coal exports during the 1950s amounted to little more than half those of the 1920s, and continued to shrink, with no significant shipments outside Europe after 1954. Ten years later – probably for the first peacetime year for centuries – no coal left the Tyne for France or Germany. Coastal shipments held up better for a while, with London taking 6.5 million tons from the North East in 1952, a good year. (Elliott 1968, 92)

There was a marked drop in employment connected with the coal trade. The collier fleet shrank and coal-shipping berths dwindled. The Tyne-side coal-loading staiths dropped from 36 in 1946 to 16 by the early 1960s and decline continued; at the time of writing only one survives. The fall in mining employment was the biggest element in loss of work within the old interdependent group of staple industries. The availability of cheap oil was important here. During the 1950s, 22,000 jobs were lost on the Great Northern Coalfield. Notwithstanding such developments, in 1961–62 mining still employed 14 per cent of the insured working population of the North East, more than any other industry, despite shrinkage in mining employment that year by 6,000, to 119,821.

There were 13 collieries at work in Cumberland at the time of nationalization in 1947, and for a while national need for coal postponed the effects of poor profitability and relative inefficiency. By 1981 only the Haig pit near Whitehaven survived, and open-cast workings in the county already produced twice its 250,000 tons output. This lone survivor closed in the aftermath of the disastrous coal strike of the early 1980s. A similar fate lay in store for the collieries of the North East. The Rising Sun Colliery at Wallsend, closed in 1969, was the last colliery working on the north bank of the Tyne; the process of decline was completed by the closure of Ellington Colliery early in 1994. (Wood 1988, 260, 284; Whitfield 1975, 106)

In the 1920s *c*.45 per cent of the Tyneside work force was employed in manufacturing or mining. By the mid-1980s, manufacturing employed only 20 per cent and mining 2 per cent. (House 1969, 106; Robinson 1988, iv, 9) By the mid-1990s there was one surviving glass-works on Wearside, and the once prosperous paper industry there was in similar straits. (Royal Commission 1992, 45) In Cumbria, depletion of iron ore reserves and costly dependence on imported ore saw the run-down of British Steel's Workington plant. By 1981 it was a relatively unimportant installation, confined to modest production of steel rails. The Backbarrow Iron Works at Newby Bridge closed in 1967. The major Hodbarrow iron-mine at Millom survived until 1968, when its closure saw local unemployment exceed 50 per cent. (Bennett 1993, 30, 37) In 1929 almost half of all employment in west Cumberland was in mining and quarrying; the figure was 18.6 per cent in 1946 and 8.8 per cent in 1966.

There was some compensation in new or extended enterprises. Although many firms established on industrial estates experienced only a transitory existence, some fared better. Survivors generally enjoyed some kind of local

394

Figure 21.1 The Thorp reprocessing plant for nuclear fuel, the most recent development on the extensive Sellafield nuclear site in West Cumbria.

advantage. In Cumbria, abundant water supply encouraged paper-making, chemicals, textiles, pharmaceuticals (in Furness), leather and pulp boards. Barrow remained dependent upon naval construction. A wartime munitions factory at Sellafield was chosen in 1947 as an 'Atomic Factory', producing fissile material for Britain's nuclear defence policy. Successive crises in international oil supplies encouraged investment in nuclear power. In 1993, at Sellafield, British Nuclear Fuels Limited directly employed 8,234 people in reprocessing nuclear fuel, waste management and the Calder Hall Magnox power station. This level of dependence represented renewed local reliance upon a single industry.

There was a shift of employment into the service sector. By 1971, there were 210,000 jobs of this kind on Tyneside, representing 53 per cent of all employment. About 80,000 of these were now in the public sector, including education, social administration, health services and public administration. In the late 1980s, the major social services complex at Longbenton, in suburban Newcastle, provided *c.*8,000 jobs. In 1978, the service sector provided 59 per cent of all Tyneside employment, 63 per cent in 1981. In west

Cumberland, the service sector expanded from 27 per cent of employment in 1929 to 43.6 per cent in 1966. (Robinson 1988, 18, 41; Whitfield 1975, 106)

Government measures other than those specifically regional in intent also affected the North. Coal, railways, electricity and gas were all nationalized. The steel industry suffered particularly from political uncertainties, being twice nationalized and denationalized. The role of the state became much more pervasive in other ways too, including a greater involvement in welfare and continuance of high levels of taxation on both individuals and corporations. Reorganization of local government in 1974, designed to improve efficiency, was at best a mixed blessing to the northern counties. Cumberland and Westmorland, with Furness and a small annexation from the West Riding, were joined in Cumbria. In the east, creation of the counties of Tyne and Wear and Cleveland involved loss of territory and revenue to Northumberland and Durham. Subsequent tinkering brought abolition of these new elements, without restoring control of those areas to the old North Eastern counties.

Results of Regional Policies

At first it seemed that government regional policies were achieving their objectives. In 1946, unemployment figures for the four northern counties were about three times the 2.4 per cent overall level of Great Britain. By 1958 the differential had shrunk – 2.1 per cent nationally and 2.3 per cent for the North East – and it was easy to believe that this convergence would continue.

West Cumberland was thought a successful test case for regional policy. In the five years after the war, the principal architect of this policy here, Jack Adams, succeeded in attracting more private capital into west Cumberland than had been seen in the previous fifty years. In retrospect, this was seen by Harold Wilson, when President of the Board of Trade, as a particularly glowing example of Labour's industrial policy. This was scarcely fair, as there was considerable consensus between parties on regional policy, and Adams also worked in close co-operation with Conservative governments. Even Wilson saw him as a 'pragmatic socialist' rather than an ideologue of more rigorous style. Adams had entered public life as a keen Labour activist, responsible for a notable local victory in 1919, when Labour took all nine seats on the Alecdon and Frizington Urban District Council. This launched him into political activity on a wider scale, but in later life he found himself working for the benefit of the region in reasonable harmony with local leaders of landed and industrial wealth whom he had strenuously opposed in earlier years. His acceptance of a peerage in 1948 (the first created in Cumbria for over 150 years) was part of a remarkable personal odyssey. It was not without parallels elsewhere in the northern counties, among them examples from trade unions, including the miners.

At the time of Adams' death in 1960, west Cumberland was as close to full employment as it was ever to be in post-war years. (Holmes 1983) Amongst the private-sector successes was creation and development of Marchon Chemicals at Whitehaven, exploiting deposits of anhydrite for manufacture of sulphuric acid, needed by the expanding detergents industry. Smaller-scale developments saw factories developed for textiles, footwear and some branches of engineering.

Any complacency on regional policies was soon checked as regional unemployment figures began to drift apart again. From the 1960s, the North's particular problem was the continued decline of major industries. Shipbuilding suffered from overseas competition and consequent unemployment. By 1961, 10 per cent of the work force was out of work, and this key industry continued to shrink as orders went elsewhere. At the beginning of the twentieth century, British shipyards had built 55 per cent of the world's new tonnage; in 1960 the figure was only 15 per cent and continued to drop. Northern yards did not even hold their share of the shrunken British total, despite some success stories, including the SD14 design from Austin & Pickersgill's Sunderland yard, which won 100 orders in the years after 1966. Shipbuilding expansion overseas would in any event have posed problems for British yards; the catastrophic scale of decline reflected failures by both management and labour. (Royal Commission 1992, 45; Roberts 1967)

To provide enduring replacements for lost employment was an intractable problem. The years 1978–81 were bad ones for the northern economy. Tyneside lost 11 per cent of total employment, and 6 per cent in 1981–84. Severe losses continued in manufacturing and mining sectors. Shipbuilding employment on Tyneside dropped from 16,000 in 1984 to *c*.4,000 in 1987; further falls followed and the loss of a key government order in 1993 saw pay-offs at Swan Hunters on the Tyne, followed by closure.

In January 1988, Tyneside's official unemployment rate was 15.4 per cent, as against a national figure of 9.6 per cent. Local variations continued. In a depressed area of west Newcastle, the unemployment rate was 39.4 per cent in April 1987; in northern suburbs Gosforth's rate was 7 per cent. (Robinson 1988, 2, 22, 25, 78)

In post-war years, governments, both Labour and Conservative, resorted to shifting and piecemeal measures to combat such trends, and achieved only limited success. As late as the 1970s it was common to find northern economic problems seen officially as temporary aberrations of a mainly cyclical nature. Both central and local authorities have been criticized for shortcomings in responses to economic and social problems. 'The experience of public policy intervention in the local economy over a long period . . . demonstrated its usefulness, but also its limitations, ameliorating conditions but not solving fundamental problems.' At its peak in 1975–76, the Rate Support Grant from national funds met two-thirds of local government expenditure in the region, but the administration of national regional policy was not always competent or consistent. (Townsend 1983, 16; Hudson 1989, 101–2, 211–330)

In the years after 1945, an unholy alliance of mining unions, National Coal Board, local authorities and central government frustrated schemes to diversify the industrial base of the coalfields. A County Durham Planning Officer's paper of March 1947 emphasized that 'Competitive industries must not be encouraged in mining areas to such an extent as to create a shortage of male labour in the mines.' The county council refused to attract alternative industries to the new town of Peterlee, persisting in viewing the project as a dormitory area for miners. (Robinson 1988, 3, 89; Hudson 1989, 133–4, 221–5)

The old depressed regions, while sharing the general improvement in the British standard of living, lagged behind prosperous regions in income and employment. Where industries saw significant technological improvement, as in the Teesside chemical industry, this often entailed a reduced work force. In 1968, the Tyneside electrical engineering firm of Reyrolles Parsons employed 22,000 workers, but by 1977, with deteriorating markets at home and abroad for heavy electrical equipment, this dropped markedly and the firm was forced into defensive amalgamation with Clarke Chapman to form NEI Parsons. At Carlisle, the engineering works of Cowan and Sheldon closed down and the site was cleared in the late 1980s. At Penrith, the Stalker engineering works ceased production in 1962. Near Keswick, the Lake District's biggest lead-mine, Greenside, closed in 1962. The Honister slate-mine closed in 1985. (Bennett 1993, 4, 8)

Enterprises attracted to northern counties by direct or indirect subsidies from public funds could prove frail in a more adverse economic climate. One of Tyneside's technically advanced plants, Churchill at Blaydon, closed in 1986 as part of its parent company Tube Investment's retrenchment programme, involving concentration on its Coventry base. The Burton clothing factories at Sunderland and Gateshead, the Plessey telecommunications works at Sunderland and the GEC plant at Hartlepool were other examples here. (Robinson 1988, 32; Townsend 1983, 102)

More exotic enterprises did something to compensate for these losses. Availability of a flexible and skilled work force, together with official inducements and access to the wider market of the European Economic Community, encouraged Japanese manufacturers to set up factories. The first car from the Nissan plant at Washington was completed in 1986, two years after the firm's arrival in County Durham. Within nine years, Nissan invested £926 million in the North East. In addition to 6,000 Nissan jobs at Washington, suppliers employed another 2,000 within the region by the end of 1993. Durham-built cars were sold in 29 countries and component-suppliers found that their skills need not be confined to this major company. The Newcastle-based Ikeda Technology took on the role of car-seat design for the whole Nissan empire. The French-owned Sommer Allibert Industrie (UK) invested £6 million in a new plant near the main Nissan Washington base to supply components for Nissan cars, delivered to the assembly line within 42 minutes of receipt of a computerized order. A few miles away, at Birtley, Komatsu manufactures earth-moving machinery, and uses local suppliers whenever possible; this connection enabled Cascade Engineering at Cramlington in Northumberland to increase output and expand its own technological base. Since 1985, Far Eastern investment has brought £2 billion investment and 17,000 new jobs to the North East. Although an over-dependence on these ventures might not be healthy, their scale played a part in regenerating the region's industrial base. A national newspaper noted part of this response: 'The region is no longer content simply to supply the Japanese . . . It is looking to sell to the Japanese in Japan.' (*Daily Telegraph*, 3/11/1993)

High technology has established a strong foothold within the region. Most of the 4,000 new jobs at the recently created Newcastle Business Park are based on information technology projects. On Team Valley, near Gateshead, Quality Software Products produces accounting software for customers, including the Bank of England and the Stock Exchange. Integrated Micro Products is another company of this kind to develop within the region; c.90 per cent of its output is exported to the USA. British Airways considered thirteen other possible sites for its £36 million installation computing flight paths, including those for Concorde, before settling on Newcastle Business Park. Grant aid here may have been as high as £5 million. The fiscal advantages derived from designation as Enterprise Zones helped centres like Newcastle, Gateshead and Sunderland to attract new sources of income and employment. Inducements have included rate 'holidays', and up to 100 per cent capital allowances against building costs. Assisted Area grants have offered up to £10,000 for each job created, local authorities have offered additional subsidies and more has come from the Regional Fund of the European Community. Time alone will tell how far such expedients can effect long-term growth, but early signs have been encouraging. The turnover at Newcastle International Airport tripled between 1988 and 1993, while profits quadrupled. A Durham University study of 155 companies in the North East painted a picture of high productivity coupled with rates of absenteeism and strikes appreciably below national averages. (*Daily Telegraph*, 17/11/1993)

Although less than 10 per cent of the work force in the Tyne/Wear district are employed in finance and business, compared with more than 12 per cent nationally, there has also been growth here. At Sunderland, The Insurance Service, a direct selling offshoot of Royal Insurance, is spending

£3 million (nearly one-third of it supplied by grants from local and central government) on offices which will employ 350 when completed. Sunderland obtained this investment in competition with Peterborough, Birmingham and Liverpool, because its package of grants, salary levels and rental costs proved the most attractive. At Newcastle Business Park, the Automobile Association's Insurance and Financial Services headquarters employs 1,200, mostly women. Economic changes in post-war decades have involved continuing decline in regional autonomy and distinctiveness, little affected by self-conscious attempts to perpetuate or recover elements in regional popular culture, such as the artificial 'Geordie cult' of the North East. Where efforts have been made to reverse this trend, they have usually been short-lived or failures, as in the case of the Northern Economic Development Council of the 1960s and the later botched attempt to increase the amount of local official expenditure met from local sources in the so-called 'poll tax' episode.

Post-War Social Improvement

The concentration on problems of the northern economy, as in inter-war years, reflects the preoccupations of much contemporary source material. However, in these years the northern counties supported a population which was generally enjoying a much higher standard of living than ever before. Regional disparities remained, but not all to the disadvantage of the northern counties. High taxation imposed to meet war expenditure provided opportunities later for maintaining higher levels of spending for social purposes than earlier generations would have tolerated. There were many wartime expressions of a determination that post-war society would inhabit a more just and wholesome environment. Medical discoveries during the war could be used after 1945 to combat some killer diseases of earlier years. Better techniques of preventive medicine and radically improved drugs contributed to virtual elimination in post-war years of such old scourges as scarlet fever and diphtheria, while the toll of others, including tuberculosis, was reduced to relatively tiny proportions. In 1938, there had been 100 deaths of children under 15 from tuberculosis on Tyneside; there were 85 in 1947, 18 in 1951, four in 1954. The 1938 figure already represented improvement on earlier figures, but the scale of the post-1945 achievement was striking. (Miller 1960, 112; Pybus Society 1993, 317–56)

In housing, peace allowed renewed progress, despite shortages of materials and other problems. Even a small local authority such as Castle Ward in Northumberland built 1,000 houses in the decade after 1945, at a cost of £1.5 million. Between 1945 and 1957, more than 40,000 new houses were built on Teesside. Much pre-1914 housing was modernized during the 1970s. In the early 1950s, some 400 miles of main cables were installed in Northumberland, bringing electricity to many rural homes for the first time. (House and Fullerton 1960, 418; Pawson 1961, 37)

Some improvements were not unmixed gain. Rapid movement of large numbers of families from overcrowded but well-established and intimate communities in slum areas brought new problems. The creation of peripheral housing estates in towns meant that social, retail and recreational facilities became more distant from homes and more expensive to reach, though this could be mitigated by improvements in public and private transport and creation of suburban shopping and community centres. Large new housing estates did not find it easy to reproduce the closeness of neighbourly communities of the older urban areas. Victorian Britain was not the classical period of urban sprawl into rural areas, and in the early twentieth century northern townspeople were not normally more than a short distance from open country. The unprecedented urban extension since 1945 has made this much less the case. It is, though, easy to exaggerate the appetite of urban populations for rural tranquillity.

The early and mid twentieth century saw a continuing decline in rural population, but now without spectacular urban expansion. No doubt decline in farm labour and rural industries played a part here, but so did social and cultural attractions missing from rural contexts before car ownership spread widely. Between 1951 and 1961 the population of North Westmorland Rural District fell by 8.3 per cent. Cumbrian employment in agriculture fell from 12,726 to 6,767 between 1951 and 1971. This trend, which affected all four northern counties, brought such blows to village communities as closure of local schools, shops, or village halls. (Capstick 1970, 4–6, 41; Structure Cumbria 1976)

The role played by the railway network declined in post-war years. This was more than compensated by increases in road transport. Like rural electrification, new roads helped to break down isolation of remote districts. Increased road freight deliveries were accompanied by acceleration in the increase of private car ownership. This reached a point where many rural bus services ceased to be viable, so that for some of those without private transport mobility actually deteriorated during the later twentieth century. The decline in less profitable railway lines began soon after the coming of peace. On the former Border Counties Railway, passenger services between Riccarton Junction and Hexham ended in October 1956, the line closed for goods traffic two years later and the nationalized railway corporation was quick to remove the track before the end of 1960. The Haltwhistle to Alston line was closed in 1976. (Slade 1975; Bennett 1993, 12)

Although social inequalities had not been eliminated, they were reduced. At mid-century a peer, the Rt Hon. John James Lawson, Baron Lawson of Beamish, was Lord Lieutenant of the County Palatine of Durham, but he had been a miner before winning a parliamentary seat for Labour. Among his deputy lieutenants in 1950 were the marquis of Londonderry, the earl of Scarbrough, and Viscount Gort. There was generally a significant increase in female employment. On Tyneside, women, who had provided *c.*20 per cent of the work force in the 1920s, occupied *c.*45 per cent of all jobs in the 1980s. The success of clothing firms like JJ Fashions and Barbour made significant contributions here. (Luxmoore 1952, 220–1; Robinson 1988, 12, 37)

Overall, improvements in social conditions effected after 1945 were substantial. Prosaic statistics from successive censuses illustrate material advances. In 1931, the proportion of households in County Durham living at a density of more than two persons per room was 13.1 per cent, and these included more than one-fifth of the population. By 1951, the figure was 3 per cent, down to one-twentieth of the population; in the same year 11 per cent of Durham households lived at a density of more than 1.5 per room, but by 1961 that had dropped to 4.9 per cent. The years 1951–61 saw an increase in dwellings of 34 per cent for Newcastle, 72 per cent in Gosforth, 57 per cent in Longbenton, 45 per cent in Whitley Bay and 45 per cent in Castle Ward Rural District on Newcastle's periphery. Much of these increases represented new suburban housing. By the 1961 census, 96.5 per cent of Durham households had their own internal cold-water supply, 78.5 per cent had a hot-water system, 72.8 per cent had a fixed bath and 92 per cent their own WC. Neighbouring counties were close to these figures. This does not indicate perfection, but higher levels of comfort than ever before.

Not everyone would agree that extension of material well-being had been paralleled by the spread of civilized values but, despite some conflicting currents, this was generally the case. There remained elements of violence, vice and crime, but that was nothing new. There was decline in support of organized religion, which came to affect a smaller proportion of the population. A study of Methodism in Cumbria concludes that despite amalgamations between different sects

> The present century has seen the decline of Cumbrian Methodism because of economic depression and emigration. The Connexions lost their dynamism and remained in their chapels with dwindling congregations instead of evangelizing as they had once had to do . . . (Burgess 1981, 149–50)

In the late 1980s, only *c.*7–9 per cent of the Tyneside population regularly attended divine service, though 83 per cent claimed denominational allegiance when filling in forms. (Robinson 1988, 195)

The spread of car ownership, like cycling in the 1890s, increased the use of Sundays for recreation rather than church-going. A greater variety of secular sources of recreation and entertainment reduced the appeal of social activities of churches and temperance organizations. Nevertheless, a diffuse Christianity continued to exercise some influence on wide reaches of society. A clear majority continued to resort to church or chapel to sanctify birth, marriage and death, despite their absence from regular worship.

Temperance organizations failed to hold their mass following for a number of reasons. Inhabitants of the northern counties continued to consume large quantities of drink, even if intake of spirits remained below the national average. Increased purchasing power meant that modest indulgence was less of a pressing danger to family life. Brutish drunkenness was still to be found, but less commonly than in the past. In 1947, there were 477 convictions for drunkenness in Newcastle, a figure which would have astonished a late Victorian Chief Constable by its moderation. (Elliston Allen 1968, 173; Spence 1954, 22)

As in previous years, political activity was not something which preoccupied most people. In terms of parliamentary elections, the northern counties came to provide the Labour Party with important support, but there was always a significant minority which thought differently. In Cumbria, the west-coast industrial belt has been a Labour stronghold, while the rural eastern and central districts evince equal polarization towards Conservatism. In some constituencies, as for example Durham's Houghton-le-Spring seat, Labour held an impressively dominant position, but this was far from universal. Tynemouth (with many voters in North Shields) retained Conservative allegiance after an isolated Labour victory in 1945. Stockton and South Shields returned Labour MPs from 1945 onwards, but there was always a substantial minority vote. Gateshead, Sunderland and most Newcastle constituencies exhibited divided loyalties. It remained impossible to relate political activism and electoral allegiances to the social status of electors in any simple way.

Some murky aspects remained, in northern counties as elsewhere. Two of the region's biggest local authorities, County Durham and Newcastle, were involved in revelations of widespread malpractices in the 1960s and early 1970s. At their heart was a web of corrupt practices involving the Labour leader of the city's council, T. Dan Smith, and a prominent architect, John Poulson, which extended widely within the region and elsewhere. Both men went to prison when the storm broke in the early 1970s, as did Andrew Cunningham, a Labour leader on Durham County Council. (Gillard and Tomkinson 1980; Fitzwalter and Taylor 1981; Potts 1994)

Prostitution was by no means dead, and may well have been encouraged by the dislocations of the war years. A report of 1944 noted that 'the women who are promiscuous or who have become prostitutes appear to form the habit very early, even as young as 16 years'. In 1953, Newcastle clinics reported 2,587 new cases of venereal disease. This persistence, despite improved medical techniques, was attributed variously to increased promiscuity or continued inhibitions in sexual matters. Conceivably it reflected both. (Anon. 1944, 7; Newcastle Hospital 1953, 21; Pybus Club 1993, 333–41)

Worries about vandalism became increasingly vocal. Some older people felt that younger contemporaries rejected social discipline. The growing display of 'youth culture' reflected the evolution of an unprecedented range of separate tastes and interests, in which northern counties took a leading role. An official report from Newcastle in 1955 noted that 'Young people seem able, through the various social techniques and therapies at their disposal, to create for themselves a society which is colourful, healthy, satisfying and harmless but lacks much contact or concern with some of the traditional virtues and values, particularly those which are roughly called "spiritual".' (Elliston Allen 1968, 42; Anon. 1955, 8)

Yet if there were worries, on balance the improvements of the post-war years outweighed any disadvantages. By 1981, there had been great progress in diminishing the region's housing problems. In terms of over crowding and poor-quality housing, Tyneside was at least up to the national average. Some mistakes were made, but the worst examples generally had short lives. At Newcastle, the unsatisfactory Noble Street flats of 1958 were demolished by 1977. This progress was particularly fortunate, in view of the steep fall in central government housing grants during the 1980s. (Robinson 1988, 123–9)

The North shared in national health improvement. Infant mortality in Newcastle had been 80 per 1,000 in 1933–35, but it was down to 8.8 per 1,000 in 1983–85. In 1930, 102 Tyneside children died of infectious diseases, only four in 1986. In 1930, 67 Tyneside women died in childbirth, only one in 1986. There were 822 TB deaths on Tyneside in 1930, 13 in 1986. In 1930, two-thirds of all Tyneside deaths were of those under 65; in 1986 this proportion was under one-quarter. (Robinson 1988, 159–84)

Educational provision expanded, both in schools and higher education, although overall the northern counties remained relatively low in national tables of children who received more than the statutory minimum of schooling. At Gateshead the proportion of children entering grammar schools was raised from 8 per cent to 40 per cent by the building of three new schools in post-war years. Over much of the region, the size of school classes was appreciably below, and spending per pupil appreciably above, the national average. (Robinson 1988, 87, 90)

Retail services grew more extensive and more sophisticated. In the late 1980s, Tyneside had c.3,000 shops, with 40 of them employing more than 100. When Newcastle's central Eldon Square shopping precinct opened in the 1970s it was the largest of its kind in Europe. Similarly Gateshead's out-of-town Metro Centre was the biggest of its kind in Europe when it opened in the following decade. (Robinson 1988, iv)

Leisure and Recreation

Facilities for recreation and entertainment saw striking growth. The availability of wireless and cinema was supplemented by television. The growth and increasing quality of working men's clubs continued. Hazlerigg and District Victory Social Club spent £16,000 on a new concert room in 1955, and then £2,000 on an Alpine Lounge in 1960. A further £8,000 provided the Beachcomber Lounge in 1967. These were not unusual ventures. Three half-yearly accounts of the early 1980s from the principal Tynemouth club, not among the biggest clubs, show takings of £15,014, £15,855 and £16,140 from gaming machines, which just about met the salary bill. In 1983, sale of 'refreshments' brought in £253,282. In the late 1980s Tyneside retained its record for significantly above average consumption of alcohol. (Robinson 1988, 45)

The extension of holidays, and then of holidays abroad, were additional indicators of higher standards of recreation and opportunity, as was the continuing spread of car ownership, even if it remained lower than in more prosperous regions. No doubt such gains cannot be simply equated with an increase in happiness, a commodity notoriously difficult to measure, but there was an increase in opportunities for happiness, in so far as these were governed by factors such as health, income, material comfort, leisure, recreation, tolerance and availability of help and support from communal resources.

Continuance of Discontent

These gains did not satisfy everybody. Many of the minority of political activists who had campaigned persistently for social improvement believed that the changes had not gone as far or as fast as they should have done, but there was more to it than that. Some radical reformers had believed or simply assumed that better material conditions were not only desirable for their own sake, but would lead to a different society, marked by cultural, intellectual, moral and ideological changes of a fundamental kind. Arthur Barton's Uncle Jim (see p. 338 above) lived to see the alleviation of the poverty and its consequences against which he had fought in earlier years. His reactions were described in an account of 1967:

> Well, he saw it come – most of it anyway, for he lived until the other day. He saw slums wiped out, churches diminished, council houses

405

> multiplied ... And he puzzled over the emptiness of heart and mind that a security beyond his modest hopes has brought ... He turned back to his pile of penny poets and his 1920 *Clarions*, an old fighter whose victory had turned sour, a rebel without a cause.
>
> 'What went wrong, hinny', he asked. (Barton 1967, 130–1)

The verdict was harsh, though perhaps understandable. Those who struggled against poverty, suffering and inequality were buoyed up by the belief that such changes would lead to the creation of a virtuous and unselfish society. This was an attractive vision, but scarcely realistic. For example, the belief that greater leisure, coupled with readier access to rural areas, would naturally inculcate a love and care for the environment, was never completely vindicated. Although the ruined castle at Mitford suffered damage when the site was used for military training during the 1939–45 war, it subsequently suffered more from picnickers and other visitors, who desecrated graves, threw tombstones into the quarry in the area of the old bailey, knocked down any loose stonework and stole the commemorative bronze plate fixed to the keep by the Ministry of Works. (Honeyman 1955, 33)

It is possible to take a more favourable view of the state of society in the northern counties in the later twentieth century if it is compared, not with a utopian dream, but with the realities of any earlier period. A more favourable notice would have to take account of conflicting factors, for the continued existence of brutality, cruelty, vandalism, vice and crime could not be denied. Yet the life expectancy and material prosperity experienced by the overwhelming majority of the region's inhabitants was higher than ever before. This was important in itself, but there was more to it. A society which had in general grown richer devoted part of this increased wealth to provision of more complex and sophisticated resources of social improvement. This represented significant advance on provisions of earlier years, and acceptance of an unprecedented level of public responsibility in dealing with wide ranges of social problems.

Soon after Victoria ascended the throne, Macaulay began to write his *History of England*. In its third chapter he accurately prophesied that the twentieth century would see unprecedented improvements in standards of living, health and life expectancy, noting,

> that numerous comforts and luxuries which are now unknown, or confined to a few, may be within the reach of every diligent and thrifty person. And yet it may then be the mode to assert that the increase of wealth and the progress of science have benefitted the few at the expense of the many.

Epilogue

It is probable that the pace of change in human affairs has been accelerating throughout the development of human society. During the millennium covered in this book, there can be no doubt that this was the case.

In AD 1000 our region was thinly populated and living at a comparatively primitive level. The organization of society in its political, economic and social aspects was simple in comparison with what was to come, even if perhaps already more sophisticated than in earlier periods. In AD 1000, establishment of the English kingdom was still incomplete, its frontiers insecure and consolidation uncertain. Even if the great period of Viking raiding was past, it still seemed possible that England would become a dependency of a Scandinavian-based empire. The experience of the northern counties of England was in future centuries to be much intertwined with that of the kingdom of the Scots, itself undergoing a comparable period of consolidation in the early part of our period. Until the Union of the Crowns in 1603, English relations with Scotland were to have a decisive influence on the four northern counties. The repeated destructive effects of border warfare played a part in retarding development of the English North, as indeed in Scottish border counties too.

The ending of the military frontier in 1603 was an abrupt change, producing acceleration in the pace of economic, social and political development. The population and its social organization, still primarily based on agriculture, was no longer shaped by the needs of defence, and this facilitated improvements in farming. By the early nineteenth century, peaceful evolution had provided a base capable of exploiting the remarkable opportunities offered to the region in the great age of Steam, Iron and Coal. In a few generations, the northern counties switched from being a relatively unimportant and remote frontier region to one of the main powerhouses of technological development and a leading agent in the making of the modern world. During the 1850–1914 period, the northern counties exercised unprecedented influence. A tenfold increase in international exchange owed much to the coal, the shipbuilding and the engineering enterprises of our region. As with

407

comparable regions elsewhere, the North of England experienced a prodigious and unforeseeable growth in population but contrived to absorb this crucial change within a framework of peaceful social and political evolution. Although firmly part of the kingdom, the North controlled much of its regional economy and continued to exhibit identifiable regional characteristics, even though these elements were declining by 1900.

The cataclysmic impact of the First World War, and a variety of other changing circumstances, meant that the primacy of regions like the four northern counties could not be maintained. During the inter-war and post-war years, old staple industries faced increasing problems, leading to the traumatic experiences of depression and mass unemployment, even if these were experienced against a background of generally improving social conditions. A variety of differing developments, including growth of the apparatus of the nation state, a more centralized economy, and the increasingly national standardization and organization of sport and recreation, accelerated a decline in regional distinctiveness and autonomy to an extent which in the later twentieth century provoked romantic and rather feeble attempts to shore up an artificial regional identity.

The region's evolution since AD 1000 has been complex, with some setbacks and conflicting trends, but overall its development has been a remarkable historical achievement. Not only has there been an enormous increase in population, but despite this the condition of the people has improved to a degree which would have astonished every century before our own.

For most of the period covered here, life has been experienced for most people on a distinctly local level. While it would be easy to underestimate the extent to which most people are still much concerned with their own immediate and local concerns, there has been a great change here. Not only have the northern counties become much more closely integrated with the rest of Britain, but that more integrated Britain is now more closely linked to the rest of the world than ever before. This process has involved a major shift in patterns of organization. In AD 1000, and for many years afterwards, the great majority of people depended upon their families and neighbours for mutual support – essentially upon those whom they knew and with whom they lived in small locally orientated communities. Especially in more recent times, this pattern has been supplanted, or perhaps to some degree only complemented, by an increasingly intricate network of different forms of interdependence which link people who do not know each other. The complex networks of services whereby contemporary society is fed, clothed, transported, entertained, for instance, vividly illustrate this crucial change. If this development has been largely concentrated in the rapid changes

---

Figure 22.1 Photograph by Herbert Bell of part of Ambleside in the 1890s, showing the mock-vernacular architecture common in nineteenth-century Lakeland, with a booking office for scenic coach trips indicating the increasingly important role of tourism and the hotel trade.

of the last two centuries, the foundations for it were laid during slower evolution in earlier years. It is not possible to cite a time at which this process began, though it may be feasible to point to contexts in which the rate of change was quickened or in some cases slowed. (McCord 1995)

In the space of a few generations, increases in population, the development of a more sophisticated and interlocking economy, and expansion of the role of the state, produced a more complex and diverse, and at the same time much more interdependent, society than that of earlier years. Even if the balance of the historical record has not always been correct, and things which have gone awry figure more prominently in it than things which have gone well, the diligent student of the region's past will find it impossible to fix upon any earlier period in which the condition of the people appears more attractive than that of the later twentieth century. Despite setbacks and fluctuations, the overall tendency of the past millennium has been one of progress and achievement rather than discord and deterioration.

Bibliography

Abbreviations

AA   *Archaeologia Aeliana*. AA3, AA4, AA5 = 3rd, 4th, 5th Series
CW   *Transactions of the Cumberland and Westmorland Antiquarian and Archaeological Society*. CW2 = New Series
NH   *Northern History*

Aird 1992. W. M. Aird, 'The Making of a Medieval Miracle Collection: The *Liber de Translationibus et Miraculis Sancti Cuthberti*', NH, XXVIII, 1992.
Airey 1979. A. and J. Airey, *The Bainbridges of Newcastle: A Family History, 1679–1976*, 1979.
Alexander and Roberts 1978. M. J. Alexander and B. K. Roberts, 'The Deserted Village of Low Buston, Northumberland: A Study in Soil Phosphate Analysis', AA5, VI, 1978.
Alfrey 1980–81. J. Alfrey, *A Social History of Housing in the Lanes, Carlisle, in the 19th Century*, Carlisle Archaeological Unit, 1980–81.
Allen 1971. E. Allen *et al.*, *The North-East Engineers' Strikes of 1871*, 1971.
Anon. 1644. Anon., *A True Relation of the Happy Success of His Majestie's Forces in Scotland under the Command of Lord James, Marquis of Montrose*, Jackson Collection, Carlisle Central Library.
Anon. 1854. Anon., *Report of the Commissioners Appointed to Inquire into the . . . Outbreak of Cholera in the Towns of Newcastle upon Tyne, Gateshead and Tynemouth*, 1854.
Anon. 1862. Anon., *Accident at New Hartley Colliery*, 1862.
Anon. 1884. Anon., *The Royal Visit to Newcastle upon Tyne*, 1884.
Anon. 1886. Anon., *Notes on the Leading Industries of the River Tyne*, 1886.
Anon. *c*.1894. Anon., *A Descriptive Account of Newcastle*, Newcastle, *c*.1894.
Anon. 1894–97. Anon., *The Northern Temperance Year Book*, 1894–97.
Anon. 1908. Anon., *Newcastle upon Tyne Police-Aided Association for the Clothing of Destitute Children*, 1908.
Anon. 1912. Anon., *Jubilee History and Handbook: Wallsend Industrial Co-operative Society*, 1912.
Anon. 1913. Anon., *A Romance of Regeneration*, 1913.
Anon. 1917. Anon., *Report of the Proceedings of the Business Jubilee of Alderman G. B. Bainbridge, JP*, 1917.

411

Anon. 1924. Anon., *Centenary of Ferguson Brothers*, Carlisle 1924.

Anon. 1929. Anon., *Dame Allan's School, Newcastle upon Tyne, 1705–1929*, 1929.

Anon. 1935. Anon., *The Cleveland Bridge and Engineering Company Ltd.*, n.d. but *c.*1935.

Anon. 1939. Anon., *The Jubilee of County Councils – Cumberland 1889–1939*, 1939.

Anon. 1940. Anon., *Durham County Police*, 1940.

Anon. 1946. Anon., *Hartlepool Gas and Water Company: 100 Years of Progress, 1846–1946*, n.d., *c.*1946.

Anon. 1949. Anon., *The County Borough of Tynemouth*, 1949.

Anon. 1944. Anon., *The Social Background of Venereal Disease*, 1944.

Anon. 1955. Anon., *Report by HM Inspectors on the Rye Hill Youth Club*, 1955.

Anon. 1956. Anon., *The Story of the Thermal Syndicate*, n.d., *c.*1956.

Anon. 1957. Anon., *Northumberland County Constabulary, 1857–1957*, n.d., *c.*1957.

Anon. 1961. Anon., *Newcastle upon Tyne Permanent Building Society, 1861–1961*, 1961.

Anon. 1969. Anon., *A Brief History of the County Borough of Tynemouth Police*, n.d., *c.*1969.

Anon. 1979. Anon., *Victor, The First Fifty Years*, Wallsend n.d. but *c.*1979.

Anon. 1985. Anon., *Railways of Sunderland*, Tyne and Wear Museums Service, 1985.

Apperley 1924. N. W. Apperley, *North Country Hunting Half a Century Ago*, 1924.

Appleby 1975. A. B. Appleby, 'Agrarian Capitalism or Seigneurial Reaction? The North-West of England, 1500–1700', *American Historical Review*, 1975.

Appleby 1978. A. B. Appleby, *Famine in Tudor and Stuart England*, Liverpool 1978.

Armitt 1908. M. L. Armitt, 'Fullers and Freeholders of the Parish of Grasmere', CW2, VIII, 1908.

Armstrong 1883. H. E. Armstrong, *Report on the Recently Increased Death Rate of the City*, Newcastle 1883.

Armstrong 1895. H. E. Armstrong, *Report on the Milk Supply*, Newcastle 1895.

Armstrong 1898. H. E. Armstrong, *Report of the MOH on the Manufacture of Ice Creams*, Newcastle 1898.

Arvanigian 1996. M. E. Arvanigian, 'Free Rents in the Palatinate of Durham, and the Crisis of the late 1430s', *AA5*, XXIV, 1996.

Ashington Coal Company 1946. Ashington Coal Company, sales brochure, March 1935.

Ashton 1991. O. R. Ashton, *W. E. Adams: Chartist Radical and Journalist*, Newcastle 1991.

Ashton and Sykes 1929. T. S. Ashton and J. Sykes, *The Coal Industry of the Eighteenth Century*, 1929.

Ashworth 1975. W. Ashworth, *A Short History of the International Economy*, 3rd ed., 1975.

Atkinson 1981. M. Atkinson, *Iron Ore Mining in Mainland Britain in the Nineteenth and Early Twentieth Centuries*, Ph.D. Thesis, Essex University, 1981.

Austin 1976. D. Austin, 'Fieldwork and Excavation at Hart, Co. Durham, 1965–1975', *AA5*, IV, 1976.

Bailey 1988. M. R. Bailey, 'The Development of the Locomotive and its Components up to 1836', *Newcomen Bulletin*, 140, April 1988.

Bailey and Culley 1797. J. Bailey and G. Culley, *A General View of the Agriculture of the Counties of Northumberland, Cumberland and Westmorland*, Newcastle 1797.

Bainbridge 1964. J. W. Bainbridge, *A Comparative Study of Two Iron Ore Mining Districts: Cleveland and West Cumberland*, M.Sc. Thesis, Durham University, 1964.

Bainbridge 1939. T. H. Bainbridge, 'Barrow in Furness: A Population Study', *Economic Geography*, Vol. 15, No. 4, 1939.

Bainbridge 1946. T. H. Bainbridge, 'Cumberland Population Movements', *Geographical Journal*, 108, 1946.

Baker 1970. L. G. D. Baker, 'The Desert in the North', *NH*, V, 1970.

Baldwin and Whyte 1985. J. R. Baldwin and I. D. Whyte (eds), *The Scandinavians in Cumbria*, Edinburgh 1985.

Balfour 1892. D. Balfour, *Report on a Scheme of Sewage Disposal for the Town of Alnwick*, 1892.

Bank of England. Newcastle Branch Correspondence, Bank of England Record Office.

Banks, Nichol and Bridge 1994. T. M. Banks, C. Nichol and D. G. Bridge, 'Lead Mines in the Manor of Kinniside', *CW2*, XCIV, 1994.

Bargett 1993. C. Bargett, *The Lonsdale Battalion or XI (Service) Battalion, Border Regiment (Lonsdale)*, 1993.

Barke 1992. M. Barke, 'The Development of Public Transport in Newcastle upon Tyne and Tyneside, 1850–1914', *J. of Regional and Local Studies*, 12, 1, 1992.

Barke and Callcott 1994. M. Barke and M. Callcott, 'Municipal Intervention in Housing: Constraints and Developments in Newcastle upon Tyne 1835–1914', in B. Lancaster (ed.), *Working Class Housing on Tyneside 1850–1939*, Whitley Bay, Bewick Press, 1994.

Barke and Turnbull 1994. M. Barke and G. Turnbull, 'Meadowell and Mythology: The Making of a "Problem Estate"', in B. Lancaster (ed.), *Working Class Housing on Tyneside 1850–1939*, Whitley Bay, Bewick Press, 1994.

Barker 1974. R. Barker, *The Houghton-le-Spring Poor Law Union*, M.Litt. Thesis, Newcastle University, 1974.

Barnes 1981. J. Barnes, *Popular Protest and Radical Politics: Carlisle 1790–1850*, Ph.D. Thesis, Lancaster University, 1981.

Barrow 1965. G. W. S. Barrow, *Robert Bruce and the Community of the Realm of Scotland*, 1965.

Barrow 1966. G. W. S. Barrow, 'The Anglo-Scottish Border', *NH*, I, 1966.

Barrow 1969. G. W. S. Barrow, 'Northern English Society in the Twelfth and Thirteenth Centuries', *NH*, IV, 1969.

Barrow 1973. G. W. S. Barrow, *The Kingdom of the Scots*, 1973.

Barrow 1995. T. Barrow (ed.), *Walks around the Old Grain Ports of Northumberland: Alnmouth, Seahouses and Berwick*, Northumberland County Library, 1995.

Barton 1967. A. Barton, *Two Lamps in our Street*, 1967.

Barton 1969. A. Barton, *The Penny World: A Boyhood Recalled*, 1969.

Batho 1957. G. R. Batho, 'The Percies and Alnwick Castle, 1557–1632', *AA4*, XXXV, 1957.

Bean 1954. J. M. Bean, 'The Percies' Acquisition of Alnwick', *AA4*, XXXII, 1954.

Bean 1957. J. M. W. Bean, 'The Percies and their Estates in Scotland', *AA4*, XXXV, 1957.

Bean 1958. J. M. W. Bean, *The Estates of the Percy Family, 1416–1537*, Oxford 1958.
Bean 1959. J. M. W. Bean, 'Henry IV and the Percies', *History*, New Series, Vol. 44, 1959.
Beard 1978. G. Beard, *The Greater House in Cumbria*, Kendal 1978.
Beard 1925. J. Beard, *Reports on the Sanitary Condition of Carlisle*, 1925.
Beckett 1975. J. V. Beckett, *Landownership in Cumbria*, Ph.D. Thesis, Lancaster University, 1975.
Beckett 1976. J. Beckett, 'Local Custom and "New Taxation" in the Seventeenth and Eighteenth Centuries: The Example of Cumberland', *NH*, XII, 1976.
Beckett 1981. J. Beckett, *Coal and Tobacco*, Cambridge 1981.
Beckett Decline. J. Beckett, 'The Decline of the Small Landowner in 18th and 19th Century England: Some Regional Considerations', *Agric. Hist. Rev.*, 30, 1982.
Beckett 1982. J. Beckett, 'English Landownership in the later 17th and 18th Centuries', *Econ. Hist. Rev.*, 2nd Ser., XXXV, 1982.
Beckett 1983. J. Beckett, 'Absentee Landownership in the Later Seventeenth and Early Eighteenth Centuries: The Case of Cumbria', *NH*, XIX, 1983.
Beckingsale 1969. B. W. Beckingsale, 'The Characteristics of the Tudor North', *NH*, IV, 1969.
Bell 1907. (Lady) F. Bell, *At the Works*, 1907.
Bell 1951. R. Bell, *Twenty-Five Years of the North Eastern Railway*, 1951.
Bell 1971. R. C. Bell, *Tyneside Pottery*, 1971.
Bell and Ollard. H. E. Bell and R. L. Ollard (eds), *Historical Essays 1600–1750 Presented to David Ogg*, 1963.
Bellenger 1982. D. Bellenger, 'The French Exiled Clergy in the North of England', *AA5*, X, 1982.
Bennett 1993. J. and J. Bennett, *A Guide to the Industrial Archaeology of Cumbria*, Assoc. for Industrial Archaeology, 1993.
Bennett, Clavering and Rounding 1990. G. Bennett, E. Clavering and A. Rounding, *A Fighting Trade: Rail Transport in Tyne Coal, 1600–1800*, 1990.
Bennison 1994. B. Bennison, 'Concentration in the Brewing Industry of Northumberland and Durham, 1890–1914', *NH*, XXX, 1994.
Bennison 1995. B. Bennison, 'Not So Common: The Public House in North East England between the Wars', *The Local Historian*, Vol. 25, 1, 1995.
Bennison Brewers 1995. B. Bennison, *Brewers and Bottlers of Newcastle upon Tyne from 1850 to the Present Day*, Newcastle 1995.
Bewick 1975. T. Bewick, *A Memoir Written by Himself*, Oxford 1975.
Binfield 1982. J. C. G. Binfield, 'The Building of a Town Centre Church: St James's Congregational Church, Newcastle upon Tyne', *NH*, XVIII, 1982.
Birley 1958. E. B. Birley, 'John Horsley and John Hodgson', *AA4*, XXXVI, 1958.
Blake 1965. J. R. Blake, 'Medieval Smuggling in the North-East: Some Fourteenth-Century Evidence', *AA4*, XLIII, 1965.
Blake 1967. J. R. Blake, 'The Medieval Coal Trade of North East England: Some Fourteenth Century Evidence', *NH*, II, 1967.
Blanchard 1973. I. S. W. Blanchard, 'Commercial Crisis and Change: Trade and the Industrial Economy of the North-East, 1509–1532', *NH*, VIII, 1973.
Board of Trade 1932. Board of Trade, *An Industrial Survey of the North East Coast Area*, 1932.

Boldon Book 1982. D. Austin (ed.), *Boldon Book*, Chichester 1982.
Bonner 1989. G. Bonner, D. Rollason and C. Stancliffe (eds), *St Cuthbert, his Cult and his Community*, 1989.
Bonsall 1960. B. Bonsall, *Sir James Lowther and Cumberland and Westmorland Elections, 1754–1775*, Manchester 1960.
Borne and Dixon 1978. P. Borne and P. Dixon, 'Halton Castle Reconsidered', *AA5*, VI, 1978.
Bouch 1948. C. M. L. Bouch, *Prelates and People of the Lake Counties*, Kendal 1948.
Bouch and Jones, 1961. C. M. L. Bouch and G. P. Jones, *The Lake Counties, 1500–1830: A Social and Economic History*, Manchester 1961.
Bowen 1970. R. Bowen, *Cricket: A History of its Growth and Development throughout the World*, 1970.
BPP 1868–69. *British Parliamentary Papers*, 1868–69, XIII.
BPP 1882. *British Parliamentary Papers*, 1882, V.
BPP 1895. *British Parliamentary Papers*, 1895, XVII.
Brader 1966. C. Brader, 'Liberty Boys in the Free City: Policing and Public Order in Carlisle 1819–1828', North East Labour History Bulletin No. 30, 1996.
Branson and Heinemann 1971. N. Branson and M. Heinemann, *Britain in the Nineteen Thirties*, 1971.
Brassley 1985. P. W. Brassley, *The Agricultural Economy of Northumberland and Durham in the Period 1640–1750*, 1985.
Brentano 1959. R. Brentano, *York Metropolitan Jurisdiction and Papal Judges Delegate (1270–1296)*, University of California, 1959.
Briggs 1968. A. Briggs, *Victorian Cities*, 1968.
Briggs 1996. A. Briggs, 'Middlesbrough: The Growth of a New Community', in A. J. Pollard (ed.), *Middlesbrough: Town and Community 1830–1950*, Stroud 1996.
Briggs 1989. G. W. D. Briggs, 'The Church of Holy Trinity, Widdrington', *AA5*, XVII, 1989.
Bright 1949. J. Bright, *History of the Northumberland Hussars Yeomanry*, 1949.
Brooks 1980. P. R. B. Brooks, *William Hedley, Locomotive Pioneer*, Newcastle 1980.
Brown 1995. H. D. Brown, 'Colliery Cottages 1830–1915: The Great Northern Coalfield', *AA5*, XXIII, 1995.
Buchan 1955. C. Buchan, *A Lifetime in Football*, 1955.
Building Societies 1906. Building Societies' Association, *Proceedings at Annual Meeting*, Newcastle 1906.
Buller 1882. T. E. Buller, *A Directory of East Cumberland*, 1882.
Bullock 1974. I. Bullock, 'The Origins of Economic Growth on Teesside, 1851–81', *NH*, IX, 1974.
Bulmer 1958. W. Bulmer, with Prof. N. Hodgson, 'The Barber-Surgeons Company of Newcastle upon Tyne', *AA4*, XXXVI, 1958.
Burgess 1979. J. Burgess, 'The Quakers, the Brethren and the Religious Census in Cumbria', *CW2*, LXXIX, 1979.
Burgess 1981. J. Burgess, 'The Growth and Development of Methodism in Cumbria: The Local History of a Denomination from its Inception to the Union of 1932 and After', *NH*, XVII, 1981.
Burgess 1984. J. Burgess, *A Religious History of Cumbria*, Ph.D. Thesis, Sheffield University, 1984.

Burn 1956. W. L. Burn, 'Newcastle upon Tyne in the Early Nineteenth Century', *AA4*, XXXIV, 1956.

Bush 1971. M. L. Bush, 'The Problem of the Far North: A Study of the Crisis of 1537 and its Consequences', *NH*, VI, 1971.

Buss 1974. L. G. Buss, *Some Aspects of Crime and Punishment in Westmorland in the Second Half of the Nineteenth Century*, MA Thesis, Lancaster University, 1974.

Butcher 1978. A. F. Butcher, 'Rent, Population and Economic Change in Late Medieval Newcastle', *NH*, XIV, 1978.

Butler 1869. J. E. Butler, *John Grey of Dilston*, 1869.

Butlin 1967. R. A. Butlin, 'Enclosure and Improvement in Northumberland in the Sixteenth Century', *AA4*, XLV, 1967.

Byrne 1994. D. Byrne, 'T. Dan Smith: The Disastrous Impact of a Liberal, Authoritarian Moderniser', *North East Labour History Bulletin*, No. 28, 1994.

Byrne Housing 1994. D. Byrne, 'Working Class Owner-Occupation and Social Differentiation on Inter-War Tyneside', in B. Lancaster (ed.), *Working Class Housing on Tyneside 1850–1939*, Whitley Bay, Bewick Press, 1994.

Cadman 1976. G. Cadman, *The Administration of the Poor Law Amendment Act, 1834, in the Hexham Poor Law Union*, M.Litt. Thesis, Newcastle University, 1976.

Callcott 1973. M. Callcott, *Parliamentary Elections in County Durham, 1929–35*, M.Litt. Thesis, Newcastle University, 1973.

Callcott 1980. M. Callcott, 'The Nature and Extent of Political Change in the Inter-War Years: The Example of County Durham', *NH*, XVI, 1980.

Callcott 1984. M. Callcott, 'The Challenge of Cholera: The Last Epidemic at Newcastle upon Tyne', *NH*, XX, 1984.

Callcott 1988. M. Callcott, *The Municipal Administration of Newcastle upon Tyne, 1835–1900*, Ph.D. Thesis, Newcastle University, 1988.

Callcott and Challinor 1983. M. Callcott and R. Challinor (eds), *Working Class Politics in North East England*, Newcastle 1983.

Cambridge 1979. E. Cambridge, 'C. C. Hodges and the Nave of Hexham Abbey', *AA5*, VII, 1979.

Campbell 1964. W. A. Campbell, *The Old Tyneside Chemical Trade*, Newcastle 1964.

Campbell 1968. W. A. Campbell, 'The Newcastle Chemical Society and its Illustrious Child', *Chemistry and Industry*, 1968.

Campbell 1969. W. A. Campbell, *A Century of Chemistry on Tyneside*, Newcastle 1969.

Campbell 1980. W. A. Campbell, 'Men of Science in Nineteenth-Century Newcastle', *AA5*, VIII, 1980.

Campbell and Dixon 1970. P. Campbell and P. Dixon, 'Two Fortified Houses in Haltwhistle', *AA4*, XLVIII, 1970.

Capstick 1970. M. Capstick, *Patterns of Rural Development*, Westmorland County Council, Kendal 1970.

Carus Wilson 1838. W. Carus Wilson, *Remarks on Certain Operations of the New Poor Law Respectfully Submitted to the Serious and Candid Consideration of the British Legislature*, Kirkby Lonsdale 1838.

Carver 1974. M. D. H. Carver, 'Excavations in New Elvet, Durham City, 1961–1973', *AA5*, II, 1974.

Chalkin and Havinden 1974. C. W. Chalkin and M. A. Havinden (eds), *Rural Change and Urban Growth, 1500–1800*, 1974.

Challinor 1972. R. Challinor, *Gun-Running from the North East Coast*, Newcastle 1972.

Challinor 1994. R. Challinor, 'T. Dan Smith: The Youthful Revolutionary', *North East Labour History Bulletin*, No. 28, 1994.

Challinor and Ripley 1968. R. Challinor and B. Ripley, *The Miners' Association: A Trade Union in the Age of the Chartists*, 1968.

Charlesworth 1952. D. Charlesworth, 'The Battle of Hexham, 1464', *AA4*, XXX, 1952.

Charlesworth 1953. D. Charlesworth, 'Northumberland in the Early Years of Edward IV', *AA4*, XXXI, 1953.

Charlesworth 1957. D. Charlesworth, 'The Raid on Haydon Bridge, 1587', *AA4*, XXXV, 1957.

Charleton 1889. R. J. Charleton, *A History of Newcastle upon Tyne*, 1889.

Charlton 1941. R. B. Charlton, *A Lifetime with Ponies*, n.d., *c.*1941.

Charlton 1987. B. Charlton, *Upper North Tynedale: A Northumbrian Valley and its People*, Newcastle 1987.

Charlton and Day 1980. D. B. Charlton and J. C. Day, 'Excavation and Field Survey in Upper Redesdale, Part II', *AA5*, VIII, 1980.

Charlton and Day 1982. D. B. Charlton and J. C. Day, 'Excavation and Field Survey in Upper Redesdale: Part IV', *AA5*, X, 1982.

Chase 1994. M. Chase, ' "Dangerous People": The Teesside Irish in the 19th Century', *North East Labour History Bulletin*, No. 28, 1994.

Chronicle 1851. Newcastle Chronicle, *Inquiry into the Condition of the Labouring Poor of Newcastle upon Tyne*, 1851.

Clack and Gosling 1976. P. A. G. Clack and P. F. Gosling, *Archaeology in the North*, HMSO 1976.

Clark 1969. J. W. Clark, 'The Copper Plate of the Goldsmiths Company of Newcastle upon Tyne', *AA4*, XLVII, 1969.

Clarke 1981. E. M. Clarke, *Special Areas Legislation with Reference to West Cumberland*, Ph.D. Thesis, McMaster University, 1981.

Clarke 1966. J. F. Clarke, *Labour Relations in Engineering and Shipbuilding on the North East Coast in the Second Half of the Nineteenth Century*, MA Thesis, Newcastle University 1966.

Clavering 1982. E. Clavering, 'Catholics and the Rise of the Durham Coal Trade', *Northern Catholic History*, 16, 1982.

Clavering and Rounding 1995. E. Clavering and A. Rounding, 'Early Tyneside Industrialism: The Lower Derwent and Blaydon Burn Valleys 1550–1700', *AA5*, XXIII, 1995.

Clay 1950. E. W. Clay, *The Path of the 50th*, 1950.

Cleansing 1911. Institute of Cleansing Superintendents, *Proceedings of 14th Annual Conference*, Newcastle 1911.

Cochrane 1909. A, Cochrane, *The Early History of Elswick*, 1909.

Cockburn 1968. J. S. Cockburn, 'The Northern Assize Circuit', *NH*, III, 1968.

Cole n.d. G. R. Cole, unpublished paper on *The Bridges of Brancepeth*, n.d.

Collingwood Bruce 1889. J. Collingwood Bruce, *Handbook to Newcastle upon Tyne*, Newcastle 1889.

Common 1938. J. Common, *Seven Shifts*, 1938.

Commissioners 1933. *Report to the Minister of Labour by the Commissioners Appointed to Administer Transitional Payments in the County of Durham*, 1933.

Conway Davies 1953. J. Conway Davies, 'Shipping and Trade in Newcastle upon Tyne', *AA4*, XXXI, 1953.

Cook 1961. M. G. Cook, 'The Last Days of the Unreformed Corporation of Newcastle upon Tyne', *AA4*, XXXIX, 1961.

Coombes 1958. L. C. Coombes, 'Lead Mining in East and West Allendale', *AA4*, XXXVI, 1958.

Coombes 1966. L. C. Coombes, 'Wigham of Coanwood', *AA4*, XLIV, 1966.

Coote Hibbert and Wells 1907. J. Coote Hibbert and W. H. Wells, 'A Sketch of the Sanitary History of Newcastle upon Tyne', *J. of R. Sanitary Institute*, XXVIII, 1907.

Corfe 1983. T. Corfe (ed.), *The Buildings of Sunderland, 1814–1914*, 1983.

Craster 1952. Sir E. Craster, 'The Early History of the Craster Family', *AA4*, XXX, 1952.

Craster 1953. Sir E. Craster, 'The Craster Family – Three Generations', *AA4*, XXXI, 1953.

Craster Peers 1953. Sir E. Craster, 'Memoir of Sir Charles Peers', *AA4*, XXXI, 1953.

Craster 1955. Sir E. Craster, 'The Contents of a Northumberland Mansion, 1772', *AA4*, XXXIII, 1955.

Craster 1956. Sir E. Craster, 'Beadnell in the Eighteenth Century', *AA4*, XXXIV, 1956.

Cressy 1978. D. Cressy, 'Social Status and Literacy in North-East England, 1560–1630', *Local Population Studies*, 21, 1978.

Crofts 1967. J. Crofts, *Packhorse, Waggon and Post*, 1967.

Cromar 1978. P. Cromar, 'The Coal Industry on Tyneside, 1715–1750', *NH*, XIV, 1978.

Crump 1947. N. Crump, *By Rail to Victory*, 1947.

Cumberland Victoria. *The Victoria History of the County of Cumberland*, Vol. I 1901, Vol. II 1905.

Cumbria County Council 1976. Cumbria County Council, *Choices for Cumbria: Structure Plan Report for Cumbria*, 1976.

Cumbria Tourist Board 1995. Cumbria Tourist Board, *Regional Tourism Facts: Cumbria*, 1995.

Curry 1986. I. Curry, 'Aspects of the Anglo-Norman Design of Durham Cathedral', *AA5*, XIV, 1986.

Curwen 1900. J. F. Curwen, *Kirkbie-Kendall: Fragments relating to its streets and yards, churches and castle, houses and inns*, 1900.

Curwen 1913. J. F. Curwen, 'Castles and Towers of Cumberland and Westmorland', *CW Extra Series*, XIII, 1913.

Dark and Dark 1996. K. R. Dark and S. P. Dark, 'New Archaeological and Palynological Evidence for a Sub-Roman Reoccupation of Hadrian's Wall', *AA5*, XXIV, 1996.

Darlington 1893. T. Darlington (ed.), *Memoir of Emerson Muschamp Bainbridge*, Edinburgh 1893.

Davidson 1946. J. F. Davidson, *'From Collier to Battleship': Palmers of Jarrow, 1852–1933*, 1946.

Davis 1966. D. Davis, *A History of Shopping*, 1966.

Day and Charlton 1981. J. Day and D. B. Charlton, 'Excavation and Field Survey in Upper Redesdale, Part III', *AA5*, IX, 1981.

Daysh 1938. G. H. J. Daysh, *West Cumberland (with Alston): A Survey of Industrial Facilities*, Whitehaven 1938.

Defoe 1928. D. Defoe, *A Tour through the whole Island of Great Britain*, Everyman Edition, 1928.

Dennis 1970. N. Dennis, *People and Planning*, 1970.

Dennison 1939. S. R. Dennison, *The Location of Industry and the Depressed Areas*, Oxford 1939.

Devyr 1882. T. R. Devyr, *The Odd Book of the Nineteenth Century*, New York 1882.

Dewsnup 1907. E. R. Dewsnup, *The Housing Problem in England*, 1907.

Dickinson 1979. H. T. Dickinson, *Radical Politics in the North-East of England in the Later Eighteenth Century*, Durham County Local History Society, 1979.

Dickinson 1852. W. Dickinson, 'Essay on the Agriculture of Cumberland', *J. of the Royal Agricultural Society*, 13, 1852.

Dilley 1972. R. S. Dilley, *Common Land in Cumberland*, Ph.D. Thesis, Cambridge University, 1972.

Dintenfass 1992. M. Dintenfass, *Managing Industrial Decline: Entrepreneurship in the British Coal Industry Between the Wars*, Ohio State University Press, 1992.

Dixon 1895. D. D. Dixon, *Whittingham Vale*, 1895.

Dobbs 1973. B. Dobbs, *Edwardians at Play: Sport 1890–1914*, 1973.

Dobson 1973. R. B. Dobson, *Durham Priory, 1400–1450*, Cambridge 1973.

Dobson 1983. R. B. Dobson, 'Cathedral Chapters and Cathedral Cities: York, Durham and Carlisle in the Fifteenth Century', *NH*, XIX, 1983.

Dobson 1992. R. B. Dobson, 'The Church of Durham and the Scottish Borders, 1378–88', in A. Goodman and A. Tuck (eds), *War and Border Societies in the Middle Ages*, 1992.

Dodd 1897. J. J. Dodd, *The History of the Urban District of Spennymoor*, 1897.

Dodds 1959. J. F. Dodds, 'Setting out on the Trail of Ancient Border Strongholds', *J. Northumberland and Newcastle Society*, May 1959.

Dodds 1915. M. H. and R. Dodds, *The Pilgrimage of Grace and the Exeter Conspiracy*, Cambridge 1915 (reprinted 1971).

Dodds, *Boroughs*, 1915. M. H. Dodds, 'The Bishops' Boroughs', *AA3*, XII, 1915.

Donald 1989. M. B. Donald, *Elizabethan Copper: The History of the Company of Mines Royal*, Whitehaven 1989.

Donaldson 1960. R. Donaldson, 'Sponsors, Patrons and Presentations to Benefices – Particularly those in the Gift of the Priors of Durham – During the Later Middle Ages', *AA4*, XXXVIII, 1960.

Dougan 1968. D. Dougan, *The History of North-East Shipbuilding*, 1968.

Dougan 1971. D. Dougan, *The Great Gun Maker*, 1971.

Dowthwaite 1991. M. Dowthwaite, 'Defenders of Lakeland: The Lake District Defence Society in the Late Nineteenth Century', in O. M. Westall (ed.), *Windermere in the Nineteenth Century*, University of Lancaster 1991.

Drury 1976. J. L. Drury, 'Early Settlement in Stanhope Park, Weardale, c.1406–79', *AA5*, IV, 1976.

Drury 1978. J. L. Drury, 'Durham Palatinate Forest Law and Administration, especially in Weardale up to 1440', *AA5*, VI, 1978.

Drury 1987. J. L. Drury, 'More Stout than Wise: Tenant Right in Weardale in the Tudor Period', in D. Marcombe (ed.), *The Last Principality: Politics, Religion and Society in the Bishopric of Durham, 1494–1660*, Nottingham 1987.

Duckham 1973. H. and B. Duckham, *Great Pit Disasters*, 1973.

Dumble 1987. W. Dumble, 'The Durham Lilburnes and the English Revolution', in D. Marcombe (ed.), *The Last Principality: Politics, Religion and Society in the Bishopric of Durham, 1494–1660*, Nottingham 1987.

Duncan 1992. A. A. Duncan, 'The War of the Scots, 1306–1323', *Tran. R. Hist. Soc.*, 6th Ser., 2, 1992.

Dunham and Hobbs 1976. R. K. Dunham and R. J. Hobbs, 'Burtree Pasture Lead Mine, Weardale', *Indust. Archaeol. Rev.*, I, 1976.

Dunkley 1974. P. Dunkley, 'The "Hungry Forties" and the New Poor Law: A Case Study', *Hist. J.*, XVII, 1974.

Dunn 1931. P. J. Dunn, *The Political and Ecclesiastical Career of William Nicholson, Bishop of Carlisle, 1702–18*, M. A. Thesis, London University, 1931.

Durham Victoria. *The Victoria History of the Counties of England; Durham*, Vol. 1 1905, Vol. 2 1907, Vol. 3 1928.

Duxbury 1994. A. H. Duxbury, 'The Decline of the Cumbrian Yeoman. Ravenstondale: A Case Study', *CW2*, XCIV, 1994.

Eaglesham 1977. A. Eaglesham, *West Cumberland Shipping, 1660–1800*, Ph.D. Thesis, Lancaster University, 1977.

Economics Dept 1935. Economics Dept, Armstrong College, Newcastle, *The Industrial Position of the North-East Coast of England*, 1935.

Edwards 1985. Ll. J. Edwards, 'The Deserted Post-Medieval Farms of the Bearpark Estate', CBA (Council for British Archaeology) Group 3, *Newsbulletin*, Vol. 3, No. 4, September 1985.

Elkins 1970. T. Elkins, *They Brewed Their Own Beer*, 1970.

Elliot 1994. D. W. Elliot, 'The Merchant Navy in Wartime: A Civilian Occupation', *North East Labour History Bulletin*, No. 28, 1994.

Elliot 1959. G. Elliot, 'The System of Cultivation and Evidence of Enclosure in Cumberland Open Fields in the 16th Century', *CW2*, LIX, 1959.

Elliot 1960. G. Elliot, 'The Enclosure of Aspatria', *CW2*, LX, 1960.

Elliot 1961. G. Elliot, 'The Decline of the Woollen Trade in Cumberland, Westmorland and Northumberland in the Late 16th Century', *CW2*, LXI, 1961.

Elliott 1968. N. R. Elliott, 'A Geographical Analysis of the Tyne Coal Trade', *Tijdschrift voor Econ. en Soc. Geografie*, March–April 1968.

Ellis 1952. H. G. Ellis, *Broughs Limited*, n.d., *c.*1952.

Ellis 1981. J. Ellis, 'A Bold Adventurer: The Business Fortunes of William Cotesworth, *c.*1668–1726', *NH*, XVII, 1981.

Ellison 1993. M. Ellison *et al.*, 'Excavations at Newcastle Quayside: Waterfront Development at the Swirle', *AA5*, XXI, 1993.

Ellison and Harbottle 1983. M. Ellison and B. Harbottle, 'The Excavation of a 17th-Century Bastion in the Castle of Newcastle upon Tyne, 1976–81', *AA5*, XI, 1983.

Elliston Allen 1968. D. Elliston Allen, *British Tastes*, 1968.

Emery 1992. N. Emery, *The Coalminers of Durham*, Stroud 1992.

English Tourist Board 1986. English Tourist Board, *Report on a Survey of Visitors in Cumbria*, 1986.

Evans 1992. C. Evans, 'Manufacturing Iron in the North-East during the Eighteenth Century: The Case of Bedlington', *NH*, XXVIII, 1992.

Evans 1988. D. H. Evans, M. G. Jarrett and S. Wrathmell, 'The Deserted Village of West Whelpington, Northumberland: Third Report, Part Two', *AA5*, XVI, 1988.

Everett 1963. B. Everett, *The Tynemouth School Board*, MA Thesis, Newcastle University, 1963.

Fairclough 1980. G. Fairclough, 'Brinkburn Priory: A Structural Analysis of the Manor House', *AA5*, VIII, 1980.

Farrer 1923. W. Farrer, *Records Relating to the Barony of Kendal*, (ed. by J. F. Curwen), Kendal 1923.

Ferguson 1871. R. S. Ferguson, *Cumberland and Westmorland MPs*, Carlisle 1871.

Fiennes 1947. C. Morris (ed.), *The Journeys of Celia Fiennes*, 1947.

Finberg 1972. H. P. R. Finberg (ed.), *The Agrarian History of England and Wales, II, AD 43–1042*, Cambridge 1972.

Fisher Cassie 1972. W. Fisher Cassie, 'Early Civil Engineering in Northumbria', *Dept of Civil Engineering Bulletin*, Newcastle University, 43, June 1972.

Fitzwalter and Taylor 1981. R. Fitzwalter and D. Taylor, *Web of Corruption: The Story of John Poulson and T. Dan Smith*, 1981.

Fletcher 1881. H. A. Fletcher, 'The Archaeology of the West Cumberland Iron Trade', *CW*, V, 1881.

Flinn 1984. *The History of the British Coal Industry*, Vol. II, Oxford 1984.

Forster 1979. A. M. C. Forster, 'An Outline History of the Catholic Church in North East England from the Sixteenth Century: V, Northumberland, 1688–1720', *Northern Catholic History*, 10, 1979.

Foster 1987. A. M. Foster, 'The Struggle for Parliamentary Representation for Durham, *c*.1600–1641', in D. Marcombe (ed.), *The Last Principality: Politics, Religion and Society in the Bishopric of Durham, 1494–1660*, Nottingham 1987.

Fox 1980. R. C. Fox, *The Demography of Sunderland*, Sunderland Polytechnic 1980.

France 1913. G. France (ed.), *Thomas Hudson Bainbridge: Reminiscences*, 1913.

Fraser 1955. C. M. Fraser, 'Gilly-Corn and the Customary of the Convent of Durham', *AA4*, XXXIII, 1955.

Fraser Officers 1957. C. M. Fraser, 'Officers of the Bishopric of Durham under Antony Bek, 1283–1311', *AA4*, XXXV, 1957.

Fraser 1957, History. C. M. Fraser, *A History of Antony Bek*, Oxford 1957.

Fraser 1959. C. M. Fraser, 'The Life and Death of John of Denton', *AA4*, XXXVII, 1959.

Fraser 1961. C. M. Fraser, 'Medieval Trading Restrictions in the North East', *AA4*, XXXIX, 1961.

Fraser 1968. C. M. Fraser (ed.), *The Northumberland Lay Subsidy Roll of 1296*, Newcastle upon Tyne, Society of Antiquaries, 1968.

Fraser 1969. C. M. Fraser, 'The Pattern of Trade in the North-East of England, 1265–1350', *NH*, IV, 1969.

Fraser 1984. C. M. Fraser, 'The Early Hostmen of Newcastle upon Tyne', *AA5*, XII, 1984.

Fraser and Emsley 1969. C. M. Fraser and K. Emsley, 'Law and Society in Northumberland and Durham, 1290 to 1350', *AA4*, XLVII, 1969.

Fraser and Emsley 1971. C. M. Fraser and K. Emsley, 'Some Early Recorders of Newcastle upon Tyne', *AA4*, XLIX, 1971.

Fraser and Emsley, Justice 1971. C. M. Fraser and K. Emsley, 'Justice in North East England, 1256–1356', *American J. of Legal History*, 1981.

Fraser and Emsley 1974. 'The Clerical Justices of the Peace in the North East, 1626–30', *AA5*, II, 1974.

Fraser and Emsley 1978. C. M. Fraser and K. Emsley, 'Newcastle Merchant Adventurers from West Yorkshire', *AA5*, VI, 1978.

Fraser and Emsley Northumbria. C. M. Fraser and K. Emsley, *Northumbria*, Chichester 1978.

Fraser 1935. K. Fraser, *Annual Report to Cumberland County Council on Health Services*, 1935.

Fraser 1939. K. Fraser, *Annual Report to Cumberland County Council on Health Services*, 1939.

Freeman 1987. J. Freeman, 'The Distribution and Use of Ecclesiastical Patronage in the Diocese of Durham, 1558–1640', in D. Marcombe (ed.), *The Last Principality: Politics, Religion and Society in the Bishopric of Durham, 1494–1660*, Nottingham 1987.

Free Trade Union, 1909. Free Trade Union, *Free Trade and the Industries of Newcastle upon Tyne*, 1909.

Galloway 1898. R. L. Galloway, *Annals of Coal Mining and the Coal Trade*, 1898.

Gammage 1894. R. G. Gammage, *History of the Chartist Movement*, revised ed., Newcastle 1894.

Gard and Shrimpton 1972. R. Gard and C. Shrimpton, *A Revolution in Agriculture* (Archive Teaching Unit), Newcastle 1972.

Garnett 1912. F. W. Garnett, *Westmorland Agriculture*, Kendal 1912.

Gatiss 1969. P. D. Gatiss, *The History of the County Borough of Gateshead Police*, 1969.

Gill 1980. M. Gill, 'The Newcastle Goldsmiths and the Capital', *AA5*, VIII, 1980.

Gillard and Tomkinson 1980. M. Gillard and M. Tomkinson, *Nothing to Declare: The Political Corruption of John Poulson*, 1980.

Gilly 1842. W. S. Gilly, *The Peasantry of the Border*, 1842.

Gittins 1976. J. Gittins, 'Soapmaking and the Excise Laws, 1711–1853', *Indust. Archaeol. Rev.*, I, 1976.

Glass 1948. R. Glass, *The Social Background of a Plan: A Study of Middlesbrough*, 1948.

Godwin 1986. J. Godwin, *Mass Football in Cumberland and Elsewhere*, unpub. study, Carlisle Record Office, 1986.

Gooch 1982. L. Gooch, 'The Vicars Apostolic of the Northern District, Part 1: 1688–1790', *Northern Catholic History*, 16, 1982.

Gooch 1983. L. Gooch, 'The Vicars Apostolic of the Northern District, Part 2: 1790–1850', *Northern Catholic History*, 17, 1983.

Gooch 1996. L. Gooch, *The Desperate Faction? The Jacobites in North-East England, 1688–1745*, Hull University Press, 1996.

Goodfellow 1940. D. M. Goodfellow, *Tyneside: The Social Facts*, 1940.

Goodman and Tuck 1992. A. Goodman and A. Tuck (eds), *War and Border Societies in the Middle Ages*, 1992.

Gotch 1955. C. Gotch, 'Robert Mylne and Tyne Bridges', *AA4*, XXXIII, 1955.

Gough 1827. J. Gough, *The Manners and Customs of Westmorland*, Kendal 1827.

Graham 1907. T. H. B. Graham, 'An Old Map of Hayton Manor', *CW2*, VII, 1907.

Grasse 1970. J. L. Grasse, 'Royal Clerks from the York Archdiocese', *NH*, V, 1970.

Green 1994. S. J. D. Green, 'Unestablished Versions: Voluntary Religion in the Victorian North', *NH*, XXX, 1994.

Gregson 1976. K. Gregson, *The Operation of the Poor Laws in the Hartlepool Poor Law Union*, M.Litt. Thesis, Newcastle University, 1976.

Gregson 1980. N. Gregson, *Continuity and Change in Agrarian Organization in North-West England, 1100–1800*, Ph.D. Thesis, Durham University, 1980.

Grierson 1972. E. Grierson, *Confessions of a County Magistrate*, 1972.

Griffin 1978. A. R. Griffin, 'The Monster Subdued: The Origins of the Miners' Safety Lamp', *Colliery Guardian*, December 1978.

Griffin 1980. A. R. Griffin, 'The Rolt Memorial Lecture, 1978', *Indust. Archaeol. Rev.*, IV, 3, Autumn 1980.

Griffin 1976. C. P. Griffin, 'Some Comments on Capital Formation in the British Coalmining Industry during the Industrial Revolution', *Indust. Archaeol. Rev.*, I, 1976.

Griffiths 1995. D. Griffiths, 'British Shipping and the Diesel Engine: The Early Years', *The Mariner's Mirror*, Vol. 81, No. 3, 1995.

Hackett 1960. B. Hackett, 'A Formal Landscape at Hesleyside in Northumberland', *AA4*, XXXVIII, 1960.

Hadfield 1977. J. Hadfield, *Health in the Industrial North East, 1919–1939*, 1977.

Halcrow 1952. Elizabeth M. Halcrow, 'Merchant Charities of Newcastle upon Tyne', *AA4*, XXX, 1952.

Halcrow 1953. E. Halcrow, 'The Town Moor of Newcastle upon Tyne', *AA4*, XXXI, 1953.

Halcrow 1955. E. Halcrow, 'The Social Position and Influence of the Priors of Durham, as illustrated by their Correspondence', *AA4*, XXXIII, 1955.

Halcrow 1956. E. Halcrow, 'Ridley Charters', *AA4*, XXXIV, 1956.

Halcrow. Charity, 1956. E. Halcrow, 'The Charity for the Relief of Poor Women Lying-in at Their Own Homes', *AA4*, XXXIV, 1956.

Halcrow 1957. E. Halcrow, 'Obedientiaries and Counsellors in Monastic Administration at Durham', *AA4*, XXXV, 1957.

Halcrow 1958. E. Halcrow, 'The Election Campaigns of Sir Charles Miles Lambert Monck', *AA4*, XXXVI, 1958.

Halcrow 1959. E. Halcrow, 'Records of the Bakers and Brewers of Newcastle upon Tyne', *AA4*, XXXVII, 1959.

Hale 1953. L. Hale, *Hedley of Newcastle*, 1953.

Hallam 1988. H. E. Hallam, *The Agrarian History of England and Wales, II, 1042–1350*, Cambridge 1988.

Halliday 1988. S. Halliday, *Landed Power in the Palatinate: A Study of the Attainment, Maintenance and Loss of Landed Elite Status in the County Palatinate of Durham between the Seventeenth and Nineteenth Centuries*, CNAA (Sunderland Polytchnic) MA Thesis, 1988.

Halliday 1994. S. Halliday, 'Social Mobility, Demographic Change and the Landed Elite of County Durham, 1610–1819: An Open or Shut Case?', *NH*, XXX, 1994.

Handloom Weavers 1840–41. Report of the House of Commons Select Committee on Handloom Weaving, 1840–41, Parliamentary Papers (Commons), Vol. 24, 1840–41, Reports from Commissioners.

Hanley 1936. J. H. Hanley, A. L. Boyd, and W. Williamson, *An Agricultural Survey of the Northern Province*, Newcastle 1936.

Harbottle 1958. B. Harbottle, 'Bishop Hatfield's Visitation of Durham Priory in 1354', *AA4*, XXXVI, 1958.

Harbottle 1966. B. Harbottle, 'Excavations at the South Curtain Wall of the Castle, Newcastle upon Tyne', *AA4*, XLIV, 1966.

Harbottle 1969. B. Harbottle, 'The Town Wall of Newcastle upon Tyne: Consolidation and Excavation in 1968', *AA4*, XLVII, 1969.

Harbottle 1995. B. Harbottle, 'Prestwick Carr: Its Draining and Enclosure', *AA5*, XXIII, 1995.

Harbottle and Ellison 1981. B. Harbottle and M. Ellison, 'An Excavation in the Castle Ditch, Newcastle upon Tyne, 1974–9', *AA5*, IX, 1981.

Harbottle and Newman 1973. B. Harbottle and T. G. Newman, 'Excavation and Survey on the Starsley Burn, North Tynedale, 1972', *AA5*, I, 1973.

Harbottle and Salway 1960. B. Harbottle and P. Salway, 'Nafferton Castle, Northumberland', *AA4*, XXXVIII, 1960.

Harbottle and Salway 1964. B. Harbottle and P. Salway, 'Excavations at Newminster Abbey, Northumberland, 1961–1963', *AA4*, XLII, 1964.

Harris 1965. A. Harris, 'Askam Iron: The Development of Askam in Furness, 1850–1920', *CW2*, LXV, 1965.

Harris 1966. A. Harris, 'Millom, a Victorian New Town', *CW2*, LXVI, 1966.

Harris 1967. A. Harris, 'Denton Holme, Part 2', *CW2*, LXVII, 1967.

Harrison 1975. J. M. Harrison, *The Pilgrimage of Grace in the Lake Counties*, M.Litt. Thesis, Lancaster University, 1975.

Harrison and Hollis 1979. R. Harrison and P. Hollis (eds), *Robert Lowery: Radical and Chartist*, 1979.

Hay 1979. D. Hay, *Whitehaven, An Illustrated History*, 1979.

Hayler 1897. G. Hayler, *The Prohibition Movement*, 1897.

Hedley 1957. W. P. Hedley, 'The Early Widdringtons of Widdrington', *AA4*, XXXV, 1957.

Hedley 1959. W. P. Hedley, 'The Origin of the Families of Heron and Swinburne', *AA4*, XXXVII, 1959.

Heesom 1974. A. J. Heesom, 'Entrepreneurial Paternalism: The Third Lord Londonderry and the Coal Trade', *Durham University J.*, LXVI, 1974.

Heesom 1979. A. J. Heesom, 'Problems of Church Extension in a Victorian New Town: The Londonderrys and Seaham Harbour', *NH*, XV, 1979.

Heesom, Duffy and Colls 1981. A. J. Heesom, B. Duffy and R. Colls, 'Coal, Class and Education in the North-East', *Past and Present*, 90, 1981.

Hennessey 1972. R. S. S. Hennessey, *The Electric Revolution*, 1972.

Heslop and Truman 1993. D. H. Heslop and L. Truman, 'The Cooperage, 32–4 The Close: A Timber-Framed Building in Newcastle upon Tyne', *AA5*, XXI, 1993.

Hicks 1978. M. A. Hicks, 'Dynastic Change and Northern Society: The Career of the Fourth Earl of Northumberland', *NH*, XIV, 1978.

Hicks 1984. M. A. Hicks, 'Edward IV, the Duke of Somerset and Lancastrian Loyalism in the North', *NH*, XX, 1984.

Higham 1978. N. J. Higham, 'Continuity Studies in the First Millennium AD in North Cumbria', *NH*, XIV, 1978.

Higham 1986. Nick Higham, *The Northern Counties to AD 1000*, 1986.

Higham CW2 1986. N. Higham, 'The Origins of Inglewood Forest', *CW2*, LXXXVI, 1986.

Higham 1993. N. J. Higham, *The Kingdom of Northumbria, AD 350–1100*, Stroud 1993.

Hilton 1977. J. A. Hilton, 'Catholicism in Elizabethan Northumberland', *NH*, XIII, 1977.

Hilton 1980. J. A. Hilton, 'The Cumbrian Catholics', *NH*, XVI, 1980.

Hiskey 1974. C. Hiskey, 'Sources for Labour History in the Durham Record Office', *Bulletin of NE Group for the Study of Labour History*, 8, 1974.

Hislop 1991. M. J. B. Hislop, 'The Date of the Warkworth Donjon', *AA5*, XIX, 1991.

Hislop 1992. M. J. B. Hislop, 'The Castle of Ralph Fourth Baron Neville at Raby', *AA5*, XX, 1992.

Hislop 1995. M. J. B. Hislop, 'John of Gaunt's Building Works at Dunstanburgh Castle', *AA5*, XXIII, 1995.

Hitchin 1962. G. Hitchin, *Pit Yacker*, 1962.

Hodgson 1907. G. B. Hodgson, *The Borough of South Shields*, 1907.

Hodgson 1975. J. Hodgson, *Changes in the Structure of Employment in the Northern Region of England, 1921–1971*, MA Thesis, Newcastle University, 1975.

Hodgson 1978. R. I. Hodgson, *Demographic Trends in County Durham, 1560–1801: Data Sources and Preliminary Findings with Particular Reference to North Durham*, Univ. of Manchester School of Geography Research Papers, 5, May 1978.

Hodnett 1994. R. M. Hodnett, *Politics and the Northumberland Miners: Liberals and Labour in Morpeth and Wansbeck, 1890–1922*, University of Teesside, 1994.

Hodson 1979. R. I. Hodson, 'The Progress of Enclosure in County Durham, 1550–1870', in H. S. A. Fox and R. A. Butlin (eds), *Change in the Countryside: Essays on Rural England, 1500–1900*, Inst. of Brit. Geographers, 1979.

Hoeppner Moran 1981. J. Hoeppner Moran, 'Literacy and Education in Northern England, 1359–1550: A Methodological Enquiry', *NH*, VI, 1971.

Holmes 1983. N. Holmes, ' "King of Cumberland": A Radio Biography of Jack Adams, Baron Adams of Ennerdale', BBC Radio Cumbria, April 1983.

Holt 1968. G. O. Holt, *A Regional History of the Railways of Great Britain: Vol. 10. The North West*, 2nd ed., Newton Abbot 1968.

Home Office 1944. *Report of the Tribunal appointed . . . to inquire into the administration by the Council of . . . Newcastle upon Tyne and its Committees and Officers of . . . functions in relation to the Fire, Police and Civil Defence services.* Cmd. 6522 of 1944.

Honeyman 1953. H. L. Honeyman, 'Three Jacobean Houses (Washington Old Hall, Ovingham Vicarage and Aydon White House)', *AA4*, XXXI, 1953.

Honeyman 1955. H. L. Honeyman, 'Mitford Castle', *AA4*, XXXIII, 1955.

Hoole 1986. K. Hoole, *A Regional History of the Railways of Great Britain: Vol. 4. The North East*, 3rd ed., Newton Abbot 1986.

Hopkinson 1973. R. Hopkinson, *Elections in Cumberland and Westmorland, 1695–1723*, Ph.D. Thesis, Newcastle University, 1973.

Hopkinson 1979. R. Hopkinson, 'The Electorate of Cumberland and Westmorland in the Late Seventeenth and Early Eighteenth Centuries', *NH*, XV, 1979.

Horden Collieries Ltd, 1946. Horden Collieries Ltd, *75,000,000 Tons of Coal*, 1946.

Hough 1966. R. Hough, *The Big Battleship*, 1966.

House 1969. J. W. House, *The North East*, 1969.

House and Fullerton 1960. J. W. House and B. Fullerton, *Teesside at Mid-Century*, 1960.

Housman 1800. J. Housman, *A Topographical Description of Cumberland, Westmorland, and Lancashire and Part of the West Riding of Yorkshire*, 1800.

Houston 1982. R. A. Houston, 'Illiteracy among Newcastle Shoemakers, 1618–1740', *AA5*, X, 1982.

Houston Durham 1982. R. A. Houston, 'Illiteracy in the Diocese of Durham, 1663–89 and 1750–62: The Evidence of Marriage Bonds', *NH*, XVIII, 1982.

Howell 1964. R. Howell, 'Newcastle's Regicide: The Parliamentary Career of John Blakiston', *AA4*, XLII, 1964.

Howell 1967. R. Howell, *Newcastle upon Tyne and the Puritan Revolution*, Oxford 1967.

Howell 1968. R. Howell, 'The Elections to the Long Parliament in Newcastle: Some New Evidence', *AA4*, XLVI, 1968.

Howell 1970. R. Howell, 'Thomas Weld of Gateshead: The Return of a New England Puritan', *AA4*, XLVIII, 1970.

Howell 1979. R. Howell, 'The Newcastle Clergy and the Quakers', *AA5*, VII, 1979.

Howell 1980. R. Howell, 'Newcastle and the Nation: The Seventeenth-Century Experience', *AA5*, VIII, 1980.

Howell 1981. R. Howell, 'The Army and the English Revolution: The Case of Robert Lilburne', *AA5*, IX, 1981.

Howlett 1975. R. Howlett, 'The Provenance, Date and Structure of *De Abbatibus*', *AA5*, III, 1975.

Hoyle 1985. R. W. Hoyle, 'Thomas Master's Narrative of the Pilgrimage of Grace', *NH*, XXI, 1985.

Hoyle 1992. R. W. Hoyle (ed.), 'Letters of the Cliffords, Lords Clifford and Earls of Cumberland, *c*.1500–*c*.1565', in *Camden Miscellany*, XXXI, 1992.

Hudson 1989. R. Hudson, *Wrecking a Region*, 1989.

Huggins 1996. M. J. Huggins, 'Leisure and Sport in Middlesbrough, 1840–1914', in A. J. Pollard (ed.), *Middlesbrough: Town and Community 1830–1950*, Stroud 1996.

Hughes 1953. E. Hughes, 'The Correspondence of Colonel Robert Ellison of Hebburn, 1733–48', *AA4*, XXXI, 1953.

Hughes 1956. E. Hughes, 'Some Clavering Correspondence', *AA4*, XXXIV, 1956.

Hughes 1952. E. Hughes, *North Country Life in the Eighteenth Century, Vol. I, The North-East 1700–1750*, Durham 1952.

Hughes 1965. E. Hughes, *North Country Life in the Eighteenth Century, Vol. II, Cumberland and Westmorland 1700–1830*, Durham 1965.

Hume 1941. W. E. Hume, 'The Royal Infirmary, Newcastle upon Tyne', *Medical Press and Circular*, 1 and 8 October 1941.

Hunt 1970. C. J. Hunt, *The Lead Miners of the Northern Pennines*, Manchester 1970.

Hunt and Isaac 1977. C. J. Hunt and P. C. G. Isaac, 'The Regulation of the Book Trade in Newcastle upon Tyne at the Beginning of the Nineteenth Century', *AA5*, V, 1977.

Hunter 1982. J. R. Hunter, 'Medieval Berwick upon Tweed', *AA5*, 1982.

Hunter Blair 1952. C. H. Hunter Blair, 'Baronys and Knights of Northumberland, AD 1166–*c*.AD 1266', *AA4*, XXX, 1952.

Hunter Blair 1955. C. H. Hunter Blair, 'The Armorials of Newcastle upon Tyne', *AA4*, XXXIII, 1955.

Hunter Blair 1958. C. H. Hunter *et al.*, 'Wall Knoll, Sallyport or Carpenters' Tower', *AA4*, XXXVI, 1958

Hurst 1864. N. E. Hurst, *Report on Proposed Superannuation Allowance*, unpub., PRO, Ministry of Health Papers, 32, vol. 47, 1864.

Hutchinson 1778. W. Hutchinson, *A View of Northumberland*, 1778.

Hutchinson 1794. W. Hutchinson, *History and Antiquities of Cumberland*, 1794.

Hutton 1759. B. G. Hutton, *A Lakeland Journey*, 1759.

Iley 1974. W. Iley, 'The Stones of St Andrew's, Corbridge', *AA5*, II, 1974.

Jackson 1947. S. F. Jackson, *A Short History of the Newcastle and Gateshead Gas Company*, 1947.

Jaffe 1989. J. A. Jaffe, 'Competition and the Size of Firms in the North-East Coal Trade, 1800–1850', *NH*, XXV, 1989.

Jalland 1976 for 1975. P. Jalland, 'The "Revolution" in Northern Borough Representation in Mid-Fifteenth Century England', *NH*, XI, 1976 for 1975.

James 1966. M. E. James, 'The First Earl of Cumberland (1493–1542) and the Decline of Northern Feudalism', *NH*, I, 1966.

James 1967. M. E. James, *Change and Continuity in the Tudor North*, York 1967.

James 1973. M. E. James, 'The Concept of Order and the Northern Rising of 1569', *Past and Present*, 60, 1973.

James 1994. S. E. James, 'Sir William Parr of Kendal: Part II, 1471–1483', *CW2*, XCIV, 1994.

Jarrett 1962. M. G. Jarrett, 'The Deserted Village of West Whelpington', *AA4*, XL, 1962.

Jarrett 1970. M. G. Jarrett, 'The Deserted Village of West Whelpington: Second Report', *AA4*, XLVIII, 1970.

Jarrett and Edwards 1961. M. G. Jarrett and B. J. N. Edwards, 'Medieval and Other Pottery from Finchale Priory, County Durham', *AA4*, XXXIX, 1961.

Jarrett and Mason 1995. M. G. Jarrett and H. Mason, '"Greater and More Splendid": Some Aspects of Romanesque Durham Cathedral', *The Antiquaries Journal*, Vol. 75, 1995.

Jarvis 1954. R. C. Jarvis, 'Cumberland Shipping in the 18th Century', *CW2*, LIV, 1954.

Jewell 1982. H. M. Jewell, '"The Bringing up of Children in Good Learning and Manners": A Survey of Secular Educational Provision in the North of England, ac. 1359–1550', *NH*, XVIII, 1982.

Jewkes and Winterbottom 1933. J. Jewkes and A. Winterbottom, *An Industrial Survey of Cumberland and Furness*, Manchester 1933.

Jobey 1967. G. Jobey, 'Excavations at Tynemouth Priory and Castle', *AA4*, XLV, 1967.

Jobey 1977. G. Jobey, 'Iron Age and Later Farmsteads on Belling Law, Northumberland', *AA5*, V, 1977.

Jobey 1986. G. Jobey, 'Millstones and Millstone Quarries in Northumberland', *AA5*, XIV, 1986.

Jobey 1992. G. Jobey, 'Cock-Fighting in Northumberland and Durham during the Eighteenth and Nineteenth Centuries', *AA5*, XX, 1992.

Jollie 1811. F. Jollie, *Sketch of Cumberland Manners and Customs*, 1811.

Jones 1962. G. P. Jones, 'The Decline of the Yeomanry in the Lake Counties', *CW2*, LXII, 1962.

Jones 1995. G. R. J. Jones, 'Some Donations to Bishop Wilfrid in Northern England', *NH*, XXXI, 1995.

Jupp 1973. P. Jupp, *British and Irish Elections, 1784–1831*, 1973.

Kapelle 1979. W. E. Kapelle, *The Norman Conquest of the North*, 1979.

Keeling 1979. S. Keeling, 'The Reformation in the Anglo-Scottish Border Counties', *NH*, XV, 1979.

Keeling 1987. S. Keeling, 'The Dissolution of the Monasteries in the Border Country', in D. Marcombe (ed.), *The Last Principality: Politics, Religion and Society in the Bishopric of Durham, 1494–1660*, Nottingham 1987.

Kelly 1925. *Kelly's Directory of Durham and Northumberland*, 1925.

Kennedy and Marshall 1962. B. C. Kennedy and P. J. Marshall, *British Bus Fleets: No. 10. North Eastern Area*, 1962.

Kershaw 1973. I. Kershaw, 'The Great Famine and Agrarian Crisis in England, 1315–1322', *Past and Present*, 60, 1973.

Killick and Thomas 1970. J. R. Killick and W. A. Thomas, 'The Stock Exchanges of the North of England, 1836–1850', *NH*, V, 1970.

Kirby 1972. D. A. Kirby, 'Population Density and Land Values in County Durham during the Mid-Seventeenth Century', *Trans. Inst. Brit. Geographers*, 57, November 1972.

Kirby 1993. M. W. Kirby, *The Origins of Railway Enterprise: The Stockton and Darlington Railway, 1821–1863*, Cambridge 1993.

Kitching 1987. C. Kitching, 'The Durham Palatinate and the Courts of Westminster under the Tudors', in D. Marcombe (ed.), *The Last Principality: Politics, Religion and Society in the Bishopric of Durham, 1494–1660*, Nottingham 1987.

Lambert 1995. A. Lambert, 'Another Time, Another Place', *National Trust Magazine*, 76, 1995.

Lancashire and Wattleworth 1977. J. Y. Lancashire and D. R. Wattleworth, *The Iron and Steel Industry of West Cumberland*, Workington 1977.

Lancashire Victoria. *The Victoria History of the County of Lancaster*, Vol. VIII, 1914.

Lancaster 1994. B. Lancaster (ed.), *Working Class Housing on Tyneside 1850–1939*, Whitley Bay, Bewick Press, 1994.

Lapsley 1900. G. T. Lapsley, *The County Palatine of Durham: A Study in Constitutional History*, Harvard 1900.

Large 1958–59. D. Large, 'The Third Marquess of Londonderry and the End of the Regulation, 1844–5', *Durham University J.*, LI, 1958–59.

Lavery 1917. F. Lavery, *Irish Heroes of the Great War*, 1917.

Lawson 1966. W. Lawson, 'The Origin of the Military Road from Newcastle to Carlisle', *AA4*, XLIV, 1966.

Lawson 1971. W. Lawson, 'The Newcastle to Carter Bar Road (A696 and A68)', *AA4*, XLIX, 1971.

Leach 1872. F. Leach, *Barrow in Furness: Its Rise and Progress*, Barrow 1872.

Leifchild 1853. Anon. (J. R. Leifchild), *Our Coal and Our Coal Pits*, 1853.

Leonard 1996. J. W. Leonard, '"City Beautiful": Planning the Future in Mid-Twentieth-Century Middlesbrough', in A. J. Pollard (ed.), *Middlesbrough: Town and Community 1830–1950*, Stroud 1996.

Le Patourel 1971. J. Le Patourel, 'The Norman Conquest of Yorkshire', *NH*, VI, 1971.

Levine and Wrightson 1991. D. Levine and K. Wrightson, *The Making of an Industrial Society: Whickham 1560–1765*, Oxford 1991.

Lewis and English 1990. P. J. Lewis and I. R. English, *Into Battle with the Durhams: 8 DLI in World War II*, 1990.

Lewis 1996. R. Lewis, 'The Evolution of a Political Culture: Middlesbrough 1850–1950', in A. J. Pollard (ed.), *Middlesbrough: Town and Community 1830–1950*, Stroud 1996.

Little 1880. H. J. Little, 'Farming in Cumberland', *J. of The Royal Agricultural Society*, 16, 1880.

Lloyd 1916. E. Lloyd, *History of the Crook Co-operative Society*, 1916.

Loades 1987, Introduction. D. Loades, 'Introduction', in D. Marcombe (ed.), *The Last Principality: Politics, Religion and Society in the Bishopric of Durham, 1494–1660*, Nottingham 1987.

Loades 1987. D. Loades, 'The Dissolution of the Diocese of Durham, 1553–4', in D. Marcombe (ed.), *The Last Principality: Politics, Religion and Society in the Bishopric of Durham, 1494–1660*, Nottingham 1987.

Loebl 1988. H. Loebl, *Government Factories and the Origins of British Regional Policy, 1934–1946*, Aldershot 1988.

Lomas 1977. R. A. Lomas, 'Developments in Land Tenure on the Prior of Durham's Estates in the Later Middle Ages', *NH*, XIII, 1977.

Lomas 1982. R. A. Lomas, 'A Northern Farm at the End of the Middle Ages: Elvethall Manor, Durham, 1443/4–1513/4', *NH*, XVIII, 1982.

Lomas 1992. R. A. Lomas, *North-East England in the Middle Ages*, Edinburgh 1992.

Lomas 1996. R. A. Lomas, *County of Conflict: Northumberland from Conquest to Civil War*, East Linton 1996.

Louw 1989. H. Louw, ' "Of Ancient Rights and Priviledges": Demarcation Disputes between the Companies of Joiners and Housecarpenters, Millwrights and Trunkmakers of Newcastle upon Tyne, *c*.1580–*c*.1740', *AA5*, XVII, 1989.

Lovecy 1976. I. Lovecy, 'The End of Celtic Britain: A Sixth Century Battle near Lindisfarne', *AA5*, IV, 1976.

Luxmoore 1952. A. A. Luxmoore, 'Lieutenancy of the County of Durham', *AA4*, XXX, 1952.

MacCaffrey 1969. W. MacCaffrey, *The Shaping of the Elizabethan Régime*, 1969.

McCord 1968. N. McCord, 'The 1815 Seamen's Strikes in North East England', *Econ. Hist. Rev.*, 2nd Ser., XXI, 1968.

McCord 1969. N. McCord, 'The Implementation of the 1834 Poor Law Amendment Act on Tyneside', *Int. Rev. Soc. Hist.*, XIV, 1969.

McCord Gateshead 1969. N. McCord, 'Gateshead Politics in the Age of Reform', *NH*, IV, 1969.

McCord 1970. N. McCord, 'The Government of Tyneside, 1800–50', *Trans. R. Hist. Soc.*, 5th Ser., 20, 1970.

McCord 1977. N. McCord (ed.), *Essays in Tyneside Labour History*, Newcastle 1977.

McCord 1979. N. McCord, *North East England: The Region's Development, 1760–1960*, 1979.

McCord 1987. N. McCord, *The Days of Visitation: An Examination of Some Durham Records, 1857–1936*, Dean and Chapter of Durham, 1987.

McCord 1994. N. McCord, 'The Engineers', in J. Philipson (ed.), *The Literary and Philosophical Society of Newcastle upon Tyne Bicentenary Lectures*, Newcastle 1994.

McCord 1995. N. McCord, 'Aspects of Change in the Nineteenth-Century North East', *NH*, XXXI, 1995.

McCord and Brewster 1968. N. McCord and D. E. Brewster, 'Some Labour Troubles of the 1790s in North East England', *Int. Rev. Soc. Hist.*, XIII, 1968.

McCord and Carrick 1966. N. McCord and A. E. Carrick, 'Northumberland in the General Election of 1852', *NH*, I, 1966.

McCord and Rowe 1977. N. McCord and D. J. Rowe, 'Industrialisation and Urban Growth in North-East England', *Int. Rev. Soc. Hist.*, XXII, 1977.

McCord and Wood 1959–60. N. McCord and P. A. Wood, 'The Sunderland Election of 1845', *Durham University J.*, New Ser., XXI, 1959–60.

McCrone 1969. G. McCrone, *Regional Policy in Britain*, 1969.

Macdonald 1974. S. Macdonald, *The Development of Agriculture and the Diffusion of Agricultural Innovation in Northumberland, 1750–1850*, Ph.D. Thesis, Newcastle University, 1974.

Macdonald 1975. S. Macdonald, 'The Role of George Culley of Fenton in the Development of Northumberland Agriculture', *AA5*, III, 1975.

Macdonald Fraser 1971. G. Macdonald Fraser, *The Steel Bonnets*, 1971.

McDonnell 1988. J. McDonnell, 'The Role of Transhumance in Northern England', *NH*, XXIV, 1988.

McDonnell 1994. J. McDonnell, 'Antecedents of Border Tenant Right', *NH*, XXX, 1994.

McGloin 1977. P. R. McGloin, *The Impact of the Railway on the Development of Keswick as a Tourist Resort*, MA Thesis, Lancaster University, 1977.

Mackenzie 1811. E. Mackenzie, *A Historical and Descriptive View of the County of Northumberland*, Newcastle 1811.

Mackenzie 1827. E. Mackenzie, *A Descriptive and Historical Account of the Town and County of Newcastle upon Tyne*, Newcastle 1827.

Mackenzie and Ross 1834. E. Mackenzie and M. Ross, *An Historical, Topographical and Descriptive View of the County Palatine of Durham*, Newcastle 1834.

McNamee 1990. C. J. McNamee, 'William Wallace's Invasion of Northern England in 1297', *NH*, XXVI, 1990.

McQuiston 1976 for 1975. J. R. McQuiston, 'The Lonsdale Connection and its Defender, William, Viscount Lowther, 1818–1830', *NH*, XI, 1976 for 1975.

Maddicott 1970. J. R. Maddicott, *Thomas of Lancaster, 1307–22: A Study in the Reign of Edward II*, Oxford 1970.

Maehl 1963. W. H. Maehl, 'Chartist Disturbances in North East England', *Int. Rev. Soc. Hist.*, Vol. VIII, Part 3, 1963.

Maidwell 1959. C. F. Maidwell, *A Short History of Paper Making in the North East*, 1959.

Malden 1991. R. J. Malden, 'The Elusive Mr. Birch', *AA5*, XIX, 1991.

Manders 1973. F. W. D. Manders, *A History of Gateshead*, 1973.

Manders 1980. F. W. D. Manders, *The Administration of the Poor Law in the Gateshead Union, 1836–1930*, M.Litt. Thesis, Newcastle University, 1980.

Manders 1991. F. W. D. Manders, *Cinemas of Newcastle: A Comprehensive History of the Cinemas of Newcastle upon Tyne*, Newcastle 1991.

Manders 1995. F. W. D. Manders, *Cinemas of Gateshead*, Gateshead 1995.

Mann 1984. J. Mann, 'Causey Arch – a Note', *AA5*, XII, 1984.

Manning 1923. F. Manning, *The Life of Sir William White*, 1923.

Marcombe 1980. D. Marcombe, 'Bernard Gilpin: Anatomy of an Elizabethan Legend', *NH*, XVI, 1980.

Marcombe 1987. D. Marcombe, 'A Rude and Heady People: The Local Community and the Rebellion of the Northern Earls', in D. Marcombe (ed.), *The Last Principality: Politics, Religion and Society in the Bishopric of Durham 1494–1660*, Nottingham 1987.

Marshall 1958. J. Marshall, *Furness and the Industrial Revolution*, 1958.

Marshall 1970. J. Marshall, 'Crime and the Countryman', *CW2*, LXX, 1970.

Marshall 1971. J. Marshall, *Old Lakeland*, Newton Abbot 1971.

Marshall 1973. J. D. Marshall, 'The Domestic Economy of the Lakeland Yeoman, 1660–1789', *CW2*, LXXIII, 1973.

Marshall 1975. J. Marshall, 'Kendal in the late 17th and 18th Centuries', *CW2*, LXXV, 1975.

Marshall 1980. J. Marshall, 'Agrarian Wealth and Social Structure in Pre-Industrial Cumbria', *Econ. Hist. Rev.*, 2nd Ser., XXX, 1980.

Marshall 1981. J. D. Marshall, 'The Study of Local and Regional "Communities": Some Problems and Possibilities', *NH*, XVII, 1981.

Marshall 1983. J. Marshall, 'The Rise and Transformation of the Cumbrian Market Town, 1660–1900', *NH*, XIX, 1983.

Marshall 1995. J. D. Marshall, 'Out of Wedlock: Perceptions of a Cumbrian Social Problem in the Victorian Context', *NH*, XXXI, 1995.

Marshall 1996. J. D. Marshall, 'Communities, Societies, Regions and Local History: Perceptions of Locality in High and Low Furness', *The Local Historian*, Vol. 26, 1, 1966.

Marshall and Davies-Shiel 1977. J. Marshall and M. Davies-Shiel, *The Industrial Archaeology of the Lake Counties*, 2nd ed., Beckermet, 1977.

Marshall and Dyhouse 1976. J. Marshall and C. A. Dyhouse, 'Social Transition in Kendal and Westmorland, *c*.1760–1860', *NH*, XII, 1976.

Marshall and Walton 1981. J. Marshall and J. Walton, *The Lake Counties from 1830 to the Mid-Twentieth Century*, Manchester 1981.

Martin and McCord 1971. S. B. Martin and N. McCord, 'The Steamship Bedlington, 1841–54', *Maritime History*, I, 1971.

Mathias 1967. P. Mathias, *Retailing Revolution*, 1967.

Maud 1862. W. Maud, *Remarks and Enquiries about Agriculture*, 1862.

Maw 1964. W. Maw, *The Story of Rutherford Grammar School*, 1964.

Mawson 1971. P. Mawson, *Poor Law Administration in South Shields, 1830–1930*, MA Thesis, Newcastle University, 1971.

Maynard 1990. W. R. Maynard, 'Pluralism and Non-Residence in the Archdeaconry of Durham, 1774–1856: The Bishop and Chapter as Patrons', *NH*, XXVI, 1990.

Meikle 1992. M. M. Meikle, 'Northumberland Divided: Anatomy of a Sixteenth-Century Bloodfeud', *AA5*, XX, 1992.

Mellor 1970. G. J. Mellor, *The Northern Music Hall*, 1970.

Middlebrook 1950. S. Middlebrook, *Newcastle upon Tyne, its Growth and Achievement*, Wakefield 1950.

Middleton 1967. P. Middleton, 'Seventeenth-Century Witchcraft in Northumberland', *AA4*, XLV, 1967.

Miller 1976 for 1975. E. Miller, 'Farming in Northern England during the Twelfth and Thirteenth Centuries', *NH*, XI, 1976 for 1975.

Miller 1986. E. Miller, 'Rulers of Thirteenth Century Towns: The Cases of York and Newcastle upon Tyne', in P. R. Coss and S. Lloyd, (eds), *Thirteenth Century England: I*, Woodbridge 1986.

Miller 1988. E. Miller, 'Social Structure: G. – Northern England', in H. E. Hallam (ed.), *The Agrarian History of England and Wales, II, 1042–1350*, Cambridge 1988.

Miller 1960. F. J. W. Miller, *Growing Up in Newcastle upon Tyne*, 1960.

Miller 1986. F. J. W. Miller, 'The Infirmary on the Forth, 1753–1906', *AA5*, XIV, 1986.

Miller 1990. F. J. W. Miller, 'The Newcastle Dispensary, 1777–1976', *AA5*, XVIII, 1990.

Miller 1976. S. Miller, 'The Iron Bridge at Sunderland: A Revision', *Indust. Archaeol. Rev.*, I, 1976.

Mills 1991. M. Mills, 'One of its Kind: The Newcastle Infirmary', *Country Life*, 10 October 1991.

Millward and Robinson 1970. R. Millward and A. Robinson, *The Lake District*, 1970.

Milne 1971. J. M. Milne, *The Newspapers of Northumberland and Durham*, Newcastle 1971.

Mitchell 1984. B. R. Mitchell, *Economic Development of the British Coal Industry*, Cambridge 1984.

Mitchell 1919. W. C. Mitchell, *History of Sunderland*, 1919.

Moore 1974. R. Moore, *Pit-Men, Preachers and Politics: The Effects of Methodism in a Durham Mining Community*, 1974.

Moorman 1948. J. R. H. Moorman, 'The Estates of the Lanercost Canons', *CW2*, XLVIII, 1948.

Moorsom 1967. N. Moorsom, *The Birth and Growth of Modern Middlesbrough*, 1967.

Morison 1925. F. H. Morison, *Report of the Medical Officer of Health for Cumberland County Council*, 1925.

Morrill 1976. J. S. Morrill, *The Revolt of the Provinces: Conservatives and Radicals in the English Civil War, 1630–1650*, 1976.

Morrill 1979. J. S. Morrill, 'The Northern Gentry and the Great Rebellion', *NH*, XV, 1979.

Morris 1992. C. J. Morris, *Marriage and Murder in Eleventh-Century Northumbria: A Study of 'De Obsessione Dunelmi'*, University of York, Borthwick Paper No. 82, 1992.

Mott 1962. R. A. Mott, 'The London and Newcastle Chaldrons for Measuring Coal', *AA4*, XL, 1962.

Mountford 1966. C. Mountford, *The Bowes Railway*, Birmingham 1966.

Mountford 1967. C. Mountford, *The History of John Bowes and Partners up to 1914*, MA Thesis, Durham Universiy, 1967.

Moyes 1969. W. A. Moyes, *Mostly Mining*, Newcastle 1969.

Muirhead 1992. G. Muirhead, *The Fishing Industry of Northumberland and Durham, 1780–1914*, Ph.D. Thesis, Newcastle University, 1992.

Mulcaster *c.*1805. MS on lead working in library of Newcastle Literary and Philosophical Society.

Munby 1985. J. Munby, 'Medieval Kendal: The First Borough Charter and its Connections', *CW2*, LXXXV, 1985.

Munden 1990. A. F. Munden, 'The First Palmerston Bishop: Henry Montagu Villiers, Bishop of Carlisle, 1856–60, and Bishop of Durham, 1860–1', *NH*, XXVI, 1990.

Municipal 1935. Anon., *Municipal Government Centenary: County Borough of Gateshead*, 1935.

Murfin 1990. L. Murfin, *Popular Leisure in the Lake Counties*, Manchester 1990.

Murray MS. Claudine Murray, *Victorian Childhood*, unpub. recollections *c.*1970, copy in Newcastle University Library.

Nef 1932. J. U. Nef, *The Rise of the British Coal Industry in the Sixteenth and Seventeenth Centuries*, 1932.

Neville 1983. C. J. Neville, 'Gaol Delivery in the Border Counties, 1439–1459: Some Preliminary Observations', *NH*, XIX, 1983.

Neville 1994. C. J. Neville, 'Keeping the Peace on the Northern Marches in the Later Middle Ages', *Eng. Hist. Rev.*, CIX, 430, 1994.

Newcastle 1930. *The Newcastle Official Year Book*, 1930.

Newcastle Council 1891. *Proceedings of the Council . . . of Newcastle upon Tyne*, 1891.

Newcastle Council 1930, 1932. Newcastle City Council, *First Annual Report of the Public Assistance Committee*, 1930; *Second Annual Report*, ibid., 1932.

Newcastle Hospital 1937. Newcastle General Hospital, *Nurses' League Journal*, 1937.

Newcastle Hospital 1953. Newcastle Hospital Management Committee, *Clinical Review for 1953*, 1953.

Newcastle Union 1880, 1889. Newcastle Poor Law Union, *Annual Statements of Receipts and Expenditure*, 1880 and 1889.

Newcastle Watch 1869. Newcastle Watch Committee, *The Borough Constable's Guide*, 1869.

Newcastle Watch 1905. Newcastle Watch Committee, *The Police and Fire Brigade Manual*, 1905.

Newman 1981. P. R. Newman, 'The Royalist North: A Rejoinder', *NH*, XVII, 1981.

Nicholas 1989. K. Nicholas, *The Social Effects of Unemployment on Teesside, 1919–1939*, Manchester 1989.

Nicholson 1861. C. Nicholson, *Annals of Kendal*, 1861.

Nicholson and Burn 1777. J. Nicholson and R. Burn, *History of Cumberland and Westmorland*, 1777.

Nicholson 1996. T. Nicholson, '"Jacky" and the Jubilee: Middlesbrough's Creation Myth', in A. J. Pollard (ed.), *Middlesbrough: Town and Community 1830–1950*, Stroud 1996.

Nicholson 1975. W. J. Nicholson, 'Ralph Peter Clavering of Callaly, 1727–1787', *Northern Catholic History*, 1, 1975.

Nicholson 1978. W. J. Nicholson, 'Catholics in Morpeth in the Eighteenth Century', *Northern Catholic History*, 8, 1978.

Nicholson 1980. W. J. Nicholson, 'Nicholas Alain Gilbert: French Emigre Priest', *Northern Catholic History*, 11, 1980.

Nicholson 1981. W. J. Nicholson, 'Warwick Bridge and Corby Castle', *Northern Catholic History*, 14, 1981.

Nicholson 1985. W. J. Nicholson, 'Irish Priests in the North East in the Nineteenth Century', *Northern Catholic History*, 21, 1985.

Noble 1925. M. D. Noble, *A Long Life*, 1925.

Nolan 1989. J. Nolan, R. Fraser, B. Harbottle and F. C. Burton, 'The Medieval Town Defences of Newcastle upon Tyne: Excavation and Survey, 1986–7', *AA5*, XVII, 1989.

Northumberland Miners 1910. Northumberland Miners' Union, *Minutes*, 1910.

Northumbrian Tourist Board 1995. Northumbrian Tourist Board, *Regional Tourist Facts – Northumbria*, 1995.

O'Brien 1989. C. O'Brien *et al.*, 'Excavations at Newcastle Quayside: The Crown Court Site', *AA5*, XVII, 1989.

Odber 1965. A. J. Odber, *Area Redevelopment Policies in Britain and the Countries of the Common Market*, US Dept. of Commerce 1965.

Offler 1967. H. S. Offler, 'A Northumberland Charter of King Henry I', *AA4*, XLV, 1967.

Offler 1988. H. S. Offler, 'Murder on Framwellgate Bridge', *AA5*, XVI.

O'Neill 1982. C. F. O'Neill, 'The "Contest for Dominion": Political Conflict and the Decline of the Lowther "Interest" in Whitehaven, 1820–1900', *NH*, XVIII, 1982.

O'Neill 1994. C. O'Neill, 'Windermere in the 1920s', *The Local Historian*, Vol. 24, 4, 1994.

Ormrod 1990. W. M. Ormrod, *The Reign of Edward III: Crown and Political Society in England, 1327–1377*, Yale University Press, 1990.

Owen 1990. H. Owen, *The Lowther Family*, 1990.

Oxberry 1924. J. Oxberry, *The Birth of a Movement*, 1924.

Palmer 1972. A. Palmer, *Local Government and Social Problems in Kendal*, MA Thesis, Lancaster University, 1972.

Palmers 1946. Palmers Hebburn Co. Ltd., *Six Years Hard Labour*, 1946.

Parker 1909. F. H. M. Parker, 'Inglewood Forest IV', *CW2*, IX, 1909.

Parson and White, Cumberland, 1829. *History, Directory and Gazetteer of the Counties of Cumberland and Westmorland*, 1829.

Parson and White, Northumberland, 1828. *History, Directory and Gazetteer of the County of Northumberland*, 1828.

Patten 1978. J. Patten, *English Towns, 1500–1700*, 1978.

Patterson 1909. W. M. Patterson, *Northern Primitive Methodism*, 1909.

Pawson 1961. H. C. Pawson, *A Survey of the Agriculture of Northumberland*, 1961.

Pearson 1991. L. F. Pearson, 'The Architecture of Entertainment Run Riot', *NH*, XXVII, 1991.

Pease 1907. Sir A. E. Pease (ed.), *The Diaries of Edward Pease*, 1907.

Pelling 1967. H. Pelling, *Social Geography of the British Electorate, 1885–1910*, 1967.

Pennant 1772. T. Pennant, *A Tour in Scotland and Voyage to the Hebrides*, 1772.

Perriam 1992. D. R. Perriam, *Carlisle: An Illustrated History*, Kendal 1992.

Perry 1889. J. J. M. Perry, *The Edlingham Burglary: Or Circumstantial Evidence*, 1889.

Philipson 1958. J. Philipson, 'The Distillation of Spirits in the Eighteenth and Early Nineteenth Centuries', *AA4*, XXXVI, 1958.

Phillips 1970. C. B. Phillips, 'County Committees and Local Government in Cumberland and Westmorland, 1642–1660', *NH*, XIV, 1970.

Phillips 1973. C. B. Phillips, *Cumberland and Westmorland Gentry, 1600–85*, Ph.D. Thesis, Lancaster University, 1973.

Phillips 1977. C. B. Phillips, 'The Cumbrian Iron Industry in the 17th Century', in W. H. Challoner and B. M. Radcliffe (eds), *Trade and Transport*, Manchester 1977.

Phillips 1978. C. B. Phillips, 'The Royalist North: The Cumberland and Westmorland Gentry, 1642–1660', *NH*, XIV, 1978.

Phillips 1979. C. B. Phillips (ed.), *Lowther Family Estate Books, 1617–1675*, Surtees Society, 1979.

Phillips 1984. C. B. Phillips, 'Town and Country: Economic Change in Kendal, *c.*1550–1700', in P. Clark (ed.), *The Transformation of English Provincial Towns, 1600–1800*, 1984.

Phillips 1994. C. B. Phillips, 'The Plague in Kendal in 1598: Some New Evidence', *CW2*, XCIV, 1994.

Phillips 1995. C. B. Phillips, 'The Corporation of Kendal under Charles II', *NH*, XXXI, 1995.

Pollard 1976 for 1975. A. J. Pollard, 'The Northern Retainers of Richard Nevill, Earl of Salisbury', *NH*, XI, 1976 for 1975.

Pollard 1989. A. J. Pollard, 'The North-Eastern Economy and the Agrarian Crisis of 1438–40', *NH*, XXV, 1989.

Pollard 1990. A. J. Pollard, *North-Eastern England during the Wars of the Roses*, Oxford 1990.

Pollard 1996. A. J. Pollard (ed.), *Middlesbrough: Town and Community 1830–1950*, Stroud 1996.

Pollard 1955. S. Pollard, 'Barrow in Furness and the Seventh Duke of Devonshire', *Econ. Hist. Rev.*, 2nd Ser., VIII, 1955.

Pollard and Marshall 1954–55. S. Pollard and J. Marshall, 'The Furness Railway and the Growth of Barrow', *J. of Transport History*, I, 1954–55.

Polley 1996. L. Polley, 'Housing the Community, 1830–1914', in A. J. Pollard (ed.), *Middlesbrough: Town and Community 1830–1950*, Stroud 1996.

Poor Law Commissioners, 1836. *Report of the Poor Law Commission*, 1836.

Porter 1970. J. H. Porter, 'David Dale and Conciliation in the Northern Manufactured Iron Trade, 1869–1914', *NH*, V, 1970.

Potts 1991. A. Potts, *Jack Casey: The Sunderland Assassin*, Newcastle 1971.

Potts 1992. A. Potts, *From Acorn to Oak: Co-operation on Tyneside, 1858–1909*, n.d., *c.*1992.

Potts 1993. A. Potts, *The Wearside Champions*, Newcastle 1993.

Potts 1994. A. Potts, 'T. Dan Smith: The Man and the Legend', *North East Labour History Bulletin*, No. 28, 1994.

Pound 1972. R. Pound, *The Fenwick Story*, 1972.

Prestwich 1988. M. Prestwich, *Edward I*, 1988.

Prevost 1961. W. E. J. Prevost, 'A Journey to Carlisle and Penrith in 1731', CW2, LXI, 1961.

Price 1993. K. Price, 'Women of Steel: Health and Safety Issues During World War Two', *North East Labour History Bulletin*, No. 27, 1993.

Price 1980. T. Price, *Defence and Public Order in Cumberland in the Age of Revolution*, undergraduate dissertation, University of Manchester, 1980.

Pringle Cumberland. A. Pringle, *A General View of the Agriculture of the County of Cumberland*, 1794.

Pringle Westmorland. A. Pringle, *A General View of the Agriculture of the County of Westmorland*, 1794.

Pugh 1978. D. R. Pugh, *The North-West in the Nineties: Press and Social Opinion in North Lancashire, Westmorland and Cumberland, 1894–9*, M.Litt. Thesis, Lancaster University, 1978.

Purdue 1974. A. W. Purdue, *Parliamentary Elections in North East England, 1900–1906: The Advent of Labour*, M.Litt. Thesis, Newcastle University, 1974.

Purdue 1982. A. W. Purdue, 'Jarrow Politics, 1885–1914: The Challenge to Liberal Hegemony', *NH*, XVIII, 1982.

Purdue 1994. A. W. Purdue, 'John and Harriet Carr: A Brother and Sister from the North-East on the Grand Tour', *NH*, XXX, 1994.

Purvis 1986. M. Purvis, 'Co-operative Retailing in England, 1830–1850: Developments Beyond Rochdale', *NH*, XXII, 1986.

Pybus Society 1993. The Pybus Society, *Medicine in Northumbria: Essays in the History of Medicine*, Newcastle 1993.

Radcliffe 1977. B. M. Radcliffe, 'Control of the Liquor Trade in Great Britain', in W. H. Chaloner and B. M. Radcliffe (eds), *Trade and Transport*, Manchester 1977.

Raimes 1955. A. L. Raimes, 'Shortflatt Tower and its Owners', *AA4*, XXXIII, 1955.

Raistrick 1977. A. Raistrick, *Two Centuries of Industrial Welfare, 1692–1905*, Buxton 1977.

Rawlinson 1850. R. Rawlinson, *Report to the General Board of Health . . . on . . . Inquiry into the Sanitary Condition . . . of Alnwick, etc.*, 1850.

Rawlinson Gateshead 1850. R. Rawlinson, *Report . . . on a Preliminary Inquiry into . . . the Borough of Gateshead*, 1850.

Rawnsley 1896. H. D. Rawnsley, *Harvey Goodwin, Bishop of Carlisle*, 1896.

Reader 1976. W. J. Reader, *Metal Box: A History*, 1976.

Readshaw 1910. T. Readshaw, *History of the Bishop Auckland Industrial Co-operative Society*, 1910.

Redmayne 1942. R. A. S. Redmayne, *Men, Mines and Memories*, 1942.

Reed 1903. A. Reed, *Bruce's School, with a Peep at Newcastle in the 'Fifties*, London and Newcastle 1903.

Reid 1845. D. B. Reid, *Report on the Sanitary Condition of Carlisle*, 1845.

Reid Newcastle 1845. D. B. Reid, *A Report on the State of Newcastle and other Towns*, 1845.

Reid 1990. D. S. Reid, *The Durham Crown Lordships in the Sixteenth and Seventeenth Centuries and the Aftermath*, Durham County Local History Society, 1990.

Reid 1906. R. R. Reid, 'The Rebellion of the Earls, 1569', *Trans. R. Hist. Soc.*, 2nd Ser., 20, 1906.

Reid 1921. R. R. Reid, *The King's Council in the North*, 1921.

Relief Fund 1885–86. *Newcastle Relief Fund, 1885–86*, volume of press cuttings, Newcastle Central Library.

Rennison 1977. R. W. Rennison, 'The Supply of Water to Newcastle upon Tyne and Gateshead, 1680–1837', *AA5*, V, 1977.

Rennison 1979. R. W. Rennison, *Water to Tyneside: A History of the Newcastle and Gateshead Water Company*, Newcastle 1979.

Rennison 1993–94. R. W. Rennison, 'The Development of the River Tees, 1808–1914', *Trans. Newcomen Soc.*, 65, 1993–94.

Report 1933. *Report to the Minister of Labour by the Commissioners Apointed to Administer Transitional Payments in the County of Durham*, 1933.

Rewcastle 1854. J. Rewcastle, *Newcastle As It Is*, Newcastle 1854.

Reynolds 1935. J. D. Reynolds, *The Governance of Blyth*, 1935.

Richardson 1923. W. Richardson, *History of the Parish of Wallsend*, 1923.

Ridley 1974. G. W. Ridley, 'The Inclosure and Division of Certain Wastes and Commons in the Manor of Hexham', *AA5*, II, 1974.

Ridley 1958. U. Ridley, *Cecilia: The Life and Letters of Cecilia Ridley, 1819–45*, 1958.

Ridley 1962. U. Ridley, 'The History of Glass-Making on the Tyne and Wear', *AA4*, XL, 1962.

Roberts 1967. G. Roberts, *Demarcation Rules in Shipbuilding and Shiprepairing*, Cambridge 1967.

Robinson 1988. F. Robinson (ed.), *Post-Industrial Tyneside: An Economic and Social Survey of Tyneside in the 1980s*, Newcastle 1988.

Robinson 1934. W. Robinson, *The Story of the Royal Infirmary, Sunderland*, 1934.

Robinson and Sadler, 1984. F. Robinson and D. Sadler, *Consett after the Closure*, Dept of Geography, Durham University, 1984.

Rogan 1956. J. Rogan, 'Episcopal Visitations in the Diocese of Durham, 1662–1671', *AA4*, XXXIV, 1956.

Rogers 1967. F. W. Rogers, 'The Unreformed Borough of Gateshead', *AA4*, XLV, 1967.

Rogers 1971. F. W. Rogers, 'Gateshead and the Public Health Act of 1848', *AA4*, XLIX, 1971.

Rollason 1994. D. Rollason, M. Harvey and M. Prestwich (eds), *Anglo-Norman Durham*, Woodbridge 1994.

Rollinson 1963. R. Rollinson, 'The Historical Geography of Settlement in Monastic Low Furness', *Naturalists' Field Club*, New Ser., 9, 1963.

Rollinson 1978. W. Rollinson, *A History of Cumberland and Westmorland*, 1978.

Rose 1971. M. E. Rose, *The English Poor Law*, Newton Abbot 1971.

Rose 1982. R. K. Rose, 'Cumbrian Society and the Anglo-Norman Church', in S. Mews (ed.), *Religion and National Identity*, Oxford 1982.

Ross 1982. C. Ross, *The Development of the Glass Industry on the Rivers Tyne and Wear*, Ph.D. Thesis, Newcastle University, 1982.

Rounding 1985. A. Rounding, 'William, 4th Lord Widdrington of Blankney, 1675–1743', *Northern Catholic History*, 22, 1985.

Rowan Hamilton 1914. G. Rowan Hamilton (ed.), *The Trial of John Alexander Dickman*, Edinburgh and London 1914.

Rowe 1971. D. J. Rowe, 'The Culleys, Northumberland Farmers, 1767–1813', *Agric. Hist. Rev.*, 19, 1971.

Rowe Bibliography 1971. D. J. Rowe, 'The Economy of the North-East in the Nineteenth Century: A Survey with a Bibliography', *NH*, VI, 1971.
Rowe Chartism 1971. D. J. Rowe, 'Some Aspects of Chartism on Tyneside', *Int. Rev. Soc. Hist*, Vol. XVI, Part 1, 1971.
Rowe 1972. D. J. Rowe (ed.), Reprint of J. Bailey and G. Culley, *A General View of the Agriculture of the Counties of Northumberland, Cumberland and Westmorland*, Newcastle 1972.
Rowe 1973. D. J. Rowe, 'Occupations in Northumberland and Durham, 1851–1911', *NH*, VIII, 1973.
Rowe 1977. D. J. Rowe, 'Tyneside Chartism', in N. McCord (ed.), *Essays in Tyneside Labour History*, Newcastle 1977.
Rowe 1990. D. J. Rowe, 'The North-East', in F. M. L. Thompson (ed.), *The Cambridge Social History of Britain 1750–1950, Vol. I, Regions and Communities*, Cambridge 1990.
Rowland 1983. J. Rowland, 'Physical Force Chartism on Tyneside in 1839', in M. Callcott and R. Challinor (eds), *Working Class Politics in North East England*, Newcastle 1983.
Royal Commission 1834. *Report of the Royal Commission on the Poor Laws*, 1834.
Royal Commission 1842. Royal Commission on the Employment of Children, First Report of Commissioners, Mines, 1842.
Royal Commission 1992. Royal Commission on the Historical Monuments of England, *An Architectural Survey of Urban Development Corporation Areas: Tyne and Wear Volume Two: Wearside*, RCHM 1992.
Runciman 1926. W. Runciman, *Collier Brigs and their Sailors*, 1926.
Rushton 1989. P. Rushton, 'The Poor Law, the Parish and the Community in North-East England', *NH*, XXV, 1989.
Russell 1913. C. E. B. Russell, *Social Problems of the North*, n.d., *c.*1913.
Russell 1910. G. W. E. Russell, *Sir Wilfrid Lawson: A Memoir*, 1910.
Ryder 1992. P. F. Ryder, 'The Gatehouse of Morpeth Castle, Northumberland', *AA5*, XX, 1992.
Ryle Elliot 1952. W. Ryle Elliot, 'The Work of Robert Adam in Northumberland', *AA4*, XXX, 1952.
Saunders 1985. D. Saunders, 'Tyneside and the Making of the Russian Revolution', *NH*, XXI, 1985.
Sawyer 1995. P. Sawyer, 'The Last Scandinavian Kings of York', *NH*, XXXI, 1995.
Scammell 1960–61. G. V. Scammell, 'War at Sea under the Tudors: Some Newcastle upon Tyne Evidence', *AA4*, XXXVIII, 1960, XXXIX, 1961.
Scott 1952. Forrest S. Scott, 'Earl Waltheof of Northumbria', *AA4*, XXX, 1952.
Scott 1959. Forrest S. Scott, 'Pre-Conquest Sculptures and the Common Seal of Hartlepool', *AA4*, XXXVII, 1959.
Scott 1962. J. D. Scott, *Vickers: A History*, 1962.
Searle 1983. C. E. Searle, *The Odd Corner of England: A Study of Rural Social Formation in Transition, c.1700–1914*, Ph.D. Thesis, Essex University, 1983.
Searle 1993. C. E. Searle, 'Customary Tenants and the Enclosure of the Cumbrian Commons', *NH*, XXIX, 1993.
Seeley 1973. J. Y. E. Seeley, *Coal-Mining Villages of Northumberland and Durham: A Study of Sanitary Conditions and Social Facilities*, MA Thesis, Newcastle University, 1973.

Semple 1936. A. Semple, *Reports on the Sanitary Condition of Carlisle*, 1936.

Sewell 1978. J. R. Sewell, 'A "Short View" of Some Northumberland Manors, 1629', *NH*, XIV, 1978.

Sharp 1980. R. Sharp, '100 Years of a Lost Cause: Nonjuring Principles in Newcastle from the Revolution to the Death of Prince Charles Edward Stuart', *AA5*, 1980.

Shaw 1920. H. Shaw, *Newcastle and Gateshead Trade and Commerce*, 1920.

Sill 1984. M. Sill, 'Landownership and Industry: The East Durham Coalfield in the Nineteenth Century', *NH*, XX, 1984.

Slade 1975. J. and M. Slade, 'Railway Structures near Falstone, on the Former Border Counties Railway', *AA5*, III, 1975.

Smailes 1968. A. E. Smailes, *North England*, 1961, revised ed. 1968.

Smith, n.d. H. J. Smith, (ed.), *A Mirthless Mirrour Mischievously Managed*, Durham County Local History Society, n.d.

Smith 1961. R. Smith, *Sea-Coal for London*, 1961.

Smith 1976. W. V. Smith, 'The Riddell Family of Gateshead as Recusants in the Seventeenth Century', *Northern Catholic History*, 3, 1976.

Smith and Holden 1947. J. W. Smith and T. S. Holden, *Where Ships are Born: Sunderland 1346–1946*, 1947.

Snape 1961. M. G. Snape, 'Some Evidence of Lollard Activity in the Diocese of Durham in the Early Fifteenth Century', *AA4*, XXXIX, 1961.

Southern 1993. J. Southern, 'Co-operation in the North-West of England, 1919–39', *J. of Regional and Local Studies*, 13, 1, 1993.

Speck 1989. W. A. Speck, 'The Revolution of 1688 in the North of England', *NH*, XXV, 1989.

Speck 1992. W. A. Speck, 'Northumberland Elections in the Eighteenth Century', *NH*, XXVIII, 1992.

Spence 1954. J. Spence *et al.*, *A Thousand Families in Newcastle upon Tyne*, 1954.

Spence 1977. R. T. Spence, 'The Pacification of the Cumberland Borders, 1593–1628', *NH*, XIII, 1977.

Spence 1979. R. T. Spence, 'Lady Anne Clifford, Countess of Dorset, Pembroke and Montgomery (1590–1676): A Reappraisal', *NH*, XV, 1979.

Spence 1980. R. T. Spence, 'The Graham Clans and Lands on the Eve of the Jacobean Pacification', *CW2*, LXXX, 1980.

Spence, 'First Sir Richard', 1980. R. T. Spence, 'The First Sir Richard Graham of Norton Conyers and Netherby, 1583–1653', *NH*, XVI, 1980.

Spence 1984. R. T. Spence, 'The Backward North Modernized? The Cliffords, Earls of Cumberland, and the Socage Manor of Carlisle, 1611–1643', *NH*, XX, 1984.

Spence 1991. R. T. Spence, 'A Royal Progress in the North: James I at Carlisle Castle and the Feast of Brougham, August 1617', *NH*, XXVII, 1991.

Spence 1995. R. T. Spence, 'Henry, Lord Clifford, and the First Bishops' War, 1639', *NH*, XXXI, 1995.

Spencer 1911. A. Spencer, *Life of Henry Watts*, 1911.

Spring 1955. D. Spring, 'A Great Agricultural Estate: Netherby under Sir James Graham, 1820–45', *Agricultural History*, XXIX, 1955.

Staddon 1973. S. A. Staddon, *Sunderland Corporation Transport*, 1973.

Stark 1972. D. Stark, *The Origins and Development of a Single Industry Town: Barrow in Furness*, MA Thesis, Lancaster University, 1972.

Steele 1976. E. D. Steele, 'The Irish Presence in the North of England, 1850–1914', *NH*, XII, 1976.
Steele 1995. E. D. Steele, 'Lord Salisbury and his Northern Audiences', *NH*, XXXI, 1995.
Stenton 1970. F. M. Stenton, 'Pre-Conquest Westmorland', in D. Stenton (ed.), *Preparatory to Anglo-Saxon England*, Oxford 1970.
Stevens Banham 1987. L. M. Stevens Benham, 'The Durham Clergy, 1494–1540: A Study in Continuity and Mediocrity among the Unbeneficed', in D. Marcombe (ed.), *The Last Principality: Politics, Religion and Society in the Bishopric of Durham, 1494–1660*, Nottingham 1987.
Stevenson 1979. J. Stevenson, *Popular Disturbances in England, 1700–1870*, 1979.
Stigant 1971. P. Stigant, 'Wesleyan Methodism and Working-Class Radicalism in the North, 1792–1821', *NH*, VI, 1971.
Storey 1961. R. L. Storey, *Thomas Langley and the Bishopric of Durham, 1406–1437*, SPCK, 1961.
Stranks 1978. C. J. Stranks, 'John Sharp at Bamburgh Castle, 1758–1792', *AA5*, VI, 1978.
Structure Cumbria. Cumbria County Council, *Structure Plan Report for Cumbria*, 1976.
Sturgess 1975. R. W. Sturgess, *Aristocrat in Business*, Durham County Local History Society, 1975.
Sturgess 1982. R. Sturgess, 'The Londonderry Trust, 1819–54', *AA5*, X, 1982.
Sullivan 1971. W. R. Sullivan, *Blyth in the Eighteenth Century*, Newcastle 1971.
Summerson 1982. H. Summerson, 'Crime and Society in Medieval Cumberland', *CW2*, LXXXII, 1982.
Summerson 1986. H. Summerson, 'The Place of Carlisle in the Commerce of Northern England in the Thirteenth Century', in P. R. Coss and S. D. Lloyd (eds), *Thirteenth Century England: I*, Woodbridge 1986.
Summerson 1992. H. Summerson, 'The King's *Clericulus*: The Life and Career of Silvester de Everdon, Bishop of Carlisle, 1247–1254', *NH*, XXVIII, 1992.
Summerson Responses 1992. H. Summerson, 'Responses to War: Carlisle and the West March in the Later Fourteenth Century', in A. Goodman and A. Tuck (eds), *War and Border Societies in the Middle Ages*, 1992.
Summerson 1993. H. Summerson, *Medieval Carlisle: The City and the Borders from the Late Eleventh to the Mid-Sixteenth Century*, Cumberland and Westmorland Antiquarian and Archaeological Society, 2 vols., 1993.
Summerson 1995. H. Summerson, 'From Border Stronghold to Railway Station: The Fortunes of Berwick Castle 1560–1850', *AA5*, XXIII, 1995.
Sunderland 1967. N. Sunderland, *A History of Darlington*, Darlington 1967.
Sutherland 1972. D. Sutherland, *The Story of the Border Regiment (1702–1959)*, 1972.
Swanton 1966. E. W. Swanton, *The World of Cricket*, 1966.
Tapper 1973. O. Tapper, *Armstrong Whitworth Aircraft Since 1913*, 1973.
Tate 1942. W. E. Tate, *A Hand List of English Enclosure Acts and Awards: Part 26, Northumberland*, Durham, Proc. Soc. Antiq. Newcastle, 4th Ser., 10, 1942.
Taylor 1992. A. Taylor, 'More Tick than Big Ben: Working Class Credit on Tyneside between the Wars', *North East Labour History Bulletin*, No. 26, 1992.
Taylor 1953. A. J. Taylor, 'Combination in the Mid-Nineteenth Century Coal Trade', *Trans. R. Hist. Soc.*, 5th Ser., 3, 1953.

Taylor 1995. D. Taylor, *A Well-Chosen Effective Body of Men: The Middlesbrough Police Force, 1841–1914*, University of Teesside, 1995.

Taylor 1996. D. Taylor, 'The Infant Hercules and the Augean Stables: A Century of Economic and Social Development in Middlesbrough *c.*1840–1939', in A. J. Pollard (ed.), *Middlesbrough; Town and Community 1830–1950*, Stroud 1996.

Taylor 1989. J. M. Taylor, *England's Border County: A History of Northumberland County Council, 1889–1989*, Northumberland County Council 1989.

Taylor 1964. M. Taylor, *The Gateshead School Board*, MA Thesis, Newcastle University, 1964.

Thirsk 1984. J. Thirsk (ed.), *The Agrarian History of England and Wales*, Vol. V, Cambridge 1984.

Thompson 1946. B. L. Thompson, *The Lake District and the National Trust*, Kendal 1946.

Thompson 1976. R. N. Thompson, *The New Poor Law in Cumberland and Westmorland*, Ph.D. Thesis, Newcastle University, 1976.

Thompson 1979. R. N. Thompson, 'The Working of the Poor Law Amendment Act in Cumbria, 1836–1871', *NH*, XV, 1979.

Thompson and Harrison 1978. D. Thompson and J. F. C. Harrison, *A Bibliography of the Chartist Movement*, 1978.

Thornthwaite 1991. S. E. Thornthwaite, 'The Border Counties Railway', *AA5*, XIX, 1991.

Thornthwaite 1992. S. E. Thornthwaite, 'On the Most Advantageous Line: The Tyne–Solway Canal', *AA5*, XX, 1992.

Tillbrook 1987. M. Tillbrook, 'Arminianism and Society in County Durham, 1617–1642', in D. Marcombe (ed.), *The Last Principality: Politics, Religion and Society in the Bishopric of Durham, 1494–1660*, Nottingham 1987.

Todd 1991. J. M. Todd, *The Lanercost Cartulary*, Ph.D. Thesis, Lancaster University, 1991.

Todd 1976. N. Todd, *A History of Labour in Lancaster and Barrow-in-Furness, c.1890–1920*, M.Litt. Thesis, Lancaster University, 1976.

Todd 1991. N. Todd, *The Militant Democracy: Joseph Cowen and Victorian Radicalism*, Newcastle 1991.

Todd 1994. N. Todd, *The People against the Blackshirts*, Newcastle 1994.

Tomlinson 1915. W. W. Tomlinson, *The North East Railway: Its Rise and Development*, 1915.

Topping 1993. P. Topping, 'Lordenshaws Hillfort and its Environs: A Survey by the Royal Commission on the Historical Monuments of England', *AA5*, XXI, 1993.

Tough 1928. D. L. W. Tough, *The Last Years of a Frontier: A History of the Borders during the Reign of Elizabeth I*, Oxford 1928 (reprinted Alnwick 1987).

Towill 1991. S. Towill, *Carlisle*, 1991.

Townsend 1983. A. R. Townsend, *The Impact of Recession on Industry, Employment and the Regions, 1976–1981*, 1983.

Trescatheric 1985. B. Trescatheric, *How Barrow was Built*, 1985.

Tuck 1968. J. A. Tuck, 'Richard II and the Border Magnates', *NH*, III, 1968.

Tuck 1971. J. A. Tuck, 'Northumbrian Society in the Fourteenth Century', *NH*, VI, 1971.

Tuck 1985. J. A. Tuck, 'War and Society in the Medieval North', *NH*, XXI, 1985.

Tuck 1986. J. A. Tuck, 'The Emergence of a Northern Nobility, 1250–1400', *NH*, XXII, 1986.

Tuck 1992. J. A. Tuck, 'The Percies and the Community of Northumberland in the Later Fourteenth Century', in A. Goodman and A. Tuck (eds), *War and Border Societies in the Middle Ages*, 1992.

Tuck 1993. J. T. Tuck, *The Collieries of Northumberland, Vol. 1*, Newcastle 1993.

Tuck R. F. 1968. R. F. Tuck, 'The Origins of the Royal Grammar School, Newcastle upon Tyne', *AA4*, XLVI, 1968.

Tucker 1987. G. Tucker, 'Millstone Making in England', *Indust. Archaeol. Rev.*, IX, 1987.

Tudor 1989. V. Tudor, 'The Cult of St Cuthbert in the Twelfth Century: The Evidence of Reginald of Durham', in B. Bonner, D. Rollason and C. Stancliffe (eds), *St Cuthbert, his Cult and his Community*, 1989.

Tufft 1976. R. Tufft, *The Social and Political Composition of the Early Cumberland County Councils, 1889–1914*, MA Thesis, Lancaster University, 1976.

Tullett and McCombie 1980. E. Tullett and G. McCombie, 'An Excavation in the Cloth Market, Newcastle upon Tyne', *AA5*, VIII, 1980.

Turnbull 1975. L. Turnbull, *The History of Lead Mining in the North East of England*, Newcastle 1975.

Turnbull 1991. J. Turnbull, *Housing Tenure and Social Structure: The Impact of Inter-War Housing Change in Carlisle, 1917–1939*, Ph.D. Thesis, Lancaster University, 1991.

Turnbull and Walsh 1994. P. Turnbull and D. Walsh, 'Recent Work at Egremont Castle', *CW2*, XCIV, 1994.

Turner 1996. J. Turner, 'The Frontier Revisited: Thrift and Fellowship in the New Industrial Town, c.1830–1914', in A. J. Pollard (ed.), *Middlesbrough: Town and Community 1830–1950*, Stroud 1966.

Tyler 1969. P. Tyler, 'The Church Courts at York and Witchcraft Prosecutions, 1567–1640', *NH*, IV, 1969.

Tyneside 1935. Tyneside Industrial Development Board, *Tyneside: The Natural Centre of Industry*, 1935.

Tyneside Scottish 1915. Tyneside Scottish Brigade Committee, *First Report of the Honorary Secretary*, 1915.

Vaughan and Wilkes 1987. D. R. Vaughan and K. Wilkes, *Tourism in Cumbria: A Study of the Economic Impact, etc., 1986*, Cumbria Tourist Board 1987.

Ville 1989. S. P. Ville, 'Patterns of Shipping Investment in the Port of Newcastle upon Tyne, 1750–1850', *NH*, XXV, 1989.

Wade 1994. J. F. Wade, 'The Overseas Trade of Newcastle upon Tyne in the Late Middle Ages', *NH*, XXX, 1994.

Waitt 1972. E. I. Waitt, *John Morley, Joseph Cowen and Robert Spence Watson: Liberal Divisions in Newcastle Politics, 1873–1895*, Ph.D. Thesis, Manchester University, 1972.

Wallace 1934. D. Euan Wallace, Durham and Tyneside Report, in *Reports of Investigations into the Industrial Conditions in Certain Depressed Areas*, Cmd. 4728 of 1934.

Walsh 1991. D. Walsh, 'Salt-Making on the Cumbrian Coast', *Archaeology North*, I, 1991.

Walton 1979. J. K. Walton, 'Railways and Resort Development in Victorian England: The Case of Silloth', *NH*, XV, 1979.

Walton 1991. J. K. Walton, 'The Windermere Tourist Trade', in O. M. Westall (ed.), *Windermere in the Nineteenth Century*, University of Lancaster 1991.

Walton and McGloin 1981. J. Walton and F. R. McGloin, 'The Tourist Trade in Victorian Lakeland', *NH*, XVII, 1981.

Ward 1967. J. T. Ward, *Sir James Graham*, 1967.

Ward 1971. J. T. Ward, 'Landowners and Mining', in J. T. Ward and R. G. Wilson (eds), *Land and Industry*, 1971.

Ward 1963. S. P. G. Ward, *Faithful: The Story of the Durham Light Infantry*, 1963.

Warren 1989. K. Warren, *Armstrongs of Elswick: Growth in Engineering to the Merger with Vickers*, 1989.

Warren 1990. K. Warren, *Consett from 1840 to 1980: A Study in Industrial Location*, Oxford 1990.

Waterson 1987. A. Waterson, 'Working Class Housing and Related Health Policies in Mid-Nineteenth Century Kendal, with particular reference to the activities of John Whitwell, MP', *CW2*, LXXXVII, 1987.

Watson 1937. A. Watson, *My Life*, 1937.

Watson 1994. D. Watson, ' "Champion Peds": Road Running on Victorian Tyneside', *North East Labour History Bulletin*, No. 28, 1994.

Watt 1971. S. J. Watt, 'Tenant-Right in Early Seventeenth Century Northumberland', *NH*, VI, 1971.

Watts 1975. S. and S. Watts, *From Border to Middle Shire: Northumberland, 1586–1625*, 1975.

Wearmouth 1958. R. F. Wearmouth, *Leaves from a Padre's Diary*, North Shields 1958.

Webster 1868. C. Webster, 'On Farming in Westmorland', *J. of the Royal Agricultural Society*, 19, 1868.

Welford 1895. R. Welford, *Men of Mark 'Twixt Tyne and Tweed*, 1895.

Welford 1905. R. Welford (ed.), *Records of the Committees for Compounding, etc., with Delinquent Royalists in Northumberland and Durham during the Civil War*, Surtees Society, III, 1905.

Wesencraft 1988. C. F. Wesencraft, *The Battle of Otterburn*, Athena Books, Doncaster 1988.

Westall 1991. O. M. Westall, 'The Retreat to Arcadia: Windermere as a Select Residential Resort in the Late Nineteenth Century', in O. M. Westall (ed.), *Windermere in the Nineteenth Century*, University of Lancaster 1991.

Whatley 1976. C. Whatley, 'The Introduction of the Newcomen Engine to Ayrshire', *Indust. Archaeol. Rev.*, I, 1976.

Whitfield 1975. J. N. Whitfield, *The Economic Problems of West Cumberland and the Effect on Regional Policy since 1945*, BA (Geography) dissertation, Durham University, 1975.

Whyte, Sheiling, 1985. I. D. Whyte, 'The Sheiling and Upland Pastoral Economy in the Lake District in Medieval and Early Modern Times', in J. R. Baldwin and I. D. Whyte (eds), *The Scandinavians in Cumbria*, Edinburgh 1985.

Wigham Richardson 1911. J. Wigham Richardson, *Memoirs*, 1911.

Williams 1951. J. E. Williams, *The Growth and Decline of the Port of Whitehaven*, MA Thesis, Leeds University, 1951.

Williams 1975. L. A. Williams, *Road Transport in Cumbria in the 19th Century*, 1975.

Williams 1963. P. Williams, 'The Northern Borderland under the Early Stuarts', in H. E. Bell and R. L. Ollard (eds), *Historical Essays, 1600–1750 Presented to David Ogg*, 1963.

Wilson 1901, 1905. J. M. Wilson, *The Victoria History of the County of Cumberland*, Vol. I 1901, Vol. II 1905.

Wilson 1983. K. Wilson, ' "Whole Hogs" and "Suckling Pigs": Chartism and the Complete Suffrage Union in Sunderland', in M. Callcott and R. Challinor (eds), *Working Class Politics in North East England*, Newcastle 1983.

Winchester 1985. A. Winchester, 'The Multiple Estate – a Framework for the Evolution of Settlement in Anglo-Saxon and Scandinavian Cumbria', in J. R. Baldwin and I. D. Whyte (eds), *The Scandinavians in Cumbria*, Edinburgh 1985.

Winchester 1986. A. Winchester, 'Medieval Cockermouth', *CW2*, LXXXVI, 1986.

Winchester 1987. A. Winchester, *Landscape and Society in Medieval Cumbria*, Edinburgh 1987.

Wood 1995. I. Wood, 'Northumbrians and Franks in the Age of Wilfrid', *NH*, XXXI, 1995.

Wood 1952. O. Wood, *The Development of the Coal, Iron and Shipbuilding Industries of West Cumberland, 1750–1914*, Ph.D. Thesis, London University, 1952.

Wood 1988. O. Wood, *West Cumberland Coal*, Kendal 1988.

Wood 1976. P. A. Wood, *The Sunderland Poor Law Union*, M.Litt. Thesis, Newcastle University, 1976.

Wood 1975. R. Wood (ed.), *The Rising in the North: The 1569 Rebellion*, Durham 1975.

Wrathmell 1975. S. Wrathmell, *Deserted Villages in Northumberland*, Ph.D. Thesis, University of Wales (Cardiff), 1975.

Wrathmell 1980. S. Wrathmell, 'Village Depopulation in the 17th and 18th Centuries: Examples from Northumberland', *Post-Medieval Archaeology*, 14, 1980.

Yarrow 1992. P. J. Yarrow, 'Mrs. Gaskell and Newcastle', *AA5*, XX, 1992.

Young 1771. A. Young, *A Six Months' Tour Through the North of England*, 1771.

Young 1994. A. Young, 'The Bishopric of Durham in Stephen's Reign', in D. Rollason, M. Harvey and M. Prestwich (eds), *Anglo-Norman Durham*, Woodbridge 1994.

Index

Abernethy, treaty of, 23, 24–5
Adams, Jack, 1st Lord, 376, 396–7
agriculture
  arable farming, 39, 40, 47–9, 52,
    117, 121, 122, 175–8, 183, 184,
    293, 309; early, 40–51, 55, 57,
    118–20; border warfare and,
    75–6, 118–20; cattle farming and
    the cattle trade, 29, 39, 40, 46–9,
    117, 118, 121, 122, 128, 178,
    179, 183, 186, 224, 292–3, 365;
    cattle plague, 117; dairy farming,
    292, 293, 265, 389; education,
    295; farm labour, 41–3, 46–7, 50,
    120, 137, 176, 186–8, 213, 294;
    female farm workers, 294, 346;
    pigs, 46, 49, 292, 293, 307, 365;
    sheep farming, 29, 40, 46, 47, 49,
    73, 104, 117, 127, 137, 181, 183,
    187, 292, 393, 365; tenurial
    changes, 47–8, 104, 114, 120–1,
    123–4, 171–5; recovery, 120–4;
    enclosures, 178–81; early modern,
    120–4, 176–88; modern, 291–5,
    365, 389, 401
Ailred, Saint, 30
Alexander I, King of Scots, 29
Alexander II, King of Scots, 36–7
almshouses, see philanthropy
Alnmouth, 177, 193
Alnwick
  church, 76; early economy, 48, 49,
    55; medieval, 28, 29, 36;

monastery, 58, 107; Percy base,
  67, 72, 88, 135; public health,
  234, 300, 305, 309–10; rebuilding
  of castle, 243; road links, 193,
  194; textiles, 220; Tudor garrison,
  93
Alston, 53, 194, 278, 401
Ambleside, 217, 224, 225, 288, 352,
  409
Appleby
  barony, 30; Civil War, 154; Earl
    of Thanet and, 184, 240–1;
    education, 138, 139; James II and,
    156; parliamentary elections,
    240–1, 247, 250; trade lost to
    Penrith, 225
Appleby, Thomas, Bishop of Carlisle,
  99, 100, 107
aristocracy
  early northern baronies, 26–32,
    37–8, 39–44, 57; importance of,
    83, 113–14, 115–16; 16th century,
    84–90, 91, 92–8, 113–17; early
    modern, 173, 174–5, 180–5;
    modern, 235–44, 245, 273–7,
    353–4, 389–90, 401–2
Armstrong, William George, 1st Lord,
  and company, 256, 272–3, 273–6,
  283–4, 354, 364, 388
Ashington, 277, 303–4, 360, 387
Aspatria, 121, 122, 286, 340
assarts, 41, 46, 55, 121, 126
Athelwold, Bishop of Carlisle, 30, 58

445

Duncan I, King of Scots, 14, 15
Duncan II, King of Scots, 23
Durham, Bishopric of
  cathedral, 7, 58; courts, 35, 115,
    161; creation of, 7; episcopal
    administration, 35, 36, 43, 45–6,
    55, 72, 100–2, 115, 136;
    episcopal boroughs, 55, 128–30;
    importance of, 54, 57, 99–102;
    lead-mining, 213; markets, 52;
    modern, 329, 381; Reformation
    and, 129–30, 148, 160; relations
    with Durham monastic
    community, 16–17, 25–6, 99,
    104–5; Restoration and, 161;
    secular power, 24, 26, 31–2, 35,
    36, 45–6, 52, 72, 99–103; wealth,
    21, 54, 118, 136, 162, 329
Durham Cathedral Priory
  administration, 11, 43, 45, 47–8,
    102–5, 122, 123; border warfare
    and, 102; cathedral, 7, 58;
    creation of, 25–6, 60; dependent
    houses, 60, 102; importance of,
    60, 102–5; relations with bishop,
    25–6, 204–5; wealth 43, 45,
    47–8, 60, 102–5, 122, 123, 301
Durham, City of
  borough, 128–9; carpet making,
    220, 278; cathedral, 58; creation,
    7; early history, 20–1, 23, 25;
    Infirmary, 323; industry, 220, 278;
    market, 56; parliamentary
    elections, 247; philanthropy, 323;
    road links, 191, 194; size, 124;
    textiles, 220, 278
Durham, County of
  corruption, 370, 371, 403;
    drunkenness, 331; economy, 350,
    393, 398; education, 322; First
    World War, 348; housing, 303–4,
    380; overcrowding, 303–4;
    parliamentary elections, 116, 247;
    police, 246, 317, 348; poor law,
    public assistance, 368, 370–1;
    population, 250–2, 291–2,
    300–1, 377; revenue, 368, 379;
    social conditions, 303–6, 331,

368, 374; unemployment, 374;
    water supply, 306
Durham, Treaty of, 32

Ealdred, Bishop of Durham, 17
Edgar, King of Scots, 28
Edgar the Atheling, 20, 22, 23
education
  medieval, 138–9; early modern,
    166–7; 18th and 19th centuries,
    229, 295, 310, 321–2; 20th
    century, 381, 404
Edward the Confessor, King, 15, 16,
  19
Edward I, King, 64–5, 68–9, 100, 126
Edward II, King, 69–71, 72, 75
Edward III, King, 100–1
Edward IV, King, 79, 81
Edward VI, King, 129
Edwin, Earl of Mercia, 17, 19, 20
Egremont, 30, 52, 56
electricity
  engineering, 276–7, 367, 398;
    generation, 276–7, 367, 395, 398;
    in mining, 262, 267, 277; lighting,
    282; power industry, 276–7, 367,
    393, 395, 396, 398; railways,
    277; rural, 401
Elizabeth I, Queen, 90, 93–8, 101,
  132, 137, 143
engineering
  complexities of, 272–3, 352;
    employment, 216, 270–1, 361–5;
    depression and, 361–5; failures,
    271, 361–5, 398; Japanese
    investment, 398–9; major firms,
    270–1, 273–5, 283–4, 354,
    362–3, 398–9; mining, 215–16;
    shipbuilding, 270–1; railways,
    215–16; trade unions, 341–2
entertainment, *see* leisure
Everdon, Sylvester de, Bishop of
  Carlisle, 101

fairs, 56, 122, 132, 292
Falaise, Treaty of, 35
farming, *see* agriculture
Fenwick, Sir John, 157

Robert I, King of Scots (Robert the
Bruce), 69, 70–1, 75–6
Robert, Duke of Normandy, 24–5
Robinson, Henry, Bishop of Carlisle, 119
Roses, Wars of the, 79–82, 115, 186

St Bees, 56, 105, 108, 139, 186
salt industry, 56, 105, 182, 195, 199,
201, 204, 205, 238
Scotland
Anglo-Scottish wars, 14–16, 17,
24–5, 27, 28, 32–3, 35, 36, 53,
65–7, 68–76, 83–5, 135, 147–50;
border, 27, 34, 37, 83; cross-
border connections, 30–1, 37–8,
45, 53, 58, 66–7, 126, 193, 201,
285; brigandage, 67, 72–3, 74,
114, 118, 143–5; succession
crises, 15–16, 65–7; Union of the
Crowns, 143–7
Seaham Harbour, 284, 328, 372
Second World War, 388–91
Sedgefield, 96
Shap Abbey, 108
shielings, 45, 47, 55, 76
shipbuilding
arbitration, 342; Armstrong
Mitchell/Armstrong Whitworth,
272, 273–4; Barrow, 269, 270,
276, 352, 363, 376; closures,
362–3, 364; complexity, 272–3,
352; depression, 362, 364, 375,
397; Doxfords, 271–2; Hurry's,
216; importance of, 271; iron,
258; *John Bowes*, 258; Leslie,
Andrew, 270–1, 273; *Mauretania*,
274–5; Mitchell, Charles, 272–3;
oil tankers, 272, 362; Palmer,
Charles Mark, 272, 342, 362–3;
Redheads, 272; Second World
War, 388; strikes, 341–2; Swan
Hunter, 275; Tees, 263, 271;
trade unions, 341–2; Tyne, 216,
271–2; wages, 275–6; Walker
Naval Yard, 275; Wigham
Richardson, 256, 272, 275; work
force, 273, 314, 341–2, 362–3,
375, 397

shipping, *see* transport
Silloth, 287–8, 376
Siward, Earl, 14–16
slums (*see also* housing), 233, 246,
271, 300, 301, 305, 379, 382,
388, 401, 405
smallpox, 305, 307
soap industry, 212, 280, 367
South Shields
air raids, 390; children, 344, 382;
coal, 203; Dean and Chapter,
301; drunkenness, 312, 331;
expansion, 301, 316; glass, 282;
housing, 301, 303, 378, 382, 384;
iron ore, 266–7; local government,
233, 316, 369, 378, 382; milk
supply, 293; overcrowding, 301,
303, 378, 384; parliamentary
elections, 247; philanthropy, 384;
poor law, 312, 320, 325, 345;
population, 369; public health,
301, 303, 344, 378, 382; public
houses, 331; Redheads, 272;
religion, 327; Second World War,
390; shipbuilding, 272–3;
tuberculosis, 378; water supply,
306; women, 345; workhouse,
320
Special Areas Acts, 1934, 1937, 374–6
sport, *see* leisure
Standard, Battle of the, 32
Stephen, King, 32–4
Stephenson, George, 196, 197, 209–10
Stephenson, Robert, 196, 215–16,
301–2
Stewart family, Marquises of
Londonderry, 184, 207, 240, 284,
328
Stockton and Darlington Railway,
196–7, 215–16, 263, 284
Stockton on Tees
bridge, 193; charter, 128; children,
382; customs, 195; leisure, 288;
local government, 128, 170;
overcrowding, 303, 382;
parliamentary elections, 372; poor
law, 170; port, 177, 195; public
health, 303, 382; railways, 196–7,